C000261941

Collins
gem

Spanish
School
Dictionary

Published by Collins
An imprint of HarperCollins
Publishers
Westerhill Road
Bishopbriggs
Glasgow G64 2QT

Third Edition 2015

10 9 8 7 6 5 4 3

© HarperCollins Publishers 2006,
2010, 2015

ISBN 978-0-00-756930-4

Collins® and Collins Gem®
are registered trademarks of
HarperCollins Publishers Limited

www.collinsdictionary.com
www.collins.co.uk/dictionaries

Typeset by Davidson Publishing
Solutions, Glasgow

Printed in Italy by Grafica Veneta
S.p.A.

A catalogue record for this book is
available from the British Library.

If you would like to comment on any
aspect of this book, please contact us
at the given address or online.
E-mail: dictionaries@harpercollins.co.uk

🅵 facebook.com/collinsdictionary

🆈 @collinsdict

Acknowledgements
We would like to thank those authors
and publishers who kindly gave
permission for copyright material
to be used in the Collins Corpus.
We would also like to thank Times
Newspapers Ltd for providing
valuable data.

EDITOR
Susie Beattie

CONTRIBUTORS
Val McNulty
Maggie Seaton

FOR THE PUBLISHER
Gerry Breslin
Helen Newstead
Ruth O'Donovan
Sheena Shanks

TECHNICAL SUPPORT
Thomas Callan
Agnieszka Urbanowicz

CONTENTS

v–vii
Using this dictionary

viii
Abbreviations used in this dictionary

ix
Time

x
Dates

xi–xii
Numbers

1–276
Spanish – English dictionary

277–566
English – Spanish dictionary

1–60
Verb Tables

Acknowledgements

We are grateful to all those teachers and students who have contributed to the development of the *Collins Spanish School Dictionary* by advising us on how to tailor it to their needs. We also gratefully acknowledge the help of the examining boards.

USING THIS DICTIONARY

The *Collins Spanish School Dictionary* is designed specifically
for anyone starting to learn Spanish, and has been carefully
researched with teachers and students. It is very straightforward,
with an accessible layout that is easy on the eye, guiding students
quickly to the right translation. It also offers essential help on
Spanish culture.

This section gives useful tips on how to use the *Collins Spanish School
Dictionary* effectively.

▷ **Make sure you look in the right side of the dictionary**
There are two sides in a bilingual dictionary. Here, the **Spanish–
English** side comes first, and the second part is **English–Spanish**.
At the top of each page there is a reminder of which side of the
dictionary you have open. The middle pages of the book have a
blue border so you can see where one side finishes and the other
one starts.

▷ **Finding the word you want**
To help you find a word more quickly, use the alphabet tabs down
the side of the page, then look at the words in blue at the top of
pages. They show the first and last words on the two pages where
the dictionary is open.

▷ **Make sure you use the right part of speech**
Some entries are split into several parts of speech. For example
'**glue**' can either be a noun ("Can I borrow your **glue**?") or a verb
("**Glue** this into your exercise book"). Parts of speech within an
entry are separated by a black triangle ▶ and are given on a new
line. They are given in their abbreviated form (*n* for noun, *adj* for
adjective, etc). For the full list of abbreviations, look at page viii.

    glue *n* pegamento *m*
      ▶ *vb* pegar [**37**] …

▷ Choosing the right translation

The main translation of a word is underlined and is shown after the part of speech. If there is more than one main translation for a word, each one is numbered. You may also sometimes find bracketed words in *italics* which give you some context. They help you to choose the translation you want.

> **pool** n **❶** *(pond)* <u>estanque</u> m
> **❷** *(swimming pool)* <u>piscina</u> f
> **❸** *(game)* <u>billar americano</u> m

Often you will see phrases in *italics*, preceded by a white triangle ▷. These are examples of the word being used in context. Examples in **bold type** are phrases which are particularly common and important. Sometimes these phrases have a completely different translation.

> **bolsa** nf **❶** <u>bag</u> ▷ *una bolsa de plástico* a plastic bag; **una bolsa de viaje** a travel bag **❷** *(Mex)* <u>handbag</u>; **la Bolsa** the Stock Exchange

Once you have found the right translation, remember that you may need to adapt the Spanish word you have found. You may need to make a noun plural, or make an **adjective** feminine or plural. Remember that the feminine form is given for nouns and irregular adjectives, and that irregular plural forms are given also.

> **lawyer** n <u>abogado</u> m, <u>abogada</u> f
> **garden** n <u>jardín</u> m *(pl* jardines)
> **bossy** adj <u>mandón</u> *(f* mandona, *pl* mandones)

You may also need to adapt the **verb**. Verbs are given in the infinitive form, but you may want to use them in the present, past or future tense. To do this, use the **verb tables** in the last section of the dictionary. Spanish verbs on both sides are usually followed by a number in square brackets. This number corresponds to a page number in the verb tables at the back of the dictionary. In the following example, **cambiar** follows the same pattern as **hablar**, shown on page 25 in the verb tables.

cambiar *vb* **[25]** **❶** to change

▷ Find out more

In the *Collins Spanish School Dictionary*, you will find lots of extra information about the Spanish language. These **usage notes** help you understand how the language works and draw your attention to false friends (words which look similar but have a different meaning).

malo, -a *adj*
 Use **mal** before a masculine noun.
 ❶ bad ▷ *un mal día* a bad day

librería *nf* **❶** bookshop
 ❷ bookshelf
 Be careful! **librería** does not mean **library**.

You can also find out more about life in Spain and Spanish-speaking countries by reading the **cultural notes**.

Nochevieja *nf* New Year's Eve
 At midnight on New Year's Eve in Spain, it is traditional to eat **las uvas de la suerte** (twelve good-luck grapes) to the chimes of Madrid's **Puerta del Sol** clock, which are broadcast live.

▷ Remember!

Never take the first translation you see without looking at the others. Always look to see if there is more than one translation, or more than one part of speech.

ABBREVIATIONS USED IN THIS DICTIONARY

abbr	abbreviation	*nf*	feminine noun
adj	adjective	*nm*	masculine noun
adv	adverb	*nmf*	masculine and
art	article		feminine noun
conj	conjunction	*nm/f*	masculine or
def art	definite article		feminine noun
excl	exclamation	*npl*	plural noun
f	feminine	*num*	number
indef art	indefinite article	*pl*	plural
inv	invariable form, the	*prep*	preposition
	same for *m*, *f* and *pl*	*pron*	pronoun
LatAm	Latin America	*sg*	singular
m	masculine	*Sp*	Spain
n	noun	*vb*	verb

SYMBOLS

▷	example
▶	new part of speech
❷	new meaning
[29]	verb table number (see Verb Tables section at the back of the dictionary)
accident	Key words which you need for your GCSE or other exams of a similar level are highlighted in light blue throughout both sides of the dictionary to help you find them more easily.

TIME

¿Qué hora es? What time is it?

Es la una

Es la una y diez

Es la una y cuarto

Es la una y media

Son las dos menos veinte

Son las dos menos cuarto

¿A qué hora? What time?

a medianoche

al mediodía

a la una (de la tarde)

a las nueve (de la noche)

las 11:15 *or* las once quince

las 20:45 *or* las veinte cuarenta
y cinco

DATES

▷ Days of the Week
lunes	Monday
martes	Tuesday
miércoles	Wednesday
jueves	Thursday
viernes	Friday
sábado	Saturday
domingo	Sunday

▷ Months of the Year
enero	January	**julio**	July
febrero	February	**agosto**	August
marzo	March	**septiembre**	September
abril	April	**octubre**	October
mayo	May	**noviembre**	November
junio	June	**diciembre**	December

▷ ¿Cuándo?
en febrero
el uno de diciembre
de 2015
en dos mil quince

▷ When?
in February
on the first of December
2015
in two thousand and fifteen

▷ ¿Qué día es hoy?
Es...
lunes, veintiséis de mayo

▷ What day is it?
It's...
Monday, 26th May *or*
Monday, the twenty-sixth
of May

NUMBERS

▷ Cardinal numbers

1	uno	22	veintidós
2	dos	30	treinta
3	tres	31	treinta y uno
4	cuatro	40	cuarenta
5	cinco	41	cuarenta y uno
6	seis	50	cincuenta
7	siete	60	sesenta
8	ocho	70	setenta
9	nueve	80	ochenta
10	diez	90	noventa
11	once	100	cien
12	doce	101	ciento uno
13	trece	200	doscientos
14	catorce	201	doscientos uno
15	quince	500	quinientos
16	dieciséis	700	setecientos
17	diecisiete	900	novecientos
18	dieciocho	1000	mil
19	diecinueve	1001	mil uno
20	veinte	1,000,000	un millón
21	veintiuno		

▷ Fractions etc

1/2	un medio	0.5	cero coma cinco
1/3	un tercio	10%	diez por ciento
1/4	un cuarto	100%	cien por cien
1/5	un quinto		

NUMBERS

▷ Ordinal numbers

1st	primero
2nd	segundo
3rd	tercero
4th	cuarto
5th	quinto
6th	sexto
7th	séptimo
8th	octavo
9th	noveno
10th	décimo
11th	undécimo
12th	decimosegundo
13th	decimotercero
14th	decimocuarto
15th	decimoquinto
16th	decimosexto
17th	decimoséptimo
18th	decimoctavo
19th	decimonoveno
20th	vigésimo
21st	vigésimo primero
30th	trigésimo
100th	centésimo
101st	centésimo primero
1000th	milésimo

The translation of **a** can depend on the verb preceding it.

▷ **Me caí al río.** I fell into the river.; **Se subieron al tejado.** They climbed onto the roof.; **Gira a la derecha.** Turn right.; **Me voy a casa.** I'm going home.; **¡A comer!** Lunch is ready!; **Al verlo, lo reconocí inmediatamente.** When I saw him, I recognized him immediately.; **Nos cruzamos al salir.** We bumped into each other as we were going out. ❷ **at**

The other main translation of **a** is **at**.

▷ **a las** 10 at 10 o'clock ▷ **a medianoche** at midnight ▷ **a los 24 años** at the age of 24 ▷ **Íbamos a más de 90 km por hora.** We were going at over 90 km an hour. ▷ **Marta llegó a la oficina.** Marta arrived at the office.; **Está a 15 km de aquí.** It's 15 km from here.; **Estamos a 9 de julio.** It's the 9th of July.; **Los huevos están a 1,50 euros la docena.** Eggs are 1.50 euros a dozen.; **una vez a la semana** once a week

The 'personal **a**' before direct objects is not translated.

▷ **Vi a Juan.** I saw Juan. ▷ **Llamé al médico.** I called the doctor.

a *prep* ❶ **to**

a is often translated as **to** when talking about direction or movement.

▷ **Fueron a Madrid.** They went to Madrid.

a is also usually translated as **to** before an infinitive.

▷ **Voy a verle.** I'm going to see him. ▷ **Vine a decírtelo.** I came to tell you. ▷ **Me obligaban a comer.** They forced me to eat.

a is usually translated by **to** or nothing in constructions with an indirect object.

▷ **Se lo di a Ana.** I gave it to Ana. ▷ **Le enseñé a Pablo el libro que me dejaste.** I showed Pablo the book you lent me.; **Se lo compré a él.** I bought it from him.

abadía *nf* abbey

abajo *adv* ❶ below ▷ **La montaña no parece tan alta desde abajo.** The mountain doesn't seem so high from below. ▷ **Mira ahí abajo.** Look down below.; **Mete las cervezas abajo del todo.** Put the beers at

the bottom.; **el estante de abajo** the bottom shelf; **la parte de abajo del contenedor** the bottom of the container ❷ downstairs
▷ *Abajo están la cocina y el salón.* The kitchen and lounge are downstairs. ▷ *Hay una fiesta en el piso de abajo.* There's a party in the flat downstairs.; **más abajo** further down; **ir calle abajo** to go down the street; **Todos los bolsos son 50 euros para abajo.** All the bags are 50 euros or under.; **abajo de** (LatAm) under

abandonado, -a adj **un pueblo abandonado** a deserted village

abandonar vb [25] ❶ to leave ▷ *Decidieron abandonar el país.* They decided to leave the country. ❷ (plan, idea) to give up

abanico nm fan

abarrotado, -a adj packed ▷ *abarrotado de gente* packed with people

abarrotería nf (Mex) grocer's

abarrotes nmpl (Mex, Chile) groceries

abastecer vb [12] **abastecer de algo a alguien** to supply somebody with something; **Nos abastecimos bien de comida para el viaje.** We stocked up with food for the trip.

abdomen nm stomach

abdominales nmpl sit-ups

abecedario nm alphabet

abeja nf bee

abeto nm fir

abierto vb see **abrir**
▶ adj ❶ open ▷ *¿Están abiertas las tiendas?* Are the shops open? ❷ on ▷ *No dejes el gas abierto.* Don't leave the gas on.

abogado, -a nm/f lawyer

abolir vb [58] to abolish

abollar vb [25] to dent; **abollarse** to get dented

abombarse vb [25] (LatAm) to go bad

abonar vb [25] ❶ to pay ❷ to fertilize; **abonarse a (1)** to take out a subscription to **(2)** to join

abono nm ❶ fertilizer ❷ season ticket

abortar vb [25] ❶ to have an abortion ❷ to miscarry

aborto nm ❶ abortion ❷ miscarriage

abrasar vb [25] to burn; **abrasarse** to be burned

abrazar vb [13] to hug ▷ *Al verme me abrazó.* He hugged me when he saw me.; **abrazarse** to hug ▷ *Se abrazaron y se besaron.* They hugged and kissed.

abrazo nm hug ▷ *¡Dame un abrazo!* Give me a hug!; **Siempre están dándose besos y abrazos.** They're always hugging and kissing.; **'un abrazo'** 'with best wishes'

abrebotellas (pl abrebotellas) nm bottle opener

abrelatas (pl abrelatas) nm tin opener

abreviatura nf abbreviation

abridor nm ❶ bottle opener ❷ tin opener

abrigar vb [37] **Ponte algo que te abrigue.** Put something warm on.; **Abriga bien al niño, que**

hace frío. Wrap the baby up well – it's cold.; **abrigarse** to wrap up well

abrigo nm coat; **ropa de abrigo** warm clothing

abril nm April

abrir vb [58, pp abierto] ❶ to open ▷ Las tiendas abren a las diez. The shops open at ten o'clock. ▷ Abre la ventana. Open the window. ❷ (tap, gas) to turn on; **abrirse** to open

abrocharse vb [25] to do up; **Abróchense los cinturones.** Please fasten your seat belts.

absoluto, -a adj absolute ▷ Nos dio garantía absoluta. He gave us an absolute guarantee.; **La operación fue un éxito absoluto.** The operation was a complete success.; **en absoluto** at all ▷ ¿Te molesta que fume? — En absoluto. Do you mind if I smoke? — Not at all.; **nada en absoluto** nothing at all

absorber vb [8] to absorb

abstemio, -a adj teetotal

abstención (pl abstenciones) nf abstention

abstenerse vb [53] to abstain

abstracto, -a adj abstract

absurdo, -a adj absurd

abuela nf grandmother ▷ mi abuela my grandmother; ¿**Dónde está la abuela?** Where's Gran?

abuelo nm grandfather ▷ mi abuelo my grandfather; ¿**Dónde está el abuelo?** Where's Granddad?; **mis abuelos** my grandparents

abultado, -a adj bulky

abultar vb [25] to be bulky; **Tus cosas apenas abultan.** Your

things hardly take up any space at all.

abundante adj ❶ plenty of ▷ Habrá comida y bebida abundante. There'll be plenty of food and drink. ❷ enormous

aburrido, -a adj ❶ bored ▷ Estaba aburrida y me marché. I was bored so I left. ❷ boring ▷ una película muy aburrida a very boring film ❸ tired

aburrimiento nm ¡Qué aburrimiento! This is such a bore!; **Estoy muerto de aburrimiento.** I'm bored stiff.

aburrirse vb [58] to get bored

abusar vb [25] abusar de alguien (1) to take advantage of somebody (2) to abuse somebody; **Está bien beber de vez en cuando pero sin abusar.** Drinking every so often is fine as long as you don't overdo it.; **No conviene abusar del aceite en las comidas.** You shouldn't use too much oil in food.

abuso nm abuse ▷ el abuso de las drogas drug abuse; **Lo que han hecho me parece un abuso.** I think what they've done is outrageous.

acá adv here; **Hay que ponerlo más acá.** You'll have to bring it closer.

acabar vb [25] to finish ▷ Ayer acabé de pintar la valla. Yesterday I finished painting the fence.; **acabar con** (1) to put an end to (2) to finish; **Acabo de ver a tu padre.** I've just seen your father. ▷ Acababa de entrar cuando sonó el teléfono. I had just come in when the phone rang.; **acabarse** to run out ▷ *Se me acabó el tabaco.* I ran out of cigarettes.

academia nf school ▷ *una academia de idiomas* a language school

académico, -a adj academic ▷ *el curso académico* the academic year

acampada nf **ir de acampada** to go camping

acampar vb [**25**] to camp

acantilado nm cliff

acariciar vb [**25**] ❶ to stroke ❷ to caress

acaso adv **por si acaso** just in case; **No necesito nada; si acaso, un poco de leche.** I don't need anything; well maybe a little milk.; **Si acaso lo vieras, dile que me llame.** If you see him, tell him to call me.

acatarrarse vb [**25**] to catch cold

acceder vb [**8**] **acceder a (1)** to agree to **(2)** to gain access to

accesible adj ❶ accessible ❷ approachable

acceso nm access; **las pruebas de acceso a la universidad** university entrance exams

accesorio nm accessory

accidentado, -a adj ❶ rough ❷ eventful

accidente nm accident; **Han tenido un accidente.** They've had a car accident.

acción (pl acciones) nf ❶ action; **entrar en acción** to go into action ❷ (in company) share

accionista nmf shareholder

aceite nm oil; **el aceite de girasol** sunflower oil; **el aceite de oliva** olive oil

aceitoso, -a adj oily

aceituna nf olive ▷ *aceitunas rellenas* stuffed olives

acelerador nm accelerator

acelerar vb [**25**] to accelerate; **¡Acelera, que no llegamos!** Speed up or we'll never get there!; **acelerar el paso** to walk faster

acelgas nfpl spinach beet sg

acento nm ❶ accent ❷ stress

acentuarse vb [**1**] to have an accent ▷ *No se acentúa.* It doesn't have an accent.

aceptable adj acceptable

aceptar vb [**25**] to accept; **aceptar hacer algo** to agree to do something

acequia nf irrigation channel

acera nf pavement

acerca adv **acerca de** about ▷ *un documental acerca de la fauna africana* a documentary about African wildlife

acercar vb [**48**] ❶ to pass ▷ *¿Me acercas los alicates?* Could you pass me the pliers? ❷ to bring over ▷ *Acerca la silla.* Bring your chair over.; **¿Acerco más la cama a la ventana?** Shall I put the bed nearer the window?; **Nos acercaron al aeropuerto.** They gave us a lift to the airport.;

acercarse (1) to come closer ▷ *Acércate, que te vea.* Come closer so that I can see you. **(2)** to go over ▷ *Me acerqué a la ventana.* I went over to the window.; **Ya se acerca la Navidad.** Christmas is coming.

acero nm steel ▷ *acero inoxidable* stainless steel

acertar vb [39] ① to get...right
▷ He acertado todas las respuestas.
I got all the answers right.; **No
acerté.** I got it wrong.; **Creo que
hemos acertado con estas
cortinas.** I think these curtains
were a good choice. ② (correctly) to
guess; **Acerté en el blanco.** I hit
the target.

ácido, -a adj acid
▶ nm acid

acierto vb see **acertar**
▶ nm ① right answer ▷ Tuve más
aciertos que fallos en el examen. I got
more right answers than wrong
ones in the exam. ② good idea
▷ Fue un acierto ir de vacaciones a la
montaña. Going to the mountains
on holiday was a good idea.

aclarar vb [25] ① (washing) to rinse
② (doubts, matter) to clear up; **Con
tantos números no me aclaro.**
There are so many numbers that
I can't get it straight.

acné nm acne

acobardarse vb [25] **No se
acobarda por nada.** He isn't
frightened by anything.

acogedor, a adj cosy ▷ un cuarto
muy acogedor a very cosy room

acoger vb [7] to receive; **Me
acogieron muy bien en Estados
Unidos.** I was made very welcome
in the United States.

acogida nf reception ▷ una fría
acogida a cold reception; **una
calurosa acogida** a warm
welcome; **tener buena acogida**
to be well received

acomodado, -a adj well-off

acomodador nm usher

acomodadora nf usherette

acompañar vb [25] ① to come
with ② to go with ▷ Me pidió que la
acompañara a la estación. She asked
me to go to the station with her.;
**¿Quieres que te acompañe a
casa?** Would you like me to see you
home? ③ to stay with ▷ Me
acompañó hasta que llegó el autobús.
He stayed with me until the bus
arrived.

aconsejar vb [25] ① to advise;
**aconsejar a alguien que haga
algo** to advise somebody to do
something; **Te aconsejo que lo
hagas.** I'd advise you to do it.
② to recommend

acontecimiento nm event

acordar vb [11] to agree on;
acordar hacer algo to agree to do
something

acordarse vb [11] to remember
▷ Ahora mismo no me acuerdo. Right
now I can't remember.; **acordarse
de** to remember ▷ ¿Te acuerdas de
mí? Do you remember me?
▷ Acuérdate de cerrar la puerta con
llave. Remember to lock the door.;
acordarse de haber hecho algo
to remember doing something

acordeón (pl acordeones) nm
accordion

acoso nm **el acoso escolar** bullying

acostado, -a adj **estar acostado**
to be in bed

acostarse vb [11] ① to lie down
② to go to bed; **acostarse con
alguien** to go to bed with
somebody

acostumbrarse vb [25]

acostumbrarse a to get used to ▷ *No me acostumbro a la vida en la ciudad.* I can't get used to city life.; **acostumbrarse a hacer algo** to get used to doing something ▷ *Ya me he acostumbrado a trabajar de noche.* I've got used to working at night now.

acróbata nmf acrobat

actitud nf attitude

actividad nf activity

activo, -a adj active

acto nm ❶ act ❷ ceremony; **acto seguido** immediately afterwards; **en el acto** instantly; **Te arreglan tus zapatos en el acto.** They will repair your shoes while you wait.

actor nm actor

actriz (pl actrices) nf actress

actuación (pl actuaciones) nf ❶ performance ❷ gig

actual adj present; **uno de los mejores pintores del arte actual** one of the greatest painters of today

⚠ Be careful! The Spanish word **actual** does not mean **actual**.

actualidad nf un repaso a la **actualidad nacional** a round-up of the national news; **un tema de gran actualidad** a very topical issue; **en la actualidad** (1) currently (2) nowadays

actualmente adv ❶ nowadays ❷ currently

⚠ Be careful! **actualmente** does not mean **actually**.

actuar vb [1] ❶ to act; **Hay que actuar con cautela.** We'll have to be cautious.; **No actuó en esa**

película. He wasn't in that film. ❷ to perform

acuarela nf watercolour

Acuario nm (sign) Aquarius; **Soy acuario.** I'm Aquarius.

acuario nm aquarium

acuático, -a adj **esquí acuático** water skiing; **aves acuáticas** waterfowl pl

acudir vb [58] ❶ to go ▷ *Acudió a un amigo en busca de consejo.* He went to a friend for advice.; **No tengo a quien acudir.** I have no one to turn to.; **acudir a una cita** to keep an appointment ❷ to come ▷ *El perro acude cuando lo llamo.* The dog comes when I call.

acuerdo vb see **acordar**
▶ nm agreement ▷ *llegar a un acuerdo* to reach an agreement; **estar de acuerdo con alguien** to agree with somebody; **ponerse de acuerdo** to agree ▷ *Al final no nos pusimos de acuerdo.* In the end we couldn't agree.; **¡De acuerdo!** All right!

acupuntura nf acupuncture

acurrucarse vb [25] to curl up

acusar vb [25] ❶ to accuse ❷ to charge

acústico, -a adj acoustic ▷ *una guitarra acústica* an acoustic guitar

adaptar vb [25] to adapt; **adaptarse** to adapt

adecuado, -a adj ❶ suitable ▷ *No es la ropa más adecuada para ir de boda.* They aren't the most suitable clothes to wear to a wedding. ❷ right ▷ *el hombre adecuado para el puesto* the right man for the job

a. de J.C. abbr (= antes de Jesucristo) B.C. (= before Christ)

adelantado, -a adj ① advanced ▷ Suecia es un país muy adelantado. Sweden is a very advanced country.; **los niños más adelantados de la clase** the children who are doing best in the class ② fast ▷ Este reloj va adelantado. This watch is fast.; **pagar por adelantado** to pay in advance

adelantar vb [25] ① to bring... forward ▷ Tuvimos que adelantar la boda. We had to bring the wedding forward. ② to overtake ▷ Adelanta a ese camión cuando puedas. Overtake that lorry when you can. ③ to put...forward ▷ El domingo hay que adelantar los relojes una hora. On Sunday we'll have to put the clocks forward an hour.; **Así no adelantas nada.** You won't get anywhere that way.; **Tu reloj adelanta.** Your watch gains.

adelantarse vb [25] to go on ahead; **adelantarse a alguien** to get ahead of somebody

adelante adv forward ▷ Se inclinó hacia adelante. He leant forward.; **¿Nos vamos adelante para ver mejor?** Shall we sit near the front to get a better view?; **más adelante (1)** further on **(2)** later; **adelante de** (LatAm) in front of; **Hay que seguir adelante.** We must go on.; **de ahora en adelante** from now on
▶ excl ① come on! ② come in!

adelanto nm advance

adelgazar vb [13] to lose weight ▷ ¡Cómo has adelgazado! What a lot of weight you've lost!; **He adelgazado cinco kilos.** I've lost five kilos.

además adv ① as well ▷ Es profesor y además es carpintero. He's a teacher and a carpenter as well. ② what's more ▷ El baño es demasiado pequeño y, además, no tiene ventana. The bathroom's too small and, what's more, it hasn't got a window. ③ besides ▷ Además, no tienes nada que perder. Besides, you've got nothing to lose.; **además de** as well as

adentro adv inside; **adentro de** (LatAm) inside

adhesivo, -a adj sticky ▷ cinta adhesiva sticky tape
▶ nm sticker

adicción (pl adicciones) nf addiction

adición (pl adiciones) nf (River Plate) bill

adicto, -a adj addicted ▷ Es adicto a la cafeína. He is addicted to caffeine.
▶ nm/f addict ▷ un adicto a las drogas a drug addict

adinerado, -a adj wealthy

adiós excl ① goodbye!; **decir adiós a alguien** to say goodbye to somebody ② (on passing) hello!

aditivo nm additive

adivinanza nf guess

adivinar vb [25] to guess ▷ Adivina quién viene. Guess who's coming.; **adivinar el futuro** to see into the future

adjetivo nm adjective

adjunto, -a adj ❶ enclosed
❷ attached ❸ deputy ▷ el director
adjunto the deputy head

administración (pl
administraciones) nf
❶ administration ▷ Master de
Administración de Empresas Master
of Business Administration ❷ civil
service ▷ Carmen trabaja en la
administración. Carmen works for
the civil service.

administrativo, -a adj
administrative
▶ nm/f clerk

admiración nf ❶ admiration
❷ amazement ▷ para admiración de
todos to everyone's amazement;
signo de admiración exclamation
mark

admirar vb [25] to admire

admitir vb [58] ❶ to admit
▷ Admite que estabas equivocado.
Admit you were wrong. ❷ to
accept; **Espero que me admitan
a la universidad.** I hope I'll get a
place at university. ❸ to allow in
▷ Aquí no admiten perros. Dogs
aren't allowed in here.

adolescente nmf teenager

adonde conj where; **la ciudad
adonde nos dirigimos** the city
we're going to

adónde adv where

adopción (pl adopciones) nf
adoption

adoptar vb [25] to adopt

adoptivo, -a adj **un hijo adoptivo**
an adopted child; **mis padres
adoptivos** my adoptive parents

adorar vb [25] ❶ to adore ❷ to
worship

adornar vb [25] to decorate

adorno nm ❶ ornament
❷ decoration ▷ Habían puesto
adornos en las calles. Decorations
had been put up in the streets. ▷ Es
solo de adorno. It's only for
decoration.

adosado, -a adj **un chalet
adosado** a terraced house

adquirir vb [2] to acquire; **adquirir
velocidad** to gain speed; **adquirir
fama** to achieve fame; **adquirir
una vivienda** to purchase a
property; **adquirir importancia**
to become important

adrede adv on purpose

aduana nf customs sg

aduanero, -a nm/f customs
officer

adulto nm adult

adverbio nm adverb

adversario, -a nm/f opponent

advertencia nf warning

advertir vb [51] ❶ to warn ▷ Ya te
advertí que no intervinieras. I warned
you not to get involved.; **advertir
a alguien de algo** to warn
somebody about something; **Te
advierto que no va a ser nada
fácil.** I must warn you that it won't
be at all easy. ❷ to notice ▷ No
advertí nada extraño en su
comportamiento. I didn't notice
anything strange about his
behaviour.

aéreo, -a adj air; **por vía aérea** by
air mail; **una fotografía aérea** an
aerial photograph

aerobic nm aerobics sg

aeromozo, -a nm/f (LatAm) flight attendant

aeropuerto nm airport

aerosol nm aerosol

afán (pl afanes) nm ❶ ambition ❷ effort; **Trabajan con mucho afán.** They put a lot of effort into their work.

afectado, -a adj upset

afectar vb [25] to affect ▷ Esto a ti no te afecta. This doesn't affect you.; **Me afectó mucho la noticia.** The news upset me terribly.

afectivo, -a adj emotional ▷ problemas afectivos emotional problems

afecto nm affection; **tener afecto a alguien** to be fond of somebody

afectuoso, -a adj affectionate; **'Un saludo afectuoso'** 'With best wishes'

afeitar vb [25] to shave; **afeitarse** to shave; **Me afeité la barba.** I shaved off my beard.

Afganistán nm Afghanistan

afiche nm (LatAm) poster

afición (pl aficiones) nf ❶ hobby ▷ Mi afición es la filatelia. My hobby is stamp collecting. ▷ por afición as a hobby; **Tengo mucha afición por el ciclismo.** I'm very keen on cycling. ❷ fans pl ▷ la afición del Athletic the Athletic fans

aficionado, -a adj ❶ keen ▷ Es muy aficionada a la pintura. She's very keen on painting. ❷ amateur ▷ un equipo de fútbol aficionado an amateur football team

▶ nm/f ❶ enthusiast ▷ un libro para los aficionados al bricolaje a book for DIY enthusiasts ❷ lover ▷ los aficionados al teatro theatre lovers ❸ amateur ▷ un partido para aficionados a game for amateurs

aficionarse vb [25] **aficionarse a algo** (1) to take up something (2) to become interested in something

afilado, -a adj sharp

afilar vb [25] to sharpen

afiliarse vb [25] **afiliarse a algo** to join something

afinar vb [25] to tune ▷ afinar un violín to tune a violin

afirmar vb [25] to affirm ▷ ... to say that ...; **Afirma haberla visto aquella noche.** He says that he saw her that night.

afirmativo, -a adj affirmative

aflojar vb [25] to loosen; **Tengo que aflojarme la corbata.** I must loosen my tie.; **aflojarse** to come loose

afónico, -a adj **Estoy afónico.** I've lost my voice.

afortunadamente adv fortunately

afortunado, -a adj lucky ▷ Es un tipo afortunado. He's a lucky guy.

África nf Africa

africano, -a adj, nm/f African

afrontar vb [25] to face up to

afuera adv outside ▷ Vámonos afuera. Let's go outside.; **afuera de** (LatAm) outside

afueras nfpl outskirts ▷ en las afueras de Barcelona on the outskirts of Barcelona

agacharse vb [25] ❶ to crouch down ❷ to bend down

agarradera nf (LatAm) handle

agarrado, -a adj stingy

agarrar vb [25] ❶ to grab ▷ Agarró al niño por el hombro. He grabbed the child by the shoulder. ❷ to hold ▷ Agarra bien la sartén. Hold the frying pan firmly. ❸ to catch ▷ Ya han agarrado al ladrón. They've already caught the thief. ❹ (LatAm) to take ▷ Agarré otro pedazo de pastel. I took another piece of cake.; **agarrarse** to hold on

agencia nf agency; **una agencia inmobiliaria** an estate agent's; **una agencia de viajes** a travel agent's

agenda nf ❶ diary ❷ address book

Be careful! The Spanish word **agenda** does not mean agenda.

agente nmf agent; **un agente de bolsa** a stockbroker; **un agente de policía** a police officer; **un agente de seguros** an insurance broker

ágil adj agile

agitado, -a adj (life) hectic

agitar vb [25] ❶ (tea, coffee) to stir ❷ to shake ▷ Agítese antes de usar. Shake before use. ❸ to wave ▷ La gente agitaba los pañuelos. People were waving their handkerchiefs.

aglomerarse vb [25] **La gente se aglomeraba a la entrada.** People were crowding around the entrance.

agobiante adj ❶ stifling ❷ overwhelming ❸ exhausting

agobiar vb [25] **Le agobian sus problemas.** His problems are getting on top of him.; **agobiarse** to worry

agosto nm August

agotado, -a adj ❶ exhausted ▷ Estoy agotado. I'm exhausted. ❷ sold out ▷ Ese modelo en concreto está agotado. That particular model is sold out.

agotador, a adj exhausting

agotar vb [25] ❶ to use up ❷ to tire out; **agotarse** to run out; **Se agotaron todas las entradas.** The tickets sold out.

agradable adj nice

agradar vb [25] **Esto no me agrada.** I don't like this.

agradecer vb [12] **agradecer algo a alguien** to thank somebody for something; **Te agradezco tu interés.** Thank you for your interest.; **Le agradecería me enviara ...** I should be grateful if you would send me ...

agradecido, -a adj **estar agradecido a alguien por algo** to be grateful to somebody for something

agrado nm **no fue de mi agrado** it was not to my liking

agredir vb [58] to attack

agresión (pl agresiones) nf ❶ attack ❷ aggression

agresivo, -a adj aggressive

agrícola adj agricultural

agricultor, a nm/f farmer

agricultura nf farming

agridulce *adj* sweet-and-sour

agrio, -a *adj* ❶ sour ❷ tart

agrupación (*pl* agrupaciones) *nf* group

agrupar *vb* [25] ❶ to group ❷ to bring together; **Los ecologistas se han agrupado en varios partidos.** The ecologists have formed several parties.; **Se agruparon en torno a su jefe.** They gathered round their boss.

agua *nf* water; **agua corriente** running water; **agua potable** drinking water; **agua dulce** fresh water; **agua salada** salt water; **agua de colonia** cologne; **agua oxigenada** peroxide

aguacate *nm* avocado

aguafiestas (*pl* aguafiestas) *nmf* spoilsport

aguanieve *nf* sleet

aguantar *vb* [25] ❶ to stand ▷ No aguanto la ópera. I can't stand opera. ❷ to take ▷ La estantería no va a aguantar el peso. The shelf won't take the weight. ▷ ¡No aguanto más! I can't take any more! ❸ to hold ▷ Aguántame el martillo un momento. Can you hold the hammer for me for a moment? ▷ Aguanta la respiración. Hold your breath. ❹ to last ▷ Este abrigo ya no aguanta otro invierno. This coat won't last another winter.; **No pude aguantar la risa.** I couldn't help laughing.; **Últimamente estás que no hay quien te aguante.** You've been unbearable lately.; **¿Puedes aguantar hasta que lleguemos a casa?** Can

you hold out until we get home?; **Si no puede venir, que se aguante.** If he can't come, he'll just have to lump it.

aguante *nm* tener aguante (1) to be patient (2) to have stamina

aguardar *vb* [25] to wait for

agudo, -a *adj* ❶ (hearing, pain) sharp ❷ (sound, voice) high-pitched ❸ (illness) acute ❹ (comment) witty

aguijón (*pl* aguijones) *nm* sting

águila *nf* eagle

aguja *nf* (for sewing) needle

agujero *nm* ❶ hole; **hacer un agujero** to make a hole ❷ pocket

agujeta *nf* (Mex) shoe lace

agujetas *nfpl* tener agujetas to be stiff

ahí *adv* ❶ there ▷ ¡Ahí están! There they are! ▷ Ahí llega el tren. There's the train.; **Ahí está el problema.** That's the problem.; **ahí arriba** up there; **Están ahí dentro.** They're in there.; **Lo tienes ahí mismo.** You've got it right there.; **de ahí que** that's why; **por ahí** over there ▷ Tú busca por ahí. You look over there. ❷ thereabouts ▷ 200 o por ahí 200 or thereabouts; **¿Las tijeras? Andarán por ahí.** The scissors? They must be somewhere around.

ahogarse *vb* [37] ❶ to drown ❷ to suffocate ❸ to get breathless

ahora *adv* now ▷ ¿Dónde vamos ahora? Where are we going now?; **Ahora te lo digo.** I'll tell you in a moment.; **ahora mismo** right now; **Ahora mismo voy.** I'm just coming.; **de ahora en adelante**

from now on; **hasta ahora (1)** so far **(2)** till now; **ahora bien** however; **por ahora** for the moment

ahorcar vb [48] to hang; **ahorcarse** to hang oneself

ahorita adv (LatAm) now

ahorrar vb [25] to save

ahorros nmpl savings

ahumado, -a adj smoked

aire nm ❶ air; **aire acondicionado** air conditioning; **tomar el aire** to get some fresh air; **al aire libre (1)** outdoors ▷ Comimos al aire libre. We had lunch outdoors. **(2)** outdoor ▷ una fiesta al aire libre an outdoor party

aislado, -a adj isolated ▷ Es un caso aislado. It's an isolated case.; **El pueblo estaba aislado por la nieve.** The village was cut off by the snow.

ajedrez (pl ajedreces) nm ❶ chess ▷ jugar al ajedrez to play chess ❷ chess set

ajeno, -a adj **No respeta la opinión ajena.** He doesn't respect other people's opinions.; **por razones ajenas a nuestra voluntad** for reasons beyond our control

ajetreado, -a adj (day) busy

ají nm (River Plate) chili sauce

ajo nm garlic

ajustado, -a adj tight

ajustar vb [25] ❶ to adjust ❷ to tighten ❸ to fit

al prep see **a**
■ **al** is the contracted form of **a** + **el**.

ala nf ❶ wing ❷ brim

alabar vb [25] to praise

alambrada nf fence ▷ una alambrada eléctrica an electric fence

alambre nm wire

álamo nm poplar

alargador nm extension lead

alargar vb [37] ❶ to lengthen ▷ Hay que alargar un poco las mangas. We'll need to lengthen the sleeves a little. ❷ to extend ▷ Decidieron alargar las vacaciones. They decided to extend their holidays. ❸ to stretch out ▷ Alargué el brazo para apagar la luz. I stretched out my arm to put out the light. ❹ to pass ▷ ¿Me alargas la llave inglesa? Will you pass me the wrench?;
alargarse (1) to get longer ▷ Ya van alargándose los días. The days are getting longer. **(2)** to go on ▷ La fiesta se alargó hasta el amanecer. The party went on into the early hours.

alarma nf alarm; **dar la voz de alarma** to raise the alarm; **alarma de incendios** fire alarm

alba nf dawn; **al alba** at dawn

albañil nmf ❶ builder ❷ bricklayer

albaricoque nm apricot

alberca nf (LatAm) swimming pool

albergue nm ❶ mountain refuge ❷ hostel; **un albergue juvenil** a youth hostel

albóndigas nfpl meatballs

albornoz (pl albornoces) nm bathrobe

alboroto nm racket ▷ ¡Vaya alboroto que estaban montando los niños! What a racket the kids were making!

álbum (pl **álbumes**) nm album

alcachofa nf ❶ artichoke ❷ shower head ❸ rose

alcalde, -esa nm/f (post holder) mayor

alcance nm ❶ range ▷ misiles de largo alcance long-range missiles ❷ scale ▷ Se desconoce el alcance de la catástrofe. The scale of the disaster isn't yet known.; **Está al alcance de todos.** It's within everybody's reach.

alcantarilla nf ❶ sewer ❷ drain

alcanzar vb [13] ❶ to catch up with ▷ La alcancé cuando salía por la puerta. I caught up with her just as she was going out of the door. ❷ to reach ▷ alcanzar la cima de la montaña to reach the top of the mountain ❸ to find ▷ alcanzar la fama to find fame ❹ to pass ▷ ¿Me alcanzas las tijeras? Could you pass me the scissors?; **Con dos botellas alcanzará para todos.** Two bottles will be enough for all of us.

alcaucil nm (River Plate) artichoke

alcoba nf bedroom

> Be careful! **alcoba** does not mean **alcove**.

alcohol nm alcohol; **cerveza sin alcohol** non-alcoholic beer

alcohólico, -a adj alcoholic

aldea nf village

aldeano, -a nm/f villager

alegrar vb [25] to cheer up; **Me alegra que hayas venido.** I'm glad you've come.; **alegrarse** to be glad; **alegrarse de algo** to be glad about something; **Me alegro de oír que estás bien.** I'm glad to hear that you're well.; **alegrarse por alguien** to be happy for somebody

alegre adj cheerful; **Estoy muy alegre.** I'm feeling very happy.

alegría nf Sentí una gran alegría. I was really happy.; **¡Qué alegría!** How lovely!

alejarse vb [25] to move away ▷ Aléjate un poco del fuego. Move a bit further away from the fire.; **El barco se iba alejando de la costa.** The boat was getting further and further away from the coast.

alemán (falemana, mpl **alemanes)** adj, nm/f German ▷ nm (language) German

Alemania nf Germany

alentador, a adj encouraging

alergia nf allergy; **la alergia al polen** hay fever

alerta adj, nf, adv alert; **dar la alerta** to give the alert; **estar alerta** to be alert

aleta nf ❶ (of fish) fin ❷ (for diving) flipper ❸ (of car) wing

alfabeto nm alphabet

alfarería nf pottery

alfarero, -a nm/f potter

alféizar nm sill

alfil nm bishop

alfiler nm pin

alfombra nf ❶ rug ❷ carpet

alfombrilla nf mat

a
b
c
d
e
f
g
h
i
j
k
l
m
n
ñ
o
p
q
r
s
t
u
v
w
x
y
z

algas nfpl seaweed sg

algo pron ❶ something ▷ *Algo se está quemando.* Something is burning. ▷ *¿Quieres algo de comer?* Would you like something to eat? ▷ *¿Te pasa algo?* Is something the matter?; **Aún queda algo de café.** There's still some coffee left. ❷ anything ▷ *¿Algo más?* Anything else? ▷ *¿Has visto algo que te guste?* Have you seen anything you like?; **algo así como** a bit like; **o algo así** or something of the sort; **Por algo será.** There must be a reason for it.
▶ adv rather

algodón (pl algodones) nm cotton ▷ *ropa de algodón* cotton clothes; **Me puse algodones en los oídos.** I put cotton wool in my ears.

alguien pron ❶ somebody ▷ *Alguien llama a la puerta.* There's somebody knocking at the door. ❷ anybody ▷ *¿Conoces a alguien aquí?* Do you know anybody here?

algún (f alguna, mpl algunos) adj ❶ some ▷ *Algún día iré.* I'll go there some day. ❷ any ▷ *¿Compraste algún cuadro?* Did you buy any pictures?; **¿Quieres alguna cosa más?** Was there anything else?; **algún que otro ...** the odd ... ▷ *He leído algún que otro libro sobre el tema.* I've read the odd book on the subject.

alguno, -a pron ❶ somebody ▷ *Siempre hay alguno que se queja.* There's always somebody who complains.; **Algunos piensan que no ocurrió así.** Some people think that it didn't happen like that.

❷ one ▷ *Tiene que haber sido alguno de ellos.* It must have been one of them. ▷ *Tiene que estar en alguna de estas cajas.* It must be in one of these boxes. ❸ some ▷ *Son tantas maletas que alguna siempre se pierde.* There are so many suitcases that some inevitably get lost.; **Solo conozco a algunos de los vecinos.** I only know some of the neighbours. ❹ any ▷ *Necesito una aspirina. ¿Te queda alguna?* I need an aspirin. Have you got any left? ▷ *Si alguno quiere irse que se vaya.* If any of them want to leave, fine. ▷ *¿Lo sabe alguno de vosotros?* Do any of you know?

aliado, -a nm/f ally

alianza nf ❶ alliance ▷ *formar una alianza* to form an alliance ❷ wedding ring

aliarse vb [21] aliarse con alguien to form an alliance with somebody

alicates nmpl pliers

aliento nm breath ▷ *Tengo mal aliento.* I've got bad breath.; **Llegué sin aliento.** I arrived out of breath.

aligerar vb [25] to make ... lighter; **¡Aligera o llegaremos tarde!** Hurry up or we'll be late!

alimentación nf diet ▷ *Hay que cuidar la alimentación.* You need to be sensible about your diet.; **una tienda de alimentación** a grocer's shop

alimentar vb [25] to feed ▷ *alimentar a un niño* to feed a child; **Esto no alimenta.** That's not very nutritious.; **alimentarse de algo** to live on something

alimento nm food; **alimentos congelados** frozen food sg; **Las legumbres tienen mucho alimento.** Pulses are very nutritious.

alineación (pl **alineaciones**) nf line-up

aliñar vb [**25**] to season

aliño nm dressing

aliviar vb [**25**] to make...better

alivio nm relief; **¡Qué alivio!** What a relief!

allá adv there ▷ allá arriba up there; **más allá** further on; **Échate un poco más allá.** Move over that way a bit.; **más allá de** beyond; **¡Allá tú!** That's up to you!; **el más allá** the next world

allanar vb [**25**] to level

allí adv there ▷ Allí está. There it is.; **Allí viene tu hermana.** Here comes your sister.; **allí abajo** down there; **allí mismo** right there; **Marta es de por allí.** Marta comes from somewhere around there.

alma nf soul; **Lo siento en el alma.** I'm really sorry.

almacén (pl **almacenes**) nm store; **unos grandes almacenes** a department store

almacenar vb [**25**] to store

almeja nf clam

almendra nf almond

almíbar nm syrup; **en almíbar** in syrup

almirante nm admiral

almohada nf pillow

almohadilla nf cushion

almorzar vb [**3**] to have lunch; **¿Qué has almorzado?** What did you have for lunch?

almuerzo vb see **almorzar**
▶ nm lunch

aló excl (LatAm) hello!

alocado, -a adj crazy ▷ una decisión alocada a crazy decision; **una chica con un poco alocada** a rather silly girl

alojamiento nm accommodation

alojarse vb [**25**] to stay

alpargata nf espadrille

Alpes nmpl the Alps

alpinismo nm mountaineering

alpinista nmf mountaineer

alquilar vb [**25**] ❶ to rent
▷ Alquilaremos un apartamento en la playa. We'll rent an apartment near the beach. ❷ to let ▷ Alquilan habitaciones a estudiantes. They let rooms to students.; **'se alquila'** 'to let' ❸ to hire ▷ Alquilamos un coche. We hired a car.

alquiler nm rent ▷ pagar el alquiler to pay the rent; **un piso de alquiler** a rented flat; **un coche de alquiler** a hire car; **alquiler de automóviles** car-hire

alrededor adv alrededor de (1) around ▷ El satélite gira alrededor de la Tierra. The satellite goes around the Earth. ▷ A su alrededor todos gritaban. Everybody around him was shouting. (2) about ▷ Deben de ser alrededor de las dos. It must be about two o'clock.

alrededores nmpl Ocurrió en los alrededores de Madrid.

It happened near Madrid.; **Hay muchas tiendas en los alrededores del museo.** There are a lot of shops in the area around the museum.

alta *nf* **dar de alta a alguien** to discharge somebody; **darse de alta** to join

altar *nm* altar

altavoz (*pl* **altavoces**) *nm* loudspeaker

alterar *vb* [25] to change ▷ *Alteraron el orden.* They changed the order.; **alterar el orden público** to cause a breach of the peace; **alterarse** to get upset

alternar *vb* [25] **alternar algo con algo** to alternate something with something; **Alterna con gente del teatro.** He mixes with people from the theatre.

alternativa *nf* alternative; **No tenemos otra alternativa.** We have no alternative.

alterno, -a *adj* alternate ▷ *en días alternos* on alternate days

altibajos *nmpl* ups and downs

altitud *nf* altitude

alto, -a *adj* ❶ tall ▷ *Es un chico muy alto.* He's a very tall boy. ▷ *un edificio muy alto* a very tall building ❷ high ▷ *El Everest es la montaña más alta del mundo.* Everest is the highest mountain in the world. ▷ *Sacó notas altas en todos los exámenes.* He got high marks in all his exams. ❸ loud ▷ *La música está demasiado alta.* The music's too loud.; **a altas horas de la noche** in

the middle of the night; **Celebraron la victoria por todo lo alto.** They celebrated the victory in style.; **alta fidelidad** hi-fi; **una familia de clase alta** an upper-class family

▷ *adv* high ▷ *subir muy alto* to go up very high; **Pepe habla muy alto.** Pepe has got a very loud voice.; **¡Más alto, por favor!** Speak up, please!; **Pon el volumen más alto.** Turn the volume up.

▷ *excl* stop!

▷ *nm* **La pared tiene dos metros de alto.** The wall is two metres high.; **en lo alto de** at the top of; **hacer un alto** to stop ▷ *A las dos haremos un alto para comer.* We'll stop to have lunch at two o'clock.; **pasar algo por alto** to overlook something; **el alto el fuego** ceasefire

altoparlante *nm* (*LatAm*) loudspeaker

altura *nf* height ▷ *La pared tiene dos metros de altura.* The wall's two metres high.; **cuando llegues a la altura del hospital** when you reach the hospital; **a estas alturas** at this stage

alubias *nfpl* beans

alucinar *vb* [25] to be amazed ▷ *Alucino con las cosas que haces.* I'm amazed at the things you do.

alud *nm* avalanche

aludir *vb* [58] to refer ▷ *No aludió a lo del otro día.* He didn't refer to that business the other day.; **No se dio por aludida.** She didn't take the hint.

aluminio nm aluminium

alumno, -a nm/f pupil

alusión (pl alusiones) nf hacer alusión a to refer to

alverja nf (LatAm) pea

alza nf rise ▷ un alza de los precios a rise in prices

alzar vb [13] to raise; **alzarse** to rise

ama nf owner; **ama de casa** housewife

Word for word, **ama de casa** means 'owner of house'.

ama de llaves housekeeper

Word for word, **ama de llaves** means 'owner of keys'.

amable adj kind ▷ Es usted muy amable. You're very kind.

amamantar vb [25] ❶ to breast-feed ❷ to suckle

amanecer vb [12] ❶ to get light ▷ Amanece a las siete. It gets light at seven. ❷ to wake up ▷ El niño amaneció con fiebre. The boy woke up with a temperature.
▶ nm dawn

amante nmf lover; **amantes del cine** cinema lovers

amapola nf poppy

amar vb [25] to love

amargado, -a adj bitter; **estar amargado por algo** to be bitter about something

amargar vb [37] to spoil; **amargar la vida a alguien** to make somebody's life a misery; **amargarse** to get upset

amargo, -a adj bitter

amarillo adj, nm yellow

amarrar vb [25] ❶ to moor ❷ to tie up ❸ (LatAm) to do up

amateur (pl amateurs) adj, nmf amateur

Amazonas nm the Amazon

ámbar nm amber

ambición (pl ambiciones) nf ambition

ambicioso, -a adj ambitious

ambientador nm air freshener

ambiente nm atmosphere ▷ Se respira un ambiente tenso. There's a tense atmosphere.; **Había un ambiente muy cargado en la habitación.** It was very stuffy in the room.; **Necesito cambiar de ambiente.** I need a change of scene.; **el medio ambiente** the environment

ambiguo, -a adj ambiguous

ámbito nm scope

ambos, -as pron both ▷ Vinieron ambos. They both came. ▷ Ambos tenéis los ojos azules. You've both got blue eyes.

ambulancia nf ambulance

ambulatorio nm out-patients' department

amén excl amen

amenace vb see **amenazar**

amenaza nf threat

amenazar vb [13] to threaten

ameno, -a adj enjoyable

América nf the Americas; **América Central** Central America; **América Latina** Latin America; **América del Sur** South America; **el español de América** Latin American Spanish

americana nf ❶ jacket ❷ American

americano adj, nm American

ametralladora nf machine gun

amígdalas nfpl tonsils

amigo, -a nm/f friend; **hacerse amigos** to become friends; **ser muy amigos** to be good friends

amistad nf friendship; **hacer amistad con alguien** to make friends with somebody; **las amistades** friends

amistoso, -a adj friendly

amo nm owner ▷ *el amo del perro* the dog's owner

amontonar vb [25] to pile up; **Se me amontona el trabajo.** My work's piling up.

amor nm love; **hacer el amor** to make love; **amor propio** self-esteem

amoratado, -a adj ❶ blue ❷ black and blue

amortiguar vb [25, gu → gü before e and i] ❶ to cushion ❷ to muffle

ampliar vb [21] ❶ to expand ❷ to enlarge ❸ to extend

amplificador nm amplifier

amplio, -a adj ❶ wide ▷ *una calle muy amplia* a very wide street ❷ spacious ▷ *una habitación amplia* a spacious room ❸ loose ▷ *ropa amplia* loose clothing

ampolla nf blister

amputar vb [25] to amputate

amueblar vb [25] to furnish; **un piso sin amueblar** an unfurnished flat

analfabeto, -a adj illiterate

analgésico nm painkiller

análisis (pl análisis) nm ❶ analysis ❸ test ▷ *un análisis de sangre* a blood test

analizar vb [13] to analyse

anarquía nf anarchy

anatomía nf anatomy

ancho, -a adj ❶ wide ▷ *una calle ancha* a wide street ❷ loose ▷ *Le gusta llevar ropa ancha.* He likes to wear loose clothing.; **Me está ancho el vestido.** The dress is too big for me.; **Es ancho de espaldas.** He's broad-shouldered. ▶ nm width ▷ *el ancho de la tela* the width of the cloth; **¿Cuánto mide de ancho?** How wide is it?; **Mide tres metros de ancho.** It's three metres wide.

anchoa nf anchovy

anchura nf width; **¿Qué anchura tiene?** How wide is it?; **Tiene tres metros de anchura.** It's three metres wide.

anciana nf elderly woman

anciano, -a adj elderly ▶ nm elderly man; **los ancianos** elderly people

ancla nf anchor

anda excl ❶ well I never! ❷ come on; **¡Anda ya!** You're not serious!

Andalucía nf Andalusia

andaluz, a (mpl andaluces) adj, nm/f Andalusian

andamio nm scaffolding

andar vb [4] ❶ to walk; **Iremos andando a la estación.** We'll walk to the station. ❷ to be ▷ *Últimamente ando muy liado.* I've been very busy lately.; **andar mal de dinero** to be short of money; **Anda por los cuarenta.** He's about forty. ❸ (clock, car) to go; **¡No andes ahí!** Keep away from there!; **Ándate con cuidado.** Take care.

andén (*pl* **andenes**) *nm* platform

Andes *nmpl* the Andes

anduve *vb see* **andar**

anécdota *nf* anecdote

anemia *nf* anaemia

anestesia *nf* anaesthetic; **poner anestesia a alguien** to give somebody an anaesthetic

anfiteatro *nm* ❶ amphitheatre ❷ lecture theatre

ángel *nm* angel

anginas *nfpl* **tener anginas** to have tonsillitis

ángulo *nm* angle

anillo *nm* ring; **un anillo de boda** a wedding ring

animado, -a *adj* ❶ cheerful ▷ *Últimamente parece que está más animada.* She has seemed more cheerful lately. ❷ lively ▷ *Fue una fiesta muy animada.* It was a very lively party.; **dibujos animados** cartoons

animador, a *nm/f* ❶ entertainments officer ❷ animator

animal *nm* animal; **los animales domésticos** pets

animar *vb* [25] ❶ (*person*) to cheer up ❷ (*team*) to cheer on ❸ (*party*) to liven up; **animar a alguien a que haga algo** to encourage somebody to do something; **animarse** to cheer up; **animarse a hacer algo** to make up one's mind to do something

ánimo *nm* **Está muy mal de ánimo.** He's in very low spirits.;

dar ánimos a alguien (**1**) to cheer somebody up (**2**) to give somebody moral support; **tener ánimos para hacer algo** to feel like doing something
▶ *excl* cheer up! ▷ *¡Ánimo, chaval, que no es el fin del mundo!* Cheer up mate, it's not the end of the world!

anís (*pl* **anises**) *nm* anisette

aniversario *nm* anniversary ▷ *su aniversario de boda* their wedding anniversary

anoche *adv* last night; **antes de anoche** the night before last

anochecer *vb* [12] to get dark ▷ *En invierno anochece muy temprano.* It gets dark very early in winter.

anónimo, -a *adj* anonymous ▶ *nm* anonymous threat

anorak (*pl* **anoraks**) *nm* anorak

anormal *adj* odd ▷ *Yo no noté nada anormal en su comportamiento.* I didn't notice anything odd about his behaviour.; **¡Soy anormal!** What a fool I am!

anotar *vb* [25] ❶ to take a note of ❷ to score

ansiedad *nf* anxiety

ansioso, -a *adj* **estar ansioso por hacer algo** to be eager to do something

Antártico *nm* the Antarctic

ante *prep* ❶ before ▷ *Le da vergüenza aparecer ante tanta gente.* She's shy about appearing before so many people. ❷ in the face of ▷ *Mantuvo la calma ante el peligro.* He remained calm in the face of danger.
▶ *nm* suede

anteanoche *adv* the night before last

anteayer *adv* the day before yesterday

antecedentes *nmpl* **antecedentes penales** criminal record *sg*

antelación *nf* **hacer una reserva con antelación** to make an advance booking; **Deben avisarle con un mes de antelación.** They must give you a month's notice.

antemano *adv* **de antemano** in advance

antena *nf* aerial; **una antena parabólica** a satellite dish

anteojos *nmpl* (LatAm) glasses; **los anteojos de sol** sunglasses

antepasados *nmpl* ancestors

anterior *adj* ❶ before ▷ *La semana anterior llovió mucho.* It rained a lot the week before. ▷ *Su boda fue anterior a la nuestra.* Their wedding was before ours. ❷ front ▷ *las extremidades anteriores* the front limbs

anteriormente *adv* previously

antes *adv* ❶ before ▷ *Esta película ya la he visto antes.* I've seen this film before. ▷ *Él estaba aquí antes que yo.* He was here before me. ▷ *la noche antes* the night before; **El supermercado está justo antes del semáforo.** The supermarket is just before the lights.; **antes de** before ▷ *antes de ir al teatro* before going to the theatre ▷ *antes de que te vayas* before you go ❷ first ▷ *Nosotros llegamos antes.* We arrived first.; **Antes no había**

tanto desempleo. There didn't use to be so much unemployment.; **cuanto antes mejor** the sooner the better; **lo antes posible** as soon as possible; **antes de nada** first and foremost; **Antes que verle prefiero esperar aquí.** I'd rather wait here than see him.

antibiótico *nm* antibiotic

anticipado, -a *adj* early ▷ *convocar elecciones anticipadas* to call early elections; **por anticipado** in advance ▷ *pagar por anticipado* to pay in advance

anticipar *vb* **[25]** ❶ to foresee ❷ (event) to bring...forward ❸ to pay...in advance; **anticiparse a alguien** to get in before somebody; **Se anticipó a su tiempo.** He was ahead of his time.

anticipo *nm* advance ▷ *pedir un anticipo* to ask for an advance; **ser un anticipo de algo** to be a foretaste of something

anticonceptivo *adj, nm* contraceptive

anticuado, -a *adj* outdated

anticuaria *nf* antique dealer

anticuario *nm* ❶ antique shop ❷ antique dealer

antifaz (*pl* antifaces) *nm* mask

antiguamente *adv* ❶ in the past ❷ formerly

antigüedad *nf* **Es un monumento de gran antigüedad.** It's a very old monument.; **en la antigüedad** in ancient times; **las antigüedades** antiques; **una tienda de antigüedades** an antique shop

antiguo, -a adj ❶ old ▷ Este reloj es muy antiguo. This clock is very old. ❷ ancient ▷ Estudia historia antigua. He studies ancient history. ❸ former ▷ el antiguo secretario general del partido the former secretary general of the party

Antillas nfpl the West Indies

antipático, -a adj unfriendly

antiséptico adj, nm antiseptic

antojarse vb ❶ to feel like; **Siempre hace lo que se le antoja.** He always does what he feels like.; **Se me ha antojado un helado.** I really fancy an ice-cream.

antorcha nf torch

antropología nf anthropology

anual adj annual

anular vb [25] ❶ to call off ▷ Anularon el partido por la lluvia. The match was called off owing to the rain. ❷ (goal) to disallow ❸ (sentence) to overturn
▸ nm ring finger

anunciar vb [25] ❶ to advertise ❷ to announce

anuncio nm ❶ advertisement; **anuncios por palabras** small ads ❷ announcement

anzuelo nm hook

añadidura nf **por añadidura** in addition

añadir vb [58] to add

añicos nmpl **hacer algo añicos** to smash something to pieces; **hacerse añicos** to smash to pieces

año nm year ▷ Estuve allí el año pasado. I was there last year.; **el año que viene** next year; **el año**

escolar the school year; **¡Feliz Año Nuevo!** Happy New Year!; **los años 80** the 80s; **¿Cuántos años tiene?** How old is he?; **Tiene 15 años.** He's 15.

apagado, -a adj ❶ switched off ▷ La tele estaba apagada. The TV was switched off.

apagar vb [37] ❶ to switch off ❷ to put out; **apagar el fuego** to put the fire out

apagón (pl apagones) nm power cut

apañado, -a adj resourceful

apañarse vb [25] to manage ▷ ¿Podrás hacerlo solo? — Ya me apañaré. Can you do it on your own? — I'll manage.; **apañarse con algo** to make do with something ▷ Nos apañaremos con la comida que sobró. We can make do with the leftovers.

aparador nm ❶ sideboard ❷ (Mex) shop window

aparato nm **No sé manejar este aparato.** I don't know how to operate this.; **un aparato de televisión** a television; **los aparatos de gimnasia** the apparatus; **Fabrican aparatos electrónicos.** They make electronic equipment.; **un aparato electrodoméstico** an electrical appliance

aparcamiento nm ❶ car park ❷ parking place

aparcar vb [48] to park; **'prohibido aparcar'** 'no parking'

aparecer vb [12] ❶ to appear ❷ to turn up ❸ to come out

aparentar vb [**25**] to appear; **Aparenta más edad de la que tiene.** He looks older than he is.

aparente adj apparent

aparentemente adv apparently

apariencia nf **Tiene la apariencia de un profesor de universidad.** He looks like a university lecturer.; **guardar las apariencias** to keep up appearances

apartado, -a adj isolated
▶ nm section; **apartado de correos** PO box

apartamento nm apartment

apartar vb [**25**] ❶ to remove ▷ Lo apartaron del equipo. They removed him from the team. ❷ to move out of the way ▷ Aparta todas las sillas. Move all the chairs out of the way.; **¡Aparta!** Stand back! ❸ to set aside; **apartarse** to stand back

aparte adv separately; **La ropa que no valga ponla aparte.** Put the clothes that aren't any use on one side.; **aparte de (1)** apart from **(2)** as well as; **punto y aparte** full stop, new paragraph
▶ adj separate

apasionante adj exciting

apasionar vb [**25**] **Le apasiona el fútbol.** He's crazy about football.

apdo. abbr (= apartado de correos) PO box (= Post Office box)

apearse vb [**25**] **apearse de** to get off

apego nm **tener apego a algo** to be attached to something

apellidarse vb [**25**] **Se apellida Pérez.** His surname is Pérez.

apellido nm surname

In the Spanish-speaking world, most people have two surnames, the first being their father's first surname and the second being their mother's first surname. So if Juan Mata Pérez marries María Valle García, any children will have Mata Valle as their surnames. Although she would keep her own surnames, their mother could also be referred to as la señora de Mata.

apenado, -a adj ❶ sad ❷ (LatAm) embarrassed

apenas adv, conj ❶ hardly ❷ hardly ever ❸ barely ❹ as soon as

apendicitis nf appendicitis

aperitivo nm aperitif

apertura nf opening ▷ el acto de apertura the opening ceremony

apestar vb [**25**] to stink; **apestar a** to stink of

apetecer vb [**12**] **¿Te apetece una tortilla?** Do you fancy an omelette?; **No, gracias, ahora no me apetece.** No, thanks, I don't feel like it just now.

apetito nm appetite ▷ Eso te va a quitar el apetito. You won't have any appetite left.; **No tengo apetito.** I'm not hungry.

apetitoso, -a adj ❶ tasty ❷ tempting

apio nm celery

aplastante adj overwhelming

aplastar vb [**25**] to squash

aplaudir vb [**58**] to clap

aplauso nm applause; **Los aplausos duraron varios minutos.** The applause lasted for several minutes.

aplazar vb [13] to postpone

aplicación (pl aplicaciones) nf application

aplicado, -a adj hard-working

aplicar vb [48] ❶ to apply ❷ to enforce

apoderarse vb [25] **apoderarse de un lugar** to take over a place; **Se apoderaron de las joyas.** They went off with the jewels.

apodo nm nickname

apogeo nm height ▷ **en el apogeo de su poder** at the height of his power; **La fiesta estaba en su apogeo.** The party was in full swing.

aportar vb [25] to provide

aposta adv on purpose

apostar vb [11] to bet; **apostar por algo** to bet on something; **¿Qué te apuestas a que ...?** What's the betting that ...

apóstrofo nm apostrophe

apoyar vb [25] ❶ to lean ▷ Apoya el espejo contra la pared. Lean the mirror against the wall. ❷ to rest ▷ Apoya la espalda en este cojín. Rest your back against this cushion. ❸ to support ▷ Todos mis compañeros me apoyan. All my colleagues support me.; **apoyarse** to lean

apoyo nm support

apreciar vb [25] **apreciar a alguien** to be fond of somebody; **Aprecio mucho mi tiempo libre.** I really value my free time.

aprecio nm **tener aprecio a alguien** to be fond of somebody

aprender vb [8] to learn; **aprender a hacer algo** to learn to do something; **aprender algo de memoria** to learn something by heart

aprendiz, a (mpl aprendices) nm/f trainee ▷ Es aprendiz de mecánico. He's a trainee mechanic.; **estar de aprendiz** to be doing an apprenticeship

aprendizaje nm learning ▷ dificultades de aprendizaje learning difficulties

aprensivo, -a adj overanxious

apresurado, -a adj hasty

apresurarse vb [25] **No nos apresuremos.** Let's not be hasty.; **Me apresuré a sugerir que ...** I hastily suggested that ...

apretado, -a adj ❶ tight ❷ cramped

apretar vb [39] ❶ to tighten ❷ to press; **apretar el gatillo** to press the trigger; **Me aprietan los zapatos.** My shoes are too tight.; **Apretaos un poco para que me siente yo también.** Move up a bit so I can sit down too.

aprieto nm **estar en un aprieto** to be in a tight spot

aprisa adv fast; **¡Aprisa!** Hurry up!

aprobar vb [11] ❶ to pass ▷ aprobar un examen to pass an exam ▷ Han aprobado una ley antitabaco. They've passed an anti-smoking law.; **aprobar por los pelos** to scrape through ❷ to approve ❸ to approve of

apropiado, -a adj suitable

aprovechar vb [25] ❶ to make good use of ▷ No aprovecha el tiempo. He doesn't make good use of his time. ❷ to use; **aprovecho la ocasión para decirles ...** I'd like to take this opportunity to tell you ...; **Aprovecharé ahora que estoy solo para llamarle.** I'll call him now while I'm on my own.; **¡Que aproveche!** Enjoy your meal!; **aprovecharse de** to take advantage of

aproximadamente adv about

aproximado, -a adj approximate

aproximarse vb [25] to approach

apruebo vb see **aprobar**

aptitud nf ❶ suitability ❷ aptitude

apto, -a adj **ser apto para algo** to be suitable for something

apuesta nf bet ▷ Hicimos una apuesta. We had a bet.

apuesto vb see **apostar**

apuntar vb [25] ❶ to write down ▷ Apúntalo o se te olvidará. Write it down or you'll forget.; **Me apuntó con el dedo.** He pointed at me.; **Luis me apuntó en el examen.** Luis gave me the answers in the exam.; **apuntarse** to put one's name down; **apuntarse a un curso** to enrol on a course; **¡Yo me apunto!** Count me in!

▌ Be careful **apuntar** does not mean to appoint.

apuntes nmpl notes; **tomar apuntes** to take notes

apuñalar vb [25] to stab

apurado, -a adj (situation) difficult; **Si estás apurado de dinero, dímelo.** If you're short of money, tell me.; **estar apurado** to feel embarrassed

apurar vb [25] to finish up ▷ Apura la cerveza que nos vamos. Finish up your beer and let's go.; **apurarse** (1) to hurry up (2) to worry

apuro nm fix ▷ El dinero de la herencia los sacó del apuro. The money they inherited got them out of the fix.; **Pasé muchos apuros para salir del agua.** I had a lot of trouble getting out of the water.; **Me da mucho apuro no llevar ningún regalo.** I feel very embarrassed about not taking a present.; **estar en apuros** to be in trouble

aquel (f **aquella**) adj that ▷ Me gusta más aquella mesa. I prefer that table.

▷ **that one**

aquello pron **aquello que hay allí** that thing over there; **Me fui; aquello era insoportable.** I left. It was just unbearable.; **¿Qué fue de aquello del viaje alrededor del mundo?** What ever happened to that round-the-world trip idea?

aquellos, -as adj pl those ▷ ¿Ves aquellas montañas? Can you see those mountains?

▷ **pron pl those ones** ▷ Aquellos de allí son mejores. Those ones over there are better.

aquí adv ❶ here; **aquí abajo** down here; **aquí arriba** up here; **aquí mismo** right here; **por aquí** (1) around here (2) this way

❷ now; **de aquí en adelante** from now on; **de aquí a siete días** a week from now; **hasta aquí (1)** up to here **(2)** up to now

árabe adj, nmf Arab
▶ nm (language) Arabic

Arabia nf Arabia **Saudí** Saudi Arabia

arado nm plough

araña nf spider

arañar vb **[25]** to scratch

arañazo nm scratch

arar vb **[25]** to plough

árbitro, -a nm/f referee

árbol nm tree; **el árbol de Navidad** the Christmas tree; **un árbol genealógico** a family tree

arbusto nm ❶ bush ❷ shrub

arca nf chest; **el Arca de Noé** Noah's Ark

arcadas nfpl **Me dieron arcadas con el olor.** The smell made me retch.

arcén (pl arcenes) nm hard shoulder

archivador nm ❶ filing cabinet ❷ file

archivar vb **[25]** to file

archivo nm ❶ archive ❷ file; **los archivos policiales** police files

arcilla nf clay

arco nm ❶ (for arrows, violin) bow ❷ arch; **el arco iris** the rainbow

Word for word, **arco iris** means 'iris arch'.

arder vb **[8]** to burn; **¡La sopa está ardiendo!** The soup's boiling hot!

ardilla nf squirrel

ardor nm passion; **Defiende sus ideas con ardor.** He defends his ideas passionately.; **tener ardor de estómago** to have heartburn

área nf ❶ area; **en distintas áreas del país** in different parts of the country; **un área de descanso** a lay-by; **un área de servicios** a service area ❷ penalty area

arena nf sand; **arenas movedizas** quicksand sg

Word for word, **arenas movedizas** means 'moving sands'.

arenque nm herring; **arenques ahumados** kippers

Argelia nf Algeria

argelino, -a adj, nm/f Algerian

Argentina nf Argentina

argentino, -a adj, nm/f Argentinian

argolla nf ring

argot (pl argots) nm ❶ slang ❷ jargon

argumento nm ❶ argument ❷ plot

árido, -a adj arid

Aries nm (sign) Aries; **Soy aries.** I'm Aries.

aristócrata nmf aristocrat

arma nf ❶ weapon; **un fabricante de armas** an arms manufacturer ❷ gun ▶ **Nos apuntaba con un arma.** He pointed a gun at us.; **un arma de fuego** a firearm

armada nf navy

armadura nf armour; **una armadura medieval** a medieval suit of armour

armamento nm (weapons) arms pl

armar vb **[25]** ❶ to arm ❷ (flatpack furniture) to assemble ❸ to make

▷ *Los vecinos de arriba arman mucho jaleo.* Our upstairs neighbours make a lot of noise.; **Si no aceptan voy a armar un escándalo.** If they don't agree I'm going to make a fuss.; **armarse un lío** to get in a muddle; **armarse de paciencia** to be patient; **armarse de valor** to summon up one's courage; **Se armó la gorda.** *(informal)* All hell broke loose.

armario *nm* ❶ cupboard; **un armario de cocina** a kitchen cupboard ❷ wardrobe

armazón *(pl* armazones*) nm* frame

armonía *nf* harmony

armónica *nf* mouth organ

aro *nm* ❶ ring ▷ **los aros olímpicos** the Olympic rings ❷ hoop

aroma *nm* aroma

aromaterapia *nf* aromatherapy

arpa *nf* harp

arqueología *nf* archaeology

arqueólogo, -a *nm/f* archaeologist

arquero, -a *nm/f (LatAm)* goalkeeper

arquitecto, -a *nm/f* architect

arquitectura *nf* architecture

arrancar *vb* **[48]** ❶ (plant) to pull up; **El viento arrancó varios árboles.** Several trees were uprooted by the wind. ❷ (nail, thorn) to pull out ❸ (page, sheet) to tear out ❹ (label, plaster) to pull off ❺ to snatch ▷ *Me lo arrancaron de las manos.* They snatched it from me.; **Arranca y vámonos.** Start

the engine and let's get going.; **arrancarle información a alguien** to drag information out of somebody

arrasar *vb* **[25]** ❶ to sweep away ❷ to destroy; **Los socialistas arrasaron en las elecciones.** The socialists swept the board in the elections.

arrastrar *vb* **[25]** ❶ to drag ❷ to sweep along ❸ to trail on the ground; **arrastrarse** to crawl

arrebatar *vb* **[25]** snatch ▷ *Me lo arrebató de las manos.* He snatched it from me.

arrecife *nm* reef; **los arrecifes de coral** coral reefs

arreglar *vb* **[25]** ❶ (appliance, object) to fix ❷ (house, room) to do up ❸ (problem) to sort out; **Deja tu cuarto arreglado antes de salir.** Leave your room tidy before going out.; **arreglarse (1)** to get ready **(2)** to work out **(3)** to manage; **arreglarse el pelo** to do one's hair; **arreglárselas para hacer algo** to manage to do something

arreglo *nm* ❶ repair; **Esta tele no tiene arreglo.** This TV is unrepairable.; **Este problema no tiene arreglo.** There's no solution to this problem. ❷ compromise ▷ *Llegamos a un arreglo.* We reached a compromise.; **con arreglo a** in accordance with

arrepentirse *vb* **[51] arrepentirse de algo** to regret something; **arrepentirse de haber hecho algo** to regret doing something

arrestar *vb* **[25]** to arrest

arresto nm arrest ▷ un arresto domiciliario house arrest

arriba adv ❶ above ▷ Visto desde arriba parece más pequeño. Seen from above it looks smaller.; **Pon esos libros arriba del todo.** Put those books on top.; **la parte de arriba del biquini** the bikini top ❷ upstairs ▷ Arriba están los dormitorios. The bedrooms are upstairs. ▷ los vecinos de arriba our upstairs neighbours.; **allí arriba** up there; **más arriba** further up; **ir calle arriba** to go up the street; **Tenemos bolsos de 20 euros para arriba.** We've got bags from 20 euros upwards.; **arriba de (1)** (LatAm) on top of **(2)** (LatAm) above; **mirar a alguien de arriba abajo** to look somebody up and down

arriesgado, -a adj risky

arriesgar vb [37] to risk ▷ Carlos arriesgó su vida para salvar a su perro. Carlos risked his life to save his dog.; **arriesgarse** to take a risk; **arriesgarse a hacer algo** to risk doing something

arrimar vb [25] to bring...closer ▷ Arrima tu silla a la mía. Bring your chair closer to mine.; **Vamos a arrimar la mesa a la pared.** Let's put the table by the wall.; **arrimarse** to get close ▷ Al aparcar procura arrimarte a la acera. Try to get close to the pavement when parking.; **Arrímate a mí.** Come closer.

arroba nf @ symbol

arrodillarse vb [25] to kneel down

arrogante adj arrogant

arrojar vb [25] ❶ to throw ❷ to dump ▷ 'Prohibido arrojar basuras' 'No dumping'

arropar vb [25] ❶ to tuck in ▷ Voy a arropar al niño. I'll go and tuck the baby in. ❷ to wrap up ▷ Arrópate bien. Wrap her up well.; **arrópate bien (1)** tuck yourself up warmly **(2)** wrap up well

arroyo nm stream

arroz (pl arroces) nm rice; **arroz blanco** white rice; **arroz con leche** rice pudding

> Word for word, **arroz con leche** means 'rice with milk'.

arruga nf ❶ (in skin) wrinkle ❷ (in paper, clothing) crease

arrugarse vb [37] ❶ (skin) to get wrinkled ❷ to get creased ▷ Procura que no se arrugue el sobre. Try not to let the envelope get creased.

arruinar vb [25] to ruin; **arruinarse** to be ruined

arte (pl artes) nm ❶ art; **el arte abstracto** abstract art; **el arte dramático** drama ❷ flair ▷ Tiene arte para la cocina. She has a flair for cooking.; **por arte de magia** by magic

artefacto nm device ▷ un artefacto explosivo an explosive device

arteria nf artery

artesana nf craftswoman

artesanía nf la artesanía local local crafts; **objetos de artesanía** hand-crafted goods

artesano nm craftsman

ártico, -a adj arctic

articulación (pl articulaciones) nf joint

artículo nm article ▷ el artículo determinado the definite article ▷ el artículo indeterminado the indefinite article; **artículos de lujo** luxury goods; **artículos de escritorio** stationery; **artículos de tocador** toiletries

artificial adj artificial

artista nmf (painter, sculptor) artist

arveja nf (LatAm) pea

arzobispo nm archbishop

as nm ▷ el as de picas the ace of spades; **ser un as de la cocina** to be a wizard at cooking

asa nf handle

asado, -a adj roast ▷ pollo asado roast chicken
▶ nm ❶ roast ❷ (LatAm) barbecue

asaltar vb [25] ❶ to storm ❷ to raid ❸ to mug

asalto nm ❶ raid ▷ un asalto a una gasolinera a raid on a petrol station; **durante el asalto al parlamento** during the storming of parliament ❷ (in boxing) round

asamblea nf ❶ meeting ❷ assembly

asar vb [25] to roast; **asar algo a la parrilla** to grill something; **Me aso de calor.** I'm boiling.; **Aquí se asa uno.** It's boiling in here.

ascender vb [20] ❶ to rise ▷ El globo comenzó a ascender. The balloon began to rise. ❷ to be promoted; **ascender a primera división** to go up to the first division

ascenso nm promotion

ascensor nm lift

asciendo vb see **ascender**

asco nm **El ajo me da asco.** I think garlic's revolting.; **¡Puaj! ¡Qué asco!** Yuk! How revolting!; **La casa está hecha un asco.** The house is filthy.

asegurar vb [25] ❶ to insure ❷ to assure ▷ No he sido yo. Te lo aseguro. It wasn't me, I assure you.; **Ella asegura que no lo conoce.** She says that she doesn't know him. ❸ to fasten securely; **asegurarse de** to make sure

aseo nm **el cuarto de aseo** the toilet

> Word for word, **cuarto de aseo** means 'room of cleanliness'.

el aseo personal personal hygiene; **los aseos** the toilets

asequible adj ❶ affordable ❷ achievable

asesinar vb [25] to murder

asesinato nm murder

asesino, -a nm/f murderer

asesor, a nm/f consultant; **asesor fiscal** tax consultant; **asesor de imagen** public relations consultant

asfalto nm tarmac

asfixia nf suffocation

asfixiarse vb [25] to suffocate

así adv ❶ like this ❷ like that; **un tomate así de grande** a tomato this big; **Así es la vida.** That's life.; **así, así** so-so; **así es** that's right; **¿No es así?** Isn't that so?; **así que ... so ...; ... o así ... or thereabouts; y así sucesivamente** and so on

Asia nf Asia

asiático, -a adj, nm/f Asian

asiento nm seat; **el asiento delantero** the front seat; **el asiento trasero** the back seat

asignatura nf subject ▷ Tiene dos asignaturas pendientes. He's got two subjects to retake.

asilo nm ❶ home; **un asilo de ancianos** an old people's home; **un asilo de pobres** a hostel for the poor ❷ asylum ▷ asilo político political asylum

asimilar vb [25] to assimilate; **El cambio es grande y cuesta asimilarlo.** It's a big change and it takes getting used to.

asistencia nf **asistencia médica (1)** medical attention **(2)** medical care; **asistencia técnica** technical support

asistenta nf cleaner

asistente nmf assistant; **asistente social** social worker; **los asistentes al acto** those present at the ceremony

asistir vb [58] ❶ to go ▷ No asistieron a la ceremonia. They didn't go to the ceremony. ❷ to treat ▷ Le asistió un médico que había de guardia. He was treated by a duty doctor.

asma nf asthma

asociación (pl asociaciones) nf association

asociar vb [25] to associate; **asociarse** to go into partnership

asolearse vb [25] (LatAm) to sunbathe

asomar vb [25] **Te asoma el pañuelo por el bolsillo.** Your handkerchief's sticking out of your pocket.; **No asomes la cabeza por la ventanilla.** Don't lean out of the window.; **Me asomé a la terraza a ver quién gritaba.** I went out onto the balcony to see who was shouting.; **Asómate a la ventana.** Look out of the window.

asombrar vb [25] to amaze ▷ Me asombra que no lo sepas. I'm amazed you don't know.; **asombrarse** to be amazed ▷ Se asombró de lo tarde que era. He was amazed at how late it was.

asombro nm amazement

asombroso, -a adj amazing

aspecto nm ❶ appearance ❷ aspect; **tener buen aspecto (1)** (person) to look well **(2)** (food) to look good

áspero, -a adj ❶ rough ❷ harsh

aspiradora nf vacuum cleaner

aspirar vb [25] ❶ to breathe in; **aspirar a hacer algo** to hope to do something ❷ (LatAm) to hoover

aspirina nf aspirin

asqueroso, -a adj ❶ (food, smell) disgusting ❷ (kitchen, hands) filthy ▷ Esta cocina está asquerosa. This kitchen is filthy. ❸ horrible ▷ Esta gente es asquerosa. They're horrible people.

astilla nf splinter

astro nm star

astrología nf astrology

astronauta nmf astronaut

astronomía nf astronomy

astuto, -a adj clever

asumir vb [58] to accept; **Asumo toda la responsabilidad.** I take full responsibility.; **No estoy dispuesta a asumir ese riesgo.** I'm not prepared to take that risk.

asunto *nm* matter ▷ *Es un asunto muy delicado.* It's a very delicate matter.; **el ministro de asuntos exteriores** the minister for foreign affairs; **No me gusta que se metan en mis asuntos.** I don't like anyone meddling in my affairs.; **¡Eso no es asunto tuyo!** That's none of your business!

asustar *vb* [25] ❶ to frighten ❷ to startle; **asustarse** to get frightened; **No te asustes.** Don't be frightened.

atacar *vb* [48] to attack

atado *nm* (River Plate) **un atado de cigarrillos** a packet of cigarettes

atajo *nm* short cut

ataque *nm* attack ▷ *un ataque contra alguien* an attack on somebody; **un ataque cardíaco** a heart attack; **Le dio un ataque de risa.** He burst out laughing.; **un ataque de nervios** a fit of panic

atar *vb* [25] to tie; **Átate los cordones.** Tie your shoelaces up.

atardecer *vb* [12] to get dark ▷ *Está atardeciendo.* It's getting dark.
 ▶ *nm* dusk; **al atardecer** at dusk

atareado, -a *adj* busy

atasco *nm* traffic jam

ataúd *nm* coffin

Atenas *nf* Athens

atención (*pl* atenciones) *nf* **Hay que poner más atención.** You should pay more attention.; **Escucha con atención.** He listens attentively.; **Me llamó la atención lo grande que era la casa.** I was struck by how big the house was.; **El director del colegio le llamó la atención.** The headmaster gave him a talking-to.; **Estás llamando la atención con ese sombrero.** You're attracting attention in that hat.
 ▶ *excl* Attention!; **¡Atención, por favor!** May I have your attention please?; **'¡Atención!'** 'Danger!'

atender *vb* [20] ❶ (in a bar, shop) to serve ▷ *¿Le atienden?* Are you being served? ❷ (in a bank, office) to attend to ▷ *Tengo que atender a un par de clientes.* I've got a couple of clients to attend to. ❸ to look after ▷ *atender a los enfermos* to look after the sick ❹ to pay attention to; **atender los consejos de alguien** to listen to somebody's advice

atentado *nm* attack ▷ *un atentado terrorista* a terrorist attack ▷ *un atentado suicida* a suicide attack

atentamente *adv* ❶ Yours sincerely ❷ Yours faithfully

atento, -a *adj* thoughtful ▷ *Es un chico muy atento.* He's a very thoughtful boy.; **Estaban atentos a las explicaciones del instructor.** They were listening attentively to the instructor's explanations.

aterrizaje *nm* landing; **un aterrizaje forzoso** an emergency landing

aterrizar *vb* [13] to land

atestado, -a *adj* packed ▷ *El local estaba atestado de gente.* The place was packed with people.

atiborrarse vb [25] to stuff oneself

ático nm top-floor flat; **un ático de lujo** a luxurious penthouse

atiendo vb see **atender**

atlántico, -a adj Atlantic; **el océano Atlántico** the Atlantic Ocean

atlas (pl atlas) nm atlas

atleta nmf athlete

atletismo nm athletics

atmósfera nf atmosphere

atolondrado, -a adj scatterbrained

atómico, -a adj atomic

átomo nm the atom

atónito, -a adj amazed; **quedarse atónito** to be amazed

atracador, a nm/f ❶ robber ❷ mugger

atracar vb [48] ❶ to hold up ▷ **atracar un banco** to hold up a bank ❷ to mug ▷ **La atracaron en la plaza.** She was mugged in the square.

atracción (pl atracciones) nf attraction ▷ **una atracción turística** a tourist attraction; **sentir atracción por algo** to be attracted to something ▷ **Sentía atracción por él.** I was attracted to him.

atraco nm ❶ hold-up ❷ mugging

atractivo, -a adj attractive ▶ nm attraction

atraer vb [54] to attract; **Esa chica me atrae mucho.** I find that girl very attractive.; **No me atrae mucho lo del viaje a Turquía.** That Turkey trip doesn't appeal to me much.

atrapar vb [25] to catch

atrás adv

▪ **atrás** is often translated as **the back**.

▷ **Los niños viajan siempre atrás.** The children always travel in the back.; **la parte de atrás** the back; **el asiento de atrás** the back seat

▪ **atrás** can also be translated as **back** when used to describe a position or a direction.

▷ **Mirar hacia atrás.** To look back.

▷ **Está más atrás.** It's further back.

▪ **atrás** can also be translated as **behind**.

▷ **El coche de atrás va a adelantarnos.** The car behind is going to overtake us. ▷ **Yo me quedé atrás porque iba muy cansado.** I stayed behind because I was very tired.; **ir para atrás** to go backwards; **años atrás** years ago

atrasado, -a adj ❶ backward ▷ **Es un país muy atrasado.** It's a very backward country. ❷ back ▷ **números atrasados de una revista** back numbers of a magazine ▷ **pagos atrasados** back payments ❸ behind ▷ **Va bastante atrasado en la escuela.** He's rather behind at school.; **Tengo mucho trabajo atrasado.** I'm very behind with my work.; **El reloj está atrasado.** The clock's slow. ❹ (LatAm) late ▷ **Siempre llega atrasada al trabajo.** She's always late for work.

atrasar vb [25] ❶ to delay ▷ **Tuvimos que atrasar nuestra salida.** We had to delay our departure. ❷ to put back ▷ **Acordaos de atrasar una hora vuestros relojes.**

Remember to put your watches back one hour.; **atrasarse** to be late ▷ *El tren se atrasó.* The train was late.

atravesar vb **[39]** ❶ to cross ▷ *Atravesamos el río.* We crossed the river. ❷ to go through ▷ *Atravesamos un mal momento.* We're going through a bad patch.

atravieso vb see **atravesar**

atreverse vb **[8]** to dare ▷ *No me atreví a decírselo.* I didn't dare tell him.; **No me atrevo.** I daren't.; **La gente no se atreve a salir de noche.** People are afraid to go out at night.

atrevido, -a adj ❶ daring ▷ *un escote muy atrevido* a very daring neckline ❷ cheeky ▷ *No seas tan atrevido con el jefe.* Don't be so cheeky to the boss.

atropellar vb **[25]** to run over

ATS abbr mf (= *Ayudante Técnico Sanitario*) Registered Nurse

atún (pl atunes) nm tuna

audaz (pl audaces) adj daring

audiencia nf audience

audiovisual adj audiovisual

auditorio nm ❶ auditorium ❷ audience

aula nf classroom

aumentar vb **[25]** to increase; **aumentar de peso** to put on weight

aumento nm increase; **Los precios van en aumento.** Prices are going up.

aun adv even ▷ *Aun sentado me duele la pierna.* Even when I'm sitting down, my leg hurts.; **aun así** even so; **aun cuando** even if

aún adv ❶ still ▷ *¿Aún te duele?* Is it still hurting? ❷ yet ▷ *¿No ha venido aún?* Hasn't he got here yet? ▷ *Y aún no me has devuelto el libro.* You still haven't given me the book back. ❸ even ▷ *La película es aún más aburrida de lo que creía.* The film's even more boring than I thought it would be.

aunque conj ❶ although ▷ *Me gusta el francés, aunque prefiero el alemán.* I like French, although I prefer German. ▷ *Estoy pensando en ir, aunque no sé cuándo.* I'm thinking of going, though I don't know when. ❷ even though ▷ *Seguí andando, aunque me dolía mucho la pierna.* I went on walking, even though my leg was hurting badly.; **No te lo daré, aunque protestes.** I won't give it to you however much you complain. ❸ even if ▷ *Pienso irme, aunque tenga que salir por la ventana.* I shall leave, even if I have to climb out of the window.

auricular nm (of telephone) receiver; **los auriculares** headphones

ausencia nf absence

ausente adj absent

Australia nf Australia

australiano, -a adj, nm/f Australian

Austria nf Austria

austriaco, -a adj, nm/f Austrian

auténtico, -a adj ❶ real ▷ *Es de cuero auténtico.* It's real leather. ❷ genuine ▷ *El cuadro era auténtico.* The painting was genuine.; **Es un auténtico campeón.** He's a real champion.

auto nm car

autobiografía nf autobiography

autobús (pl autobuses) nm bus; **en autobús** by bus; **un autobús de línea** a coach

autocar nm coach

autoedición nf desktop publishing

autoescuela nf driving school

autógrafo nm autograph

automático, -a adj automatic

automóvil nm car

automovilista nmf motorist

autonomía nf ❶ autonomy ❷ autonomous region

autonómico, -a adj regional

autónomo, -a adj ❶ autonomous ▷ las comunidades autónomas the autonomous regions ❷ self-employed ▷ Ser autónomo tiene sus ventajas. Being self-employed has its advantages.

autopista nf motorway; **autopista de peaje** toll motorway

autor, a nm/f author; **el autor del cuadro** the painter; **los presuntos autores del crimen** the suspected killers

autorizado, -a adj authorized

autorizar vb [13] to authorize; **Eso no te autoriza a tratarlo así.** That doesn't give you the right to treat him this way.

autoservicio nm ❶ supermarket ❷ self-service restaurant

autostop nm hitch-hiking; **hacer autostop** to hitch-hike

autostopista nmf hitch-hiker

autovía nf dual carriageway

auxilio nm help ▷ una llamada de auxilio a call for help; **los primeros auxilios** first aid ▶ excl help!

avanzar vb [13] to make progress; **¿Qué tal avanza el proyecto?** How's the project coming on?

avaro, -a adj miserly

Avda. abbr (= Avenida) Ave. (= Avenue)

AVE abbr f (= Alta Velocidad Española) high-speed train

ave nf bird; **un ave de rapiña** a bird of prey; **aves de corral** poultry sg

avellana nf hazelnut

avena nf oats pl

avenida nf avenue

aventajar vb [25] **El Salamanca aventaja en tres puntos al Córdoba.** Salamanca has a three-point lead over Córdoba.

aventar vb [39] (Mex) to throw

aventón (pl aventones) nm (Mex) lift ▷ Le di un aventón. I gave him a lift.

aventura nf ❶ adventure ❷ affair

avergonzar vb [13] to embarrass; **Me avergüenzan estas situaciones.** I find this sort of situation embarrassing.; **No me avergüenza nuestra relación.** I'm not ashamed of our relationship.; **avergonzarse de algo** to be ashamed of something ▷ No hay de qué avergonzarse. There's nothing to be ashamed of.; **Me avergüenzo de haberme portado tan mal.** I'm ashamed of myself for behaving so badly.

a b c d e f g h i j k l m n ñ o p q r s t u v w x y z

avería nf **El coche tiene una avería.** The car has broken down.

averiarse vb [**21**] to break down

averiguar vb [**25, gu → gü** before **e** and **i**] to find out

avestruz (pl avestruces) nm ostrich

aviación (pl aviaciones) nf ❶ aviation ❷ air force

aviento vb see **aventar**

avión (pl aviones) nm plane; **ir en avión** to fly

avioneta nf light aircraft

avisar vb [**25**] ❶ to warn ❷ to let... know ▷ *Avísanos si hay alguna novedad.* Let us know if there's any news. ❸ to call ▷ *avisar al médico* to call the doctor

aviso nm ❶ warning ▷ *El árbitro le dio un aviso.* The referee gave him a warning. ❷ notice ▷ *Había un aviso en la puerta.* There was a notice on the door.; **hasta nuevo aviso** until further notice

avispa nf wasp

ay excl ❶ owl ▷ *¡Ay! ¡Me has pisado!* Owl You've stepped on my toe! ❷ oh no! ▷ *¡Ay! ¡Creo que nos han engañado!* Oh no! I think they've cheated us!

ayer adv yesterday; **antes de ayer** the day before yesterday; **ayer por la mañana** yesterday morning; **ayer por la tarde** (1) yesterday afternoon (2) yesterday evening; **ayer por la noche** last night

ayuda nf help; **la ayuda humanitaria** humanitarian aid

ayudante nmf assistant

ayudar vb [**25**] to help ▷ *¿Me ayudas con los ejercicios?* Could you help me with these exercises?; **ayudar a alguien a hacer algo** to help somebody do something

ayuntamiento nm ❶ council ▷ *El ayuntamiento recauda sus propios impuestos.* The council collects its own taxes. ❷ town hall ❸ city hall

azafata nf air hostess; **una azafata de congresos** a conference hostess

azar nm chance ▷ *Nos encontramos por azar.* We met by chance.; **al azar** at random ▷ *Escoge uno al azar.* Pick one at random.

azotar vb [**25**] to whip

azotea nf roof

azteca adj, nmf Aztec

azúcar nm sugar; **azúcar moreno** brown sugar; **un caramelo sin azúcar** a sugar-free sweet

azul adj, nm blue ▷ *una puerta azul* a blue door ▷ *Yo iba de azul.* I was dressed in blue.; **azul celeste** sky blue; **azul marino** navy blue

azulejo nm tile

b

babero *nm* bib
baca *nf* roof rack
bacalao *nm* cod
bache *nm* ❶ pothole ❷ bump
Bachillerato *nm*
  • The **Bachillerato** is a two-year
  ◦ secondary school course leading
  ◦ to university.
bacteria *nf* bacterium
bafle *nm* loudspeaker
bahía *nf* bay
bailar *vb* [**25**] to dance
bailarín (*f* bailarina, *mpl*
  bailarines) *nm/f* dancer
baile *nm* dance
baja *nf* darse de baja to leave ▷ Se
  dieron de baja en el club. They left the
  club.; **estar de baja** to be on sick
  leave
bajada *nf* drop ▷ Hubo una bajada

de las temperaturas. There was a
drop in temperature.; **Me caí en
la bajada de la montaña.** I fell
going down the mountain.; **La
bajada hasta la playa es muy
pronunciada.** The road down to
the beach is very steep.
bajar *vb* [**25**] ❶ to go down ▷ Bajó
la escalera muy despacio. He went
down the stairs very slowly.
❷ to come down ▷ Baja y ayúdame.
Come down and help me. ▷ Han
bajado los precios. Prices have come
down.; **Los coches han bajado
de precio.** Cars have come down
in price. ❸ to take down ▷ ¿Has
bajado la basura? Have you taken
the rubbish down? ❹ to bring
down ▷ ¿Me bajas el abrigo? Hace
frío aquí fuera. Could you bring my
coat down, it's cold out here.
❺ to get down ▷ ¿Me bajas la
maleta del armario? Could you get
me the suitcase down from the
wardrobe? ❻ to put down ▷ ¿Bajo
la persiana? Shall I put the blind
down? ▷ Los comercios han bajado
los precios. Businesses have put
their prices down.; **¡Baja la voz,
que no estoy sordo!** Keep your
voice down, I'm not deaf! ❼ to
turn down ▷ Baja la radio que no
oigo nada. Turn the radio down,
I can't hear a thing. ❽ (*from
internet*) to download; **bajarse
de** (1) (*bus, train, plane*) to get off
▷ Se bajó del autobús antes que yo.
He got off the bus before me.
(2) (*car*) to get out of ▷ ¡Bájate del
coche! Get out of the car! (3) to get

down from ▷ *¡Bájate de ahí!* Get down from there!

bajo, -a adj ▶ ❶ low ▷ *una silla muy baja* a very low chair; **la temporada baja** the low season ❷ short ▷ *Mi hermano es muy bajo.* My brother is very short.; **Hablaban en voz baja.** They spoke quietly.
▶ prep under ▷ *Juan llevaba un libro bajo el brazo.* Juan was carrying a book under his arm.; **bajo tierra** underground
▶ adv ❶ low ▷ *El avión volaba muy bajo.* The plane was flying very low. ❷ quietly ▷ *¡Habla bajo!* Speak quietly!
▶ nm ❶ bass ❷ ground floor

bala nf bullet
balcón (pl balcones) nm balcony
baldosa nf tile
baldosín (pl baldosines) nm tile
balear adj Balearic
Baleares nfpl the Balearic Islands
ballena nf whale
ballet (pl ballets) nm ballet
balneario nm spa
balón (pl balones) nm ball
baloncesto nm basketball
balonmano nm handball
balonvolea nm volleyball
balsa nf raft
banana nf (LatAm) banana
bancario, -a adj bank
banco nm ❶ (financial) bank ❷ bench ❸ pew
banda nf ❶ band ❷ gang ❸ sash; **la banda ancha** broadband; **la banda sonora** the soundtrack

Word for word, **banda sonora** means 'sound band'.

bandeja nf tray
bandera nf flag
bandido nm bandit
bando nm side
banqueta nf ❶ stool ❷ (Mex) pavement
banquete nm banquet; **el banquete de bodas** the wedding reception
banquillo nm bench
bañador nm ❶ swimming trunks pl ❷ swimming costume
bañarse vb [25] ❶ to have a bath ❷ to go for a swim
bañera nf bath
baño nm bathroom; **darse un baño (1)** to have a bath **(2)** to go for a swim
bar nm bar
baraja nf pack of cards
barandilla nf ❶ banisters pl ❷ railing
barata nf (Mex) sale
barato, -a adj cheap ▷ *Esta marca es más barata que aquella.* This brand is cheaper than that one.
▶ adv cheaply ▷ *Aquí se come muy barato.* You can eat really cheaply here.
barba nf beard; **dejarse barba** to grow a beard
barbacoa nf barbecue
barbaridad nf atrocity; **Pablo come una barbaridad.** Pablo eats an awful lot.; **decir barbaridades** to talk nonsense; **¡Qué barbaridad!** Good grief!
barbilla nf chin

barca nf boat

barco nm ❶ ship; **un barco de guerra** a warship ❷ boat; **un barco de vela** a sailing boat

barda nf (Mex) fence

barniz (pl **barnices**) nm varnish

barnizar vb [13] to varnish

barra nf bar ▷ *Me tomé un café en la barra.* I had a coffee at the bar.; **una barra de pan** a French loaf; **una barra de labios** a lipstick; **las barras paralelas** the parallel bars

barraca nf small farmhouse; **una barraca de feria** a fairground stall

barranco nm ravine

barrer vb [8] to sweep

barrera nf barrier; **una barrera de seguridad** a safety barrier

barriga nf belly; **Me duele la barriga.** I have a sore stomach.

barril nm barrel

barrilete nm (River Plate) kite

barrio nm (of town, city) area; **la pescadería del barrio** the local fishmonger's; **el barrio chino** the red-light district

barro nm ❶ mud ❷ clay ▷ *una vasija de barro* a clay pot

barrote nm bar

barullo nm ❶ racket; **armar barullo** to make a racket ❷ mess

basarse vb [25] **Mi conclusión se basa en los datos.** My conclusion is based on the facts.; **¿En qué te basas para decir eso?** What grounds have you got for saying that?; **Para la novela me basé en la vida de mi abuela.** I based the novel on the life of my grandmother.

báscula nf scales pl

base nf ❶ base ❷ basis; **Lo consiguió a base de mucho trabajo.** She managed it through hard work.; **una base militar** a military base; **una base de datos** a database

básico, -a adj basic

bastante adj, pron ❶ enough ▷ *No tengo bastante dinero.* I haven't enough money. ▷ *Ya hay bastantes libros en casa.* There are enough books in the house. ▷ *¿Hay bastante?* Is there enough? ❷ quite a lot of ▷ *Vino bastante gente.* Quite a lot of people came.; **Se tarda bastante tiempo en llegar.** It takes quite a while to get there.; **Voy a tardar bastante.** I'm going to take quite a while.

▶ adv ❶ quite ▷ *Son bastante ricos.* They are quite rich. ▷ *Juegas bastante bien.* You play quite well. ❷ quite a lot ▷ *Sus padres ganan bastante.* Their parents earn quite a lot.

bastar vb [25] to be enough; **¡Basta!** That's enough!; **bastarse** to manage ▷ *Yo me basto solo.* I can manage on my own.

basto, -a adj coarse

bastón (pl **bastones**) nm stick; **un bastón de esquí** a ski stick

bastos nmpl clubs

⠿ **Bastos** are clubs, one of the suits in the Spanish card deck.

basura nf ❶ rubbish ▷ *Eso es basura.* That's rubbish.; **tirar algo a la basura** to put something in the bin ❷ litter ▷ *Hay mucha* *basura en la calle.* There's a lot of litter in the street.

basurero *nm* ① dustman ② rubbish dump ③ (*Chile, Mex*) rubbish bin

bata *nf* ① dressing gown ② lab coat

batalla *nf* battle

batería *nf* ① battery ② drums *pl*; **una batería de cocina** a set of kitchen equipment ③ drummer ▶ *nm* drummer

batido *nm* milkshake ▷ *un batido de fresa* a strawberry milkshake

batidora *nf* mixer

batir *vb* [**58**] ① (*eggs*) to beat ② (*cream*) to whip ③ (*a record*) to break

baúl *nm* ① chest ② trunk ③ (*River Plate*) boot

bautizo *nm* christening

bayeta *nf* cloth

bebe, -a *nm/f* (*River Plate*) baby

bebé (*pl* bebés) *nm* baby

bebedero *nm* (*Chile, Mex*) drinking fountain

beber *vb* [**8**] to drink

bebida *nf* drink; **bebidas alcohólicas** alcoholic drinks

bebido, -a *adj* drunk; **estar bebido** to be drunk

beca *nf* ① grant ② scholarship

becario, -a *nm/f* ① grant holder ② scholarship holder ③ intern

béisbol *nm* baseball

belén *nm* (*pl* belenes) *nm* crib

belga *adj, nmf* Belgian

Bélgica *nf* Belgium

belleza *nf* beauty

bello, -a *adj* beautiful; **bellas artes** fine art *sg*

bendecir *vb* [**15**] to bless

bendición (*pl* bendiciones) *nf* blessing

beneficiar *vb* [**25**] to benefit; **beneficiarse de algo** to benefit from something

beneficio *nm* profit; **sacar beneficio de algo** to benefit from something; **a beneficio de** in aid of

benéfico, -a *adj* charity ▷ *un concierto benéfico* a charity concert

berberecho *nm* cockle

berenjena *nf* aubergine

bermudas *nfpl* Bermuda shorts

berza *nf* cabbage

besar *vb* [**25**] to kiss; **Ana y Pepe se besaron.** Ana and Pepe kissed each other.

beso *nm* kiss; **dar un beso a alguien** to give somebody a kiss

bestia *nf* beast
▶ *adj* ¡**Qué bestia eres!** (*informal*) You're too rough!

besugo *nm* sea bream

betún *nm* shoe polish

biberón (*pl* biberones) *nm* baby's bottle; **Voy a dar el biberón al niño.** I'm going to give the baby his bottle.

Biblia *nf* Bible

biblioteca *nf* library

bicarbonato *nm* bicarbonate

bicho *nm* insect

bici *nf* bike

bicicleta *nf* bicycle; **una bicicleta de montaña** a mountain bike

bidé (*pl* bidés) *nm* bidet

bidón (pl **bidones**) nm drum

bien nm ❶ good ▷ Lo digo por tu bien. I'm telling you for your own good.; **los bienes** possessions
▶ adv ❶ well ▷ Habla bien el español. He speaks Spanish well. ❷ good; **Lo pasamos muy bien.** We had a very good time. ❸ very ▷ un café **bien caliente** a very hot coffee; **¿Estás bien?** Are you OK?; **¡Está bien! Lo haré.** OK! I'll do it.; **¡Eso no está bien!** That's not very nice!; **Hiciste bien en decírselo.** You were right to tell him.; **¡Ya está bien!** That's enough!; **¡Qué bien!** Excellent!

bienestar nm well-being

bienvenida nf **dar la bienvenida a alguien** to welcome somebody

bienvenido, -a adj welcome
▷ Siempre serás bienvenido aquí. You will always be welcome here.
▶ excl welcome!

bife nm (Chile, River Plate) steak

bifurcación (pl **bifurcaciones**) nf fork

bigote nm moustache

bikini nm bikini

bilingüe adj bilingual

billar nm billiards sg; **el billar americano** pool

billete nm ❶ ticket ▷ un billete de metro an underground ticket; **sacar un billete** to buy a ticket; **un billete de ida y vuelta** a return ticket

> Word for word, **billete de ida y vuelta** means 'ticket for going and coming back'.

un billete electrónico an e-ticket ❷ note ▷ un billete de veinte euros a twenty-euro note

billón (pl **billones**) nm **un billón** a million million

bingo nm ❶ bingo ▷ jugar al bingo to play bingo ❷ bingo hall

biodegradable adj biodegradable

biografía nf biography

biología nf biology

biológico, -a adj ❶ organic ❷ biological

biquini nm bikini

birome nf (River Plate) ballpoint pen

bisabuela nf great-grandmother

bisabuelo nm great-grandfather; **mis bisabuelos** my great-grandparents

bisagra nf hinge

bisiesto, -a adj **un año bisiesto** a leap year

bisnieta nf great-granddaughter

bisnieto nm great-grandson; **tus bisnietos** your great-grandchildren

bistec (pl **bistecs**) nm steak

bisutería nf costume jewellery

bizco, -a adj cross-eyed

bizcocho nm sponge cake

blanco, -a adj white ▷ un vestido blanco a white dress
▶ nm white; **dar en el blanco** to hit the target; **dejar algo en blanco** to leave something blank; **Cuando iba a responder me quedé en blanco.** Just as I was about to reply my mind went blank.

a b c d e f g h i j k l m n ñ o p q r s t u v w x y z

blando, -a adj ❶ soft ▷ *Este colchón es muy blando.* This mattress is very soft. ❷ easy

bloc (pl **blocs**) nm writing pad; **un bloc de dibujo** a drawing pad

blog nm blog

bloguero, -a nm/f blogger

bloque nm block; **un bloque de pisos** a block of flats

bloquear vb [25] to block

blusa nf blouse

bobada nf **hacer bobadas** to do stupid things; **decir bobadas** to talk nonsense

bobina nf reel

bobo, -a adj silly

boca nf mouth ▷ *No debes hablar con la boca llena.* You shouldn't talk with your mouth full.; **boca abajo** face down; **boca arriba** face up; **Me quedé con la boca abierta.** I was dumbfounded.; **la boca del metro** the entrance to the underground

bocacalle nf **Es una bocacalle del Paseo Central.** It's a side street of the Paseo Central.

bocadillo nm **Ya me he comido el bocadillo.** I've already had my roll.; **un bocadillo de queso** a cheese baguette

bocado nm ❶ bite; **No he probado bocado desde ayer.** I haven't had a bite to eat since yesterday. ❷ mouthful

bocata nm = **bocadillo**

bochorno nm **Hace bochorno.** It's muggy.

bocina nf ❶ horn ❷ (Chile, River Plate) receiver

boda nf wedding; **las bodas de oro** golden wedding sg; **las bodas de plata** silver wedding sg

bodega nf ❶ cellar ❷ wine cellar ❸ wine shop ❹ (of plane) hold

bofetada nf slap ▷ *dar una bofetada a alguien* to give somebody a slap

boicot (pl **boicots**) nm boycott

boina nf beret

bola nf ball; **una bola de nieve** a snowball

bolera nf bowling alley

boletería nf (LatAm) ticket office

boletín (pl **boletines**) nm bulletin; **un boletín informativo** a news bulletin

boleto nm ticket ▷ *un boleto de lotería* a lottery ticket; **un boleto de quinielas** a pools coupon

boli nm pen

bolígrafo nm pen

bolillo nm (Mex) bun

Bolivia nf Bolivia

boliviano, -a adj, nm/f Bolivian

bollería nf pastries pl

bollo nm ❶ bun ❷ dent

bolos nmpl ❶ bowls sg ❷ tenpin bowling sg

bolsa nf ❶ bag ▷ *una bolsa de plástico* a plastic bag; **una bolsa de viaje** a travel bag ❷ (Mex) handbag; **la Bolsa** the Stock Exchange

bolsillo nm pocket ▷ *Sacó las llaves del bolsillo.* He took the keys out of his pocket.; **un libro de bolsillo** a paperback

> Word for word, **libro de bolsillo** means 'book for the pocket'.

bolso nm bag

bomba nf ❶ bomb ❷ pump ▷ *una bomba de agua* a water pump; **pasarlo bomba** to have a brilliant time

bombacha nf (River Plate) panties pl

bombardear vb [25] to bombard

bombero, -a nm/f firefighter; **llamar a los bomberos** to call the fire brigade

bombilla nf lightbulb

bombita nf (River Plate) lightbulb

bombo nm bass drum

bombón (pl bombones) nm chocolate

bombona nf gas cylinder

bondad nf kindness; **¿Tendría la bondad de …?** Would you be so kind as to …?

boniato nm sweet potato

bonito, -a adj pretty
▶ nm tuna

bonobús (pl bonobuses) nm bus pass

boquerón (pl boquerones) nm anchovy

boquete nm hole

borda nf echar algo por la borda to throw something overboard

bordar vb [25] to embroider

borde nm edge ▷ *al borde de la mesa* at the edge of the table; **estar al borde de algo** to be on the verge of something
▶ adj **¡No seas borde!** Don't be so horrible!

bordillo nm kerb

bordo nm subir a bordo to get on board

borrachera nf coger una borrachera to get drunk

borracho, -a adj drunk ▷ *Estás borracho.* You're drunk.

borrador nm ❶ rough draft ❷ duster ▷ *Usó un trapo como borrador.* He used a rag as a duster.

borrar vb [25] ❶ to rub out ❷ to clean ▷ *Borra la pizarra.* Clean the blackboard. ❸ to wipe ▷ *No borres esa cinta.* Don't wipe that tape.; **borrarse de (1)** to take one's name off ▷ *Voy a borrarme de la lista.* I'm going to take my name off the list. **(2)** to leave

borrasca nf Viene una borrasca por el Atlántico. There's an area of low pressure over the Atlantic.

borrón (pl borrones) nm stain

borroso, -a adj blurred

Bosnia nf Bosnia

bosnio, -a adj, nm/f Bosnian

bosque nm ❶ wood ❷ forest

bostezar vb [13] to yawn

bota nf boot; **unas botas de agua** a pair of wellingtons

> Word for word, **botas de agua** means 'boots of water'.

una bota de vino a wineskin

botana nf (Mex) snack

botánica nf botany

botánico, -a adj botanical

botar vb [25] ❶ to bounce ❷ to jump ❸ (LatAm) to throw out

bote nm ❶ can ❷ tin ❸ jar ❹ boat; **un bote salvavidas** a lifeboat; **pegar un bote** to jump

botella nf bottle

botellín (pl botellines) nm bottle

a
b
c
d
e
f
g
h
i
j
k
l
m
n
ñ
o
p
q
r
s
t
u
v
w
x
y
z

botijo nm
- A **botijo** is an earthenware
- water container with spouts.

botín (pl botines) nm ❶ ankle boot
❷ haul

botiquín (pl botiquines) nm
❶ medicine cupboard ❷ first-aid
kit ❸ sick bay

botón (pl botones) nm button;
pulsar un botón to press a button

bóveda nf vault

boxeador, a nm/f boxer

boxear vb [25] to box

boxeo nm boxing

bragas nfpl knickers; **unas bragas**
a pair of knickers

bragueta nf fly

brasa nf carne a la brasa
barbecued meat; **las brasas** the
embers

brasier nm (Mex) bra

Brasil nm Brazil

brasileño, -a adj, nm/f Brazilian

brasilero, -a adj, nm/f (LatAm)
= **brasileño**

bravo, -a adj un toro bravo
a fighting bull
▶ excl well done!

braza nf breaststroke; **nadar a
braza** to do the breaststroke

brazalete nm bracelet

brazo nm arm ▷ Me duele el brazo.
My arm hurts. ▷ Estaba sentada con
los brazos cruzados. She was sitting
with her arms folded.; **ir del brazo**
to walk arm-in-arm; **un brazo de
gitano** a swiss roll

brecha nf opening

breve adj ❶ brief ▷ por breves
momentos for a few brief moments

❷ short ▷ un relato breve a short
story; **en breve** shortly

bricolaje nm DIY

brillante adj ❶ shiny; **blanco
brillante** brilliant white
❷ outstanding
▶ nm diamond

brillar vb [25] ❶ to shine ❷ to
sparkle

brillo nm ❶ shine ❷ sparkle;
La pantalla tiene mucho brillo.
The screen is too bright.; **sacar
brillo a algo** to polish something

brincar vb [48] to jump up and
down; **brincar de alegría** to jump
for joy

brinco nm pegar un brinco to
jump; **Bajé tres escalones de un
brinco.** I jumped down three
steps.

brindar vb [25] brindar por to
drink a toast to; **brindarse a
hacer algo** to offer to do
something

brindis (pl brindis) nm toast;
hacer un brindis to make a toast

brisa nf breeze

británico, -a adj British
▶ nm/f British person; **los
británicos** the British

brocha nf ❶ paintbrush ❷ shaving
brush

broche nm ❶ brooch ❷ clasp

broma nf joke; **gastar una broma
a alguien** to play a joke on
someone; **decir algo en broma** to
say something as a joke; **una
broma pesada** a practical joke

bromear vb [25] to joke

bromista nmf joker

bronca nf ❶ row; **echar una bronca a alguien** to tell somebody off ❷ fuss; **armar una bronca** to kick up a fuss

bronce nm bronze

bronceado, -a adj tanned
▶ nm suntan

bronceador nm suntan lotion

bronquitis nf bronchitis

brotar vb [25] to sprout

bruces adv **Me caí de bruces.** I fell flat on my face.

bruja nf witch

brujo nm wizard

brújula nf compass

bruma nf mist

brusco, -a adj ❶ sudden ❷ abrupt

bruto, -a adj gross ▷ **el salario bruto** gross salary; **¡No seas bruto!** Don't be so rough!

bucear vb [25] to dive

buen adj = **bueno**

bueno, -a adj good

> **bueno** is shortened to **buen** before masculine singular nouns.

▷ **Es un buen libro.** It's a good book. ▷ **Hace buen tiempo.** The weather's good. ▷ **Es buena persona.** He's a good person.; **ser bueno para** to be good for ▷ **Esta bebida es buena para la salud.** This drink is good for your health.; **Está muy bueno este bizcocho.** This sponge cake is lovely.; **Lo bueno fue que ni siquiera quiso venir.** The best thing was that he didn't even want to come.; **¡Bueno! (1)** OK! **(2)** (Mex) Hello!; **Bueno. ¿Y qué?** Well?; **¡Buenas!** Hello!; **Irás por las**

buenas o por las malas. You'll go whether you like it or not.

buey nm ox

bufanda nf scarf

bufete nm **un bufete de abogados** a legal practice

buffet (pl **buffets**) nm buffet

buhardilla nf attic

búho nm owl

buitre nm vulture

bujía nf spark plug

Bulgaria nf Bulgaria

búlgaro, -a adj, nm/f Bulgarian
▶ nm (language) Bulgarian

bulto nm ❶ lump ▷ **Tengo un bulto en la frente.** I have a lump on my forehead. ❷ figure ▷ **Solo vi un bulto.** I only saw a figure.; **Llevábamos muchos bultos.** We were carrying a lot of bags.

buñuelo nm doughnut

buque nm ship; **un buque de guerra** a warship

burbuja nf bubble; **un refresco sin burbujas** a still drink; **un refresco con burbujas** a fizzy drink

burlarse vb [25] **burlarse de alguien** to make fun of someone

buró (pl **burós**) nm (Mex) bedside table

burocracia nf bureaucracy

burrada nf (informal) **hacer burradas** to do stupid things ▷ **No hagas burradas con el coche.** Don't do anything stupid with the car.

burro nm ❶ donkey ❷ idiot ▷ **Eres un burro.** You're an idiot.
▶ adj ❶ thick ❷ rough

busca nf **en busca de** in search of
▶ nm bleeper

buscador *nm* search engine

buscar *vb* [**48**] to look for ▷ *Ana busca trabajo.* Ana's looking for work.; **Te voy a buscar a la estación.** I'll come and get you at the station.; **buscar una palabra en el diccionario** to look up a word in the dictionary; **Él se lo ha buscado.** He was asking for it.

búsqueda *nf* search

butaca *nf* **①** armchair **②** seat

butano *nm* bottled gas

buzo *nm* diver

buzón (*pl* buzones) *nm* **①** letterbox **②** postbox; **echar una carta al buzón** to post a letter; **buzón de voz** voice mail

Word for word, **buzón de voz** means 'box of voice'.

C

C/ *abbr* (= *calle*) St (= *Street*)

caballero *nm* gentleman; **¿Dónde está la sección de caballeros?** Where is the men's department?; **'Caballeros'** 'Gents'

caballo *nm* **①** horse; **¿Te gusta montar a caballo?** Do you like riding?; **un caballo de carreras** a racehorse **②** (*in chess*) knight

cabaña *nf* hut

cabello *nm* hair

caber *vb* [**47**, *pres* **yo quepo**] to fit ▷ *No cabe en mi armario.* It won't fit in my cupboard.; **En mi coche caben dos maletas más.** There's room for two more suitcases in my car.; **No cabe nadie más.** There's no room for anyone else.

cabeza nf head ▷ Se rascó la cabeza. He scratched his head.; **Se tiró al agua de cabeza.** He dived headfirst into the water.; **estar a la cabeza de la clasificación** to be at the top of the league

cabina nf ❶ phone box ❷ booth ❸ cockpit ❹ cubicle

cable nm cable

cabo nm ❶ cape; **Cabo Verde** Cape Verde ❷ corporal; **al cabo de dos días** after two days; **llevar algo a cabo** to carry something out

cabra nf goat

cabrá vb see **caber**

cabreado, -a adj annoyed

caca nf **hacer caca (1)** to do a poo **(2)** to go to the loo

cacahuate nm (Mex) peanut

cacahuete nm peanut

cacao nm ❶ cocoa ❷ lipsalve

cacerola nf saucepan

cacharro nm **los cacharros** the pots and pans

cachondeo nm **Las clases eran un cachondeo.** (informal) The classes were a joke.; **No le hagas caso, está de cachondeo.** (informal) Don't pay any attention to him, he's having you on.

cachorro, -a nm/f ❶ puppy ❷ cub

cactus (pl cactus) nm cactus

cada adj ❶ each ▷ Cada libro es de un color distinto. Each book is a different colour.; **cada uno** each one ❷ every ▷ cada año every year ▷ cada vez que la veo every time I see her ▷ uno de cada diez one out of every ten; **Viene cada vez más gente.** More and more people are coming.; **Viene cada vez menos.** He comes less and less often.; **Cada vez hace más frío.** It's getting colder and colder.; **¿Cada cuánto vas al dentista?** How often do you go to the dentist?

cadáver nm corpse

cadena nf ❶ chain ▷ una cadena de oro a gold chain; **una reacción en cadena** a chain reaction; **tirar de la cadena del wáter** to flush the toilet; **la cadena de montaje** the assembly line ❷ channel ▷ Por la cadena 3 ponen una película. There's a film on channel 3.; **cadena perpetua** life imprisonment

cadera nf hip

caducar vb [48] to expire; **Esta leche está caducada.** This milk is past its sell-by date.

caer vb [5] to fall; **El avión cayó al mar.** The plane came down in the sea.; **Su cumpleaños cae en viernes.** Her birthday falls on a Friday.; **caerse** to fall; **El niño se cayó de la cama.** The child fell out of bed.; **No te vayas a caer del caballo.** Be careful not to fall off the horse.; **Se me cayeron las monedas.** I dropped the coins.; **Su hermano me cae muy bien.** I really like his brother.

café (pl cafés) nm ❶ coffee; **un café con leche** a white coffee; **un café solo** a black coffee

┃ Word for word, **café solo** means 'coffee alone'.

❷ café

cafetera nf coffee pot

cafetería nf café

caída nf fall

caigo vb see **caer**

caimán (pl caimanes) nm alligator

caja nf ❶ box ▷ una caja de zapatos a shoe box ❷ case ❸ crate ❹ checkout ❺ till ❻ cash desk; **la caja de ahorros** the savings bank; **la caja de cambios** the gearbox; **la caja fuerte** the safe

cajero, -a nm/f **Trabajo de cajera en un supermercado.** I work on the checkout in a supermarket. ▶ nm **un cajero automático** a cash dispenser

cajón (pl cajones) nm ❶ drawer ❷ crate ❸ (LatAm) coffin

cajuela nf (Mex) boot

cala nf cove

calabacín (pl calabacines) nm courgette

calabacita nf (Mex) courgette

calabaza nf pumpkin

calado, -a adj soaked ▷ Estaba calado hasta los huesos. He was soaked to the skin.

calamar nm squid; **calamares a la romana** squid fried in batter

calambre nm ❶ cramp ▷ Tengo un calambre en la pierna. I've got cramp in my leg. ❷ electric shock ▷ Si tocas el cable te dará calambre. If you touch the cable you'll get an electric shock.

calar vb [25] to soak ▷ La lluvia me caló hasta los huesos. I got soaked to the skin in the rain.

calavera nf skull

calcar vb [48] to trace

calcetín (pl calcetines) nm sock

calcio nm calcium

calculadora nf calculator

calcular vb [25] to calculate; **Calculo que nos llevará unos tres días.** I reckon that it will take us around three days.

cálculo nm calculation

caldo nm broth; **una pastilla de caldo** a stock cube

calefacción nf heating ▷ calefacción central central heating

calendario nm calendar

calentador nm heater

calentamiento nm el **calentamiento global** global warming; **ejercicios de calentamiento** warm-up exercises

calentar vb [39] ❶ to heat up ❷ to warm up; **calentarse (1)** to heat up (2) to warm up

calentura nf ❶ temperature ❷ cold sore

calidad nf quality

caliente vb see **calentar** ▶ adj ❶ hot ▷ Esta sopa está muy caliente. This soup is very hot. ❷ warm ▷ ¡Esta cerveza está caliente! This beer is warm!

calificación (pl calificaciones) nf mark; **boletín de calificaciones** school report

calificar vb [48] to mark; **Me calificó con sobresaliente.** He gave me an A.

callado, -a adj quiet ▷ Estuvo callado bastante rato. He was quiet for quite a while.

callar vb [25] to be quiet; **callarse (1)** to keep quiet (2) to stop talking; **¡Cállate!** (informal) Shut up!

calle nf ❶ street ▷ *Viven en la calle Peñalver, 13.* They live at number 13, Peñalver Street.; **Hoy no he salido a la calle.** I haven't been out today.; **una calle peatonal** a pedestrian precinct ❷ (on racetrack, in pool) lane

callejero nm street map

callejón (pl **callejones**) nm alley

calma nf calm; **Todo estaba en calma.** Everything was calm.; **Logró mantener la calma.** He managed to keep calm.; **Piénsalo con calma.** Think about it calmly.; **Tómatelo con calma.** Take it easy.

calmante nm ❶ painkiller ❷ tranquillizer

calmar vb [25] ❶ to calm down ▷ *¡Cálmate!* Calm down! ❷ (pain) to relieve

calor nm heat ▷ *No se puede trabajar con este calor.* It's impossible to work in this heat.; **Hace calor.** It's hot.; **Tengo calor.** I'm hot.

caloría nf calorie

caluroso, -a adj hot

calvo, -a adj bald ▷ *Se está quedando calvo.* He's going bald.

calzado nm footwear

calzoncillos nmpl underpants

calzones nmpl (Chile) panties

cama nf bed; **hacer la cama** to make the bed; **Está en la cama.** He's in bed.; **meterse en la cama** to get into bed

cámara nf ❶ camera; **una cámara digital** a digital camera; **a cámara lenta** in slow motion ❷ inner tube

camarera nf ❶ waitress ❷ maid

camarero nm ❶ waiter ❷ bellboy

camarote nm cabin

cambiar vb [25] ❶ to change ▷ *No has cambiado nada.* You haven't changed a bit.; **Quiero cambiar este abrigo por uno más grande.** I want to change this coat for a larger size.; **Tenemos que cambiar de tren en París.** We have to change trains in Paris.; **He cambiado de idea.** I've changed my mind. ❷ to swap ▷ *Te cambio mi bolígrafo por tu goma.* I'll swap my ballpoint for your rubber.; **cambiarse** to get changed; **Se han cambiado de coche.** They have changed car.; **cambiarse de sitio** to move; **cambiarse de casa** to move house

cambio nm ❶ change ▷ *un cambio brusco de temperatura* a sudden change in temperature ▷ *¿Tiene cambio de veinte euros?* Have you got change of twenty euros? ▷ *¿Te han dado bien el cambio?* Have they given you the right change?; **el cambio climático** climate change ❷ small change ▷ *Necesito cambio.* I need small change. ❸ exchange ▷ *¿A cómo está el cambio?* What's the exchange rate?; **Me lo regaló a cambio del favor que le hice.** He gave it to me in return for the favour I did him.; **en cambio** on the other hand

camello nm ❶ camel ❷ drug pusher

camilla nf ❶ stretcher ❷ couch

caminar vb [25] to walk

caminata nf long walk

camino nm **❶** path; **un camino de montaña** a mountain track **❷** way ▷ ¿Sabes el camino a su casa? Do you know the way to his house?; **A medio camino paramos a comer.** Half-way there, we stopped to eat.; **La farmacia me queda de camino.** The chemist's is on my way.

camión (pl **camiones**) nm **❶** lorry; **un camión cisterna** a tanker; **el camión de la basura** the dustcart **❷** (Mex) bus

camionero, -a nm/f lorry driver

camioneta nf van

camisa nf shirt

camiseta nf **❶** T-shirt **❷** vest **❸** shirt

camisón (pl **camisones**) nm nightdress

camote nm (Mex) sweet potato

campamento nm camp

campana nf bell

campaña nf campaign; **la campaña electoral** the election campaign

campeón (**campeona**) nm/f champion

campeonato nm championship

campesino, -a nm/f **❶** country person **❷** peasant

camping (pl **campings**) nm **❶** camping ▷ ir de camping to go camping **❷** campsite

campo nm **❶** country ▷ Prefiero vivir en el campo. I prefer living in the country. **❷** countryside ▷ El campo se pone verde en primavera. The countryside turns green in

springtime.; **Corrían campo a través.** They were running cross-country.; **el trabajo del campo** farm work **❸** pitch; **un campo de deportes** a sports ground; **un campo de golf** a golf course

cana nf grey hair; **Tiene canas.** He's got grey hair.; **Le están saliendo canas.** He's going grey.

Canadá nm Canada

canadiense adj, nmf Canadian

canal nm **❶** channel ▷ Por el canal 2 ponen una película. They're showing a film on channel 2.; **el Canal de la Mancha** the English Channel **❷** canal ▷ un canal de riego an irrigation canal; **el Canal de Panamá** the Panama Canal

canapé (pl **canapés**) nm canapé

Canarias nfpl the Canaries; **las Islas Canarias** the Canary Islands

canario nm canary

canasta nf basket

cancelar vb [**25**] to cancel

Cáncer nm (sign) Cancer; **Soy cáncer.** I'm Cancer.

cáncer nm cancer ▷ cáncer de mama breast cancer

cancha nf **❶** court **❷** (LatAm) pitch

canción (pl **canciones**) nf song; **una canción de cuna** a lullaby

candado nm padlock; **Estaba cerrado con candado.** It was padlocked.

candidato, -a nm/f candidate

canela nf cinnamon

canelones nmpl cannelloni sg

cangrejo nm ❶ crab ❷ crayfish

canguro nm kangaroo
▶ nmf baby-sitter; **hacer de canguro** to baby-sit

canica nf marble; **jugar a las canicas** to play marbles

canilla nf (River Plate) tap

canoa nf canoe

cansado, -a adj ❶ tired ▷ Estoy muy cansado. I'm very tired. ❷ tiring ▷ Es un trabajo muy cansado. It's a very tiring job.

cansancio nm ¡Qué cansancio! I'm so tired!

cansar vb [**25**] Es un viaje que cansa. It's a tiring journey.; **cansarse** to get tired; **Me cansé de esperarlo y me marché.** I got tired of waiting for him and I left.

cantante nmf singer

cantar vb [**25**] to sing

cantidad nf ❶ amount ▷ una cierta cantidad de dinero a certain amount of money ❷ quantity; **¡Qué cantidad de gente!** What a lot of people! **Había cantidad de turistas.** There were loads of tourists.

cantimplora nf water bottle

canto nm ❶ edge ❷ singing ❸ song

caña nf cane; **caña de azúcar** sugar cane; **Me tomé dos cañas.** I had two beers.; **una caña de pescar** a fishing rod

cañería nf pipe

caos nm chaos

capa nf ❶ layer; **la capa de ozono** the ozone layer ❷ cloak

capacidad nf ❶ ability ❷ capacity

capaz (pl capaces) adj capable
▷ Es capaz de olvidarse el pasaporte. He's quite capable of forgetting his passport.; **Por ella sería capaz de cualquier cosa.** He would do anything for her.

capilla nf chapel

capital nf capital

capitán (f capitana) nm/f captain

capítulo nm ❶ chapter ❷ episode

capricho nm whim; **Lo compré por capricho.** I bought it on a whim.; **Decidí viajar en primera para darme un capricho.** I decided to travel first class to give myself a treat.

Capricornio nm (sign) Capricorn; **Soy capricornio.** I'm Capricorn.

capturar vb [**25**] to capture

capucha nf ❶ hood ❷ top

caqui (pl caquis) adj khaki

cara nf ❶ face ▷ Tiene la cara alargada. He has a long face.; **Tienes mala cara.** You don't look well.; **Tenía cara de pocos amigos.** He looked very unfriendly.; **No pongas esa cara.** Don't look like that. ❷ cheek ▷ ¡Qué cara! What a cheek! ❸ side ▷ un folio escrito por las dos caras a sheet written on both sides; **¿Cara o cruz?** Heads or tails?

◼ Word for word, **¿Cara o cruz?** means 'Face or cross?'

caracol nm ❶ snail ❷ winkle

carácter (pl caracteres) nm nature; **tener buen carácter** to be good-natured; **tener mal carácter** to be bad-tempered.

La chica tiene mucho carácter.
The girl has a strong personality.
característica nf characteristic
caramba excl goodness!
caramelo nm sweet
caravana nf caravan; **Había una
caravana de dos kilómetros.**
There was a two kilometre
tailback.
carbón nm coal; **carbón de leña**
charcoal
carcajada nf **soltar una carcajada**
to burst out laughing; **reírse a
carcajadas** to roar with laughter
cárcel nf prison ▷ **Todavía está en la
cárcel.** He's still in prison.
cardenal nm ❶ bruise ❷ cardinal
cardiaco, -a adj cardiac ▷ **ataque
cardiaco** cardiac arrest
careta nf mask
carga nf ❶ load ▷ **carga máxima**
maximum load ❷ burden ❸ refill
cargado, -a adj ❶ loaded ❷ stuffy
❸ strong; **Venía cargada de
paquetes.** She was laden with
parcels.
cargamento nm ❶ cargo ❷ load
cargar vb [37] ❶ to load ▷ **Cargaron
el coche de maletas.** They loaded the
car with suitcases. ❷ (pen, lighter)
to fill ❸ (battery) to charge; **Tuve
que cargar con todo.** I had to take
responsibility for everything.
cargo nm post ▷ **un cargo de mucha
responsabilidad** a very responsible
post; **Está a cargo de la
contabilidad.** He's in charge of
keeping the books.
Caribe nm the Caribbean
caribeño, -a adj, nm/f Caribbean

caricatura nf caricature
caricia nf caress; **Le hacía caricias
al bebé.** She was caressing the
baby.
caridad nf charity
caries (pl caries) nf ❶ tooth decay
❷ cavity
cariño nm affection; **Les tengo
mucho cariño.** I'm very fond of
them.; **Ven aquí, cariño.** Come
here, darling.
cariñoso, -a adj affectionate
carnaval nm carnival
  * The **carnaval** is the traditional
    period of celebrating prior to the
    start of Lent.
carne nf meat ▷ **No como carne.**
I don't eat meat.; **carne de cerdo**
pork; **carne de puerco** (Mex) pork;
carne de cordero lamb; **carne
molida** (LatAm) mince; **carne
picada** (Mex) mince; **carne de ternera**
veal; **carne de vaca** beef; **carne
de res** (Mex) beef
carnet (pl carnets) nm card;
el carnet de identidad identity
card; **un carnet de conducir** a
driving licence
carnicería nf butcher's
carnicero, -a nm/f butcher
caro, -a adj, adv expensive ▷ **Las
entradas me costaron muy caras.** The
tickets were very expensive.
carpeta nf folder
carpintería nf ❶ carpenter's shop
❷ carpentry
carpintero, -a nm/f carpenter
carrera nf ❶ race ▷ **una carrera de
caballos** a horse race; **Me di una
carrera para alcanzar el**

a

autobús. I had to run to catch the bus. ❷ **degree** ▷ *Está haciendo la carrera de derecho.* He's doing a law degree. ❸ **career** ▷ *Estaba en el mejor momento de su carrera.* He was at the height of his career. ❹ *(in tights)* **ladder**

carrete nm ❶ **film** ❷ **reel**

carretera nf **road**; **una carretera nacional** an A-road; **una carretera de circunvalación** a bypass

carretilla nf **wheelbarrow**

carril nm ❶ **lane** ❷ **rail**

carril-bici (pl **carriles-bici**) nm **cycle lane**

carrito nm **trolley**

carro nm ❶ **cart** ❷ **trolley** ❸ *(LatAm)* **car**

carroza nf ❶ **coach** ❷ **float**

carta nf ❶ **letter** ▷ *Le he escrito una carta a Juan.* I've written Juan a letter.; **echar una carta** to post a letter ❷ **card** ▷ *jugar a las cartas* to play cards ❸ *(in restaurant)* **menu**; **la carta de vinos** the wine list

cartel nm ❶ **poster** ❷ **sign**

cartelera nf ❶ **billboard** ❷ **listings** pl; **Estuvo tres años en la cartelera.** It ran for three years.

cartera nf ❶ **wallet** ❷ **briefcase** ❸ **satchel** ❹ *(LatAm)* **handbag** ❺ **postwoman**

cartero nm **postman**

cartón (pl **cartones**) nm ❶ **cardboard** ▷ *una caja de cartón* a cardboard box ❷ **carton**

cartucho nm **cartridge**

cartulina nf **card**

casa nf ❶ **house** ▷ *una casa de dos plantas* a two-storey house ❷ **home** ▷ *Estábamos en casa.* We were at home. ▷ *Le dolía la cabeza so se fue a casa.* She had a headache so she went home.; **Estábamos en casa de Juan.** We were at Juan's.; **una casa de discos** a record company

casado, -a adj **married** ▷ *una mujer casada* a married woman; **Está casado con una francesa.** He's married to a French woman.

casarse vb **[25]** to **get married**; **Se casó con una periodista.** He married a journalist.

cascabel nm **small bell**

cascada nf **waterfall**

cascar vb **[48]** *(nut, egg)* to **crack**

cáscara nf ❶ **shell** ❷ **skin**

casco nm **helmet** ▷ *El ciclista llevaba casco.* The cyclist was wearing a helmet.; **el casco antiguo de la ciudad** the old part of the town; **el casco urbano** the town centre; **los cascos** headphones

casero, -a adj **homemade**

caseta nf ❶ **kennel** ❷ **bathing hut** ❸ **stall**

casete nm ❶ **cassette player** ❷ **cassette**

casi adv **almost** ▷ *Casi me ahogo.* I almost drowned. ▷ *Son casi las cinco.* It's almost five o'clock. ▷ **No queda casi nada en la nevera.** There's hardly anything left in the refrigerator.; **Casi nunca se equivoca.** He hardly ever makes a mistake.

b

c

d

e

f

g

h

i

j

k

l

m

n

ñ

o

p

q

r

s

t

u

v

w

x

y

z

casilla nf ❶ box ❷ square; **Casilla de Correos** (River Plate) post-office box (number)

casino nm casino

caso nm case; **en ese caso** in that case; **En caso de que llueva, iremos en autobús.** If it rains, we'll go by bus.; **El caso es que no me queda dinero.** The thing is, I haven't got any money left.; **No le hagas caso.** Don't take any notice of him.; **Hazle caso que ella tiene más experiencia.** Listen to her, she has more experience:

caspa nf dandruff

cassette = **casete**

castaña nf chestnut

castaño, -a adj chestnut ▷ Mi hermana tiene el pelo castaño. My sister has chestnut hair.

castañuelas nfpl castanets

castellano, -a adj, nm/f Castilian
▶ nm (language) Spanish

Since the language we know as Spanish originated in Castile, it is commonly referred to as **castellano**, especially by Catalans, Basques and Galicians, who have their own regional official languages too.

castigar vb [37] to punish

castigo nm punishment

Castilla nf Castile

castillo nm castle

casualidad nf coincidence; **¡Qué casualidad!** What a coincidence!; **Nos encontramos por casualidad.** We met by chance.;

Da la casualidad que nacimos el mismo día. It so happens that we were born on the same day.

catalán (f catalana, mpl catalanes) adj, nm/f Catalan
▶ nm (language) Catalan

catálogo nm catalogue

Cataluña nf Catalonia

catarata nf waterfall

catarro nm cold ▷ Vas a pillar un catarro. You're going to catch a cold.

catástrofe nf catastrophe

catedral nf cathedral

catedrático, -a nm/f ❶ professor ❷ principal teacher

categoría nf category; **un hotel de primera categoría** a first-class hotel; **un puesto de poca categoría** a low-ranking position

católico, -a adj, nm/f Catholic
▷ Soy católico. I am a Catholic.

catorce adj, pron fourteen; **el catorce de enero** the fourteenth of January

caucho nm rubber

causa nf cause; **a causa de** because of

causar vb [25] to cause; **Su visita me causó mucha alegría.** His visit made me very happy.; **Rosa me causó buena impresión.** Rosa made a good impression on me.

cava nm cava (sparkling wine)

cavar vb [25] to dig

caverna nf cave

cayendo vb see caer

caza nf ❶ hunting ❷ shooting

cazador nm hunter

cazadora nf ❶ jacket ❷ hunter

cazar vb [13] ❶ to hunt ❷ to shoot

cazo nm ❶ saucepan ❷ ladle

cazuela nf pot

CD (pl CDs) nm CD

CD-ROM (pl CD-ROMs) nm CD-ROM

cebo nm bait

cebolla nf onion

cebolleta nf ❶ spring onion ❷ pickled onion

cebra nf zebra; **un paso de cebra** a zebra crossing

ceder vb [8] ❶ to give in ▷ Al final tuve que ceder. Finally I had to give in. ❷ to give way ▷ La estantería cedió por el peso de los libros. The shelves gave way under the weight of the books.; **'Ceda el paso'** 'Give way'

ceguera nf blindness

ceja nf eyebrow

celda nf cell

celebración (pl celebraciones) nf celebration

celebrar vb [25] ❶ to celebrate ❷ to hold

celo nm Sellotape®

celofán nm cellophane

celos nmpl jealousy sg ▷ Lo hizo por celos. He did it out of jealousy.; **Tiene celos de su mejor amiga.** She's jealous of her best friend.; **Lo hace para darle celos.** He does it to make her jealous.

celoso, -a adj jealous

célula nf cell

cementerio nm cemetery; **un cementerio de coches** a scrapyard

cemento nm ❶ cement; **el cemento armado** reinforced concrete ❷ (LatAm) glue

cena nf dinner ▷ La cena es a las nueve. Dinner is at nine o'clock.

cenar vb [25] to have dinner; **¿Qué quieres cenar?** What do you want for dinner?

cenicero nm ashtray

ceniza nf ash

censura nf censorship

centavo nm (division of dollar) cent

centésima nf **una centésima de segundo** a hundredth of a second

centígrado, -a adj centigrade

centímetro nm centimetre

céntimo nm (division of euro) cent

central adj central
  ▶ nf head office; **una central eléctrica** a power station; **una central nuclear** a nuclear power station

centralita nf switchboard

céntrico, -a adj central ▷ Está en un barrio céntrico. It's in a central area.; **Un piso céntrico.** The flat is in the centre of town.

centro nm centre ▷ en pleno centro de la ciudad right in the town centre; **Fui al centro a hacer unas compras.** I went into town to do some shopping.; **un centro comercial** a shopping centre; **un centro médico** a hospital

centroamericano, -a adj, nm/f Central American

ceñido, -a adj tight

cepillar vb [25] to brush; **Se está cepillando los dientes.** He's brushing his teeth.

cepillo nm brush; **un cepillo de dientes** a toothbrush

cera nf wax

cerámica nf pottery ▷ *Me gusta la cerámica.* I like pottery.; **una cerámica** a piece of pottery

cerca adv near ▷ *El colegio está muy cerca.* The school is very near.; **¿Hay algún banco por aquí cerca?** Is there a bank nearby?; **cerca de la iglesia** near the church; **cerca de dos horas** nearly two hours; **Quería verlo de cerca.** I wanted to see it close up.

cercanías nfpl outskirts

cercano, -a adj nearby ▷ *Viven en un pueblo cercano.* They live in a nearby village.; **una de las calles cercanas a la catedral** one of the streets close to the cathedral

cerdo nm ❶ pig ❷ pork

cereal nm cereal; **Los niños desayunan cereales.** The children have cereal for breakfast.

cerebro nm brain

ceremonia nf ceremony

cereza nf cherry

cerilla nf match

cerillo nm (Mex) match

cero nm zero; **Estamos a cinco grados bajo cero.** It's five degrees below zero.; **cero coma tres** zero point three; **Van dos a cero.** The score is two-nil!.; **Empataron a cero.** It was a no-score draw.; **quince a cero** fifteen-love

cerquillo nm (LatAm) fringe

cerrado, -a adj closed ▷ *Las tiendas están cerradas.* The shops are closed.; **una curva muy cerrada** a very sharp bend

cerradura nf lock

cerrar vb [**39**] ❶ to close ▷ *Cerró el libro.* He closed the book. ❷ to turn off ▷ *Cierra el grifo.* Turn off the tap.; **Cerré la puerta con llave.** I locked the door.; **La puerta se cerró de golpe.** The door slammed shut.

cerrojo nm bolt; **echar el cerrojo** to bolt the door

certificado, -a adj registered; **Mandé el paquete certificado.** I sent the parcel by registered post. ▶ nm certificate

cervecería nf bar

cerveza nf beer; **la cerveza de barril** draught beer

cesar vb [**25**] to stop; **No cesa de hablar.** He never stops talking.; **No cesaba de repetirlo.** He kept repeating it.

césped nm grass ▷ *'no pisar el césped'* 'keep off the grass'

cesta nf basket; **una cesta de Navidad** a Christmas hamper

cesto nm basket

chabacano nm (Mex) apricot

chabola nf shack; **un barrio de chabolas** a shantytown

chaleco nm waistcoat; **un chaleco salvavidas** a life jacket

chalet (pl chalets) nm ❶ cottage ❷ villa ❸ house

champán (pl champanes) nm champagne

champiñón (pl champiñones) nm mushroom

champú (pl champús) nm shampoo

chancho, -a nm/f (River Plate) pig

chancleta nf flip-flop; **unas chancletas** a pair of flip-flops

chándal (pl chándals) nm tracksuit

chantaje nm blackmail; **hacer chantaje a alguien** to blackmail somebody

chapa nf ❶ badge ❷ (of bottle) top ❸ (of metal) sheet ❹ panel ❺ (LatAm) number plate

chapado, -a adj chapado en oro gold-plated

chaparrón (pl chaparrones) nm ▷ **Anoche cayó un buen chaparrón.** There was a real downpour last night.; **Es solo un chaparrón.** It's just a shower.

chapuza nf botched job; **hacer chapuzas** to do odd jobs

chapuzón (pl chapuzones) nm **darse un chapuzón** to go for a dip

chaqueta nf ❶ cardigan ❷ jacket

charca nf pond

charco nm puddle

charcutería nf (specializing in cold meats) delicatessen

charla nf ❶ chat ▷ **Estuvimos de charla.** We had a chat. ❷ talk ▷ **Dio una charla sobre teatro clásico.** He gave a talk on classical theatre.

charlar vb ❶ to chat

chasco nm **llevarse un chasco** to be disappointed

chat nm chatroom

chatarra nf scrap metal

chava nf (Mex) girl

chavo nm (Mex) boy

checar vb [48] (Mex) to check

checo, -a adj, nm/f Czech; **la República Checa** the Czech Republic

▶ nm (language) Czech

chef (pl chefs) nm chef

cheque nm cheque; **los cheques de viaje** traveller's cheques

chequeo nm check-up ▷ **hacerse un chequeo** to have a check-up

chévere adj, adv (LatAm) great

chica nf girl

chícharo nm (Mex) pea

chichón (pl chichones) nm bump ▷ **Me ha salido un chichón en la frente.** I've got a bump on my forehead.

chicle nm chewing gum

chico, -a adj small

▶ nm ❶ boy ▷ **los chicos de la clase** the boys in the class ❷ guy ▷ **Me parece un chico muy guapo.** I think he's a cute guy.

Chile nm Chile

chileno, -a adj, nm/f Chilean

chillar vb [25] ❶ to scream ❷ to squeak ❸ to squeal ❹ to screech

chimenea nf ❶ chimney ❷ fireplace

chimpancé (pl chimpancés) nm chimpanzee

China nf China

china nf Chinese woman

chinche nf (Mex, River Plate) drawing pin

chincheta nf drawing pin

chino, -a adj Chinese

▶ nm ❶ Chinese man; **los chinos** the Chinese ❷ (language) Chinese

Chipre nm Cyprus

chirimoya nf custard apple

chirriar vb [21] to squeak

chisme nm ❶ thing ❷ piece of gossip

chismorrear vb **[25]** to gossip

chismoso, -a adj ¡No seas chismoso! Don't be such a gossip!

chiste nm ❶ joke ▷ contar un chiste to tell a joke; **un chiste verde** a dirty joke

▪ Word for word, **chiste verde** means 'green joke'.

❷ cartoon

chocar nm **[48]** chocar contra (1) to hit (2) to bump into; **chocar con algo** to crash into something; **Los trenes chocaron de frente.** The trains crashed head-on.; **Me choca que no sepas nada.** I'm shocked that you don't know anything about it.

chocolate nm chocolate ▷ chocolate con leche milk chocolate; **Nos tomamos un chocolate.** We had a cup of hot chocolate.

chocolatina nf chocolate bar

chófer nmf ❶ driver ❷ chauffeur

chopo nm black poplar

choque nm ❶ crash ❷ clash

chorizo nm

▪ **Chorizo** is a kind of spicy sausage.

chorrito nm dash ▷ Échame un chorrito de leche. Just a dash of milk, please.

chorro nm **salir a chorros** to gush out

choza nf hut

chubasco nm heavy shower

chubasquero nm cagoule

chuche nf (informal) sweetie

chuleta nf chop ▷ una chuleta de cerdo a pork chop

chulo, -a adj ❶ (informal) cocky ❷ (informal) neat ▷ ¡Qué mochila más chula! What a neat rucksack!

chupar vb **[25]** to suck

chupete nm dummy

churro nm

▪ A **churro** is a type of fritter typically served with a cup of hot chocolate at cafés or **churrerías** (churro stalls/ shops).

cibercafé nm Internet café

cicatriz (pl cicatrices) nf scar

ciclismo nm cycling; **Mi hermano hace ciclismo.** My brother is a cyclist.

ciclista nmf cyclist

ciclo nm cycle

ciega nf blind woman

ciego, -a adj blind; **quedarse ciego** to go blind

▶ nm blind man; **los ciegos** blind people

cielo nm ❶ sky ❷ heaven

cien adj, pron a hundred ▷ Había unos cien invitados en la boda. There were about a hundred guests at the wedding. ▷ cien mil a hundred thousand; **cien por cien** a hundred percent ▷ Es cien por cien algodón. It's a hundred percent cotton.

ciencia nf science ▷ Me gustan mucho las ciencias. I really enjoy science. ▷ ciencias sociales social sciences; **ciencias empresariales** business studies

ciencia-ficción nf science fiction

científica nf scientist

científico, -a adj scientific
▶ nm scientist

ciento adj, pron a hundred; **ciento cuarenta y dos libras** a hundred and forty-two pounds; **Recibimos cientos de cartas.** We received hundreds of letters.; **el diez por ciento de la población** ten percent of the population

cierre nm ❶ clasp ❷ closing-down; **un cierre relámpago** (River Plate) a zip

cierro vb see **cerrar**

cierto, -a adj ❶ true ▷ No, eso no es cierto. No, that's not true. ❷ certain ▷ Viene ciertos días a la semana. He comes certain days of the week.; **por cierto** by the way

ciervo nm deer

cifra nf figure ▷ un número de cuatro cifras a four-figure number

cigarrillo nm cigarette

cigarro nm cigarette

cigüeña nf stork

cima nf top

cimientos nmpl foundations

cinco adj, pron five; **Son las cinco.** It's five o'clock.; **el cinco de enero** the fifth of January

cincuenta adj, pron fifty; **el cincuenta aniversario** the fiftieth anniversary

cine nm cinema; **ir al cine** to go to the cinema; **una actriz de cine** a film actress

cínico, -a adj cynical

cinta nf ❶ ribbon ❷ tape; **una cinta de vídeo** a videotape; **cinta**

aislante insulating tape; **una cinta transportadora** a conveyor belt

cintura nf waist ▷ ¿Cuánto mides de cintura? What's your waist size?

cinturón (pl cinturones) nm belt; **el cinturón de seguridad** the safety belt

ciprés (pl cipreses) nm cypress

circo nm circus

circuito nm ❶ track ❷ circuit; **circuito cerrado de televisión** closed-circuit television

circulación nf ❶ traffic ▷ un accidente de circulación a traffic accident ❷ circulation

circular vb [25] ❶ to drive; **¡Circulen!** Move along please! ❷ to circulate ❸ to go round

círculo nm circle

circunferencia nf circumference

circunstancia nf circumstance

ciruela nf plum; **una ciruela pasa** a prune

cirugía nf surgery; **hacerse la cirugía plástica** to have plastic surgery

cirujano, -a nm/f surgeon

cisne nm swan

cisterna nf cistern

cita nf ❶ appointment ▷ Tengo cita con el Sr. Pérez. I've got an appointment with Mr. Pérez. ❷ date ▷ No llegues tarde a la cita. Don't be late for your date. ❸ quotation ▷ una cita de Quevedo a quotation from Quevedo

citar vb [25] ❶ to quote ▷ Siempre está citando a los clásicos. He's always quoting the classics.

❷ to mention ▷ Citó el caso que ocurrió el otro día. He mentioned as an example what happened the other day.; **Nos han citado a las diez.** We've been given an appointment for ten o'clock.; **Me he citado con Elena.** I've arranged to meet Elena.

ciudad nf ❶ city ❷ town; **la ciudad universitaria** the university campus

ciudadano, -a nm/f citizen

civil adj civil ▷ la guerra civil the Civil War

civilización (pl civilizaciones) nf civilization

civilizado, -a adj civilized

clara nf (of egg) white

clarinete nm clarinet

claro, -a adj ❶ clear ▷ Lo quiero mañana. ¿Está claro? I want it tomorrow. Is that clear?; **Está claro que esconden algo.** It's obvious that they are hiding something.; **No tengo muy claro lo que quiero hacer.** I'm not very sure about what I want to do.; ❷ light ▷ una camisa azul claro a light blue shirt
▷ adv clearly ▷ Lo oí muy claro. I heard it very clearly.; **Quiero que me hables claro.** I want you to be frank with me.; **No he sacado nada en claro de la reunión.** I'm none the wiser after that meeting.; **¡Claro! (1)** Sure! **(2)** Of course!

clase nf ❶ class ▷ A las diez tengo clase de física. I have a physics class at ten.; **Mi hermana da clases de**

inglés. My sister teaches English.; **Hoy no hay clase.** There's no school today.; **clases de conducir** driving lessons; **clases particulares** private classes ❷ classroom ❸ kind ▷ Había juguetes de todas clases. There were all kinds of toys.; **la clase media** the middle class

clásico, -a adj ❶ classical ▷ Me gusta la música clásica. I like classical music. ❷ classic ▷ Es el clásico ejemplo de malnutrición. It's the classic case of malnutrition.

clasificación (pl clasificaciones) nf classification; **estar a la cabeza de la clasificación** to be at the top of the table

clasificar vb [48] to classify; **Esperan clasificarse para la final.** They hope to qualify for the final.; **Se clasificaron en tercer lugar.** They came third.

clavar vb [25] clavar una punta en algo to hammer a nail into something; **Las tablas están mal clavadas.** The boards aren't properly nailed down.; **Me he clavado una espina en el dedo.** I got a thorn in my finger.

clave nf ❶ code; **un mensaje en clave** a coded message ❷ key ▷ la clave del éxito the key to success; **la clave de sol** the treble clef

clavel nm carnation

clavícula nf collar bone

clavo nm nail

clic nm click; **hacer clic en** to click on

clicar *vb* **[49]** to click; **clicar dos veces** to double-click

cliente, -a *nm/f* **①** customer **②** client **③** guest

clima *nm* climate

climatizado, -a *adj* **①** air-conditioned **②** heated

clínica *nf* hospital

clínico, -a *adj* clinical

clip (*pl* **clips**) *nm* **①** paper clip **②** clip

cloaca *nf* sewer

cloro *nm* chlorine

club (*pl* **clubs**) *nm* club ▷ **el club de tenis** the tennis club

cobarde *adj* cowardly
▶ *nmf* coward

cobaya *nf* guinea pig

cobija *nf* (*LatAm*) blanket

cobrar *vb* **[25]** to charge ▷ **Me cobró treinta euros por la reparación.** He charged me thirty euros for the repair.; **cuando cobre el sueldo de este mes** when I get my wages this month; **¿Me cobra los cafés?** How much do I owe for the coffees?; **¡Cóbrese, por favor!** Can I pay, please?; **cobrar un cheque** to cash a cheque

cobre *nm* copper

cobro *nm* **llamar a cobro revertido** to reverse the charges

cocaína *nf* cocaine

cocer *vb* **[6]** **①** to boil **②** to cook; **Tarda diez minutos en cocerse.** It takes ten minutes to cook.

coche *nm* **①** car ▷ **Fuimos a Sevilla en coche.** We went to Seville by car.; **un coche de carreras** a racing car; **los coches de choque** bumper

cars **②** pram **③** carriage ▷ **Fuimos en coche cama.** We took the sleeper.; **un coche de bomberos** a fire engine

cochino, -a *adj* filthy
▶ *nm* pig

cocido *nm* stew
 The **cocido madrileño** is a stew of chickpeas, vegetables and meat.

cocina *nf* **①** kitchen **②** cooker ▷ *una cocina de gas* a gas cooker; **la cocina vasca** Basque cuisine; **un libro de cocina** a cookery book

cocinar *vb* **[25]** to cook ▷ *No sabe cocinar.* He can't cook.; **Cocinas muy bien.** You're a very good cook.

cocinero, -a *nm/f* cook

coco *nm* coconut

cocodrilo *nm* crocodile

código *nm* code; **el código de la circulación** the highway code; **el código postal** the postcode

codo *nm* elbow

codorniz (*pl* **codornices**) *nf* quail

coger *vb* **[7]** **①** to take ▷ *Coja la primera calle a la derecha.* Take the first street on the right. **②** to catch; **coger un resfriado** to catch a cold **③** to pick up **④** to get ▷ *¿Nos coges dos entradas?* Would you get us two tickets? **⑤** to borrow ▷ *¿Te puedo coger el bolígrafo?* Can I borrow your pen?; **Voy a coger el autobús.** I'm going to get the bus.; **Iban cogidos de la mano.** They were walking hand in hand.

cohete *nm* rocket; **un cohete espacial** a rocket

cohibido, -a adj inhibited;
sentirse cohibido to feel inhibited

coincidencia nf coincidence;
¡Qué coincidencia! What a
coincidence!

coincidir vb [58] to match ▷ Las
huellas dactilares coinciden. The
fingerprints match.; **Coincidimos
en el tren.** We happened to meet
on the train.; **Es que esas fechas
coinciden con mi viaje.** The
problem is, those dates clash with
my trip.

cojear vb [25] ① to limp ② to be
lame ③ (furniture) to wobble

cojín (pl cojines) nm cushion

cojo vb see **coger**
▸ adj ① lame; **Está cojo.** He's lame.
② (furniture) wobbly

col nf cabbage; **las coles de
Bruselas** Brussels sprouts

cola nf ① tail ② queue ▷ Había
mucha cola para el baño. There was a
long queue for the toilets.; **hacer
cola** to queue ③ glue

colaborar vb [25] **Todo el pueblo
colaboró.** Everyone in the village
joined in.

colador nm ① strainer ② sieve

colar vb [11] to strain; **colarse**
(informal) to push in; **Nos colamos
en el cine.** We sneaked into the
cinema without paying.

colcha nf bedspread

colchón (pl colchones) nm
mattress; **un colchón de aire** an
air bed

colchoneta nf ① mat ② air bed

colección (pl colecciones) nf
collection

coleccionar vb [25] to collect

colecta nf collection

colectivo nm (River Plate) bus

colega nmf ① colleague
② (informal) mate

colegio nm school ▷ Voy al colegio en
bicicleta. I cycle to school. ▷ ¿Todavía
vas al colegio? Are you still at
school?; **un colegio de curas** a
Catholic boys' school; **un colegio
de monjas** a convent school; **un
colegio público** a state school; **un
colegio mayor** a hall of residence

coleta nf ponytail; **La niña llevaba
coletas.** The girl wore her hair in
bunches.

colgado, -a adj hanging ▷ Había
varios cuadros colgados en la pared.
There were several pictures
hanging on the wall.; **Debe
tener el teléfono mal colgado.**
He must have the telephone off
the hook.

colgante nm pendant

colgar vb [28] ① to hang ② to
upload; **¡No dejes la chaqueta en
la silla, cuélgala!** Don't leave your
jacket on the chair, hang it up!;
Me colgó el teléfono. He hung up
on me.; **¡Cuelga, por favor, que
quiero hacer una llamada!** Hang
up, please. I want to use the
phone!; **No cuelgue, por favor.**
Please hold.

coliflor nf cauliflower

colilla nf cigarette end

colina nf hill

colisión nf collision

collar nm ① necklace ② collar

colmena nf beehive

colmillo nm ❶ canine tooth ❷ fang ❸ tusk

colmo nm ¡Esto ya es el colmo! This really is the last straw!; **Para colmo de males, empezó a llover.** To make matters worse, it started to rain.

colocar vb [48] ❶ to put ❷ to arrange; **colocarse** (1) to get a job (2) (informal) to get plastered (3) (informal) to get high; ¡Colocaos en fila! Get into a line!; **El equipo se ha colocado en quinto lugar.** The team are now in fifth place.

Colombia nf Colombia

colombiano, -a adj, nm/f Colombian

colonia nf ❶ perfume ❷ colony ❸ (Mex) district; **una colonia de verano** a summer camp

colonizar vb [13] to colonize

color nm colour ▷ ¿De qué color son? What colour are they?; **un vestido de color azul** a blue dress; **una televisión en color** a colour television

colorado, -a adj red; **ponerse colorado** to blush

columna nf column; **la columna vertebral** the spine

columpio nm swing

coma nf comma ▷ palabras separadas por comas words separated by commas; **cero coma ocho** zero point eight

▶ nm coma; **estar en coma** to be in a coma

comadrona nf midwife

comandante nmf major

comba nf skipping rope; **saltar a la comba** to skip

combate nm battle; **un piloto de combate** a fighter pilot; **un combate de boxeo** a boxing match

combinar vb [25] ❶ to combine ❷ to match ▷ colores que combinan con el azul colours which match with blue

combustible nm fuel

comedia nf comedy

comedor nm ❶ dining room ❷ refectory ❸ canteen

comentar vb [25] ❶ to say ❷ to discuss; **Me han comentado que es una película muy buena.** I've been told that is a very good film.

comentario nm comment

comentarista nmf commentator

comenzar vb [19] to begin; **Comenzó a llover.** It began to rain.

comer vb [8] ❶ to eat; **Me comí una manzana.** I had an apple. ❷ to have lunch; **Hemos comido paella.** We had paella for lunch.; ¿Qué hay para comer? What is there for lunch? ❸ (LatAm) to have dinner; **Le estaba dando de comer a su hijo.** She was feeding her son.; **No te comas el coco por eso.** (informal) Don't worry too much about it.

comercial adj ❶ business ❷ trade ❸ commercial

comerciante nmf shopkeeper

comercio nm ❶ trade ❷ shop

cometa nm comet

▶ nf kite

cometer vb [8] ❶ to commit
❷ to make

cómic (pl **cómics**) nm comic

cómico, -a adj ❶ comical ▷ Fue muy
cómico. It was very comical.
❷ comic ▷ un actor cómico a comic
actor

comida nf ❶ food; **la comida
basura** junk food ❷ lunch ▷ La
comida es a la una y media. Lunch is
at half past one. ❸ (LatAm) supper
❹ meal ▷ Es la comida más
importante del día. It's the most
important meal of the day.

comienzo vb see **comenzar**

comillas nfpl quotation marks;
entre comillas in quotation marks

comisaría nf police station

comité (pl **comités**) nm
committee

como adv, conj ❶ like ▷ Tienen un
perro como el nuestro. They've got a
dog like ours.; **Sabe como a
cebolla.** It tastes a bit like onion.
❷ as ▷ Lo usé como cuchara. I used it
as a spoon. ▷ blanco como la nieve as
white as snow ▷ Como ella no
llegaba, me fui. As she didn't arrive,
I left.; **Hazlo como te dijo ella.** Do
it the way she told you.; **Es tan
alto como tú.** He is as tall as you.;
tal como lo había planeado just
as I had planned it; **como si** as if
❸ if ▷ Como lo vuelvas a hacer se lo
digo a tu madre. If you do it again I'll
tell your mother. ❹ about
▷ Vinieron como unas diez personas.
About ten people came.

cómo adv how; **¿A cómo están las
manzanas?** How much are the

apples?; **¿Cómo es de grande?**
How big is it?; **¿Cómo es su novio?**
(1) What's her boyfriend like?
(2) What does her boyfriend look
like?; **Perdón, ¿cómo has dicho?**
Sorry, what did you say?; **¡Cómo!
¿Mañana?** What? Tomorrow?;
¡Cómo corría! Boy, was he
running!

cómoda nf chest of drawers

comodidad nf ❶ comfort
❷ convenience

cómodo, -a adj ❶ comfortable
❷ convenient

compact disc (pl **compact discs**)
nm ❶ compact disc ❷ compact
disc player

compadecer vb [12] to feel sorry
for

compañero, -a nm/f
❶ classmate ❷ workmate
❸ partner; **un compañero de
piso** a flatmate

compañía nf company ▷ una
compañía de seguros an insurance
company; **Ana vino a hacerme
compañía.** Ana came to keep me
company.; **una compañía aérea**
an airline

comparación (pl
comparaciones) nf comparison;
**Mi coche no tiene comparación
con el tuyo.** There's no
comparison between my car and
yours.; **Mi cuarto es
pequeñísimo en comparación
con el tuyo.** My room is tiny
compared to yours.

comparar vb [25] to compare

compartir vb [58] to share

compás (pl **compases**) nm compass; **bailar al compás de la música** to dance in time to the music

compatible adj compatible

compensar vb [**25**] ❶ (lack, loss) to make up for ❷ to compensate; **No compensa viajar tan lejos por tan poco tiempo.** It's not worth travelling that far for such a short time.

competencia nf ❶ rivalry ❷ competition; **No quiere hacerle la competencia a su mejor amigo.** He doesn't want to compete with his best friend.

competente adj competent

competición (pl **competiciones**) nf competition

competir vb [**38**] to compete; **competir por un título** to compete for a title

complacer vb [**12**] to please

complejo nm complex

completar vb [**25**] to complete

completo, -a adj ❶ complete ▷ las obras completas de Lorca the complete works of Lorca ❷ full ▷ Los hoteles estaban completos. The hotels were full.; **Me olvidé por completo.** I completely forgot.

complicado, -a adj complicated

complicar vb [**48**] to complicate; **complicarse** to get complicated; **No quiero complicarme la vida.** I don't want to make life more difficult for myself.

cómplice nmf accomplice

componer vb [**41**] to compose

comportamiento nm behaviour

comportarse vb [**25**] to behave

compra nf shopping; **hacer la compra** to do the shopping; **ir de compras** to go shopping

comprar vb [**25**] to buy; **Le compré el coche a mi amigo.** I bought my friend's car.; **Quiero comprarme unos zapatos.** I want to buy a pair of shoes.

comprender vb [**8**] to understand

comprensivo, -a adj understanding

compresa nf sanitary towel

comprimido nm pill

comprobante nm receipt

comprobar vb [**11**] to check

comprometerse vb [**8**] **Me he comprometido a ayudarlos.** I have promised to help them.; **No quiero comprometerme por si después no puedo ir.** I don't want to commit myself in case I can't go.

compromiso nm engagement ▷ El ministro canceló sus compromisos. The minister cancelled his engagements. ▷ Se iban a casar pero rompieron el compromiso. They were going to get married but they broke their engagement.; **Puede probarlo sin ningún compromiso.** You can try it with no obligation.; **Iba a ir pero solamente por compromiso.** I was going to go but only out of duty.; **poner a alguien en un compromiso** to put someone in a difficult situation

compruebo vb see **comprobar**

a
b
c
d
e
f
g
h
i
j
k
l
m
n
ñ
o
p
q
r
s
t
u
v
w
x
y
z

compuesto vb see **componer**
▶ adj **un jurado compuesto de seis miembros** a jury made up of six members

computador nm (LatAm) computer; **un computador portátil** a laptop

computadora nf (LatAm) computer; **una computadora de escritorio** a desktop computer

común adj common ▷ **un apellido muy común** a very common surname; **No tenemos nada en común.** We have nothing in common.; **Hicimos el trabajo en común.** We did the work between us.; **las zonas de uso común** the communal areas

comunicación (pl comunicaciones) nf communication; **Se ha cortado la comunicación.** We've been cut off.

comunicar vb [48] to be engaged; **comunicarse** to communicate; **Los dos despachos se comunican.** The two offices are connected.

comunidad nf community; **una comunidad autónoma** an autonomous region

comunión (pl comuniones) nf communion; **Voy a hacer la primera comunión.** I'm going to make my first communion.

comunista adj, nmf communist

con prep with ▷ **¿Con quién vas a ir?** Who are you going with?; **Lo he escrito con bolígrafo.** I wrote it in pen.; **Voy a hablar con Luis.**

I'll talk to Luis.; **café con leche** white coffee; **Ábrelo con cuidado.** Open it carefully.; **Con estudiar un poco apruebas.** With a bit of studying you should pass.; **Con que me digas tu teléfono basta.** If you just give me your phone number that'll be enough.; **con tal de que no llegues tarde** as long as you don't arrive late

concejal, a nm/f town councillor

concentrarse vb [25] ❶ to concentrate ▷ **Me cuesta concentrarme.** I find it hard to concentrate. ❷ to gather ▷ **Los manifestantes se concentraron en la plaza.** The demonstrators gathered in the square.

concertar vb [39] to arrange

concha nf shell

conciencia nf conscience; **Lo han estudiado a conciencia.** They've studied it thoroughly.

concierto nm ❶ concert ❷ concerto

conclusión (pl conclusiones) nf conclusion

concreto, -a adj ❶ specific ▷ **por poner un ejemplo concreto** to take a specific example ❷ definite ▷ **Todavía no hay fechas concretas.** There are no definite dates yet.; **No me refiero a nadie en concreto.** I don't mean anyone in particular.; **Todavía no hemos decidido nada en concreto.** We still haven't decided anything definite.

concurrido, -a adj (street, place) busy

concursante *nmf* competitor

concurso *nm* ❶ game show ❷ competition ▷ *un concurso de poesía* a poetry competition; **un concurso de belleza** a beauty contest

conde *nm* count

condecoración (*pl* **condecoraciones**) *nf* decoration

condena *nf* sentence; **cumplir una condena** to serve a sentence

condenar *vb* [25] to sentence

condesa *nf* countess

condición (*pl* **condiciones**) *nf* condition; **a condición de que apruebes** on condition that you pass; **El piso está en muy malas condiciones.** The flat is in a very bad state.; **No está en condiciones de viajar.** He's not fit to travel.

condón (*pl* **condones**) *nm* condom

conducir *vb* [9] ❶ to drive; **No sé conducir.** I can't drive. ❷ to ride; **Enfadarse no conduce a nada.** Getting angry won't get you anywhere.

conducta *nf* behaviour

conductor, a *nm/f* driver

conduzco *vb see* **conducir**

conectar *vb* [25] to connect

conejillo *nm* **un conejillo de Indias** a guinea pig

conejo *nm* rabbit

conexión (*pl* **conexiones**) *nf* connection

conferencia *nf* ❶ lecture ❷ conference ❸ long-distance call

confesar *vb* [39] ❶ to confess to ❷ to admit; **confesarse** to go to confession

confeti *nm* confetti

confianza *nf* trust; **Tengo confianza en ti.** I trust you.; **No tiene confianza en sí mismo.** He has no self-confidence.; **un empleado de confianza** a trusted employee; **Se lo dije porque tenemos mucha confianza.** I told her about it because we're very close.; **Los alumnos se toman muchas confianzas con él.** The pupils take too many liberties with him.

confiar *vb* [21] to trust ▷ *No confío en ella.* I don't trust her.; **Confiaba en que su familia le ayudaría.** He was confident that his family would help him.; **No hay que confiarse demasiado.** You mustn't be over-confident.

confidencial *adj* confidential

confieso *vb see* **confesar**

confirmar *vb* [25] to confirm

confitería *nf* cake shop

conflicto *nm* conflict

conformarse *vb* [25] **conformarse con** to be satisfied with; **Se conforman con poco.** They're easily satisfied.; **Tendrás que conformarte con uno más barato.** You'll have to make do with a cheaper one.

conforme *adj* satisfied ▷ *No quedó muy conforme con esa explicación.* He wasn't very satisfied with that explanation.; **estar conforme** to agree

confortable *adj* comfortable

confundir *vb* [58] ❶ to mistake ❷ to confuse; **Confundí las**

fechas. I got the dates mixed up.;
¡Vaya! ¡Me he confundido! Oh!
I've made a mistake!; **Me
confundí de piso.** I got the wrong
flat.

confusión (pl **confusiones**) nf
confusion

confuso, -a adj confused

congelado, -a adj frozen

congelador nm freezer

congelar vb [25] to freeze; **Me
estoy congelando.** I'm freezing.

congestionado, -a adj ❶ blocked
❷ congested

congreso nm conference; **un
congreso médico** a medical
conference; **el Congreso de los
Diputados** The Lower Chamber of
the Spanish Parliament.

conjunción (pl **conjunciones**) nf
conjunction

conjunto nm ❶ collection ▷ El libro
es un conjunto de poemas de amor.
The book is a collection of love
poems. ❷ group ▷ un conjunto de
música pop a pop group; **un
conjunto de falda y blusa** a
matching skirt and blouse; **Hay
que estudiar esos países en
conjunto.** You have to study these
countries as a whole.

conmemorar vb [25] to
commemorate

conmigo pron with me ▷ ¿Por qué
no vienes conmigo? Why don't you
come with me?; **Rosa quiere
hablar conmigo.** Rosa wants to
talk to me.

conmovedor, a adj moving

conmover vb [33] to move

cono nm cone; **el Cono Sur** the
Southern Cone

conocer vb [12] ❶ to know; **Nos
conocemos desde el colegio.**
We know each other from school.;
Me encantaría conocer China.
I would love to visit China. ❷ (for
the first time) to meet

conocida nf acquaintance

conocido, -a adj well-known
▶ nm acquaintance

conocimiento nm consciousness;
perder el conocimiento to lose
consciousness; **Tengo algunos
conocimientos de francés.** I have
some knowledge of French.

conozco vb see **conocer**

conque conj so ▷ Hemos terminado,
conque podéis iros. We've finished,
so you may leave now.

conquistar vb [25] ❶ to conquer
❷ to win...over

consciente adj conscious ▷ El
enfermo no estaba consciente. The
patient wasn't conscious.; **Es
plenamente consciente de sus
limitaciones.** He's fully aware of
his shortcomings.

consecuencia nf consequence
▷ Todo es una consecuencia de su falta
de disciplina. Everything is a
consequence of his lack of
discipline.; **Perdió el
conocimiento a consecuencia
del golpe.** He lost consciousness
as a result of the blow.

consecutivo, -a adj consecutive

conseguir vb [50] ❶ to get ▷ Él me
consiguió el trabajo. He got me the
job. ❷ to achieve; **Después de**

muchos intentos, al final lo **consiguió.** After many attempts, he finally succeeded.; **Finalmente conseguí convencerla.** I finally managed to convince her.; **No conseguí que se lo comiera.** I couldn't get him to eat it.

consejo nm advice ▷ Fui a pedirle consejo. I went to ask him for advice.; **¿Quieres que te dé un consejo?** Would you like me to give you some advice?

consentir vb [51] **①** to allow **②** to spoil

conserje nmf **①** caretaker **②** janitor **③** porter

conserva nf No comemos muchas conservas. We don't eat much tinned food.; **atún en conserva** tinned tuna

conservador, a adj conservative

conservar vb [25] **①** to keep ▷ Debe conservarse en la nevera. It should be kept in the fridge. **②** to preserve; **Enrique se conserva joven.** Enrique looks good for his age.

conservatorio nm music school

considerable adj considerable

considerado, -a adj considerate; **Está muy bien considerada entre los profesores.** She's very highly regarded among the teachers.

considerar vb [25] to consider

consiento vb see **consentir**

consigna nf left-luggage office

consigo vb see **conseguir**
▶ pron **①** with him **②** with her **③** with you

consiguiendo vb see **conseguir**

consintiendo vb see **consentir**

consistir vb [58] **El menú consiste en tres platos.** The menu consists of three courses.; **¿En qué consiste el trabajo?** What does the job involve?; **En eso consiste el secreto.** That's the secret.

consola nf console; **consola de videojuegos** games console

consolar vb [11] to console; **Para consolarme me compré un helado.** I bought an ice cream to cheer myself up.

consonante nf consonant

constante adj constant

constantemente adv constantly

constar vb [25] **La obra consta de siete relatos.** The work consists of seven stories.; **¡Que conste que yo pagué mi parte!** Don't forget that I paid my share!

constipado, -a adj **estar constipado** to have a cold

▌ Be careful! **constipado** does not mean **constipated**.

▶ nm cold ▷ coger un constipado to catch a cold

constitución (pl **constituciones**) nf constitution

construcción (pl **construcciones**) nf construction

constructor, a nm/f builder

construir vb [10] to build

consuelo vb see **consolar**
▶ nm consolation

cónsul nmf consul

consulado nm consulate

consulta nf surgery; **horas de consulta** surgery hours; **un libro de consulta** a reference book

consultar vb [**25**] to consult
consumición (pl **consumiciones**)
nf drink ▷ *Con la entrada tienes una
consumición.* The admission price
includes a drink.
consumir vb [**58**] ❶ to use ▷ *Mi
coche consume mucha gasolina.* My
car uses a lot of petrol. ❷ to drink;
**No podemos estar en el bar sin
consumir.** We can't stay in the pub
without buying a drink.; **Solo
piensan en consumir.** Spending
money is all they think about.
consumo nm consumption; **una
charla sobre el consumo de
drogas** a talk on drug use; **la
sociedad de consumo** the
consumer society
contabilidad nf accountancy
contable nmf accountant
contactar vb [**25**] **contactar con
alguien** to contact someone
contacto nm ❶ contact ❷ touch
▷ *Nos mantenemos en contacto por
teléfono.* We keep in touch by
phone. ▷ *Me puse en contacto con su
familia.* I got in touch with her
family.
contado adv **al contado** ▷ *Lo pagué
al contado.* I paid cash for it.
contador nm meter ▷ *el contador de
la luz* the electricity meter
▶ nm/f (LatAm) accountant
contagiar vb [**25**] **No quiero
contagiarte.** I don't want to give
it to you.; **Tiene la gripe y no
quiere que los niños se
contagien.** He has the flu and
doesn't want the children to
catch it.

contagioso, -a adj infectious
contaminación nf pollution
contaminar vb [**25**] to pollute
contar vb [**11**] ❶ to count ▷ *Sabe
contar hasta diez.* He can count to
ten. ❷ to tell ▷ *Cuéntame lo que
pasó.* Tell me what happened.;
Cuento contigo. I'm counting on
you.; **¿Qué te cuentas?** (informal)
How's things?
contendrá vb see **contener**
contenedor nm ❶ container
❷ recycling bin
contener vb [**53**] to contain;
contenerse to control oneself
contenido nm contents pl
contentarse vb [**25**] **Se contenta
con cualquier juguete.** She is
happy with any toy.; **Tuve que
contentarme con el segundo
premio.** I had to be satisfied with
second prize.
contento, -a adj happy ▷ *Estaba
contento porque era su cumpleaños.*
He was happy because it was his
birthday.; **estar contento con
algo** to be pleased with
something
contestación (pl
contestaciones) nf reply; **No me
des esas contestaciones.** Don't
answer back.
contestador nm **el contestador
automático** the answering
machine
contestar vb [**25**] to answer;
**Les he llamado varias veces y
no contestan.** I've phoned them
several times and there's no
answer.; **Me escribieron y tengo**

que contestarles. They wrote to me and I have to reply to them.

contigo *pron* with you ▷ *Quiero ir contigo.* I want to go with you.; *Necesito hablar contigo.* I need to talk to you.

continente *nm* continent

continuamente *adv* constantly

continuar *vb* [1] to continue; *Continuó estudiando toda la noche.* He carried on studying right through the night.

continuo, -a *adj* **1** constant **2** continuous

contra *prep* against ▷ *Eran dos contra uno.* They were two against one.; *Me choqué contra una farola.* I bumped into a lamppost.; *Estoy en contra de la pena de muerte.* I'm against the death penalty.

contrabajo *nm* double bass

contrabando *nm* smuggling ▷ *el contrabando de drogas* drug smuggling; *Lo trajeron al país de contrabando.* They smuggled it into the country.

contradecir *vb* [15] to contradict

contradicción (*pl* **contradicciones**) *nf* contradiction

contraria *nf* llevar la contraria a alguien (1) to contradict somebody (2) to do the opposite of what somebody wants

contrario, -a *adj* **1** opposing **2** opposite ▷ *Los dos coches iban en dirección contraria.* The two cars were travelling in opposite

directions.; *Ella opina lo contrario.* She thinks the opposite.; *Al contrario, me gusta mucho.* On the contrary, I like it a lot.; *De lo contrario, tendré que castigarte.* Otherwise, I will have to punish you.

contraseña *nf* password

contrastar *vb* [25] to contrast

contraste *nm* contrast

contratar *vb* [25] **1** to hire **2** to sign up

contrato *nm* contract

contribución (*pl* **contribuciones**) *nf* **1** contribution **2** tax ▷ *la contribución municipal* local tax

contribuir *vb* [10] to contribute

contribuyente *nmf* taxpayer

contrincante *nmf* opponent

control *nm* **1** control **2** road-block; **el control de pasaportes** passport control

controlar *vb* [25] to control; *Tuve que controlarme para no pegarle.* I had to control myself, otherwise I would have hit him.; *No te preocupes, todo está controlado.* Don't worry, everything is under control.

convencer *vb* [12] **1** to convince; *No me convence nada la idea.* I'm not convinced by the idea. **2** to persuade ▷ *La convencimos para que nos acompañara.* We persuaded her to go with us.

convencional *adj* conventional

conveniente *adj* convenient; *Sería conveniente que se lo dijeras.* It would be advisable to tell him.

convenir vb [56] to suit ▷ *el método que más le convenga* the method that suits you best; **Te conviene descansar un poco.** You ought to get some rest.; **Quizá convenga recordar que ...** It might be appropriate to recall that ...

conversación (pl **conversaciones**) nf conversation

convertir vb [51] to turn ▷ *Convirtieron la casa en colegio.* They turned the house into a school.; **convertirse** to convert ▷ *Se convirtió al cristianismo.* He converted to Christianity.; **convertirse en (1)** to become ▷ *Se convirtió en un hombre rico.* He became a rich man. ▷ *El convento se convirtió en hotel.* The convent became a hotel. **(2)** to turn into ▷ *Se convirtió en una pesadilla.* It turned into a nightmare. ▷ *La oruga se convierte en mariposa.* The caterpillar turns into a butterfly.

convocar vb [48] to call

coñac (pl **coñacs**) nm brandy

cooperación nf cooperation

cooperar vb [25] to cooperate

copa nf ❶ glass ▷ *Solo tomé una copa de champán.* I only had one glass of champagne. ❷ drink; **Fuimos a tomar unas copas.** We went for a few drinks. ❸ (of tree) top

  ⁞ **copas** are goblets, one of the
  ⁞ suits in the Spanish card deck.

copia nf copy ▷ *hacer una copia* to make a copy; **una copia impresa** a printout

copiar vb [25] to copy; **to copy and paste** copiar y pegar

copo nm un copo de nieve a snowflake

corazón (pl **corazones**) nm heart ▷ *Está mal del corazón.* He has heart trouble.; **Tiene muy buen corazón.** He is very kind-hearted.

corbata nf tie

corcho nm cork; **un tapón de corcho** a cork

cordel nm cord

cordero nm lamb ▷ *Comimos chuletas de cordero.* We had lamb chops.

cordón (pl **cordones**) nm ❶ shoelace ❷ cable

corneta nf bugle

coro nm ❶ choir ❷ chorus

corona nf crown; **una corona de flores** a garland

coronel nm colonel

corporal adj ❶ body ❷ corporal ❸ personal

corral nm ❶ farmyard ❷ playpen

correa nf ❶ belt ❷ lead ❸ strap

correcto, -a adj correct

corredor, a nm/f runner

corregir vb [18] ❶ to correct ❷ to mark

correo nm post ▷ *Me lo mandó por correo.* He sent it to me by post.; **Correos** post office ▷ *Fui a Correos a comprar sellos.* I went to the post office to buy stamps.; **el servicio de correos** the postal service; **correo electrónico** email; **correo basura** spam

correr vb [8] ❶ to run; **El ladrón echó a correr.** The thief started to run. **③ to hurry** ▷ *Corre que llegamos tarde.* Hurry or we'll be late.; **No corras que te equivocarás.** Don't rush or you'll make a mistake. **③ to go fast** ▷ *No corras tanto, que hay hielo en la carretera.* Don't go so fast, the road's icy. **④ to move;** **¿Quieres que corra la cortina?** Do you want me to draw the curtains?

correspondencia *nf* correspondence

corresponder *vb* [**8**] **Me pagó lo que me correspondía.** He paid me my share.; **Estas fotos corresponden a otro álbum.** These photos belong to another album.; **No me corresponde a mí hacerlo.** It's not for to me to do it.

correspondiente *adj* relevant; **los datos correspondientes al año pasado** the figures for last year

corresponsal *nmf* correspondent

corrida *nf* bullfight

corriente *adj* common ▷ *Pérez es un apellido muy corriente.* Pérez is a very common surname.; **Es un caso poco corriente.** It's an unusual case.; **Tengo que ponerle al corriente de lo que ha pasado.** I have to let him know what has happened.
▶ *nf* **①** current; **Te va a dar corriente.** You'll get an electric shock. **②** draught

corrijo *vb* see **corregir**

corro *nm* ring ▷ *Los niños hicieron un corro.* The children formed a ring.

corrupción *nf* corruption

cortado, -a *adj* **①** (*milk*) sour **②** chapped **③** (*street, road*) closed; **Juan estaba muy cortado con mis padres.** Juan was very shy with my parents.
▶ *nm* white coffee
　　A **cortado** is a small white coffee with only a little milk.

cortar *vb* [**25**] **①** to cut ▷ *Corta la manzana por la mitad.* Cut the apple in half.; **Te vas a cortar.** You're going to cut yourself. **②** to cut off **③** to close; **Fui a cortarme el pelo.** I went to get my hair cut.; **De repente se cortó la comunicación.** Suddenly we were cut off.

cortaúñas (*pl* **cortaúñas**) *nm* nail clippers

corte *nm* cut; **un corte de pelo** a haircut; **Me da corte pedírselo.** I'm embarrassed to ask him.

cortés, a (*mpl* **corteses**) *adj* polite

cortesía *nf* courtesy; **por cortesía** as a courtesy

corteza *nf* **①** crust **②** rind **③** bark

cortina *nf* curtain

corto, -a *adj* short ▷ *Susana tiene el pelo corto.* Susana has short hair.; **ser corto de vista** to be short-sighted
▶ *abbr m* (= *cortometraje*) short film

cortocircuito *nm* short-circuit

cosa *nf* thing ▷ *Cogí mis cosas y me fui.* I picked up my things and left.; **cualquier cosa** anything; **¿Me puedes decir una cosa?** Can you tell me something?; **¡Qué cosa más rara!** How strange!

cosecha nf harvest

cosechar vb [25] to harvest

coser vb [8] to sew

cosmético nm cosmetic

cosquillas nfpl **hacer cosquillas a alguien** to tickle someone; **Tiene muchas cosquillas.** He's very ticklish.

costa nf coast ▷ *Pasamos el verano en la costa.* We spend the summer on the coast.

costado nm side; **Estaba tumbado de costado.** He was lying on his side.

costar vb [11] to cost ▷ *¿Cuánto cuesta?* How much does it cost? ▷ *Me costó diez euros.* It cost me ten euros.; **Las matemáticas le cuestan mucho.** He finds maths very difficult.; **Me cuesta hablarle.** I find it hard to talk to him.

Costa Rica nf Costa Rica

costarricense adj, nmf Costa Rican

costarriqueño, -a adj, nm/f Costa Rican

coste nm cost ▷ *el coste de la vida* the cost of living

costilla nf rib

costo nm cost

costoso, -a adj expensive

costra nf ❶ scab ❷ crust

costumbre nf ❶ habit ❷ custom; **Se le olvidó, como de costumbre.** He forgot, as usual.; **Nos sentamos en el sitio de costumbre.** We sat in our usual place.

costura nf ❶ seam ❷ sewing

cotidiano, -a adj everyday ▷ *la vida cotidiana* everyday life

cotilla nmf gossip

cotillear vb [25] to gossip

cotilleo nm gossip

cráneo nm skull

creación (pl **creaciones**) nf creation

crear vb [25] to create; **No quiero crearme problemas.** I don't want to create problems for myself.

creativo, -a adj creative

crecer vb [12] ❶ to grow ❷ to grow up

crecimiento nm growth

crédito nm ❶ loan ▷ *Pedí un crédito al banco.* I asked the bank for a loan. ❷ credit ▷ *comprar algo a crédito* to buy something on credit

creencia nf belief

creer vb [30] ❶ to believe; **Eso no se lo cree nadie.** No one will believe that. ❷ to think ▷ *No creo que pueda ir.* I don't think I'll be able to go.; **Se cree muy lista.** She thinks she's pretty clever.; **Creo que sí.** I think so.; **Creo que no.** I don't think so.

creído, -a adj **Es muy creído.** He's so full of himself.

crema nf cream ▷ *Me pongo crema en las manos.* I put cream on my hands.; **la crema de afeitar** shaving cream; **crema de champiñones** cream of mushroom soup; **una blusa de color crema** a cream-coloured blouse

cremallera nf zip ▷ *Súbete la cremallera.* Pull up your zip.

crematorio nm crematorium

creyendo vb see creer

creyente nmf believer

crezco vb see crecer

cría nf ❶ baby; **una cría de cebra** a baby zebra; **La leona tuvo dos crías.** The lioness had two cubs. ❷ girl

criada nf maid

criado nm servant

criar vb [21] ❶ to raise ❷ to breed ❸ to bring up ▷ **Me criaron mis abuelos.** My grandparents brought me up.; **Me crie en Sevilla.** I grew up in Seville.

crimen (pl **crímenes**) nm ❶ murder ❷ crime

criminal nmf criminal

crío nm ❶ baby; **¡No seas crío!** Don't be such a baby! ❷ boy; **los críos** the children

crisis (pl **crisis**) nf crisis; **una crisis nerviosa** a nervous breakdown

cristal nm ❶ glass ▷ **una botella de cristal** a glass bottle; **Me corté con un cristal.** I cut myself on a piece of broken glass.; **En el suelo había cristales rotos.** There was some broken glass on the floor. ❷ window pane; **limpiar los cristales** to clean the windows ❸ crystal

cristiano, -a adj, nm/f Christian

Cristo nm Christ

crítica nf ❶ criticism ❷ review ▷ **La película ha tenido muy buenas críticas.** The film got very good reviews. ❸ critic

criticar vb [48] to criticize

crítico, -a adj critical
  ▶ nm critic

croissant (pl **croissants**) nm croissant

cromo nm picture card

crónico, -a adj chronic

cronometrar vb [25] to time

cronómetro nm stopwatch

croqueta nf croquette ▷ **croquetas de pollo** chicken croquettes

cruce nm crossroads; **un cruce de peatones** a pedestrian crossing

crucial adj crucial

crucifijo nm crucifix

crucigrama nm crossword

crudo, -a adj ❶ raw ❷ underdone ▷ **El filete estaba crudo.** The fillet was underdone.

cruel adj cruel

crueldad nf cruelty

crujiente adj ❶ crunchy ❷ crusty

crujir vb [58] ❶ to rustle ❷ to creak ❸ to crunch

cruz (pl **cruces**) nf cross; **la Cruz Roja** the Red Cross

cruzado, -a adj **Había un tronco cruzado en la carretera.** There was a tree trunk lying across the road.

cruzar vb [13] ❶ to cross ❷ to fold; **Nos cruzamos en la calle.** We passed each other in the street.

cuaderno nm notebook

cuadra nf ❶ stable ❷ (LatAm) block

cuadrado adj, nm square; **dos metros cuadrados** two square metres

cuadrar vb [25] to tally

cuadriculado, -a adj **papel cuadriculado** squared paper

cuadro nm ❶ painting ▷ un cuadro de Picasso a painting by Picasso ❷ picture; **un mantel a cuadros** a checked tablecloth

cuajar vb [25] ❶ to set ❷ to lie; **cuajarse** to curdle

cual pron ❶ who ▷ el primo del cual te estuve hablando the cousin who I was speaking to you about ❷ which ▷ la ventana desde la cual nos observaban the window from which they were watching us; **lo cual** which ▷ Se ofendió, lo cual es comprensible. He took offence, which is understandable.; **con lo cual** with the result that; **sea cual sea la razón** whatever the reason may be

cuál pron ❶ what ▷ ¿Cuál es la solución? What is the solution? ▷ No sé cuál es la solución. I don't know what the solution is. ❷ which one ▷ ¿Cuál te gusta más? Which one do you like best? ▷ ¿Cuáles quieres? Which ones do you want?

cualidad nf quality

cualquier adj see **cualquiera**

cualquiera adj any

> **cualquiera** is shortened to **cualquier** before singular nouns.

▷ en cualquier ciudad española in any Spanish town ▷ Puedes usar un bolígrafo cualquiera. You can use any pen.; **No es un empleo cualquiera.** It's not just any job.; **cualquier cosa** anything; **cualquier persona** anyone; **en cualquier sitio** anywhere

▶ pron ❶ anyone ▷ Cualquiera puede

hacer eso. Anyone can do that.; **cualquiera que le conozca** anyone who knows him ❷ any one ▷ Me da igual, cualquiera. It doesn't matter, any one.; **en cualquiera de las habitaciones** in any one of the rooms; **cualquiera que elijas** whichever one you choose ❸ either ▷ ¿Cuál de los dos prefieres? — Cualquiera. Which of the two do you prefer? — Either.

cuando conj when ▷ cuando vienen a vernos when they come to see us ▷ Lo haré cuando tenga tiempo. I'll do it when I have time.; **Puedes venir cuando quieras.** You can come whenever you like.

cuándo adv when ▷ No sabe cuándo ocurrió. He doesn't know when it happened.; **¿Desde cuándo trabajas aquí?** Since when have you worked here?

cuanto, -a adj, pron **Termínalo cuanto antes.** Finish it as soon as possible.; **Cuanto más lo pienso menos lo entiendo.** The more I think about it, the less I understand it.; **Cuantas menos personas haya mejor.** The fewer people the better.; **En cuanto oí su voz me eché a llorar.** As soon as I heard his voice I began to cry.; **Había solo unos cuantos invitados.** There were only a few guests.; **en cuanto a** as for

cuánto, -a adj, pron ❶ how much ▷ ¿Cuánto dinero? How much money? ▷ ¿Cuánto le debo? How much do I owe you? ▷ Me dijo cuánto costaba. He told me how much it was. ❷ how many ▷ ¿Cuántas sillas? How many chairs?; ¿A cuántos estamos? What's the date?; ¡Cuánta gente! What a lot of people!; ¿Cuánto hay de aquí a Bilbao? How far is it from here to Bilbao?; ¿Cuánto tiempo llevas estudiando inglés? How long have you been studying English?

cuarenta adj, pron forty; **el cuarenta aniversario** the fortieth anniversary

cuartel nm barracks; **el cuartel general** the headquarters

cuarto, -a adj, pron fourth ▷ Vivo en el cuarto piso. I live on the fourth floor.
▶ nm ❶ room; **el cuarto de estar** the living room; **el cuarto de baño** the bathroom ❷ quarter ▷ un cuarto de hora a quarter of an hour; **Son las once y cuarto.** It's a quarter past eleven.; **A las diez menos cuarto.** At a quarter to ten.; **Es un cuarto para las diez.** (LatAm) It's a quarter to ten.

cuatro adj, pron four; **Son las cuatro.** It's four o'clock.; **el cuatro de julio** the fourth of July

cuatrocientos, -as adj, pron four hundred

Cuba nf Cuba

cubano, -a adj, nm/f Cuban

cubertería nf cutlery

cúbico, -a adj cubic

cubierta nf ❶ cover ❷ tyre ❸ deck

cubierto vb see cubrir
▶ adj covered ▷ Estaba todo cubierto de nieve. Everything was covered in

snow.; **una piscina cubierta** an indoor swimming pool

cubiertos nmpl cutlery sg

cubito de hielo nm ice cube

cubo nm bucket; **el cubo de la basura** the dustbin

cubrir vb [58, pp cubierto] to cover; **Las mujeres se cubren la cara con un velo.** The women cover their faces with a veil.

cucaracha nf cockroach

cuchara nf spoon

cucharada nf spoonful

cucharilla nf teaspoon

cucharón (pl cucharones) nm ladle

cuchichear vb [25] to whisper

cuchilla nf blade; **una cuchilla de afeitar** a razor blade

cuchillo nm knife

cuclillas adv en cuclillas squatting; **ponerse en cuclillas** to squat down

cucurucho nm cone

cuelgo vb see colgar

cuello nm ❶ neck ❷ collar

cuenta nf ❶ bill ❷ account; **una cuenta corriente** a current account; **Ahora trabaja por su cuenta.** He's self-employed now.; **una cuenta de correo** an email account; **darse cuenta (1)** to realize ▷ Perdona, no me daba cuenta de que eras vegetariano. Sorry, I didn't realize you were a vegetarian. **(2)** to notice ▷ ¿Te has dado cuenta de que han cortado el árbol? Did you notice they've cut down that tree?; **tener algo en cuenta** to bear something in mind

a
b
c
d
e
f
g
h
i
j
k
l
m
n
ñ
o
p
q
r
s
t
u
v
w
x
y
z

cuento *vb see* **contar**

▶ *nm* story; **un cuento de hadas** a fairy tale

cuerda *nf* ❶ rope ❷ string; **dar cuerda a un reloj** to wind up a watch

cuerno *nm* horn

cuero *nm* leather ▷ *una chaqueta de cuero* a leather jacket

cuerpo *nm* body ▷ *el cuerpo humano* the human body; **el cuerpo de bomberos** the fire brigade

cuervo *nm* raven

cuesta *vb see* **costar**

▶ *nf* slope; **ir cuesta abajo** to go downhill; **ir cuesta arriba** to go uphill; **Llevaba la caja a cuestas.** He was carrying the box on his back.

cuestión (*pl* **cuestiones**) *nf* matter ▷ *Eso es otra cuestión.* That's another matter.

cueva *nf* cave

cuezo *vb see* **cocer**

cuidado *nm* care ▷ *Pone mucho cuidado en su trabajo.* He takes great care over his work.; **Conducía con cuidado.** He was driving carefully.; **Debes tener mucho cuidado al cruzar la calle.** You must be very careful crossing the street.; **¡Cuidado!** Careful!; **Carlos está al cuidado de los niños.** Carlos looks after the children.; **cuidados intensivos** intensive care *sg*

cuidadoso, -a *adj* careful

cuidar *vb* [25] to look after; **cuidarse** to look after oneself; **¡Cuídate!** Take care!

culebra *nf* snake

culebrón (*pl* **culebrones**) *nm* (*informal*) soap (opera)

culo *nm* (*informal*) bum

culpa *nf* fault ▷ *La culpa es mía.* It's my fault.; **Tú tienes la culpa de todo.** It's all your fault.; **Siempre me echan la culpa a mí.** They're always blaming me.; **por culpa del mal tiempo** because of the bad weather

culpable *adj* guilty ▷ *Se siente culpable de lo que ha pasado.* He feels guilty about what has happened.

▶ *nmf* culprit; **Ella es la culpable de todo.** She is to blame for everything.

cultivar *vb* [25] to grow to farm

culto, -a *adj* ❶ cultured ❷ formal

cultura *nf* culture

culturismo *nm* bodybuilding

cumbre *nf* summit

cumpleaños (*pl* **cumpleaños**) *nm* birthday; **¡Feliz cumpleaños!** Happy birthday!

cumplir *vb* [58] ❶ to carry out ❷ to keep ❸ to observe ❹ to serve; **Mañana cumplo dieciséis años.** I'll be sixteen tomorrow.; **El viernes se cumple el plazo para entregar las solicitudes.** Friday is the deadline for handing in applications.

cuna *nf* cradle

cuneta *nf* ditch

cuñada *nf* sister-in-law

cuñado *nm* brother-in-law

cuota *nf* fee

cupo *vb see* **caber**

cupón (pl **cupones**) nm ❶ voucher ❷ ticket

cura nf ❶ cure ❷ therapy
▶ nm priest

curar vb [25] ❶ to cure ❷ to treat;
Espero que te cures pronto.
I hope that you get better soon.

curiosidad nf curiosity; **Lo preguntté por curiosidad.** I asked out of curiosity.; **Tengo curiosidad por saber cuánto gana.** I'm curious to know how much he earns.

curioso, -a adj ❶ curious; **¡Qué curioso!** How odd! ❷ nosy

curita nf (LatAm) sticking plaster

cursillo nm course ▷ **un cursillo de cocina** a cookery course

curso nm ❶ year ▷ **un chico de mi curso** a boy in my year ▷ **Hago segundo curso.** I'm in the second year.; **el curso académico** the academic year ❷ course

curva nf ❶ bend ❷ curve

cuyo, -a adj whose ▷ **El marido, cuyo nombre era Ricardo, estaba jubilado.** The husband, whose name was Ricardo, was retired. ▷ **la señora en cuya casa me hospedé** the lady whose house I stayed in

d

dado nm dice; **jugar a los dados** to play dice

dama nf lady ▷ **Damas y caballeros ...** Ladies and gentlemen ...; **las damas** draughts ▷ **jugar a las damas** to play draughts

damasco nm (LatAm) apricot

danés (f **danesa**, mpl **daneses**) adj Danish
▶ nm/f Dane
▶ nm (language) Danish

dañar vb [25] ❶ to damage ❷ to hurt; **Se dañó la pierna.** She hurt her leg.

daño nm damage; **ocasionar daños** to cause damage; **hacer daño a alguien** to hurt somebody; **hacerse daño** to hurt oneself

dar vb [14] ❶ to give ▷ **Le dio un bocadillo a su hijo.** He gave his son a sandwich. ▷ *Se lo di a Teresa.* I gave it to Teresa.; **Me dio mucha alegría verla.** I was very pleased to see her.; **Déme 2 kilos.** 2 kilos please. ❷ *to strike* ▷ *El reloj dio las 6.* The clock struck 6.; **dar a** to look out onto; **dar con** to find; **Al final di con la solución.** I finally came up with the answer.; **El sol me da en la cara.** The sun's shining in my face.; **¿Qué más te da?** What does it matter to you?; **Se han dado muchos casos.** There have been a lot of cases.; **Se me dan bien las ciencias.** I'm good at science.; **darse un baño** to have a bath; **darse por vencido** to give up

dátil nm date

dato nm *Ese es un dato importante.* That's an important piece of information.; **Necesito más datos para poder juzgar.** I need more information to be able to judge.; **reunir datos para un proyecto de investigación** to gather data for a research project; **los datos personales** personal details

de prep ❶ *of* ▷ *un paquete de caramelos* a packet of sweets; **una copa de vino (1)** a glass of wine **(2)** a wine glass; **la casa de Isabel** Isabel's house; **las clases de inglés** English classes; **un anillo de oro** a gold ring; **una máquina de coser** a sewing machine; **es de ellos** it's theirs; **a las 8 de la mañana** at 8 o'clock in the morning ❷ *from* ▷ *Soy de Gijón.* I'm from Gijón.; **salir del**

cine to leave the cinema ❸ *than* ▷ *see* **dar**
▷ *Es más difícil de lo que creía.* It's more difficult than I thought it would be.; **más de 500 personas** over 500 people; **De haberlo sabido ...** If I'd known ...

dé vb *see* **dar**

debajo adv underneath ▷ *Levanta la maceta, la llave está debajo.* Lift up the flowerpot, the key's underneath.; **debajo de** under

debate nm debate

debatir vb **[58]** to debate

deber nm duty ▷ *Solo cumplí con mi deber.* I simply did my duty.; **los deberes** homework ▷ *see*
▶ vb **[8]** ❶ *must* ▷ *Debo intentar verla.* I must try to see her. ▷ *No debes preocuparte.* You mustn't worry.; **Debería dejar de fumar.** I should stop smoking.; **No deberías haberla dejado sola.** You shouldn't have left her alone.; **como debe ser** as it should be; **deber de** must ▷ *Debe de ser canadiense.* He must be Canadian.; **No debe de tener mucho dinero.** He can't have much money.
❷ *to owe* ▷ *¿Cuánto le debo?* How much do I owe you?; **deberse a** to be due to ▷ *El retraso se debió a una huelga.* The delay was due to a strike.

debido, -a adj debido a owing to ▷ *Debido al mal tiempo, el vuelo se suspendió.* Owing to the bad weather, the flight was cancelled.; **Habla como es debido.** Speak properly.

débil adj weak

debilidad nf weakness

debilitar vb **[25]** to weaken

década nf decade

decena nf ten ▷ decenas de miles de: tens of thousands of; **Habrá una decena de libros.** There must be about ten books.

decente adj decent

decepción (pl **decepciones**) nf disappointment

> Be careful! **decepción** does not mean **deception**.

decepcionar vb **[25]** to disappoint; **La película me decepcionó.** The film was disappointing.

decidido, -a adj determined ▷ Estoy decidido a hacerlo. I'm determined to do it.

decidir vb **[58]** to decide; **decidirse a hacer algo** to decide to do something; **decidirse por algo** to decide on something; **¡Decídete!** Make up your mind!

decimal adj, nm decimal

décimo, -a adj, pron tenth; **Vivo en el décimo.** I live on the tenth floor.

decir vb **[15]** ❶ to say ▷ ¿Qué dijo? What did he say? ▷ ¿Cómo se dice 'casa' en inglés? How do you say 'casa' in English?; **es decir** that's to say; **es un decir** it's a manner of speaking; **¡Diga!** Hello? ❷ to tell; **decirle a alguien que haga algo** to tell somebody to do something; **¡No me digas!** Really?; **querer decir** to mean

decisión (pl **decisiones**) nf decision ▷ tomar una decisión to take a decision

decisivo, -a adj decisive

declaración (pl **declaraciones**) nf ❶ statement ❷ evidence ▷ Prestó declaración ante el juez. He gave evidence before the judge.; **una declaración de amor** a declaration of love; **la declaración de la renta** the income tax return

declarar vb **[25]** to declare ▷ ¿Algo que declarar? Anything to declare? ❷ to give evidence; **declarar culpable a alguien** to find somebody guilty; **declararse (1)** to declare oneself ▷ Se declaró partidario de hacerlo. He declared himself in favour of doing it. **(2)** to break out ▷ Se declaró un incendio en el bosque. A fire broke out in the forest.; **declararse a alguien** to propose to somebody

decorador, a nm/f interior decorator

decorar vb **[25]** to decorate

decreto nm decree

dedal nm thimble

dedicar vb **[48]** ❶ to devote ❷ to dedicate; **¿A qué se dedica?** What does he do for a living?; **Ayer me dediqué a arreglar los armarios.** I spent yesterday tidying the cupboards.

dedo nm ❶ finger ▷ Lleva un anillo en el dedo meñique. She wears a ring on her little finger.; **hacer dedo** to hitch a lift; **no mover un dedo** not to lift a finger ❷ toe; **el dedo gordo (1)** the thumb **(2)** the big toe

deducir vb [**9**] to deduce

defecto nm ❶ defect ❷ fault

defender vb [**20**] to defend;
defenderse to defend oneself; **Me
defiendo en inglés.** I can get by in
English.

defensa nf defence; **salir en
defensa de alguien** to come to
somebody's defence; **en defensa
propia** in self-defence

defensor, a nm/f defender

deficiente adj poor ▷ Su trabajo es
muy deficiente. His work is very
poor.

definición (pl definiciones) nf
definition

definir vb [**58**] to define

definitivo, -a adj definitive; **en
definitiva** in short

defraudar vb [**25**] ❶ to disappoint
❷ to defraud

dejar vb [**25**] ❶ to leave ▷ He dejado
las llaves en la mesa. I've left the
keys on the table.; **¡Déjalo ya!**
Don't worry about it!; **Deja
mucho que desear.** It leaves a lot
to be desired. ❷ to let ▷ Mis padres
no me dejan salir de noche. My
parents won't let me go out at
night.; **dejar caer** to drop ▷ Dejó
caer la bandeja. She dropped the
tray. ❸ to lend ▷ Le dejé mi libro de
matemáticas. I lent him my maths
book. ❹ to give up ▷ Dejó el esquí
después del accidente. He gave up
skiing after the accident.; **dejar de**
to stop ▷ dejar de fumar to stop
smoking; **dejarse** to leave ▷ Se dejó
el bolso en un taxi. She left her bag in
a taxi.

del prep see **de**
del is the contracted form of
de + **el**.

delantal nm apron

delante adv in front; **de delante**
front; **la parte de delante** the
front; **delante de (1)** in front of
(2) opposite; **pasar por delante
de** to go past; **hacia delante**
forward

delantero, -a adj front ▷ los
asientos delanteros the front seats;
la parte delantera del coche the
front of the car

delegación (pl delegaciones) nf
(Mex) police station

delegado, -a nm/f delegate;
el delegado de clase the class
representative

deletrear vb [**25**] to spell out

delfín (pl delfines) nm dolphin

delgado, -a adj ❶ slim ❷ thin

delicado, -a adj ❶ delicate ▷ Estas
copas son muy delicadas. These
glasses are very delicate. ▷ Se trata
de un asunto muy delicado. It's a very
delicate subject. ❷ thoughtful
▷ Enviarte flores ha sido un gesto muy
delicado. Sending you flowers was
a very thoughtful gesture.

delicioso, -a adj delicious

delincuente nmf criminal; **un
delincuente juvenil** a juvenile
delinquent

delito nm crime

demanda nf demand; **presentar
una demanda contra alguien** to
sue somebody

demás adj other ▷ los demás niños
the other children

▶ pron **los demás** the others; **lo demás** the rest ▷ *Yo limpio las ventanas y lo demás lo limpias tú.* I'll clean the windows and you clean the rest.; **todo lo demás** everything else

demasiado, -a adj too much
▷ *demasiado vino* too much wine
▷ *demasiados libros* too many books
▶ adv ❶ too ▷ *Es demasiado pesado para levantarlo.* It's too heavy to lift.
▷ *Caminas demasiado deprisa.* You walk too quickly. ❷ too much ▷ *Hablas demasiado.* You talk too much.

democracia nf democracy

democrático, -a adj democratic

demonio nm devil

demostración (pl **demostraciones**) nf
❶ demonstration ❷ proof

demostrar vb [11] ❶ to demonstrate ❷ to prove

densidad nf density

denso, -a adj ❶ (fog, smoke) thick ❷ (book) heavy

dentadura nf teeth pl; la **dentadura postiza** false teeth pl

dentífrico nm toothpaste

dentista nmf dentist

dentro adv inside ▷ *¿Qué hay dentro?* What's inside?; **por dentro** inside; **Está aquí dentro.** It's in here.; **dentro de** in; **dentro de poco** soon; **dentro de lo que cabe** as far as it goes

denuncia nf **Voy a ponerle una denuncia por hacer tanto ruido.** I'm going to report him for making

so much noise.; **Le pusieron una denuncia por verter residuos en el río.** He was reported to the authorities for tipping waste into the river.

denunciar vb [25] to report

departamento nm
❶ department ❷ compartment
❸ (LatAm) flat

depender vb [8] **depender de** to depend on; **Depende.** It depends.; **No depende de mí.** It's not up to me.

dependiente, -a nm/f sales assistant

deporte nm sport ▷ *No hago mucho deporte.* I don't do much sport.
▷ *los deportes de invierno* winter sports

deportista adj sporty ▷ *Alicia es poco deportista.* Alicia is not very sporty.
▶ nm sportsman
▶ nf sportswoman

deportivo, -a adj ❶ sports ▷ *un club deportivo* a sports club
❷ sporting

depósito nm ❶ tank ❷ deposit

depresión (pl **depresiones**) nf
❶ depression; **tener una depresión** to be suffering from depression ❷ hollow

deprimido, -a adj depressed

deprimir vb [58] to depress; **deprimirse por algo** to get depressed about something

deprisa adv quickly; **¡Deprisa!** Hurry up!; **Lo hacen todo deprisa y corriendo.** They do everything in a rush.

derecha nf ❶ right hand ▷ Escribo con la derecha. I write with my right hand. ❷ right ▷ doblar a la derecha to turn right; **ser de derechas** to be right-wing ▷ un partido de derechas a right-wing party; **a la derecha** on the right ▷ la segunda calle a la derecha the second turning on the right; **conducir por la derecha** to drive on the right

derecho, -a adj ❶ right ▷ Me duele el ojo derecho. I've got a pain in my right eye. ❷ right ▷ Escribo con la mano derecha. I write with my right hand.; **a mano derecha** on the right-hand side ▷ ¡Ponte derecho! Stand up straight!
▶ adv straight ▷ Siga derecho. Carry straight on.
▶ nm ❶ right ▷ tener derecho a hacer algo to have the right to do something ▷ No tienes derecho a decir eso. You have no right to say that. ▷ los derechos humanos human rights; **¡No hay derecho!** It's not fair! ❷ law ▷ Estudio derecho. I'm studying law.

derramar vb [25] to spill

derrapar vb [25] to skid

derretir vb [38] to melt; **derretirse** to melt ▷ El hielo se está derritiendo. The ice is melting.; **derretirse de calor** to be melting

derribar vb [25] ❶ (building) to demolish ❷ (plane) to shoot down ❸ (government) to overthrow

derrota nf defeat

derrotar vb [25] to defeat

derrumbar vb [25] to pull down; **derrumbarse** to collapse

desabrochar vb [25] to undo; **desabrocharse** (1) to undo ▷ Me desabroché la blusa. I undid my blouse. (2) to come undone

desacuerdo nm disagreement

desafiar vb [21] to challenge

desafío nm challenge

desafortunado, -a adj unfortunate

desagradable adj unpleasant

desagradecido, -a adj ungrateful

desagüe nm ❶ waste pipe ❷ drain

desahogarse vb [37] Se desahogó conmigo. He poured out his heart to me.; **Lloraba para desahogarse.** He was crying to let off steam.

desalojar vb [25] to clear

desanimado, -a adj ❶ downhearted ❷ dull

desanimar vb [25] to discourage; **desanimarse** to lose heart

desaparecer vb [12] to disappear; **¡Desaparece de mi vista!** Get out of my sight!

desaparición (pl desapariciones) nf disappearance

desapercibido, -a adj pasar desapercibido to go unnoticed

desaprovechar vb [25] to waste

desarme nm disarmament ▷ el desarme nuclear nuclear disarmament

desarrollar vb [25] to develop; **desarrollarse** (1) to develop (2) to take place

desarrollo nm development; **un país en vías de desarrollo** a developing country

desastre nm disaster

desastroso, -a adj disastrous

desatar vb [25] ❶ to undo ❷ to untie; **desatarse** (1) to come undone (2) to get loose (3) to break

desayunar vb [25] ❶ to have breakfast ❷ to have...for breakfast ▷ *Desayuné café con leche y un bollo.* I had coffee and a roll for breakfast.

desayuno nm breakfast

descalzarse vb [13] to take one's shoes off

descalzo, -a adj barefoot; **No entres en la cocina descalzo.** Don't come into the kitchen in bare feet.

descampado nm open space

descansar vb [25] ❶ to rest ❷ to sleep ▷ *¡Que descanses!* Sleep well!

descansillo nm landing

descanso nm ❶ rest ▷ *He caminado mucho, necesito un descanso.* I've done a lot of walking, I need a rest. ❷ break ▷ *Cada dos horas me tomo un descanso.* I have a break every two hours. ❸ relief ▷ *¡Qué descanso!* What a relief! ❹ (in performance) interval ❺ (at a match) half time; **tomarse unos días de descanso** to take a few days off

descapotable nm convertible

descarado, -a adj cheeky

descargar vb [37] ❶ to unload ▷ *Me ayudó a descargar los muebles de la camioneta.* He helped me unload the furniture from the van. ❷ to take out ▷ *Descarga su mal humor sobre mí.* He takes his bad moods out on me. ❸ to download; **descargarse** to go flat

descaro nm nerve ▷ *¡Qué descaro!* What a nerve!

descender vb [20] to go down; **descender de** to be descended from

descendiente nmf descendant

descenso nm ❶ drop ▷ *Va a haber un descenso de las temperaturas.* There's going to be a drop in temperature. ❷ descent ▷ *Los ciclistas iniciaron el descenso del puerto.* The cyclists began the descent from the mountain pass. ❸ relegation ▷ *el descenso a segunda división* relegation to the second division

descolgar vb [28] ❶ to take down ❷ to pick up the phone; **descolgar el teléfono** to pick up the phone

descomponerse vb [41] (LatAm) to break down

desconcertar vb [39] to disconcert; **desconcertarse** to be disconcerted

desconectar vb [25] ❶ to unplug ❷ to disconnect

desconfianza nf distrust

desconfiar vb [21] **Desconfío de él.** I don't trust him.; **Desconfía siempre de las apariencias.** Always beware of appearances.

descongelar vb [25] to defrost; **descongelarse** to defrost

desconocido, -a nm/f stranger ▶ adj unknown ▷ *un actor desconocido* an unknown actor

descontar vb [11] to deduct; **Descuentan el 5% si se paga en metálico.** They give a 5% discount if you pay cash.

a
b
c
d
e
f
g
h
i
j
k
l
m
n
ñ
o
p
q
r
s
t
u
v
w
x
y
z

descontento, -a adj unhappy
▷ *Están descontentos de mis notas.*
They're unhappy with my marks.
descoser vb [8] to unpick;
descoserse to come apart at the
seams
descremado, -a adj skimmed
describir vb [58, pp **descrito**] to
describe
descripción (pl **descripciones**) nf
description
descubierto nm overdraft
descubrimiento nm discovery
descubrir vb [58, pp **descubierto**]
❶ to discover ❷ to find out
descuento nm discount
descuidado, -a adj ❶ careless
▷ *Es muy descuidada con sus
juguetes.* She's very careless with
her toys. ❷ neglected ▷ *El jardín
estaba descuidado.* The garden was
neglected.
descuidar vb [25] to neglect;
Descuida, que yo lo haré. Don't
worry, I'll do it.; **descuidarse** to let
one's attention wander
descuido nm oversight
desde prep ❶ from ▷ *Desde Burgos
hasta mi casa hay 30 km.* It's 30km
from Burgos to my house. ▷ *Te
llamaré desde la oficina.* I'll ring you
from the office. ❷ since ▷ *Desde que
llegó no ha salido.* He hasn't been
out since he arrived. ▷ *La conozco
desde niño.* I've known her since I
was a child. ▷ *desde entonces* since
then; **¿desde cuándo vives aquí?**
How long have you been living
here?; **desde hace tres años** for
three years; **desde ahora en**

adelante from now on; **desde
luego** of course
desdichado, -a adj ❶ ill-fated
❷ unlucky
desdoblar vb [25] to unfold
desear vb [25] to wish ▷ *Te deseo
mucha suerte.* I wish you lots of
luck.; **Estoy deseando que esto
termine.** I'm longing for this to
finish.; **¿Qué desea?** What can
I do for you?; **dejar mucho que
desear** to leave a lot to be
desired
desechable adj disposable
desechos nmpl waste sg
desembarcar vb [48] ❶ to
disembark ❷ to unload
desembarco nm landing
desembocar vb [48]
desembocar en (1) to flow into
(2) to lead into
desempacar vb [48] (LatAm) to
unpack
desempate nm play-off; **el
partido de desempate** the
deciding match
desempleado, -a nm/f
unemployed person; **los
desempleados** the unemployed
desempleo nm unemployment
desenchufar vb [25] to unplug
desengañar vb [25] **Su traición
la desengañó.** His betrayal
opened her eyes.; **¡Desengáñate!
No está interesada en ti.** Stop
fooling yourself! She isn't
interested in you.
desengaño nm disappointment
desenredar vb [25] ❶ to untangle
❷ to resolve

desenrollar vb [25] ❶ to unwind
❷ to unroll

desenroscar vb [48] to unscrew

desenvolver vb [59] to unwrap;
desenvolverse to cope

deseo nm wish ▷ Pide un deseo.
Make a wish.

desequilibrado, -a adj
unbalanced

desértico, -a adj desert ▷ una
región desértica a desert region

desesperado, -a adj desperate
▶ nm/f Corría como un
desesperado. He was running like
mad.

desesperar vb [25] ❶ to drive...
mad ▷ Los atascos me desesperan.
Traffic jams drive me mad. ❷ to
despair ▷ No desesperes y sigue
intentándolo. Don't despair, just
keep trying.; **desesperarse** to get
exasperated

desfavorable adj unfavourable

desfiladero nm gorge

desfilar vb [25] to parade

desfile nm parade; **un desfile de
modas** a fashion show

desgana nf ❶ loss of appetite
❷ reluctance; **hacer algo con
desgana** to do something
reluctantly

desgarrar vb [25] to tear up;
desgarrarse to rip

desgarrón (pl **desgarrones**) nm
rip

desgastar vb [25] ❶ to wear out
❷ to wear away; **desgastarse** to
get worn out

desgaste nm ❶ wear and tear
❷ erosion

desgracia nf tragedy; **Ha tenido
una vida llena de desgracias.**
He's had a lot of misfortune in his
life.; **por desgracia (1)** sadly
(2) unfortunately

desgraciado, -a adj ❶ unhappy
▷ Desde que Ana le dejó ha sido muy
desgraciado. He has been very
unhappy since Ana left him.
❷ tragic ▷ Murió en un desgraciado
accidente. He died in a tragic
accident.

deshabitado, -a adj
❶ uninhabited ❷ unoccupied

deshacer vb [26] ❶ to untie
❷ (case) to unpack ❸ (ice, butter)
to melt ❹ (sewing, knitting) to
unpick; **deshacerse (1)** (knot,
sewing) to come undone **(2)** to
melt; **deshacerse de algo** to get
rid of something

deshecho, -a adj ❶ (knot) undone
❷ (bed) unmade ❸ broken
❹ melted; **Estoy deshecho.**
(1) I'm shattered. **(2)** I'm
devastated.

deshielo nm thaw

deshinchar vb [25] to let down;
deshincharse (1) (balloon) to go
down **(2)** (tyre) to go flat

desierto, -a adj deserted
▶ nm desert

desigual adj ❶ (size) different
❷ (land, writing) uneven ❸ (fight)
unequal

desilusión (pl **desilusiones**) nf
disappointment; **llevarse una
desilusión** to be disappointed

desilusionar vb [25] to
disappoint; **Su conferencia me**

desilusionó. His lecture was disappointing.; **desilusionarse** to be disappointed

desinfectante nm disinfectant

desinfectar vb [25] to disinfect

desinflar vb [25] to let down

desinterés nm lack of interest

deslizarse vb [13] to slide

deslumbrar vb [25] to dazzle

desmayarse vb [25] to faint

desmayo nm faint; **sufrir un desmayo** to faint

desmontar vb [25] ❶ (furniture) to take apart ❷ (tent) to take down ❸ to trip down ❹ to dismount

desnatado, -a adj ❶ skimmed ❷ low-fat

desnudar vb [25] to undress; **desnudarse** to get undressed

desnudo, -a adj ❶ naked; **Duerme desnudo.** He sleeps in the nude. ❷ bare

desobedecer vb [12] to disobey

desobediente adj disobedient

desodorante nm deodorant

desorden (pl **desórdenes**) nm mess ▷ Hay mucha desorden en esta casa. This whole house is in a mess.; **los desórdenes callejeros** street disturbances

desordenado, -a adj untidy

desordenar vb [25] to mess up

desorganización nf disorganization

desorientar vb [25] to confuse; **desorientarse** to lose one's way

despachar vb [25] ❶ to sell ❷ to serve ❸ to dismiss

despacho nm ❶ office; **una mesa de despacho** a desk ❷ study; **un**

despacho de billetes a booking office

despacio adv slowly; **¡Despacio!** Take it easy!

despectivo, -a adj ❶ contemptuous ▷ Me habló en un tono muy despectivo. He spoke to me in a very contemptuous tone. ❷ pejorative ▷ 'Mujerzuela' es una palabra despectiva. 'Mujerzuela' is a pejorative term.

despedida nf Le hicimos una buena despedida a Marta. We gave Marta a good send-off.; **una fiesta de despedida** a farewell party; **una despedida de soltero** a stag party; **una despedida de soltera** a hen party

despedir vb [38] ❶ to say goodbye to; **Fueron a despedirlo al aeropuerto.** They went to the airport to see him off. ❷ to dismiss; **despedirse** to say goodbye

despegar vb [37] (plane) to take off; **despegarse** to come unstuck

despegue nm takeoff

despeinar vb [25] **despeinar a alguien** to mess somebody's hair up

despejado, -a adj (sky, day, mind) clear

despejar vb [25] to clear; **¡Despejen!** Move along!; **Tomaré un café para despejarme.** I'll have a coffee to wake myself up.

despellejar vb [25] to skin

despensa nf larder

desperdiciar vb [25] ❶ to waste ❷ to throw away

desperdicio nm waste ▷ *Tirar toda esta comida es un desperdicio.* It's a waste to throw away all this food.; **los desperdicios** scraps; **El libro no tiene desperdicio.** It's an excellent book from beginning to end.

desperezarse vb [13] to stretch

desperfecto nm flaw; **sufrir desperfectos** to get damaged

despertador nm alarm clock

despertar vb [39] ① to wake up ▷ *No me despiertes hasta las once.* Don't wake me up until eleven o'clock. ② to arouse; **despertarse** to wake up

despido nm dismissal

despierto, -a adj ① awake ② bright ▷ *Es un niño muy despierto.* He's a very bright boy.

despistado, -a nm/f scatterbrain ▶ adj absent-minded ▷ *Es tan despistado que siempre se olvida las llaves.* He's so absent-minded that he's always forgetting his keys.

despistar vb [25] ① to shake off ② to be misleading; **Me despisté y salí de la autopista demasiado tarde.** I wasn't concentrating and I turned off the motorway too late.

despiste nm absent-mindedness

desplazar vb [13] ① to move ② to take the place of

desplegar vb [34] ① to unfold ② to spread; **desplegarse** to be deployed

desplomarse vb [25] to collapse

despreciar vb [25] to despise

desprecio nm contempt

despreocuparse vb [25] to stop worrying; **despreocuparse de todo** to show no concern for anything

desprevenido, -a adj pillar a **alguien desprevenido** to catch somebody unawares

después adv ① afterwards ▷ **Primero cenaré y después saldré.** I'll have dinner first and go out after that. ② later ▷ *un año después* a year later ③ next ▷ *¿Qué viene después?* What comes next?; **después de** after; **después de todo** after all

destacar vb [48] ① to stress ② to stand out

destapador nm (LatAm) bottle opener

destapar vb [25] ① to open ② to take the lid off; **destaparse** to lose the covers

desteñir vb [45] ① to run ② to fade; **desteñirse** to fade

desternillarse vb [25] **desternillarse de risa** (informal) to split one's sides laughing

destinar vb [25] ① (person) to post ② (funds) to earmark; **El libro está destinado al público infantil.** The book is aimed at children.

destinatario, -a nm/f addressee

destino nm ① destination ▷ *Por fin llegamos a nuestro destino.* We finally arrived at our destination.; **el tren con destino a Valencia** the train to Valencia; **salir con destino a** to leave for ② posting ▷ *Cada dos años me cambian de destino.* They give me a new

a
b
c
d
e
f
g
h
i
j
k
l
m
n
ñ
o
p
q
r
s
t
u
v
w
x
y
z

posting every two years. ❸ use
▷ *Quiero saber qué destino tendrá este dinero.* I want to know what use will be made of this money.

destornillador nm screwdriver

destornillar vb [25] to unscrew

destreza nf skill

destrozar vb [13] to wreck; **La noticia le destrozó el corazón.** The news broke his heart.

destrozos nmpl damage sg

destrucción nf destruction

destruir vb [10] ❶ to destroy ❷ to ruin ❸ to demolish

desvalijar vb [25] ❶ to burgle ❷ to rob

desván (pl **desvanes**) nm attic

desventaja nf disadvantage; **estar en desventaja** to be at a disadvantage

desviar vb [21] to divert

desvío nm ❶ turning ▷ *Coge el primer desvío a la derecha.* Take the first turning on the right. ❷ diversion

detalle nm detail ▷ *No recuerdo todos los detalles.* I don't remember all the details.; **¡Qué detalle!** How thoughtful!

detectar vb [25] to detect

detective nmf detective ▷ *un detective privado* a private detective

detener vb [53] ❶ to stop ❷ to arrest; **detenerse** to stop ▷ *Nos detuvimos en el semáforo.* We stopped at the lights.; **¡Deténgase!** Stop!

detergente nm detergent

deteriorar vb [25] to damage; **deteriorarse** to deteriorate

determinación nf determination; **tomar una determinación** to take a decision

determinado, -a adj ❶ certain ▷ *En determinadas ocasiones es mejor callarse.* There are certain occasions when it's better to say nothing.; **No hemos quedado a una hora determinada.** We haven't fixed a definite time. ❷ particular ▷ *¿Buscas algún libro determinado?* Are you looking for a particular book?

determinar vb [25] ❶ to determine ▷ *Trataron de determinar la causa del accidente.* They tried to determine the cause of the accident. ❷ to fix ▷ *determinar la fecha de una reunión* to fix the date of a meeting ❸ to bring about ▷ *Aquello determinó la caída del gobierno.* That brought about the fall of the government. ❹ to state ▷ *El reglamento determina que ...* The rules state that ...

detestar vb [25] to detest

detrás adv behind; **detrás de** behind ▷ *Se escondió detrás de un árbol.* He hid behind a tree.; **uno detrás de otro** one after another; **La critican por detrás.** They criticize her behind her back.

deuda nf debt; **contraer deudas** to get into debt

devolución (pl **devoluciones**) nf ❶ (of letter, book) return ❷ (of money) repayment; **No se admiten devoluciones.** Goods cannot be returned.

devolver vb [59] ❶ to give back;
Me devolvieron mal el cambio.
They gave me the wrong change.;
**Te devolveré el favor cuando
pueda.** I'll return the favour when I
can. ❷ (goods) to take back
❸ (vomit: informal) to throw up

devorar vb [25] to devour;
devorar un bocadillo to wolf
down a sandwich

di vb see **decir**

día nm day ▷ **Duerme de día y trabaja
de noche.** He sleeps during the day
and works at night.; **Es de día.** It's
daylight.; **¿Qué día es hoy?**
(1) What's the date today?
(2) What day is it today?; **el día de
mañana** tomorrow; **al día
siguiente** the following day;
todos los días every day; **un día
de estos** one of these days; **un día
sí y otro no** every other day;
¡Buenos días! Good morning!;
un día de fiesta a public holiday;
un día feriado (LatAm) a public
holiday; **un día laborable** a
working day; **pan del día** fresh
bread

diabético, -a adj, nm/f diabetic

diablo nm devil

diagnóstico nm diagnosis

diagonal adj, nf diagonal; **en
diagonal** diagonally

dialecto nm dialect

dialogar vb [37] dialogar con
alguien to hold talks with
somebody

diálogo nm conversation

diamante nm diamond;
diamantes diamonds

diámetro nm diameter

diana nf ❶ bull's-eye ▷ **dar en la
diana** to get a bull's-eye
❷ dartboard

diapositiva nf slide

diario, -a adj daily ▷ **la rutina diaria**
the daily routine; **la ropa de diario**
everyday clothes; **a diario** every
day ▷ **Va al gimnasio a diario.** He
goes to the gym every day.
▸ nm ❶ newspaper ❷ diary

diarrea nf diarrhoea

dibujante nmf ❶ artist
❷ cartoonist ❸ draughtsman

dibujar vb [25] to draw ▷ **No sé
dibujar.** I can't draw.

dibujo nm drawing ▷ **el dibujo
técnico** technical drawing; **los
dibujos animados** cartoons

diccionario nm dictionary

dicho vb see **decir**
▸ adj **en dichos países** in the
countries mentioned above;
mejor dicho or rather; **dicho y
hecho** no sooner said than done
▸ nm saying

dichoso, -a adj ❶ happy ❷ lucky;
¡Dichoso ruido! (informal)
Damned noise!

diciembre nm December

diciendo vb see **decir**

dictado nm dictation ▷ **La maestra
nos hizo un dictado.** The teacher
gave us a dictation.

dictador, a nm/f dictator

dictadura nf dictatorship

dictar vb [25] to dictate; **dictar
sentencia** to pass sentence

diecinueve adj, pron nineteen
▷ **Tengo diecinueve años.** I'm

nineteen.; **el diecinueve de julio** the nineteenth of July

dieciocho adj, pron eighteen
▷ **Tengo dieciocho años.** I'm eighteen.; **el dieciocho de abril** the eighteenth of April

dieciséis adj, pron sixteen ▷ **Tengo dieciséis años.** I'm sixteen.; **el dieciséis de febrero** the sixteenth of February

diecisiete adj, pron seventeen ▷ **Tengo diecisiete años.** I'm seventeen.; **el diecisiete de enero** the seventeenth of January

diente nm tooth ▷ **lavarse los dientes** to clean one's teeth; **un diente de ajo** a clove of garlic

dieta nf diet; **estar a dieta** to be on a diet; **ponerse a dieta** to go on a diet; **dietas** expenses

diez adj, pron ten ▷ **Tengo diez años.** I'm ten.; **Son las diez.** It's ten o'clock.; **el diez de agosto** the tenth of August

diferencia nf difference; **a diferencia de** unlike ▷ **A diferencia de su hermana, a ella le encanta viajar.** Unlike her sister, she loves travelling.

diferenciar vb [25] ¿**En qué se diferencian?** What's the difference between them?; **Solo se diferencian en el tamaño.** The only difference between them is their size.; **Se diferencia de los demás por su bondad.** His kindness sets him apart from the rest.; **No diferencia el color rojo del verde.** He can't tell the difference between red and green.

diferente adj different

difícil adj difficult ▷ **Es un problema difícil de entender.** It's a difficult problem to understand. ▷ **Resulta difícil concentrarse.** It's difficult to concentrate.

dificultad nf difficulty ▷ **con dificultad** with difficulty; **tener dificultades para hacer algo** to have difficulty doing something

dificultar vb [25] to make... difficult ▷ **La niebla dificultaba la visibilidad.** The fog made visibility difficult.

digerir vb [51] to digest

digestión nf digestion; **hacer la digestión** to digest

digestivo, -a adj digestive

digital adj digital ▷ **un reloj digital** a digital watch; **una huella digital** a fingerprint

dignidad nf dignity

digno, -a adj ❶ decent
❷ honourable; **digno de mención** worth mentioning

digo vb see **decir**

dije vb see **decir**

diluir vb [10] to dilute

diluviar vb [25] **Está diluviando.** It's pouring with rain.

diluvio nm downpour

dimensión (pl dimensiones) nf dimension

diminutivo nm diminutive

diminuto, -a adj tiny

dimisión (pl dimisiones) nf resignation ▷ **presentar la dimisión** to hand in one's resignation

dimitir vb [58] to resign

Dinamarca nf Denmark

dinámico, -a adj dynamic

dinero nm money ▷ No tengo más dinero. I haven't got any more money.; **andar mal de dinero** to be short of money; **dinero suelto** loose change

dinosaurio nm dinosaur

dio vb see **dar**

Dios nm God ▷ ¡Gracias a Dios! Thank God! ▷ ¡Dios mío! My God!; ¡**Por Dios!** For God's sake!; **¡Si Dios quiere!** God willing!; **No vino ni Dios.** (informal) Nobody turned up.

diploma nm diploma

diplomacia nf diplomacy

diplomático, -a adj diplomatic ▶ nm/f diplomat

diputado, -a nm/f Member of Parliament

dirá vb see **decir**

dirección (pl direcciones) nf ❶ direction ▷ Íbamos en dirección equivocada. We were going in the wrong direction.; **Tienes que ir en esta dirección.** You have to go this way.; **una calle de dirección única** a one-way street; 'dirección prohibida' 'no entry'; 'todas direcciones' 'all routes' ❷ address ❸ management ▷ la dirección de la empresa the management of the company

directo, -a adj ❶ direct ▷ Hay un tren directo a Valencia. There's a direct train to Valencia. ❷ straight ▷ Se fue directa a casa. She went straight home.; **transmitir en directo** to broadcast live

director, a nm/f ❶ manager ❷ headteacher ❸ director ❹ conductor ❺ editor

directorio nm ❶ directory ❷ (LatAm) phone book

dirigente nmf ❶ leader ❷ manager

dirigir vb [16] ❶ (company) to manage ❷ (expedition) to lead ❸ to aim at ▷ Este anuncio va dirigido a los niños. This advertisement is aimed at children.; **no dirigir la palabra a alguien** not to speak to somebody ❹ (film) to direct ❺ (orchestra) to conduct; **dirigirse a (1)** to address **(2)** to write to **(3)** to make one's way to

discapacitada nf disabled woman

discapacitado, -a adj disabled ▶ nm disabled man

discar vb [48] (LatAm) to dial

disciplina nf discipline

disco nm ❶ (for playing) record ❷ (traffic light) light ❸ discus; **un disco compacto** a compact disc; **el disco duro** the hard disk

discoteca nf discotheque

discreción nf discretion

discreto, -a adj discreet

discriminación nf la discriminación racial racial discrimination

disculpa nf pedir disculpas a alguien por algo to apologize to somebody for something

disculpar vb [25] to excuse ▷ Disculpa ¿me dejas pasar? Excuse me, can I go past?; **disculparse** to apologize

discurso nm speech

discusión (pl **discusiones**) nf
discussion; **tener una discusión
con alguien** to have an argument
with somebody

discutir vb [**58**] ❶ to quarrel
▷ *Siempre discuten por dinero.*
They're always quarrelling about
money. ❷ to discuss ▷ *Tenemos que
discutir el nuevo proyecto.* We've got
to discuss the new project.

diseñar vb [**25**] to design

diseño nm ❶ design ❷ drawing

disfraz (pl **disfraces**) nm
❶ disguise ❷ costume; **una
fiesta de disfraces** a fancy-dress
party

disfrazarse vb [**13**] **disfrazarse de
(1)** to disguise oneself as **(2)** to
dress up as

disfrutar vb [**25**] to enjoy oneself
▷ *Disfruté mucho en la fiesta.* I really
enjoyed myself at the party.;
Disfruto leyendo. I enjoy
reading.; **disfrutar de buena
salud** to enjoy good health

disgustado, -a adj upset

▌ Be careful! **disgustado** does
not mean **disgusted**.

disgustar vb [**25**] to upset;
disgustarse to get upset;
disgustarse con alguien to fall
out with somebody

disgusto nm **dar un disgusto a
alguien** to upset somebody;
llevarse un disgusto to get upset

disimular vb [**25**] to hide; **No
disimules, sé que has sido tú.**
Don't bother pretending, I know
it was you.

disminución (pl **disminuciones**)
nf fall

disminuido, -a nm/f un
disminuido mental a person with
learning difficulties; **un
disminuido físico** a person with a
physical disability

disminuir vb [**10**] to fall

disolver vb [**33**] ❶ to dissolve
❷ to break up; **disolverse** to
break up

disparar vb [**25**] to shoot; **disparar
a alguien** to shoot at somebody;
Disparó dos tiros. He fired two
shots.

disparate nm silly thing; **¡Qué
disparate!** How absurd!

disparo nm shot

disponer vb [**41**] to arrange;
disponer de to have; **disponerse
a hacer algo** to get ready to do
something

disponible adj available

dispuesto, -a adj ❶ prepared
▷ *estar dispuesto a hacer algo* to be
prepared to do something ❷ ready
▷ *Todo está dispuesto para la fiesta.*
Everything's ready for the party.

disputa nf dispute

distancia nf distance;
mantenerse a distancia to keep
at a distance; **¿Qué distancia hay
entre Madrid y Barcelona?** How
far is Madrid from Barcelona?;
**¿A qué distancia está la
estación?** How far's the station?;
a 20 kilómetros de distancia
20 kilometres away

distinción (pl **distinciones**) nf
distinction

distinguido, -a adj distinguished

distinguir vb [58, gu→g before a and o] ① to distinguish; **Se parecen tanto que no los distingo.** They're so alike that I can't tell them apart. ② to make out; **distinguirse** to stand out

distinto, -a adj ① different ▷ *Carlos es distinto a los demás.* Carlos is different from other people.; **distintos** several ▷ *distintas clases de coches* several types of car

distracción (pl **distracciones**) nf pastime; **En el pueblo hay pocas distracciones.** There isn't much to do in the village.

distraer vb [54] ① to keep... entertained ▷ *Les pondré un DVD para distraerlos.* I'll put a DVD on to keep them entertained. ② to distract ▷ *No me distraigas, que tengo trabajo.* Don't distract me. I've got work to do.; **Me distrae mucho escuchar música.** I really enjoy listening to music.; **Me distraje un momento y me pasé de parada.** I let my mind wander for a minute and missed my stop.

distraído, -a adj absent-minded; **Perdona, estaba distraído.** Sorry, I wasn't concentrating.

distribución (pl **distribuciones**) nf ① layout ② distribution

distribuir vb [10] to distribute

distrito nm district

diversión (pl **diversiones**) nf entertainment

⚠ Be careful! **diversión** does not mean **diversion**.

diverso, -a adj different

divertido, -a adj ① funny ② enjoyable; **Fue muy divertido.** It was great fun.

divertir vb [51] to entertain; **divertirse** to have a good time

dividir vb [58] to divide; **dividirse** (1) to divide (2) to share

divierto vb see **divertir**

divino, -a adj divine

división (pl **divisiones**) nf division

divorciarse vb [25] to get divorced

divorcio nm divorce

divulgar vb [37] to spread

DNI abbr m (= *Documento Nacional de Identad*) ID card

doblar vb [25] ① to double ▷ *Le han doblado el sueldo.* They've doubled his salary. ② to fold ▷ *Dobla los pañuelos y guárdalos.* Fold the handkerchiefs and put them away. ③ to turn ▷ *Cuando llegues al cruce, dobla a la derecha.* When you reach the junction, turn right. ④ to dub ▷ *Doblan todas las películas extranjeras.* All foreign films are dubbed. ⑤ to toll ▷ *Las campanas de la iglesia estaban doblando.* The church bells were tolling.

doble adj double ▷ *una habitación doble* a double room
▶ nm twice as much ▷ *Su sueldo es el doble del mío.* His salary's twice as much as mine. ▷ *Comes el doble que yo.* You eat twice as much as I do.; **Trabaja el doble que tú.** He works twice as hard as you do.; **jugar un partido de dobles** to play doubles

doce adj, pron twelve ▷ Tengo doce años. I'm twelve.; **Son las doce.** It's twelve o'clock.

docena nf dozen

doctor, a nm/f doctor

doctrina nf doctrine

documental nm documentary

documento nm document; **el documento nacional de identidad** the identity card

All Spanish nationals over 14 must have an identity card including their photo, personal details and fingerprint. In Spain this card is also known as the **DNI** or **carnet (de identidad)**, while in Latin American countries a similar card is called the **cédula de identidad**.

un **documento adjunto** an attachment

dólar nm dollar

doler vb [33] to hurt; **Me duele la cabeza.** I've got a headache.; **Me duele el pecho.** I've got a pain in my chest.; **Me duele la garganta.** I've got a sore throat.

dolor nm pain; Tengo dolor de cabeza. I've got a headache.; Tengo dolor de estómago. I've got stomach ache.; **Tengo dolor de muelas.** I've got toothache.; **Tengo dolor de oídos.** I've got earache.; **Tengo dolor de garganta.** I've got a sore throat.

doméstico, -a adj domestic; **las tareas domésticas** the housework; **un animal doméstico** a pet

domicilio nm residence ▷ su domicilio particular their private residence; **servicio a domicilio** home delivery

dominar vb [25] ❶ to dominate ❷ (temper) to control ❸ (language) to be fluent in ❹ (fire) to bring under control; **dominarse** to control oneself

domingo nm Sunday ▷ el domingo pasado last Sunday ▷ el domingo que viene next Sunday

dominicano, -a adj, nm/f Dominican

dominio nm ❶ (of subject) command ❷ rule ❸ control

dominó nm ❶ domino ❷ dominoes sg ▷ jugar al dominó to play dominoes

don nm gift ▷ Tiene un don para la música. He has a gift for music.; **tener don de gentes** to be good with people; **don Juan Gómez** Mr Juan Gómez; **Es un don nadie.** He's a nobody.

dona nf (Mex) doughnut

donante nmf donor

donativo nm donation

donde adv where ▷ La nota está donde la dejaste. The note's where you left it.

dónde adv where ▷ ¿Dónde vas? Where are you going? ▷ ¿Sabes dónde está? Do you know where he is?; ¿**De dónde eres?** Where are you from?; ¿**Por dónde se va al cine?** How do you get to the cinema?

doña nf doña Marta García Mrs Marta García

dorado, -a adj golden

dormir vb [17] to sleep; **Se me ha dormido el brazo.** My arm has gone to sleep.; **dormir la siesta** to have a nap; **dormir como un tronco** to sleep like a log; **estar medio dormido** to be half asleep; **dormirse** to fall asleep

dormitorio nm ❶ bedroom ❷ dormitory

dorso nm back ▷ Se apuntó el teléfono en el dorso de la mano. He wrote the telephone number on the back of his hand.; **'véase al dorso'** 'see over'

dos adj, pron ❶ two ▷ ¿Tienes los dos libros que te dejé? Have you got the two books I lent you? ▷ Tiene dos años. He's two.; **Son las dos.** It's two o'clock.; **de dos en dos** in twos; **el dos de enero** the second of January; **cada dos por tres** every five minutes ❷ both ▷ Al final vinieron los dos. In the end they both came. ▷ Los hemos invitado a los dos. We've invited both of them.

doscientos, -as adj, pron two hundred ▷ doscientos cincuenta two hundred and fifty

dosis (pl dosis) nf dose

doy vb see **dar**

dragón (pl dragones) nm dragon

drama nm drama

dramático, -a adj dramatic

droga nf drug ▷ las drogas blandas soft drugs ▷ las drogas duras hard drugs

drogadicto, -a nm/f drug addict

drogar vb [37] to drug; **drogarse** to take drugs

droguería nf
▪ This is a shop selling cleaning
▪ materials, paint and toiletries.

ducha nf shower ▷ darse una ducha to have a shower

ducharse vb [25] to have a shower

duda nf doubt; **Tengo mis dudas.** I have my doubts.; **sin duda** no doubt; **no cabe duda** there's no doubt about it; **Tengo una duda.** I have a query.; **¿Alguna duda?** Any questions?

dudar vb [25] to doubt; **Dudo que sea cierto.** I doubt if it's true.; **Dudó si comprarlo o no.** He wasn't sure whether to buy it or not.

dudoso, -a adj ❶ doubtful ▷ Es dudoso que vengan. It's doubtful whether they'll come. ❷ dubious

duelo vb see **doler**

dueño, -a nm/f owner

duermo vb see **dormir**

Duero nm the Douro

dulce adj ❶ sweet ❷ gentle
▶ nm sweet

duración nf length; **una pila de larga duración** a long-life battery

duradero, -a adj ❶ lasting
❷ hard-wearing

durante adv during; **durante toda la noche** all night long; **Habló durante una hora.** He spoke for an hour.

durar vb [25] to last ▷ La película dura dos horas. The film lasts two hours. ▷ Solo duró dos meses como director. He only lasted two months as manager. ▷ Todavía le dura el enfado. He's still angry.

durazno *nm (LatAm)* peach
dureza *nf* ❶ hardness ❷ harshness
❸ callus
durmiendo *vb see* **dormir**
duro, -a *adj* ❶ hard ▷ *Los diamantes son muy duros.* Diamonds are very hard. ❷ tough ▷ *Esta carne está dura.* This meat's tough. ❸ harsh ▷ *El clima es muy duro.* The climate is very harsh.; **a duras penas** with great difficulty; **ser duro de oído** to be hard of hearing
▶ *adv* hard ▷ *trabajar duro* to work hard
▶ *nm* five-peseta coin
DVD *abbr m* (= *Disco de Vídeo Digital*) DVD

e *conj*

e is used instead of **y** in front of words beginning with 'i' and 'hi', but not 'hie'.

and ▷ *Pablo e Inés.* Pablo and Inés.
echar *vb* **[25]** ❶ to throw ▷ *Échame las llaves.* Throw me the keys over.; **Eché la carta en el buzón.** I posted the letter. ❷ to put ▷ *Tengo que echar gasolina.* I need to put petrol in the car.; **¿Te echo más whisky?** Shall I pour you some more whisky? ❸ to throw out ▷ *Me echó de su casa.* He threw me out of the house. ❹ to expel ▷ *Lo han echado del colegio.* He's been expelled from school.; **La echaron del trabajo.** They sacked her.; **¿Qué echan hoy en la tele?** What's on TV today?; **echar de menos a alguien** to miss

somebody; **echar una ojeada (a)** to browse; **echarse (1)** to lie down **(2)** to jump

eco *nm* echo

ecología *nf* ecology

ecológico, -a *adj* ❶ ecological ❷ organic; **un producto ecológico** an environmentally friendly product

ecologista *adj* environmental ▸ *nmf* environmentalist

economía *nf* ❶ economy ❷ economics *sg*

económico, -a *adj* ❶ economic ▷ *una profunda crisis económica* a deep economic crisis ❷ economical ▷ *un motor económico* an economical engine ❸ inexpensive ▷ *Ese restaurante es muy económico.* That restaurant's very inexpensive.

economista *nmf* economist

economizar *vb* [**13**] to economize

Ecuador *nm* Ecuador

ecuatoriano, -a *adj, nm/f* Ecuadorean

edad *nf* age ▷ *Tenemos la misma edad.* We're the same age.; *¿Qué edad tienen?* How old are they?; **Está en la edad del pavo.** She's at that difficult age.

edición (*pl* **ediciones**) *nf* edition

edificar *vb* [**48**] to build

edificio *nm* building

Edimburgo *nm* Edinburgh

editar *vb* [**25**] to publish

editor, a *nm/f* publisher

editorial *nf* publisher

edredón (*pl* **edredones**) *nm* ❶ eiderdown ❷ duvet

educación *nf* ❶ education; **educación física** PE ❷ upbringing; **Señalar es de mala educación.** It's rude to point.; **Se lo pedí con educación.** I asked her politely.

educado, -a *adj* polite; **Me contestó de forma educada.** He answered me politely.

educar *vb* [**48**] ❶ to educate ❷ to bring up

educativo, -a *adj* educational

EE.UU. *abbr* (= *Estados Unidos*) USA

efectivamente *adv* **Efectivamente, estaba donde tú decías.** You were right, he was where you said.; **Entonces, ¿Es usted su padre? — Efectivamente.** So, are you his father? — That's right.

efectivo, -a *adj* effective; **pagar en efectivo** to pay in cash

efecto *nm* effect; **hacer efecto** to take effect; **en efecto** indeed

efectuar *vb* [**1**] to carry out

eficaz *adj* ❶ effective ❷ efficient

eficiente *adj* efficient

egipcio, -a *adj, nm/f* Egyptian

Egipto *nm* Egypt

egoísmo *nm* selfishness

egoísta *adj* selfish ▸ *nmf* **María es una egoísta.** Maria's very selfish.

Eire *nm* Eire

eje *nm* ❶ axle ❷ axis

ejecución (*pl* **ejecuciones**) *nf* execution

ejecutar *vb* [**25**] ❶ to carry out ❷ to execute

ejecutivo, -a *nm/f* executive

ejemplar *nm* copy

ejemplo nm example; **por ejemplo** for example

ejercer vb [**6**, no vowel change] **Ejerce de abogado.** He's a practising lawyer.; **Ejerce mucha influencia sobre sus hermanos.** He has a lot of influence on his brothers.

ejercicio nm exercise; **hacer ejercicio** to exercise

ejército nm army

ejote nm (Mex) green bean

el (fsg la, mpl los, fpl las) art the
▷ Perdí el autobús. I missed the bus.

Look how the English possessive corresponds to the article in the following.
▷ Ayer me lavé la cabeza. I washed my hair yesterday. ▷ Me puse el abrigo. I put my coat on. ▷ Tiene un coche bonito, pero prefiero el de Juan. He's got a nice car, but I prefer Juan's.

The article is not always translated; for example when making generalizations, in certain time expressions, and with titles such as **Mr**, **Mrs**, and **Dr**.
▷ No me gusta el pescado. I don't like fish. ▷ Vendrá el lunes que viene. He's coming next Monday. ▷ Ha llamado el Sr. Sendra. Mr Sendra called.; **el del sombrero rojo** the one in the red hat; **Yo fui el que lo encontró.** I was the one who found it.

él pron ❶ he ▷ Me lo dijo él. He told me. ❷ him ▷ Se lo di a él. I gave it to him. ▷ Su mujer es más alta que él.

His wife is taller than him.; **él mismo** himself; **de él** his ▷ El coche es de él. The car's his.

elaborar vb [**25**] to produce

elástico, -a adj **un tejido elástico** a stretchy material; **una goma elástica** an elastic band

elección (pl elecciones) nf ❶ election ▷ Han convocado elecciones generales. General elections have been called. ❷ choice ▷ No tuve elección. I had no choice.

electoral adj **la campaña electoral** the election campaign

electricidad nf electricity

electricista nmf electrician

eléctrico, -a adj ❶ electric ▷ una guitarra eléctrica an electric guitar ❷ electrical ▷ a causa de un fallo eléctrico due to an electrical fault

electrodoméstico nm domestic appliance

electrónica nf electronics sg

electrónico, -a adj electronic; **el correo electrónico** email

elefante nm elephant

elegante adj smart

elegir vb [**18**] ❶ to choose ❷ to elect

elemento nm element

elevado, -a adj high

elevar vb [**25**] to raise

eligiendo vb see **elegir**

elijo vb see **elegir**

eliminar vb [**25**] ❶ to remove ❷ to eliminate

elixir bucal nm mouthwash

ella pron ❶ she ▷ Ella no estaba en casa. She was not at home.

2 her ▷ *El regalo es para ella.* The present's for her. ▷ *Él estaba más nervioso que ella.* He was more nervous than her.; **ella misma** herself; **de ella** hers ▷ *Este abrigo es de ella.* This coat's hers.

ellos, -as *pron pl* **1** they ▷ *Ellos todavía no lo saben.* They don't know yet. **2** them ▷ *Yo me iré con ellas.* I'll leave with them. ▷ *Somos mejores que ellos.* We're better than them.; **ellos mismos** themselves ▷ *Me lo dijeron ellos mismos.* They told me themselves.; **de ellos** theirs ▷ *El coche era de ellos.* The car was theirs.

elogiar *vb* [25] to praise

elote *nm* (Mex) **1** corncob **2** sweetcorn

e-mail *nm* **1** (message, system) email **2** email address

embajada *nf* embassy

embajador, a *nm/f* ambassador

embalar *vb* [25] to pack

embalse *nm* reservoir

embarazada *adj* pregnant ▷ *Estaba embarazada de cuatro meses.* She was four months pregnant.; **quedarse embarazada** to get pregnant

Be careful! **embarazada** does not mean **embarrassed**.

embarazoso, -a *adj* embarrassing

embarcar *vb* [48] to board

embargo *nm* embargo; **sin embargo** nevertheless

emborracharse *vb* [25] to get drunk

embotellado, -a *adj* bottled

embotellamiento *nm* traffic jam

embrague *nm* clutch

embrollarse *vb* [25] **1** to get tangled up **2** to get muddled up

embrollo *nm* tangle

embrujado, -a *adj* haunted

embutido *nm* cold meats

emergencia *nf* emergency; **la salida de emergencia** the emergency exit

emigrar *vb* [25] **1** to emigrate **2** to migrate

emisión (*pl* emisiones) *nf* **1** broadcast **2** emission

emitir *vb* [58] **1** to broadcast **2** to give off

emoción (*pl* emociones) *nf* **1** emotion; **Su carta me produjo gran emoción.** I was very moved by his letter.; **¡Qué emoción!** How exciting!

emocionado, -a *adj* **1** moved **2** excited

emocionante *adj* **1** moving **2** exciting

emotivo, -a *adj* **1** moving **2** emotional

empacharse *vb* [25] to get a tummy upset

empalagoso, -a *adj* sickly

empalmar *vb* [25] **1** to connect **2** to join

empanada *nf* pasty

empañarse *vb* [25] to get steamed up

empapar *vb* [25] to soak; **estar empapado hasta los huesos** to be soaked to the skin

empapelar *vb* [25] to paper

empaquetar *vb* [25] to pack

emparedado nm (LatAm) sandwich

emparejar vb [25] to pair up

empastar vb [25] **Me han empastado dos muelas.** I've had two fillings.

empaste nm filling

empatar vb [25] to draw

empate nm ① draw ② tie

empedernido, -a adj **un fumador empedernido** a chronic smoker; **Es un lector empedernido.** He's a compulsive reader.

empeñado, -a adj determined

empeñarse vb [25] **empeñarse en hacer algo** (1) to be determined to do something (2) to insist on doing something

empeorar vb [25] ① to get worse ▷ Empeoró tras la operación. He got worse after the operation. ② to make…worse ▷ Tu comentario solo empeorará las cosas. Your comment will only make matters worse.

empezar vb [19] to start; **empezar a hacer algo** to start doing something; **volver a empezar** to start again

empinado, -a adj steep

empleado, -a nm/f ① employee ② (LatAm) shop assistant

emplear vb [25] ① to use ② to employ

empleo nm job; **estar sin empleo** to be unemployed; **'modo de empleo'** 'how to use'

empollar vb [25] to swot

empollón (f **empollona**, mpl **empollones**) nm/f swot

empresa nf firm

empresaria nf businesswoman

empresario nm businessman

empujar vb [25] to push

empujón (pl **empujones**) nm **Me dieron un empujón y me caí.** They pushed me and I fell.; **abrirse paso a empujones** to shove one's way through

en prep ① in ▷ en el armario in the wardrobe ▷ Viven en Granada. They live in Granada. ▷ Nació en invierno. He was born in winter. ▷ Lo hice en dos días. I did it in two days. ▷ Hablamos en inglés. We speak in English. ▷ Está en el hospital. She's in hospital. ② into ▷ Entré en el banco. I went into the bank. ▷ Me metí en la cama a las diez. I got into bed at ten o'clock. ③ on ▷ Las llaves están en la mesa. The keys are on the table. ▷ Lo encontré tirado en el suelo. I found it lying on the floor. ▷ La librería está en la calle Pelayo. The bookshop is on Pelayo Street. ▷ La oficina está en el quinto piso. The office is on the fifth floor.; **Mi cumpleaños cae en viernes.** My birthday falls on a Friday. ④ at ▷ Yo estaba en casa. I was at home. ▷ Te veo en el cine. See you at the cinema. ▷ Vivía en el número 17. I was living at number 17. ▷ en ese momento at that moment ▷ en Navidades at Christmas ⑤ by ▷ Vinimos en avión. We came by plane.; **ser el primero en llegar** to be the first to arrive

enamorado, -a adj **estar enamorado de alguien** to be in love with somebody

enamorarse vb [25] to fall in love

encabezar vb [13] to head

encaminarse vb [25] **Nos encaminamos hacia el pueblo.** We headed towards the village.

encantado, -a adj ❶ delighted ▷ **Está encantada con su nuevo coche.** She's delighted with her new car. ❷ enchanted; **¡Encantado de conocerle!** Pleased to meet you!

encantador, a adj lovely

encantar vb [25] to love

encanto nm charm; **Eugenia es un encanto.** Eugenia is charming.

encarcelar vb [25] to imprison

encargado, -a nm/f manager ▷ **Quiero hablar con el encargado.** I'd like to talk to the manager.

encargar vb [37] ❶ to order ❷ to ask

encariñarse vb [25] **encariñarse con** to grow fond of

encendedor nm lighter

encender vb [20] ❶ to light ❷ to switch on

encendido, -a adj ❶ on ▷ **La tele estaba encendida.** The telly was on. ❷ (fire) lit

encerado nm blackboard

encerrar vb [39] ❶ to shut up ❷ to lock up

enchilada nf (Mex) stuffed tortilla

enchufado, -a nm/f **Amelia es la enchufada del profesor.** (informal) Amelia's the teacher's pet.

enchufar vb [25] to plug in

enchufe nm ❶ plug ❷ socket

encía nf gum

enciclopedia nf encyclopaedia

enciendo vb see **encender**

encierro vb see **encerrar**

encima adv on ▷ **Pon el cenicero aquí encima.** Put the ashtray on there. ▷ **No llevo dinero encima.** I haven't got any money on me.; **encima de** (1) on ▷ **Ponlo encima de la mesa.** Put it on the table. (2) on top of ▷ **Mi maleta está encima del armario.** My case is on top of the wardrobe.; **Lo leí por encima.** I glanced at it.; **por encima de** (1) above (2) over; **¡Y encima no te da ni las gracias!** And on top of it he doesn't even thank you!

encina nf oak tree

encoger vb [7] to shrink; **Antonio se encogió de hombros.** Antonio shrugged his shoulders.

encontrar vb [11] to find ▷ **Mi hermano ha encontrado trabajo.** My brother has found a job. ▷ **Lo encuentro un poco arrogante.** I find him a bit arrogant.; **No encuentro las llaves.** I can't find the keys.; **encontrarse (1)** to feel ▷ **Ahora se encuentra mejor.** Now she's feeling better. **(2)** to meet ▷ **Nos encontramos en el cine.** We met at the cinema.; **Me encontré con Manolo en la calle.** I bumped into Manolo in the street.

encuentro nm ❶ meeting ❷ match

encuesta nf survey

enderezar vb [13] to straighten

endulzar vb [13] to sweeten

endurecer vb [12] (muscles) to tone up

enemigo, -a adj, nm/f enemy

enemistarse vb [25] to fall out

energía nf energy; **la energía solar** solar power; **la energía eléctrica** electricity

enérgico, -a adj energetic

enero nm January

enfadado, -a adj angry ▷ *Mi padre estaba muy enfadado conmigo.* My father was very angry with me.; **Ana y su novio están enfadados.** Ana and her boyfriend have fallen out.

enfadarse vb [25] to be angry ▷ *Papá se va a enfadar mucho contigo.* Dad will be very angry with you.; **Mi hermana y su novio se han enfadado.** My brother and his girlfriend have fallen out.

enfado nm **Ya se le ha pasado el enfado.** He isn't angry any more.

enfermarse vb [25] (LatAm) to get sick

enfermedad nf ① illness ② disease

enfermería nf sick bay

enfermero, -a nm/f nurse

enfermo, -a adj ill ▷ *He estado enferma toda la semana.* I've been ill all week.; **¿Cuándo te pusiste enfermo?** When did you get ill? ▷ nm/f patient

enfocar vb [48] ① to focus on ② to approach

enfrentarse vb [25] **enfrentarse a algo** to face something

enfrente adv opposite; **La panadería está enfrente.** The baker's is across the street.; **de enfrente** opposite ▷ *la casa de enfrente* the house opposite; **enfrente de** opposite

enfriarse vb [21] ① to get cold ② to cool down ③ to catch cold

enganchar vb [25] to hook; **engancharse** to get caught

engañar vb [25] ① to cheat ② to lie ③ to cheat on; **Las apariencias engañan.** Appearances can be deceptive.

engaño nm ① con ② deception

engordar vb [25] ① to put on weight; **He engordado dos kilos.** I've put on two kilos. ② to be fattening

engreído, -a adj conceited

enhorabuena nf **¡Enhorabuena!** Congratulations!; **Me dieron la enhorabuena por el premio.** They congratulated me on winning the prize.

enlace nm ① connection ② (in computing) link

enlatado, -a adj tinned

enlazar vb [13] to connect

enmarcar vb [48] to frame

enmoquetado, -a adj carpeted

enojado, -a adj angry ▷ *Mi padre estaba muy enojado conmigo.* My father was very angry with me.; **Ana y su novio están enojados.** Ana and her boyfriend have fallen out.

enojarse vb [25] to be angry

enorme adj enormous

enredarse vb [25] ① to get tangled up ▷ *Se me ha enredado el pelo.* My hair's got all tangled up. ② to get into a tangle

enrevesado, -a adj difficult

enriquecerse vb [12] to get rich

enrollar vb [25] to roll up

enroscar vb [48] **①** to screw in **②** to coil

ensalada nf salad

ensaladilla nf **una ensaladilla rusa** a Russian salad

ensanchar vb [25] to widen; **ensancharse** to stretch

ensayar vb [25] to rehearse

ensayo nm rehearsal

enseguida adv straight away; **Enseguida te atiendo.** I'll be with you in a minute.

enseñanza nf **①** teaching **②** education; **la enseñanza primaria** primary education

enseñar vb [25] **①** to teach ▷ Mi padre me enseñó a nadar. My father taught me to swim. **②** to show; **Les enseñé el colegio.** I showed them round the school.

ensuciar vb [25] to get...dirty ▷ Vas a ensuciar el sofá. You'll get the sofa dirty.; **ensuciarse** to get dirty; **Te has ensuciado de barro los pantalones.** You've got mud on your trousers.

entender vb [20] to understand ▷ ¿Lo entiendes? Do you understand?; **Creo que lo he entendido mal.** I think I've misunderstood.; **Mi primo entiende mucho de coches.** My cousin knows a lot about cars.; **entenderse (1)** to get on ▷ Mi hermana y yo no nos entendemos. My sister and I don't get on. **(2)** to communicate; **Dio a entender que no le gustaba.** He implied that he didn't like it.

entendido, -a nm/f expert

enterarse vb [25] **①** to find out; **Se enteraron del accidente por la tele.** They heard about the accident on the TV.; **Me sacaron una muela y ni me enteré.** They took out a tooth and I didn't feel a thing. **②** to understand

entero, -a adj whole ▷ Se pasó la noche entera estudiando. He spent the whole night studying.; **la leche entera** full-cream milk

enterrar vb [39] to bury

entierro nm **①** burial ▶ nm funeral

entonces adv **①** then ▷ Me recogió y entonces fuimos al cine. He picked me up and then we went to the cinema. **②** so ▷ ¿Entonces, vienes o te quedas? So, are you coming or staying?; **desde entonces** since then; **para entonces** by then

entorno nm surroundings pl

entrada nf **①** entrance; **'entrada libre'** 'free admission' **②** ticket ▷ Tengo entradas para el teatro. I've got tickets for the theatre. **③** entry; **'prohibida la entrada'** 'no entry' **④** deposit

entrante nm starter

entrar vb [25] **①** to go in ▷ Abrí la puerta y entré. I opened the door and went in. ▷ Mi amiga entró al banco. My friend went into the bank.; **Pedro entra a trabajar a las 8.** Pedro starts work at 8 o'clock.; **No me dejaron entrar por ser menor de 16 años.** They wouldn't let me in because I was under 16. **②** to come in ▷ ¿Se puede?

— Sí, entra. May I? — Yes, come in.
▷ *Entraron en mi cuarto mientras yo dormía.* They came into my room while I was asleep. ❸ to fit ▷ *Estos zapatos no me entran.* These shoes don't fit me. ▷ *La maleta no entra en el maletero.* The case won't fit in the boot.; **El vino no entra en el precio.** The wine is not included in the price.; **Le entraron ganas de reír.** She wanted to laugh.; **De repente le entró sueño.** He suddenly felt sleepy.; **Me ha entrado hambre al verte comer.** Watching you eat has made me hungry.

entre *prep* ❶ between ▷ *Vendrá entre las diez y las once.* He'll be coming between ten and eleven. ❷ among ▷ *Las mujeres hablaban entre sí.* The women were talking among themselves.; **Le compraremos un regalo entre todos.** We'll buy her a present between all of us. ❸ by ▷ *15 dividido entre 3 es 5.* 15 divided by 3 is 5.

entreabierto, -a *adj* ajar
entregar *vb* [37] ❶ to hand in ❷ to deliver ❸ to present with ▷ *El director le entregó la medalla.* The director presented him with the medal.; **El ladrón se entregó a la policía.** The thief gave himself up.
entremeses *nmpl* appetizers
entrenador, -a *nm/f* coach
entrenamiento *nm* training
entrenarse *vb* [25] to train
entretanto *adv* meanwhile
entretener *vb* [53] ❶ to entertain; **La tele entretiene mucho.** TV is

very entertaining. ❷ to keep ▷ *Una vecina me entretuvo hablando en las escaleras.* A neighbour kept me talking on the stairs.;
entretenerse *vb* to amuse oneself ▷ *Se entretienen viendo los dibujos animados.* They amuse themselves by watching cartoons.; **No os entretengáis jugando.** Don't hang about playing.
entretenido, -a *adj* entertaining
entrevista *nf* interview; **hacer una entrevista a alguien** to interview somebody
entrevistador, a *nm/f* interviewer
entrevistar *vb* [25] to interview
entrometerse *vb* [8] to meddle
entusiasmado, -a *adj* excited
entusiasmarse *vb* [25] to get excited
entusiasmo *nm* enthusiasm; **con entusiasmo** enthusiastically
enumerar *vb* [25] to list
envase *nm* container; **'envase no retornable'** 'non-returnable bottle'
envejecer *vb* [12] to age
enviar *vb* [21] to send; **Juan me envió el regalo por correo.** Juan posted me the present.
envidia *nf* envy; **¡Qué envidia!** I'm so jealous!; **Le tiene envidia a Ana.** She's jealous of Ana.; **Le da envidia que mi coche sea mejor.** He's jealous that my car is better.
envidiar *vb* [25] to envy
envidioso, -a *adj* envious
envolver *vb* [59] to wrap up
envuelto *vb see* **envolver**

epidemia nf epidemic

episodio nm episode

época nf time ▷ En aquella época vivíamos en Alicante. At that time we were living in Alicante. ▷ en esta época del año at this time of year

equilibrado, -a adj balanced

equilibrio nm balance ▷ Perdí el equilibrio y me caí. I lost my balance and fell over. ▷ Luis podía mantener el equilibrio en la cuerda floja. Luis managed to keep his balance on the tightrope.

equipaje nm luggage; **equipaje de mano** hand luggage

equipo nm ① team ▷ un equipo de baloncesto a basketball team ② equipment ▷ Me robaron todo el equipo de esquí. They stole all my skiing equipment.; **el equipo de música** the stereo

> Word for word, **equipo de música** means 'music equipment'.

equitación nf riding

equivaler vb [55] equivalent to; **equivaler a algo** to be equivalent to something

equivocación (pl equivocaciones) nf mistake

equivocado, -a adj wrong ▷ Estás equivocada. You're wrong.

equivocarse vb [48] ① to make a mistake ② to be wrong; **Perdone, me he equivocado de número.** Sorry, wrong number.; **Se equivocaron de tren.** They caught the wrong train.

era vb see ser

eres vb see ser

erizo nm hedgehog; **un erizo de mar** a sea urchin

error nm mistake

eructar vb [25] to burp

eructo nm burp

es vb see ser

esa adj see ese

> **pron** see ese

esbelto, -a adj slender

escala nf ① scale ▷ a escala nacional on a national scale ② stopover ▷ Tenemos una escala de tres horas en Bruselas. We've got a three-hour stopover in Brussels.

escalar vb [25] to climb

escalera nf stairs pl ▷ bajar las escaleras to go down the stairs; **una escalera de mano** a ladder

> Word for word, **escalera de mano** means 'hand stairs'.

la **escalera de incendios** the fire escape; **una escalera mecánica** an escalator

escalofrío nm Tengo escalofríos. I'm shivering.

escalón (pl escalones) nm step

escama nf scale

escandalizarse vb [13] to shock

escándalo nm ① scandal ② racket ▷ ¿Qué escándalo es éste? What's all this racket?

escandaloso, -a adj noisy

escandinavo, -a nm/f Scandinavian; **los escandinavos** the Scandinavians

escáner nm ① scanner ② scan ▷ hacerse un escáner to have a scan

escapar vb [25] to escape; **escaparse** to escape; **Se me escapó un eructo.** I let out a burp.

escaparate *nm* shop window; **ir de escaparates** to go window-shopping

escape *nm* leak ▷ *Había un escape de gas.* There was a gas leak.

escaquearse *vb* [**25**] **escaquearse de clase** to skip school

escarabajo *nm* beetle

escarbar *vb* [**25**] to dig

escarcha *nf* frost

escasez *nf* shortage

escaso, -a *adj* scarce ▷ *Los alimentos eran muy escasos.* Food was scarce.; **Habrá escasa visibilidad en las carreteras.** Visibility on the roads will be poor.; **Duró una hora escasa.** It lasted barely an hour.

escayola *nf* plaster

escayolar *vb* [**25**] **Le escayolaron la pierna.** They put his leg in plaster.

escena *nf* scene

escenario *nm* stage

escéptico, -a *adj* sceptical

esclavo, -a *nm/f* slave

escoba *nf* broom

escocer *vb* [**6**] to sting

escocés (*f* **escocesa**, *mpl* **escoceses**) *adj* Scottish; **el whisky escocés** Scotch whisky; **una falda escocesa** a kilt
▶ *nm* Scotsman ▷ *los escoceses* Scottish people

escocesa *nf* Scotswoman

Escocia *nf* Scotland

escoger *vb* [**7**] to choose

escolar *adj* school ▷ *el uniforme escolar* school uniform

escombros *nmpl* rubble *sg*

esconder *vb* [**8**] to hide; **Me escondí debajo de la cama.** I hid under the bed.

escondidas *nfpl* **a escondidas** in secret

escondite *nm* jugar al escondite to play hide-and-seek

escopeta *nf* shotgun

Escorpio *nm* (*sign*) Scorpio; **Soy escorpio.** I'm Scorpio.

escorpión (*pl* **escorpiones**) *nm* scorpion

escribir *vb* [**58**, *pp* **escrito**] to write
▷ *Les escribí una carta.* I wrote them a letter.; **Nos escribimos de vez en cuando.** We write to each other from time to time.; **¿Cómo se escribe tu nombre?** How do you spell your name?; **escribir a máquina** to type

escrito, -a *adj* written

escritor, a *nm/f* writer

escritorio *nm* ❶ desk ❷ (*LatAm*) office

escritura *nf* writing

escrupuloso, -a *adj* fussy

escuchar *vb* [**25**] to listen ▷ *Me gusta escuchar música.* I like listening to music.

escudo *nm* ❶ shield ❷ badge

escuela *nf* school; **la escuela primaria** primary school

esc[u]lcar *vb* [**48**] (*Mex*) to search

escultura *nf* sculpture

escupir *vb* [**58**] to spit

escurridizo, -a *adj* slippery

escurridor *nm* ❶ colander ❷ plate rack

escurrir *vb* [**58**] ❶ to wring ❷ to drain

ese adj that ▷ Dame ese libro. Give me that book.
▶ pron that one

esencial adj essential

esforzarse vb [3] to make an effort

esfuerzo nm effort

esfumarse vb [25] to vanish

esguince nm sprain; **Me hice un esguince en el tobillo.** I've sprained my ankle.

esmalte nm el esmalte de uñas nail varnish

ESO abbr f (= Enseñanza Secundaria obligatoria)
  ◆ ESO is the compulsory
  ◆ secondary education course
  ◆ done by 12 to 16 year-olds.

eso pron that ▷ Eso es mentira. That's a lie. ▷ ¡Eso es! That's it!; **a eso de las cinco** at about five; **En eso llamaron a la puerta.** Just then there was a ring at the door.; **Por eso te lo dije.** That's why I told you.

esos, -as adj pl those ▷ Trae esas sillas aquí. Bring those chairs over here.
▶ pron pl those ones

espabilar vb [25] = despabilar

espacio nm ❶ room ▷ El piano ocupa mucho espacio. The piano takes up a lot of room. ❷ space; **un espacio en blanco** a gap; **viajar por el espacio** to travel in space

espada nf sword
  ▲ Be careful! **espada** does not
  mean **spade**.

espaguetis nmpl spaghetti sg

espalda nf back ▷ Me duele la espalda. My back aches.; **Estaba tumbada de espaldas.** She was lying on her back.; **Ana estaba de espaldas a mí.** Ana had her back to me.; **Me encanta nadar a espalda.** I love swimming backstroke.

espantapájaros (pl espantapájaros) nm scarecrow

espantar vb [25] ❶ to frighten ❷ to frighten off ❸ to horrify ▷ Me espantan los zapatos de tacón. I hate high heels.; **espantarse** to get frightened

espantoso, -a adj awful; **Hacía un frío espantoso.** It was awfully cold.

España nf Spain

español, a adj Spanish
  ▶ nm/f Spaniard; **los españoles** the Spanish
  ▶ nm (language) Spanish

esparadrapo nm plaster

espárrago nm asparagus

especia nf spice

especial adj special; **en especial** particularly ▷ ¿Desea ver a alguien en especial? Is there anybody you particularly want to see?

especialidad nf speciality

especialista nmf specialist

especializarse vb [13] Rosario se especializó en pediatría. Rosario specialized in paediatrics.

especialmente adv ❶ especially ❷ specially

especie nf species

específico, -a adj specific

espectacular, a adj spectacular

espectáculo nm performance; Dio el espectáculo delante de

todo el mundo. He made a spectacle of himself in front of everyone.

espectador, a nm/f spectator; **los espectadores** the audience

espejo nm mirror ▷ Me miré en el espejo. I looked at myself in the mirror.; **el espejo retrovisor** rearview mirror

espeluznante adj hair-raising

espera nf wait ▷ tras una espera de tres horas after a three-hour wait; **estar a la espera de algo** to be expecting something

esperanza nf hope; **No tengo esperanzas de aprobar.** I have no hope of passing.; **No pierdas las esperanzas.** Don't give up hope.

esperar vb [25] ① to wait ▷ Espera en la puerta, ahora mismo voy. Wait at the door. I'm just coming.; **Espera un momento, por favor.** Hang on a moment, please. ② to wait for ▷ No me esperéis. Don't wait for me.; **Me hizo esperar una hora.** He kept me waiting for an hour. ③ to expect ▷ Llegaron antes de lo que yo esperaba. They arrived sooner than I expected. ▷ Esperaban que Juan les pidiera perdón. They were expecting Juan to apologize. ▷ Llamará cuando menos lo esperes. He'll call when you're least expecting it. ▷ No esperes que venga a ayudarte. Don't expect him to come and help you.; **esperar un bebé** to be expecting a baby; **Me espera un largo día de trabajo.** I've got a long day of work

ahead of me.; **Era de esperar que no viniera.** He was bound to not to come. ④ to hope ▷ Espero que no sea nada grave. I hope it isn't anything serious.; **¿Vendrás a la fiesta? — Espero que sí.** Are you coming to the party? — I hope so.; **¿Crees que Carmen se enfadará? — Espero que no.** Do you think Carmen will be angry? — I hope not.; **Fuimos a esperarla a la estación.** We went to the station to meet her.

espeso, -a adj thick

espía nmf spy

espiar vb [21] to spy on

espina nf ① thorn ② bone

espinaca nf spinach

espinilla nf ① shin ② blackhead

espionaje nm spying; **una novela de espionaje** a spy story

espíritu nm spirit

espiritual adj spiritual

espléndido, -a adj splendid

esponja nf sponge

esponjoso, -a adj spongy

espontáneo, -a adj spontaneous; **de manera espontánea** spontaneously

esposa nf wife; **las esposas** handcuffs

esposo nm husband

espuma nf ① foam ② (on beer) head; **la espuma de afeitar** shaving cream

espumoso, -a adj vino espumoso sparkling wine

esqueleto nm skeleton

esquema nm ③ outline ② diagram

esquí (*pl* **esquís**) *nm* ❶ skiing; **el esquí acuático** water skiing; **una pista de esquí** a ski slope ❷ ski

esquiar *vb* [**21**] to ski

esquimal *adj*, *nmf* Inuit

esquina *nf* corner; **doblar la esquina** to turn the corner

esquivar *vb* [**25**] to dodge

esta *adj* see **este**

▶ *pron* see **este**

está *vb* see **estar**

estable *adj* stable

establecer *vb* [**12**] to establish; **Han logrado establecer contacto con el barco.** They've managed to make contact with the boat.; **La familia se estableció en Madrid.** The family settled in Madrid.

establecimiento *nm* establishment

establo *nm* stable

estación (*pl* **estaciones**) *nf* ❶ station ▷ *la estación de autobuses* the bus station ▷ *la estación de ferrocarril* the railway station ❷ season ▷ *las cuatro estaciones del año* the four seasons of the year; **una estación de esquí** a ski resort; **una estación de servicio** a service station

estacionar *vb* [**25**] to park

estacionarse *vb* [**25**] (Chile, River Plate, Mex) to park

estadía *nf* (LatAm) stay

estadio *nm* stadium

estado *nm* state; **El Estado Español** The Spanish State; **estado civil** marital status; **María está en estado.** María is expecting.

Estados Unidos *nmpl* the United States ▷ *en Estados Unidos* in the United States

estadounidense *adj*, *nmf* American

estafar *vb* [**25**] to swindle

estallar *vb* [**25**] ❶ (bomb) to explode ❷ (tyre, balloon) to burst ❸ (war) to break out

estampilla *nf* (LatAm) stamp

estancado, -a *adj* stagnant

estancia *nf* ❶ stay ❷ ranch

estanco *nm* tobacconist's

In Spain, an **estanco** is a government-licensed tobacconist's, recognizable by its brown and yellow "T" sign. The **estanco** also sells stamps, stationery, official forms and coupons for the **quiniela** or football pools.

estándar *adj* standard

estanque *nm* pond

estante *nm* shelf

estantería *nf* ❶ shelves *pl* ❷ bookshelves *pl* ❸ shelf unit

estaño *nm* tin

estar *vb* [**22**] ❶ to be ▷ *¿Dónde estabas?* Where were you? ▷ *Madrid está en el centro de España.* Madrid is in the centre of Spain.; **¿Está Mónica?** Is Mónica there?; **¿Cómo estás?** How are you? ▷ *Estoy muy cansada.* I'm very tired.; **¿Estás casado o soltero?** Are you married or single?; **Estamos de vacaciones.** We're on holiday.; **Hoy no estoy para bromas.** I'm not in the mood for jokes today.; **¿A cuánto está el kilo de**

naranjas? How much are oranges a kilo?; **Estamos a treinta de enero.** It's the thirtieth of January.; **Estábamos a 30°C.** The temperature was 30°C.; **Estamos esperando a Manolo.** We're waiting for Manolo.; **María estaba sentada en la arena.** María was sitting on the sand.; **La radio está rota.** The radio's broken.; **¡Ya está! Ya sé lo que podemos hacer.** That's it! I know what we can do.; **estarse** to be ▷ En la cama se está muy bien. It's nice being in bed. ▷ ¡Estáte quieto! Keep still! ➋ to look ▷ ¡Qué guapa estás esta noche! You're looking really pretty tonight! ▷ Ese vestido te está muy bien. That dress looks very good on you.

estas adj pl see **estos**
  ▶ pron pl see **estos**

estatal adj state

estatua nf statue

estatura nf height ▷ ¿Cuál es tu estatura? What height are you?; **Tiene casi dos metros de estatura.** He's well over six feet tall.

este nm, adj east ▷ en el este de España in the East of Spain
  ▶ adj this ▷ este libro this book
  ▶ pron this one

esté vb see **estar**

estera nf mat

estéreo (pl estéreos) nm stereo

esterlina adj diez libras esterlinas ten pounds sterling

estético, -a adj Se ha hecho la cirugía estética. He's had plastic surgery.

estiércol nm manure

estilo nm style; **un estilo de vida similar al nuestro** a similar lifestyle to ours

estima nf Lo tengo en gran estima. I think very highly of him.

estimado, -a adj Estimado señor Pérez Dear Mr Pérez

estimulante adj stimulating

estimular vb [25] ➊ to encourage ➋ to stimulate

estirar vb [25] to stretch

esto pron this ▷ ¿Para qué es esto? What's this for?; **En esto llegó Juan.** Just then Juan arrived.

estofado nm stew

estómago nm stomach ▷ Me dolía el estómago. I had stomach ache.

estorbar vb [25] to be in the way

estornudar vb [25] to sneeze

estos, -as adj pl these; **estas maletas** these cases
  ▶ pron pl these ones

estoy vb see **estar**

estrangular vb [25] to strangle

estratégico, -a adj strategic

estrechar vb [25] to take in ▷ ¿Me puedes estrechar esta falda? Can you take in this skirt for me?; **La carretera se estrecha en el puente.** The road gets narrower over the bridge.; **Se estrecharon la mano.** They shook hands.

estrecho, -a adj ➊ narrow ➋ tight ▷ La falda me va muy estrecha. The skirt is very tight on me.
  ▶ nm strait; **el estrecho de Gibraltar** the straits of Gibraltar

estrella nf star; **una estrella de cine** a film star

estrellarse vb [**25**] to smash

estrenar vb [**25**] to premiere;
Mañana estrenaré el vestido.
I'll wear the dress for the first
time tomorrow.

estreno nm premiere

estreñido, -a adj constipated

estrés nm stress

estricto, -a adj strict

estridente adj loud

estropajo nm scourer

estropeado, -a adj ❶ broken
❷ broken down

estropear vb [**25**] ❶ to break ❷ to
ruin ▷ La lluvia nos estropeó las
vacaciones. The rain ruined our
holidays.; **estropearse** to break ▷ Se
nos ha estropeado la tele. The TV's
broken.; **Se me estropeó el coche
en la autopista.** My car broke down
on the motorway.; **La fruta se
está estropeando con este calor.**
The fruit's going off in this heat.

estructura nf structure

estrujar vb [**25**] ❶ to squeeze
❷ to wring

estuche nm case

estudiante nmf student

estudiar vb [**25**] ❶ to study ❷ to
learn

estudio nm ❶ studio ❷ studio flat;
Ha dejado los estudios. He's
given up his studies.

estudioso, -a adj studious

estufa nf ❶ heater ❷ (Mex) stove

estupendamente adv **Me
encuentro estupendamente.**
I feel great.; **Nos lo pasamos
estupendamente.** We had a
great time.

estupendo, -a adj great ▷ Pasamos
unas Navidades estupendas. We had
a great Christmas.; **¡Estupendo!**
Great!

estupidez (pl estupideces) nf **No
dice más que estupideces.** He
just talks rubbish.; **Lo que hizo
fue una estupidez.** What he did
was stupid.

estúpido, -a adj stupid
▶ nm/f idiot

estuve vb see **estar**

etapa nf stage ▷ Lo hicimos por
etapas. We did it in stages.

etc. abbr (= etcétera) etc

eterno, -a adj eternal

ética nf ❶ ethics pl ❷ ethics

ético, -a adj ethical

Etiopía nf Ethiopia

etiqueta nf label; **traje de
etiqueta** formal dress

étnico, -a adj ethnic

ETT abbr (= Empresa de Trabajo
Temporal) temp agency

eufórico, -a adj ecstatic

euro nm euro

Europa nf Europe

europeo, -a adj, nm/f European

Euskadi n the Basque Country

euskera nm Basque

> Basque is one of Spain's four
> official languages, and there is
> Basque-language radio and
> television. It is not from the
> same family of languages as
> Spanish.

evacuar vb [**25**] to evacuate

evadir vb [**58**] ❶ to avoid ❷ to evade

evaluación (pl evaluaciones) nf
assessment

evaluar vb [1] to assess

evangelio nm gospel

evaporarse vb [25] to evaporate

evasivo, -a adj evasive

eventual adj **un trabajo eventual** a temporary job

evidencia nf evidence

evidente adj obvious

evidentemente adv obviously

evitar vb [25] ❶ to avoid ▷ *Intento evitar a Luisa.* I'm trying to avoid Luisa.; **No pude evitarlo.** I couldn't help it. ❷ to save ▷ *Esto nos evitará muchos problemas.* This will save us a lot of problems.

evolución (pl **evoluciones**) nf progress; **la teoría de la evolución** the theory of evolution

evolucionar vb [25] ❶ to develop ❷ to evolve

ex prefix ex; **su ex-marido** her ex-husband

exactamente adv exactly

exactitud nf **No lo sabemos con exactitud.** We don't know exactly.

exacto, -a adj ❶ exact ▷ *el precio exacto* the exact price; **El tren salió a la hora exacta.** The train left bang on time. ❷ accurate ▷ *Tus conclusiones no son muy exactas.* Your conclusions aren't very accurate.; **Tenemos que defender nuestros derechos. — ¡Exacto!** We have to stand up for our rights. — Exactly!

exageración (pl **exageraciones**) nf exaggeration

exagerar vb [25] to exaggerate

examen (pl **exámenes**) nm exam; **el examen de conducir** driving test

examinar vb [25] to examine; **Mañana me examino de inglés.** Tomorrow I've got an English exam.

excavadora nf digger

excavar vb [25] to dig

excelente adj excellent

excéntrico, -a adj eccentric

excepción (pl **excepciones**) nf exception; **a excepción de** except for

excepcional adj exceptional

excepto prep except for

excesivo, -a adj excessive

exceso nm **exceso de equipaje** excess luggage

excitarse vb [25] **Se excitó mucho en la discusión.** He got very worked up in the argument.

exclamar vb [25] to exclaim

excluir vb [10] to exclude

exclusivo, -a adj exclusive

excluyendo vb *see* **excluir**

excursión (pl **excursiones**) nf trip ▷ *Mañana vamos de excursión con el colegio.* Tomorrow we're going on a school trip.

excusa nf excuse

exhibición (pl **exhibiciones**) nf exhibition

exhibir vb [58] to exhibit; **Le gusta mucho exhibirse.** He likes drawing attention to himself.

exigente adj demanding

exigir vb [16] ❶ to demand; **La maestra nos exige demasiado.** Our teacher is too demanding. ❷ to require; **Exigen tres años de experiencia para el puesto.** They're asking for three years' experience for the job.

exiliado, -a nm/f exile

existir vb [58] to exist; **Existen dos maneras de hacerlo.** There are two ways of doing it.

éxito nm success; **Su película tuvo mucho éxito.** His film was very successful.

exótico, -a adj exotic

expansión (pl expansiones) nf expansion

expedición (pl expediciones) nf expedition

expediente nm file; **expediente académico** student record

expendio nm (LatAm) shop

expensas nfpl **a expensas de su salud** at the cost of her health

experiencia nf experience; **con experiencia** experienced

experimental adj experimental

experimentar vb [25] ① to experiment ② to experience

experimento nm experiment

experto, -a nm/f expert

explicación (pl explicaciones) nf explanation

explicar vb [48] to explain; **¿Me explico?** Do I make myself clear?; **No me lo explico.** I can't understand it.

explorador, a nm/f explorer

explorar vb [25] to explore

explosión (pl explosiones) nf explosion; **El artefacto hizo explosión.** The device exploded.

explosivo nm explosive

explotación (pl explotaciones) nf exploitation

explotar vb [25] ① to exploit ② to explode

exponer vb [41] ① to display ② to present

exportación (pl exportaciones) nf export

exportar vb [25] to export

exposición (pl exposiciones) nf exhibition ▷ **montar una exposición** to put on an exhibition

expresamente adv ① specifically ② specially

expresar vb [25] to express

expresión (pl expresiones) nf expression

expresivo, -a adj expressive

expreso nm ① (train) express ② (coffee) espresso

exprimir vb [58] to squeeze

expuesto vb see **exponer**

expulsar vb [25] ① to expel ② to send off

expulsión (pl expulsiones) nf expulsion

exquisito, -a adj delicious

éxtasis nm ecstasy

extender vb [20] to spread ▷ **El fuego se extendió rápidamente.** The fire spread quickly.; **extender los brazos** to stretch one's arms out

extendido, -a adj outstretched

extensión (pl extensiones) nf area ▷ **una enorme extensión de tierra** an enormous area of land; **¿Me pone con la extensión 212, por favor?** Can you put me through to extension 212, please?

extenso, -a adj extensive

exterior adj ① (world) outside ② (policy, trade) foreign
▶ nm outside; **Salimos al exterior**

para ver qué pasaba. We went outside to see what was going on.

externo, -a adj ❶ outside ❷ outer

extiendo vb see **extender**

extinción nf (of fire) putting out; **una especie en vías de extinción** an endangered species

extinguidor nm (LatAm) fire extinguisher

extinguir vb [**58**, **gu → g** before a and **o**] to put out; **extinguirse** to become extinct; **El fuego se fue extinguiendo lentamente.** The fire was slowly going out.

extinto, -a adj extinct

extintor nm fire extinguisher

extra adj extra ▷ **una manta extra** an extra blanket; **chocolate de calidad extra** top quality chocolate
▶ nmf extra

extractor nm extractor fan

extraer vb [**54**] ❶ to extract ❷ to draw

extraescolar adj **actividades extraescolares** extracurricular activities

extraigo vb see **extraer**

extranjero, -a adj foreign
▶ nm **vivir en el extranjero** to live abroad; **viajar al extranjero** to travel abroad
▶ nm/f foreigner

extrañar vb [**25**] to miss ▷ **Extraña mucho a sus padres.** He misses his parents a lot.; **Me extraña que no haya llegado.** I'm surprised he hasn't arrived.; **¡Ya me extrañaba a mí!** I thought it was strange!;

extrañarse de algo to be surprised at something

extrañeza nf **Nos miró con extrañeza.** He looked at us in surprise.

extraño, -a adj strange; **¡Qué extraño!** How strange!

extraordinario, -a adj extraordinary

extravagante adj extravagant

extraviado, -a adj ❶ lost ❷ missing

extremista adj, nmf extremist

extremo, -a adj extreme
▶ nm (of rope, street) end; **pasar de un extremo a otro** to go from one extreme to the other

extrovertido, -a adj outgoing

exuberante adj lush

f

fábrica _nf_ factory

fabricante _nmf_ manufacturer

fabricar _vb_ **[48]** to make; **'fabricado en China'** 'made in China'

fachada _nf_ **la fachada del edificio** the front of the building

fácil _adj_ easy ▷ _El examen fue muy fácil._ The exam was very easy.; **Es fácil de entender.** It's easy to understand.; **Es fácil que se le haya perdido.** He may have lost it.

facilidad _nf_ **Se me rompen las uñas con facilidad.** My nails break easily.; **Pepe tiene facilidad para los idiomas.** Pepe has a gift for languages.; **Te dan facilidades de pago.** They offer credit facilities.

facilitar _vb_ **[25]** to make...easier ▷ _Un ordenador facilita mucho el trabajo._ A computer makes work much easier.; **El banco me facilitó la información.** The bank provided me with the information.

factor _nm_ factor

factura _nf_ bill

facturar _vb_ **[25]** to check in

facultad _nf_ **❶** faculty; **la Facultad de Derecho** the Faculty of Law **❷** university; **ir a la facultad** to go to university

faena _nf_ work; **las faenas domésticas** the housework

falda _nf_ skirt

fallar _vb_ **[25]** (_brakes, engine, sight_) to fail; **Fallé el tiro.** I missed.

fallecer _vb_ **[12]** to die

fallo _nm_ **❶** fault ▷ _un pequeño fallo eléctrico_ a small electrical fault **❷** failure ▷ _debido a un fallo de motor_ due to engine failure **❸** mistake ▷ _¡Qué fallo!_ What a stupid mistake!; **Fue un fallo humano.** It was human error.

falsificar _vb_ **[48]** to forge

falso, -a _adj_ **❶** false **❷** forged; **Los diamantes eran falsos.** The diamonds were fakes.; **Eso es falso.** That's not true.

falta _nf_ **❶** lack ▷ _la falta de dinero_ lack of money **❷** foul ▷ _Ha sido falta._ It was a foul.; **Eso es una falta de educación.** That's bad manners.; **una falta de ortografía** a spelling mistake; **Me falta un ordenador.** I need a computer.; **No hace falta que vengáis.** You don't need to come.

faltar vb [**25**] ① to be missing ▷ *Me falta un bolígrafo.* One of my pens is missing.; **Faltan varios libros del estante.** There are several books missing from the shelf.; **No podemos irnos. Falta Manolo.** We can't go. Manolo isn't here yet.; **A la sopa le falta sal.** There isn't enough salt in the soup.; **Falta media hora para comer.** There's half an hour to go before lunch.; **¿Te falta mucho?** Will you be long?; **faltar al colegio** to miss school

fama nf fame; **llegar a la fama** to become famous; **tener mala fama** to have a bad reputation; **Tiene fama de mujeriego.** He has a reputation for being a womanizer.

familia nf family; **una familia numerosa** a large family

familiar adj ① family ▷ *la vida familiar* family life ② familiar
▶ nmf relative ▷ *un familiar mío* a relative of mine

famoso, -a adj famous
▶ nm/f celebrity

fan (pl **fans**) nmf fan

fantasía nf fantasy ▷ *un mundo de fantasía* a fantasy world ▷ *Son fantasías infantiles.* They're just children's fantasies.; **las joyas de fantasía** costume jewellery sg

fantasma nm ghost

fantástico, -a adj fantastic

farmacéutico, -a nm/f chemist

farmacia nf chemist's; **una farmacia de guardia** a duty chemist's

faro nm ① lighthouse ② headlight ③ lamp; **los faros antiniebla** foglamps

farol nm ① streetlamp ② lantern

farola nf ① streetlamp ② lamppost

fascículo nm part

fascinante adj fascinating

fascista adj, nmf fascist

fase nf phase

fastidiar vb [**25**] ① to annoy; **Esa actitud me fastidia mucho.** I find this attitude very annoying. ② to pester ▷ *¡Deja ya de fastidiarme!* Will you stop pestering me! ③ to spoil ▷ *El accidente nos fastidió las vacaciones.* The accident spoilt our holidays.

fastidio nm **¡Qué fastidio!** What a nuisance!

fatal adj awful ▷ *Me siento fatal.* I feel awful. ▷ *La obra estuvo fatal.* The play was awful.; **Me parece fatal que le trates así.** I think it's rotten of you to treat him like that.
▶ adv **Lo pasé fatal.** I had an awful time.; **Lo hice fatal.** I made a mess of it.

favor nm favour ▷ *¿Puedes hacerme un favor?* Can you do me a favour?; **por favor** please; **¡Haced el favor de callaros!** Will you please be quiet!; **estar a favor de algo** to be in favour of something

favorecer vb [**12**] (dress, hairstyle) to suit

favorito, -a adj favourite

fax (pl **fax**) nm fax; **mandar algo por fax** to fax something

fe nf faith

febrero nm February

fecha nf date ▷ *¿En qué fecha estamos?* What's the date today?; **La carta tiene fecha del 21 de enero.** The letter is dated the 21st of January.; **la fecha de caducidad** the use-by date; **la fecha límite** the closing date; **la fecha tope** the deadline; **su fecha de nacimiento** his date of birth

felicidad nf happiness; **¡Felicidades! (1)** Happy birthday! **(2)** Congratulations!

felicitación (pl **felicitaciones**) nf congratulations pl

felicitar vb [25] to congratulate; **¡Te felicito!** Congratulations!; **felicitar a alguien por su cumpleaños** to wish somebody a happy birthday

feliz (pl **felices**) adj happy ▷ *Se la ve muy feliz.* She looks very happy.; **¡Feliz cumpleaños!** Happy birthday!; **¡Feliz Año Nuevo!** Happy New Year!; **¡Felices Navidades!** Happy Christmas!

felpudo nm doormat

femenino, -a adj ❶ (clothes, behaviour, pronoun) feminine ❷ (body, sex) female ❸ (team, sport) women's ▷ *el tenis femenino* women's tennis
▶ nm feminine ▷ *El femenino de 'lobo' es 'loba'.* The feminine of 'lobo' is 'loba'.

fenomenal adj, adv great ▷ *Nos hizo un tiempo fenomenal.* We had great weather.; **Lo pasé fenomenal.** I had a great time.

feo, -a adj ugly

féretro nm coffin

feria nf ❶ fair; **una feria de muestras** a trade fair ❷ (Mex) small change ❸ (Chile, River Plate) street market

ferretería nf ironmonger's

ferrocarril nm railway

fértil adj fertile

fertilizante nm fertilizer

festejar vb [25] (LatAm) to celebrate

festival nm festival

festivo, -a adj festive; **un día festivo** a holiday

feto nm foetus

fiable adj reliable

fiambres nmpl cold meats

fianza nf deposit

fiar vb [21] **Es un hombre de fiar.** He's completely trustworthy.; **fiarse de alguien** to trust somebody

fibra nf fibre

ficha nf ❶ index card ❷ counter; **una ficha de dominó** a domino

fichar vb [25] ❶ to clock in ❷ to clock out ❸ to sign up

fichero nm ❶ filing cabinet ❷ card index ❸ file

fideos nmpl ❶ noodles ❷ (River Plate) pasta sg

fiebre nf ❶ temperature ▷ *Le bajó la fiebre.* His temperature came down.; **tener fiebre** to have a temperature ❷ fever ▷ *la fiebre amarilla* yellow fever

fiel adj faithful; **ser fiel a alguien** to be faithful to somebody

fiera nf wild animal

fiesta nf ❶ party; **una fiesta de cumpleaños** a birthday party

figura | 118

❷ holiday ▷ *El lunes es fiesta.* Monday is a holiday.

figura nf figure

figurar vb [25] to appear; **figurarse** to imagine; **¡Ya me lo figuraba!** I thought as much!

fijar vb [25] to fix; **fijarse** (1) to pay attention ▷ *Tienes que fijarte más en lo que haces.* You must pay more attention to what you're doing. (2) to notice ▷ *No me fijé en la ropa que llevaba.* I didn't notice what she was wearing.; **¡Fíjate en esos dos!** Just look at those two!

fijo, -a adj ❶ fixed ▷ *Gano un sueldo fijo.* I earn a fixed salary. ❷ permanent; **Está fija en la empresa.** She's got a permanent job in the company.

fila nf ❶ row ▷ *Estábamos sentados en segunda fila.* We were sitting in the second row. ❷ line ▷ *Los niños se pusieron en fila.* The children got into line.

filete nm ❶ steak ▷ *un filete con patatas fritas* steak and chips ❷ fillet ▷ *un filete de merluza* a hake fillet

Filipinas nfpl the Philippines

filmar vb [25] to film; **filmar una película** to shoot a film

filo nm **Tiene poco filo.** It isn't very sharp.

filoso, -a adj (LatAm) sharp

filosofía nf philosophy

filtrar vb [25] to filter; **filtrarse** (1) to seep (2) to filter

filtro nm filter

fin nm end ▷ *el fin de una era* the end of an era; **a fines de** at the end of

▷ *a fines de abril* at the end of April; **al fin** finally ▷ *Al fin llegaron a un acuerdo.* They finally reached an agreement.; **al fin y al cabo** after all; **En fin, ¡qué le vamos a hacer!** Oh well, what can we do about it!; **por fin** at last ▷ *¡Por fin hemos llegado!* We've got here at last!; **el fin de año** New Year's Eve; **el fin de semana** the weekend

final adj final ▷ *el resultado final* the final result
  ▶ nm end ▷ *Al final de la calle hay un colegio.* At the end of the street there's a school.; **a finales de mayo** at the end of May; **al final** in the end ▷ *Al final tuve que darle la razón.* In the end I had to admit that he was right.; **un final feliz** a happy ending
  ▶ nf final ▷ *la final de la copa* the cup final

finca nf country house

fingir vb [16] to pretend

finlandés (finlandesa, mpl finlandeses) adj Finnish
  ▶ nm/f Finn
  ▶ nm (language) Finnish

Finlandia nf Finland

fino, -a adj ❶ (paper, layer) thin ❷ (hair, point, sand) fine ❸ (fingers, neck) slender

firma nf signature

firmar vb [25] to sign

firme adj ❶ steady ▷ *Mantén la escalera firme.* Can you hold the ladder steady? ❷ firm ▷ *Se mostró muy firme con ella.* He was very firm with her.

fiscal nmf public prosecutor

fisgar *vb* [**37**] to snoop

física *nf* ❶ physics *sg* ❷ physicist

físico, -a *adj* physical
▶ *nm* physicist

flaco, -a *adj* thin

flama *nf* (*Mex*) flame

flamenco *nm* flamenco

flan *nm* crème caramel

flash (*pl* **flashes**) *nm* flash

flauta *nf* ❶ recorder ❷ flute

flecha *nf* arrow

flechazo *nm* **Fue un flechazo.** It was love at first sight.

flecos *nmpl* fringe *sg* ▷ *los flecos de la cortina* the curtain fringe

flequillo *nm* fringe

flexible *adj* flexible

flojo, -a *adj* ❶ (*knot, screw*) loose ❷ (*cable, rope*) slack ❸ (*tea, student, patient*) weak ❹ (*LatAm*) lazy; **Todavía tengo las piernas muy flojas.** My legs are still very weak.; **Está flojo en matemáticas.** He's weak at maths.

flor *nf* flower ▷ *un ramo de flores* a bunch of flowers

florero *nm* vase

floristería *nf* florist's

flotador *nm* ❶ rubber ring ❷ armband

flotar *vb* [**25**] to float

flote *adv* **a flote** afloat

fluir *vb* [**10**] to flow

fluorescente *adj* fluorescent

fluyendo *vb* *see* **fluir**

foca *nf* seal

foco *nm* ❶ spotlight ❷ floodlight ❸ (*LatAm*) headlight ❹ (*Mex*) light bulb; **el foco de atención** the focus of attention

folio *nm* sheet of paper

folklore *nm* folklore

folleto *nm* ❶ brochure ❷ leaflet

fomentar *vb* [**25**] to promote

fonda *nf* ❶ boarding house ❷ restaurant

fondo *nm* ❶ bottom ▷ *el fondo de la cazuela* the bottom of the pan; **en el fondo del mar** at the bottom of the sea ❷ end ▷ *Mi habitación está al fondo del pasillo.* My room's at the end of the corridor.; **estudiar una materia a fondo** to study a subject in depth; **un corredor de fondo** a long-distance runner; **en el fondo** deep down; **recaudar fondos** to raise funds

fontanero, -a *nm/f* plumber

footing *nm* jogging ▷ *Hago footing todas las mañanas.* I go jogging every morning.

forestal *adj* forest ▷ *un incendio forestal* a forest fire

forma *nf* ❶ shape; **en forma de pera** pear-shaped ❷ way ▷ *Me miraba de una forma extraña.* She was looking at me in a strange way. ❸ fitness; **de todas formas** anyway; **estar en forma** to be fit

formación (*pl* **formaciones**) *nf* training; **formación profesional** vocational training

formal *adj* responsible ▷ *un chico muy formal* a very responsible boy; **Sé formal y pórtate bien.** Be good and behave yourself.

formar *vb* [**25**] (*club*) to start; **Se formó una cola enorme en la puerta.** A huge queue formed at the door.; **estar formado por** to be made up of; **formar parte de algo** to be part of something

formidable *adj* fantastic

fórmula *nf* formula

formulario *nm* form

forrar *vb* [25] ❶ to line ❷ to cover

forro *nm* ❶ lining ❷ cover

fortuna *nf* fortune ▷ *Vale una fortuna.* It's worth a fortune.; **por fortuna** luckily

forzar *vb* [3] to force; **Estás forzando la vista.** You're straining your eyes.

fosa *nf* ❶ ditch ❷ grave

fósforo *nm* match

foto *nf* photo ▷ *Les hice una foto a los niños.* I took a photo of the children.

fotocopia *nf* photocopy

fotocopiadora *nf* photocopier

fotocopiar *vb* [25] to photocopy

fotografía *nf* ❶ photograph ▷ *una fotografía de mis padres* a photograph of my parents ❷ photography

fotógrafo *nm* photographer

fracasar *vb* [25] to fail

fracaso *nm* failure

fracción (*pl* **fracciones**) *nf* fraction

fractura *nf* fracture

frágil *adj* fragile

fraile *nm* friar

frambuesa *nf* raspberry

francés (*f* **francesa**, *mpl* **franceses**) *adj* French
▶ *nm* ❶ Frenchman; **los franceses** the French ❷ (*language*) French

francesa *nf* Frenchwoman

Francia *nf* France

franco, -a *adj* frank; **para serte franco ...** to be frank with you ...
▶ *nm* franc

franqueo *nm* postage

frasco *nm* bottle ▷ *un frasco de perfume* a bottle of perfume

frase *nf* sentence; **una frase hecha** a set phrase

fraude *nm* fraud

frazada *nf* (*LatAm*) blanket

frecuencia *nf* frequency; **Nos vemos con frecuencia.** We often see each other.; **¿Con qué frecuencia tienen estos síntomas?** How often do they get these symptoms?

frecuente *adj* ❶ common ❷ frequent

fregadero *nm* sink

fregar *vb* [34] to wash; **fregar los platos** to wash the dishes; **Yo estaba en la cocina fregando.** I was in the kitchen washing the dishes.; **fregar el suelo** to mop the floor

fregona *nf* mop

freír *vb* [23] to fry

frenar *vb* [25] to brake

frenazo *nm* **Tuve que dar un frenazo.** I had to brake suddenly.

freno *nm* brake ▷ *Me quedé sin frenos.* My brakes failed.; **el freno de mano** the handbrake

frente *nf* forehead
▶ *nm* front ▷ *un frente común* a united front; **frente a** opposite ▷ *Frente al hotel hay un banco.* There's a bank opposite the hotel.; **Los coches chocaron de frente.** The cars collided head on.;

Viene un coche de frente. There's a car coming straight for us.; **hacer frente a algo** to face up to something

fresa nf strawberry

fresco, -a adj ❶ (place, drink, fabric) cool ❷ (fish, vegetables) fresh; **hace fresco (1)** it's chilly **(2)** it's cool ▷ nm **Hace fresco.** It's a bit chilly.

friego vb see **fregar**

frigorífico nm fridge

frijol nm (LatAm) bean

frío see **freír**
▷ adj cold ▷ **Tengo las manos frías.** My hands are cold.; **Estuvo muy frío conmigo.** He was very cold towards me.
▷ nm **Hace frío.** It's cold.; **Tengo mucho frío.** I'm very cold.

frito vb see **freír**
▷ adj fried ▷ **huevos fritos** fried eggs

frontera nf border ▷ **Nos pararon en la frontera.** We were stopped at the border.

frontón (pl **frontones**) nm
❶ pelota court ❷ pelota

> **pelota** is a game in which two players use baskets or wooden rackets to hit a ball against a specially marked wall.

frotar vb [25] to rub; **El niño se frotaba las manos para calentarse.** The child was rubbing his hands to get warm.

fruncir vb [58, c → z before a and o] **fruncir el ceño** to frown

frustrado, -a adj frustrated

fruta nf fruit

frutería nf greengrocer's

frutilla nf (River Plate) strawberry

fruto nm fruit; **los frutos secos** nuts

fue vb see **ir**; **ser**

fuego nm fire ▷ **encender el fuego** to light the fire; **prender fuego a algo** to set fire to something; **Puse la cazuela al fuego.** I put the pot on to heat.; **cocinar algo a fuego lento** to cook something on a low heat; **¿Tiene fuego, por favor?** Have you got a light, please?; **fuegos artificiales** fireworks

> Word for word, **fuegos artificiales** means 'artificial fires'.

fuente nf ❶ fountain ❷ dish

fuera vb see **ir**; **ser**
▷ adv ❶ outside ▷ **Los niños estaban jugando fuera.** The children were playing outside. ▷ **Por fuera es blanco.** It is white on the outside.; **¡Estamos aquí fuera!** We are out here!; **Hoy vamos a cenar fuera.** We're going out for dinner tonight. ❷ away; **El enfermo está fuera de peligro.** The patient is out of danger.; **fuera de mi casa** outside my house

fuerte adj ❶ (material, smell, character) strong ❷ (noise) loud ❸ (knock) hard ❹ (pain, cold) bad; **'un beso muy fuerte'** 'lots of love'
▷ adv loudly; **Agárrate fuerte.** Hold on tight.; **No le pegues tan fuerte.** Don't hit him so hard.

fuerza nf strength ▷ **No le quedaban fuerzas.** He had no strength left.; **tener mucha fuerza** to be very strong; **Solo lo conseguirás a fuerza de practicar.** You'll only manage it by practising.; **No te lo comas la fuerza.** Don't force yourself to eat it.; **la fuerza de gravedad** the force of gravity; **la fuerza de voluntad** willpower

fuerzo vb *see* **forzar**

fugarse vb [**25**] to escape

fui vb *see* **ir**; **ser**

fumador, a nm/f smoker; **sección para no fumadores** non-smoking section

fumar vb [**25**] to smoke

función (pl **funciones**) nf
① function ② role ③ show ▷ *Los niños representan una función en el colegio.* The children are putting on a show at school.

funcionar vb [**25**] to work ▷ *El ascensor no funciona.* The lift isn't working.; **'no funciona'** 'out of order'; **Funciona con pilas.** It runs on batteries.

funcionario, -a nm/f civil servant

funda nf cover; **una funda de almohada** a pillowcase

fundamental adj basic; **Es fundamental que entendamos el problema.** It is essential that we understand the problem.

fundar vb [**25**] to found

fundirse vb [**58**] to melt; **Se han fundido los fusibles.** The fuses have blown.

funeral nm funeral

funeraria nf undertaker's

furgoneta nf van

furia nf fury

furioso, -a adj furious ▷ *Mi padre estaba furioso conmigo.* My father was furious with me.

fusible nm fuse ▷ *Han saltado los fusibles.* The fuses have blown.

fusil nm rifle

fútbol nm football ▷ *jugar al fútbol* to play football

futbolín (pl **futbolines**) nm table football

futbolista nmf footballer

futuro adj, nm future ▷ *su futuro marido* your future husband; **la futura madre** the mother-to-be

g

gabardina *nf* raincoat

gabinete *nm* **1** office; **el gabinete de prensa** press office **2** *(in government)* cabinet

gafas *nfpl* **1** glasses ▷ *Tengo que llevar gafas.* I have to wear glasses.; **las gafas de sol** sunglasses **2** goggles

gaita *nf* bagpipes *pl*

gajo *nm* segment

galaxia *nf* galaxy

galería *nf* gallery ▷ *una galería de arte* an art gallery; **una galería comercial** a shopping centre

Gales *nm* Wales; **el País de Gales** Wales

galés *(f* **galesa,** *mpl* **galeses)** *adj* Welsh
▶ *nm* **1** Welshman; **los galeses** the Welsh **2** *(language)* Welsh

galesa *nf* Welshwoman

galgo *nm* greyhound

Galicia *nf* Galicia

gallego, -a *adj, nm/f* Galician
▶ *nm* *(language)* Galician

galleta *nf* biscuit

gallina *nmf* **¡Eres un gallina!** *(informal)* You're chicken!
▶ *nf* hen; **Solo pensarlo me pone la carne de gallina.** It gives me goosepimples just thinking about it.; **jugar a la gallina ciega** to play blind man's buff

gallinero *nm* **1** henhouse **2** *(informal)* madhouse

gallo *nm* cock; **en menos que canta un gallo** in an instant

Word for word, **en menos que canta un gallo** means 'in less than a cock crows'.

galopar *vb* [**25**] to gallop

gama *nf* range ▷ *una amplia gama de ordenadores* a wide range of computers

gamba *nf* prawn

gamberro, -a *nm/f* hooligan

gana *nf* **Me visto como me da la gana.** I dress the way I want to.; **¡No me da la gana!** I don't want to!; **hacer algo de mala gana** to do something reluctantly; **tener ganas de hacer algo** to feel like doing something

ganadería *nf* cattle

ganado *nm* livestock; **el ganado vacuno** cattle

ganador, a *adj* winning ▷ *el equipo ganador* the winning team
▶ *nm/f* winner

ganancia nf profit

ganar vb [25] ❶ to earn; **ganarse la vida** to earn a living ❷ to win ❸ to beat; **Con eso no ganas nada.** You won't achieve anything by doing that.; **ganar tiempo** to save time; **¡Te lo has ganado!** You deserve it!; **salir ganando** to do well

ganchillo nm crochet ▷ una aguja de ganchillo a crochet hook; **hacer ganchillo** to crochet

gancho nm ❶ hook ▷ Colgué el abrigo de un gancho. I hung the coat on a hook.; **Maradona tiene gancho.** Maradona is a crowd-puller. ❷ (LatAm) hanger

gandul, -a adj lazy
▸ nm/f good-for-nothing

ganga nf bargain

gángster (pl gángsters) nm gangster

ganso, -a nm/f goose

garabato nm ❶ doodle ❷ scribble

garaje nm garage; **una plaza de garaje** a parking space

garantía nf guarantee ▷ La lavadora está todavía en garantía. The washing machine is still under guarantee.

garantizar vb [13] to guarantee

garbanzo nm chick pea

garganta nf throat ▷ Me duele la garganta. I've got a sore throat.

gargantilla nf necklace

gárgaras nfpl **hacer gárgaras** to gargle

garita nf sentry box

garra nf ❶ claw ❷ talon

garrafa nf carafe
  A **garrafa** is also a large bottle with handles.
vino de garrafa cheap wine

garúa nf (LatAm) drizzle

gas (pl gases) nm gas; **agua mineral sin gas** still mineral water; **una bebida sin gas** a still drink; **agua mineral con gas** sparkling mineral water; **los gases del tubo de escape** exhaust fumes; **El niño tiene muchos gases.** The baby's got a lot of wind.; **Pasó una moto a todo gas.** A motorbike shot past at full speed.

gasa nf gauze

gaseosa nf
  A **gaseosa** is a drink of sweet fizzy water.

gasoil nm diesel oil

gasóleo nm diesel oil

gasolina nf petrol ▷ Tengo que echar gasolina. I have to fill up with petrol.; **gasolina súper** four-star petrol; **gasolina sin plomo** unleaded petrol

gasolinera nf petrol station

gastado, -a adj worn ▷ La moqueta está muy gastada. The carpet is very worn.

gastar vb [25] ❶ to spend; **Javier gasta mucho en ropa.** Javier spends a lot of money on clothes. ❷ to use; **Gasté toda una caja de cerillas.** I used up a whole box of matches.; **¿Qué numero de zapato gastas?** What size shoes do you take?; **Le gastamos una broma a Juan.** We played a joke on Juan.; **Se han gastado las pilas.** The batteries have run out.; **Se me han gastado las suelas.** The soles of my shoes have worn out.

gasto nm expense ▷ *Este año hemos tenido muchos gastos.* We've had a lot of expenses this year.; **gastos de envío** postage and packing sg

> Word for word, **gastos de envío** means 'sending expenses'.

gatear vb [**25**] to crawl

gato nm ① cat ② jack

gaviota nf seagull

gay (pl **gays**) adj, nm gay

gazpacho nm

> **Gazpacho** is a refreshing soup made from tomatoes, cucumber, garlic, peppers, oil and vinegar and served cold.

gel nm gel ▷ *gel de baño* bath gel

gelatina nf jelly

gemelo, -a adj, nm/f identical twin ▷ *Son gemelos.* They're identical twins. ▷ *mi hermano gemelo* my identical twin

gemelos nmpl ① binoculars ② cufflinks

Géminis nm (sign) Gemini; **Soy géminis.** I'm Gemini.

gen nm gene

generación (pl **generaciones**) nf generation

general adj general; **en general** in general; **por lo general** generally ▷ *Por lo general me acuesto temprano.* I generally go to bed early.

▶ nmf general

generalizar vb [**13**] to generalize

generalmente adv generally

generar vb [**25**] to generate

género nm ① gender ② kind ▷ *¿Qué género de música prefieres?* What kind of music do you prefer? ③ material; **el género humano** the human race

generosidad nf generosity

generoso, -a adj generous

genial adj brilliant ▷ *Antonio tuvo una idea genial.* Antonio had a brilliant idea. ▷ *El concierto estuvo genial.* It was a brilliant concert.

genio nm ① temper ▷ *¡Menudo genio tiene tu padre!* Your father has got such a temper!; **tener mal genio** to have a bad temper ② genius ▷ *¡Eres un genio!* You're a genius! ③ genie

genitales nmpl genitals

genoma nm genome

gente nf people pl ▷ *Había poca gente en la sala.* There were few people in the room. ▷ *La gente está cansada de promesas.* People are tired of promises.; **Son buena gente.** They're good people.; **Óscar es buena gente.** Óscar's a good sort.; **la gente de la calle** the people in the street

geografía nf geography

geología nf geology

geometría nf geometry

geranio nm geranium

gerente nmf manager

germen (pl **gérmenes**) nm germ

germinar vb [**25**] to germinate

gesto nm Hizo un gesto de alivio. He looked relieved.; **Me hizo un gesto para que me sentara.** He made a sign for me to sit down.

gestoría nf
° A **gestoría** is a private agency which deals with government departments on behalf of its clients.

Gibraltar nm Gibraltar

gibraltareño, -a adj, nm/f Gibraltarian

gigante nmf giant

gigantesco, -a adj gigantic

gimnasia nf gymnastics sg; **Mi madre hace gimnasia todas las mañanas.** My mother does exercises every morning.

gimnasio nm gym

gimnasta nmf gymnast

ginebra nf gin

ginecólogo, -a nm/f gynaecologist

gira nf tour ▷ Hicimos una gira por toda Europa. We did a tour all round Europe.; **estar de gira** to be on tour

girar vb [25] ❶ to turn ▷ Al llegar al semáforo gira a la derecha. When you get to the lights turn right. ▷ Giré la cabeza para ver quién era. I turned my head to see who it was. ❷ to rotate ▷ La Tierra gira alrededor de su eje. The Earth rotates on its axis.; **La Luna gira alrededor de la Tierra.** The moon revolves around the Earth.

girasol nm sunflower

giro nm ❶ turn ▷ El avión dio un giro de 90 grados. The plane did a 90 degree turn. ❷ postal order

gitano, -a nm/f gypsy

glándula nf gland

global adj global

globo nm balloon; **un globo terráqueo** a globe

glorieta nf roundabout

glotón, -a (f glotona, mpl glotones) adj greedy

gobernar vb [39] to govern

gobierno nm government

gol nm goal; **meter un gol** to score a goal

golf nm golf; **jugar al golf** to play golf

golfo nm gulf

golondrina nf swallow

golosina nf sweet

goloso, -a adj ser goloso to have a sweet tooth

golpe nm knock ▷ Oímos un golpe en la puerta. We heard a knock at the door.; **Me he dado un golpe en el codo.** I banged my elbow.; **Se dio un golpe contra la pared.** He hit the wall.; **El coche de atrás nos dio un golpe.** The car behind ran into us.; **Di unos golpecitos a la puerta antes de entrar.** I tapped on the door before going in.; **de golpe** suddenly ▷ De golpe decidió dejar el trabajo. He suddenly decided to give up work.; **La puerta se cerró de golpe.** The door slammed shut.; **no dar golpe** to be bone idle

golpear vb [25] ❶ to hit ❷ to bang; **Me golpeé la cabeza contra el armario.** I banged my head on the cupboard.

goma nf ❶ rubber ▷ *unos guantes de goma* a pair of rubber gloves; **una goma de borrar** (eraser) a rubber ❷ elastic band

gordo, -a adj ❶ fat ▷ *Estoy muy gordo.* I'm very fat. ❷ thick ❸ big ▷ *Debe de ser algo bastante gordo.* It must be something pretty big.; **Su mujer me cae gorda.** I can't stand his wife.

gorila nm gorilla

gorra nf cap

gorrión (pl **gorriones**) nm sparrow

gorro nm hat; **un gorro de baño** a swimming cap

gorrón (f **gorrona**, mpl **gorrones**) nm/f scrounger

gota nf drop; **Están cayendo cuatro gotas.** It's spitting.

gotear vb [**25**] ❶ to drip ❷ to leak

gotera nf leak

gozar vb [**13**] **gozar de algo** to enjoy something

grabación (pl **grabaciones**) nf recording

grabadora nf recorder

grabar vb [**25**] ❶ to record ❷ to engrave; **Lo tengo grabado en la memoria.** It's etched on my memory.

gracia nf **tener gracia** to be funny; **Yo no le veo la gracia.** I don't see what's so funny.; **Me hizo mucha gracia.** It was so funny.; **No me hace gracia tener que salir con este tiempo.** I'm not too pleased about having to go out in this weather.; **¡Muchas gracias!** Thanks very

much!; **dar las gracias a alguien por algo** to thank somebody for something ▷ *Vino a darme las gracias por las flores.* He came to thank me for the flowers.; **Ni siquiera me dio las gracias.** He didn't even say thank you.; **gracias a** thanks to

gracioso, -a adj funny ▷ *¡Qué gracioso!* How funny!

gradas nfpl terraces

grado nm degree ▷ *Estaban a diez grados bajo cero.* It was ten degrees below zero.

graduado, -a adj **gafas graduadas** prescription glasses

gradual adj gradual

graduar vb [**1**] to adjust; **Tengo que graduarme la vista.** I've got to have my eyes tested.; **Se graduó en Medicina hace dos años.** He graduated in Medicine two years ago.

gráfica nf graph

gráfico, -a adj graphic ▶ nm table

gramática nf grammar

gramo nm gram

gran adj see **grande**

granada nf pomegranate; **una granada de mano** a hand grenade

granate adj maroon

When **granate** is used as an adjective, it never changes its ending.

▷ *una bufanda granate* a maroon scarf

Gran Bretaña nf Great Britain

grande adj ❶ big ▷ *Viven en una casa muy grande.* They live in a big

house.; **¿Cómo es de grande?**
How big is it?; **La camisa me está
grande.** The shirt is too big for me.
② large ▷ *un gran número de
visitantes* a large number of visitors
▷ *grandes sumas de dinero* large
sums of money **③** great ▷ *un gran
pintor* a great painter ▷ *Es una
ventaja muy grande.* It's a great
advantage.; **Me llevé una
alegría muy grande.** I felt very
happy.; **Lo pasamos en grande.**
We had a great time.; *unos
grandes almacenes* a
department store

> Word for word, **grandes
> almacenes** means 'big
> warehouses'.

granel *adv* **a granel** in bulk
granero *nm* barn
granizado *nm*

> A **granizado** is a crushed ice
> drink.

granizar *vb* [**13**] to hail ▷ *Está
granizando.* It's hailing.
granizo *nm* hail
granja *nf* farm
granjero, -a *nm/f* farmer
grano *nm* **①** (of sand, rice) grain
② (of coffee) bean **③** spot ▷ *Me ha
salido un grano en la frente.* I've got a
spot on my forehead.; **ir al grano**
to get to the point
grapa *nf* staple
grapadora *nf* stapler
grasa *nf* **①** fat ▷ *No me va bien tanta
grasa.* So much fat isn't good for
me. **②** grease; **La cocina está
llena de grasa.** The cooker's really
greasy.

grasiento, -a *adj* greasy
graso, -a *adj* greasy
gratis (*pl* **gratis**) *adj, adv* **①** free
▷ *La entrada es gratis.* Entry is free.
② for free
gratuito, -a *adj* free
grava *nf* gravel
grave *adj* **①** serious ▷ *Tenemos un
problema grave.* We've got a serious
problem.; **Su padre está grave.**
His father is seriously ill. **②** low
gravedad *nf* gravity ▷ *la ley de la
gravedad* the law of gravity; **estar
herido de gravedad** to be
seriously injured
gravemente *adv* seriously
Grecia *nf* Greece
griego, -a *adj, nm/f* Greek
▶ *nm* (language) Greek
grieta *nf* crack
grifo *nm* tap ▷ *abrir el grifo* to turn
on the tap ▷ *cerrar el grifo* to turn
off the tap
grillo *nm* cricket
gripe *nf* flu ▷ *tener la gripe* to have
the flu
gris *adj, nm* grey ▷ *una puerta gris* a
grey door
gritar *vb* [**25**] **①** to shout **②** to
scream
grito *nm* **①** shout; **¡No des esos
gritos!** Stop shouting like that!
② scream ▷ *Oímos un grito en la
calle.* We heard a scream outside.;
Es el último grito. It's all the rage.
grosella *nf* redcurrant
grosero, -a *adj* rude
grosor *nm* thickness; **La pared
tiene 30cm de grosor.** The wall is
30cm thick.

grúa nf crane

grueso, -a adj ❶ thick ❷ stout

grumo nm lump

gruñir vb [45] to grumble

grupo nm ❶ group ▷ Se dividieron en grupos. They divided into groups.; **el grupo sanguíneo** blood group; **Los alumnos trabajan en grupo.** The students work in groups. ❷ band ▷ un grupo de rock a rock band

guacho, -a nm/f (Andes, River Plate) homeless child

guajolote nm (Mex) turkey

guante nm glove; **unos guantes** a pair of gloves

guapo, -a adj ❶ handsome ❷ pretty ❸ beautiful; **¡Ven, guapo!** Come here, love!

guarda nmf keeper; **guarda jurado** armed security guard

guardabarros (pl guardabarros) nm mudguard

guardaespaldas (mpl guardaespaldas) nmf bodyguard

guardar vb [25] ❶ to put away ▷ Los niños guardaron los juguetes. The children put away their toys. ❷ to keep ▷ Guarda el recibo. Keep the receipt.; **No les guardo rencor.** I don't bear them a grudge.; **guardar las apariencias** to keep up appearances; **guardar un fichero** to save a file

guardarropa nm cloakroom

guardería nf nursery

guardia nf de guardia on duty ▷ Estoy de guardia. I'm on duty.; **la Guardia Civil** the Civil Guard ▶ nmf police officer

guarro, -a nm/f (informal) **¡Eres un guarro!** You're disgusting!

guay adj (informal) cool ▷ ¡Qué moto más guay! What a cool bike!

güero, -a adj (Mex) blonde

guerra nf war; **estar en guerra** to be at war

guía nmf guide ▷ El guía vino a recogernos al aeropuerto. The guide came to pick us up at the airport.
▶ nf guidebook; **una guía de hoteles** a hotel guide; **una guía telefónica** a telephone directory

guiar vb [21] to guide; **Nos guiamos por un mapa que teníamos.** We found our way using a map that we had.

guijarro nm pebble

guinda nf cherry

guindilla nf chilli pepper

guiñar vb [25] to wink; **Me guiñó el ojo.** He winked at me.

guion nm ❶ hyphen ❷ dash ❸ script

guisante nm pea

guisar vb [25] to cook

guitarra nf guitar

gusano nm ❶ worm ❷ maggot ❸ caterpillar

gustar vb [25] **Me gustan las uvas.** I like grapes.; **¿Te gusta viajar?** Do you like travelling?; **Me gustó como hablaba.** I liked the way he spoke.; **Me gustaría conocerla.** I would like to meet her.; **Me gusta su hermana.** I fancy his sister.; **Le gusta más llevar pantalones.** She prefers to wear trousers.

a b c d e f g h i j k l m n ñ o p q r s t u v w x y z

gusto nm taste ▷ *No tiene gusto para vestirse.* He has no taste in clothes. ▷ *He decorado la habitación a mi gusto.* I've decorated the room to my taste.; **un comentario de mal gusto** a tasteless remark; **Le noto un gusto a almendras.** It tastes of almonds.; **¡Con mucho gusto!** With pleasure!; **¡Mucho gusto en conocerle!** I'm very pleased to meet you!; **sentirse a gusto** to feel at ease

ha vb see **haber**
haba nm broad bean
Habana n **La Habana** Havana
haber vb [24] to have ▷ *He comido.* I've eaten. ▷ *Hemos comido.* We've eaten. ▷ *Había comido.* I'd eaten. ▷ *Se ha sentado.* She's sat down.; **De haberlo sabido, habría ido.** If I'd known, I would have gone.; **¡Haberlo dicho antes!** You should have said so before!; **hay (1)** there is ▷ *Hay una iglesia en la esquina.* There's a church on the corner. ▷ *Hubo una guerra.* There was a war. **(2)** there are ▷ *Hay treinta alumnos en mi clase.* There are thirty pupils in my class. ▷ *¿Hay entradas?* Are there any tickets?; **¡No hay de qué!** Don't mention it!; **¿Qué hay?** (informal) How are things?;

¿Qué hubo? (Mex: informal) How are things?; **¡Habrá que decírselo!** We'll have to tell him!

hábil adj skilful ▷ Es un jugador muy hábil. He's a very skilful player.; **Es muy hábil con las manos.** He's very good with his hands.; **Es muy hábil para los negocios.** He's a very able businessman.

habilidad nf skill; **Tiene mucha habilidad para los idiomas.** She's very good at languages.

habitación (pl habitaciones) nf ❶ bedroom ❷ room; **una habitación doble** a double room; **una habitación individual** a single room

habitante nmf inhabitant; **los habitantes de la zona** people living in the area

habitar vb [25] to live in; **La casa está todavía sin habitar.** The house is still unoccupied.

hábito nm habit

habitual adj usual; **un cliente habitual** a regular customer

habla nm speech; **Ha perdido el habla.** He's lost the power of speech.; **países de habla inglesa** English-speaking countries; **¿Señor López? — Al habla.** Señor López? — Speaking.

hablador, a adj ❶ chatty ❷ gossipy

habladurías nfpl gossip sg

hablante nmf speaker

hablar vb [25] ❶ to speak ▷ ¿Hablas español? Do you speak Spanish?; **¿Quién habla?** Who's calling? ❷ to talk ▷ Estuvimos hablando toda la tarde. We were talking all afternoon.; **hablar con alguien** (1) to speak to someone ▷ ¿Has hablado ya con el profesor? Have you spoken to the teacher yet? (2) to talk to someone ▷ Necesito hablar contigo. I need to talk to you.; **hablar de algo** to talk about something; **¿Vas a ayudarle en la mudanza? — ¡Ni hablar!** Are you going to help him with the move? — No way!

habré vb see **haber**

hacer vb [26] ❶ to make ▷ Tengo que hacer la cama. I've got to make the bed. ▷ Voy a hacer una tortilla. I'm going to make an omelette. ▷ Están haciendo mucho ruido. They're making a lot of noise. ❷ to do ▷ ¿Qué haces? What are you doing? ▷ Estoy haciendo los deberes. I'm doing my homework. ▷ Hago mucho deporte. I do a lot of sport. ▷ ¿Qué hace tu padre? What does your father do? ❸ to be ▷ Hace calor. It's hot. ▷ Ojalá haga buen tiempo. I hope the weather's nice. ▷ Hizo dos grados bajo cero. It was two degrees below zero.; **hace ...** (1) ago ▷ Terminé hace una hora. I finished an hour ago. (2) for ▷ Hace un mes que voy. I've been going for a month.; **¿Hace mucho que esperas?** Have you been waiting long?; **hacer hacer algo** to have something done ▷ Hicieron pintar la fachada del colegio. They had the front of the school painted.; **hacer a alguien hacer algo** to make someone do

SPANISH > ENGLISH

something; **hacerse** to become;
Ya se está haciendo viejo. He's
getting old now.

hacha nf axe

hacia prep ❶ towards ▷ Venía hacia
mí. He was coming towards me.
❷ at about ▷ Volveremos hacia las
tres. We'll be back at about three.;
hacia adelante forwards; **hacia
atrás** backwards; **hacia dentro**
inside; **hacia fuera** outside; **hacia
abajo** down; **hacia arriba** up

hada nm fairy; **un hada madrina** a
fairy godmother; **un cuento de
hadas** a fairy tale

hago vb see **hacer**

hala excl come on!

halagar vb [37] to flatter

hallar vb [25] to find; **hallarse** to
be

hamaca nf ❶ hammock
❷ deckchair ❸ (River Plate) swing

hambre nm hunger; **tener
hambre** to be hungry ▷ Tengo
mucha hambre. I'm very hungry.

hamburguesa nf hamburger

hámster (pl **hámsters**) nm
hamster

hardware nm hardware

haré vb see **hacer**

harina nf flour

hartar vb [25] **hartarse** to get
fed up; **Me harté de pasteles.**
I stuffed myself with cakes.;
¡Me estás hartando! You're
getting on my nerves!

harto, -a adj ❶ fed up; **estar harto
de algo** to be fed up with
something ▷ Estábamos hartos de
repetirlo. We were fed up with

repeating it. ▷ ¡Me tienes harto! I'm
fed up with you! ❷ (LatAm) a lot of
▷ Había harta comida. There was a
lot of food.
▶ adv (LatAm) ❶ very ▷ Es un idioma
harto difícil. It's a very difficult
language. ❷ a lot ▷ Tenemos harto
que estudiar. We've got a lot to
study.

hasta adv even ▷ Estudia hasta
cuando está de vacaciones. He even
studies when he's on holiday.
▶ prep, conj ❶ till ▷ Está abierto
hasta las cuatro. It's open till four
o'clock.; **¿Hasta cuándo?** How
long? ▷ ¿Hasta cuándo te quedas? —
Hasta la semana que viene. How
long are you staying? — Till next
week.; **Hasta ahora no ha
llamado nadie.** No one has called
up to now.; **hasta que** until
▷ Espera aquí hasta que te llamen.
Wait here until you're called.
❷ up to ▷ Caminamos hasta la
puerta. We walked up to the door.
❸ as far as ▷ Desde aquí se ve
hasta el pueblo de al lado. From here
you can see as far as the next
town.; **¡Hasta luego!** See you!;
¡Hasta el sábado! See you on
Saturday!

hay vb see **haber**

haz vb see **hacer**

he vb see **haber**
▶ adv **He aquí un ejemplo.** Here's
an example.; **He aquí unos
ejemplos.** Here are some
examples.; **he aquí por qué ...**
that's why ...

hebilla nf buckle

hebreo, -a adj, nm/f Hebrew
▶ nm (language) Hebrew

hechizo nm spell

hecho vb see **hacer**
▶ adj made ▷ ¿De qué está hecho?
What's it made of?; **hecho a mano**
handmade; **hecho a máquina**
machine-made; **Me gusta la
carne bien hecha.** I like my meat
well done.; **un filete poco hecho** a
rare steak; **¡Bien hecho!** Well
done!
▶ nm ❶ fact ▷ el hecho de que ... the
fact that ... ▷ el hecho es que ... the
fact is that ... ❷ event; **de hecho** in
fact

helada nf frost

heladera nf (River Plate)
refrigerator

heladería nf ice-cream parlour

helado, -a adj ❶ frozen ▷ El lago
está helado. The lake's frozen over.
❷ freezing ▷ Este cuarto está helado.
This room's freezing. ▷ ¡Estoy
helado! I'm freezing!
▶ nm ice cream ▷ un helado de
chocolate a chocolate ice cream

helar vb [39] to freeze; **helarse** to
freeze; **Anoche heló.** There was a
frost last night.

helecho nm fern

helicóptero nm helicopter

hembra adj, nf female ▷ un elefante
hembra a female elephant

hemos vb see **haber**

heredar vb [25] to inherit

heredera nf heiress

heredero nm heir

herencia nf inheritance

herida nf ❶ wound ❷ injury

herido, -a adj ❶ wounded
❷ injured

herir vb [51] ❶ to wound ❷ to injure

hermana nf sister

hermanastra nf ❶ stepsister
❷ half-sister

hermanastro nm ❶ stepbrother
❷ half-brother; **mis
hermanastros** (1) my
stepbrothers (2) my stepbrothers
and stepsisters

hermano nm brother; **mis
hermanos** (1) my brothers (2) my
brothers and sisters

hermético, -a adj airtight

hermoso, -a adj beautiful

hermosura nf beauty; **¡Qué
hermosura de paisaje!** What a
beautiful landscape!

héroe nm hero

heroína nf heroine

heroinómano, -a nm/f heroin
addict

herradura nf horseshoe

herramienta nf tool

herrero nm blacksmith

hervir vb [51] to boil; **hervir agua**
to boil water

heterosexual adj, nmf
heterosexual

hice vb see **hacer**

hielo vb see **helar**
▶ nm ice

hierba nf ❶ grass ❷ herb; **una
mala hierba** a weed

> Word for word, **mala hierba**
> means 'bad grass'.

hierbabuena nf mint

hierro nm iron ▷ una caja de hierro
an iron box

hígado nm liver

higiene nf hygiene

higiénico, -a adj hygienic; **poco higiénico** unhygienic

higo nm fig; **un higo chumbo** a prickly pear

higuera nf fig tree

hija nf daughter; **Soy hija única.** I'm an only child.; **Sí, hija mía, tienes razón.** Yes, my dear, you're right.

hijastra nf stepdaughter

hijastro nm stepson; **mis hijastros (1)** my stepsons **(2)** my stepchildren

hijo nm son ▷ su hijo mayor his oldest son; **mis hijos (1)** my sons **(2)** my children; **Soy hijo único.** I'm an only child.

hilera nf ❶ row ❷ line ▷ ponerse en hilera to get into a line

hilo nm ❶ thread ▷ hilo de coser sewing thread ❷ linen; **los hilos del teléfono** the telephone wires

himno nm hymn; **el himno nacional** the national anthem

hincha nmf fan ▷ los hinchas del fútbol football fans

hinchado, -a adj swollen

hipermercado nm hypermarket

hipo nm hiccups ▷ **Tengo hipo.** I've got hiccups.

hipócrita adj hypocritical; **¡No seas hipócrita!** Don't be such a hypocrite!
▶ nmf hypocrite

hipódromo nm racecourse

hipopótamo nm hippo

hipoteca nf mortgage

hiriendo vb see herir

hirviendo vb see hervir

hispanohablante adj Spanish-speaking ▷ los países hispanohablantes Spanish-speaking countries
▶ nmf Spanish speaker

historia nf ❶ history ▷ la historia de España Spanish history ❷ story ▷ El libro cuenta la historia de dos niños. The book tells the story of two children.

historial nm record

histórico, -a adj ❶ historic ▷ una ciudad histórica a historic city ❷ historical ▷ un personaje histórico a historical character

historieta nf comic strip

hizo vb see hacer

hobby nm hobby; **Lo hago por hobby.** I do it as a hobby.
▌The 'h' in **hobby** is pronounced like Spanish 'j'.

hockey nm hockey; **el hockey sobre hielo** ice hockey
▌The 'h' in **hockey** is pronounced like Spanish 'j'.

hogar nm home ▷ en todos los hogares españoles in every Spanish home; **productos para el hogar** household products

hoguera nf bonfire

hoja nf ❶ leaf ❷ sheet ▷ una hoja de papel a sheet of paper; **una hoja de cálculo** a spreadsheet; **una hoja de solicitud** an application form ❸ page; **una hoja de afeitar** a razor blade

hojaldre nm puff pastry

hojear vb [25] to leaf through

hola excl hello!

Holanda nf Holland

holandés (fholandesa, mpl holandeses) adj Dutch
▶nm ❶ Dutchman; los holandeses the Dutch
❷ (language) Dutch

holandesa nf Dutchwoman

holgazán (fholgazana, mpl holgazanes) adj lazy

hollín nm soot

hombre nm man; un hombre de negocios a businessman; la historia del hombre sobre la tierra the history of mankind on earth

hombro nm shoulder; encogerse de hombros to shrug one's shoulders

homenaje nm tribute; en homenaje a in honour of

homosexual adj, nmf homosexual

hondo, -a adj deep ▷ un pozo muy hondo a very deep well ▷ Se ha tirado por la parte honda de la piscina. He dived into the deep end of the pool.

Honduras nf Honduras

hondureño, -a adj, nm/f Honduran

honestidad nf ❶ honesty
❷ decency

honesto, -a adj honest

hongo nm ❶ fungus ❷ (LatAm) mushroom

honor nm honour

honradez nf honesty

honrado, -a adj honest

hora nf ❶ hour ▷ El viaje dura una hora. The journey lasts an hour.
❷ time ▷ ¿Qué hora es? What's the time? ▷ ¿Tienes hora? Have you got the time?; ¿A qué hora llega? What time is he arriving?; llegar a la hora to arrive on time; la hora de cenar dinner time; a última hora at the last minute ❸ period; Después de inglés tenemos una hora libre. After English we have a free period. ❹ appointment ▷ Tengo hora para el dentista. I've got an appointment at the dentist's.; horas extras overtime sg; en mis horas libres in my spare time

horario nm timetable; el horario de trenes the train timetable; horario de visitas visiting hours pl

horchata nf
● Horchata is a milky looking
● drink made from tiger nuts and
● served with ice.

horizontal adj horizontal

horizonte nm horizon

hormiga nf ant

hormigón nm concrete

hormigueo nm pins and needles

horno nm oven; pescado al horno baked fish; pollo al horno roast chicken; un horno microondas a microwave oven

horóscopo nm horoscope

horquilla nf hairgrip

horrible adj awful ▷ El tiempo ha estado horrible. The weather has been awful.

horror nm horror; tener horror a algo to be terrified of something ▷ Les tengo horror a las arañas. I'm terrified of spiders.; ¡Qué horror! How awful!

horroroso, -a adj ❶ horrific ▷ un accidente horroroso a horrific accident ❷ hideous

hortaliza nf vegetable

hortera adj (informal) naff ▷ Tiene un gusto muy hortera. He's got really naff taste.

hospedarse vb [25] to stay

hospital nm hospital

hospitalidad nf hospitality

hostal nm small hotel

hostia nf host

hotel nm hotel

hoy adv today; desde hoy en adelante from now on; hoy en día nowadays; hoy por la mañana this morning

hoyo nm hole

hube vb see haber

hucha nf moneybox

hueco, -a adj hollow
  ▶ nm ❶ space ▷ Deja un hueco para la respuesta. Leave a space for the answer.; Hazme un hueco para sentarme. Make a bit of room so that I can sit down. ❷ free period ▷ Los lunes tengo un hueco entre clase y clase. I have a free period between classes on Mondays.; Entró por un hueco que había en la valla. He got in through a gap in the fence.

huelga nf strike; estar en huelga to be on strike; declararse en huelga to go on strike

huelguista nmf striker

huella nf footprint; huellas tracks; Desapareció sin dejar huella. He disappeared without trace.; huella digital fingerprint

huelo vb see oler

huérfano, -a adj un niño huérfano an orphan; ser huérfano to be an orphan; es huérfano de padre he's lost his father; quedarse huérfano to be orphaned
  ▶ nm/f orphan

huerta nf ❶ vegetable garden ❷ orchard

huerto nm ❶ kitchen garden ❷ orchard

hueso nm ❶ bone ❷ (in plum, peach) stone; aceitunas sin hueso pitted olives

huésped nmf guest

huevo nm egg; un huevo duro a hard-boiled egg; un huevo escalfado a poached egg; un huevo frito a fried egg; huevos revueltos scrambled eggs; un huevo pasado por agua a soft-boiled egg

huida nf escape

huir vb [10] to escape ▷ Huyó de la cárcel. He escaped from prison.; Huyeron del país. They fled the country.; salir huyendo to run away

hule nm ❶ oilcloth ❷ (Mex) rubber ▷ una liga de hule a rubber band

humanidad nf humanity

humano, -a adj human ▷ el cuerpo humano the human body; los seres humanos human beings
  ▶ nm human being

humareda nf cloud of smoke

humedad nf ❶ dampness ❷ humidity

húmedo, -a *adj* **①** damp ▷ *La ropa está húmeda todavía.* The clothes are still damp. **②** humid ▷ *El día estaba muy húmedo.* It was a very humid day.

humilde *adj* humble ▷ *Era de familia humilde.* She was from a humble background.

humo *nm* smoke

humor *nm* mood; **estar de buen humor** to be in a good mood; **estar de mal humor** to be in a bad mood; **Tiene un gran sentido del humor.** He has got a good sense of humour.; **humor negro** black humour

hundirse *vb* [58] **①** to sink **②** to collapse

húngaro, -a *adj, nm/f* Hungarian ▸ *nm (language)* Hungarian

Hungría *nf* Hungary

huracán *nm* hurricane

hurgar *vb* [37] to rummage; **hurgarse la nariz** to pick one's nose

huyendo *vb see* **huir**

I.B. *abbr* (= *Instituto de Bachillerato*)
- In Spain the **Institutos de Bachillerato** are state secondary schools for 12- to 18-year-olds.

iba *vb see* **ir**

iberoamericano, -a *adj, nm/f* Latin American

iceberg (*pl* icebergs) *nm* iceberg

icono *nm* icon

ida *nf* single ▷ *¿Cuánto cuesta la ida?* How much does a single cost?; **un billete de ida y vuelta** a return ticket; **un boleto de ida y vuelta** (*LatAm*) a return ticket; **a la ida** on the way there; **El viaje de ida duró dos horas.** The journey there took two hours.

idea nf idea ▷ ¡Qué buena idea!
What a good idea! ▷ No tengo ni
idea. I haven't the faintest idea.;
cambiar de idea to change one's
mind

ideal adj ideal
▶ nm ideal

idear vb **[25]** to devise

idéntico, -a adj identical ▷ Tiene
una falda idéntica a la mía. She has
an identical skirt to mine.; **Es
idéntica a su padre.** She's the
spitting image of her father.

identificar vb **[48]** to identify;
identificarse con alguien to
identify with somebody

idioma nm language

idiota adj stupid ▷ ¡No seas tan
idiota! Don't be so stupid!
▶ nmf idiot

idiotez (pl idioteces) nf Deja de
decir idioteces. Stop talking
nonsense.

ídolo nm idol

iglesia nf church; **la Iglesia
católica** the Catholic Church

ignorante adj ignorant

ignorar vb **[25]** ❶ not to know
▷ Ignoramos su paradero. We don't
know his whereabouts. ❷ to
ignore ▷ Es mejor ignorarla. It's best
to ignore her.

igual adj ❶ equal; **X es igual a Y.**
X is equal to Y. ❷ the same
▷ Todas las casas son iguales. All
the houses are the same.; **Es
igual a su madre.** (1) She looks
just like her mother. (2) She's just
like her mother.; **Tengo una falda
igual que la tuya.** I've got a skirt

just like yours.; **ir iguales** to be
even; **Van quince iguales.** It's
fifteen all.; **Es igual hoy que
mañana.** Today or tomorrow,
it doesn't matter.; **Me da igual.**
I don't mind.
▶ adv ❶ the same ▷ Se visten
igual. They dress the same.
❷ maybe ▷ Igual no lo saben
todavía. Maybe they don't know
yet. ❸ anyway ▷ No hizo nada pero
la castigaron igual. She didn't do
anything but they punished her
anyway.

igualdad nf equality ▷ la igualdad
racial racial equality; **la igualdad
de oportunidades** equal
opportunities

igualmente adv the same to you
▷ ¡Feliz Navidad! — Gracias,
igualmente. Happy Christmas! —
Thanks, the same to you.

ilegal adj illegal

ilegible adj illegible

ileso, -a adj unhurt; **Todos
resultaron ilesos.** No one was
hurt.

iluminación nf lighting; **Se
cortó la iluminación del estadio.**
The stadium floodlighting went
out.

iluminar vb **[25]** to light ▷ Unas
velas iluminaban la habitación.
The room was lit by candles.;
El flash le iluminó el rostro.
The flash lit up his face.; **Esta
lámpara ilumina muy poco.**
This lamp gives out very little
light.; **Se le iluminó la cara.** His
face lit up.

ilusión (pl **ilusiones**) nf ❶ hope ▷ No te hagas muchas ilusiones. Don't build your hopes up. ❷ dream ▷ Mi mayor ilusión es llegar a ser médico. My dream is to become a doctor. ❸ illusion ▷ una ilusión óptica an optical illusion; **Le hace mucha ilusión que vengas.** He's really looking forward to you coming.; **Tu regalo me hizo mucha ilusión.** I was delighted to get your present.; **¡Qué ilusión!** How wonderful!

ilusionado, -a adj excited

ilusionar vb [25] **Me ilusiona mucho la idea.** I'm really excited about the idea.; **ilusionarse** to build up one's hopes; **ilusionarse con algo** to get really excited about something

ilustración (pl **ilustraciones**) nf illustration

imagen (pl **imágenes**) nf ❶ image; **ser la viva imagen de alguien** to be the spitting image of somebody ❷ picture

imaginación (pl **imaginaciones**) nf imagination; **Esas son imaginaciones tuyas.** You're imagining things.; **Ni se me pasó por la imaginación.** It never even occurred to me.

imaginarse vb [25] to imagine ▷ No te imaginas lo mal que me sentí. You can't imagine how bad I felt. ▷ Me imagino que seguirá en Madrid. I imagine that he's still in Madrid.; **Me imagino que sí.** I imagine so.; **Me imagino que no.** I wouldn't

think so.; **¿Se enfadó mucho?** — **¡Imagínate!** Was he very angry? — What do you think!

imán (pl **imanes**) nm magnet

imbécil adj stupid

imitación (pl **imitaciones**) nf ❶ impression ▷ Es muy buena haciendo imitaciones. She's very good at doing impressions. ❷ imitation ▷ Aprendemos a hablar por imitación. We learn to speak by imitation. ▷ los diamantes de imitación imitation diamonds ▷ Es imitación de cuero. It's imitation leather.

imitar vb [25] to copy; **imitar a alguien** to do an impression of somebody; **imitar un acento** to imitate an accent

impaciente adj impatient ▷ Se estaba empezando a poner impaciente. He was beginning to get impatient. ▷ Estarás impaciente por saberlo. You'll be impatient to know.

impar adj odd ▷ un número impar an odd number
▶ nm odd number

imparcial adj impartial

impecable adj impeccable

impedir vb [38] ❶ to prevent ▷ impedir que alguien haga algo to prevent somebody from doing something ❷ to stop ❸ to block ▷ Un camión nos impedía el paso. A lorry was blocking our way.

imperdible nm safety pin

imperio nm empire

impermeable adj waterproof
▶ nm raincoat

SPANISH > ENGLISH

impersonal adj impersonal
impertinente adj impertinent
impidiendo vb see **impedir**
impido vb see **impedir**
imponer vb [**41**] to impose;
imponerse (1) to triumph (2) to
assert oneself
importación (pl importaciones)
nf import ▷ una empresa de
importación/exportación an
import-export business; **los
artículos de importación**
imported goods
importancia nf importance ▷ un
asunto de suma importancia a
matter of great importance; **dar
importancia a algo** to attach
importance to something ▷ Les
da demasiada importancia a los
detalles. He attaches too much
importance to details.; **darse
importancia** to give oneself airs;
**La educación tiene mucha
importancia.** Education is very
important.; **¡Me he olvidado tu
libro! — No tiene importancia.**
I've forgotten your book! — It
doesn't matter.; **cuestiones sin
importancia** unimportant
matters
importante adj important; **lo
importante** the important thing
▷ Lo importante es que vengas.
The important thing is that you
come.
importar vb [**25**] ❶ (goods) to
import ▷ Importa especias de la
India. He imports spices from
India. ❷ to matter ▷ ¿Y eso qué
importa? And what does that

matter?; **no importa (1)** it doesn't
matter ▷ No importa lo que piensen
los demás. It doesn't matter what
other people think. **(2)** never mind
▷ No importa, podemos hacerlo
mañana. Never mind, we can do it
tomorrow.; **No me importa
levantarme temprano.** I don't
mind getting up early. ▷ ¿Le
importa que fume? Do you mind if
I smoke?; **¿Y a ti qué te importa?**
What's it to you?; **Me importan
mucho mis estudios.** My studies
are very important to me.; **Me
importa un bledo.** I couldn't
care less.
imposible adj impossible ▷ Es
imposible predecir quién ganará.
It's impossible to predict who
will win.; **Es imposible que lo
sepan.** They can't possibly
know.
impostor, a nm/f impostor
imprescindible adj essential
impresión (pl impresiones) nf
impression ▷ Le causó muy buena
impresión a mis padres. He made a
very good impression on my
parents.; **Tengo la impresión de
que no va a venir.** I have a feeling
that he won't come.
impresionante adj ❶ impressive
❷ amazing ❸ striking
impresionar vb [**25**] ❶ to shock
▷ Me impresionó mucho su palidez.
I was really shocked at how pale
he was. ❷ to impress; **Impresiona
lo rápido que es.** His speed is
impressive.; **impresionarse** to be
impressed

impreso nm form ▷ un impreso de solicitud an application form

impresora nf printer ▷ una impresora láser a laser printer

imprevisible adj ❶ unforeseeable ❷ unpredictable

imprevisto, -a adj unexpected ▷ nm si no surge algún imprevisto if nothing unexpected comes up

imprimir vb [58] to print

improvisar vb [25] to improvise

imprudencia nf Saltar la tapia fue una imprudencia. It was unwise to jump over the wall.; El accidente fue debido a una imprudencia del conductor. The accident was caused by reckless driving.

imprudente adj unwise; conductores imprudentes reckless drivers

impuesto vb see **imponer** ▷ nm tax; el impuesto sobre la renta income tax; libre de impuestos duty-free

impulsar vb [25] to drive

impulso nm impulse ▷ Actué por impulso. I acted on impulse.; Mi primer impulso fue salir corriendo. My first instinct was to run away.

inaceptable adj unacceptable

inadecuado, -a adj unsuitable

inadvertido, -a adj pasar inadvertido to go unnoticed

inapropiado, -a adj unsuitable

inauguración (pl inauguraciones) nf opening ▷ la ceremonia de inauguración the opening ceremony

inaugurar vb [25] to open

incapacidad nf inability; la incapacidad física physical disability; la incapacidad mental learning difficulties

incapaz (pl incapaces) adj incapable ▷ Es incapaz de estarse callado. He is incapable of keeping quiet.; Hoy soy incapaz de concentrarme. I can't concentrate today.

incendiarse vb [25] to catch fire

incendio nm fire

incentivo nm incentive

incidente nm incident

incierto, -a adj uncertain

inclinar vb [25] to tilt ▷ Inclina un poco más la sombrilla. Can you tilt the sun umbrella a bit more?; inclinar la cabeza to nod; inclinarse (1) to bend down ▷ Se inclinó para besarlo. She bent down to kiss him. (2) to lean ▷ inclinarse sobre algo to lean over something ▷ inclinarse hacia delante to lean forward ▷ inclinarse hacia atrás to lean back (3) to bow ▷ inclinarse ante alguien to bow to somebody

incluido, -a adj included ▷ El servicio no está incluido en el precio. Service is not included.

incluir vb [10] to include

inclusive adv ❶ inclusive ▷ Está abierto de lunes a sábado inclusive. It's open from Monday to Saturday inclusive. ❷ including

incluso adv even

incluyendo vb see **incluir**

incómodo, -a adj uncomfortable

incompetente adj incompetent

incompleto, -a adj incomplete

incomprensible adj incomprehensible

inconsciente adj ❶ unconscious ❷ thoughtless

inconveniente adj inconvenient
▶ nm ❶ problem ▷ Ha surgido un inconveniente. A problem has come up. ❷ drawback ▷ El plan tiene sus inconvenientes. The plan has its drawbacks.; **No tengo ningún inconveniente.** I have no objection.; **No tengo inconveniente en preguntárselo.** I don't mind asking him.; **¿Tienes algún inconveniente en que le dé tu teléfono?** Do you mind if I give him your telephone number?

incorrecto, -a adj ❶ incorrect ❷ impolite

increíble adj incredible

inculto, -a adj ignorant

incurable adj incurable

indeciso, -a adj indecisive; **Estoy indecisa, no sé cuál comprar.** I can't make up my mind, I don't know which to buy.

indefenso, -a adj defenceless

indemnización (pl indemnizaciones) nf compensation ▷ Recibieron mil dólares de indemnización. They received a thousand dollars compensation.

indemnizar vb [13] to compensate; **Nos tienen que indemnizar.** They've got to pay us compensation.

independencia nf independence

independiente adj ❶ independent ❷ self-contained

independientemente adv independently

independizarse vb [13] to become independent

India nf La India India

india nf Indian

indicación (pl indicaciones) nf sign; **Nos hizo una indicación para que siguiéramos.** He signalled to us to go on.; **indicaciones (1)** instructions **(2)** directions ▷ Me dio indicaciones de cómo llegar. He gave me directions for getting there.

indicar vb [48] ❶ to indicate ❷ to tell ▷ Un guardia me indicó el camino. A police officer told me the way. ❸ to advise ▷ El médico me indicó que no fumara. The doctor advised me not to smoke.

índice nm ❶ index ❷ index finger

indiferencia nf indifference

indiferente adj indifferent; **Es indiferente que viva en Glasgow o Edimburgo.** It makes no difference whether he lives in Glasgow or Edinburgh.; **Me es indiferente hacerlo hoy o mañana.** I don't mind whether I do it today or tomorrow.

indígena adj indigenous
▶ nmf native

indigestión nf indigestion

indignado, -a adj angry

indignar vb [25] to infuriate; **indignarse por algo** to get angry about something; **indignarse con alguien** to be furious with somebody

indio adj, nm Indian

indirecta nf hint ▷ **lanzar una indirecta** to drop a hint

indirecto, -a adj indirect

indispensable adj essential

individual adj ❶ individual ❷ (bed, room) single
▶ nm singles pl ▷ **la final del individual femenino** the ladies' singles final

individuo nm individual

industria nf industry ▷ **la industria pesada** heavy industry ▷ **la industria petrolífera** the oil industry

industrial adj industrial
▶ nmf industrialist

ineficiente adj inefficient

inesperado, -a adj unexpected

inestable adj ❶ unsteady ❷ changeable

inevitable adj inevitable

inexacto, -a adj inaccurate

inexperto, -a adj inexperienced

inexplicable adj inexplicable

infantil adj ❶ (clothing, playground, programme) children's ❷ childish ▷ **¡No seas tan infantil!** Don't be so childish!

infarto nm heart attack ▷ **Le dio un infarto.** He had a heart attack.

infección (pl **infecciones**) nf infection

infeliz (pl **infelices**) adj unhappy

inferior adj ❶ lower ❷ inferior; **un número inferior a nueve** a number below nine

infierno nm hell

infinitivo nm infinitive

inflable adj inflatable

inflación nf inflation

inflamable adj inflammable

inflar vb [25] ❶ to blow up ❷ to inflate

influencia nf influence

influenciar vb [25] to influence

influir vb [10] **dos hombres que influyeron en su vida** two men who influenced his life; **Mis padres influyeron mucho en mí.** My parents had a great influence on me.; **El cansancio ha influido en su rendimiento.** Tiredness has affected his work.

información (pl **informaciones**) nf ❶ information; **una información muy importante** a very important piece of information ❷ news sg ▷ **Este canal tiene mucha información deportiva.** There's a lot of sports news on this channel. ❸ directory enquiries ▷ **Llama a información y pide que te den el número.** Call directory enquiries and ask them for the number.; **Pregunta en información de dónde sale el tren.** Ask at the information desk which platform the train leaves from.

informal adj ❶ informal; **Prefiero la ropa informal.** I prefer casual clothes. ❷ (person) unreliable

informar vb [25] to inform; **Les han informado mal.** You've been misinformed.; **¿Me podría**

informar sobre los cursos de inglés? Could you give me some information about English courses?; **informarse de algo** to find out about something

informática nf computing

informático, -a adj computer ▷ **un programa informático** a computer program
▶ nm computer expert

informe nm report; **según mis informes** according to my information; **pedir informes** to ask for references

infusión (pl **infusiones**) nf herbal tea; **una infusión de manzanilla** a camomile tea

ingeniar vb [25] to devise; **ingeniárselas** to manage

ingeniera nf engineer ▷ **Quiere ser ingeniera.** She wants to be an engineer.

ingeniería nf engineering

ingeniero nm engineer

ingenio nm ❶ ingenuity ❷ wit; **un ingenio azucarero** (LatAm) a sugar refinery

ingenioso, -a adj ❶ ingenious ❷ witty

ingenuo, -a adj naïve

Inglaterra nf England

inglés (f **inglesa**, mpl **ingleses**) adj English ▷ **la comida inglesa** English food
▶ nm ❶ Englishman; **los ingleses** the English ❷ (language) English ▷ **El inglés le resulta difícil.** He finds English difficult.

inglesa nf Englishwoman

ingrediente nm ingredient

ingresar vb [25] to pay in ▷ **ingresar un cheque en una cuenta** to pay a cheque into an account; **ingresar en el hospital** to go into hospital; **Han vuelto a ingresar a mi abuela.** They've taken my grandmother into hospital again.; **ingresar en un club** to join a club

ingreso nm admission; **un examen de ingreso** an entrance exam; **los ingresos** income sg ▷ **Tiene unos ingresos muy bajos.** He has a very low income.

inicial nf initial

iniciativa nf initiative ▷ **Lo hizo por iniciativa propia.** He did it on his own initiative.

injusticia nf injustice

injusto, -a adj unfair

inmaduro, -a adj ❶ immature ❷ unripe

inmediatamente adv immediately

inmediato, -a adj immediate; **inmediato a algo** next to something ▷ **en el edificio inmediato a la embajada** in the building next to the embassy; **de inmediato** immediately

inmenso, -a adj immense; **la inmensa mayoría** the vast majority

inmigración nf immigration

inmigrante nmf immigrant

inmoral adj immoral

inmortal adj immortal

inmóvil adj motionless ▷ **Se quedó inmóvil.** He remained motionless.

innecesario, -a adj unnecessary

inocente adj innocent ▷ Es
inocente. He's innocent.; **El jurado
la declaró inocente.** The jury
found her not guilty.

inofensivo, -a adj harmless

inolvidable adj unforgettable

inquietante adj worrying

inquietar vb [**25**] to worry;
inquietarse to worry ▷ ¡No te
inquietes! Don't worry!

inquieto, -a adj ❶ worried
❷ restless

inquilino, -a nm/f ❶ tenant
❷ lodger

insatisfecho, -a adj dissatisfied

inscribirse vb [**58**, pp **inscrito**]
to enrol

inscripción (pl inscripciones) nf
❶ enrolment ❷ inscription

inscrito vb see **inscribirse**

insecto nm insect

inseguridad nf insecurity ▷ la
inseguridad en el trabajo job
insecurity; **la inseguridad
ciudadana** the lack of safety on
the streets

inseguro, -a adj ❶ insecure
❷ unsafe

insensato, -a adj foolish

insensible adj insensitive

insignia nf badge

insignificante adj insignificant

insinuar vb [**1**] to hint at;
¿Insinúas que miento? Are you
insinuating that I'm lying?

insípido, -a adj insipid

insistir vb [**58**] to insist

insolación nf sunstroke

insolente adj insolent

insoportable adj unbearable

inspector, a nm/f inspector

instalaciones nfpl facilities

instalar vb [**25**] ❶ to install
❷ to set up; **instalarse** to settle
▷ Decidieron instalarse en el centro.
They decided to settle in the town
centre.

instantáneo, -a adj
❶ instantaneous; **el café
instantáneo** instant coffee

instante nm moment ▷ por un
instante for a moment; **A cada
instante suena el teléfono.**
The phone rings all the time.;
al instante right away

instinto nm instinct

institución (pl instituciones) nf
institution

instituto nm institute; **un
instituto de enseñanza
secundaria** a secondary school

instrucciones nfpl instructions

instructivo, -a adj educational

instructor, a nm/f instructor
▷ un instructor de esquí a ski
instructor ▷ un instructor de
autoescuela a driving instructor

instrumento nm instrument

insuficiente adj insufficient
▶ nm Sacó un insuficiente en
francés. He got an F in French.

insulina nf insulin

insultar vb [**25**] to insult

insulto nm insult

intelectual adj, nmf intellectual

inteligencia nf intelligence

inteligente adj intelligent

intención (pl intenciones) nf
intention ▷ No tengo la más mínima

intención de hacerlo. I haven't got the slightest intention of doing it.; **tener intención de hacer algo** to intend to do something

intensivo, -a *adj* intensive

intenso, -a *adj* intense

intentar *vb* **[25]** to try

intento *nm* attempt ▷ *Aprobó al primer intento.* He passed at the first attempt.

intercambiar *vb* **[25]** ❶ to exchange ❷ to swap

intercambio *nm* exchange

interés (*pl* **intereses**) *nm* interest ▷ *Tienes que poner más interés en tus estudios.* You must take more of an interest in your studies.; **tener interés en hacer algo** to be keen to do something

interesante *adj* interesting

interesar *vb* **[25]** to interest ▷ *Eso es algo que siempre me ha interesado.* That's something that has always interested me.; **Me interesa mucho la física.** I'm very interested in physics.; **interesarse por algo** to ask about something

interfono *nm* intercom

interior *adj* ❶ (lane, pocket) inside ❷ (world) inner
▶ *nm* **El tren se detuvo en el interior del túnel.** The train stopped inside the tunnel.

interiorista *nmf* interior designer

intermedio, -a *adj*
❶ intermediate ❷ medium
▶ *nm* interval

interminable *adj* endless

intermitente *adj* ❶ intermittent ❷ (light) flashing
▶ *nm* indicator

internacional *adj* international

internado *nm* boarding school

internauta *nmf* internet user

Internet *nmf* the internet ▷ *en Internet* on the internet

interno, -a *adj* **estar interno en un colegio** to be a boarder at a school
▶ *nm/f* ❶ boarder ❷ houseman

interpretación (*pl* **interpretaciones**) *nf* interpretation; **Todo fue producto de una mala interpretación.** It was all the result of a misunderstanding.

interpretar *vb* **[25]** ❶ to interpret ❷ to play ▷ *Interpreta el papel de Victoria.* She plays the part of Victoria. ❸ (piece) to perform; **No me interpretes mal.** Don't misunderstand me.

intérprete *nmf* interpreter

interrogar *vb* **[37]** to question

interrumpir *vb* **[58]** ❶ (person) to interrupt ❷ (holidays) to cut short ❸ to block ▷ *Estás interrumpiendo el paso.* You're blocking the way.

interrupción (*pl* **interrupciones**) *nf* interruption

interruptor *nm* switch

interurbano, -a *adj* long-distance

intervalo *nm* interval

intervenir *vb* **[56]** ❶ to take part ▷ *No intervino en el debate.* He did not take part in the debate. ❷ to intervene

intimidad nf ❶ private life ❷ privacy; **La boda se celebró en la intimidad.** It was a private wedding.

intimidar vb [25] to intimidate

íntimo, -a adj intimate; **Es un amigo íntimo.** He's a close friend.

introducción (pl **introducciones**) nf introduction

introducir vb [9] ❶ to insert ▷ Introdujo la moneda en la ranura. He inserted the coin in the slot. ❷ to bring in ▷ Quieren introducir un nuevo sistema de trabajo. They want to bring in new working methods.; **Han introducido cambios en el horario.** They've made changes to the timetable.

introvertido, -a adj introverted

intruso, -a nm/f intruder

intuición nf intuition

inundación (pl **inundaciones**) nf flood

inundar vb [25] to flood; **inundarse** to be flooded

inútil adj useless ▷ Es inútil tratar de hacerle entender. It's useless trying to make him understand.; **Es inútil que esperes.** There's no point in your waiting.
▶ nmf ¡Es un inútil! He's useless!

invadir vb [58] to invade

inválido, -a adj disabled

invasión (pl **invasiones**) nf invasion

inventar vb [25] ❶ to invent ❷ (story) to make up

invento nm invention

inventor, a nm/f inventor

invernadero nm greenhouse; **el efecto invernadero** the greenhouse effect

invernar vb [39] to hibernate

inverosímil adj unlikely

inversión (pl **inversiones**) nf investment

inverso, -a adj reverse ▷ en orden inverso in reverse order; **a la inversa** the other way round

invertir vb [51] ❶ (money) to invest ❷ (time) to spend ❸ (order) to reverse

investigación (pl **investigaciones**) nf ❶ research ▷ Está haciendo una investigación sobre Internet. He's doing some research on the internet. ❷ (by police) investigation ❸ inquiry ▷ Se hará una investigación pública. There will be a public inquiry.

invierno nm winter ▷ en invierno in winter

invisible adj invisible

invitación (pl **invitaciones**) nf invitation

invitado, -a nm/f guest ▷ Es el invitado de honor. He's the guest of honour.

invitar vb [25] to invite ▷ Me invitó a una fiesta. He invited me to a party.; **Te invito a un café.** I'll buy you a coffee.; **Esta vez invito yo.** This time it's on me.

inyección (pl **inyecciones**) nf injection ▷ ponerle una inyección a alguien to give someone an injection

inyectar vb [25] **Le tuvieron que inyectar insulina.** They had to

a b c d e f g h i j k l m n ñ o p q r s t u v w x y z

give him insulin injections.;
inyectarse algo to inject oneself
with something
ir vb **[27] ❶** to go ▷ *Anoche fuimos al
cine.* We went to the cinema last
night. ▷ *¿A qué colegio vas?* What
school do you go to?; **ir de
vacaciones** to go on holiday; **ir a
por** to go and get ▷ *Voy a por el
paraguas.* I'll go and get the
umbrella. ▷ *Ha ido a por el médico.*
She has gone to get the doctor.;
Voy a hacerlo mañana. I'm going
to do it tomorrow.; **vamos** let's go
▷ *Vamos a casa.* Let's go home.;
¡Vamos a ver! Let's see! **❷** to be
▷ *Iba con su madre.* He was with his
mother. ▷ *como iba diciendo* as I was
saying ▷ **❸** to come ▷ *¡Ahora voy!* I'm
just coming! ▷ *¿Puedo ir contigo?*
Can I come with you?; **ir a pie** to
walk; **ir en avión** to fly; **¿Cómo te
va?** How are things?; **¿Cómo te va
en los estudios?** How are you
getting on with your studies?;
¡Que te vaya bien! Take care of
yourself!; **¡Qué va!** What are you
talking about!; **¡Vaya! ¿Qué haces
tú por aquí?** Well, what a surprise!
What are you doing here?; **¡Vaya
coche!** What a car!; **irse (1)** to
leave ▷ *Acaba de irse.* He has just
left. **(2)** to go out ▷ *Se ha ido la luz.*
The lights have gone out.;
¡vámonos! Let's go!; **¡Vete!** Go
away!; **Vete a hacer los deberes.**
Go and do your homework.
Irak nm Iraq
Irán nm Iran
iraní (pl **iraníes**) adj, nmf Iranian

iraquí (pl **iraquíes**) adj, nmf Iraqi
Irlanda nf Ireland ▷ **Irlanda del Norte**
Northern Ireland
irlandés (f **irlandesa**, mpl
irlandeses) adj ❶ Irish ▷ *un café
irlandés* an Irish coffee
▸ nm ❶ Irishman; **los irlandeses**
the Irish **❷** (language) Irish
irlandesa nf Irishwoman
irónico, -a adj ironic
irracional adj irrational
irrelevante adj irrelevant
irresistible adj irresistible
irresponsable adj irresponsible
irritante adj irritating
irritar vb **[25]** to irritate
irrompible adj unbreakable
isla nf island
Islam nm Islam
islámico, -a adj Islamic
islandés (f **islandesa**, mpl
islandeses) adj ❶ Icelandic
▸ nm/f Icelander
▸ nm (language) Icelandic
Islandia nf Iceland
isleño nm islander
Israel nm Israel
israelí (pl **israelíes**) adj, nmf Israeli
Italia nf Italy
italiano, -a adj, nm/f Italian
▸ nm (language) Italian
itinerario nm ❶ route **❷** itinerary
▷ *Me gustaría incluir Roma en el
itinerario.* I'd like to include Rome
on our itinerary.
IVA abbr m (= Impuesto sobre el Valor
Añadido) VAT (= Value Added Tax)
izar vb **[13]** to hoist
izquierda nf ❶ left hand; **Escribo
con la izquierda.** I write with my

left hand. **2** left ▷ *doblar a la izquierda* to turn left; **ser de izquierdas** to be left-wing ▷ *un partido de izquierdas* a left-wing party; **a la izquierda** on the left ▷ *la segunda calle a la izquierda* the second turning on the left; **conducir por la izquierda** to drive on the left

izquierdo, -a *adj* left ▷ *Levanta la mano izquierda.* Raise your left hand.; **a mano izquierda** on the left-hand side

jabón (pl **jabones**) nm soap
jaiba nf (LatAm) crab
jalar vb [**25**] (LatAm) **1** to pull ▷ *No le jales el pelo.* Don't pull his hair. **2** to take ▷ *Jaló un folleto de la mesa.* He took a leaflet from the table.
jamás adv never
jamón (pl **jamones**) nm ham ▷ *un bocadillo de jamón* a ham sandwich; **jamón serrano** cured ham; **jamón de York** boiled ham
Japón nm Japan
japonés (f **japonesa**, mpl **japoneses**) adj, nm/f Japanese ▶ nm (language) Japanese
jarabe nm syrup; **jarabe para la tos** cough syrup
jardín (pl **jardines**) nm garden; **el jardín de infancia** nursery school

jardinera nf ❶ gardener
❷ window box
jardinería nf gardening
jardinero nm gardener
jarra nf ❶ jug ❷ beer glass
jarro nm jug
jarrón (pl jarrones) nm vase
jaula nf cage
jefe, -a nm/f ❶ boss ▷ Carlos es mi
jefe. Carlos is my boss. ❷ head
▷ El jefe de la empresa dimitió. The
head of the company resigned.;
el jefe del departamento the
head of department; **jefe de
estado** head of state; **el jefe del
grupo guerrillero** the leader of the
guerrilla group
jerez nm sherry
jeringuilla nf syringe
jersey (pl jerséis) nm jumper
Jesús excl ❶ Bless you! ❷ Good
God!
jinete nm jockey
jirafa nf giraffe
jitomate nm (Mex) tomato
jornada nf jornada de trabajo
working day; **trabajar a jornada
completa** to work full-time;
trabajar a media jornada to work
part-time
joven (pl jóvenes) adj young ▷ un
chico joven a young boy
▶ nmf un joven a young man; **una
joven** a young woman; **los
jóvenes** young people
joya nf jewel; **Me han robado mis
joyas.** My jewellery has been stolen.
joyería nf jeweller's
joyero nm ❶ jeweller ❷ jewellery
box

jubilación (pl jubilaciones) nf
❶ retirement ▷ La edad de
jubilación es a los 65 años. The
retirement age is 65. ❷ pension
▷ cobrar la jubilación to get one's
pension
jubilado, -a adj retired; **estar
jubilado** to be retired
▶ nm/f pensioner
jubilarse vb [25] to retire
judía nf Jew; **judía blanca** haricot
bean; **judía verde** green bean
judío, -a adj Jewish
▶ nm Jew
judo nm judo
juego vb see jugar
▶ nm ❶ game ▷ un juego de
ordenador a computer game;
juegos de cartas card games;
juegos de mesa board games
❷ gambling ▷ Lo perdió todo en el
juego. He lost everything through
gambling. ❸ set ▷ un juego de café a
coffee set; **Las cortinas hacen
juego con el sofá.** The curtains go
with the sofa.
juerga nf irse de juerga to go out
on the town
jueves (pl jueves) nm Thursday
juez, a (mpl jueces) nm/f judge;
juez de línea linesman
jugador, a nm/f player
jugar vb [28] ❶ to play; **jugar al
fútbol** to play football ❷ to
gamble; **jugar a la lotería** to do
the lottery
jugo nm ❶ juice ❷ gravy
juguete nm toy; **un avión de
juguete** a toy plane
juguetería nf toy shop

juicio nm trial; **llevar a alguien a juicio** to take someone to court

julio nm July

jungla nf jungle

junio nm June

junta nf committee; **La junta directiva tiene la última palabra.** The board of management have the final say.

juntar vb [25] ❶ to put together ▷ Vamos a juntar los pupitres. Let's put the desks together. ❷ to gather together ▷ Consiguieron juntar a mil personas. They managed to gather together one thousand people.; **juntarse (1)** to move closer together **(2)** to meet up ▷ Nos juntamos los domingos para comer. We meet up for dinner on Sundays.

junto, -a adj ❶ close together ▷ Los muebles están demasiado juntos. The furniture is too close together. ❷ together ▷ Cuando estamos juntos apenas hablamos. We hardly talk when we're together.; **todo junto** all together ▷ Ponlo todo junto en una sola bolsa. Put it all together in one bag.
▶ adv **junto a** by; **junto con** together with; **Mi apellido se escribe todo junto.** My surname is all in one word.

jurado nm ❶ jury ❷ (in competition) panel

jurar vb [25] to swear

justicia nf justice

justificar vb [48] to justify

justo, -a adj ❶ fair ▷ Tuvo un juicio justo. He had a fair trial. ❷ right

❸ tight ▷ Me están muy justos estos pantalones. These trousers are tight on me. ❹ just enough ▷ Tengo el dinero justo para el billete. I have just enough money for the ticket.
▶ adv **just** ▷ La vi justo cuando entrábamos. I saw her just as we came in.; **Me dio un puñetazo justo en la nariz.** He punched me right on the nose.

juvenil adj young; **la literatura juvenil** young people's literature

juventud nf ❶ youth ▷ Fue soldado en su juventud. He was a soldier in his youth. ❷ youngsters pl ▷ La juventud viene aquí a divertirse. Youngsters come here to have fun.

juzgado nm court

juzgar vb [37] (in court) to try

k l

kárate nm karate
kilo nm kilo
kilogramo nm kilogram
kilómetro nm kilometre
kiosco nm news stand

la art the ▷ la pared the wall

Look how the English possessive corresponds to the article in the following.

▷ Ayer me lavé la cabeza. I washed my hair yesterday. ▷ Abróchate la camisa. Do your shirt up. ▷ Tiene una casa bonita, pero prefiero la de Juan. He's got a lovely house, but I prefer Juan's.

The article is not always translated; for example when making generalizations, in certain time expressions, and with titles such as **Mrs** and **Dr**.

▷ No me gusta la fruta. I don't like fruit. ▷ Vendrá la semana que viene. He's coming next week. ▷ Me he encontrado a la Sra. Sendra. I met

Mrs Sendra.; **la del sombrero rojo** the girl in the red hat; **Yo fui la que te desperté.** It was I who woke you up.

▶ *pron* **①** her ▷ *La quiero.* I love her.; **La han despedido.** She has been sacked. **②** you

la can also refer to **usted**, the formal form meaning **you**.

▷ *La acompaño hasta la puerta.* I'll see you out. **③** it ▷ *No la toques.* Don't touch it.

labio *nm* lip

labor *nf* work; **las labores domésticas** the housework

laborable *adj* día laborable working day

laboral *adj* **①** (conditions, day) working **②** labour **③** industrial

laboratorio *nm* laboratory

laca *nf* **①** hairspray **②** lacquer; **la laca de uñas** nail varnish

lácteo, -a *adj* **los productos lácteos** dairy products

ladera *nf* hillside

lado *nm* side ▷ *a los dos lados de la carretera* on both sides of the road; **Hay gente por todos lados.** There are people everywhere.; **Tiene que estar en otro lado.** It must be somewhere else.; **Mi casa está aquí al lado.** My house is right nearby.; **la mesa de al lado** the next table; **al lado de** beside ▷ *La silla que está al lado del armario.* The chair beside the wardrobe.; **Felipe se sentó a mi lado.** Felipe sat beside me.; **por un lado ..., por otro lado ...** on the one hand ..., on the other hand ...

ladrar *vb* [**25**] to bark

ladrillo *nm* brick

ladrón (ladrona) *nm/f* **①** thief **②** burglar **③** robber

lagarto *nm* lizard

lago *nm* lake

lágrima *nf* tear

laguna *nf* lake

lamentar *vb* [**25**] **Lamento lo ocurrido.** I am sorry about what happened.; **lamentarse** to complain ▷ *De nada vale lamentarse.* There's no use complaining.

lamer *vb* [**8**] to lick

lámpara *nf* lamp

lana *nf* wool; **una bufanda de lana** a woollen scarf

lancha *nf* motorboat; **una lancha de salvamento** a lifeboat

langosta *nf* **①** lobster **②** locust

langostino *nm* king prawn

lanzar *vb* [**13**] **①** (stone, ball, grenade) to throw **②** (rocket, product) to launch; **lanzarse** to dive

lapicero *nm* pencil

lápida *nf* gravestone

lápiz (pl lápices) *nm* pencil ▷ *Escribió mi dirección a lápiz.* He wrote my address in pencil.; **los lápices de colores** crayons; **un lápiz de labios** a lipstick; **un lápiz de ojos** an eyeliner

largo, -a *adj* long ▷ *Fue una conferencia muy larga.* It was a very long conference. ▷ *Esta cuerda es demasiado larga.* This piece of string is too long.

▶ *nm* length; **¿Cuánto mide de largo?** How long is it?; **Tiene nueve metros de largo.** It's nine metres long.; **a lo largo del río** along the river; **a lo largo de la semana** throughout the week; **Pasó de largo sin saludar.** He passed by without saying hello.

> Be careful! **largo** does not mean **large**.

las *art* the ▶ **las paredes** the walls

> Look how the English possessive corresponds to the article in the following.

▷ *Me duelen las piernas.* My legs hurt. ▷ *Poneos las bufandas.* Put on your scarves. ▷ *Estas fotos son bonitas, pero prefiero las de Pedro.* These photos are nice, but I prefer Pedro's.

> The plural article is not always translated, for example when making generalizations and when talking about the time. ▷ *No me gustan las arañas.* I don't like spiders. ▷ *Vino a las seis de la tarde.* He came at six in the evening.; **las del estante de arriba** the ones on the top shelf

▶ *pron* ❶ them ▷ *Las vi por la calle.* I saw them in the street.; **Las han despedido.** They've been sacked. ❷ you

> **las** can also refer to **ustedes**, the formal form meaning **you**. ▷ *Las acompañaré hasta la puerta, señoras.* I'll see you out, ladies.

láser *nm* laser

lástima *nf* **Me da lástima de ella.** I feel sorry for her.; **Es una lástima**

que no puedas venir. It's a shame you can't come.; **¡Qué lástima!** What a shame!

lata *nf* ❶ tin ❷ can; **Deja de dar la lata.** Stop being a pain.

lateral *adj* side ▷ *la puerta lateral* the side door

latido *nm* beat

látigo *nm* whip

latín *nm* Latin

Latinoamérica *nf* Latin America

latinoamericano, -a *adj, nm/f* Latin American

latir *vb* [58] to beat

laurel *nm* laurel; **una hoja de laurel** a bay leaf

lavabo *nm* ❶ sink ❷ toilet

lavado *nm* wash; **el lavado en seco** dry cleaning

lavadora *nf* washing machine

lavandería *nf* launderette

lavaplatos (*pl* lavaplatos) *nm* ❶ dishwasher ❷ (*Mex*) sink

lavar *vb* [25] to wash; **lavar la ropa** to do the washing; **lavarse** to wash; **Ayer me lavé la cabeza.** I washed my hair yesterday.; **Lávate los dientes.** Brush your teeth.

lavarropas (*pl* lavarropas) *nm* (*Mex*) washing machine

lavavajillas (*pl* lavavajillas) *nm* ❶ dishwasher ❷ washing-up liquid

lazo *nm* ❶ bow ❷ ribbon

le *pron* ❶ him ▷ *Le mandé una carta.* I sent him a letter. ▷ *Le miré con atención.* I watched him carefully.; **Le abrí la puerta.** I opened the door for him. ❷ her ▷ *Le mandé una* carta. I sent her a letter.; **No le hablé de ti.** I didn't speak to her about you.; **Le busqué el libro.** I looked out the book for her.

① you

> le can also refer to **usted**, the formal form meaning **you**.
> *Le presento a la Señora Gutiérrez.* Let me introduce you to Mrs Gutiérrez.; **Le he arreglado el ordenador.** I've fixed the computer for you.

> When le is used in combination with an article and a part of the body or an item of clothing, it is usually translated using the possessive in English.
> *Le huelen los pies.* His feet smell.
> *Le arrastra la falda.* Her skirt is trailing on the floor.

lealtad *nf* loyalty

lección (*pl* **lecciones**) *nf* lesson

leche *nf* milk; **la leche desnatada** skimmed milk; **la leche en polvo** powdered milk

lechuga *nf* lettuce

lector, a *nm/f* **①** reader **②** language assistant
> **un lector de CD** a CD player

lectura *nf* reading

leer *vb* [**30**] to read

legal *adj* legal

legumbre *nf* pulse

lejano, -a *adj* distant > **un sitio muy lejano** a very distant place

lejía *nf* bleach

lejos *adv* far; **De lejos parecía un avión.** From a distance it looked like a plane.

lencería *nf* lingerie

lengua *nf* **①** tongue > *Me he mordido la lengua.* I've bitten my tongue. **②** language > *Habla varias lenguas.* He speaks several languages.; **mi lengua materna** my mother tongue

lenguado *nm* sole

lenguaje *nm* language

lente *nf* lens; **las lentes de contacto** contact lenses

lenteja *nf* lentil

lentes *nmpl* (*LatAm*) glasses; **los lentes de sol** sunglasses

lentilla *nf* contact lens

lento, -a *adj* slow > **un proceso lento** a slow progress
> *adv* slowly

leña *nf* firewood

Leo *nm* (*sign*) Leo; **Soy leo.** I'm Leo.

león (*pl* **leones**) *nm* lion

leona *nf* lioness

leopardo *nm* leopard

leotardos *nmpl* woolly tights

les *pron* **①** them > *Les mandé una carta.* I sent them a letter. > *Les miré con atención.* I watched them carefully.; **Les abrí la puerta.** I opened the door for them.; **Les eché de comer a los gatos.** I gave the cats something to eat.

② you

> les can also refer to **ustedes**, the formal form meaning **you**.
> *Les presento a la Señora Gutiérrez.* Let me introduce you to Mrs Gutiérrez.; **Les he arreglado el ordenador.** I've fixed the computer for you.

When **les** is used in combination with an article and a part of the body or an item of clothing, it is usually translated using the possessive in English.

▷ *Les huelen los pies.* Their feet smell. ▷ *Les arrastraban los abrigos.* Their coats were trailing on the floor.

lesbiana nf lesbian

lesión (pl **lesiones**) nf injury

lesionado, -a adj injured

letra nf ❶ letter ▷ *la letra 'a'* the letter 'a' ❷ handwriting ▷ *Tengo muy mala letra.* My handwriting's very poor. ❸ lyrics pl

letrero nm sign

levantar vb [25] to lift; **Levantad la mano si tenéis alguna duda.** Raise your hand if you are unclear.; **levantarse** to get up

leve adj minor ▷ *Solo tiene heridas leves.* He only has minor injuries. ▷ *Cometió una falta leve.* He made a minor mistake.

ley (pl **leyes**) nf law

leyendo vb see **leer**

liar vb [21] ❶ (parcel) to tie up ❷ to confuse ▷ *Me liaron con tantas explicaciones.* They confused me with all their explanations.; **liarse** to get muddled up

Líbano nm Lebanon

liberal adj, nmf liberal

liberar vb [25] to free

libertad nf freedom; **No tengo libertad para hacer lo que quiera.** I'm not free to do what

I want.; **poner a alguien en libertad** to release somebody

Libra nm (sign) Libra; **Soy libra.** I'm Libra.

libra nf pound; **libra esterlina** pound sterling

librarse vb [25] **librarse de** (1) to get out of (2) to get rid of

libre adj free ▷ *¿Está libre este asiento?* Is this seat free? ▷ *El martes estoy libre, así que podemos quedar.* I'm free on Tuesday so we can meet up.; **los 100 metros libres** the 100 metres freestyle

librería nf ❶ bookshop ❷ bookshelf

> Be careful! **librería** does not mean library.

librero nm (Chile, Mex) bookcase

libreta nf notebook

libro nm book; **un libro de bolsillo** a paperback; **un libro de texto** a text book

licencia nf licence; **estar de licencia** (LatAm) to be on leave

licenciado, -a nm/f graduate

licenciatura nf degree

licor nm liqueur; **Bebimos cerveza y licores.** We drank beer and spirits.

líder nmf leader

liebre nf hare

liga nf ❶ league ❷ garter

ligar vb [37] *Ayer ligué con una chica.* (informal) I got off with a girl yesterday.

ligero, -a adj ❶ light ▷ *Me gusta llevar ropa ligera.* I like to wear light clothing. ▷ *Comimos algo ligero.* We ate something light. ❷ slight

▷ Tengo un ligero dolor de cabeza. I have a slight headache.; **Andaba a paso ligero.** He walked quickly.

lila nf lilac

lima nf ❶ file ▷ una lima de uñas a nail file ❷ (fruit) lime

limitar vb [**25**] to limit; **España limita con Francia.** Spain has a border with France.; **Yo me limité a observar.** I just watched.

límite nm ❶ limit ▷ el límite de velocidad the speed limit; **fecha límite** deadline ❷ boundary

limón (pl limones) nm lemon

limonada nf lemonade

limosna nf **pedir limosna** to beg

limpiaparabrisas (pl limpiaparabrisas) nm windscreen wiper

limpiar vb [**25**] ❶ to clean ❷ to wipe

limpieza nf cleaning ▷ Yo hago la limpieza los sábados. I do the cleaning on Saturdays.; **limpieza en seco** dry cleaning

limpio, -a adj clean ▷ El baño está muy limpio. The bathroom's very clean.

lindo, -a adj ❶ pretty ❷ (LatAm) nice ▷ un día muy lindo a very nice day

línea nf line; **Vaya en línea recta.** Go straight ahead.; **una línea aérea** an airline; **en línea** online

lino nm linen

linterna nf torch

lío nm **En mi mesa hay un lío enorme de papeles.** My desk is in a real muddle with all these papers.; **hacerse un lío** to get

muddled up ▷ Se hizo un lío con tantos nombres. He got muddled up with all the names.; **Esta ecuación es un lío.** This equation is a real headache.; **Si sigues así te vas a meter en un lío.** If you carry on like that you'll get yourself into a real mess.

liquidación nf sale

líquido adj, nm liquid

Lisboa nf Lisbon

liso, -a adj ❶ (surface) smooth ❷ (hair) straight ❸ (colour) plain

lista nf list ▷ la lista de espera the waiting list; **pasar lista** to call the register; **la lista de correo** mailing list

listo, -a adj ❶ clever ▷ Es una chica muy lista. She's a very clever girl. ❷ ready ▷ ¿Estás listo? Are you ready?

litera nf ❶ bunk bed ❷ berth

literatura nf literature

litro nm litre

liviano, -a adj light

llaga nf sore

llama nf flame

llamada nf call; **hacer una llamada telefónica** to make a phone call

llamar vb [**25**] ❶ to call ▷ Me llamaron mentiroso. They called me a liar. ▷ llamar a la policía to call the police ❷ to ring ❸ to knock; **llamar por teléfono a alguien** to phone somebody; **¿Cómo te llamas?** What's your name?; **Me llamo Adela.** My name's Adela.

llano, -a adj flat

llave nf ① key; **Echa la llave de la puerta cuando salgas.** Lock the door when you go out.; **una llave inglesa** a spanner

> Word for word, **llave inglesa** means 'English key'.

② (LatAm) tap

llavero nm keyring

llegada nf ① (of train, plane, passengers) arrival ② (of race) finish

llegar vb [37] ① to get to; **¿A qué hora llegaste a casa?** What time did you get home? ② to arrive; **No llegues tarde.** Don't be late.; **Con tres euros no me llega.** Three euros isn't enough. ③ to reach; **El agua me llegaba hasta las rodillas.** The water came up to my knees.; **llegar a ser** to become

llenar vb [25] (container) to fill

lleno, -a adj full ▷ **El restaurante estaba lleno de gente.** The restaurant was full of people.

llevar vb [25] ① to take ▷ **¿Llevas los vasos a la cocina?** Can you take the glasses to the kitchen? ▷ **No llevará mucho tiempo.** It won't take long. ② to wear ▷ **María llevaba un abrigo muy bonito.** María was wearing a nice coat. ③ to give a lift ▷ **Sofía nos llevó a casa.** Sofía gave us a lift home. ④ to carry ▷ **Yo te llevo la maleta.** I'll carry your case. ; **Solo llevo diez euros.** I've only got ten euros on me.; **¿Cuánto tiempo llevas aquí?** How long have you been here?; **Llevo horas esperando aquí.** I've been waiting here for hours.; **Mi hermana**

mayor me lleva ocho años. My elder sister is eight years older than me.; **llevarse algo** to take something ▷ **Llévatelo.** Take it with you. ▷ **¿Le gusta? — Sí, me lo llevo.** Do you like it? — Yes, I'll take it!; **Me llevo bien con mi hermano.** I get on well with my brother.; **Nos llevamos muy mal.** We get on very badly.

llorar vb [25] to cry

llover vb [31] to rain; **llover a cántaros** to pour down

lloviznar vb [25] to drizzle

llueve vb see **llover**

lluvia nf rain ▷ **bajo la lluvia** in the rain; **la lluvia ácida** acid rain

lluvioso, -a adj rainy

lo art **Lo peor fue que no pudimos entrar.** The worst thing was we couldn't get in.; **No me gusta lo picante.** I don't like spicy things.; **Pon en mi habitación lo de Pedro.** Put Pedro's things in my room.; **Lo mío son las matemáticas.** Maths is my thing.; **Lo de vender la casa no me parece bien.** I don't like this idea of selling the house.; **Olvida lo de ayer.** Forget what happened yesterday.; **¡No sabes lo aburrido que es!** You don't know how boring he is!; **lo que (1)** what ▷ **Lo que más me gusta es nadar.** What I like most is swimming. **(2)** whatever ▷ **Ponte lo que quieras.** Wear whatever you like.; **más de lo que** more than ▷ **Cuesta más de lo que crees.** It costs more than you think.

▶ pron ❶ him ▷ No lo conozco. I don't know him.; **Lo han despedido.** He's been sacked. ❷ you

lo can also refer to **usted**, the formal form meaning "you"
▷ Yo a usted lo conozco. I know you.
❸ it ▷ No lo veo. I can't see it. ▷ Voy a pensarlo. I'll think about it.; **No lo sabía.** I didn't know.; **No parece lista pero lo es.** She doesn't seem clever but she is.

lobo nm wolf

loca nf madwoman

local adj local ▷ un producto local a local product
▶ nm premises pl

localidad nf ❶ town ❷ (in theatre) seat

localizar vb [13] ❶ to reach ▷ Me puedes localizar en este teléfono. You can reach me at this number. ❷ to locate ▷ No han conseguido localizar a las víctimas. They have been unable to locate the victims.

loción (pl lociones) nf lotion

loco, -a adj ❶ mad ▷ volverse loco to go mad ❷ crazy ▷ ¿Estás loco? Are you crazy? ▷ Está loco con su moto nueva. He's crazy about his new motorbike.; **volver loco a alguien** to drive somebody mad; **Me vuelve loco el marisco.** I'm crazy about seafood.
▶ nm madman

locura nf madness ▷ Es una locura ir solo. It's madness to go on your own.

locutor, a nm/f newsreader

lógico, -a adj ❶ logical ❷ natural; **Es lógico que no quiera venir.** It's

only natural he doesn't want to come.

lograr vb [25] ❶ to get ▷ Lograron lo que se proponían. They got what they wanted. ❷ to manage ▷ Logré que me concediera una entrevista. I managed to get an interview with him.

lombriz (pl lombrices) nf worm

lomo nm ❶ back ❷ loin ❸ spine

lona nf canvas

loncha nf slice

Londres nm London

longitud nf length; **Tiene tres metros de longitud.** It's three metres long.

loro nm parrot

los art ▷ los barcos the boats; **los de las bufandas rojas** the people in the red scarves

Look how the English possessive corresponds to the article in the following.

▷ Se lavaron los pies en el río. They washed their feet in the river. ▷ Abrochaos los abrigos. Button up your coats. ▷ Me gustan sus cuadros, pero prefiero los de Ana. I like his paintings, but I prefer Ana's.

The plural article is not always translated, as, for example, when making generalizations.

▷ No me gustan los melocotones. I don't like peaches.; **Solo vienen los lunes.** They only come on Mondays.

▶ pron ❶ them ▷ Los vi por la calle. I saw them in the street.; **Los han despedido.** They've been sacked.

❷ you
  los can also refer to **ustedes**, the formal form meaning **you**.
  ▷ *Los acompaño hasta la puerta, señores.* I'll see you to the door, gentlemen.

lotería *nf* lottery ▷ *Le tocó la lotería.* He won the lottery.

lucha *nf* fight; **lucha libre** wrestling
  Word for word, **lucha libre** means 'free fight'.

luchar *vb* [**25**] to fight

lucir *vb* [**9**] to shine

luego *adv* ❶ then ▷ *Primero se puso de pie y luego habló.* First he stood up and then he spoke. ❷ later ▷ *Mi mujer viene luego.* My wife's coming later.; **desde luego** of course; **¡Hasta luego!** See you! ❸ (*Chile, Mex*) soon
  ▶ *conj* therefore

lugar *nm* place ▷ *Este lugar es muy bonito.* This is a lovely place.; **Llegó en último lugar.** He came last.; **en lugar de** instead of; **tener lugar** to take place

lujo *nm* luxury; **un coche de lujo** a luxury car

lujoso, -a *adj* luxurious

luna *nf* ❶ moon ❷ window pane ❸ window; **la luna de miel** honeymoon

lunar *nm* mole; **una corbata de lunares** a spotted tie

lunes (*pl* **lunes**) *nm* Monday ▷ *el lunes pasado* last Monday ▷ *el lunes que viene* next Monday ▷ *Jugamos los lunes.* We play on Mondays.

lupa *nf* magnifying glass

luto *nm* **estar de luto por alguien** to be in mourning for somebody

Luxemburgo *nm* Luxembourg

luz (*pl* **luces**) *nf* ❶ light ▷ *Enciende la luz, por favor.* Put on the light please. ❷ electricity ▷ *No hay luz en todo el edificio.* There's no electricity in the whole building.; **dar a luz** to give birth

m

macarrones *nmpl* macaroni *sg*

macedonia *nf* fruit salad

maceta *nf* flowerpot

machacar *vb* [48] ❶ to crush ❷ to thrash

macho *adj, nm* male ▷ *un conejo macho* a male rabbit

madera *nf* wood; **un juguete de madera** a wooden toy; **Tiene madera de profesor.** He's got the makings of a teacher.

madrastra *nf* stepmother

madre *nf* mother; **¡Madre mía!** Goodness!

Madrid *nm* Madrid

madrileño, -a *adj* from Madrid ▷ *Soy madrileño.* I'm from Madrid.

madrina *nf* ❶ godmother ❷ matron of honour

madrugada *nf* early morning; **levantarse de madrugada (1)** to get up early **(2)** to get up at daybreak; **a las 4 de la madrugada** at 4 o'clock in the morning

madrugar *vb* [37] to get up early

maduro, -a *adj* ❶ mature ❷ ripe

maestro, -a *nm/f* teacher; **un maestro de escuela** a schoolteacher

magia *nf* magic

mágico, -a *adj* magic ▷ *una varita mágica* a magic wand

magisterio *nm* **Estudia magisterio.** He's training to be a teacher.

magnífico, -a *adj* splendid

mago, -a *nm/f* magician; **los Reyes Magos** the Three Wise Men

maíz (*pl* **maíces**) *nm* ❶ maize ❷ sweetcorn; **una mazorca de maíz** a corn cob

majestad *nf* **Su Majestad (1)** His Majesty **(2)** Her Majesty

majo, -a *adj* ❶ nice ❷ pretty

mal *adj* = **malo**
▷ *adv* ❶ badly; **Esta habitación huele mal.** This room smells bad.; **Lo pasé muy mal.** I had a very bad time.; **Me entendió mal.** He misunderstood me.; **hablar mal de alguien** to speak ill of someone ❷ wrong ▷ *Han escrito mal mi apellido.* They've spelt my surname wrong.
▷ *nm* evil ▷ *el bien y el mal* good and evil

mala *nf* **la mala de la película** the villain in the film

malcriado, -a adj badly brought up

maldito, -a adj damned; **¡Maldita sea!** Damn it!

maleducado, -a adj bad-mannered

malentendido nm misunderstanding

malestar nm discomfort

maleta nf suitcase; **hacer la maleta** to pack

maletero nm boot

maletín (pl **maletines**) nm briefcase

malgastar vb [25] to waste

malhumorado, -a adj bad-tempered; **Hoy parece malhumorado.** He appears to be in a bad mood today.

malicia nf ❶ malice ❷ mischief

malicioso, -a adj malicious

malla nf ❶ mesh ❷ leotard; **una malla de baño** (River Plate) a swimsuit; **mallas** (1) tights (2) leggings

Mallorca nf Majorca

malo, -a adj

▌ Use **mal** before a masculine noun.

❶ bad ▷ un mal día a bad day ▷ Este programa es muy malo. This is a very bad programme. ▷ Soy muy mala para las matemáticas. I'm very bad at maths.; **Hace malo.** The weather's bad.; **Lo malo es que ...** The trouble is that ... ❷ naughty ▷ ¿Por qué eres tan malo? Why are you so naughty? ❸ off ▷ Esta carne está mala. This meat's off. ❹ ill ▷ Mi hija está mala. My daughter's ill. ▷ Se puso malo después de comer. He started to feel ill after lunch.

maltratar vb [25] to ill-treat; **los niños maltratados** abused children

malvado, -a adj evil

mama nf ❶ breast ❷ mum

mamá (pl **mamás**) nf mum ▷ tu mamá your mum ▷ ¡Hola, mamá! Hi Mum!

mamífero nm mammal

manantial nm (of water) spring

mancha nf stain

manchar vb [25] to stain; **mancharse** to get dirty; **Me he manchado el vestido de tinta.** I've got ink stains on my dress.

mandar vb [25] ❶ to order; **Nos mandó callar.** He told us to be quiet.; **Aquí mando yo.** I'm the boss here. ❷ to send ▷ Se lo mandaremos por correo. We'll send it to you by post. ▷ Me mandaron a hacer un recado. They sent me on an errand.; **mandar llamar a alguien** (LatAm) to send for someone; **mandar a arreglar algo** (LatAm) to have something repaired; **¿Mande?** (Mex) Pardon?

mandarina nf tangerine

mandíbula nf jaw

mando nm un alto mando a high-ranking officer; **Está al mando del proyecto.** He's in charge of the project.; **el mando a distancia** the remote control; **los mandos** the controls

manecilla nf hand ▷ las manecillas del reloj the hands of the clock

manejable adj ❶ manoeuvrable ❷ easy to use

manejar vb [25] ❶ (machine) to operate ❷ (business) to manage ❸ (LatAm) to drive; **un examen de manejar** (LatAm) a driving test

manera nf way ▷ Lo hice a mi manera. I did it my way.; **de todas maneras** anyway; **No hay manera de convencerla.** There's nothing one can do to convince her.; **de manera que (1)** so ▷ No has hecho los deberes, de manera que no hay tele. You haven't done your homework so there's no TV. **(2)** so that ▷ Lo puse de manera que pudieran verlo. I put it so that they could see it.; **¡De ninguna manera!** Certainly not!

manga nf sleeve; **de manga corta** short-sleeved; **de manga larga** long-sleeved

mango nm ❶ handle ❷ mango

manguera nf hose

manía nf Tiene la manía de repetir todo lo que digo. He has an irritating habit of repeating everything I say.; **El profesor me tiene manía.** (informal) The teacher has it in for me.

maniático, -a adj Es una maniática del orden. She's obsessed with keeping things tidy.

manifestación (pl **manifestaciones**) nf demonstration

manifestante nmf demonstrator

manifestarse vb [39] to demonstrate

manillar nm handlebars pl

maniobra nf manoeuvre

manipular vb [25] ❶ (food) to handle ❷ (opinion, person) to manipulate

maniquí (pl **maniquíes**) nmf model
▶ nm dummy

manivela nf crank

mano nf hand ▷ Dame la mano. Give me your hand.; **tener algo a mano** to have something to hand; **hecho a mano** handmade; **de segunda mano** secondhand; **echar una mano** to lend a hand; **estrechar la mano a alguien** to shake somebody's hand; **la mano de obra** labour; **una mano de pintura** a coat of paint

> Word for word, **mano de obra** means 'hand of work'.

manojo nm bunch

manopla nf mitten; **una manopla de cocina** an oven glove

manso, -a adj tame

manta nf blanket

manteca nf (River Plate) butter; **manteca de cerdo** lard

mantel nm tablecloth

mantener vb [53] ❶ to keep ▷ mantener la calma to keep calm ❷ to support ▷ Mantiene a su familia. He supports his family.; **mantener una conversación** to have a conversation; **mantenerse** to support oneself; **mantenerse en forma** to keep fit

mantenimiento nm maintenance; **ejercicios de mantenimiento** keep-fit exercises

mantequilla nf butter

mantuve vb see **mantener**

manual adj, nm manual

manubrio nm (LatAm) handlebars pl

manuscrito nm manuscript

manzana nf ❶ apple ❷ (of buildings) block

manzano nm apple tree

mañana nf morning ▷ Llegó a las nueve de la mañana. He arrived at nine o'clock in the morning.; **Por la mañana voy al gimnasio.** In the mornings I go to the gym.; **a media mañana** mid-morning ▶ adv tomorrow; **pasado mañana** the day after tomorrow; **mañana por la mañana** tomorrow morning; **mañana por la noche** tomorrow night

mapa nm map ▷ un mapa de carreteras a road map

maqueta nf model

maquillaje nm make-up sg

maquillarse vb [25] to put one's make-up on

máquina nf machine ▷ una máquina de coser a sewing machine ▷ una máquina expendedora a vending machine ▷ una máquina tragaperras a fruit machine; **una máquina de afeitar** an electric razor; **escrito a máquina** typed; **una máquina fotográfica** a camera

maquinilla nf razor ▷ una maquinilla eléctrica an electric razor

mar nm sea; **por mar** by sea

    Note that in certain idiomatic phrases, **mar** is feminine.

en alta mar on the high seas; **Lo hizo de mar de bien.** He did it really well.

maratón (pl maratones) nm marathon

maravilla nf ¡Qué maravilla de casa! What a wonderful house!; **ser una maravilla** to be wonderful; **Se llevan de maravilla.** They get on wonderfully well together.

maravilloso, -a adj marvellous

marca nf ❶ mark ▷ Había marcas de neumático en la arena. There were tyre marks in the sand. ❷ make ▷ ¿De qué marca es tu coche? What make's your car? ❸ brand; **la ropa de marca** designer clothes

marcador nm ❶ scoreboard ❷ (for webpage) bookmark

marcar vb [48] ❶ to mark ❹ to brand ❸ (number) to dial ❹ (goal) to score ❺ (hair) to set; **Mi reloj marca las 2.** It's 2 o'clock according to my watch.; **marcar algo con una equis** to put a cross on something

marcha nf ❶ departure ❷ gear ▷ cambiar de marcha to change gear; **salir de marcha** to go out on the town; **a toda marcha** at full speed; **estar en marcha** (1) to be running (2) to be underway; **dar marcha atrás** to reverse; **No te subas nunca a un tren en marcha.** Never get onto a moving train.

marcharse vb [25] to leave

marco nm frame

marea nf tide; **una marea negra** an oil slick

Word for word, **marea negra** means 'black tide'.

mareado, -a adj Estoy mareado. **(1)** I feel dizzy. **(2)** I feel sick.

marear vb [25] to make...feel sick; **marearse (1)** to get dizzy **(2)** to get seasick **(3)** to get carsick; **¡No me marees!** Stop going on at me!

mareo nm ❶ seasickness ❷ car sickness; **Le dio un mareo a causa del calor.** The heat made her feel ill.

marfil nm ivory

margarina nf margarine

margarita nf daisy

margen (pl **márgenes**) nm margin

marido nm husband

marinero nm sailor

mariposa nf butterfly

marisco nm shellfish ▷ No me gusta el marisco. I don't like shellfish.

mármol nm marble

marrón (pl **marrones**) adj brown ▷ un traje marrón a brown suit

Marruecos nm Morocco

martes (pl **martes**) nm Tuesday ▷ el martes pasado last Tuesday ▷ el martes que viene next Tuesday

martillo nm hammer

marzo nm March ▷ en marzo in March

más adj, adv more ▷ Ahora salgo más. I go out more these days. **Últimamente nos vemos más.** We've been seeing more of each other lately. **¿Quieres más?** Would you like some more?; **No tengo más dinero.** I haven't got any more money.

In comparisons **más** is sometimes translated by -er on the end of a short English adjective or adverb.
▷ barato – más barato cheap – cheaper ▷ joven – más joven young – younger ▷ largo – más largo long – longer ▷ grande – más grande big – bigger ▷ contento – más contento happy – happier ▷ rápido – más rápido fast – faster ▷ temprano – más temprano early – earlier; **lejos – más lejos** far – further

In other comparisons **más** is translated by **more**.
▷ hermoso – más hermoso beautiful – more beautiful ▷ guapo – más guapo handsome – more handsome ▷ deprisa – más deprisa quickly – more quickly; **Es más grande que el tuyo.** It's bigger than yours.; **Corre más rápido que yo.** He runs faster than I do.; **Trabaja más que yo.** He works harder than I do.; **más de mil libros** more than a thousand books; **No tiene más de dieciséis años.** He isn't more than sixteen.; **más de lo que yo creía** more than I thought

the ... -est and **the most ...** are used to translate the Spanish superlative construction.
▷ el bolígrafo más barato the cheapest pen ▷ el niño más joven the youngest child ▷ el coche más grande the biggest car ▷ la persona más feliz the happiest person ▷ el más inteligente de todos the most

intelligent of all of them; **su película más innovadora** his most innovative film; **Paco es el que come más.** Paco's the one who eats the most.; **Fue el que más trabajó.** He was the one who worked the hardest.; **el punto más lejano** the furthest point; **¿Qué más?** What else?; **¡Qué perro más sucio!** What a filthy dog!; **Tenemos uno de más.** We have one too many.; **Por más que estudio no apruebo.** However hard I study I don't pass.; **más o menos** more or less; **2 más 2 son 4** 2 and 2 are 4; **14 más 20 menos 12 es igual a 22** 14 plus 20 minus 12 equals 22

masa nf ❶ dough ▷ *la masa de pan* bread dough ❷ mass; **las masas** the masses; **en masa (1)** mass ▷ *la producción en masa* mass production **(2)** en masse ▷ *Fueron en masa a recibir al futbolista.* They went en masse to greet the footballer.

masaje nm massage

máscara nf mask

mascota nf pet

masculino, -a adj ❶ (body, sex) male ❷ (team, sport) men's ▷ *la ropa masculina* men's clothing ❸ (voice, pronoun) masculine

masticar vb [48] to chew

matar vb [25] to kill; **matarse** to be killed

matasellos (pl matasellos) nm postmark

mate adj matt
  ▶ nm ❶ checkmate ❷ maté

matemáticas nfpl mathematics sg

materia nf ❶ matter ▷ *materia orgánica* organic matter ❷ material ▷ *la materia prima* raw material ❸ subject ▷ *Es un experto en la materia.* He's an expert on the subject.

material adj, nm material

materno, -a adj maternal; **mi lengua materna** my mother tongue

matiz (pl matices) nm shade

matorral nm bushes pl

matrícula nf registration; **la matrícula del coche (1)** the registration number of the car **(2)** the number plate of the car

matricular vb [25] to register; **matricularse** to enrol

matrimonio nm ❶ marriage ▷ *El matrimonio se celebró en la iglesia del pueblo.* The marriage took place in the village church. ❷ couple ▷ *Eran un matrimonio feliz.* They were a happy couple.

maullar vb [25] to miaow

máximo, -a adj maximum
  ▶ nm maximum; **como máximo (1)** at the most **(2)** at the latest

mayo nm May ▷ *en mayo* in May

mayonesa nf mayonnaise

mayor adj, pron ❶ older ▷ *Paco es mayor que Nacho.* Paco is older than Nacho. ▷ *Es tres años mayor que yo.* He is three years older than me.; **el hermano mayor (1)** the older brother **(2)** the oldest brother; **Soy el mayor. (1)** I'm the older. **(2)** I'm the oldest.; **Nuestros hijos**

ya son mayores. Our children are grown-up now.; **la gente mayor** elderly people ❷ bigger ▷ *Necesitamos una casa mayor.* We need a bigger house.; **la mayor iglesia del mundo** the biggest church in the world ▸ **un mayor de edad** an adult; **los mayores** grown-ups

mayoría *nf* majority; **La mayoría de los estudiantes son pobres.** Most students are poor.; **la mayoría de nosotros** most of us

mayúscula *nf* capital letter ▷ *Empieza cada frase con mayúscula.* Start each sentence with a capital letter.

mazapán (*pl* mazapanes) *nm* marzipan

me *pron* ❶ me ▷ *Me quiere.* He loves me. ▷ *Me regaló una pulsera.* He gave me a bracelet.; **Me lo dio.** He gave it to me.; **¿Me echas esta carta?** Will you post this letter for me? ❷ myself ▷ *No me hice daño.* I didn't hurt myself.; **me dije a mí mismo** I said to myself; **Me duelen los pies.** My feet hurt.; **Me puse el abrigo.** I put my coat on.

mecánica *nf* ❶ mechanic ❷ mechanics *sg*

mecánico, -a *adj* mechanical ▸ *nm* mechanic

mecanismo *nm* mechanism

mecanografía *nf* typing

mecha *nf* ❶ wick ❷ fuse

mechero *nm* cigarette lighter

medalla *nf* medal

media *nf* ❶ average ▷ *Trabajo una media de seis horas diarias.* I work an

average of six hours a day. ❷ (*LatAm*) sock; **medias** (1) stockings (2) tights; **medias bombachas** (*River Plate*) tights; **a las cuatro y media** at half past four

mediados *npl* **a mediados de** around the middle of

mediano, -a *adj* medium ▷ *de mediana estatura* of medium height; **de tamaño mediano** medium-sized; **el hijo mediano** the middle son

medianoche *nf* midnight ▷ *a medianoche* at midnight

medicamento *nm* medicine

medicina *nf* medicine

médico, -a *nm/f* doctor ▷ *Quiere ser médica.* She wants to be a doctor. ▷ *el médico de cabecera* the family doctor; **ir al médico** to go to the doctor's

medida *nf* measure ▷ *tomar medidas contra la inflación* to take measures against inflation; **El sastre le tomó las medidas.** The tailor took his measurements.; **un traje a medida** a made-to-measure suit; **a medida que ...** as ... ▷ *Saludaba a los invitados a medida que iban llegando.* He greeted the guests as they arrived.

medio, -a *adj* ❶ half ▷ *medio litro* half a litre ▷ *media hora* half an hour ▷ *una hora y media* an hour and a half; **Son las ocho y media.** It's half past eight. ❷ average ▷ *la temperatura media* the average temperature ▸ *adv* half

▶ nm ❶ middle ▷ Está en el medio.
It's in the middle.; **en medio de** in
the middle of ❷ means ▷ un medio
de transporte a means of transport;
por medio de by means of;
medios ▷ por medios
pacíficos by peaceful means; **los
medios de comunicación** the
media; **el medio ambiente** the
environment

mediodía nm **al mediodía (1)** at
midday **(2)** at lunchtime

medir vb **[38]** to measure ▷ ¿Has
medido la ventana? Have you
measured the window?; **¿Cuánto
mides? —** Mido 1.50 m. How tall
are you? — I'm 1.5 m tall.; **¿Cuánto
mide esta habitación? —** Mide
3 m por 4. How big is this room?
— It measures 3 m by 4.

Mediterráneo nm the
Mediterranean

mediterráneo, -a adj
Mediterranean

medusa nf jellyfish

mega nm (informal) meg

mejilla nf cheek

mejillón (pl mejillones) nm mussel

mejor adj ❶ better ▷ Este es mejor
que el otro. This one is better than
the other one.; **Es el mejor de los
dos.** He's the better of the two.
❷ best ▷ mi mejor amiga my best
friend ▷ el mejor de la clase the best
in the class ▷ Es el mejor de todos.
He's the best of the lot.

▶ adv ❶ better ▷ La conozco mejor
que tú. I know her better than you
do. ❷ best ▷ ¿Quién lo hace mejor?
Who does it best?; **a lo mejor**

probably; **Mejor nos vamos.** We
had better go.

mejora nf improvement

mejorar vb **[25]** to improve; **¡Que
te mejores!** Get well soon!

mejoría nf improvement

melena nf ❶ long hair ▷ Lleva una
melena rubia. She has long blond
hair. ❷ (lion's) mane

mellizo, -a adj, nm/f twin ▷ Son
mellizos. They're twins.

melocotón (pl melocotones) nm
peach

melodía nf tune

melón (pl melones) nm melon

memoria nf memory; **aprender
algo de memoria** to learn
something by heart

memorizar vb **[13]** to memorize

mencionar vb **[25]** to mention

mendigo, -a nm/f beggar

menor adj, pron ❶ younger ▷ Es tres
años menor que yo. He's three years
younger than me. ▷ Juanito es
menor que Pepe. Juanito is younger
than Pepe.; **el hermano menor
(1)** the younger brother **(2)** the
youngest brother; **Yo soy el
menor. (1)** I'm the younger. **(2)** I'm
the youngest. ❷ smaller ▷ una talla
menor a smaller size; **No tiene la
menor importancia.** It's not in
the least important.

▶ nmf ❶ un menor de edad a minor;
los menores the under-18s

Menorca nf Minorca

menos adj, adv ❶ less ▷ Fernando
está menos deprimido. Fernando is
less depressed. ▷ Ahora salgo
menos. I go out less these days.;

Últimamente nos vemos menos. We've been seeing less of each other recently.

menos is translated by **fewer** rather than **less** in comparisons involving plural nouns.

▷ *menos harina* less flour ▷ *menos gatos* fewer cats ▷ *menos gente* fewer people; **menos...que** less... than ▷ *Me gusta menos que el otro.* I like it less than the other one. ▷ *Lo hizo menos cuidadosamente que ayer.* He did it less carefully than yesterday.; **Trabaja menos que yo.** He doesn't work as hard as I do.; **menos de 50 cajas** fewer than 50 boxes; **Tiene menos de dieciocho años.** He's under eighteen. ❷ least ▷ *el chico menos desobediente de la clase* the least disobedient boy in the class; **Fue el que menos trabajó.** He was the one who worked the least hard.

menos is translated by **fewest** rather than **least** in superlative constructions involving plural nouns.

▷ *el método que lleva menos tiempo* the method which takes the least time ▷ *el examen con menos errores* the exam paper with the fewest mistakes; **No quiero verle y menos visitarle.** I don't want to see him, let alone visit him.; **¡Menos mal!** Thank goodness!; **al menos** at least; **por lo menos** at least; **¡Ni mucho menos!** No way!

▷ *prep* except ▷ *todos menos él* everyone except him; **5 menos 2 son tres** 5 minus 2 is three; **a menos que** unless

mensaje *nm* message; **un mensaje de texto** a text message; **el envío de mensajes con foto** picture messaging

mensajero, -a *nm/f* messenger

mensual *adj* monthly; **50 dólares mensuales** 50 dollars a month

menta *nf* mint ▷ *un caramelo de menta* a mint sweet

mentalidad *nf* mentality; **Tiene una mentalidad muy abierta.** He has a very open mind.

mente *nf* mind ▷ *No me lo puedo quitar de la mente.* I can't get it out of my mind.; **tener en mente hacer algo** to be thinking of doing something

mentir *vb* [**51**] to lie

mentira *nf* lie ▷ *No digas mentiras.* Don't tell lies.; **Parece mentira que aún no te haya pagado.** It's incredible that he still hasn't paid you.; **una pistola de mentira** a toy pistol

mentiroso, -a *nm/f* liar

menú *nm* (*pl* menús) menu; **el menú del día** the set meal

menudo, -a *adj* slight ▷ *Es una chica muy menuda.* She's a very slight girl.; **¡Menudo lío!** What a mess!; **a menudo** often

meñique *nm* little finger

mercado *nm* market

mercancía *nf* commodity

mercería *nf* haberdasher's

a
b
c
d
e
f
g
h
i
j
k
l
m
n
ñ
o
p
q
r
s
t
u
v
w
x
y
z

merecer vb [12] to deserve; **merece la pena** it's worthwhile

merendar vb [39] to have tea

merengue nm meringue

merienda nf tea

mérito nm merit

merluza nf hake

mermelada nf jam

mero adv (Mex) almost

mes (pl meses) nm month ▷ el mes que viene next month ▷ a final de mes at the end of the month

mesa nf table; **poner la mesa** to lay the table; **quitar la mesa** to clear the table

mesera nf (LatAm) waitress

mesero nm (LatAm) waiter

mesilla nf una mesilla de noche a bedside table

meta nf ❶ aim ❷ finishing line ❸ goal

metal nm metal

metálico, -a adj metal ▷ un objeto metálico a metal object; **en metálico** in cash

> Word for word, **en metálico** means 'in metallic'.

meter vb [8] to put; **meterse en** to go into; **meterse en política** to go into politics; **No te metas donde no te llaman.** Don't poke your nose in where it doesn't belong.; **meterse con alguien** to pick on somebody

método nm method

metro nm ❶ underground ▷ coger el metro to take the underground ❷ metre ▷ Mide tres metros de largo. It's three metres long.

mexicano, -a adj, nm/f Mexican

México nm Mexico

mezcla nf mixture

mezclar vb [25] to mix; **mezclarse en algo** to get mixed up in something

mezquino, -a adj mean

mezquita nf mosque

mi (pl mis) adj my ▷ mis hermanas my sisters

mí pron me ▷ para mí for me; **Para mí que ...** I think that ...; **Por mí no hay problema.** There's no problem as far as I'm concerned.

microbio nm microbe

micrófono nm microphone

microondas (pl microondas) nm microwave ▷ un horno microondas a microwave oven

microscopio nm microscope

midiendo vb see **medir**

miedo nm fear ▷ el miedo a la oscuridad fear of the dark; **tener miedo** to be afraid ▷ Le tenía miedo a su padre. He was afraid of his father. ▷ Tenemos miedo de que nos ataquen. We're afraid that they may attack us.; **dar miedo a** to scare ▷ Me daba miedo hacerlo. I was scared of doing it.; **pasarlo de miedo** (informal) to have a fantastic time

miedoso, -a adj ¡No seas tan miedoso! Don't be such a coward!; **Mi hijo es muy miedoso.** My son gets frightened very easily.

miel nf honey

miembro nm limb
▶ nm/f member

mientras adv, conj while; **Seguiré conduciendo mientras pueda.** I'll carry on driving for as long as

I can.; **mientras que** while;
mientras tanto meanwhile

miércoles (pl **miércoles**) nm
Wednesday ▷ el miércoles pasado
last Wednesday ▷ el miércoles que
viene next Wednesday

miga nf crumb; **hacer buenas
migas** (informal) to hit it off
Word for word, **hacer buenas
migas** means 'to make good
breadcrumbs'.

mil adj, pron thousand ▷ miles de
personas thousands of people
▷ dos mil euros two thousand
euros; **miles de veces** hundreds
of times

milagro nm miracle ▷ No hos hemos
matado de milagro. It was a miracle
we weren't killed.

mili nf military service

milímetro nm millimetre

militar nmf soldier; **los militares**
the military
▶ adj military

milla nf mile

millón (pl **millones**) nm million
▷ millones de personas millions of
people; **mil millones** a billion

millonario, -a nm/f millionaire

mimado, -a adj spoiled

mina nf mine

mineral adj, nm mineral

minero, -a nm/f miner

miniatura nf miniature; **una casa
en miniatura** a miniature house

minifalda nf miniskirt

mínimo, -a adj minimum ▷ el
salario mínimo the minimum wage;
No tienes ni la más mínima idea.
You haven't the faintest idea.

▶ nm minimum ▷ un mínimo de
10 euros a minimum of 10 euros;
lo mínimo que puede hacer the
least he can do; **Como mínimo
podrías haber llamado.** You could
at least have called.

ministerio nm ministry

ministro, -a nm/f minister

minoría nf minority

minucioso, -a adj thorough

minúscula nf small letter

minusválida nf disabled woman

minusválido nm disabled man;
los minusválidos people with
disabilities

minuto nm minute ▷ Espera un
minuto. Wait a minute.

mío, -a adj, pron mine ▷ Estos
caballos son míos. These horses are
mine. ▷ ¿De quién es esta bufanda?
— Es mía. Whose scarf is this? — It's
mine. ▷ El mío está en el armario.
Mine's in the cupboard. ▷ Este es el
mío. This one's mine.; **un amigo
mío** a friend of mine

miope adj short-sighted

mirada nf look ▷ con una mirada de
odio with a look of hatred; **echar
una mirada a algo** to have a look
at something

mirar vb [25] to look; **mirar algo** to
look at something; **mirar por la
ventana** to look out of the
window; **mirar algo fijamente** to
stare at something; **¡Mira que es
tonto!** What an idiot!; **mirarse al
espejo** to look at oneself in the
mirror; **Se miraron asombrados.**
They looked at each other in
amazement.

a
b
c
d
e
f
g
h
i
j
k
l
m
n
ñ
o
p
q
r
s
t
u
v
w
x
y
z

misa nf mass ▷ *la misa del gallo* midnight mass ▷ *ir a misa* to go to mass

miseria nf ❶ poverty ❷ pittance

misión (pl **misiones**) nf mission

misionero, -a nm/f missionary

mismo, -a adj same ▷ *Nos gustan los mismos libros.* We like the same books.; **yo mismo** myself ▷ *Lo hice yo mismo.* I did it myself.
▶ adv **Hoy mismo le escribiré.** I'll write to him today.; **Nos podemos encontrar aquí mismo.** We can meet right here.; **enfrente mismo del colegio** right opposite the school
▶ pron **lo mismo** the same ▷ *Yo tomaré lo mismo.* I'll have the same.; **Da lo mismo.** It doesn't matter.; **No ha llamado pero lo mismo viene.** He hasn't phoned but he may well come.

misterio nm mystery

misterioso, -a adj mysterious

mitad nf half ▷ *Se comió la mitad del pastel.* He ate half the cake. ▷ *más de la mitad de los trabajadores* more than half the workers; **La mitad son chicas.** Half of them are girls.; **a mitad de precio** half-price; **a mitad de camino** halfway there; **Corta el pan por la mitad.** Cut the loaf in half.

mito nm myth

mixto, -a adj mixed

mobiliario nm furniture

mochila nf rucksack

moco nm **Límpiate los mocos.** Wipe your nose.; **tener mocos** to have a runny nose

moda nf fashion; **estar de moda** to be in fashion; **pasado de moda** old-fashioned

modales nmpl manners ▷ *buenos modales* good manners

modelo adj, nmf model ▷ *una niña modelo* a model child ▷ *Quiero ser modelo.* I want to be a model.

moderado, -a adj moderate

modernizar vb [13] to modernize; **modernizarse** to get up to date

moderno, -a adj modern

modestia nf modesty

modesto, -a adj modest

modificar vb [48] to modify

modisto, -a nm/f dressmaker

modo nm way ▷ *Le gusta hacerlo todo a su modo.* She likes to do everything her own way.; **de todos modos** anyway; **de modo que** (1) so ▷ *No has hecho los deberes, de modo que no puedes salir.* You haven't done your homework so you can't go out. (2) so that ▷ *Mueve la tele de modo que todos la podamos ver.* Move the TV so that we can all see it.; **los buenos modos** good manners; **los malos modos** bad manners; **'modo de empleo'** 'instructions for use'

moho nm ❶ mould ❷ rust

mojado, -a adj wet

mojar vb [25] to get...wet ▷ *¡No mojes la alfombra!* Don't get the carpet wet!; **Moja el pan en la salsa.** Dip the bread into the sauce.; **mojarse** to get wet

molde nm mould

moler vb [33] to grind; **Estoy molido.** (informal) I'm knackered.

molestar vb [25] ❶ to bother ❷ to disturb; **molestarse** to get upset; **molestarse en hacer algo** to bother to do something

molestia nf **tomarse la molestia de hacer algo** to take the trouble to do something; **'perdonen las molestias'** 'we apologize for any inconvenience'

molesto, -a adj (noise, cough) annoying; **estar molesto** to be annoyed

molinillo nm **un molinillo de café** a coffee grinder

molino nm mill ▷ **un molino de viento** a windmill

momento nm moment ▷ *Espera un momento.* Wait a moment. ▷ **en un momento** in a moment; **en este momento** at the moment; **de un momento a otro** any moment now; **por el momento** for the moment; **Llegó el momento de irnos.** The time came for us to go.

momia nf mummy

monarca nmf monarch

monarquía nf monarchy

monasterio nm monastery

moneda nf coin ▷ **una moneda de dos euros** a two-euro coin; **la moneda extranjera** foreign currency

monedero nm purse

monitor, a nm/f instructor
▶ nm monitor

monja nf nun

monje nm monk

mono, -a adj pretty ▷ *¡Qué piso tan mono!* What a pretty flat!; *¡Qué niña tan mona!* What a sweet little girl!
▶ nm ❶ monkey ❷ overalls pl
❸ dungarees pl

monopatín (pl **monopatines**) nm skateboard

monótono, -a adj monotonous

monstruo nm monster

montaña nf mountain; **la montaña rusa** the roller coaster

Word for word, **montaña rusa** means 'Russian mountain'.

montañoso, -a adj mountainous

montar vb [25] ❶ (machinery, furniture) to assemble ❷ (business) to set up; **montar una tienda** to put up a tent; **montar a caballo** to ride a horse; **montar en bici** to ride a bike; **montarse** to get on

monte nm mountain

montón (pl **montones**) nm pile; **un montón de ...** loads of ... ▷ **un montón de gente** loads of people

monumento nm monument

moño nm bun ▷ *Mi abuela siempre lleva moño.* My grandmother always wears her hair in a bun.

moqueta nf carpet

mora nf ❶ blackberry ❷ mulberry

morado, -a adj purple ▷ **un vestido morado** a purple dress

moral adj moral
▶ nf ❶ morale; **levantar la moral a alguien** to cheer somebody up; **estar bajo de moral** to be down ❷ morals pl ▷ *No tienen moral.* They have no morals.

moraleja nf moral

morcilla nf black pudding

morder vb [33] to bite; **morderse las uñas** to bite one's nails

mordisco nm bite ▷ Dame un mordisco de tu bocadillo. Let me have a bite of your sandwich.; **dar un mordisco** to bite ▷ Me dio un mordisco. He bit me.

moreno, -a adj ❶ dark; **Es moreno.** (1) He has dark hair. (2) He is dark-skinned.; **ponerse moreno** to get brown ❷ (bread, sugar) brown

morir vb [32] to die; **morirse de hambre** to starve; **morirse de vergüenza** to die of shame; **Me muero de ganas de ir a nadar.** I'm dying to go for a swim.

mortal adj ❶ (accident, injury) fatal ❷ (enemy, danger) mortal

mosca nf fly; **por si las moscas** just in case

> Word for word, **por si las moscas** means 'for if the flies'.

mosquito nm mosquito

mostaza nf mustard

mostrador nm counter

mostrar vb [11] to show; **mostrarse amable** to be kind

mote nm nickname

motivo nm ❶ reason ▷ Dejó el trabajo por motivos personales. He left the job for personal reasons.; **sin motivo** for no reason ❷ motive ▷ ¿Cuál fue el motivo del crimen? What was the motive for the crime?

moto nf motorbike

motocicleta nf motorbike

motor nm motor

motorista nmf motorcyclist

mover vb [33] to move; **moverse** to move

móvil adj (phone) mobile
> nm ❶ mobile ❷ (for murder) motive

movimiento nm movement

moza nf girl

mozo nm ❶ youth ❷ waiter; **un mozo de estación** a porter

MP3 nm MP3 ▷ un reproductor de MP3 an MP3 player

muchacha nf ❶ girl ❷ maid

muchacho nm boy

muchedumbre nf crowd

mucho, -a adj ❶ a lot of ▷ Había mucha gente. There were a lot of people. ▷ Tiene muchas plantas. He has got a lot of plants. ❷ much ▷ No tenemos mucho tiempo. We haven't got much time. ❸ many ▷ ¿Conoces a mucha gente? Do you know many people? ▷ Muchas personas creen que ... Many people think that ...; **no hace mucho tiempo** not long ago; **Hace mucho calor.** It's very hot.; **Tengo mucho frío.** I'm very cold.; **Tengo mucha hambre.** I'm very hungry.; **Tengo mucha sed.** I'm very thirsty.

> pron ❶ a lot ▷ Tengo mucho que hacer. I've got a lot to do. ▷ ¿Cuántos había? — Muchos. How many were there? — A lot. ❷ much ▷ No tengo mucho que hacer. I haven't got much to do. ❸ many ▷ ¿Hay manzanas? — Sí, pero no muchas. Are there any apples? — Yes, but not many.; **¿Vinieron muchos?** Did many people come?; **Muchos dicen que ...** Many people say that ...

> adv ❶ very much ▷ Te quiero

mucho. I love you very much. ▷ *No me gusta mucho la carne.* I don't like meat very much. ▷ *Me gusta mucho el jazz.* I really like jazz. ❷ **a lot** ▷ *Come mucho.* He eats a lot.; **mucho más** a lot more; **mucho antes** long before; **No tardes mucho.** Don't be long.; **Como mucho leo un libro al mes.** At most I read one book a month.; **Fue, con mucho, el mejor.** He was by far the best.; **Por mucho que lo quieras no debes mimarlo.** No matter how much you love him, you shouldn't spoil him.

mudanza *nf* move

mudarse *vb* [**25**] to move; **mudarse de casa** to move house

mudo, -a *adj* with a speech impairment; **quedarse mudo de asombro** to be dumbfounded

mueble *nm* un mueble a piece of furniture; **los muebles** furniture *sg*; **seis muebles** six pieces of furniture

muela *nf* tooth; **una muela del juicio** a wisdom tooth

muelle *nm* ❶ (in mattress) spring ❷ **quay**

muelo *vb see* **moler**

muerdo *vb see* **morder**

muerta *nf* dead woman

muerte *nf* death ▷ *Lo condenaron a muerte.* He was sentenced to death.; **Nos dio un susto de muerte.** He nearly frightened us to death.; **un hotel de mala muerte** a grotty hotel

muerto *vb see* **morir**
▶ *adj* dead; **Está muerto de** cansancio. (*informal*) He's dead tired.
▶ *nm* dead man; **los muertos** the dead; **Hubo tres muertos.** Three people were killed.; **hacer el muerto** to float

muestra *nf* ❶ **sample** ❷ **sign** ▷ *dar muestras de* to show signs of ❸ **token** ▷ *Me lo regaló como muestra de afecto.* She gave it to me as a token of affection.

muestro *vb see* **mostrar**

muevo *vb see* **mover**

mujer *nf* ❶ **woman** ❷ **wife**

muleta *nf* crutch

    ● In bullfighting, the **muleta** is a
    ● special stick with a red cloth
    ● attached to it that the matador
    ● uses.

multa *nf* fine ▷ *una multa de 50 euros* a 50-euro fine; **poner una multa a alguien** to fine somebody

múltiple *adj* **múltiples** many ▷ *un sistema con múltiples inconvenientes* a system with many drawbacks

multiplicar *vb* [**48**] to multiply; **la tabla de multiplicar** the multiplication tables *pl*

multitud *nf* crowd; **multitud de** lots of

mundial *adj* ❶ (war, history) world ❷ (problem, recognition) worldwide
▶ *nm* world championship

mundo *nm* world; **todo el mundo** everybody; **No lo cambiaría por nada del mundo.** I wouldn't change it for anything in the world.

municipal *adj* ❶ (office, employee) council ❷ (tax) local ❸ (baths) public

municipio nm ❶ municipality
❷ town council

muñeca nf ❶ wrist ❷ doll

muñeco nm ❶ doll; **un muñeco de
peluche** a soft toy ❷ figure

muralla nf city wall

murciélago nm bat

murmullo nm murmur

muro nm wall

músculo nm muscle

museo nm museum; **un mueso de
arte** an art gallery

música nf ❶ music ▷ *la música pop*
pop music ❷ musician

músico nm musician

muslo nm thigh

musulmán (f **musulmana**, mpl
musulmanes) adj, nm/f Muslim

mutuo, -a adj mutual ▷ *de mutuo
acuerdo* by mutual agreement

muy adv very ▷ *muy bonito* very
pretty; **Eso es muy español.**
That's typically Spanish.; **No me
gusta por muy guapa que sea.**
However pretty she is, I still don't
like her.

nabo nm turnip

nacer vb [12] to be born ▷ *Nació en
1964.* He was born in 1964.

nacimiento nm ❶ birth ❷ crib

nación (pl **naciones**) nf nation;
las Naciones Unidas the United
Nations

nacional adj ❶ national ❷ home;
vuelos nacionales domestic
flights

nacionalidad nf nationality

nacionalismo nm nationalism

nacionalista adj, nmf
nationalist

nada pron ❶ nothing ▷ *¿Qué has
comprado? — Nada.* What have you
bought? — Nothing. ▷ *No dijo nada.*
He said nothing. ❷ anything ▷ *No
quiero nada.* I don't want anything.;
No dijo nada más. He didn't say

anything else.; **Quiero uno nada más.** I only want one, that's all.; **Encendió la tele nada más llegar.** He turned on the TV as soon as he came in.; **¡Gracias! — De nada.** Thanks! — Don't mention it.; **Se lo advertí, pero como si nada.** I warned him but he paid no attention.; **No sabe nada de español.** He knows no Spanish at all.; **No me dio nada de nada.** He gave me absolutely nothing.
▶ *adv* at all ▷ **Esto no me gusta nada.** I don't like this at all. ▷ **No está nada triste.** He isn't sad at all.

nadar *vb* [25] to swim

nadie *pron* **❶** nobody ▷ **Nadie habló.** Nobody spoke. ▷ **No había nadie.** There was nobody there.
❷ anybody ▷ **No quiere ver a nadie.** He doesn't want to see anybody.

nafta *nf* (River Plate) petrol

naipe *nm* playing card

nalgas *nfpl* buttocks

nana *nf* lullaby

naranja *adj* (colour, fruit) orange

> When **naranja** is used as an adjective, it never changes its ending.

▷ **un anorak naranja** an orange anorak
▶ *nm* (colour) orange
▶ *nf* (fruit) orange

narcotráfico *nm* drug trafficking

nariz (*pl* narices) *nf* nose; **No metas las narices en mis asuntos.** Don't poke your nose into my business.; **estar hasta las narices de algo** to be totally fed up with something

narración (*pl* narraciones) *nf* story

narrar *vb* [25] to tell

narrativa *nf* fiction

nata *nf* **❶** cream **❷** skin; **la nata líquida** single cream; **la nata montada** whipped cream

natación *nf* swimming

natal *adj* home ▷ **su pueblo natal** his home town

natillas *nfpl* custard *sg*

nato, -a *adj* **un actor nato** a born actor

natural *adj* natural ▷ **Comes mucho y es natural que estés gordo.** You eat a lot, so it's only natural you're fat.; **Es natural de Alicante.** He's from Alicante.

naturaleza *nf* nature; **Es despistado por naturaleza.** He's naturally absent-minded.

naufragio *nm* shipwreck

náuseas *nfpl* tener náuseas to feel sick

náutico, -a *adj* club náutico yacht club

navaja *nf* clasp knife; **una navaja de afeitar** a razor

Navarra *nf* Navarre

nave *nf* ship; **una nave espacial** a spaceship

navegador *nm* browser; **un navegador de Web** a web browser

navegar *vb* [37] to sail; **navegar por Internet** to surf the Net

Navidad *nf* Christmas; **¡Feliz Navidad!** Happy Christmas!

neblina *nf* mist

necesario, -a *adj* necessary ▷ **No estudié más de lo necesario.** I didn't

a b c d e f g h i j k l m n ñ o p q r s t u v w x y z

study any more than necessary.; **No es necesario que vengas.** You don't have to come.

necesidad nf ❶ need ▷ *No hay necesidad de hacerlo.* There is no need to do it. ❷ necessity; **Hizo sus necesidades.** He did his business.

necesitar vb **[25]** to need ▷ *Necesito cien euros.* I need a hundred euros.; **'Se necesita camarero'** 'Waiter wanted'

negar vb **[34]** ❶ to deny; **negar con la cabeza** to shake one's head ❷ to refuse; **Se negó a pagar la multa.** He refused to pay the fine.

negativo, -a adj negative ▶ nm negative

negociación nf negotiation

negociar vb **[25]** Su empresa **negocia con armas.** His company deals in arms.; **Los dos gobiernos están negociando un acuerdo.** The two governments are negotiating an agreement.

negocio nm business ▷ *Hemos montado un negocio de videojuegos.* We set up a video games business.; **el mundo de los negocios** the business world

negra nf black woman

negro, -a adj (colour) black ▷ *una chaqueta negra* a black jacket ▶ nm ❶ (colour) black ❷ black man

nervio nm nerve; **Me pone de los nervios.** He gets on my nerves.

nerviosismo nm Me entra **nerviosismo cuando la veo.** I get nervous when I see her.

nervioso, -a adj nervous ▷ *Me pongo muy nervioso en los exámenes.*

I get very nervous during exams.; **¡Me pone nervioso!** He gets on my nerves!

neumático nm tyre

neutral adj neutral

nevada nf snowfall

nevar vb **[39]** to snow

nevera nf refrigerator

ni conj ❶ or ▷ *No bebe ni fuma.* He doesn't drink or smoke. ❷ neither ▷ *Ella no fue, ni yo tampoco.* She didn't go and neither did I.; **ni ... ni** neither ... nor ▷ *No vinieron ni Carlos ni Sofía.* Neither Carlos nor Sofía came.; **No me gustan ni el bacalao ni el hígado.** I don't like either cod or liver.; **No compré ni uno ni otro.** I didn't buy either of them.; **Ni siquiera me saludó.** He didn't even say hello.

Nicaragua nf Nicaragua

nicaragüense adj, nmf Nicaraguan

nido nm nest

niebla nf fog; **Hay niebla.** It's foggy.

niego vb see **negar**

nieta nf granddaughter

nieto nm grandson; **los nietos** grandchildren

nieva vb see **nevar**

nieve nf snow

NIF abbr (= número de identificación fiscal)
  This is an ID number used for tax purposes in Spain.

ningún pron see **ninguno**

ninguno, -a adj, pron ❶ no ▷ *No tengo ningún interés en ir.* I have no interest in going. ❷ any ▷ *No vimos* *ninguna serpiente en el río.* We didn't see any snakes in the river. ❸ **none** ▷ *¿Cuál eliges? — Ninguno.* Which do you want? — None of them. ▷ *No me queda ninguno.* I have none left. ▷ *Ninguno de nosotros va a ir a la fiesta.* None of us are going to the party.; **No lo encuentro por ningún sitio.** I can't find it anywhere.; **ninguno de los dos** (1) neither of them ▷ *A ninguna de las dos les gusta el café.* Neither of them likes coffee. (2) either of them ▷ *No me gusta ninguno de los dos.* I don't like either of them.

niña *nf* girl

niñera *nf* nursemaid

niñez *nf* childhood

niño, -a *adj* young
▶ *nm* boy; **de niño** as a child; **los niños** children

nitrógeno *nm* nitrogen

nivel *nm* ❶ level ▷ *el nivel del agua* the water level ❷ standard; **el nivel de vida** the standard of living

no *adv* no ▷ *¿Quieres venir? — No.* Do you want to come? — No.; *¿Te gusta? — No mucho.* Do you like it? — Not really.

> Spanish verbs can be made negative by simply adding **no** while **don't**, **didn't** and so on are needed in English.

▷ *No me gusta.* I don't like it. ▷ *María no habla inglés.* María doesn't speak English. ▷ *No puedo venir esta noche.* I can't come tonight.; **No tengo tiempo.** I haven't got time.; **No debes preocuparte.** You

mustn't worry.; **No hace frío.** It isn't cold.

> Unlike in English, two negative words are often combined in Spanish.

▷ *No conozco a nadie.* I don't know anyone.

> Note the use of **¿no?** in Spanish where in English **isn't it?**, **didn't they?** and so on are used.

▷ *Esto es tuyo, ¿no?* This is yours, isn't it? ▷ *Fueron al cine, ¿no?* They went to the cinema, didn't they?; **¿Puedo salir esta noche? — ¡Que no!** Can I go out tonight? — I said no!; **los no fumadores** non-smokers

noble *adj* noble

noche *nf* night; **¡Buenas noches!** (1) Good evening! (2) Goodnight!; **esta noche** tonight; **hoy por la noche** tonight; **por la noche** at night ▷ *Estudia por la noche.* He studies at night. ▷ *el sábado por la noche* on Saturday night; **Era de noche cuando llegamos a casa.** It was night time when we got back home.; **No me gusta conducir de noche.** I don't like driving at night.

Nochebuena *nf* Christmas Eve

Nochevieja *nf* New Year's Eve

> At midnight on New Year's Eve in Spain it is traditional to eat **las uvas de la suerte** (twelve good-luck grapes) to the chimes of Madrid's **Puerta del Sol** clock, which are broadcast live.

a
b
c
d
e
f
g
h
i
j
k
l
m
n
ñ
o
p
q
r
s
t
u
v
w
x
y
z

nociones *nfpl* **Tengo nociones de informática.** I know a little about computers.

nocturno, -a *adj* ❶ **night** ❷ **evening**

nomás *adv* (LatAm) **just; así nomás** just like that

nombrar *vb* [**25**] ❶ **to appoint** ❷ **to mention**

nombre *nm* ❶ **name; nombre de pila** first name; **nombre y apellidos** full name ❷ **noun**

nómina *nf* **pay slip; estar en nómina** to be on the payroll

nordeste *nm* **northeast**

noreste *nm* **northeast**

noria *nf* **big wheel**

norma *nf* **rule**

normal *adj* ❶ **normal** ▷ *una persona normal* a normal person ▷ *Es normal que quiera divertirse.* It's only normal that he wants to enjoy himself. ❷ **ordinary** ▷ *¿Es guapo? — No, normal.* Is he handsome? — No, just ordinary.

normalmente *adv* **normally**

noroeste *nm* **northwest**

norte *nm* **north**

norteamericano, -a *adj, nm/f* **American**

Noruega *nf* **Norway**

noruego, -a *adj, nm/f* **Norwegian** ▶ *nm* (language) **Norwegian**

nos *pron* ❶ **us** ▷ *Nos vinieron a ver.* They came to see us. ▷ *Nos dio un consejo.* He gave us some advice.; **Nos lo dio.** He gave it to us.; **Nos tienen que arreglar el ordenador.** They have to fix the computer for us. ❷ **ourselves** ▷ *Tenemos que defendernos.* We must defend

ourselves.; **Nos levantamos a las ocho.** We got up at eight o'clock. ❸ **each other** ▷ *No nos hablamos desde hace tiempo.* We haven't spoken to each other for a long time.; **Nos dolían los pies.** Our feet were hurting.; **Nos pusimos los abrigos.** We put our coats on.

nosotros, -as *pron* ❶ **we** ▷ *Nosotros no somos italianos.* We are not Italian. ❷ **us** ▷ *¿Quién es? — Somos nosotros.* Who is it? — It's us. ▷ *Tu hermano vino con nosotros.* Your brother came with us. ▷ *Llegaron antes que nosotros.* They arrived before us.; **nosotros mismos** ourselves

nota *nf* ❶ **mark** ▷ *Saca muy malas notas.* He gets very bad marks. ❷ **note** ▷ *Tomó muchas notas en la conferencia.* He took a lot of notes during the lecture.

notar *vb* [**25**] ❶ **to notice** ❷ **to feel; Se nota que has estudiado mucho este trimestre.** You can tell that you've studied a lot this term.

notario, -a *nm/f* **notary**

noticia *nf* **news** *sg* ▷ *Tengo una buena noticia que darte.* I've got some good news for you.; **Fue una noticia excelente para la economía.** It was an excellent piece of news for the economy.; **Vi las noticias de las nueve.** I watched the nine o'clock news.; **No tengo noticias de Juan.** I haven't heard from Juan.

▋ Be careful! **noticia** does not mean **notice**.

notificar vb [48] to notify

novato, -a nm/f beginner

novecientos, -as adj, pron nine hundred

novedad nf Las últimas novedades en moda infantil. The latest in children's fashions.; ¿Cómo sigue tu hijo? — Sin novedad. How's your son? — There's no change.

novela nf novel; una novela policíaca a detective story

noveno, -a adj, pron ninth; Vivo en el noveno. I live on the ninth floor.

noventa adj, pron ninety; el noventa aniversario the ninetieth anniversary

novia nf ❶ girlfriend ❷ fiancée ❸ bride

noviazgo nm relationship

noviembre nm November ▷ en noviembre in November

novillos nmpl hacer novillos to play truant

novio nm ❶ boyfriend ❷ fiancé ❸ bridegroom; los novios the bride and groom

nube nf cloud

nublado, -a adj cloudy

nublarse vb [25] to cloud over

nuboso, -a adj cloudy

nuca nf nape

nuclear adj nuclear; una central nuclear a nuclear power station

núcleo nm el núcleo urbano the city centre

nudo nm knot; atar con un nudo to tie in a knot

nuera nf daughter-in-law

nuestro, -a adj, pron ❶ our ▷ nuestro perro our dog ▷ nuestras bicicletas our bicycles ❷ ours ▷ ¿De quién es esto? — Es nuestro. Whose is this? — It's ours. ▷ Esta casa es la nuestra. This house is ours.; un amigo nuestro a friend of ours

nueve adj, pron nine; Son las nueve. It's nine o'clock.; el nueve de marzo the ninth of March

nuevo, -a adj new ▷ Necesito un ordenador nuevo. I need a new computer.; Tuve que leer el libro de nuevo. I had to read the book again.

nuez (pl nueces) nf ❶ walnut ❷ Adam's apple; la nuez moscada nutmeg

número nm ❶ number ❷ size ❸ issue; Calle Aribau, sin número. Aribau Street, no number.; número de teléfono telephone number; montar un número to make a scene

nunca adv ❶ never; No le veré nunca más. I'll never see him again. ❷ ever ▷ Casi nunca me escribe. He hardly ever writes to me.

nutria nf otter

nylon nm nylon

a
b
c
d
e
f
g
h
i
j
k
l
m
n
ñ
o
p
q
r
s
t
u
v
w
x
y
z

ñoño *adj* soppy
ñu *nm* gnu

o *conj* or ▷ *¿Quieres té o café?*
Would you like tea or coffee?;
o ... o ... either ... or ... ▷ *O ha salido
o no coge el teléfono.* Either he's
out or he's not answering the
phone.; **O te callas o no sigo
hablando.** If you're not quiet
I won't go on.
obedecer *vb* [**12**] to obey;
obedecer a alguien to obey
someone
obediente *adj* obedient
obeso, -a *adj* obese
obispo *nm* bishop
objeción (*pl* **objeciones**) *nf*
objection
objetivo *nm* objective; **Nuestro
principal objetivo es ganar las
elecciones.** Our main aim is to
win the elections.

objeto nm object; ¿Cuál es el objeto de su visita? What's the reason for your visit?; **los objetos de valor** valuables

obligación (pl **obligaciones**) nf obligation

obligado, -a adj **verse obligado a hacer algo** to be forced to do something ▷ Se vieron obligados a vender su casa. They were forced to sell their house.; **No estás obligado a venir si no quieres.** You don't have to come if you don't want to.

obligar vb [37] ❶ to force ▷ Nadie te obliga a aceptar este empleo. Nobody's forcing you to accept this job. ❷ to make ▷ No puedes obligarme a ir. You can't make me go.

obligatorio, -a adj compulsory

obra nf ❶ work; **una obra de arte** a work of art; **la obra completa de Neruda** the complete works of Neruda; **una obra de teatro** a play; **una obra maestra** a masterpiece ❷ building site; **'obras'** roadworks'

obrero, -a nm/f worker

obsequio nm gift ▷ como obsequio as a gift

observación (pl **observaciones**) nf ❶ observation ❷ comment

observador, a adj observant

observar vb [25] ❶ to observe ❷ to remark

obsesión (pl **obsesiones**) nf obsession

obsesionar vb [25] **Es un tema que le obsesiona.** He's obsessed by the subject.

obstáculo nm obstacle ▷ Nos puso muchos obstáculos. He put many obstacles in our way.

obstante adv **no obstante** nevertheless

obstinado, -a adj obstinate

obstinarse vb [25] to insist ▷ ¿Por qué te obstinas en hacerlo? Why do you insist on doing it?

obtener vb [53] to obtain

obvio, -a adj obvious

oca nf goose

ocasión (pl **ocasiones**) nf ❶ opportunity ❷ occasion ▷ en varias ocasiones on several occasions; **un libro de ocasión** a secondhand book

ocasionar vb [25] to cause

occidental adj western; **los países occidentales** the West

occidente nm **el Occidente** the West

océano nm ocean ▷ el océano Atlántico the Atlantic Ocean

ochenta adj, pron eighty ▷ Tiene ochenta años. He's eighty.; **el ochenta aniversario** the eightieth anniversary

ocho adj, pron eight; **Son las ocho.** It's eight o'clock.; **el ocho de agosto** the eighth of August

ochocientos, -as adj, pron eight hundred

ocio nm **en mis ratos de ocio** in my spare time

octavo, -a adj, pron eighth; **Vivo en el octavo.** I live on the eighth floor.

octubre nm October ▷ en octubre in October

oculista *nmf* eye specialist ▷ *Es oculista.* He's an eye specialist.

ocultar *vb* [25] to conceal; **No nos oculte la verdad.** Don't try to hide the truth from us.; **ocultarse** to hide

ocupación (*pl* ocupaciones) *nf*
❶ activity ❷ occupation

ocupado, -a *adj* ❶ busy ▷ *Estoy muy ocupado.* I'm very busy.
❷ engaged ▷ *La línea está ocupada.* The line's engaged.; **'ocupado'** 'engaged'; **¿Está ocupado este asiento?** Is this seat taken?

ocupar *vb* [25] ❶ to occupy ❷ to take up ▷ *Ocupa casi todo mi tiempo.* It takes up almost all my time.; **ocuparse de algo** to look after something; **Yo me ocuparé de decírselo.** I'll tell him.

ocurrencia *nf* **Juan tuvo la ocurrencia de decírselo a la cara.** Juan had the bright idea to tell her to her face.; **¡Qué ocurrencia!** Him and his crazy ideas!

ocurrir *vb* [58] to happen; **¿Qué te ocurre?** What's the matter?; **Se nos ocurrió una idea brillante.** We had a brilliant idea.

odiar *vb* [25] to hate

odio *nm* hate

oeste *nm, adj* west ▷ *en la costa oeste* on the west coast; **Viajábamos hacia el oeste.** We were travelling west.; **una película del oeste** (*film*) a western

ofender *vb* [8] to offend; **ofenderse** to take offence

ofensa *nf* insult

oferta *nf* offer; **una oferta especial** a special offer; **estar de oferta** to be on special offer; **'ofertas de trabajo'** 'situations vacant'

oficial *adj* official
▶ *nmf* officer ▷ *Es oficial de marina.* He's an officer in the navy.

oficina *nf* office; **la oficina de turismo** the tourist office; **la oficina de empleo** the job centre; **la oficina de correos** the post office; **la oficina de objetos perdidos** the lost property office

oficio *nm* trade ▷ *Es carpintero de oficio.* He's a carpenter by trade.

ofrecer *vb* [12] to offer; **ofrecerse para hacer algo** to offer to do something; **¿Qué se le ofrece?** What can I get you?

ofrecimiento *nm* offer

oído *nm* ❶ hearing ❷ ear; **tener buen oído** to have a good ear

oír *vb* [35] ❶ to hear ❷ to listen to; **oír la radio** to listen to the radio; **¡Oye!** Hey!; **¡Oiga, por favor!** Excuse me!

ojalá *excl* ❶ I hope ▷ *¡Ojalá Toni venga hoy!* I hope Toni comes today! ❷ if only ▷ *¡Ojalá pudiera!* If only I could!

ojeras *nfpl* **tener ojeras** to have bags under one's eyes

ojo *nm* eye; **ir con ojo** to keep one's eyes open for trouble; **costar un ojo de la cara** to cost an arm and a leg; **¡Ojo! Es muy mentiroso.** Be careful! He's an awful liar.

ola *nf* wave

oler vb [36] to smell; **Huele a tabaco.** It smells of cigarette smoke.; **oler bien** to smell good; **oler mal** to smell awful

olfato nm sense of smell

Olimpiadas nfpl the Olympics

olímpico, -a adj Olympic; **los Juegos Olímpicos** the Olympic Games

oliva nf olive; **el aceite de oliva** olive oil

olivo nm olive tree

olla nf pot; **una olla a presión** a pressure cooker

olor nm smell ▷ un olor a tabaco a smell of cigarette smoke; **¡Qué mal olor!** What a horrible smell!

olvidar vb [25] ① to forget ▷ No olvides comprar el pan. Don't forget to buy the bread.; **olvidarse de hacer algo** to forget to do something; **Se me olvidó por completo.** I completely forgot. ② to leave ▷ Olvidé las llaves en la mesa. I left the keys on the table.

olvido nm **Ha sido un olvido imperdonable.** It was an unforgivable oversight.

ombligo nm navel

omitir vb [58] to leave out

once adj, pron eleven ▷ Tengo once años. I'm eleven.; **Son las once.** It's eleven o'clock.; **el once de agosto** the eleventh of August

onda nf wave; **onda corta** short wave

ondear vb [25] to fly

ondulado, -a adj wavy

ONU nf (= Organización de las Naciones Unidas) UN (= United Nations)

opaco, -a adj ① opaque ② (not shiny) dull

opción (pl **opciones**) nf option ▷ No tienes otra opción. You have no option.

ópera nf opera

operación (pl **operaciones**) nf operation

operar vb [25] to operate on; **Me van a operar del corazón.** I'm going to have a heart operation.; **operarse** to have an operation

opinar vb [25] to think

opinión (pl **opiniones**) nf opinion; **en mi opinión** in my opinion

oponerse vb [41] to oppose; **No me opongo.** I don't object.

oportunidad nf chance ▷ No tuvo la oportunidad de hacerlo. He didn't have a chance to do it.; **dar otra oportunidad a alguien** to give someone another chance

oportuno, -a adj **en el momento oportuno** at the right time

oposición (pl **oposiciones**) nf opposition; **las oposiciones** public examinations

> **Oposiciones** are exams held periodically for posts in the public sector, state education and the judiciary. Such posts are permanent, so the number of candidates is high and the exams are very hard.

optar vb [25] **optar por hacer algo** to choose to do something

optativo, -a adj optional ▷ las asignaturas optativas optional subjects

óptica nf optician's

optimismo nm optimism

optimista adj optimistic
▶ nmf optimist

óptimo, -a adj optimum

opuesto, -a adj ❶ conflicting
❷ opposite

opuse vb see **oponerse**

oración (pl **oraciones**) nf ❶ prayer
❷ (phrase) sentence

orador, a nm/f speaker

oral adj oral; **por vía oral** orally;
un examen oral an oral exam

orden nm order; **por orden
alfabético** in alphabetical order;
La casa está en orden. The house
is tidy.
▶ nf order; **¡Deja de darme
órdenes!** Stop bossing me about!

ordenado, -a adj tidy

ordenador nm computer; **un
ordenador portátil** a laptop

ordenar vb [25] ❶ to tidy up ❷ to
order ▷ El policía nos ordenó que
saliéramos del edificio. The police
officer ordered us to get out of the
building.

ordeñar vb [25] to milk

ordinario, -a adj ❶ common
❷ ordinary; **de ordinario** usually

oreja nf ear

orgánico, -a adj organic

organismo nm organization

organización (pl
organizaciones) nf
organization

organizar vb [13] to organize;
organizarse to organize oneself

órgano nm organ

orgullo nm pride

orgulloso, -a adj proud

orientación (pl **orientaciones**) nf
tener sentido de la orientación
to have a good sense of direction;
la orientación profesional
careers advice

oriente nm **el Oriente** the East

origen (pl **orígenes**) nm origin

original adj original

originalidad nf originality

orilla nf ❶ shore ❷ bank; **a orillas
de (1)** on the shores of **(2)** on the
banks of; **un paseo a la orilla del
mar** a walk along the seashore

orina nf urine

orinar vb [25] to urinate

oro nm gold ▷ un collar de oro a gold
necklace

orquesta nf orchestra; **una
orquesta de jazz** a jazz band

ortodoxo, -a adj orthodox

ortografía nf spelling

oruga nf caterpillar

os pron ❶ you ▷ No os oigo. I can't
hear you. ▷ Os he comprado un libro
a cada uno. I've bought each of you
a book.; **Os lo doy.** I'll give it to
you.; **¿Os han arreglado ya el
ordenador?** Have they fixed the
computer for you yet?
❷ yourselves ▷ ¿Os habéis hecho
daño? Did you hurt yourselves?;
**Os tenéis que levantar antes
de las ocho.** You have to get up
before eight. ❸ each other
▷ Quiero que os pidáis perdón. I want
you to say sorry to each other.;
**No hace falta que os quitéis el
abrigo.** You don't need to take
your coats off.; **Lavaos las
manos.** Wash your hands.

oscilar vb [25] to range

oscurecer vb [12] to get dark

oscuridad nf darkness; **Estaban hablando en la oscuridad.** They were talking in the dark.

oscuro, -a adj dark ▷ una habitación muy oscura a very dark room; **azul oscuro** dark blue; **a oscuras** in darkness

oso, -a nm/f bear; **un oso de peluche** a teddy bear

ostión (pl ostiones) nm (Mex) oyster

ostra nf oyster; **¡Ostras!** Good grief!

OTAN nf (= Organización del Tratado del Atlántico Norte) NATO (= North Atlantic Treaty Organization)

otoño nm autumn ▷ en otoño in autumn

otro, -a adj, pron ❶ another ▷ otro coche another car ▷ ¿Me das otra manzana, por favor? Can you give me another apple, please?; **¿Has perdido el lápiz? — No importa, tengo otro.** Have you lost your pencil? — It doesn't matter, I've got another one.; **¿Hay alguna otra manera de hacerlo?** Is there any other way of doing it?; **otra vez** again; **otros tres libros** another three books ❷ other ▷ Tengo otros planes. I have other plans.; **Quiero otra cosa.** I want something else.; **No quiero este, quiero el otro.** I don't want this one, I want the other one.; **Que lo haga otro.** Let someone else do it.; **Están enamorados el uno del otro.** They're in love with each other.

ovalado, -a adj oval

oveja nf sheep

ovillo nm ball ▷ un ovillo de lana a ball of wool

OVNI nm (= objeto volador no identificado) UFO (= unidentified flying object)

oxidado, -a adj rusty

oxidarse vb [25] to go rusty

oxígeno nm oxygen

oyendo vb see **oír**

oyente nmf ❶ listener ❷ occasional student

a
b
c
d
e
f
g
h
i
j
k
l
m
n
ñ
o
p
q
r
s
t
u
v
w
x
y
z

p

paciencia nf patience; **¡Ten paciencia!** Be patient!

paciente adj, nmf patient

Pacífico nm the Pacific

pacífico, -a adj peaceful

pacifista adj, nmf pacifist; **el movimiento pacifista** the peace movement

pacto nm agreement ▷ **hacer un pacto** to make an agreement

padecer vb [12] ❶ to suffer from; **Padece del corazón.** He has heart trouble. ❷ to suffer

padrastro nm stepfather

padre nm father; **Es padre de familia.** He's a family man.; **mis padres** my parents; **rezar el Padre Nuestro** to say the Lord's Prayer

padrino nm godfather; **mis padrinos** my godparents

The **padrino** is also the person who escorts the bride down the aisle and gives her away at a wedding, usually her father.

paella nf paella

paga nf ❶ pocket money ❷ pay

pagar vb [37] ❶ to pay; **Se puede pagar con tarjeta de crédito.** You can pay by credit card. ❷ to pay for

página nf page; **una página web** a web page

pago nm payment

país (pl **países**) nm country; **el País Vasco** the Basque Country; **los Países Bajos** the Netherlands

paisaje nm ❶ landscape ❷ scenery

paja nf ❶ straw ▷ **un sombrero de paja** a straw hat ❷ padding ▷ **El resto del texto es solo paja.** The rest of the text is just padding.

pajarita nf bow tie

pájaro nm bird

pajita nf drinking straw

pala nf ❶ spade ❷ shovel ❸ (for table tennis) bat ❹ blade

palabra nf word ▷ **Cumplió su palabra.** He was true to his word. ▷ **sin decir palabra** without a word; **No me dirige la palabra.** He doesn't speak to me.

palabrota nf swearword; **soltar palabrotas** to swear

palacio nm palace

paladar nm palate

palanca nf lever; **la palanca de cambio** gear lever

palangana nf washbasin

palco nm box

Palestina nf Palestine

palestino, -a adj, nm/f Palestinian

paleta nf ❶ trowel ❷ (painter's) palette

pálido, -a adj pale ▷ Se puso pálida. She turned pale.

palillo nm ❶ toothpick ❷ chopstick

paliza nf ❶ beating ❷ thrashing ▷ Si mi padre se entera me va a dar una paliza. If my father finds out he'll give me a thrashing.; **Sus clases son una paliza.** His classes are a real pain.

palma nf palm; **dar palmas** to clap

palmera nf palm tree

palo nm ❶ stick ❷ (golf) club ❸ (cards) suit; **una cuchara de palo** a wooden spoon

paloma nf pigeon ▷ una paloma mensajera a carrier pigeon; **la paloma de la paz** the dove of peace

palomitas nfpl **las palomitas de maíz** popcorn sg

Word for word, **palomitas de maíz** means 'little pigeons of corn'.

palpar vb [25] to feel

palpitación (pl **palpitaciones**) nf palpitation

palpitar vb [25] ❶ to pound ▷ El corazón me palpitaba de miedo. My heart was pounding with fear. ❷ to beat ▷ Su corazón dejó de palpitar. His heart stopped beating.

palta nf (Chile, River Plate) avocado

pan nm ❶ bread ▷ pan con mantequilla bread and butter ▷ pan integral wholemeal bread ▷ pan de molde sliced bread ▷ una barra de pan a loaf of bread; **pan rallado** breadcrumbs pl; **pan tostado** toast ❷ loaf ▷ Compré dos panes. I bought two loaves.

pana nf corduroy

panadera nf baker

panadería nf bakery

panadero nm baker ▷ Es panadero. He's a baker.

Panamá nm Panama

panameño, -a adj, nm/f Panamanian

pancarta nf banner

pancito nm (LatAm) bread roll

panda nm panda

pandereta nf tambourine

pandilla nf gang

panfleto nm pamphlet

pánico nm panic; **Me entró pánico.** I panicked.

pantaletas nfpl (Mex) panties

pantalla nf ❶ screen ❷ lampshade

pantalones nmpl trousers; **unos pantalones** a pair of trousers; **pantalones cortos** shorts; **pantalones vaqueros** jeans

pantano nm reservoir

pantera nf panther

pantimedias nfpl (Mex) tights

pantis nmpl tights

pantorrilla nf calf

pants nmpl (Mex) tracksuit sg

pañal nm nappy

paño nm cloth; **un paño de cocina** a dishcloth

pañuelo nm ❶ handkerchief ❷ scarf ❸ headscarf

a b c d e f g h i j k l m n ñ o p q r s t u v w x y z

papa nm ❶ pope; **el Papa** the Pope
▶ nf (LatAm) potato; **pescado frito
con papas fritas** fish and chips;
un paquete de papas fritas a
packet of crisps

papá (pl **papás**) nm dad; **mis
papás** my mum and dad; **Papá
Noel** Father Christmas

papalote nm (Mex) kite

papel nm ❶ paper ▷ una bolsa de
papel a paper bag ❷ piece of paper
▷ Lo escribí en un papel. I wrote it on
a piece of paper.; **papel de
aluminio** tinfoil; **papel higiénico**
toilet paper

> Word for word, **papel
higiénico** means 'hygienic
paper'.

papel pintado wallpaper

> Word for word, **papel
pintado** means 'painted
paper'.

❸ role ▷ Le han dado el papel
principal. They gave her the leading
role. ▷ Jugó un papel muy importante
en las negociaciones. He played a
very important part in the
negotiations.; **¿Qué papeles te
piden para sacar el pasaporte?**
What documents do you need to
get a passport?

papeleo nm paperwork

papelera nf ❶ wastepaper bin
❷ litter bin

papelería nf stationer's

papeleta nf ❶ (with exam results)
results slip ❷ ballot paper ❸ raffle
ticket

paperas nfpl mumps

papilla nf ❶ baby food ❷ pap

paquete nm ❶ (of biscuits,
cigarettes) packet ❷ parcel ▷ Me
mandaron un paquete por correo.
I got a parcel in the post.

Paquistán nm Pakistan

paquistaní (pl **paquistaníes**) adj,
nmf Pakistani

par adj número par even number
▶ nm ❶ couple ▷ un par de horas
al día a couple of hours a day
❷ pair ▷ un par de calcetines a pair
of socks; **Abrió la ventana de par
en par.** He opened the window
wide.

para prep ❶ for ▷ Es para ti. It's for
you. ▷ Tengo muchos deberes para
mañana. I have a lot of homework
to do for tomorrow. ▷ el autobús
para Marbella the bus for Marbella.
¿Para qué lo quieres? What do
you want it for?; **¿Para qué sirve?**
What's it for?; **para siempre**
forever; **Para entonces ya era
tarde.** It was already too late by
then. ❷ to ▷ Estoy ahorrando para
comprarme una moto. I'm saving up
to buy a motorbike. ▷ Son cinco
para las ocho. (LatAm) It's five to
eight.; **Entré despacito para no
despertarla.** I went in slowly so as
not to wake her.; **para que te
acuerdes de mí** so that you
remember me

parabólica nf satellite dish

parabrisas (pl **parabrisas**) nm
windscreen

paracaídas (pl **paracaídas**) nm
parachute

paracaidista nmf ❶ paratrooper
❷ parachutist

parachoques (pl **parachoques**) nm bumper

parada nf stop; **una parada de autobús** a bus stop; **una parada de taxis** a taxi rank

paradero nm (LatAm) bus stop

parado, -a adj unemployed ▷ Hace seis meses que está parada. She's been unemployed for six months.; **No te quedes ahí parado.** Don't just stand there.; **Estuve toda la mañana parado.** (LatAm) I was standing all morning.

parador nm
 The **paradores** are a group of luxury Spanish hotels occupying castles, monasteries and other historical buildings and sited in scenic areas.

paraguas (pl **paraguas**) nm umbrella

Paraguay nm Paraguay

paraguayo, -a adj, nm/f Paraguayan

paraíso nm paradise

paralelo adj, nm parallel

parálisis (pl **parálisis**) nf paralysis

paralítico, -a adj Está paralítico. He's paralyzed.

parapente nm ❶ paragliding ▷ paraglider

parar vb [25] to stop; **Nos equivocamos de tren y fuimos a parar a Manchester.** We got on the wrong train and ended up in Manchester.; **hablar sin parar** to talk non-stop; **pararse** (1) to stop (2) (LatAm) to stand up

pararrayos (pl **pararrayos**) nm lightning conductor

parcela nf plot of land

parche nm patch

parchís nm Spanish version of ludo

parcial adj ❶ partial; **a tiempo parcial** part time ❷ biased
▶ nm mid-term exam

parecer vb [12] ❶ to seem
▷ Parece muy simpática. She seems very nice.; **Parece mentira que ya haya pasado tanto tiempo.** I can't believe it has been so long. ❷ to look ▷ Parece más joven. He looks younger.; **Parece una modelo.** She looks like a model.; **Parece que va a llover.** It looks as if it's going to rain. ❸ to think; **¿Qué te pareció la película?** What did you think of the film?; **Me parece que sí.** I think so.; **Me parece que no.** I don't think so.; **si te parece bien** if that's all right with you; **parecerse** to look alike; **parecerse a** to look like

parecido, -a adj similar ▷ Tu blusa es parecida a la mía. Your blouse is similar to mine.; **o algo parecido** or something like that

pared nf wall

pareja nf ❶ couple ▷ Había varias parejas bailando. There were several couples dancing. ❷ pair ▷ En este juego hay que formar parejas. For this game you have to get into pairs. ❸ partner ▷ Vino con su pareja. He came with his partner.

parejo, -a adj (LatAm) even

paréntesis (pl **paréntesis**) nm bracket ▷ entre paréntesis in brackets

a
b
c
d
e
f
g
h
i
j
k
l
m
n
ñ
o
p
q
r
s
t
u
v
w
x
y
z

pariente nmf relative ▷ Es pariente mío. He's a relative of mine.

Be careful! **pariente** does not mean **parent**.

París nm Paris

parisiense adj, nmf Parisian

parisino, -a adj, nm/f Parisian

parking (pl parkings) nm car park

parlamento nm parliament

parlanchín (f parlanchina, mpl parlanchines) adj chatty

parlante nm (LatAm) loudspeaker

paro nm ❶ unemployment ▷ Ha bajado el paro. Unemployment has come down.; **Mi hermano está en paro.** My brother is unemployed.; **cobrar el paro** to claim unemployment benefit ❷ strike ▷ un paro de tres días a three-day strike

parpadear vb [25] to blink

párpado nm eyelid

parque nm park; **un parque de atracciones** an amusement park; **un parque infantil** a children's playground; **un parque temático** a theme park; **un parque zoológico** a zoo

parquímetro nm parking meter

parra nf vine

párrafo nm paragraph

parrilla nf grill; **carne a la parrilla** grilled meat

parrillada nf grill

párroco nm parish priest

parroquia nf parish

parte nf ❶ part ▷ ¿De qué parte de Inglaterra eres? What part of England are you from? ❷ share

▷ mi parte de la herencia my share of the inheritance ▷ Tengo que haberlo dejado en alguna parte. I must have left it somewhere. ▷ por todas partes everywhere; **en parte** partly ▷ Se debe en parte a su falta de experiencia. It's partly due to his lack of experience.; **la mayor parte de los españoles** most Spanish people; **la parte delantera** the front; **la parte de atrás** the back; **la parte de arriba** the top; **la parte de abajo** the bottom; **por una parte ..., por otra ...** on the one hand ..., on the other hand ...; **Llamo de parte de Juan.** I'm calling on behalf of Juan.; **¿De parte de quién?** Who's calling please?; **Estoy de tu parte.** I'm on your side.

participar vb [25] to take part

participio nm participle

particular adj private ▷ clases particulares private classes; **El vestido no tiene nada de particular.** The dress is nothing special.; **en particular** in particular

partida nf ❶ game ▷ echar una partida de cartas to have a game of cards ▷ certificate ▷ partida de nacimiento birth certificate

partidario, -a adj ser partidario de algo to be in favour of something

▶ nm/f supporter

partido nm ❶ (political) party ❷ (football, tennis) match ❸ (LatAm) game ▷ un partido de ajedrez a game of chess

partir vb [58] ❶ (cake, melon) to cut ❷ (nut) to crack ❸ (branch, piece of chocolate) to break off ❹ to leave ▷ *La expedición partirá mañana de París.* The expedition is to leave from Paris tomorrow.; **a partir de enero** from January; **partirse** to break; **partirse de risa** to split one's sides laughing

partitura nf score

parto nm birth; **estar de parto** to be in labour

pasa nf raisin

pasado, -a adj ❶ last ▷ *el verano pasado* last summer ❷ after ▷ *Pasado el semáforo, verás un cine.* After the traffic lights you'll see a cinema. ▷ *Volvió pasadas las tres de la mañana.* He returned after three in the morning.; **pasado mañana** the day after tomorrow; **un sombrero pasado de moda** an old-fashioned hat
▶ nm past ▷ *en el pasado* in the past

pasador nm ❶ hair slide ❷ tiepin

pasaje nm ❶ ticket ❷ passage

pasajero, -a adj ❶ (pain, upset) temporary ❷ (fashion, phase) passing
▶ nm/f passenger

pasamanos (pl pasamanos) nm banister

pasaporte nm passport

pasar vb [25] ❶ to pass ▷ *Cuando termines pásasela a Isabel.* When you've finished pass it on to Isabel. ▷ *La foto fue pasando de mano en mano.* The photo was passed around.; **Un momento, te paso con Pedro.** Just a

moment, I'll put you on to Pedro. ❷ to go past ▷ *Pasaron varios coches.* A number of cars went past.; **¡Pase, por favor!** Please come in.; **El tiempo pasa deprisa.** Time goes so quickly.; **Pasaron cinco años.** Five years went by.; **Ya ha pasado una hora.** It's been an hour already. ❸ to spend ▷ *Me pasé el fin de semana estudiando.* I spent the weekend studying. ❹ to happen ▷ *pase lo que pase* whatever happens; **¿Qué pasa? (1)** What's the matter? **(2)** What's happening?; **¿Qué le pasa a Juan?** What's the matter with Juan?; **pasarlo bien** to have a good time; **pasarlo mal** to have a bad time; **Hemos pasado mucho frío.** We were very cold.; **Están pasando hambre.** They are starving.; **¡Paso de todo!** I couldn't care less!; **pasar por (1)** to go through ▷ *No pasamos por la ciudad.* We don't go through the city. **(2)** to go past; **Podrían perfectamente pasar por gemelos.** They could easily pass for twins.; **No puedo pasar sin teléfono.** I can't get by without a telephone.; **pasarse de moda** to go out of fashion

pasatiempo nm hobby

Pascua nf Easter; **¡Felices Pascuas!** Happy Christmas!

pase nm pass ▷ *un pase gratis* a free pass; **un pase de modelos** a fashion show

pasear vb [25] to walk; **ir a pasear** to go for a walk

paseo nm walk ▷ Salimos a dar un paseo. We went out for a walk.; **ir de paseo** to go for a walk; **un paseo en barco** a boat trip; **un paseo en bicicleta** a bike ride; **el paseo marítimo** the promenade

> Word for word, **paseo marítimo** means 'maritime walk'.

pasillo nm ❶ corridor ❷ (in cinema, plane) aisle

pasión (pl pasiones) nf passion

pasivo, -a adj passive

pasmado, -a adj amazed

paso nm ❶ step ▷ Dio un paso hacia atrás. He took a step backwards. ▷ paso a paso step by step; **He oído pasos.** I heard footsteps.; **Vive a un paso de aquí.** He lives very near here. ❷ way ▷ **Han cerrado el paso.** They've blocked the way.; **'Ceda el paso'** 'Give way'; **'Prohibido el paso'** 'No entry'; **El banco me pilla de paso.** The bank is on my way.; **Están de paso por Barcelona.** They're just passing through Barcelona.; **un paso de peatones** a pedestrian crossing; **un paso de cebra** a zebra crossing; **un paso a nivel** a level crossing

pasta nf ❶ pasta ❷ dosh; **pastas de té** biscuits; **pasta de dientes** toothpaste

pastar vb [25] to graze

pastel nm cake

pastelería nf patisserie

pastilla nf ❶ pill; **pastillas para la tos** cough sweets ❷ (of soap) bar ❸ (of chocolate) piece; **pastillas de caldo** stock cubes

pasto nm (LatAm) grass

pastor nm shepherd; **un pastor alemán** an Alsatian; **un perro pastor** a sheepdog

pastora nf shepherdess

pata nf leg; **¡He vuelto a meter la pata!** I've gone and put my foot in it again!; **Me parece que he metido la pata en el examen de física.** I think I messed up my physics exam.

patada nf **Me dio una patada.** He kicked me.

Patagonia nf Patagonia

patata nf potato; **un filete con patatas fritas** steak and chips; **una bolsa de patatas fritas** a bag of crisps

paté (pl patés) nm pâté

patera nf small boat

paterno, -a adj paternal

patilla nf ❶ sideburn ❷ (of glasses) arm

patín (pl patines) nm ❶ roller skate ❷ skate ❸ pedal boat

patinaje nm ❶ roller skating ❷ ice skating; **patinaje artístico** figure skating

patinar vb [25] ❶ to roller-skate ❷ to skate ❸ to skid

patinete nm scooter

patio nm ❶ playground ❷ courtyard; **el patio de butacas** the stalls pl

pato nm duck

patoso, -a adj clumsy

patria nf homeland

patriota adj patriotic

patrocinador, a nm/f sponsor

patrocinar vb [25] to sponsor

patrón (pl patrones) nm ❶ patron saint ❷ boss

patrona nf ❶ patron saint ❷ landlady

patrulla nf patrol ⊳ **estar de patrulla** to be on patrol

pausa nf ❶ (during speech, reading) pause ❷ (in meeting, programme) break

pavimento nm ❶ paving ❷ surface

pavo nm turkey; **un pavo real** a peacock

payaso, -a nm/f clown; **Deja de hacer el payaso.** Stop clowning around.

paz (pl paces) nf peace; **¡Déjame en paz!** Leave me alone!; **Ha hecho las paces con su novio.** She's made it up with her boyfriend.

PC abbr m PC

P.D. abbr (= posdata) P.S.

peaje nm toll

peatón (pl peatones) nm pedestrian

peca nf freckle

pecado nm sin

pecar vb [48] to sin

pecho nm ❶ chest ❷ breast; **dar el pecho a un niño** to breastfeed a baby

pechuga nf breast

pedal nm ❶ pedal ⊳ **el pedal del freno** the brake pedal

pedalear vb [25] to pedal

pedante adj pedantic

pedazo nm ❶ piece ⊳ **un pedazo de pan** a piece of bread; **hacer pedazos (1)** to smash **(2)** to tear up

pediatra nmf paediatrician

pedido nm order ⊳ **hacer un pedido** to place an order

pedir vb [38] ❶ to ask for ⊳ **Le pedí dinero a mi padre.** I asked my father for some money. ❷ to ask ⊳ **¿Te puedo pedir un favor?** Can I ask you a favour? ⊳ **Pedí que me enviaran la información por correo.** I asked them to mail me the information. ❸ to order ⊳ **Yo pedí paella.** I ordered paella.; **Le pedí disculpas.** I apologized to him.; **Tuve que pedir dinero prestado.** I had to borrow some money.

pega nf snag; **Me pusieron muchas pegas.** They made things very difficult for me.

pegadizo, -a adj catchy

pegajoso, -a adj ❶ sticky ❷ (LatAm) catchy

pegamento nm glue

pegar vb [37] ❶ to hit ⊳ **Andrés me ha pegado.** Andrés hit me. ❷ to stick ⊳ **Lo puedes pegar con celo.** You can stick it on with sellotape. ❸ to give; **Pegó un grito.** He shouted.; **Le pegaron un tiro.** They shot him. ❹ to look right ⊳ **Esta camisa no pega con el traje.** This shirt doesn't look right with the suit.; **El niño se pegó a su madre.** The boy clung to his mother.

pegatina nf sticker

peinado nm hairstyle

peinar vb [25] ❶ to comb ⊳ **Péinate antes de salir.** Comb your hair before you go out. ❷ to brush; **Mañana voy a peinarme.** I'm going to have my hair done tomorrow.

peine nm comb

p.ej. abbr (= por ejemplo) e.g.

pelar vb [25] **1** to peel **2** to shell; **Se me está pelando la espalda.** My back is peeling.; **Hace un frío que pela.** It's bitterly cold.

peldaño nm **1** step **2** rung

pelea nf **1** fight **2** argument ▷ Tuvo una pelea con su novio. She had an argument with her boyfriend.

peleado, -a adj Están peleados. They've fallen out.

pelear vb [25] **1** to fight **2** to argue

pelícano nm pelican

película nf film ▷ A las ocho ponen una película. There's a film on at eight.; **una película de dibujos animados** a cartoon; **una película del oeste** a western; **una película de suspense** a thriller

peligro nm danger ▷ Está fuera de peligro. He's out of danger.

peligroso, -a adj dangerous

pelirrojo, -a adj Es pelirrojo. He has red hair.

pellejo nm skin; **arriesgar el pellejo** to risk one's neck

pellizcar vb [48] to pinch

pellizco nm pinch ▷ un pellizco de sal a pinch of salt

pelmazo, -a nm/f bore

pelo nm hair ▷ Tiene el pelo rizado. He has curly hair.; **No perdí el avión por un pelo.** I only just caught the plane.; **Se me pusieron los pelos de punta.** It made my hair stand on end.; **Me estás tomando el pelo.** You're pulling my leg.

pelota nf ball ▷ jugar a la pelota to play ball
▶ nmf (informal) creep

peluca nf wig

peludo, -a adj hairy

peluquera nf hairdresser

peluquería nf hairdresser's

peluquero nm hairdresser

pena nf shame ▷ Es una pena que no puedas venir. It's a shame you can't come. ▷ ¡Qué pena! What a shame!; **Me dio tanta pena el pobre animal.** I felt so sorry for the poor animal.; **Me da pena tener que marcharme.** I'm so sad to have to go away.; **No tengas pena.** (LatAm) Don't be embarrassed.; **Vale la pena.** It's worth it.; **No vale la pena gastarse tanto dinero.** It's not worth spending so much money.; **la pena de muerte** the death penalty

penalty (pl penaltys) nm penalty

pendiente adj Tenemos un par de asuntos pendientes. We have a couple of matters to sort out.; **Tiene una asignatura pendiente.** He has to resit one subject.; **Estaban pendientes de ella.** They were watching her intently.
▶ nm earring
▶ nf slope

pene nm penis

penetrar vb [25] penetrar en to find one's way into

penicilina nf penicillin

península nf peninsula; **la Península Ibérica** the Iberian Peninsula

penique nm penny

pensamiento nm ❶ thought ❷ pansy

pensar vb [39] ❶ to think ▷ ¿Qué piensas de Manolo? What do you think of Manolo?; ¿Qué piensas del aborto? What do you think about abortion? ❷ to think about ▷ Tengo que pensarlo. I'll have to think about it.; Estaba pensando en ir al cine esta tarde. I was thinking of going to the cinema this evening.; ¡Ni pensarlo! (informal) No way!; pensándolo bien ... on second thoughts ...; Piénsatelo. Think it over.

pensativo, -a adj thoughtful

pensión (pl pensiones) nf ❶ pension ❷ guest house; pensión completa full board; media pensión half board

pensionista nmf pensioner

penúltimo, -a adj la penúltima estación the last station but one ▶ nm/f Soy el penúltimo. I'm second to last.

peñón (pl peñones) nm el Peñón de Gibraltar the Rock of Gibraltar

peón (pl peones) nm ❶ labourer ❷ pawn

peonza nf spinning top

peor adj, adv worse ▷ Su caso es peor que el nuestro. His case is worse than ours. ▷ Hoy me siento peor. I feel worse today. ❷ worst ▷ el peor día de mi vida the worst day of my life; el restaurante donde peor se come the restaurant with the worst food; y lo peor es que ... and the worst

thing is that ...; Si no viene, peor para ella. If she doesn't come, too bad for her.

pepinillo nm gherkin

pepino nm cucumber; Me importa un pepino lo que piense. I couldn't care less what he thinks.

pepita nf ❶ (in fruit) pip ❷ (of gold) nugget

pequeño, -a adj small ▷ Prefiero los coches pequeños. I prefer small cars. ▷ Estos zapatos me quedan pequeños. These shoes are too small for me.; ¿Cuál prefieres? — El pequeño. Which one do you prefer? — The small one.; mi hermana pequeña my younger sister; La pequeña estudia medicina. The youngest is studying medicine.; Tuvimos un pequeño problema. We had a slight problem.

pequinés nm Pekinese

pera nf pear

percha nf ❶ coat hanger ❷ coat hook

perchero nm ❶ coat rack ❷ coat stand

percibir vb [58] ❶ to notice ❷ to see ❸ to sense

percusión nf percussion

perdedor, a adj losing ▷ la pareja perdedora the losing pair ▶ nm/f loser ▷ Eres mal perdedor. You're a bad loser.

perder vb [20] ❶ to lose ▷ He perdido el monedero. I've lost my purse.; Se le perdieron las llaves. He lost his keys. ❷ to miss; ¡No te lo pierdas! Don't miss it!; ¡Me estás haciendo perder el tiempo!

You're wasting my time!; **Ana es la que saldrá perdiendo.** Ana is the one who will lose out.; **Tenía miedo de perderme.** I was afraid of getting lost.

pérdida nf ❶ loss ❷ (of liquid, gas) leak; **Fue una pérdida de tiempo.** It was a waste of time.

perdido, -a adj ❶ lost ▷ la oficina de objetos perdidos the lost property office ❷ remote ▷ un pueblecito perdido en la montaña a remote little village in the mountains

perdigón (pl **perdigones**) nm pellet

perdiz (pl **perdices**) nf partridge

perdón nm **Le pedí perdón.** I apologized to him.; **¡Perdón!** (1) Sorry! (2) Excuse me!

perdonar vb [25] to forgive; **¡Perdona! ¿Tienes hora?** Excuse me, do you have the time?; **¡Perdona! ¿Te he hecho daño?** I'm so sorry. Did I hurt you?

peregrino, -a nm/f pilgrim

perejil nm parsley

pereza nf laziness; **¡Qué pereza tengo!** I feel so lazy!; **Me da pereza levantarme.** I can't be bothered to get up.

perezoso, -a adj lazy

perfeccionar vb [25] to improve

perfectamente adv perfectly

perfecto, -a adj perfect

perfil nm profile

perfume nm perfume

perfumería nf perfume shop

periódico, -a adj periodic
▶ nm newspaper

periodismo nm journalism

periodista nmf journalist

periodo nm period

periquito nm budgerigar

perjudicar vb [48] ❶ to damage ❷ to be harmful to; **El cambio ha perjudicado sus estudios.** The change has had an adverse effect on his studies.

perjudicial adj damaging; **El tabaco es perjudicial para la salud.** Smoking damages your health.

perla nf pearl

permanecer vb [12] to remain

permanente adj permanent
▶ nf perm; **hacerse la permanente** to have a perm

permiso nm ❶ permission; **¡Con permiso!** Excuse me. ❷ leave ▷ **Mi hermano está de permiso.** My brother is on leave. ❸ permit ▷ **Necesitas un permiso de trabajo.** You need a work permit.; **un permiso de conducir** a driving licence

permitir vb [58] to allow; **No me lo puedo permitir.** I can't afford it.; **¿Me permite?** May I?

pero conj but

perpendicular adj at right angles

perplejo, -a adj puzzled

perrera nf dogs' home

perrito nm **un perrito caliente** a hot dog

perro nm dog; **un perro callejero** a stray dog; **un perro guardián** a guard dog

perseguir vb [50] ❶ to chase ❷ to persecute

persiana nf blind

persiguiendo vb see **perseguir**

persona nf person ▷ Es una persona encantadora. He's a charming person.; **en persona** in person; **personas** people ▷ Había unas diez personas en la sala. There were about ten people in the hall.

personaje nm ❶ character ❷ figure ▷ un personaje público a public figure

personal adj personal
▶ nm staff

personalidad nf personality

personalmente adv personally

perspectiva nf perspective ▷ en perspectiva in perspective; **perspectivas** prospects ▷ buenas perspectivas económicas good economic prospects

persuadir vb [58] to persuade

pertenecer vb [12] pertenecer a to belong to

pertenencias nfpl belongings

pértiga nf pole; **el salto con pértiga** the pole vault

Perú nm Peru

peruano, -a adj, nm/f Peruvian

perverso, -a adj wicked

pervertido, -a nm/f pervert

pesa nf weight; **hacer pesas** to do weight training

pesadez nf Es una pesadez tener que madrugar. (informal) It's such a pain having to get up early.; ¡Qué pesadez de película! What a boring film!

pesadilla nf nightmare

pesado, -a adj ❶ heavy ❷ tiring ❸ boring; ¡No seas pesado!

Don't be a pain in the neck!
▶ nm/f Mi primo es un pesado. My cousin is a pain in the neck.

pésame nm condolences pl ▷ Fuimos a darle el pésame. We went to offer our condolences.

pesar vb [25] ❶ to weigh ▷ ¿Cuánto pesas? How much do you weigh? ▷ Tengo que pesarme. I must weigh myself. ❷ to be heavy; **pesar poco** to be very light; **Me pesa haberlo hecho.** I regret having done it.; **a pesar del mal tiempo** in spite of the bad weather; **a pesar de que la quiero** even though I love her

pesca nf fishing ▷ ir de pesca to go fishing

pescadería nf fishmonger's

pescadilla nf whiting

pescado nm fish

pescador nm fisherman

pescar vb [48] ❶ to fish ❷ to catch

pesero nm (Mex) minibus

peseta nf peseta

pesimista adj pessimistic; **No seas pesimista.** Don't be a pessimist.
▶ nmf pessimist

pésimo, -a adj terrible ▷ La comida era pésima. The food was terrible.

peso nm ❶ weight; **ganar peso** to gain weight ▷ Ha perdido mucho peso. He's lost a lot of weight.; **La fruta se vende a peso.** Fruit is sold by weight. ❷ scales pl ❸ peso

pesquero, -a adj fishing ▷ un pueblecito pesquero a fishing village

pestaña nf ❶ eyelash ❷ tab

pestañear vb [25] to blink

peste nf ❶ plague ❷ stink

pesticida nm pesticide

pestillo nm ❶ bolt ❷ latch

pétalo nm petal

petardo nm firecracker

petición (pl **peticiones**) nf
❶ request ▷ a petición de la pareja at the request of the couple
❷ petition ▷ firmar una petición to sign a petition

petirrojo nm robin

petróleo nm oil

petrolero nm oil tanker

pez (pl **peces**) nm fish; **un pez de colores** a goldfish

> Word for word, **pez de colores** means 'fish of colours'.

Se sentía como el pez en el agua. He felt in his element.

pezuña nf hoof

pianista nmf pianist

piano nm piano; **un piano de cola** a grand piano

piar vb [**21**] to chirp

pibe, -a nm/f (River Plate: informal) kid

picada nf (LatAm) **El avión cayó en picada.** The plane nose-dived.

picado, -a adj ❶ (tooth) bad ❷ (sea) choppy; **El avión cayó en picado.** The plane nose-dived.

picadura nf ❶ bite ❷ sting

picante adj (food, sauce) hot

picaporte nm door handle

picar vb [**48**] ❶ (insect, snake) to bite ❷ to sting ❸ to chop up ❹ to mince; **La salsa pica bastante.** The sauce is quite hot.; **Saqué algunas cosas para picar.** I put out some nibbles.; **Me pica la**

espalda. I've got an itchy back.; **Me pica la garganta.** My throat tickles.

pichi nm pinafore

picnic (pl **picnics**) nm picnic

pico nm ❶ beak ❷ (of mountain) peak ❸ (tool) pick; **Eran las tres y pico.** It was just after three.; **doscientos y pico euros** just over two hundred euros; **cuello de pico** V-neck; **la hora pico** (LatAm) the rush hour

picoso, -a adj (Mex: food) hot

pidiendo vb see **pedir**

pie nm foot ▷ Fuimos a pie. We went on foot. ▷ Al pie de la página hay una explicación. There's an explanation at the foot of the page.; **Estaba de pie junto a mi cama.** He was standing next to my bed.; **ponerse de pie** to stand up; **de pies a cabeza** from head to foot

piedad nf mercy

piedra nf stone; **una piedra preciosa** a precious stone

piel nf ❶ skin ▷ Tengo la piel grasa. I have greasy skin. ❷ fur ▷ un abrigo de pieles a fur coat ❸ leather ▷ un bolso de piel a leather bag ❹ peel

pienso vb see **pensar**

pierdo vb see **perder**

pierna nf leg; **una pierna de cordero** a leg of lamb

pieza nf piece; **una pieza de recambio** a spare part

pijama nm pyjamas pl

pijo, -a adj posh

pila nf ❶ battery ❷ pile ▷ una pila de revistas a pile of magazines ❸ sink

pilar nm pillar

píldora nf pill

pileta nf (River Plate) sink

pillar vb [25] ① to catch; **Se pilló los dedos en la puerta.** He caught his fingers in the door. ② to hit ▷ La pilló una moto. She was hit by a motorbike.; **La estación nos pilla cerca de casa.** The station is pretty close to our house.

pillo, -a adj ① crafty ② naughty

piloto nm/f ① pilot ② driver; **piloto de carreras** racing driver

pimentón nm paprika

pimienta nf pepper ▷ pimienta negra black pepper

pimiento nm pepper ▷ un pimiento morrón a red pepper

pin (pl pins) nm badge

pincel nm paintbrush

pinchadiscos (pl pinchadiscos) nm/f disc jockey

pinchar vb [25] ① to prick ▷ Me pinché con un alfiler. I pricked myself on a pin.; **Los cactus pinchan.** Cactuses are prickly.; **Me pincharon en el brazo.** They gave me an injection in the arm. ② to burst; **Se me pinchó una rueda.** I had a puncture.

pinchazo nm ① puncture ▷ Tuve un pinchazo en la autopista. I got a puncture on the motorway. ② sharp pain

pincho nm ① thorn ② snack; **un pincho moruno** a kebab

ping-pong nm table tennis ▷ jugar al ping-pong to play table tennis

pingüino nm penguin

pino nm pine tree; **hacer el pino** to do a headstand

▌ Word for word, **hacer el pino** means 'to do the pine tree'.

pinta nf tener buena pinta to look good; **Con esas gafas tienes pinta de maestra.** You look like a teacher with those glasses on.

pintadas nfpl graffiti

pintalabios (pl pintalabios) nm lipstick

pintar vb [25] ① to paint ② to colour in; **Nunca me pinto.** I never wear makeup.; **pintarse los labios** to put on lipstick; **pintarse las uñas** to paint one's nails

pintor, a nm/f painter

pintoresco, -a adj picturesque

pintura nf ① paint ▷ Tengo que comprar más pintura. I've got to buy some more paint. ② painting ▷ Me gusta la pintura abstracta. I like abstract painting. ▷ varias pinturas al óleo several oil paintings

pinza nf ① clothes peg ② hairgrip ③ pincer; **unas pinzas** a pair of tweezers

piña nf ① pine cone ② pineapple

piñón (pl piñones) nm ① pine nut ② sprocket

piojo nm louse

pipa nf ① pipe ▷ Fuma en pipa. He smokes a pipe. ② seed; **comer pipas** to eat sunflower seeds

pipí nm wee ▷ hacer pipí to have a wee

piragua nf canoe

piragüismo nm canoeing

pirámide nf pyramid

pirata adj pirate
▶ nmf pirate; **un pirata informático** a hacker

Pirineos nmpl the Pyrenees

piropo nm compliment

pirulí (pl **pirulís**) nm lollipop

pisada nf ❶ footprint ❷ footstep

pisapapeles (pl **pisapapeles**) nm paperweight

pisar vb [25] ❶ to walk on ▷ ¿Se puede pisar el suelo de la cocina? Can I walk on the kitchen floor? ❷ to tread on ▷ Perdona, te he pisado. Sorry, I trod on your foot.; **Pisé el acelerador a fondo.** I put my foot down.

piscina nf swimming pool

Piscis nm (sign) Pisces; **Soy piscis.** I'm Pisces.

piso nm ❶ flat ▷ Vivimos en un piso céntrico. We live in a flat in the town centre. ❷ floor ▷ Su oficina está en el segundo piso. His office is on the second floor. ▷ El piso estaba lleno de papeles. The floor was covered in pieces of paper.

pista nf ❶ clue ▷ ¿Te doy una pista? Shall I give you a clue? ❷ (of animal) track ❸ (sport) court; **la pista de aterrizaje** the runway; **la pista de baile** the dance floor; **la pista de carreras** the racetrack; **la pista de esquí** the ski slope; **la pista de patinaje** the ice rink

pistola nf pistol

pitar vb [25] ❶ to blow one's whistle ❷ to hoot; **Salió pitando.** He was off like a shot.

pitear vb [25] (LatAm) to whistle

pito nm whistle; **Me importa un pito.** I don't care a hoot.

piyama nm (LatAm) pyjamas pl

pizarra nf ❶ blackboard; **una pizarra digital** an interactive whiteboard ❷ slate

pizca nf pinch

pizza nf pizza

placa nf ❶ plaque ❷ badge ❸ hotplate; **una placa de matrícula** a number plate

placer nm pleasure

plaga nf ❶ pest ❷ plague

plan nm plan ▷ ¿Qué planes tienes para este verano? What are your plans for the summer?; **viajar en plan económico** to travel cheap; **Lo dije en plan de broma.** I said it as a joke.; **el plan de estudios** the syllabus

plancha nf iron; **pescado a la plancha** grilled fish

planchar vb [25] ❶ to iron ❷ to do the ironing

planeador nm glider

planear vb [25] ❶ to plan ❷ to glide

planeta nm planet

planificar vb [48] to plan

plano, -a adj flat
▶ nm ❶ street plan ❷ plan; **en primer plano** in close-up

planta nf ❶ plant ❷ floor ▷ la planta baja the ground floor; **la planta del pie** the sole of the foot

plantado, -a adj **dejar a alguien plantado** to stand someone up

plantar vb [25] to plant

plantilla nf ❶ insole ❷ staff

plástico nm plastic

plastilina® nf Plasticine®

plata nf ❶ silver ❷ (LatAm) money

plataforma nf ❶ platform; **una plataforma petrolífera** an oil rig

plátano nm banana

platicar vb [48] (Mex) ❶ to talk ❷ to tell

platillo nm **un platillo volante** a flying saucer; **los platillos** the cymbals

platino nm platinum

plato nm ❶ plate ❷ dish; **el plato del día** the dish of the day ❸ course ▷ ¿Qué hay de segundo plato? What's for the main course?; **un plato combinado** a main course with vegetables included ❹ saucer

playa nf ❶ beach ❷ seaside

playera nf ❶ canvas shoe ❷ (Mex) T-shirt

plaza nf ❶ square ▷ la plaza mayor the main square ❷ market ▷ No había pescado en la plaza. There was no fish at the market. ❸ place ▷ Todavía quedan plazas. There are still some places left.; **una plaza de toros** a bullring

plazo nm ❶ period ▷ en un plazo de diez días within a period of ten days; **El viernes se cumple el plazo.** Friday is the deadline. ❷ instalment ▷ pagar a plazos to pay in instalments; **una solución a corto plazo** a short-term solution

plegable adj folding

plegar vb [34] to fold

pleno, -a adj **en pleno verano** in the middle of summer; **a plena luz del día** in broad daylight

pletina nf tape deck

pliegue vb see plegar
▶ nm ❶ fold ❷ pleat

plomero, -a nm/f (LatAm) plumber

plomo nm lead; **gasolina sin plomo** unleaded petrol; **Se han fundido los plomos.** The fuses have blown.

pluma nf ❶ feather ❷ pen; **una pluma atómica** (LatAm) a ballpoint pen; **una pluma estilográfica** a fountain pen

plural adj, nm plural

población (pl poblaciones) nf ❶ population ❷ town

pobre adj poor ▷ Somos pobres. We're poor.; **¡Pobre Pedro!** Poor Pedro!; **los pobres** the poor

pobreza nf poverty

poco, -a adj, adv, pron not much ▷ Hay poca leche. There isn't much milk. ▷ Tenemos poco tiempo. We haven't got very much time.; **Sus libros son poco conocidos aquí.** His books are not very well known here.; **un poco** a bit ▷ ¿Me das un poco? Can I have a bit?; **Tomé un poco de vino.** I had a little wine.; **unos pocos** a few ▷ Me llevé unos pocos. I took a few with me.; **poco a poco** little by little; **poco después** shortly after; **dentro de poco** in a short time; **hace poco** not long ago; **por poco** nearly ▷ Por poco me caigo. I nearly fell.

podar vb [25] to prune

podcast nm podcast

poder nm power ▷ estar en el poder to be in power

▶ *vb* [**40**] ❶ can ▷ ¡No puede ser!
That can't be true! ▷ ¿Puedo usar tu
teléfono? Can I use your phone?
▷ Pudiste haberte hecho daño. You
could have hurt yourself. ▷ ¡Me lo
podías haber dicho! You could have
told me! ▷ Aquí no se puede fumar.
You can't smoke here. ❷ to be able
to ▷ Creo que mañana no voy a poder
ir. I don't think I'll be able to come
tomorrow. ; **¿Se puede?** May I?;
Puede que llegue mañana. He
might arrive tomorrow. ; **Puede
ser.** It's possible. ; **No puedo con
tanto trabajo.** I can't cope with so
much work.

poderoso, -a *adj* powerful

podólogo, -a *nm/f* chiropodist

podrido, -a *adj* rotten

podrirse *vb* [**58**] = **pudrirse**

poema *nm* poem

poesía *nf* ❶ poetry ❷ poem

poeta *nmf* poet

póker *nm* poker

polaco, -a *adj* Polish
▶ *nm/f* Pole; **los polacos** the Poles
▶ *nm* (language) Polish

polémica *nf* controversy

polémico, -a *adj* controversial

polen *nm* pollen; **alergia al polen**
hay fever

policía *nm* police officer
▶ *nf* ❶ police ▷ Llamamos a la
policía. We called the police.
❷ police officer

policíaco, -a *adj* **una novela
policíaca** a detective novel

polideportivo *nm* sports centre

polilla *nf* moth

polio *nf* polio

política *nf* ❶ politics *sg* ❷ policy
❸ politician

político, -a *adj* political
▶ *nm* politician

pollo *nm* chicken; **pollo asado**
roast chicken

polluelo *nm* chick

polo *nm* ❶ ice lolly ❷ polo shirt;
el Polo Norte the North Pole;
el Polo Sur the South Pole

Polonia *nf* Poland

polvo *nm* dust; **quitar el polvo** to
do the dusting; **quitar el polvo a
algo** to dust something; **en polvo**
powdered ▷ leche en polvo
powdered milk; **polvos de talco**
talcum powder; **Estoy hecho
polvo.** I'm shattered.

pólvora *nf* gunpowder

pomada *nf* ointment

pomelo *nm* grapefruit

pomo *nm* handle

pompa *nf* ❶ bubble ▷ pompas de
jabón soap bubbles ❷ pomp

pómulo *nm* cheekbone

ponchar *vb* [**25**] (Mex) **Se nos
ponchó una llanta.** We had a
puncture.

ponche *nm* punch

poncho *nm* poncho

pondrá *vb* see **poner**

poner *vb* [**41**] ❶ to put ▷ ¿Dónde
pongo mis cosas? Where shall I put
my things? ❷ to put on ▷ Me puse el
abrigo. I put on my coat. ▷ ¿Pongo
música? Shall I put some music on?;
No sé que ponerme. I don't know
what to wear. ; **Ponlo más alto.**
Turn it up. ; **¿Ponen alguna
película esta noche?** Is there a

film on tonight? ❸ **to set** ▷ *Puse el despertador para las siete.* I set the alarm for seven o'clock. ▷ *poner la mesa* to set the table ❹ **to put in** ▷ *Queremos poner calefacción.* We want to put in central heating.; **¿Me pone con el Sr. García, por favor?** Could you put me through to Mr Garcia, please?; **Le pusieron Mónica.** They called her Monica.; **¿Qué te pongo?** What can I get you?; **Cuando se lo dije se puso muy triste.** He was very sad when I told him.; **¡Qué guapa te has puesto!** You look beautiful!; **Se puso a mi lado en clase.** He sat down beside me in class.; **ponerse a hacer algo** to start doing something

poney (pl **poneys**) nm pony

pongo vb see **poner**

pop (pl **pop**) adj pop ▷ *música pop* pop music

popote nm (Mex) straw

popular adj popular

por prep ❶ **for** ▷ *Lo hice por mis padres.* I did it for my parents. ▷ *Lo vendió por 100 euros.* He sold it for 100 euros. ▷ *Me castigaron por mentir.* I was punished for lying. ❷ **through** ▷ *La conozco por mi hermano.* I know her through my brother. ▷ *por la ventana* through the window ▷ *Pasamos por Valencia.* We went through Valencia. ❸ **by** ▷ *Fueron apresados por la policía.* They were captured by the police. ▷ *por correo* by post ▷ *Me agarró por el brazo.* He grabbed me by the arm. ❹ **along** ▷ *Paseábamos por la*

playa. We were walking along the beach. ❺ **around** ▷ *viajar por el mundo* to travel around the world ▷ *Viven por esta zona.* They live around this area. ❻ **because of** ▷ *Tuvo que suspenderpor el mal tiempo.* It had to be cancelled because of bad weather. ❼ **per** ▷ *100 kilómetros por hora* 100 kilometres per hour ▷ *diez euros por persona* ten euros per person; **por aquí cerca** near here; **por escrito** in writing; **por la mañana** in the morning; **por la noche** at night; **por mí ...** as far as I'm concerned ...; **¿por qué?** Why?

porcelana nf porcelain

porcentaje nm percentage

porche nm porch

porción (pl **porciones**) nf portion

pornografía nf pornography

poro nm ❶ pore ❷ (Mex) leek

poroto nm (Chile, River Plate) bean

porque conj because

porquería nf **Este CD es una porquería.** This CD's rubbish.

porra nf truncheon

porrazo nm **Me di un porrazo en la rodilla.** I banged my knee.; **Daba porrazos en la puerta.** He was banging on the door.

portada nf ❶ front page ❷ cover

portal nm ❶ hallway ❷ (on internet) portal; **el portal de Belén** the nativity scene

portarse vb [25] **portarse bien** to behave well; **portarse mal** to behave badly; **Se portó muy bien conmigo.** He treated me very well.

portátil *adj* portable

portavoz (*pl* **portavoces**) *nm* spokesman
▶ *nf* spokeswoman

portazo *nm* **Dio un portazo.** He slammed the door.

portera *nf* ❶ caretaker
❷ goalkeeper

portería *nf* goal

portero *nm* ❶ caretaker
❷ goalkeeper; **un portero automático** an entryphone

Word for word, **portero automático** means 'automatic doorman'.

portorriqueño, -a *adj, nm/f* Puerto Rican

Portugal *nm* Portugal

portugués (*f* **portuguesa**, *mpl* **portugueses**) *adj, nm/f* Portuguese
▶ *nm* (language) Portuguese

porvenir *nm* future

posar *vb* [25] to pose; **posarse** to land

posdata *nf* postscript

poseer *vb* [30] to possess

posguerra *nf* **durante la posguerra** during the postwar period

posibilidad *nf* ❶ possibility ▷ Es una posibilidad. It's a possibility.
❷ chance ▷ Tendrás la posibilidad de viajar. You'll have the chance to travel.; **Tiene muchas posibilidades de ganar.** He has a good chance of winning.

posible *adj* possible ▷ Es posible. It's possible.; **hacer todo lo posible** to do everything possible;

Es posible que ganen. They might win.

posición (*pl* **posiciones**) *nf* position; **Está en primera posición.** He's in first place.

positivo, -a *adj* positive

posponer *vb* [41] to postpone

posta *adv* **a posta** on purpose

postal *nf* postcard

poste *nm* ❶ post ❷ pole

póster (*pl* **pósters**) *nm* poster

posterior *adj* rear ▷ los asientos posteriores the rear seats; **la parte posterior** the rear

postizo, -a *adj* false
▶ *nm* hairpiece

postre *nm* dessert ▷ De postre tomé un helado. I had ice cream for dessert. ▷ ¿Qué hay de postre? What's for dessert?

postura *nf* position

potable *adj* **agua potable** drinking water

potaje *nm* stew

potencia *nf* power

potencial *adj* potential

potente *adj* powerful

potro *nm* ❶ colt ❷ horse

pozo *nm* well

práctica *nf* practice ▷ No tengo mucha práctica. I haven't had much practice.; **en la práctica** in practice

prácticamente *adv* practically

practicante *adj* practising
▶ *nmf* nurse

practicar *vb* [48] to practise; **No practico ningún deporte.** I don't do any sports.

práctico, -a *adj* practical

prado nm meadow

precaución (pl **precauciones**) nf precaution ▷ tomar precauciones to take precautions; **con precaución** with caution

precavido, -a adj **Es muy precavida.** She's always very well-prepared.

precinto nm seal

precio nm price ▷ **Han subido los precios.** Prices have gone up.; **¿Qué precio tiene?** How much is it?

preciosidad nf **La casa es una preciosidad.** The house is beautiful.

precioso, -a adj beautiful ▷ ¡Es precioso! It's beautiful!

precipicio nm precipice

precipitarse vb [25] **No hay que precipitarse.** There's no need to rush into anything.

precisamente adv precisely

precisar vb [25] **¿Puedes precisar un poco más?** Can you be a little more specific?; **Precisó que no se trataba de un virus.** He said specifically that it was not a virus.

preciso, -a adj ❶ precise ▷ en ese preciso momento at that precise moment ❷ accurate ▷ un reloj muy preciso a very accurate watch; **si es preciso** if necessary; **No es preciso que vengas.** There's no need for you to come.

precoz (pl **precoces**) adj precocious

predecir vb [15] to predict

predicar vb [48] to preach

predicción (pl **predicciones**) nf prediction

predicho vb see **predecir**

preescolar adj pre-school

prefabricado, -a adj prefabricated

preferencia nf ❶ preference ▷ No tengo ninguna preferencia. I have no preference. ❷ priority ▷ Tienen preferencia los coches que vienen por la derecha. Cars coming from the right have priority.

preferido, -a adj favourite

preferir vb [51] to prefer; **Prefiero ir mañana.** I'd rather go tomorrow.

prefiero vb see **preferir**

prefijo nm code ▷ ¿Cuál es el prefijo de Andorra? What is the code for Andorra?

pregunta nf question ▷ hacer una pregunta to ask a question

preguntar vb [25] to ask ▷ Siempre me preguntas lo mismo. You're always asking me the same question.; **Me preguntó por ti.** He asked after you.; **Me pregunto si estará enterado.** I wonder if he's heard yet.

prehistórico, -a adj prehistoric

prejuicio nm prejudice; **Yo no tengo prejuicios.** I'm not prejudiced.

prematuro, -a adj premature

premiar vb [25] ❶ to award a prize to; **el director premiado** the award-winning director ❷ to reward

premio nm ❶ prize ▷ llevarse un premio to get a prize ❷ reward; **el premio gordo** the jackpot

prenda nf garment

prender vb [8] ❶ (match, cigarette) to light ❷ (LatAm) to switch on; **prender fuego a algo** to set fire to something

prensa nf press ⊳ *una rueda de prensa* a press conference

preocupación (pl **preocupaciones**) nf worry

preocupado, -a adj worried; **estar preocupado por algo** to be worried about something

preocupar vb [25] to worry; **preocuparse por algo** to worry about something; **Si llego un poco tarde se preocupa.** If I arrive a bit late he gets worried.

preparar vb [25] ❶ to prepare ❷ to prepare for ⊳ *¿Te has preparado el examen?* Have you prepared for the exam? ❸ to cook; **Me estaba preparando para salir.** I was getting ready to go out.

preparativos nmpl preparations

presa nf ❶ dam ❷ prey ❸ prisoner

prescindir vb [58] **prescindir de** to do without

presencia nf presence ⊳ *en presencia de un sacerdote* in the presence of a priest

presenciar vb [25] to witness

presentador, a nm/f ❶ presenter ❷ newsreader

presentar vb [25] ❶ to introduce ❷ to hand in ❸ to present; **presentarse (1)** to turn up **(2)** to introduce oneself; **presentarse a un examen** to sit an exam

presente adj, nm present ⊳ *Juan no estaba presente en la reunión.* Juan was not present at the meeting.;

el presente the present; **los presentes** those present; **¡Presente!** Present!

presentimiento nm premonition

preservativo nm condom

presidenta nf ❶ president ❷ chairperson

presidente nm ❶ president ❷ chairman

presión (pl **presiones**) nf pressure; **la presión sanguínea** blood pressure

presionar vb [25] ❶ to put pressure on ❷ to press

preso, -a adj **Estuvo tres años preso.** He was in prison for three years.; **llevarse a alguien preso** to take someone prisoner ▶ nm prisoner

prestado, -a adj **La cinta no es mía, es prestada.** It's not my tape, someone lent it to me.; **Le pedí prestada la bicicleta.** I asked if I could borrow his bicycle.; **Me dejó el coche prestado.** He lent me his car.

préstamo nm loan ⊳ *Pidieron un préstamo al banco.* They asked the bank for a loan.

prestar vb [25] to lend ⊳ *Un amigo me prestó el traje.* A friend lent me the suit.; **¿Me prestas el boli?** Can I borrow your pen?; **Tienes que prestar atención.** You must pay attention.

prestigio nm prestige

presumido, -a adj vain

presumir vb [58] to show off; **Luis presume de guapo.** Luis thinks he's really handsome.

presupuesto nm ❶ budget
❷ estimate

pretender vb [8] ❶ to intend;
¿Qué pretendes decir con eso?
What do you mean by that? ❷ to
expect ▷ *¡No pretenderás que te
pague la comida!* You're not
expecting me to pay for your meal,
are you?

> Be careful! **pretender** does not
> mean to pretend

pretexto nm excuse ▷ *Era solo un
pretexto.* It was only an excuse.;
*Vino con el pretexto de ver al
abuelo.* He came in order to see
Granddad, or so he said.

prevención nf prevention

prevenir vb [56] ❶ to prevent ❷ to
warn

prever vb [57] ❶ to foresee; *Han
previsto nevadas en el norte.*
Snow is forecast for the north.
❷ to plan; *Tienen previsto
acabar el metro para el 2016.*
They plan to finish the metro by
the year 2016.

previo, -a adj previous

previsible adj foreseeable

previsto vb see **prever**
▷ adj *Tengo previsto volver
mañana.* I plan to return
tomorrow.; *El avión tiene
prevista su llegada a las dos.* The
plane is due in at two o'clock.;
Como estaba previsto, ganó él.
As expected, he was the winner.

prima nf ❶ cousin ❷ bonus

primario, -a adj primary ▷ *la
educación primaria* primary
education

primavera nf spring ▷ *en primavera*
in spring

primer see **primero**

primero, -a adj, pron first ▷ *el
primer día* the first day ▷ *Primer
plato: sopa.* First course: soup.
▷ *Primero vamos a comer.* Let's eat
first.; *en primera fila* in the front
row; *En primer lugar, veamos los
datos.* Firstly, let's look at the
facts.; *primer ministro* prime
minister; *Vivo en el primero.* I live
on the first floor.; *Fui la primera
en llegar.* I was the first to arrive.;
Lo primero es la salud. The most
important thing is your health.;
*El examen será a primeros de
mayo.* The exam will be at the
beginning of May.

primitivo, -a adj primitive

primo nm cousin; *primo segundo*
second cousin

princesa nf princess

principal adj main; *Lo principal es
estar sano.* The main thing is to
stay healthy.

principalmente adv mainly

príncipe nm prince

principiante nmf beginner

principio nm ❶ beginning; *Al
principio parecía fácil.* It seemed
easy at first.; *a principios de año*
at the beginning of the year
❷ principle; *En principio me
parece una buena idea.* On the
face of it, it's a good idea.

prioridad nf priority

prisa nf rush; *Con las prisas me
olvidé el paraguas.* In the rush I
forgot my umbrella.; *¡Date prisa!*

Hurry up!; **Tengo prisa.** I'm in a hurry.

prisión (pl **prisiones**) nf prison

prisionero, -a nm/f prisoner

prismáticos nmpl binoculars

privado, -a adj private ▷ **un colegio privado** a private school

privarse vb [**25**] **En vacaciones no me privo de nada.** When I'm on holiday I really spoil myself.

privilegio nm privilege

pro nm **los pros y contras** the pros and cons

probabilidades nfpl **Tiene muchas probabilidades de ganar.** He has a very good chance of winning.; **No tengo muchas probabilidades de aprobar.** I don't have much chance of passing.

probable adj likely ▷ **Es muy probable.** It's very likely.; **Es probable que llegue tarde.** He'll probably arrive late.

probablemente adv probably

probador nm changing room

probar vb [**11**] ❶ to prove ▷ **La policía no pudo probarlo.** The police could not prove it. ❷ to taste ▷ **Probé la sopa para ver si le faltaba sal.** I tasted the soup to see if it needed more salt. ❸ to try ▷ **Pruébalo antes para ver si funciona bien.** Try it first and see if it works properly.; **Me probé un vestido.** I tried on a dress.

probeta nf test tube; **un niño probeta** a test-tube baby

problema nm problem; **Este coche nunca me ha dado problemas.** This car has never given me any trouble.; **tener problemas de estómago** to have stomach trouble

procedente adj procedente de from ▷ **el tren procedente de Barcelona** the train from Barcelona

procesador nm processor; **un procesador de textos** a word processor

procesión (pl **procesiones**) nf procession

proceso nm process; **el proceso de datos** data processing

proclamar vb [**25**] to proclaim

procurar vb [**25**] to try; **Procura terminarlo mañana.** Try to finish it tomorrow.

producción (pl **producciones**) nf production; **la producción en serie** mass production

producir vb [**9**] ❶ to produce ❷ to cause; **¿Cómo se produjo el accidente?** How did the accident happen?

producto nm product; **los productos del campo** farm produce

productor, a nm/f producer

profesión (pl **profesiones**) nf profession

profesional adj, nmf professional

profesor, a nm/f teacher; **mi profesor particular** my private tutor; **un profesor universitario** a university lecturer

Be careful! The Spanish word **profesor** does not mean **professor**.

profundamente adv ① deeply ② soundly

profundidad nf depth; **Tiene dos metros de profundidad.** It's two metres deep.

profundo, -a adj deep; **una piscina poco profunda** a shallow pool

programa nm ① programme ▷ un programa de televisión a television programme; **un programa-concurso** a quiz show; **el programa de estudios** the syllabus ② (on computer) program

programación nf ① programmes pl ② programming

programador, a nm/f programmer

programar vb [25] to programme

progresar vb [25] to progress

progreso nm progress; **Carmen ha hecho muchos progresos este trimestre.** Carmen has made great progress this term.

prohibir vb [42] to ban; **Queda terminantemente prohibido.** It is strictly forbidden.; **'prohibido fumar'** 'no smoking'

prolijo, -a adj (River Plate) neat

prólogo nm prologue

prolongar vb [37] to extend

promedio nm average

promesa nf promise

prometer vb [8] to promise; **¡Te lo prometo!** I promise!

promoción nf promotion; **Está en promoción.** It's on offer.

pronombre nm pronoun

pronosticar vb [48] to forecast

pronóstico nm **el pronóstico del tiempo** the weather forecast

pronto adv ① soon; **lo más pronto posible** as soon as possible; **¡Hasta pronto!** See you soon! ② early; **De pronto, empezó a nevar.** All of a sudden it began to snow.

pronunciar vb [25] to pronounce

propaganda nf ① advertising; **Han hecho mucha propaganda del concierto.** The concert has been well-advertised. ② junk mail

propagarse vb [37] to spread

propiedad nf property

propietario, -a nm/f owner

propina nf tip

propio adj ① own ▷ Tengo mi propia habitación. I have my own room. ② himself ▷ Lo anunció el propio ministro. It was announced by the minister himself. ③ typical; **un nombre propio** a proper noun

proponer vb [41] ① to suggest; **Me propuso un trato.** He made me a proposition. ② to nominate; **Se ha propuesto adelgazar.** He's decided to lose some weight.

proporción (pl proporciones) nf proportion

proporcional adj proportional

proporcionar vb [25] to provide

propósito nm purpose ▷ ¿Cuál es el propósito de su visita? What is the purpose of your visit?; **A propósito, ya tengo los billetes.** By the way, I've got the tickets.; **Lo hizo a propósito.** He did it deliberately.

propuesta nf proposal

propuesto vb see **proponer**

prórroga nf ① extension ② extra time

prospecto nm leaflet

prosperar vb [25] to do well

próspero, -a adj ¡Próspero Año Nuevo! A prosperous New Year!

prostituta nf prostitute

protagonista nmf main character; El protagonista es Tom Cruise. Tom Cruise plays the lead.

protección nf protection

protector, a adj protective ▷ una funda protectora a protective cover

proteger vb [7] to protect; Nos protegimos de la lluvia en la cabaña. We sheltered from the rain in the hut.

protesta nf protest ▷ como protesta por los despidos as a protest against redundancies

protestante adj, nmf Protestant

protestar vb [25] ① to protest ② to complain

provecho nm ¡Buen provecho! Enjoy your meal!; Sacó mucho provecho del curso. He got a lot out of the course.

proverbio nm proverb

provincia nf province

provisional adj provisional

provisiones nfpl provisions

provocar vb [48] ① to provoke ② to cause; El incendio fue provocado. The fire was started deliberately.

provocativo, -a adj provocative

próximo, -a adj next ▷ Lo haremos la próxima semana. We'll do it next week. ▷ la próxima vez next time ▷ la próxima calle a la izquierda the next street on the left

proyecto nm ① plan ▷ ¿Tienes algún proyecto a la vista? Have you got any plans? ② project ▷ el proyecto en el que estamos trabajando the project we are working on; un proyecto de ley a bill

proyector nm projector

prudente adj wise ▷ Lo más prudente sería esperar. It would be wisest to wait.; Debería ser más prudente. He should be more careful.

prueba vb see **probar**
▷ nf ① test ▷ El médico me hizo más pruebas. The doctor did some more tests.; pruebas nucleares nuclear tests ② proof ▷ Eso es la prueba de que lo hizo él. This is the proof that he did it.; El fiscal presentó nuevas pruebas. The prosecutor presented new evidence. ③ heat ▷ la prueba de los cien metros valla the hundred metres hurdles heat; a prueba de balas bullet-proof

pruebo vb see **probar**

psicóloga nf psychologist

psicología nf psychology

psicológico, -a adj psychological

psicólogo nm psychologist

psiquiatra nmf psychiatrist

psiquiátrico, -a adj psychiatric

ptas. abbr (= pesetas) pesetas

púa nf ① plectrum ② (of comb) tooth

pub (pl pubs) nm bar

publicar vb [48] to publish

publicidad nf ❶ advertising ❷ publicity

público, -a adj public
▶ nm ❶ public ❷ (at concert, play) audience ❸ (at match) spectators pl

pude vb see **poder**

pudrirse vb [**58**] to rot

pueblo nm ❶ village ❷ town ❸ people pl

puedo vb see **poder**

puente nm bridge; **el puente aéreo** the shuttle service

Word for word, **puente aéreo** means 'air bridge'.

hacer puente to make a long weekend of it

When a public holiday falls on a Tuesday or Thursday people often take off Monday or Friday as well to give themselves a long weekend.

puerco nm ❸ pig ❷ (Mex) pork

puerro nm leek

puerta nf ❶ door ▷ Llaman a la puerta. Somebody's at the door.; **Susana me acompañó a la puerta.** Susana saw me out. ❷ gate; **la puerta de embarque** boarding gate

puerto nm port ▷ un puerto pesquero a fishing port; **un puerto deportivo** a marina; **un puerto de montaña** a mountain pass

Puerto Rico nm Puerto Rico

puertorriqueño, -a adj, nm/f Puerto Rican

pues conj ❶ then ▷ Tengo sueño. —¡Pues vete a la cama! I'm tired. —Then go to bed! ❷ well ▷ Pues, como te iba contando ... Well,

as I was saying ... ▷ ¡Pues no lo sabía! Well I didn't know!; **¡Pues claro!** Yes, of course!

puesta nf **la puesta de sol** sunset; **la puesta en libertad de dos presos** the release of two prisoners

puesto vb see **poner**
▶ nm ❶ place ▷ Acabé la carrera en primer puesto. I finished in first place. ❷ stall ▷ un puesto de verduras a vegetable stall; **un puesto de trabajo** a job; **un puesto de socorro** a first aid station; **puesto que** since ▷ Puesto que no lo querías, se lo di a Pedro. Since you didn't want it, I gave it to Pedro.

pulga nf flea

pulgada nf inch

pulgar nm thumb

pulir vb [**58**] to polish

pulmón (pl pulmones) nm lung

pulpería nf (LatAm) shop

púlpito nm pulpit

pulpo nm octopus

pulsar vb [**25**] to press

pulsera nf bracelet; **un reloj de pulsera** a wrist watch

pulso nm pulse

pulverizador nm spray

punta nf ❶ (metal) nail ❷ (of finger, tongue) tip ❸ (of pen, knife) point; **Sácale punta al lápiz.** Sharpen your pencil.; **Vivo en la otra punta del pueblo.** I live at the other end of the town.; **la hora punta** the rush hour

puntapié (pl puntapiés) nm **Le dio un puntapié a la piedra.** He kicked the stone.

puntería nf **tener buena puntería** to be a good shot

puntiagudo, -a adj pointed

puntilla nf lace edging; **andar de puntillas** to tiptoe; **ponerse de puntillas** to stand on tiptoe

punto nm ❶ point ▷ *desde ese punto de vista* from that point of view ❷ stitch ❸ dot ❹ full stop; **punto y seguido** full stop, new sentence; **punto y aparte** full stop, new paragraph; **punto y coma** semi-colon; **dos puntos** colon; **Estábamos a punto de salir cuando llamaste.** We were about to go out when you phoned.; **Estuve a punto de perder el tren.** I very nearly missed the train.; **a la una en punto** at one o'clock sharp; **Me gusta hacer punto.** I like knitting.

puntuación (pl **puntuaciones**) nf ❶ punctuation ❷ score

puntual adj ❶ punctual ▷ *Sé puntual.* Be punctual.; **Jamás llega puntual.** He never arrives on time. ❷ specific

puntualidad nf punctuality

puntuar vb [1] **Este trabajo no puntúa para la nota final.** This essay doesn't count towards the final mark.; **un profesor que puntúa muy bajo** a teacher who gives very low marks

puñado nm handful

puñal nm dagger

puñalada nf **Le dieron una puñalada.** He was stabbed.

puñetazo nm punch; **Le pegó un puñetazo.** He punched him.

puño nm ❶ fist ❷ cuff

pupitre nm desk

puré (pl **purés**) nm **puré de verduras** puréed vegetables; **puré de patatas** mashed potato

puro, -a adj pure ▷ *por pura casualidad* by pure chance; **Es la pura verdad.** That's the absolute truth.
 ▶ nm cigar

puse vb see **poner**

q

que *conj* **❶** than ▷ *Es más alto que tú.* He's taller than you.; **Yo que tú, iría.** I'd go if I were you. **❷** that ▷ *José sabe que estás aquí.* José knows that you're here.

Unlike **que** in Spanish, *that* is often omitted.

▷ *Dijo que vendría.* He said he'd come.; **Dile a Rosa que me llame.** Ask Rosa to call me.; **¡Que te mejores!** Get well soon!; **¿De verdad que te gusta? — ¡Que sí!** Do you really like it? — Of course I do!

▶ *pron* **❶** which ▷ *la película que ganó el premio* the film which won the award

When not used as a subject, **que** isn't always translated.

▷ *el sombrero que te compraste* the

hat you bought ▷ *el libro del que hablé* the book I spoke to you about **❷** who ▷ *el hombre que vino ayer* the man who came yesterday

When not used as a subject, **que** isn't always translated.

▷ *la chica que conocí* the girl I met

qué *adj, adv, pron* **❶** what ▷ *¿Qué fecha es hoy?* What's today's date? ▷ *No sabe qué es.* He doesn't know what it is. ▷ *No sé qué hacer.* I don't know what to do.; **¿qué?** what? **❷** which ▷ *¿Qué película quieres ver?* Which film do you want to see?; **¡Qué asco!** How revolting!; **¡Qué día más bonito!** What a glorious day!; **¿Qué tal?** How are things?; **¿Qué tal está tu madre?** How's your mother?; **No lo he hecho. ¿Y qué?** I haven't done it. So what?

quebrado *nm* fraction

quebrar *vb* **[39]** to go bankrupt; **quebrarse** *(LatAm)* to break

quedar *vb* **[25]** **❶** to be left; **Me quedan quince euros.** I've got 15 euros left. ▷ *Eso queda muy lejos de aquí.* That's a long way from here. **❸** to arrange to meet ▷ *He quedado con ella en el cine.* I've arranged to meet her at the cinema.; **¿Quedamos en la parada?** Shall we meet at the bus stop? **❹** to suit ▷ *No te queda bien ese vestido.* That dress doesn't suit you.; **quedarse** to stay; **quedarse atrás** to fall behind; **quedarse sordo** to go deaf; **quedarse con algo** to keep something ▷ *Quédate con el cambio.* Keep the change.

quehaceres nmpl los
  quehaceres de la casa the
  household chores

queja nf complaint

quejarse vb [25] to complain;
  quejarse de algo to complain
  about something; **quejarse de
  que ...** to complain that ...

quejido nm ❶ moan ❷ whine

quemado, -a adj burnt

quemadura nf burn;
  quemaduras de sol sunburn sg

quemar vb [25] ❶ to burn ❷ to be
  burning hot; **quemarse** to burn
  oneself

quepa vb see **caber**

querer vb [43] ❶ to want ▷ No
  quiero ir. I don't want to go.;
  Quiero que vayas. I want you to
  go.; **¿Quieres un café?** Would you
  like some coffee? ❷ to love ▷ Ana
  quiere mucho a sus hijos. Ana loves
  her children dearly. ❸ to mean
  ▷ No quería hacer daño. I didn't
  mean to hurt you. ▷ Lo hice sin
  querer. I didn't mean to do it.;
  querer decir to mean ▷ ¿Qué
  quieres decir? What do you mean?

querido, -a adj dear

querré vb see **querer**

queso nm cheese

quicio nm **sacar a alguien de
  quicio** to drive somebody up the
  wall

quiebra nf **ir a la quiebra** to go
  bankrupt

quien pron who ▷ Fue Juan quien nos
  lo dijo. It was Juan who told us.

  When not used as a subject,
  quien is often not translated.

  ▷ Vi al chico con quien sales. I saw
  the boy you're going out with.

quién pron who ▷ ¿Quién es esa?
  Who's that? ▷ ¿A quién viste? Who
  did you see? ▷ No sé quién es. I don't
  know who he is.; **¿De quién es ...?**
  Whose is ...? ▷ ¿De quién es este libro?
  Whose is this book? **¿Quién es?**
  (1) Who's there? **(2)** Who's calling?

quiero vb see **querer**

quieto, -a adj still; **¡Estáte quieto!**
  Keep still!

química nf ❶ chemistry ❷ chemist

químico nm chemist

quince adj, pron fifteen; **el quince
  de enero** the fifteenth of January;
  quince días a fortnight

quinceañero, -a nm/f teenager

quincena nf fortnight

quincenal adj fortnightly

quiniela nf football pools pl

quinientos, -as adj, pron five
  hundred

quinto, -a adj, pron fifth; **Vivo en
  el quinto.** I live on the fifth floor.

quiosco nm ❶ news stand
  ❷ drinks stand ❸ flower stall
  ❹ bandstand

quirófano nm operating theatre

quirúrgico, -a adj surgical; **una
  intervención quirúrgica** an
  operation

quise vb see **querer**

quitaesmalte nm nail polish
  remover

quitamanchas (pl
  quitamanchas) nm stain
  remover

quitanieves (pl **quitanieves**) nf
  snowplough

quitar vb [25] ❶ to remove ❷ to take away; **Me han quitado la cartera.** I've had my wallet stolen.; **Esto te quitará el dolor.** This will relieve the pain.; **quitarse** to take off; **¡Quítate de en medio!** Get out of the way!

quizá adv = **quizás**

quizás adv perhaps

rábano nm radish; **¡Me importa un rábano!** I don't give a monkey's!

rabia nf ❶ rage ▷ Lo hizo por rabia. He did it out of rage.; **Me da mucha rabia.** It's really annoying. ❷ rabies sg

rabieta nf tantrum

rabo nm tail

racha nf **una racha de buen tiempo** a spell of good weather; **una racha de viento** a gust of wind; **pasar una mala racha** to go through a bad patch

racial adj racial

racimo nm bunch

ración (pl **raciones**) nf portion

racismo nm racism

racista adj, nmf racist

radar nm radar

radiación nf radiation

radiactividad nf radioactivity

radiactivo, -a adj radioactive

radiador nm radiator

radio nf radio ▷ *Por la mañana escucho la radio.* In the morning I listen to the radio.; **Lo oí por la radio.** I heard it on the radio.
▶ nm ❶ radius ❷ (LatAm) radio ❸ spoke

radiocasete nm radio cassette player

radiografía nf X-ray; **Tengo que hacerme una radiografía.** I've got to have to have an X-ray.

raíl nm rail

raíz (pl **raíces**) nf root; **La planta está echando raíces.** The plant's taking root.; **a raíz de** as a result of

raja nf ❶ crack ❷ (in fabric) tear ❸ slice

rajarse vb [25] ❶ to crack ❷ to split

rallar vb [25] to grate

rally (pl **rallys**) nm rally

rama nf branch

ramo nm bunch ▷ *un ramo de claveles* a bunch of carnations

rampa nf ramp

rana nf frog

rancho nm ranch

rancio, -a adj rancid

rango nm rank; **políticos de alto rango** high-ranking politicians

ranura nf slot ▷ *Introduzca la moneda en la ranura.* Put the coin in the slot.

rapar vb [25] ❶ to crop ❷ to shave

rape nm monkfish

rápidamente adv quickly

rapidez nf speed; **con rapidez** quickly

rápido, -a adj ❶ fast ▷ *un coche muy rápido* a very fast car ❷ quick ▷ *Fue una visita muy rápida.* It was a very quick visit.
▶ adv fast; **Lo hice tan rápido como pude.** I did it as quickly as I could.; **¡Rápido!** Hurry up!

raptar vb [25] to kidnap

rapto nm kidnapping

raqueta nf ❶ racket ❷ bat

raramente adv rarely

raro, -a adj ❶ strange; **¡Qué raro!** How strange!; **Sabe un poco raro.** It tastes a bit funny. ❷ rare; **Es raro que haga tan buen tiempo.** It's unusual to have such good weather.; **rara vez** seldom

rascacielos (pl **rascacielos**) nm skyscraper

rascar vb [48] ❶ to scratch ❷ to scrape; **rascarse** to scratch

rasgar vb [37] to rip

rasgo nm feature

rasguño nm scratch

rastrillo nm ❶ rake ❷ (Mex) razor

rastro nm ❶ trail ❷ trace ▷ *Desaparecieron sin dejar rastro.* They vanished without trace. ❸ fleamarket

rasurarse vb [25] (LatAm) to shave

rata nf rat

rato nm while ▷ *después de un rato* after a while; **Estaba aquí hace un rato.** He was here a few minutes ago.; **al poco rato** shortly after; **pasar el rato** to while away the time; **pasar un buen rato** to have a good time; **Pasamos un mal rato.** We had a dreadful time.; **en mis ratos libres** in my free time

ratón (pl **ratones**) nm <u>mouse</u>

raya nf ❶ line ▷ **trazar una raya** to draw a line; **pasarse de la raya** to overstep the mark ❷ <u>stripe</u>; **un jersey a rayas** a striped jumper ❸ parting ▷ **Me hago la raya en medio.** I have my parting in the middle. ❹ crease ❺ dash

rayar vb [**25**] <u>to scratch</u>

rayo nm ❶ lightning ▷ **Cayó un rayo en la torre de la iglesia.** The church tower was struck by lightning. ❷ ray ▷ **un rayo de luz** a ray of light; **los rayos X** X-rays

raza nf ❶ race ▷ **la raza humana** the human race ❷ breed ▷ **¿De qué raza es tu gato?** What breed's your cat?; **un perro de raza** a pedigree dog

razón (pl **razones**) nf reason ▷ **¿Cuál era la razón de su visita?** What was the reason for his visit?; **tener razón** to be right; **dar la razón a alguien** to agree that somebody is right; **no tener razón** to be wrong

razonable adj reasonable

reacción (pl **reacciones**) nf reaction

reaccionar vb [**25**] to react

reactor nm ❶ jet plane ❷ jet engine; **un reactor nuclear** a nuclear reactor

real adj ❶ real; **La película está basada en hechos reales.** The film is based on actual events. ❷ royal

realidad nf reality; **en realidad** actually; **Mi sueño se hizo realidad.** My dream came true.; **realidad virtual** virtual reality

realista adj realistic

realizar vb [**13**] ❶ to carry out; **Has realizado un buen trabajo.** You've done a good job. ❷ to realize; **realizarse** to come true

realmente adv ❶ really ❷ actually

rebaja nf ❶ discount ▷ **Me hizo una rebaja por pagar al contado.** He gave me a discount for paying cash. ❷ reduction; **las rebajas** the sales; **Todos los grandes almacenes están de rebajas.** There are sales on in all the department stores.

rebajar vb [**25**] to reduce

rebanada nf slice

rebaño nm flock ▷ **un rebaño de ovejas** a flock of sheep

rebeca nf cardigan

rebelarse vb [**25**] to rebel

rebelde adj rebellious

▶ nmf rebel

rebelión (pl **rebeliones**) nf rebellion

rebobinar vb [**25**] to rewind

rebotar vb [**25**] to bounce; **La pelota rebotó en el poste.** The ball bounced off the post.

rebozado, -a adj ❶ breaded ❷ battered

recado nm ❶ message ▷ **Dejé recado de que me llamara.** I left a message for him to call me. ❷ errand ▷ **Fui a hacer unos recados.** I went to do some errands.

recaída nf relapse

recalcar vb [**48**] to stress

recámara nf (Mex) bedroom

recambio nm ❶ spare ▷ *la rueda de recambio* the spare wheel; **una pieza de recambio** a spare part ❷ refill

recargar vb [37] ❶ to recharge ❷ to fill up

recargo nm **El taxista me cobró un recargo por el equipaje.** The taxi driver charged me extra for my luggage.

recaudar vb [25] to collect

recepción (pl recepciones) nf reception

recepcionista nmf receptionist

receptor nm receiver

recesión (pl recesiones) nf recession

receta nf ❶ recipe ▷ *Me dio la receta de los raviolis.* He gave me the recipe for the ravioli. ❷ prescription ▷ *Los antibióticos solo se venden con receta.* Antibiotics are only available on prescription.

 ▌Be careful! **receta** does not mean **receipt**.

recetar vb [25] to prescribe

rechazar vb [13] ❶ to reject ❷ to turn down

rechoncho, -a adj stocky

recibidor nm entrance hall

recibir vb [58] ❶ to receive; **Recibí muchos regalos.** I got a lot of presents. ❷ to meet ▷ *Vinieron a recibirnos al aeropuerto.* They came and met us at the airport.; **El director me recibió en su despacho.** The manager saw me in his office.

recibo nm ❶ receipt ❷ bill

reciclaje nm recycling

reciclar vb [25] to recycle

recién adv just ▷ *El comedor está recién pintado.* The dining room has just been painted.; **Recién se fueron.** (LatAm) They've just left.; **los recién casados** the newly-weds; **un recién nacido** a newborn baby; **'recién pintado'** 'wet paint'

reciente adj recent; **pan reciente** fresh bread

recientemente adv recently

recipiente nm container

recital nm recital

recitar vb [25] to recite

reclamación (pl reclamaciones) nf complaint ▷ *presentar una reclamación* to make a complaint; **el libro de reclamaciones** the complaints book

reclamar vb [25] ❶ to complain ❷ to demand

reclamo nm (LatAm) complaint

recluta nmf recruit

recogedor nm dustpan

recoger vb [7] ❶ to pick up; **recoger fruta** to pick fruit ❷ to collect ❸ to clear up; **Recogí los platos y los puse en el fregadero.** I cleared away the plates and put them in the sink.; **recoger la mesa** to clear the table

recogida nf collection

recomendación (pl recomendaciones) nf ❶ recommendation ▷ *Fuimos a ese restaurante por recomendación de un amigo.* We went to that restaurant

on the recommendation of a friend.; **una carta de recomendación** a letter of recommendation ❷ **advice**
▷ *Hago régimen por recomendación del médico.* I'm on a diet on my doctor's advice.

recomendar vb **[39]** to recommend

recompensa nf reward

reconciliarse vb **[25]**
reconciliarse con alguien to make it up with somebody

reconocer vb **[12]** ❶ to recognize ❷ to admit

reconocimiento nm check-up
▷ *hacerse un reconocimiento médico* to have a check-up

reconquista nf reconquest

reconstruir vb **[10]** to rebuild

récord (pl **récords**) nm record

recordar vb **[25]** ❶ to remember ▷ *No recuerdo dónde lo puse.* I can't remember where I put it. ❷ to remind ▷ *Recuérdame que hable con Daniel.* Remind me to speak to Daniel. ▷ *Me recuerda a su padre.* He reminds me of his father.

> Be careful! **recordar** does not mean to record.

recorrer vb **[8]** ❶ to travel around ❷ to do

recorrido nm ¿Qué recorrido hace este autobús? Which route does this bus take?; **un recorrido turístico** a tour; **un tren de largo recorrido** an inter-city train

recortar vb **[25]** to cut out; **recortar gastos** to cut costs

recorte nm **recortes de prensa** press cuttings; **recortes de personal** staff cutbacks

recostarse vb **[11]** to lie down

recreo nm break ▷ *Tenemos 20 minutos de recreo.* We have a 20-minute break.

recta nf straight line; **la recta final** the home straight

rectangular adj rectangular

rectángulo nm rectangle

recto, -a adj, adv straight ▷ *una línea recta* a straight line; **todo recto** straight on ▷ *Siga todo recto.* Go straight on.

recuadro nm box

recuerdo vb see **recordar**
▷ nm ❶ memory ❷ souvenir; **un recuerdo de familia** a family heirloom; **¡Recuerdos a tu madre!** Give my regards to your mother!; **Dale recuerdos de mi parte.** Give him my regards.

recuperación (pl **recuperaciones**) nf ❶ recovery ❷ resit

recuperar vb **[25]** to get back; **recuperar fuerzas** to get one's strength back; **recuperarse de (1)** to get over **(2)** to recover from; **recuperar el tiempo perdido** to make up for lost time

recurrir vb **[58]** recurrir a algo to resort to something; **recurrir a alguien** to turn to somebody

recurso nm como último recurso as a last resort; **recursos** resources ▷ *recursos naturales* natural resources

red nf ❶ net ❷ network; **la Red** the Net; **una red de tiendas** a chain of shops

redacción (pl **redacciones**) nf essay; **hacer una redacción sobre algo** to write an essay on something; **el equipo de redacción** the editorial staff

redactar vb [25] to write

redactor, a nm/f editor

redada nf raid

redondo, -a adj round ▷ una mesa redonda a round table; **Todo salió redondo.** Everything worked out perfectly.

reducción (pl **reducciones**) nf reduction

reducir vb [9] ❶ to reduce ❷ to cut

reembolsar vb [25] to refund

reembolso nm refund; **enviar algo contra reembolso** to send something cash on delivery

reemplazar vb [13] to replace

referencia nf reference; **con referencia a** with reference to; **hacer referencia a** to refer to; **referencias** references

referéndum (pl **referéndums**) nm referendum

referente adj referente a concerning

referirse vb [51] referirse a to refer to; **¿A qué te refieres?** (1) What exactly do you mean? (2) What are you referring to?

refinería nf refinery

refiriendo vb see referirse

reflejar vb [25] to reflect

reflejo nm reflection; **reflejos** reflexes ▷ Estás bien de reflejos. You have good reflexes.

reflexión (pl **reflexiones**) nf reflection

reflexionar vb [25] to think; Reflexiona bien antes de tomar una decisión. Think it over carefully before taking a decision.

reflexivo, -a adj reflexive

reforma nf ❶ reform ❷ alteration ▷ Estamos haciendo reformas en el piso. We're having alterations made to the flat.; **'Cerrado por reformas'** 'Closed for refurbishment'

reformar vb [25] ❶ to reform ❷ to do up

refrán (pl **refranes**) nm saying

refrescante adj refreshing

refrescar vb [48] To get cooler; refrescarse to freshen up

refresco nm soft drink

refrigerador nm fridge

refugiado, -a nm/f refugee

refugiarse vb [25] ❶ to shelter ❷ to take refuge

refugio nm refuge ▷ un refugio de montaña a mountain refuge; **un refugio antiaéreo** an air-raid shelter

regadera nf ❶ watering can ❷ (Mex) shower; **estar como una regadera** to be as mad as a hatter

regalar vb [25] ❶ to give ▷ ¿Y si le regalamos un libro? What about giving him a book?; **Ayer fue mi cumpleaños. — ¿Qué te regalaron?** It was my birthday

yesterday. — What did you get?
❷ to give away ▷ *La tele vieja la vamos a regalar.* We're going to give the old TV away.

regaliz *nm* liquorice

regalo *nm* present ▷ *hacer un regalo a alguien* to give somebody a present; **una tienda de regalos** a gift shop; **papel de regalo** wrapping paper; **de regalo** free ▷ *Te dan un CD de regalo.* They give you a free CD.

regañadientes *adv* a regañadientes reluctantly

regañar *vb* [25] to tell off

regar *vb* [34] to water

regata *nf* yacht race

regatear *vb* [25] ❶ to haggle ❷ to dodge past

régimen (*pl* regímenes) *nm* ❶ diet; **estar a régimen** to be on a diet; **ponerse a régimen** to go on a diet ❷ regime

regimiento *nm* regiment

región (*pl* regiones) *nf* region

regional *adj* regional

registrar *vb* [25] ❶ to search ▷ *Me registraron.* They searched me. ❷ to register ❸ to check in; **Me registré en el hotel.** I checked into the hotel.

registro *nm* ❶ search; **realizar un registro en un lugar** to carry out a search of a place ❷ register; **el registro civil** the registry office

regla *nf* ❶ rule ▷ *saltarse las reglas* to break the rules ❷ period ▷ *Estoy con la regla.* I've got my period. ❸ ruler ▷ *Trazó la línea con una regla.* He drew the line with a ruler.; **por**

regla general generally; **tener todo en regla** to have everything in order

reglamento *nm* regulations *pl*

regresar *vb* [25] ❶ to go back ❷ to come back; **Regresamos tarde.** We got back late. ❸ (*LatAm*) to give back; **regresarse (1)** (*LatAm*) to go back **(2)** (*LatAm*) to come back

regreso *nm* return; **a nuestro regreso** on our return; **de regreso** on the way back

regulable *adj* adjustable

regular *adj* regular ▷ *un verbo regular* a regular verb ▷ *a intervalos regulares* at regular intervals; **La obra estuvo regular.** The play was pretty ordinary.
▶ *adv* **El examen me fue regular.** My exam didn't go brilliantly.; **¿Cómo te encuentras? — Regular.** How are you? — Not too bad.

rehacer *vb* [26] to redo

rehén (*pl* rehenes) *nmf* hostage

reina *nf* queen

reinado *nm* reign

reino *nm* kingdom

Reino Unido *nm* the United Kingdom

reír *vb* [44] to laugh; **echarse a reír** to burst out laughing; **Siempre nos reímos con él.** We always have a good laugh with him.; **reírse** to laugh; **reírse de** to laugh at

reivindicación (*pl* reivindicaciones) *nf* claim

reja *nf* grille; **estar entre rejas** to be behind bars

a
b
c
d
e
f
g
h
i
j
k
l
m
n
ñ
o
p
q
r
s
t
u
v
w
x
y
z

relación (pl **relaciones**) nf ❶ link ❷ relationship; **con relación a** in relation to; **relaciones públicas** public relations

relacionar vb [25] to link; **Le gusta relacionarse con niños mayores que él.** He likes mixing with older children.; **No se relaciona mucho con la gente.** He doesn't mix much.

relajado, -a adj ❶ relaxed ▷ ¿Estás relajado? Are you feeling relaxed? ❷ laid-back ▷ Es un tipo muy relajado. He's a very laid-back guy.

relajante adj relaxing

relajar vb [25] to relax ▷ ¡Relájate! Relax!

relámpago nm flash of lightning; **No me gustan los relámpagos.** I don't like lightning.

relativamente adv relatively

relativo, -a adj relative; **en lo relativo a** concerning

relato nm story

relevo nm **una carrera de relevos** a relay race; **tomar el relevo a alguien** to take over from somebody

religión (pl **religiones**) nf religion

religioso, -a adj religious

rellano nm landing

rellenar vb [25] ❶ to stuff ❷ to fill in

relleno, -a adj stuffed ▷ aceitunas rellenas stuffed olives; **relleno de algo** filled with something

reloj nm ❶ clock; **un reloj despertador** an alarm clock; **un reloj de cuco** a cuckoo clock; **contra reloj** against the clock

❷ watch ▷ Se me ha parado el reloj. My watch has stopped.; **un reloj digital** a digital watch; **un reloj de sol** a sundial

relojera nf watchmaker

relojería nf watchmaker's

relojero nm watchmaker

relucir vb [9] to shine

remar vb [25] ❶ to paddle ❷ to row

remediar vb [25] to solve; **Me eché a reír, no lo pude remediar.** I began to laugh, I couldn't help it.

remedio nm remedy ▷ un remedio contra la tos a cough remedy; **No tuve más remedio que hacerlo.** I had no choice but to do it.

remite nm name and address of sender

remitente nmf sender

remo nm ❶ oar ❷ rowing

remojar vb [25] to soak

remojo nm **poner algo en remojo** to leave something to soak

remolacha nf beetroot

remolcar vb [48] to tow

remolque nm trailer

remordimiento nm remorse sg

remoto, -a adj remote

remover vb [33] ❶ (coffee, cooking) to stir ❷ (salad) to toss ❸ (earth) to turn over

renacuajo nm tadpole

rencor nm ill-feeling; **guardar rencor a alguien** to bear a grudge against somebody

rencoroso, -a adj **No soy rencoroso.** I don't bear grudges.

rendido, -a adj worn out ▷ Estaba rendido de tanto andar. I was worn out after so much walking.

rendija nf **1** crack **2** gap

rendimiento nm performance

rendir vb [38] Este negocio no rinde. This business doesn't pay.; **rendirse (1)** to give up **(2)** to surrender

renglón (pl renglones) nm line

reno nm reindeer

renovable adj renewable

renovar vb [11] **1** to renew **2** to renovate **3** to change

renta nf **1** income **2** rent

rentable adj profitable ▷ Es una empresa rentable. It's a profitable business.

rentar vb [25] (Mex) to rent

reñido, -a adj hard-fought

reñir vb [45] **1** to tell somebody off **2** to quarrel **3** to fall out

reparación (pl reparaciones) nf repair; 'reparaciones en el acto' 'repairs while you wait'

reparar vb [25] to repair

repartir vb [58] **1** to hand out **2** to share out **3** to deliver **4** to deal

reparto nm **1** delivery; **reparto a domicilio** home delivery service **2** cast ▷ un reparto estelar a star cast

repasar vb [25] **1** to check **2** to revise; repasar para un examen to revise for an exam

repaso nm revision; Tengo que darles un repaso a los apuntes. I must revise my notes.

repente adv de repente suddenly

repentino, -a adj sudden

repertorio nm repertoire

repetición (pl repeticiones) nf repetition

repetidamente adv repeatedly

repetir vb [38] **1** to repeat **2** to have a second helping

repetitivo, -a adj repetitive

repisa nf shelf; **la repisa de la chimenea** the mantelpiece

> Word for word, repisa de la chimenea means 'shelf of the chimney'.

repitiendo vb see **repetir**

repollo nm cabbage

reportaje nm **1** documentary **2** article

reposacabezas (pl reposacabezas) nm headrest

reposición (pl reposiciones) nf **1** (on television) repeat **2** (in theatre) revival

repostar vb [25] to refuel

repostería nf confectionery

representación (pl representaciones) nf performance

representante nmf **1** representative **2** agent

representar vb [25] **1** to represent **2** to put on ▷ Los niños van a representar una obra de teatro. The children are going to put on a play. **3** to play ▷ Representa el papel de Don Juan. He's playing the part of Don Juan.

representativo, -a adj representative

reprobar vb [11] (LatAm) to fail

reprochar vb [25] Me reprochó que no la hubiera invitado. He reproached me for not having invited her.

reproducción (pl reproducciones) nf reproduction

reproducirse vb [9] to reproduce

reproductor nm **un reproductor de CD** a CD player

reptil nm reptile

república nf republic

República Dominicana nf the Dominican Republic

republicano, -a adj, nm/f republican

repuesto nm spare part; **de repuesto** spare ▷ *la rueda de repuesto* the spare wheel

repugnante adj revolting

reputación (pl **reputaciones**) nf reputation; **tener buena reputación** to have a good reputation

requesón nm cottage cheese

requisito nm requirement

resaca nf hangover; **tener resaca** to have a hangover

resaltar vb [25] ① to stand out ② to highlight

resbaladizo, -a adj slippery

resbalar vb [25] ① to be slippery ② to skid; **resbalarse** to slip

rescatar vb [25] to rescue

rescate nm ① rescue ▷ *un equipo de rescate* a rescue team ② ransom; **pedir un rescate por alguien** to hold somebody to ransom

reserva nmf reserve ▷ nf ① reservation; **Tengo mis reservas al respecto.** I've got reservations about it. ② reserve ▷ *una reserva natural* a nature reserve

reservado, -a adj reserved

reservar vb [25] to reserve

resfriado, -a adj **estar resfriado** to have a cold ▶ nm cold; **agarrarse un resfriado** to catch a cold

resfriarse vb [21] to catch a cold

resguardo nm ① ticket ② receipt

residencia nf residence ▷ *un permiso de residencia* a residence permit; **una residencia de ancianos** an old people's home; **una residencia de estudiantes** a hall of residence; **una residencia sanitaria** a hospital

residencial adj residential

residuos nmpl waste sg ▷ *residuos radiactivos* radioactive waste

resistencia nf resistance; **resistencia física** stamina

resistente adj tough; **resistente al calor** heat-resistant

resistir vb [58] ① to resist ② to take ③ to stand; **Se resisten a cooperar.** They are refusing to cooperate.

resolver vb [33] to solve

respaldar vb [25] to back up

respaldo nm back

respectivamente adv respectively

respecto nm **con respecto a** with regard to

respetable adj respectable

respetar vb [25] ① to respect ② to obey

respeto nm respect; **tener respeto a alguien** to respect somebody; **No le faltes al respeto.** Don't be disrespectful to him.

respiración nf breathing;
quedarse sin respiración to be out of breath; **la respiración boca a boca** the kiss of life; **la respiración artificial** artificial respiration

respirar vb [25] to breathe

responder vb [8] ❶ to answer
▷ *Eso no responde a mi pregunta.* That doesn't answer my question. ❷ to reply ❸ to respond

responsabilidad nf responsibility

responsable adj responsible
▷ *Cada cual es responsable de sus acciones.* Everybody is responsible for their own actions.
▶ nmf **Tú eres la responsable de lo ocurrido.** You're responsible for what happened.; **Los responsables serán castigados.** Those responsible will be punished.; **Juan es el responsable de la cocina.** Juan is in charge of the kitchen.

respuesta nf answer

resquebrajarse vb [25] to crack

resta nf subtraction

restante adj remaining

restar vb [25] to subtract

restauración (pl **restauraciones**) nf restoration

restaurante nm restaurant

restaurar vb [25] to restore

resto nm rest ▷ *Yo haré el resto.* I'll do the rest.; **los restos** (1) the leftovers (2) the wreckage sg

restregar vb [37] to rub

restricción (pl **restricciones**) nf restriction

resuelto vb see **resolver**

resuelvo vb see **resolver**

resultado nm ❶ result ❷ score;
dar resultado to work

resultar vb [25] to turn out; **Me resultó violento decírselo.** I found it embarrassing to tell him.

resumen (pl **resúmenes**) nm summary; **hacer un resumen de algo** to summarize something; **en resumen** in short

resumir vb [58] to summarize;
Dijo, resumiendo, que el viaje había sido un desastre. He said, in short, that the trip had been a disaster.

retar vb [25] ❶ to challenge ❷ (Chile, River Plate) to tell off

retirar vb [25] ❶ to take away ❷ to withdraw; **retirarse** to retire

reto nm challenge

retorcer vb [6] to twist;
retorcerse de risa to double up with laughter

retransmisión (pl **retransmisiones**) nf broadcast

retransmitir vb [58] to broadcast

retrasado, -a adj ❶ behind ▷ *Voy retrasado con este trabajo.* I'm behind with this work. ❷ slow ▷ *Este reloj va retrasado veinte minutos.* This clock is twenty minutes slow.; **Tienen un hijo un poco retrasado.** They've got a son with learning difficulties.

retrasar vb [25] ❶ to postpone ❷ to delay ❸ to put back;
retrasarse to be late; **Tu reloj se retrasa.** Your watch is slow.

retraso nm delay; **Perdonad por el retraso.** Sorry I'm late.; **ir con**

retraso to be running late; **llegar con retraso** to be late

retrato nm portrait; **hacer un retrato a alguien** to paint somebody's portrait

retrete nm toilet

retroceder vb [8] to go back

retrovisor nm rear-view mirror

retuerzo vb see **retorcer**

reúma nm rheumatism

reunión (pl **reuniones**) nf
❶ meeting ❷ gathering

reunir vb [46] ❶ to bring together
❷ to satisfy ❸ to raise; **reunirse**
(1) to gather (2) to get together
(3) to meet

revelar vb [25] ❶ to develop; **Llevé los carretes a revelar.** I took the films to be developed. ❷ to reveal

reventar vb [39] to burst

revés (pl **reveses**) nm backhand;
al revés (1) the other way round
(2) inside out ▷ **Te has puesto los calcetines al revés.** You've put your socks on inside out. (3) back to front (4) upside down ▷ **El dibujo está al revés.** The picture's upside down.

reviento vb see **reventar**

revisar vb [25] ❶ to check; **Tengo que ir a que me revisen el coche.** I must take my car for a service.
❷ (LatAm) to search

revisión (pl **revisiones**) nf service
▷ **He llevado el coche a revisión.** I've taken the car for a service.; **una revisión médica** a check-up

revisor, a nm/f ticket inspector

revista nf magazine

revoltoso, -a adj naughty

revolución (pl **revoluciones**) nf revolution

revolucionario, -a nm/f revolutionary

revolver vb [59] ❶ to mess up;
No revuelvas mis papeles.
Don't muddle my papers up.
❷ to turn upside down ❸ to rummage in

revólver (pl **revólveres**) nm revolver

revuelto vb see **revolver**
▷ adj in a mess; **Las fotos están revueltas.** The photos are muddled up.; **El tiempo está muy revuelto.** The weather's very unsettled.; **Tengo el estómago revuelto.** I've got an upset stomach.

rey (pl **reyes**) nm king; **Los reyes visitaron China.** The King and Queen visited China.; **los Reyes Magos** the Three Wise Men
As part of the Christmas festivities, the Spanish celebrate **el día de Reyes** (Epiphany) on 6th of January, when the Three Wise Men bring presents to children.

Word for word, **Reyes Magos** means 'Magician Kings'.

rezar vb [13] to pray; **rezar el Padrenuestro** to say the Lord's Prayer

ría nf estuary

riachuelo nm stream

ribera nf bank

rica nf rich woman

rico, -a adj ❶ rich ▷ **Son muy ricos.** They're very rich. ❷ delicious

▷ **¡Qué rico!** How delicious!

▶︎ nm rich man; **los ricos** the rich

ridiculizar vb [13] to ridicule

ridículo, -a adj ridiculous; **hacer el ridículo** to make a fool of oneself; **poner a alguien en ridículo** to make a fool of somebody

riel nm rail

riendas nfpl reins

riendo vb see **reír**

riesgo nm risk; **correr riesgos** to take risks; **Corres el riesgo de que te despidan.** You run the risk of being dismissed.; **un seguro a todo riesgo** a fully comprehensive insurance policy

rifa nf raffle

rifle nm rifle

rígido, -a adj ① stiff ② strict

riguroso, -a adj ① strict ② severe

rima nf rhyme

rimel nm mascara

rincón (pl **rincones**) nm corner

rinoceronte nm rhinoceros

riña nf ① row ② brawl

riñendo vb see **reñir**

riñón (pl **riñones**) nm kidney; **Me duelen los riñones.** I've got a pain in my lower back.

riñonera nf bum bag

río vb see **reír**

▶︎ nm river ▷ **el río Támesis** the River Thames

riqueza nf ① wealth ② richness

risa nf laugh ▷ **una risa contagiosa** an infectious laugh; **Me da risa.** It makes me laugh.; **¡Qué risa!** What a laugh!; **partirse de risa** to split one's sides laughing

ritmo nm ① rhythm; **Daban palmas al ritmo de la música.** They were clapping in time to the music. ② pace

ritual nm ritual

rival adj, nmf rival

rivalidad nf rivalry

rizado, -a adj curly

rizar vb [13] ① to curl ② to perm

rizo nm curl

robar vb [25] ① to steal ▷ **Me han robado la cartera.** My wallet has been stolen. ② to rob ③ to break into

roble nm oak

robo nm ① theft ② robbery ③ burglary; **¡Estos precios son un robo!** This is daylight robbery!

robot (pl **robots**) nm robot; **el robot de cocina** the food processor

robusto, -a adj strong

roca nf rock

rociar vb [21] to spray

rocío nm dew

rodaja nf slice ▷ **cortar algo en rodajas** to cut something into slices

rodaje nm shooting

rodar vb [11] ① to roll ② to shoot

rodear vb [25] to surround; **rodeado de** surrounded by

rodilla nf knee; **ponerse de rodillas** to kneel down

rodillo nm ① rolling pin ② roller

rogar vb [28] ① to beg ② to pray; **'Se ruega no fumar'** 'Please do not smoke'

rojo, -a adj, nm red ▷ **Va vestida de rojo.** She's wearing red.; **ponerse rojo** to go red

a
b
c
d
e
f
g
h
i
j
k
l
m
n
ñ
o
p
q
r
s
t
u
v
w
x
y
z

rollo nm roll ▷ *un rollo de papel higiénico* a roll of toilet paper; **La conferencia fue un rollo.** The lecture was really boring.; **¡Qué rollo de película!** What a boring film.; **Nos soltó el rollo de siempre.** He gave us the same old lecture.

Roma nf Rome

romano, -a adj, nm/f Roman

romántico, -a adj, nm/f romantic

rombo nm rhombus

rompecabezas (pl **rompecabezas**) nm ❶ jigsaw ❷ puzzle

romper vb [58, pp **roto**] ❶ to break ❷ to tear up; **Se ha roto una sábana.** A sheet has got torn.; **Se me han roto los pantalones.** I've torn my trousers.; **romper con alguien** to finish with somebody

ron nm rum

roncar vb [48] to snore

ronco, -a adj hoarse; **quedarse ronco** to go hoarse

ronda nf round ▷ *Esta ronda la pago yo.* I'll get this round.; **hacer la ronda** to be on patrol

ronquido nm snore

ronronear vb [25] to purr

ropa nf clothes pl ▷ *Voy a cambiarme de ropa.* I'm going to change my clothes.; **la ropa interior** underwear

> Word for word, **ropa interior** means 'interior clothes'.

ropa de deporte sportswear; **la ropa de cama** bed linen; **la ropa sucia** the dirty washing

rosa adj, nm (colour) pink

> When **rosa** is used as an adjective, it never changes its ending.

▷ *Va vestida de rosa.* She's wearing pink. ▷ *Llevaba unos calcetines rosa.* He was wearing pink socks.
► nf rose

rosado, -a adj ❶ pink ❷ (wine) rosé

rosal nm rosebush

rostro nm face

roto vb see **romper**
► adj ❶ broken ❷ torn ❸ worn out
► nm hole

rotonda nf roundabout

rotulador nm ❶ felt-tip pen ❷ highlighter pen

rótulo nm sign

rozar vb [13] to rub against

rubio, -a adj fair ▷ *Luis tiene el pelo rubio.* Luis has got fair hair.; **Es rubia con los ojos azules.** She has got fair hair and blue eyes.

ruborizarse vb [13] to blush

rudimentario, -a adj basic

rueda nf wheel ▷ *la rueda delantera* the front wheel ▷ *la rueda trasera* the back wheel; **Se te ha pinchado la rueda.** You've got a puncture.; **una rueda de prensa** a press conference

ruedo vb see **rodar**

ruego vb see **rogar**

rugby nm rugby ▷ *jugar al rugby* to play rugby

rugir vb [16] to roar

ruido nm noise ▷ *No hagáis tanto ruido.* Don't make so much noise.

ruidoso, -a adj noisy

ruina *nf* **Su socio lo llevó a la ruina.** His business partner ruined him financially.; **las ruinas** the ruins ▷ *El castillo está en ruinas.* The castle is in ruins.

rulo *nm* roller

rulot (*pl* **rulots**) *nf* caravan

rumana *nf* Romanian

Rumanía *nf* Romania

rumano *adj, nm* Romanian

rumba *nf* rumba

rumor *nm* ❶ rumour ❷ murmur

rural *adj* rural

rusa *nf* Russian

Rusia *nf* Russia

ruso *adj, nm* Russian

ruta *nf* route

rutina *nf* routine ▷ *la rutina diaria* the daily routine; **un chequeo de rutina** a routine check-up

S

sábado *nm* Saturday ▷ *La vi el sábado.* I saw her on Saturday.

sábana *nf* sheet

saber *vb* [47] ❶ to know ▷ *No lo sé.* I don't know.; **Lo dudo, pero nunca se sabe.** I doubt it, but you never know. ❷ to find out ▷ *En cuanto lo supimos fuimos a ayudarle.* As soon as we found out, we went to help him.; **No sé nada de ella.** I haven't heard from her.; **que yo sepa** as far as I know ❸ can ▷ *No sabe nadar.* She can't swim. ❹ to taste ▷ *Sabe a pescado.* It tastes of fish.; **saberse** to know

sabio, -a *adj* wise

sabor *nm* ❶ taste ❷ flavour

sabotaje *nm* sabotage

sabré *vb see* **saber**

sabroso, -a *adj* tasty

sacacorchos (pl **sacacorchos**) nm corkscrew

sacapuntas (pl **sacapuntas**) nm pencil sharpener

sacar vb [48] ❶ to take out ▷ *Voy a sacar dinero del cajero.* I'm going to take some money out of the machine. ▷ *Se sacó las llaves del bolsillo.* He took the keys out of his pocket. ▷ *sacar la basura* to take the rubbish out; **Me han sacado una muela.** I've had a tooth taken out.; **sacar a pasear al perro** to take the dog out for a walk; **sacar a alguien a bailar** to get somebody up for a dance ❷ to get ▷ *Yo sacaré las entradas.* I'll get the tickets. ▷ *sacar buenas notas* to get good marks ❸ to release ▷ *Han sacado un nuevo disco.* They've released a new record.; **sacar algo adelante** to conclude; **sacar una foto a alguien** to take a photo of somebody; **sacar la lengua a alguien** to stick your tongue out at somebody; **sacarse el carnet de conducir** to pass one's driving test; **sacarse el título de abogado** to qualify as a lawyer; **sacarse las botas** to take off one's boots

sacarina nf saccharin

sacerdote nm priest

saco nm ❶ sack ▷ *un saco de harina* a sack of flour; **un saco de dormir** a sleeping bag ❷ (LatAm) jacket

sacrificio nm sacrifice

sacudir vb [58] to shake

Sagitario nm Sagittarius; **Soy sagitario.** I'm Sagittarius.

sagrado, -a adj ❶ sacred ❷ holy

sal nf salt

sala nf ❶ room ❷ ward ❸ hall; **sala de embarque** departure lounge; **sala de espera** waiting room; **sala de estar** living room; **sala de fiestas** nightclub

salado, -a adj ❶ salty ▷ *La carne está muy salada.* The meat's very salty. ❷ savoury ▷ *¿Es dulce o salado?* Is it sweet or savoury?

salario nm pay

salchicha nf sausage

salchichón (pl **salchichones**) nm spiced salami sausage

saldo nm balance; **saldos** sales

saldré vb see **salir**

salero nm salt cellar

salgo vb see **salir**

salida nf ❶ exit ▷ *salida de emergencia* emergency exit; **a la salida del teatro** on the way out of the theatre ❷ departure ❸ (of race) start; **la salida del sol** sunrise

salir vb [49] ❶ to come out ❷ to go out; **Ha salido.** She's out.; **salir con alguien** to go out with somebody ❸ to get out ❹ to leave ❺ to appear ▷ *Su foto salió en todos los periódicos.* Her picture appeared in all the newspapers.; **Sale a 15 euros por persona.** It works out at 15 euros each.; **Me está saliendo una muela del juicio.** One of my wisdom teeth is coming through.; **No sé cómo vamos a salir adelante.** I don't know how we're going to go on.; **salir bien** to work out well; **Espero que todo salga bien.** I hope everything works out all right.; **Les salió mal el proyecto.** Their plan didn't work out.; **¡Qué mal me ha salido el dibujo!** My drawing hasn't come out very well, has it!; **salirse (1)** to boil over ▷ *Se ha salido la leche.* The milk's boiled over. **(2)** to leak ▷ *Se salía el aceite del motor.* Oil was leaking out of the engine. **(3)** to come off ▷ *Nos salimos de la carretera.* We came off the road. **(4)** to come out ▷ *Se ha salido el enchufe.* The plug has come out.

saliva nf saliva

salmón (pl **salmones**) nm salmon; **rosa salmón** salmon pink

salón (pl **salones**) nm ❶ living room; **salón de actos** meeting hall; **salón de belleza** beauty salon; **salón de juegos recreativos** amusement arcade ❷ (Mex) classroom

salpicadera nf (Mex) mudguard

salpicadero nm dashboard

salpicar vb [48] to splash

salsa nf ❶ sauce ▷ *salsa de tomate* tomato sauce ❷ salsa

saltamontes (pl **saltamontes**) nm grasshopper

saltar vb [25] to jump; **hacer saltar algo por los aires** to blow something up; **saltarse** to skip; **saltarse un semáforo en rojo** to go through a red light

salto nm ❶ jump ❷ dive; **dar un salto** to jump; **salto de altura** high jump; **salto de longitud** long jump; **salto mortal** somersault

■ Word for word, **salto mortal** means 'mortal jump'.

salud nf health

▶ excl ❶ cheers! ❷ bless you!

saludable adj healthy

saludar vb [25] ❶ to say hello ❷ to greet; **Lo saludé desde la otra acera.** I waved to him from the other side of the street. ❸ to salute

saludo nm ❶ greeting ❷ regards ▷ *Carolina te manda un saludo.* Carolina sends her regards. ▷ *Saludos cordiales.* Kind regards.; **¡Saludos a Teresa de mi parte!** Say hello to Teresa for me!

salvaje adj wild

salvapantallas nm screensaver

salvar vb [25] to save

salvavidas (pl **salvavidas**) nm lifebelt

salvo prep except ▷ *todos salvo yo* everyone except me; **salvo que** unless; **estar a salvo** to be safe; **Consiguieron ponerse a salvo.** They managed to reach safety.

San adj Saint ▷ *San Pedro* Saint Peter

sandalia nf sandal

sandía nf watermelon

sándwich (pl **sándwiches**) nm ❶ sandwich ❷ toasted sandwich

sangrar vb [25] to bleed

sangre nf blood; **echar sangre** to bleed

sangría nf sangria

sanidad nf public health

sano, -a adj healthy; **sano y salvo** safe and sound

■ Be careful! **sano** does not mean **sane**.

santa nf saint ▷ *Santa Clara* Saint Clara

santo, -a adj holy
> ▶ nm ❶ saint ▷ *Santo Domingo* Saint Dominic ❷ name day
- Besides birthdays, some Spaniards also celebrate the feast day of the saint they are named after.

sapo nm toad

saque nm service; **saque de esquina** corner; **saque inicial** kick-off

sarampión (pl **sarampiones**) nm measles sg

sarcástico, -a adj sarcastic

sardina nf sardine

sargento nmf sergeant

sarpullido nm rash ▷ *Le ha salido un sarpullido en la cara.* His face has come out in a rash.

sarro nm tartar

sarta nf *Nos contó una sarta de mentiras.* He told us a pack of lies.

sartén (pl **sartenes**) nm (LatAm) frying pan
> ▶ nf frying pan

sastre nm tailor

satélite nm satellite

satisfacción (pl **satisfacciones**) nf satisfaction

satisfacer vb [26] to satisfy

satisfactorio, -a adj satisfactory

satisfecho, -a adj satisfied ▷ *No estoy satisfecho con el resultado.* I'm not satisfied with the result.

sauna nf sauna

saxofón (pl **saxofones**) nm saxophone

sazonar vb [25] to season

se pron each other ▷ *Se dieron un beso.* They gave each other a kiss.

> When used in combination with a direct-object pronoun, **se** can mean **to him**, **to her**, **to them** or **to you**, depending on the context. Sometimes the **to** is omitted and sometimes it is replaced by **for**.

▷ *Pedro necesitaba la calculadora y se la dejé.* Pedro needed the calculator and I lent it to him. ▷ *He hablado con mis padres y se lo he explicado.* I've talked to my parents and explained it to them. ▷ *No quiero que Rosa lo sepa. No se lo digas.* I don't want Rosa to know. Don't tell her. ▷ *Aquí tiene el libro. ¿Se lo envuelvo, señor?* Here's your book. Shall I wrap it for you, sir?

> **se** is not translated when used together with **a** and a name or other noun referring to a person or people.

▷ *Dáselo a Enrique.* Give it to Enrique. ▷ *No se lo digas a Susana.* Don't tell Susana. ▷ *¿Se lo has preguntado a tus padres?* Have you asked your parents about it?

> When used reflexively, **se** can translate as **himself**, **herself**, **itself**, **themselves**, **yourself** or **yourselves**, depending on the context, but often a non-reflexive construction is used in English instead.

▷ *Marcos se ha cortado con un cristal.* Marcos cut himself on a piece of broken glass. ▷ *Margarita se estaba preparando para salir.* Margarita was getting herself ready to go out. ▷ *La calefacción se apaga sola.*

The heating turns itself off automatically. ▷ *¿Se ha hecho usted daño?* Have you hurt yourself? ▷ *Se está afeitando.* He's shaving. ▷ *Mi hermana nunca se queja.* My sister never complains.

> When **se** is used in combination with an article and a part of the body or an item of clothing, it is usually translated using the possessive in English.

▷ *Pablo se lavó los dientes.* Pablo brushed his teeth. ▷ *Carmen no podía abrocharse el vestido.* Carmen couldn't do up her dress.

> When **se** is used impersonally, it is usually translated using **one** or **it**.

▷ *Es lo que pasa cuando se come tan deprisa.* That's what happens when you eat so fast. ▷ *Se cree que el tabaco produce cáncer.* It is believed that smoking causes cancer.; '**se vende**' 'for sale'

sé vb see **saber**

sea vb see **ser**

secador nm hair dryer

secadora nf ① tumble dryer ② (Mex) hair dryer

secar vb [48] to dry; **secarse** to dry; *¿Se ha secado ya la ropa?* Is the washing dry yet?; **Se han secado las plantas.** The plants have dried up.

sección (pl **secciones**) nf ① section ② department

seco, -a adj ① dry ▷ *El suelo ya está seco.* The floor's dry now. ② dried ▷ *flores secas* dried flowers

secretario, -a nm/f secretary

secreto, -a adj secret
▶ nm secret; **en secreto** in secret

secta nf sect

sector nm sector

secuencia nf sequence

secuestrador, a nm/f ① kidnapper ② hijacker

secuestrar vb [25] ① to kidnap ② to hijack

secuestro nm ① kidnapping ② hijack

secundario, -a adj secondary

sed nf thirst; **tener sed** to be thirsty

seda nf silk ▷ *una camisa de seda* a silk shirt

sedal nm fishing line

sedante nm sedative

sede nf ① headquarters pl ② venue

sediento, -a adj thirsty

segar vb [34] ① to reap ② to mow

seguido, -a adj ① in a row ▷ *La he visto tres días seguidos.* I've seen her three days in a row.; **en seguida** straight away; **en seguida termino.** I'm just about to finish.; **todo seguido** straight on ▷ *Vaya todo seguido hasta la plaza y luego ...* Go straight on until the square and then ...

seguidor, a nm/f follower ▷ *Tiene muchos seguidores en Twitter.* She has a lot of followers on Twitter.

seguir vb [50] ① to carry on ▷ *¡Sigue, por favor!* Carry on, please! ▷ *El ordenador seguía funcionando.* The computer carried on working.; **El ascensor sigue estropeado.** The lift's still not

working.; **Sigo sin comprender.**
I still don't understand.; **Sigue
lloviendo.** It's still raining. ❷ to
follow ▷ *Tú ve primero que yo te sigo.*
You go first and I'll follow you.;
seguir a alguien en Twitter to
follow somebody on Twitter;
seguir adelante to go ahead ▷ *Los
Juegos Olímpicos siguieron adelante a
pesar del atentado.* The Olympics
went ahead despite the attack.

según *prep* ❶ according to ▷ *Según
tú, no habrá problemas de entradas.*
According to you there won't be
any problems with the tickets.
❷ depending on ▷ *Iremos o no,
según esté el tiempo.* We might go,
depending on the weather.

segundo, -a *adj, pron* second; **el
segundo plato** the main course;
Vive en el segundo. He lives on
the second floor.
▶ *nm* second ▷ *Es un segundo nada
más.* It'll only take a second.

seguramente *adv* probably

seguridad *nf* ❶ safety ❷ security
▷ *Las medidas de seguridad son muy
estrictas.* The security measures
are very strict. ❸ certainty ▷ *con
toda seguridad* with complete
certainty; **seguridad en uno
mismo** self-confidence; **la
seguridad social** social security

seguro, -a *adj* ❶ safe ▷ *Este avión es
muy seguro.* This plane is very safe.
▷ *Aquí estaremos seguros.* We'll be
safe here. ❷ sure ▷ *Estoy segura de
que ganaremos.* I'm sure we'll win.
▷ *Está muy seguro de sí mismo.* He's
very sure of himself. ❸ certain

▷ *No es seguro que vayan a venir.* It's
not certain that they're going to
come.
▶ *nm* insurance ▷ *el seguro del coche*
car insurance; **seguro de vida** life
assurance

seis *adj, pron* six; **Son las seis.** It's
six o'clock.; **el seis de enero** the
sixth of January

seiscientos, -as *adj, pron* six
hundred

selección (*pl* **selecciones**) *nf*
❶ selection ❷ team

seleccionar *vb* [25] to pick

selectividad *nf* university
entrance exam

sellar *vb* [25] ❶ (*letter, parcel*) to seal
❷ (*passport*) to stamp ❸ (*for
unemployment benefit*) to sign on

sello *nm* ❶ stamp ▷ *Colecciona
sellos.* He collects stamps. ❷ seal

selva *nf* jungle; **la selva tropical**
the rainforest

semáforo *nm* traffic lights *pl*; **un
semáforo en rojo** a red light

semana *nf* week ▷ *dentro de una
semana* in a week's time ▷ *una vez a
la semana* once a week; **entre
semana** during the week;
Semana Santa Holy Week

semanal *adj* weekly

sembrar *vb* [39] ❶ to plant ❷ to
sow

semejante *adj* ❶ similar ❷ such
▷ *Nunca he dicho semejante cosa.*
I've never said such a thing.

semicírculo *nm* semicircle

semifinal *nf* semi-final

semilla *nf* seed

senado *nm* senate

senador, a nm/f senator

sencillamente adv simply

sencillo, -a adj ❶ simple ▷ Es muy sencillo. It's really simple. ❷ modest
▶ nm ❶ (record) single ❷ (LatAm) small change

senderismo nm trekking

sendero nm path

sensación (pl **sensaciones**) nf feeling ▷ Tengo la sensación de que mienten. I get the feeling they're lying. ▷ una sensación de escozor a burning feeling

sensacional adj sensational

sensato, -a adj sensible

sensible adj sensitive

Be careful! The Spanish word **sensible** does not mean **sensible**.

sensual adj sensuous

sentado, -a adj estar sentado to be sitting down

sentar vb [39] ❶ to suit ▷ Ese vestido te sienta muy bien. That dress really suits you. ❷ to agree with ▷ No me sienta bien cenar tanto. Having so much dinner doesn't agree with me.; **Le ha sentado mal que no lo invitaras a la boda.** He was put out that you didn't invite him to the wedding.; **sentarse** to sit down

sentencia nf sentence

sentido nm ❶ sense ❷ meaning; **sentido común** common sense; **sentido del humor** sense of humour; **una calle de sentido único** a one-way street; **en algún sentido** in some respects

sentimental adj sentimental

sentimiento nm feeling

sentir vb [51] ❶ to feel ▷ Sentí un dolor en la pierna. I felt a pain in my leg. ❷ to hear ❸ to be sorry ▷ Lo siento mucho. I'm very sorry.; **sentirse** to feel

seña nf sign ▷ Les hice una seña. I made a sign to them.; **señas** address

señal nf ❶ sign; **señal de tráfico** road sign; **señal indicadora** signpost; **señal de llamada** dialling tone ❷ signal ❸ deposit

señalar vb [25] to mark; **señalar con el dedo** to point

señalizar vb [13] ❶ to indicate ❷ to signpost

señor nm ❶ man ▷ Este señor ha llegado antes que yo. This man was before me.; **¿Le ocurre algo, señor?** Is there something the matter?; ¿Qué le pongo, señor? What would you like, sir? ❷ Mr ▷ el señor Delgado Mr Delgado ❸ lord; **Muy señor mío ...** Dear Sir ...; **el señor alcalde** the mayor

señora nf ❶ lady ▷ Deja pasar a esta señora. Let the lady past.; ¿Le ocurre algo, señora? Is there something the matter?; ¿Qué le pongo, señora? What would you like, madam? ❷ Mrs ▷ la señora Delgado Mrs Delgado ❸ wife ▷ Vino con su señora. He came with his wife.

señorita nf young lady ▷ Deja pasar a esta señorita. Let the young lady past. ▷ la señorita Delgado Miss Delgado

sepa vb *see* **saber**

separación (pl separaciones) nf ❶ separation ❷ gap

separado, -a adj ❶ separate; **por separado** separately ❷ separated ▷ *Está separado de su mujer.* He's separated from his wife.

separar vb [**25**] to separate; **separarse (1)** to separate **(2)** to split up

septiembre nm September

séptimo, -a adj, pron seventh; **Vivo en el séptimo.** I live on the seventh floor.

sequía nf drought

ser vb [**52**] to be ▷ *Es muy alto.* He's very tall. ▷ *Es médico.* He's a doctor. ▷ *La fiesta va a ser en su casa.* The party's going to be in her house. ▷ *Fue construido en 1960.* It was built in 1960. ▷ *Era de noche.* It was night. ▷ **Soy Lucía.** (when identifying oneself) It's Lucía.; **Son las seis y media.** It's half past six.; **Somos tres.** There are three of us.; **Son ocho.** There are eight of them.; **Éramos cinco en el coche.** There were five of us in the car.; **¡Es cierto!** That's right!; **Me es imposible asistir.** It's impossible for me to attend.; **ser de (1)** to be from ▷ *¿De dónde eres?* Where are you from? **(2)** to be made of ▷ *Es de piedra.* It's made of stone.; **Es de Joaquín.** It's Joaquín's.; **a no ser que ...** unless ... ▷ *a no ser que salgamos mañana* unless we leave tomorrow; **O sea, que no vienes.** So you're not coming.; **mis hijos, o sea, Juan y Pedro** my children, that is, Juan and Pedro

▶ nm being; **un ser humano** a human being; **un ser vivo** a living being

serie nf series

serio, -a adj serious; **en serio** seriously ▷ *No hablaba en serio.* I wasn't speaking seriously.; **¿Lo dices en serio?** Do you really mean it?

sermón (pl sermones) nm sermon

serpiente nf snake; **una serpiente de cascabel** a rattlesnake

serrar vb [**39**] to saw

serrucho nm saw

servicial adj helpful

servicio nm ❶ service ▷ *El servicio no va incluido.* Service is not included.; **estar de servicio** to be on duty ❷ toilet ▷ *Está en el servicio.* He's in the toilet.; **el servicio de caballeros** the gents; **el servicio de señoras** the ladies

servidor nm server

servilleta nf napkin

servir vb [**38**] ❶ to be useful for; **¿Para qué sirve esto?** What's this for?; **Esta radio aún sirve.** This radio still works. ❷ to serve; **Sírveme un poco más de vino.** Give me a little bit more wine.; **no servir para nada** to be useless; **¿En qué puedo servirlo?** How can I help you?

sesenta adj, pron sixty ▷ *Tiene sesenta años.* He's sixty.; **el sesenta aniversario** the sixtieth anniversary

sesión (pl sesiones) nf ❶ session ❷ showing

seta nf mushroom; **seta venenosa** toadstool

setecientos, -as adj, pron seven hundred

setenta adj, pron seventy ▷ *Tiene setenta años.* He's seventy.; **el setenta aniversario** the seventieth anniversary

seto nm hedge

seudónimo nm pseudonym

severo, -a adj ❶ strict ❷ harsh

Sevilla nf Seville

sexista adj, nmf sexist

sexo nm sex

sexto, -a adj, pron sixth; **Vivo en el sexto.** I live on the sixth floor.

sexual adj sexual

sexualidad nf sexuality

si conj ❶ if ▷ *Si quieres, te dejo el coche.* I'll lend you the car if you like. ▷ *¿Sabes si hemos cobrado ya?* Do you know if we've been paid yet?; **¿Y si llueve?** And what if it rains?; **Si me hubiera tocado la lotería ...** If only I had won the lottery ... ❷ whether ▷ *No sé si ir o no.* I don't know whether to go or not.; **si no** (1) otherwise ▷ *Ponte crema. Si no, te quemarás.* Put some cream on, otherwise you'll get sunburnt. (2) if ... not ▷ *Avisadme si no podéis venir.* Let me know if you can't come.

sí adv yes ▷ *¿Te apetece un café? — Sí, gracias.* Do you fancy a coffee? — Yes, please.; *¿Te gusta? — Sí.* Do you like it? — Yes, I do.; **Creo que sí.** I think so.; **Él no quiere pero yo sí.** He doesn't want to but I do.

▶ pron

sí can mean **himself, herself, itself, themselves, yourself** or **yourselves.**

▷ *Solo habla de sí mismo.* He only talks about himself. ▷ *Se perjudica a sí misma.* She's harming herself. ▷ *Pregúntese a sí mismo el motivo.* Ask yourself the reason. ▷ *La pregunta en sí no era difícil.* The question itself wasn't difficult. ▷ *Hablaban entre sí.* They were talking among themselves. ▷ *Es mejor aprender las cosas por sí mismo.* It's better to learn things by yourself.; **La Tierra gira sobre sí misma.** The Earth turns on its own axis.

Sicilia nf Sicily

sida nm AIDS

sidra nf cider

siego vb see **segar**

siembro vb see **sembrar**

siempre adv always; **como siempre** as usual; **para siempre** forever; **siempre y cuando** provided

siendo vb see **ser**

siento vb see **sentir**

sierra nf ❶ saw ❷ mountain range

siesta nf nap; **echarse la siesta** to have a nap

siete adj, pron seven; **Son las siete.** It's seven o'clock.; **el siete de marzo** the seventh of March

siglas nfpl abbreviation sg

siglo nm century ▷ *el siglo XX* the 20th century

significado nm meaning

significar vb [48] ❶ to mean ❷ to stand for

significativo, -a adj significant

signo nm sign; **¿De qué signo del zodíaco eres?** What star sign are you?; **signo de admiración** exclamation mark; **signo de interrogación** question mark

siguiendo vb see **seguir**

siguiente adj next ▷ el siguiente vuelo the next flight ▷ Al día siguiente visitamos Toledo. The next day we visited Toledo.; **¡Que pase el siguiente, por favor!** Next please!

sílaba nf syllable

silbar vb [25] to whistle

silbato nm whistle

silbido nm whistle

silencio nm silence; **guardar silencio** to keep quiet; **¡Silencio!** Quiet!

silencioso, -a adj silent

silla nf chair; **silla de montar** saddle; **silla de paseo** pushchair; **silla de ruedas** wheelchair

sillín (pl sillines) nm saddle

sillón (pl sillones) nm armchair

silueta nf outline; **Tiene una silueta perfecta.** She has a perfect figure.

símbolo nm symbol

simpatía nf ❶ kindness ❷ friendly nature; **Les tengo simpatía.** I like them.

simpático, -a adj nice ▷ Estuvo muy simpática con todos. She was very nice to everybody. ▷ Los cubanos son muy simpáticos. Cubans are very nice people.;

Me cae simpático. I think he's really nice.

■ Be careful! **simpático** does not mean **sympathetic**.

simple adj simple

simplemente adv simply

simultáneo, -a adj simultaneous

sin prep without ▷ Es peligroso ir en moto sin casco. It's dangerous to ride a motorbike without a helmet. ▷ Salió sin hacer ruido. She went out without making a noise. ▷ sin que él se diera cuenta without him realising; **la gente sin hogar** the homeless

sincero, -a adj honest

sindicalista nmf trade unionist

sindicato nm trade union

sinfonía nf symphony

singular adj, nm singular

siniestro, -a adj sinister

sino conj but ▷ No son inglesas sino galeses. They're not English, but Welsh.; **No hace sino pedirnos dinero.** All he does is ask us for money.; **No solo nos ayudó, sino que también nos invitó a cenar.** He didn't just help us, he also bought us dinner.

sintético, -a adj synthetic

sintiendo vb see **sentir**

síntoma nm symptom

sinvergüenza nmf crook; **Es una sinvergüenza.** She's shameless.

siquiera adv ni siquiera not even

sirena nf ❶ siren ❷ mermaid

sirviendo vb see **servir**

sirvienta nf maid

sirviente nm servant

sistema nm system

sitio nm ❶ place; **cambiar algo de sitio** to move something around; **en cualquier sitio** anywhere; **en algún sitio** somewhere; **en ningún sitio** nowhere ❷ room ▷ *Hay sitio de sobra.* There's room to spare.; **un sitio web** a website

situación (pl **situaciones**) nf situation

situado, -a adj **está situado en ...** it's situated in ...

SMS nm text message; **enviar un SMS a alguien** to text somebody

sobaco nm armpit

soborno nm ❶ bribery ❷ bribe

sobra nf **Tenemos comida de sobra.** We've got more than enough food.; **Sabes de sobra que yo no he ido.** You know full well that it wasn't me.; **las sobras** the leftovers

sobrar vb [**25**] ❶ to be left over ❷ to be spare; **Este ejemplo sobra.** This example is unnecessary.; **Con este dinero sobrará.** This money will be more than enough.

sobre prep ❶ on ▷ *Dejó el dinero sobre la mesa.* He left the money on the table. ❷ about ▷ *información sobre vuelos* information about flights; **sobre las seis** at about six o'clock; **sobre todo** above all ▶ nm envelope

sobredosis (pl **sobredosis**) nf overdose

sobrenatural adj supernatural

sobresaliente nm distinction

sobrevivir vb [**58**] to survive

sobrina nf niece

sobrino nm nephew; **mis sobrinos** (1) my nephews (2) my nieces and nephews

sobrio, -a adj sober

socia nf ❶ partner ❷ member

social adj social

socialismo nm socialism

socialista adj, nmf socialist

sociedad nf society; **una sociedad anónima** a limited company

socio nm ❶ (in business) partner ❷ (of club, organization) member

sociología nf sociology

socorrista nmf lifeguard

socorro nm help; **pedir socorro** to ask for help ▶ excl help!

soda nf soda

sofá (pl **sofás**) nm sofa; **un sofá-cama** a sofa bed

sofisticado, -a adj sophisticated

software nm software

sois vb see **ser**

soja nf soya

sol nm sun; **Hace sol.** It's sunny.; **tomar el sol** to sunbathe

solamente adv only

soldado nm soldier

soleado, -a adj sunny

soledad nf loneliness

soler vb [**33**] **Suele salir a las ocho.** He usually leaves at eight.; **Solíamos ir todos los años a la playa.** We used to go to the beach every year.

solicitar vb [**25**] ❶ to ask for ❷ to apply for

solicitud nf ❶ application ❷ request

sólido, -a adj solid

solitario, -a adj solitary

sollozar vb [13] to sob

solo, -a adj ① alone ▷ ¡Déjame solo! Leave me alone! ▷ Me quedé solo. I was left alone.; **¿Estás solo?** Are you on your own?; **Lo hice solo.** I did it on my own. ② lonely ③ single ▷ No hubo una sola queja. There wasn't a single complaint.; **Habla solo.** He talks to himself.; **un café solo** a black coffee
▶ nm solo
▶ adv only

solomillo nm sirloin

soltar vb [25] ① to let go of; **¡Suéltame!** Let me go! ② to put down ▷ Soltó la bolsa de la compra en un banco. She put her shopping bag down on a bench. ③ to release ▷ Han soltado a los rehenes. They've released the hostages. ④ (sigh) to let out

soltera nf single woman

soltero, -a adj single ▷ Es soltero. He's single.
▶ nm single man

solución (pl soluciones) nf ① solution ② answer

solucionar vb [25] to solve; **un problema sin solucionar** an unsolved problem

sombra nf ① shade ▷ Prefiero quedarme a la sombra. I prefer to stay in the shade. ② shadow; **sombra de ojos** eye shadow

sombrero nm hat

sombrilla nf ① parasol ② sunshade

somier nm mattress base

somnífero nm sleeping pill

sonajero nm rattle

sonar vb [11] ① to sound; **Escríbelo tal y como suena.** Write it down just the way it sounds. ② (music) to play ③ (bell, telephone) to ring ④ (alarm clock) to go off; **Me suena esa cara.** That face rings a bell.; **sonarse la nariz** to blow one's nose

sondeo nm un sondeo de opinión an opinion poll

sonido nm sound

sonreír vb [44] to smile

sonrisa nf smile

sonrojarse vb [25] to blush

soñar vb [11] to dream

sopa nf soup ▷ sopa de pescado fish soup

soplar vb [25] to blow

soportar vb [25] to stand
⚠ Be careful! **soportar** does not mean **to support**.

soprano nf soprano

sorber vb [8] to sip

sordo, -a adj deaf; **quedarse sordo** to go deaf

sordomudo, -a adj (with inability to speak) deaf

sorprendente adj surprising

sorprender vb [8] to surprise; **Me sorprendí al verlo allí.** I was surprised to see him there.

sorpresa nf surprise; **coger a alguien de sorpresa** to take somebody by surprise

sorteo nm draw

sortija nf ring

soso, -a adj ① dull ② bland

sospecha nf suspicion

sospechar vb [25] to suspect; **Sospechan de él.** They suspect him.

sospechoso, -a adj suspicious
▸ nm/f suspect

sostén (pl**sostenes**) nm bra

sostener vb [53] ❶ to support ❷ to hold; **¿Puedes sostener la puerta un momento?** Can you hold the door open for a moment?

sota nf jack

sótano nm ❶ basement ❷ cellar

soy vb see **ser**

spot nm **un spot publicitario** a commercial

Sr. abbr Mr

Sra. abbr Mrs

Sres. abbr Messrs

Srta. abbr Miss

su adj ❶ his ▸ su máquina de afeitar his razor ▸ sus padres his parents ❷ her ▸ su falda her skirt ▸ sus amigas her friends ❸ its ▸ un oso y su cachorro a bear and its cub ▸ el coche y sus accesorios the car and its fittings ❹ their ▸ su equipo favorito their favourite team ▸ sus amigos their friends ❺ your ▸ Su abrigo, señora. Your coat, madam. ▸ No olviden sus paraguas. Don't forget your umbrellas.

suave adj ❶ (skin, surface) smooth ❷ (hair) soft ❸ (breeze, voice, squeeze) gentle ❹ (climate, temperature) mild

suavizante nm ❶ conditioner ❷ fabric conditioner

subasta nf auction

subcampeón (f**subcampeona**, mpl**subcampeones**) nm/f runner-up

subdesarrollado, -a adj underdeveloped

subdirector, a nm/f ❶ deputy head ❷ deputy director ❸ deputy manager

subida nf ❶ rise ▸ una subida de los precios a rise in prices ❷ ascent

subir vb [58] ❶ to go up ▸ Subimos la cuesta. We went up the hill. ▸ La gasolina ha vuelto a subir. Petrol's gone up again. ❷ to come up ▸ Sube, que te voy a enseñar unas fotos. Come up, I've got some photos to show you. ❸ to climb ▸ subir una montaña to climb a mountain ❹ to take up ▸ ¿Me puedes ayudar a subir las maletas? Can you help me to take up the cases? ❺ (prices, fares) to put up ▸ Los taxistas han subido sus tarifas. Taxi drivers have put their fares up. ❻ to raise ▸ Sube los brazos. Raise your arms. ❼ (volume, radio) to turn up ▸ Sube la radio, que no se oye. Turn the radio up, I can't hear it. ❽ to upload ▸ subir una foto a una página web to upload a photo to a web page; **subirse a** (1) (car) to get into (2) (bike) to get onto (3) (bus, train, plane) to get on; **subirse a un árbol** to climb a tree

subjuntivo nm subjunctive

submarino nm submarine

subrayar vb [25] to underline

subsidio nm subsidy ▸ subsidio de paro unemployment benefit

subte nm (River Plate) underground

subterráneo, -a adj underground

subtitulado, -a adj subtitled

subtítulos nmpl subtitles

suburbio nm slum area

subvención (pl **subvenciones**) nf subsidy

subvencionar vb [**25**] to subsidize

suceder vb [**8**] to happen

suceso nm ❶ event ❷ incident; **Acudieron rápidamente al lugar del suceso.** They rushed to the scene.

> ⚠️ Be careful! **suceso** does not mean **success**.

suciedad nf dirt

sucio, -a adj dirty ▷ **Tienes las manos sucias.** You've got dirty hands.

sucursal nf branch

sudadera nf sweatshirt

Sudáfrica nf South Africa

Sudamérica nf South America

sudamericano, -a adj, nm/f South American

sudar vb [**25**] to sweat

sudeste nm southeast

sudoeste nm southwest

sudor nm sweat

sudoroso, -a adj sweaty

sueca nf Swede

Suecia nf Sweden

sueco, -a adj Swedish
> ▶ nm ❶ Swede ❷ (language) Swedish

suegra nf mother-in-law

suegro nm father-in-law

suela nf sole

sueldo nm ❶ salary ❷ wages pl

suelo nm ❶ floor ❷ ground; **Me caí al suelo.** I fell over.
> ▶ vb see **soler**

suelto vb see **soltar**
> ▶ adj loose ▷ **Lleva el pelo suelto.** She

wears her hair loose. ▷ **No dejes al perro suelto.** Don't let the dog loose.
> ▶ nm change

sueno vb see **sonar**

sueño vb see **soñar**
> ▶ nm ❶ dream ❷ sleep; **Tengo sueño.** I'm sleepy.

suerte nf luck; **por suerte** luckily; **Tuvo suerte.** She was lucky.; **¡Qué suerte!** How lucky!; **¡Qué mala suerte!** What bad luck!

suéter nm sweater

suficiente adj enough ▷ **No tenía dinero suficiente.** I didn't have enough money.

suficientemente adv sufficiently

sufrir vb [**58**] ❶ to have ▷ **Sufrió un ataque al corazón.** He had a heart attack. ❷ to suffer; **sufrir un colapso** to collapse

sugerencia nf suggestion; **hacer una sugerencia** to make a suggestion

sugerir vb [**51**] to suggest

sugiero vb see **sugerir**

suicidio nm suicide

Suiza nf Switzerland

suizo, -a adj, nm/f Swiss; **los suizos** the Swiss

sujetador nm bra

sujetar vb [**25**] ❶ to hold ❷ to fasten

sujeto nm subject

suma nf sum ▷ **una suma de dinero** a sum of money; **hacer una suma** to do a sum

sumar vb [**25**] to add up

suministrar vb [**25**] to supply

suministro nm supply

supe vb see **saber**

súper adj **gasolina súper** four-star petrol

superar vb [25] ① (illness, crisis) to get over ② (record) to beat ③ (test) to pass

superficie nf ① surface ② area

superior adj ① upper ▷ el labio superior the upper lip ② top ▷ el piso superior the top floor; **superior a** superior to; **Su inteligencia es superior a la media.** He has above-average intelligence.; **un curso de inglés de nivel superior** an advanced level English course

supermercado nm supermarket

superviviente nmf survivor

suplemento nm supplement

suplente nmf ① reserve ② supply teacher ③ locum

suplicar vb [48] to beg

suponer vb [41] ① to suppose; **Supongo que sí.** I suppose so. ② to think ▷ Supusimos que no vendrías. We didn't think you would be coming. ③ to involve ▷ Tener un coche supone más gastos. Having a car involves more expenses.

supositorio nm suppository

suprimir vb [58] to delete

supuesto vb see **suponer**
  ▶ nm ¿Y en el supuesto de que no venga? And supposing he doesn't come?; **por supuesto** of course; **¡Por supuesto que no!** Of course not!

supuse vb see **suponer**

sur nm, adj south

sureño, -a adj southern

sureste nm southeast

surf nm surfing; **surf a vela** windsurfing; **practicar el surf** to surf

surgir vb [16] to come up

suroeste nm southwest

surtido, -a adj assorted ▷ pasteles surtidos assorted cakes; **estar bien surtido** to have a good selection
  ▶ nm selection

surtidor nm petrol pump

suscripción (pl suscripciones) nf subscription

suspender vb [8] ① to call off ② to postpone; **El partido se suspendió a causa de la lluvia.** The game was rained off. ③ to fail

suspense nm suspense ▷ una película de suspense a thriller

suspenso nm (LatAm) suspense ▷ una película de suspenso a thriller; **Tengo un suspenso en inglés.** I failed English.

suspicaz (pl suspicaces) adj suspicious

suspirar vb [25] to sigh

suspiro nm sigh

sustancia nf substance

sustantivo nm noun

sustituir vb [10] ① to replace ② to stand in for

sustituto, -a nm/f ① replacement ② substitute

sustituyendo vb see **sustituir**

susto nm fright ▷ ¡Qué susto! What a fright!; **dar un susto a alguien** to give somebody a fright

susurrar vb [25] to whisper

sutil adj subtle

suyo, -a *pron, adj* ❶ his ▷ *Todas estas tierras son suyas.* All this land is his. ▷ *¿Es este su cuarto? — No, el suyo está abajo.* Is this his room? — No, his is downstairs.; **un amigo suyo** a friend of his ❷ hers ▷ *Es suyo.* It's hers. ▷ *¿Es este su abrigo? — No, el suyo es marrón.* Is this her coat? — No, hers is brown.; **un amigo suyo** a friend of hers ❸ theirs ▷ *Es suyo.* It's theirs. ▷ *¿Es esta su casa? — No, la suya está más adelante.* Is this their house? — No, theirs is further on.; **un amigo suyo** a friend of theirs ❹ yours

▌ **suyo** can also refer to **usted** or **ustedes**, the formal forms meaning **you**.

▷ *Todos estos libros son suyos.* All these books are yours. ▷ *¿Es esta nuestra habitación? — No, la suya está arriba.* Is this our room? — No, yours is upstairs.; **un amigo suyo** a friend of yours

t

tabaco *nm* ❶ tobacco ❷ cigarettes *pl*

taberna *nf* bar

tabique *nm* partition

tabla *nf* plank; **la tabla de multiplicar** the multiplication table; **una tabla de cocina** a chopping board; **la tabla de planchar** the ironing board; **la tabla de surf** the surfboard; **quedar en tablas** to draw

tablero *nm* board; **el tablero de ajedrez** the chessboard; **el tablero de mandos** the dashboard

tableta *nf* ❶ *(of chocolate)* bar ❷ *(pill)* tablet

tablón *(pl* tablones*)* *nm* plank; **el tablón de anuncios** the notice board

tabú (pl **tabúes**) nm taboo

taburete nm stool

tacaño, -a adj mean
▷ nm/f skinflint

tachar vb [**25**] to cross out

taco nm ❶ rawlplug ❷ stud ❸ cube ❹ cue ❺ swearword; **soltar tacos** to swear ❻ (Chile, River Plate) heel

tacón (pl **tacones**) nm heel; **zapatos de tacón** high-heeled shoes

táctica nf tactics pl

tacto nm ❶ touch ❷ tact; **Lo dijo con mucho tacto.** He said it very tactfully.

tajada nf slice

tajante adj ❶ emphatic ❷ (tone) sharp

tal adj, pron such ▷ En tales casos es mejor consultar con un médico. In such cases it's better to see a doctor. ▷ ¡En el aeropuerto había tal confusión! There was such confusion at the airport!; **Lo dejé tal como estaba.** I left it just as it was.; **con tal de que** as long as ▷ con tal de que regreses antes de las once as long as you get back before eleven; **¿Qué tal?** How are things?; **¿Qué tal has dormido?** How did you sleep?; **tal vez** perhaps

taladradora nf ❶ pneumatic drill ❷ punch

taladrar vb [**25**] to drill

taladro nm drill

talento nm talent

talla nf size

tallar vb [**25**] ❶ to carve ❷ to sculpt ❸ (Chile, River Plate) to scrub

tallarines nmpl noodles

taller nm ❶ garage ▷ Tengo el coche en el taller. My car is in the garage. ❷ workshop

tallo nm stem

talón (pl **talones**) nm ❶ heel ❷ cheque ▷ cobrar un talón to cash a cheque

talonario nm ❶ chequebook ❷ book of tickets ❸ receipt book

tamaño nm size; **¿Qué tamaño tiene?** What size is it?

tambalearse vb [**25**] ❶ to wobble ❷ to stagger

también adv also ▷ Canta flamenco y también baila. He sings flamenco and also dances.; **Tengo hambre. — Yo también.** I'm hungry. — So am I.; **Yo estoy de acuerdo. — Nosotros también.** I agree. — So do we.

tambor nm drum

Támesis nm the Thames

tamiz (pl **tamices**) nm sieve

tampoco adv ❶ either ▷ Yo tampoco lo compré. I didn't buy it either. ❷ neither ▷ Yo no la vi. — Yo tampoco. I didn't see her. — Neither did I. ▷ Nunca he estado en París. — Yo tampoco. I've never been to Paris. — Neither have I.

tampón (pl **tampones**) nm tampon

tan adv ❶ so ▷ No creí que fueras a venir tan pronto. I didn't think you'd come so soon. ▷ ¡No es tan difícil! It's not so difficult!; **¡Qué hombre tan amable!** What a kind man!; **tan ... que ...** so ... that ... ▷ Habla tan deprisa que no la entiendo. She talks so fast that I can't understand her. ❷ **such** ▷ *No era una idea tan buena.* It wasn't such a good idea. ▷ *¡Tiene unos amigos tan simpáticos!* He has such nice friends!; **tan ... como ...** as ... as ... ▷ *No es tan guapa como su madre.* She's not as pretty as her mother. ▷ *Vine tan pronto como pude.* I came as soon as I could.

tanque *nm* tank

tantear *vb* [**25**] to weigh up

tanto, -a *adj, adv, pron* ❶ **so much** ▷ *Ahora no bebo tanta leche.* I don't drink so much milk now. ▷ *Se preocupa tanto que no puede dormir.* He worries so much that he can't sleep. ▷ *¡Tengo tantas cosas que hacer hoy!* I have so many things to do today!; **Vinieron tantos que no cabían en la sala.** So many people came that they couldn't fit into the room.; **No recibe tantas llamadas como yo.** He doesn't get as many calls as I do.; **Gano tanto como tú.** I earn as much as you. ❷ **so often** ▷ *Ahora no la veo tanto.* Now I don't see her so often.; **¡No corras tanto!** Don't run so fast!; **tanto tú como yo** both you and I; **tanto si viene como si no** whether he comes or not; **¡Tanto gusto!** How do you do?; **entre tanto** meanwhile; **por lo tanto** therefore

▶ *nm* ❶ **goal** ▷ *Juárez marcó el segundo tanto.* Juárez scored the second goal. ❷ **amount** ▷ *Me paga un tanto fijo cada semana.* He pays me a fixed amount each week.; **un tanto por ciento** a percentage;

Había cuarenta y tantos invitados. There were forty-odd guests.; **Manténme al tanto.** Keep me informed.

tapa *nf* ❶ **lid** ❷ **top** ❸ **cover** ❹ **tapa** ▷ *Pedimos unas tapas en el bar.* We ordered some tapas in the bar.

tapadera *nf* lid

tapado *nm* (River Plate) coat

tapar *vb* [**25**] to cover; **Tapa la olla.** Put the lid on the pan.; **Me estás tapando el sol.** You're keeping the sun off me.; **Tápate bien que hace frío.** Wrap up well as it's cold.

tapete *nm* ❶ **embroidered tablecloth** ❷ (Mex) rug

tapia *nf* wall

tapicería *nf* ❶ **upholstery** ❷ **upholsterer's**

tapiz (*pl* tapices) *nm* tapestry

tapizar *vb* [**13**] to upholster

tapón (*pl* tapones) *nm* ❶ **plug** ❷ **top** ❸ **cork**; **tapón de rosca** screw top

taquigrafía *nf* shorthand

taquilla *nf* ❶ **box office** ❷ **ticket office** ❸ **locker**

tararear *vb* [**25**] to hum

tardar *vb* [**25**] to be late; **Tardaron una semana en contestar.** They took a week to reply.; **En avión se tarda dos horas.** The plane takes two hours.

tarde *adv* late ▷ *Se está haciendo tarde.* It's getting late.; **más tarde** later; **tarde o temprano** sooner or later; **Llegaré a las nueve como muy tarde.** I'll arrive at nine at the latest.

▶ nf **①** afternoon ▷ *a las tres de la tarde* at three in the afternoon ▷ ¡Buenas tardes! Good afternoon! ▷ *por la tarde* in the afternoon ▷ *hoy por la tarde* this afternoon **②** evening ▷ *a las ocho de la tarde* at eight in the evening ▷ ¡Buenas tardes! Good evening! ▶ *por la tarde* in the evening ▷ *hoy por la tarde* this evening

tarea nf task; **las tareas domésticas** the household chores; **las tareas** (LatAm) homework

tarifa nf **①** rate **②** fare; **tarifa de precios** price list

tarima nf platform

tarjeta nf card ▷ *Me mandó una tarjeta de Navidad.* He sent me a Christmas card.; **una tarjeta de cajero automático** a cash card; **una tarjeta de crédito** a credit card; **una tarjeta telefónica** a phonecard; **una tarjeta de embarque** a boarding pass; **una tarjeta electrónica** an e-card

tarro nm **①** jar **②** (Mex) mug

tarta nf **①** cake ▷ *una tarta de cumpleaños* a birthday cake **②** tart

tartamudear vb [**25**] to stammer

tartamudo, -a adj ser tartamudo to stutter

tasa nf rate ▷ *la tasa de natalidad* the birth rate

tasar vb [**25**] to value

tasca nf tavern

tata nm (LatAm) **①** daddy **②** grandpa

tatuaje nm tattoo

tatuar vb [**1**] to tattoo

Tauro nm (sign) Taurus; **Soy tauro.** I'm Taurus.

taxi nm taxi ▷ *tomar un taxi* to take a taxi

taxímetro nm taximeter

taxista nmf taxi driver

taza nf **①** cup ▷ *Tomamos una taza de café.* We had a cup of coffee. **②** cupful ▷ *una taza de arroz* a cupful of rice **③** (of toilet) bowl

tazón (pl tazones) nm bowl

te pron **①** you ▷ *Te quiero.* I love you. ▷ *Te voy a dar un consejo.* I'm going to give you some advice. ▷ **Me gustaría comprártelo.** I'd like to buy it for you. **②** yourself ▷ *¿Te has hecho daño?* Have you hurt yourself?; **¿Te duelen los pies?** Do your feet hurt?; **Te tienes que poner el abrigo.** You should put your coat on.

té (pl tés) nm tea; **Me hice un té.** I made myself a cup of tea.

teatro nm theatre; **una obra de teatro** a play

tebeo nm comic

techo nm **①** ceiling **②** (LatAm) roof

tecla nf key; **pulsar una tecla** to press a key

teclado nm keyboard

teclear vb [**25**] to type

técnica nf **①** technique **②** technology **③** technician

técnico, -a adj technical
▶ nm **①** technician ▷ *un técnico de laboratorio* a laboratory technician **②** repairman

tecno nm techno

tecnología nf technology

tecnológico, -a adj technological

teja nf tile

tejado nm roof

tejanos nmpl jeans

tejer vb [8] ❶ to weave ❷ to knit

tejido nm ❶ fabric ❷ tissue

tel. abbr (= teléfono) tel.

tela nf fabric; **tela metálica** wire netting

telaraña nf cobweb

tele nf TV ▷ Estábamos viendo la tele. We were watching TV.

telecomunicaciones nfpl telecommunications

telediario nm news sg

teledirigido, -a adj remote-controlled

teleférico nm cable car

telefonear vb [25] to phone

telefónico, -a adj telephone; **la guía telefónica** the telephone directory

telefonista nmf telephonist

teléfono nm telephone; **No tengo teléfono.** I don't have a telephone.; **Hablamos por teléfono.** We spoke on the phone.; **Está hablando por teléfono.** He's on the phone.; **colgar el teléfono a alguien** to hang up the phone on somebody; **un teléfono de tarjeta** a card phone; **un teléfono con cámara** a camera phone; **un teléfono fijo** a landline (phone); **un teléfono móvil** a mobile phone

telegrama nm telegram

telenovela nf soap opera

telepatía nf telepathy

telerrealidad nf reality TV

telescopio nm telescope

telesilla nm chairlift

telespectador, a nm/f viewer

telesquí (pl telesquís) nm ski-lift

teletexto nm Teletext®

televentas nfpl telesales

televisar vb [25] to televise

televisión (pl televisiones) nf television; **¿Qué ponen en la televisión esta noche?** What's on the television tonight?; **la televisión por cable** cable television; **la televisión digital** digital TV

televisor nm television set

telón (pl telones) nm curtain ▷ Subió el telón. The curtain rose.

tema nm ❶ topic ❷ subject ▷ Luego hablaremos de ese tema. We'll talk about that subject later.; **cambiar de tema** to change the subject; **temas de actualidad** current affairs

temblar vb [39] to tremble; **temblar de miedo** to tremble with fear; **temblar de frío** to shiver

temblor de tierra nm earthquake

tembloroso, -a adj trembling

temer vb [8] ❶ to be afraid ❷ to be afraid of ▷ Le teme al profesor. He's afraid of the teacher.

temible adj fearsome

temor nm fear ▷ el temor a la oscuridad fear of the dark

temperamental adj temperamental

temperamento nm temperament

temperatura nf temperature

tempestad nf storm

templado, -a adj ❶ (water, meal) lukewarm ❷ (climate) mild

templo nm temple

temporada nf season ▷ la temporada alta the high season ▷ la temporada baja the low season

temporal adj temporary ▶ nm storm

temporario, -a adj (LatAm) temporary

temprano adv early; **por la mañana temprano** early in the morning

ten vb see **tener**

tenaz (pl tenaces) adj tenacious

tenazas nfpl pliers

tendedero nm ① clothes line ② clothes horse

tendencia nf tendency

tender vb [**20**] ① to hang out ② to lay out; **Me tendió la mano.** He stretched out his hand to me.; **tender a hacer algo** to tend to do something; **tenderse en el sofá** to lie down on the sofa; **tender la cama** (LatAm) to make the bed; **tender la mesa** (LatAm) to lay the table

tendero, -a nm/f shopkeeper

tendido, -a adj **La ropa estaba tendida.** The washing was hanging out.; **Lo encontré tendido en el suelo.** I found him lying on the floor.

tendón (pl tendones) nm tendon

tendrá vb see **tener**

tenedor nm fork

tener vb [**53**] ① to have ▷ Tengo dos hermanas. I have two sisters.; **¿Cuántos años tienes?** How old are you?; **Tiene cinco metros de largo.** It's five metres long.; **Ten**

cuidado. Be careful.; **No tengas miedo.** Don't be afraid.; **Tenía el pelo mojado.** His hair was wet. ② to hold ▷ Tenía el pasaporte en la mano. He was holding his passport in his hand.; **tener que hacer algo** to have to do something; **Tendrías que comer más.** You should eat more.; **No tienes por qué ir.** There's no reason why you should go.; **Eso no tiene nada que ver.** That's got nothing to do with it.; **¡Tenga!** Here you are!; **tenerse en pie** to stand

tenga vb see **tener**

teniente nmf lieutenant

tenis nm tennis; **¿Juegas al tenis?** Do you play tennis?; **tenis de mesa** table tennis

tenista nmf tennis player

tenor nm tenor

tensar vb [**25**] to tighten

tensión (pl tensiones) nf ① tension ② blood pressure ▷ El médico me tomó la tensión. The doctor took my blood pressure.

tenso, -a adj ① tense ② taut

tentación (pl tentaciones) nf temptation; **caer en la tentación** to give in to temptation

tentador, a adj tempting

tentar vb [**39**] to tempt; **No me tienta la idea.** The idea isn't very tempting.

tentativa nf attempt

tentempié (pl tentempiés) nm snack

tenue adj faint

teñir vb [**45**] to dye

teología nf theology

teoría nf theory ▷ En teoría es fácil. In theory it's easy.

teórico, -a adj theoretical

terapéutico, -a adj therapeutic

terapia nf therapy

tercer see **tercero**

tercero, -a adj, pron third

> **tercero** is shortened to **tercer** before masculine singular nouns.

▷ la tercera vez the third time ▷ Llegué el tercero. I arrived third.; **una tercera parte de la población** a third of the population; **Vivo en el tercero.** I live on the third floor.; **el Tercer Mundo** the Third World

tercio nm third

terciopelo nm velvet

terco, -a adj obstinate

tergiversar vb [25] to distort

terminal nm (computer) terminal
▶ nf (in airport) terminal

terminante adj ❶ categorical ❷ strict

terminantemente adv strictly

terminar vb [25] ❶ to finish; **cuando terminó de hablar** when he finished talking ❷ to end; **Terminaron peleándose.** They ended up fighting.; **Se nos ha terminado el café.** We've run out of coffee.; **He terminado con Andrés.** I've broken up with Andrés.

término nm term ▷ un término médico a medical term; **por término medio** on average

termita nf termite

termo® nm Thermos flask®

termómetro nm thermometer; **Le puse el termómetro.** I took his temperature.

termostato nm thermostat

ternera nf ❶ (animal) calf ❷ veal

ternero nm (animal) calf

ternura nf tenderness; **con ternura** tenderly

terrateniente nmf landowner

terraza nf ❶ balcony ❷ roof terrace

terremoto nm earthquake

terreno nm ❶ land; **un terreno** a piece of land ❷ field; **el terreno de juego** the pitch; **Lo decidiremos sobre el terreno.** We'll decide as we go along.

terrestre adj land

terrible adj terrible; **Tenía un cansancio terrible.** I was awfully tired.

terrier (pl terriers) nm terrier

territorio nm territory

terrón (pl terrones) nm lump

terror nm terror; **Les tiene terror a los perros.** He's terrified of dogs.; **una película de terror** a horror film

terrorismo nm terrorism

terrorista adj, nmf terrorist; **un terrorista suicida** a suicide bomber

tesis (pl tesis) nf thesis

tesón nm determination

tesorero, -a nm/f treasurer

tesoro nm treasure; **Ven aquí, tesoro.** Come here, darling.

test (pl tests) nm test ▷ Hoy nos han hecho un test. We had a test today.

testamento nm will; **hacer testamento** to make one's will; **el Antiguo Testamento** the Old Testament; **el Nuevo Testamento** the New Testament

testarudo, -a adj stubborn

testigo nmf witness; **Fui testigo del accidente.** I witnessed the accident.

testimonio nm evidence

tétanos nm tetanus

tetera nf ① teapot ② (Chile, Mex) kettle ③ (Mex) baby's bottle

tetina nf teat

textil adj textile

texto nm text; **un libro de texto** a textbook

textura nf texture

tez nf complexion

ti pron you ▷ una llamada para ti a call for you; **Solo piensas en ti mismo.** You only think of yourself.

tía nf ① aunt ▷ mi tía my aunt ② girl ▷ Es una tía majísima. She's a really nice girl.

tibio, -a adj lukewarm

tiburón (pl tiburones) nm shark

tic nm tic ▷ un tic nervioso a nervous tic

tictac nm tick-tock

tiemblo vb see temblar

tiempo nm ① time ▷ No tengo tiempo. I don't have time. ▷ ¿Qué haces en tu tiempo libre? What do you do in your spare time? ▷ Me llevó bastante tiempo. It took me quite a long time. ¿**Cuánto tiempo hace que vives aquí?** How long have you been living here?; **Hace mucho tiempo que**

no la veo. I haven't seen her for a long time.; **al mismo tiempo** at the same time; **perder el tiempo** to waste time; **al poco tiempo** soon after; **a tiempo** in time ▷ Llegamos a tiempo de ver la película. We got there in time to see the film. ② weather; **¿Qué tiempo hace ahí?** What's the weather like there?; **Hizo buen tiempo.** The weather was fine. ③ half; **Metieron el gol durante el segundo tiempo.** They scored the goal during the second half.

tienda nf shop; **una tienda de comestibles** a grocer's shop; **ir de tiendas** to go shopping; **una tienda de campaña** a tent

tiendo vb see tender

tiene vb see tener

tiento vb see tentar

tierno, -a adj ① tender ② fresh

tierra nf ① land; **la Tierra Santa** the Holy Land; **tierra adentro** inland ② soil; **la Tierra** the Earth

tieso, -a adj ① stiff ② straight ▷ Ponte tiesa. Stand up straight.

tiesto nm flowerpot

tigre nm tiger

tijeras nfpl scissors

timar vb [25] ① to con ② to rip off

timbrazo nm ring

timbre nm ① bell ▷ Ya ha sonado el timbre. The bell has already gone.; **llamar al timbre** to ring the bell ③ (Mex) stamp

timidez nf shyness

tímido, -a adj shy

timo nm ① con ② rip off; **¡Vaya timo!** What a rip-off!

tinta nf ink; **tinta China** Indian ink
　Word for word, **tinta china**
　means 'Chinese ink'.
　sudar tinta to sweat blood
tinte nm dye
tintero nm inkwell
tinto nm red wine
tintorería nf dry cleaner's
tiñendo vb see **teñir**
tío nm ① uncle; **mis tíos** my uncle
　and aunt ② guy ▷ Es un tío muy
　simpático. He's a really nice guy.
tiovivo nm merry-go-round
típicamente adv typically
típico, -a adj typical
tipo nm ① kind ▷ No me gusta este
　tipo de fiestas. I don't like this kind
　of party.; **todo tipo de ...** all sorts
　of ... ② figure ▷ Marisa tiene un tipo
　muy bonito. Marisa has a lovely
　figure. ③ bloke ▷ un tipo de aspecto
　sospechoso a suspicious-looking
　bloke
tíquet (pl **tíquets**) nm ① ticket
　② receipt
tira nf strip ▷ una tira de papel a strip
　of paper ▷ una tira cómica a comic
　strip
tirada nf ① print run ② circulation;
　de una tirada in one go
tirado, -a adj ① dirt-cheap ② dead
　easy
tirador nm handle
tirana nf tyrant
tiránico, -a adj tyrannical
tirano nm tyrant
tirante adj ① tight ② tense
　▶ nm strap; **tirantes** braces
tirar vb [**25**] ① to throw ② to throw
　away; **tirar algo a la basura** to

throw something out; **tirar al
suelo** to knock over ③ to knock
down ④ to drop; **tirar a la derecha**
to turn right; **tirar de algo** to pull
something; **tirar la cadena**
(LatAm) to pull the chain; **Vamos
tirando.** We're getting by.; **tirarse
al agua** to plunge into the water;
tirarse de cabeza to dive in head
first; **tirarse en el sofá** (LatAm) to
lie down on the sofa; **Se tiró toda
la mañana estudiando.** He spent
the whole morning studying.
tirita nf plaster
tiritar vb [**25**] to shiver; **tiritar de
frío** to shiver with cold
tiro nm shot; **Lo mataron de un
tiro.** They shot him dead.; **tiro al
blanco** target practice; **un tiro
libre** a free kick
tiroteo nm shoot-out
títere nm puppet
titubear vb [**25**] to hesitate
titulado, -a adj qualified
titular vb [**25**] to call; **¿Cómo vas a
titular el trabajo?** What title are
you going to give the essay?
　▶ nm headline
　▶ nmf ① holder ② owner
título nm ① title ② qualification
　▷ Tiene el título de enfermera. She
　has a nursing qualification.
　③ certificate
tiza nf chalk; **una tiza** a piece of
chalk
toalla nf towel
tobillo nm ankle ▷ Me he torcido el
tobillo. I've twisted my ankle.
tobogán (pl **toboganes**) nm
　① slide ② toboggan

tocadiscos (pl **tocadiscos**) nm record player

tocador nm dressing table

tocar vb [48] ❶ to touch ❷ (instrument, waltz) to play ❸ (bell) to ring ❹ (horn) to blow; **tocar a la puerta** (LatAm) to knock on the door; **Te toca fregar los platos.** It's your turn to do the dishes.; **Le tocó la lotería.** He won the lottery.

tocino nm pork fat

todavía adv ❶ still ▷ ¿Todavía estás en la cama? Are you still in bed? ❷ yet ▷ Todavía no han llegado. They haven't arrived yet.

todo, -a adj, pron ❶ all ▷ todos los niños all the children ▷ Todos son caros. They're all expensive. ▷ el más bonito de todos the prettiest of all; **toda la noche** all night; **todos vosotros** all of you; **todos los que quieran venir** all those who want to come ❷ every ▷ todos los días every day ❸ the whole ▷ He limpiado toda la casa. I've cleaned the whole house.; **Ha viajado por todo el mundo.** He has travelled all over the world.; **Todo el mundo lo sabe.** Everybody knows. ❹ everything ▷ Lo sabemos todo. We know everything. ▷ todo lo que me dijeron everything they told me ❺ everybody ▷ Todos estaban de acuerdo. Everybody agreed.; **Vaya todo seguido.** Keep straight on.; **todo lo contrario** quite the opposite

toldo nm ❶ sun blind ❷ awning ❸ sunshade

tolerar vb [25] to tolerate; **Sus padres le toleran demasiado.** His parents let him get away with too much.

tomar vb [25] ❶ to take; **tomarse algo a mal** to take something badly ❷ to have ▷ ¿Qué quieres tomar? What are you going to have? ▷ De postre tomé un helado. I had an ice cream for dessert.; **Toma, esto es tuyo.** Here, this is yours.; **tomar el pelo a alguien** to pull somebody's leg; **tomar el aire** to get some fresh air; **tomar el sol** to sunbathe; **tomar nota de algo** to note something down

tomate nm tomato; **ponerse como un tomate** to turn as red as a beetroot

tomillo nm thyme

tomo nm volume

tonel nm barrel

tonelada nf ton

tónica nf tonic

tono nm ❶ tone ▷ Lo dijo en tono cariñoso. He said it in an affectionate tone.; **un tono de llamada** a ringtone ❷ (of colour) shade

tontería nf silly thing; **tonterías** nonsense ▷ ¡Eso son tonterías! That's nonsense! ▷ ¡No digas tonterías! Don't talk nonsense!

tonto, -a adj silly ▷ ¡Qué error más tonto! What a silly mistake! ▶ nm fool; **hacer el tonto** to act the fool; **hacerse el tonto** to act dumb

toparse vb [25] **toparse con alguien** to bump into somebody

topes nmpl **El autobús iba hasta los topes.** The bus was packed.

tópico nm cliché

topo nm mole

toque nm **dar los últimos toques a algo** to put the finishing touches to something

torcedura nf **una torcedura de tobillo** a sprained ankle

torcer vb [6] ❶ to twist; **torcerse el tobillo** to sprain one's ankle ❷ to turn ▷ **torcer a la derecha** to turn right

torcido, -a adj ❶ crooked ❷ bent

torear vb [25] to fight

toreo nm bullfighting

torero, -a nm/f bullfighter

tormenta nf ❶ storm; **Hubo tormenta.** There was a storm.; **un día de tormenta** a stormy day

torneo nm tournament

tornillo nm ❶ screw; **A tu hermana le falta un tornillo.** Your sister's got a screw loose. ❷ bolt

toro nm bull; **los toros** bullfighting; **ir a los toros** to go to a bullfight

toronja nf (LatAm) grapefruit

torpe adj ❶ clumsy ❷ dim

torre nf ❶ tower ▷ **la torre de control** the control tower ❷ pylon ❸ (in chess) rook

torta nf ❶ small flat cake ❷ (LatAm) pie ❸ (Mex) filled roll; **pegar una torta a alguien** to give somebody a slap; **No entiendo ni torta.** I don't understand a thing.

tortilla nf ❶ omelette; **una tortilla de patatas** a Spanish omelette ❷ tortilla

tortuga nf ❶ tortoise ❷ turtle

torturar vb [25] to torture

tos (pl toses) nf cough; **Tengo mucha tos.** I have a bad cough.

toser vb [8] to cough

tostada nf ❶ piece of toast; **tostadas** toast ▷ **Tomé café con tostadas.** I had coffee and toast. ❷ (Mex) fried corn tortilla

tostado, -a adj ❶ toasted ❷ roasted ❸ tanned

tostador nm toaster

tostar vb [11] ❶ to toast ❷ to roast

total adj total; **un cambio total** a complete change; **En total éramos catorce.** There were fourteen of us altogether.
  ▶ n total
  ▶ adv Total, que perdí mi trabajo. So, in the end, I lost my job.

totalitario, -a adj totalitarian

totalmente adv ❶ totally ▷ **Mario es totalmente distinto a Luis.** Mario is totally different from Luis. ❷ completely ▷ **Estoy totalmente de acuerdo.** I completely agree.; **¿Estás seguro? — Totalmente.** Are you sure? — Absolutely.

tóxico, -a adj toxic

toxicómano, -a nm/f drug addict

tozudo, -a adj obstinate

trabajador, a adj hard-working
  ▶ nm/f worker

trabajar vb [25] to work; **¿En qué trabajas?** What's your job?; **Trabajo de camarero.** I work as a waiter.; **trabajar jornada completa** to work full-time; **trabajar media jornada** to work part-time

trabajo nm ❶ work; **estar sin trabajo** to be unemployed; **trabajo en equipo** teamwork; **el trabajo de la casa** the housework; **trabajos manuales** handicrafts ❷ job ▷ *No encuentro trabajo.* I can't find a job.; **quedarse sin trabajo** to find oneself out of work ❸ essay ▷ *Tengo que entregar dos trabajos mañana.* I have to hand in two essays tomorrow.

tractor nm tractor

tradición (pl **tradiciones**) nf tradition

tradicional adj traditional

traducción (pl **traducciones**) nf translation

traducir vb [9] to translate

traductor, a nm/f translator

traer vb [54] ❶ to bring ▷ *He traído el paraguas por si acaso.* I've brought the umbrella just in case. ❷ to carry; **El periódico trae un artículo sobre eso.** There's an article about this in the newspaper. ❸ to wear ▷ *Traía un vestido nuevo.* She was wearing a new dress.

traficante nmf dealer ▷ *traficantes de armas* arms dealers

tráfico nm traffic; **un accidente de tráfico** a road accident; **tráfico de drogas** drug-trafficking

tragar vb [37] to swallow; **No la trago.** I can't stand her.

tragedia nf tragedy

trágico, -a adj tragic

trago nm drink ▷ *¿Te apetece un trago?* Do you fancy a drink?; **de un trago** in one gulp

traición (pl **traiciones**) nf ❶ betrayal ❷ treason

traicionar vb [25] to betray

traicionero, -a adj treacherous

traidor, -a nm/f traitor

traigo vb see **traer**

tráiler (pl **tráilers**) nm ❶ trailer ❷ articulated lorry

traje nm ❶ suit; **un traje de chaqueta** a suit ❷ dress; **el traje de novia** the bridal gown; **un traje de baño (1)** a pair of swimming trunks **(2)** a swimsuit

trama nf plot

tramitar vb [25] **Estoy tramitando un préstamo con el banco.** I'm negotiating a loan with the bank.; **Estamos tramitando el divorcio.** We are going through the divorce proceedings.

tramo nm ❶ (of road) section ❷ (of stairs) flight

trampa nf trap ▷ *caer en la trampa* to fall into the trap; **Les tendió una trampa.** He set a trap for them.; **hacer trampa** to cheat

trampolín (pl **trampolines**) nm ❶ diving board ❷ trampoline

tramposo, -a nm/f cheat

tranquilamente adv calmly

tranquilidad nf peace and quiet; **Respondió con tranquilidad.** He answered calmly.; **Llévatelo a casa y léelo con tranquilidad.** Take it home with you and read it at your leisure.

tranquilizar vb [13] to calm down

tranquilo, -a adj ❶ calm ❷ peaceful

transatlántico nm ocean liner

transbordador nm ferry; **el transbordador espacial** the space shuttle

transbordo nm **Hay que hacer transbordo en París.** You have to change trains in Paris.

transcurrir vb [**58**] to pass

transeúnte nmf passer-by

transferencia nf transfer
▷ **transferencia bancaria** bank transfer

transformación (pl **transformaciones**) nf transformation

transformar vb [**25**] to transform
▷ **La cirugía estética lo ha transformado completamente.** Plastic surgery has completely transformed him.; **Hemos transformado el garaje en sala de estar.** We've converted the garage into a living room.; **El príncipe se transformó en un monstruo.** The prince turned into a monster.

transfusión (pl **transfusiones**) nf **Me hicieron una transfusión de sangre.** They gave me a blood transfusion.

transgénico, -a adj genetically modified

tránsito nm traffic; **los pasajeros en tránsito para Moscú** transfer passengers to Moscow

transmisión (pl **transmisiones**) nf broadcast ▷ **una transmisión en directo** a live broadcast

transmitir vb [**58**] ❶ to transmit ❷ to broadcast

transparente adj transparent

transpiración nf perspiration

transportar vb [**25**] to carry

transporte nm transport; **el transporte público** public transport

transportista nmf carrier

tranvía nm tram

trapo nm cloth; **un trapo de cocina** a dishcloth; **Pásale un trapo al espejo.** Give the mirror a wipe over.; **el trapo del polvo** the duster

tráquea nf windpipe

tras prep after ▷ **Salimos corriendo tras ella.** We ran out after her. ▷ **semana tras semana** week after week

trasero, -a adj back ▷ **la rueda trasera de la bici** the back wheel of the bike
▶ nm bottom

trasladar vb [**25**] ❶ to move ❷ to transfer

traslado nm move; **He pedido traslado a Barcelona.** I've asked for a transfer to Barcelona.; **los gastos de traslado de la oficina** the office's relocation expenses

trasluz nm **al trasluz** against the light

trasnochar vb [**25**] to stay up late

trasplante nm transplant

trastero nm storage room

trastes nmpl (Mex) pots and pans; **lavar los trastes** to do the washing up

trasto nm piece of junk; **El desván está lleno de trastos.** The loft is full of junk.

trastornado, -a adj disturbed

trastorno nm disruption ▷ La huelga ha causado muchos trastornos. The strike has caused a lot of disruption.; **trastornos mentales** mental disorders

tratado nm treaty

tratamiento nm treatment; **Está en tratamiento médico.** He's having medical treatment.; **tratamiento de datos** data processing

tratar vb [25] ❶ to treat ❷ to deal with ▷ Trataremos este tema en la reunión. We'll deal with this subject in the meeting.; **Trato con todo tipo de gente.** I deal with all sorts of people.; **tratar de hacer algo** to try to do something; **¿De qué se trata?** What's it about?; **La película trata de un adolescente en Nueva York.** The film is about a teenager in New York.

trato nm deal ▷ hacer un trato to make a deal; **¡Trato hecho!** It's a deal!; **No tengo mucho trato con él.** I don't have much to do with him.; **recibir malos tratos de alguien** to be treated badly by somebody

trauma nm trauma

través prep a través de (1) across ▷ Nadó a través del río. He swam across the river. (2) through ▷ Se enteraron a través de un amigo. They found out through a friend.

travesía nf ❶ crossing ❷ side street

travesura nf prank; **hacer travesuras** to get up to mischief

travieso, -a adj naughty

trayecto nm ❶ journey ❷ way; **¿Qué trayecto hace el 34?** What way does the 34 go?

trazar vb [13] ❶ to draw ❷ to draw up

trébol nm clover; **tréboles** clubs

trece adj, pron thirteen ▷ Tengo trece años. I'm thirteen.; **el trece de enero** the thirteenth of January

treinta adj, pron thirty ▷ Tiene treinta años. He's thirty.; **el treinta aniversario** the thirtieth anniversary

tremendo, -a adj ❶ terrible; **Hacía un frío tremendo.** It was terribly cold. ❷ tremendous

tren nm train; **viajar en tren** to travel by train; **Tomé un tren directo.** I took a through train.; **con este tren de vida** with such a hectic life

trenza nf plait; **Le hice una trenza.** I plaited her hair.

trepadora nf climber

trepar vb [25] to climb; **trepar a un árbol** to climb a tree

tres adj, pron three; **Son las tres.** It's three o'clock.; **el tres de febrero** the third of February

trescientos, -as adj, pron three hundred

triángulo nm triangle

tribu nf tribe

tribuna nf ❶ platform ❷ stand

tribunal nm ❶ court ❷ board of examiners

tridimensional adj three-dimensional

trigo nm wheat

trillizos (trillizas) nm/f triplets

trimestral adj quarterly; **los exámenes trimestrales** the end-of-term exams

trimestre nm term

trinchar vb [25] to carve

trineo nm ❶ sledge ❷ sleigh

trío nm trio

tripa nf gut

triple nm **Esta habitación es el triple de grande.** This room is three times as big.; **Gastan el triple que nosotros.** They spend three times as much as we do.

triplicar vb [48] to treble

tripulación (pl tripulaciones) nf crew

triste adj ❶ sad ▷ Me puse muy triste cuando me enteré. I was very sad when I heard.; **El invierno me pone triste.** Winter makes me miserable. ❷ gloomy

tristeza nf sadness

triturar vb [25] ❶ to crush ❷ to grind

triunfar vb [25] to triumph

triunfo nm triumph

trivial adj trivial

trocear vb [25] to cut up

trofeo nm trophy

trombón (pl trombones) nm trombone

trompa nf ❶ (of elephant) trunk ❷ (musical instrument) horn

trompeta nf trumpet

tronar vb [11] to thunder

troncharse vb [25] **Yo me tronchaba de risa.** I was killing myself laughing.

tronco nm ❶ trunk ❷ log; **dormir como un tronco** to sleep like a log

trono nm throne

tropas nfpl troops

tropezar vb [19] to trip; **tropezar con una piedra** to trip on a stone; **tropezar contra un árbol** to bump into a tree; **Me tropecé con Juan en el banco.** I bumped into Juan in the bank.

tropezón (pl tropezones) nm trip; **dar un tropezón** to trip

tropical adj tropical

tropiece vb see **tropezar**

trotar vb [25] to trot

trozo nm piece ▷ un trozo de madera a piece of wood

trucha nf trout

truco nm trick; **Ya le he cogido el truco.** I've got the hang of it already.

truena vb see **tronar**

trueno nm **Oímos un trueno.** We heard a clap of thunder.; **Me despertaron los truenos.** The thunder woke me up.

tu adj your ▷ tu coche your car ▷ tus familiares your relations

tú pron you ▷ Cuando tú quieras. Whenever you like. ▷ Llegamos antes que tú. We arrived before you.

tubería nf pipe ▷ Ha reventado una tubería. A pipe has burst.

tubo nm ❶ pipe ▷ el tubo de escape the exhaust pipe; **el tubo de desagüe** the drainpipe ❷ tube

tuerca nf nut

tuerzo vb see **torcer**

tuétano nm marrow

tuit nm tweet

tulipán (pl tulipanes) nm tulip

tumba nf ❶ grave ❷ tomb

tumbar vb [25] to knock down;
tumbarse to lie down

tumbona nf deck chair

tumor nm tumour

túnel nm tunnel; **un túnel de
lavado** a car wash

> Word for word, **túnel de
> lavado** means 'washing
> tunnel'.

Túnez nm ❶ Tunisia ❷ Tunis

turbante nm turban

turbina nf turbine

turbio, -a adj cloudy

turbulento, -a adj turbulent

turco, -a adj Turkish
  ▶ nm/f Turk
  ▶ nm (language) Turkish

turismo nm ❶ tourism; **casas de
turismo rural** holiday cottages;
la oficina de turismo the
tourist office ❷ tourists pl ▷ En
verano hay mucho turismo. In
summer there are a lot of tourists.
❸ car

turista nmf tourist

turístico, -a adj tourist

turnarse vb [25] to take it in turns
▷ Nos turnamos para fregar los
platos. We take it in turns to do the
washing-up.

turno nm ❶ turn ▷ cuando me tocó el
turno when it was my turn ❷ shift
▷ Hago el turno de tarde. I do the
afternoon shift.

turquesa adj, nf turquoise ▷ un
anorak turquesa a turquoise
anorak

Turquía nf Turkey

turrón (pl **turrones**) nm nougat

tutear vb [25]

> **tutear** means to address
> somebody using the familiar **tú**
> form rather than the more
> formal **usted** form.
>
> ▷ Se tutean con el jefe. They address
> the boss in familiar terms.

tutor, a nm/f ❶ tutor ❷ guardian

tuve vb see **tener**

tuyo, -a adj, pron yours ▷ ¿Es tuyo
este abrigo? Is this coat yours? ▷ La
tuya está en el armario. Yours is in
the cupboard. ▷ mis amigos y los
tuyos my friends and yours; **un
amigo tuyo** a friend of yours

a
b
c
d
e
f
g
h
i
j
k
l
m
n
ñ
o
p
q
r
s
t
u
v
w
x
y
z

u

u *conj* or

▌u is used instead of **o** before words starting with **o-** or **ho-**. ▷ ¿Minutos u horas? Minutes or hours?

ubicado, -a *adj* situated

Ud. *abbr* (= usted) you

Uds. *abbr* (= ustedes) you

UE *abbr f* (= Unión Europea) EU

uf *excl* ❶ phew! ❷ ugh!

úlcera *nf* ulcer

últimamente *adv* recently

ultimátum (*pl* ultimátums) *nm* ultimatum

último, -a *adj* ❶ last ▷ la última vez que hablé con ella the last time I spoke to her ❷ top ▷ No llego al último estante. I can't reach the top shelf. ❸ back ▷ Nos sentamos en la última fila. We sat in the back row.;

la última moda the latest fashion; a última hora at the last minute; llegar en último lugar to arrive last

▶ *nm/f* the last one; a últimos de mes towards the end of the month; por último lastly

ultra *nmf* right-wing extremist

ultrasónico, -a *adj* ultrasonic

ultravioleta *adj* ultraviolet

un, a *art* ❶ a ▷ una silla a chair ❷ an ▷ un paraguas an umbrella ❸ (in plural) some ▷ Fui con unos amigos. I went with some friends.; Tiene unas uñas muy largas. He has very long nails.; Había unas 20 personas. There were about 20 people.; Me he comprado unos zapatos de tacón. I have bought a pair of high heels.

unánime *adj* unanimous

undécimo, -a *adj, pron* eleventh

únicamente *adv* only

único, -a *adj, nm/f* ❶ only ▷ el único día que tengo libre the only day I have free; Soy hija única. I'm an only child.; el único que me queda the only one I've got left; Lo único que no me gusta ... The only thing I don't like ...

unidad *nf* ❶ unit; unidad de cuidados intensivos intensive care unit ❷ unity

unido, -a *adj* close ▷ una familia muy unida a very close family

uniforme *adj* even ▷ una superficie uniforme an even surface

▶ *nm* uniform ▷ Llevaba el uniforme del colegio. He was wearing his school uniform.

unión (pl **uniones**) nf union; **la Unión Europea** the European Union

unir vb [58] ❶ to link ▷ *Este pasaje une los dos edificios.* This passage links the two buildings. ❷ to join ▷ *Unió los dos extremos con una cuerda.* He joined the two ends with some string. ❸ to unite ▷ *Los unió en matrimonio.* He united them in marriage. ❹ to bring together ▷ *La enfermedad de la madre ha unido a los hijos.* The mother's illness has brought the children together.; **unirse a algo** to join something ▷ *Andrés se unió a la expedición.* Andrés joined the expedition.; **Más adelante los dos caminos se unen.** The two paths join further on.; **Los dos bancos se han unido.** The two banks have merged.

universal adj universal

universidad nf university; **Universidad a Distancia** Open University

universitario, -a adj university ▷ *estudiantes universitarios* university students
▶ nm/f ❶ university student ❷ graduate

universo nm universe

uno, -a adj, pron one ▷ *Vivo en el número uno.* I live at number one. ▷ *Uno de ellos era mío.* One of them was mine.; **unos pocos** a few; **uno mismo** oneself; **Entraron uno a uno.** They came in one by one.; **unas diez personas** about ten people; **el uno de abril** the

first of April; **Es la una.** It's one o'clock.; **Unos querían ir, otros no.** Some of them wanted to go, others didn't.; **Se miraron uno al otro.** They looked at each other.

untar vb [25] **untar algo con algo** to spread something on something; **Te has untado las manos de chocolate.** You've got chocolate all over your hands.; **unta el molde con aceite** grease the baking dish with oil

uña nf ❶ nail ❷ claw

uranio nm uranium

urbanización (pl **urbanizaciones**) nf housing estate

urgencia nf emergency ▷ *en caso de urgencia* in an emergency ▷ *los servicios de urgencia* the emergency services; **urgencias** accident and emergency; **Tuvimos que ir a urgencias.** We had to go to casualty.; **con urgencia** urgently

urgente adj urgent; **Lo mandé por correo urgente.** I sent it express.

urna nf ballot box

Uruguay nm Uruguay

uruguayo, -a adj, nm/f Uruguayan

usado, -a adj ❶ secondhand ▷ *una tienda de ropa usada* a secondhand clothes shop ❷ worn ▷ *Estas zapatillas están ya muy usadas.* These slippers are very worn now.

usar vb [25] ❶ to use ▷ *Uso una maquinilla eléctrica.* I use an electric razor. ❷ to wear ▷ *¿Qué número de zapato usas?* What size shoe do you take?

a
b
c
d
e
f
g
h
i
j
k
l
m
n
ñ
o
p
q
r
s
t
u
v
w
x
y
z

uso nm use ▷ *instrucciones de uso* instructions for use

usted pron you ▷ *Quisiera hablar con usted en privado.* I'd like to speak to you in private.

ustedes pron pl you ▷ *Quisiera hablar con ustedes en privado.* I'd like to speak to you in private.

usual adj usual

usuario, -a nm/f user

utensilio nm utensil

útil adj useful

utilizar vb [13] to use

uva nf grape

va vb see **ir**

vaca nf ❶ cow ❷ beef ▷ *No como carne de vaca.* I don't eat beef.

vacaciones nfpl holidays; **las vacaciones de Navidad** the Christmas holidays; **La secretaria está de vacaciones.** The secretary is on holiday.; **En agosto me voy de vacaciones.** I'm going on holiday in August.

vacante adj ❶ vacant ❷ unoccupied
▸ nf vacancy

vaciar vb [21] to empty

vacilar vb [25] to hesitate; **sin vacilar** without hesitating

vacío, -a adj empty
▸ nm void

vacuna nf vaccine

vacunar vb [25] to vaccinate

vado nm **'vado permanente'** 'no parking – in constant use'

vagabunda nf tramp

vagabundo, -a adj stray
▶ nm tramp

vagar vb **[37]** to wander

vago, -a adj ❶ lazy ❷ vague
▶ nm layabout; **hacer el vago** to laze around

vagón (pl **vagones**) nm carriage; **vagón cama** sleeper; **vagón restaurante** restaurant car

vaho nm steam

vainilla nf vanilla

vajilla nf dishes pl ▷ La vajilla está en el lavaplatos. The dishes are in the dishwasher.; **Me regaló una vajilla de porcelana.** She gave me a china dinner service.

vale nm ❶ voucher ▷ un vale de regalo a gift voucher; **un vale de descuento** a money-off coupon ❷ credit note

valenciano, -a adj, nm/f Valencian

valentía nf bravery; **con valentía** bravely

valer vb **[55]** ❶ to cost ▷ ¿Cuánto vale? How much does it cost? ❷ to be worth ▷ El terreno vale más que la casa. The land is worth more than the house.; **No vale mirar.** You're not allowed to look.; **¡Eso no vale!** That's not fair!; **Vale la pena.** It's worth it.; **Vale la pena hacer el esfuerzo.** It's worth the effort.; **No vale la pena.** It's not worth it.; **No vale la pena gastar tanto dinero.** It's not worth spending that much money.; **Este cuchillo no vale para nada.** This knife is

useless.; **Yo no valdría para enfermera.** I'd make a hopeless nurse.; **¿Vale?** OK?; **¿Vamos a tomar algo?** — **¡Vale!** Shall we go for a drink? — OK!; **Más vale que te lleves el abrigo.** You'd better take your coat.; **No puede valerse por sí mismo.** He can't look after himself.

válido, -a adj valid

valiente adj brave

valija nf (River Plate) suitcase

valioso, -a adj valuable

valla nf ❶ fence; **valla publicitaria** hoarding; **los cien metros vallas** the hundred metre hurdles

valle nm valley

valor nm ❶ value; **una pulsera de gran valor** an extremely valuable bracelet ❷ courage ▷ armarse de valor to pluck up courage; **objetos de valor** valuables

valorar vb **[25]** to value

vals nm waltz; **bailar un vals** to waltz

válvula nf valve

vampiro, -a nm/f vampire

vandalismo nm vandalism

vanguardia nf avant-garde; **de vanguardia** avant-garde

vanidad nf vanity

vanidoso, -a adj vain

vano, -a adj vain ▷ un intento vano a vain attempt; **en vano** in vain

vapor nm steam; **plancha de vapor** steam iron; **al vapor** steamed

vaquero, -a adj denim ▷ una falda vaquera a denim skirt
▶ nm cowboy; **una película de**

vaqueros a western; **vaqueros** jeans

variable adj variable

variado, -a adj varied

variar vb [21] to vary; **Decidí ir en tren, para variar.** I decided to go by train for a change.

varicela nf chickenpox

variedad nf variety

varilla nf rod; **la varilla del aceite** the dipstick

varios, -as adj, pron several ▷ Estuve enfermo varios días. I was ill for several days. ▷ Le hicimos un regalo entre varios. Several of us clubbed together to get him a present.

variz (pl **varices**) nf varicose vein

varón (pl **varones**) adj male ▷ los herederos varones the male heirs ▶ nm ▷ Tiene dos hembras y un varón. She has two girls and a boy.; **Sexo: varón.** Sex: male.

Varsovia nf Warsaw

vasca nf Basque

vasco adj, nm (language) Basque; **el País Vasco** the Basque Country

vasija nf vessel

vaso nm glass ▷ Bebí un vaso de leche. I drank a glass of milk.; **un vaso de plástico** a plastic cup; **un vaso sanguíneo** a blood vessel

váter nm (informal) loo

Vaticano nm Vatican

vatio nm watt

vaya vb see **ir**

Vd. abbr (= usted) you

Vds. abbr (= ustedes) you

ve vb see **ir**; **ver**

vecina nf ❶ neighbour ❷ inhabitant

vecindario nm neighbourhood

vecino, -a adj neighbouring ▷ las ciudades vecinas the neighbouring towns ▶ nm ❶ neighbour ▷ los vecinos de al lado the next door neighbours ❷ inhabitant ▷ todos los vecinos de Torrevieja all the inhabitants of Torrevieja

vegetación (pl **vegetaciones**) nf vegetation

vegetal adj, nm vegetable ▷ aceite vegetal vegetable oil

vegetariano, -a adj, nm/f vegetarian

vehículo nm vehicle

veinte adj, pron twenty ▷ Tiene veinte años. He's twenty.; **el veinte de enero** the twentieth of January; **el siglo veinte** the twentieth century

vejez nf old age

vejiga nf bladder

vela nf ❶ candle ❷ sail ❸ sailing; **un barco de vela** a yacht; **Pasé la noche en vela.** I had a sleepless night.

velarse vb [25] **Se han velado las fotos.** The photos got exposed by accident.

velero nm yacht

vello nm ❶ hair ▷ Tiene mucho vello. He's very hairy. ❷ (on face) down

velo nm veil

velocidad nf ❶ speed ▷ Pasó una moto a toda velocidad. A motorbike went past at full speed.; **¿A qué velocidad ibas?** How fast were

you going? ❷ gear ▷ **cambiar de velocidad** to change gear
velocímetro nm speedometer
velocista nmf sprinter
velódromo nm cycle track
veloz (pl **veloces**) adj swift
ven vb see **ir**; **ver**
vena nf vein
vencedor, a adj winning ▷ **el equipo vencedor** the winning team ▶ nm/f winner
vencer vb [6, no vowel change] ❶ to defeat ❷ (fear, obstacle) to overcome ❸ to expire ▷ **El pasaporte me vence mañana.** My passport expires tomorrow.
vencido, -a adj **darse por vencido** to give up
venda nf ❶ bandage; **Me pusieron una venda en el brazo.** They bandaged my arm. ❷ blindfold
vendar vb [25] to bandage; **vendar los ojos a alguien** to blindfold someone
vendedor nm salesman; **vendedor ambulante** pedlar; **vendedor de periódicos** newspaper seller
vender vb [8] to sell; **Venden la oficina de arriba.** The office upstairs is for sale.; **'se vende'** 'for sale'; **venderse por** to sell for
vendimia nf grape harvest
vendré vb see **venir**
veneno nm ❶ poison ❷ venom
venenoso, -a adj poisonous
venezolano, -a adj, nm/f Venezuelan
Venezuela nf Venezuela

venganza nf revenge
vengarse vb [37] to take revenge; **vengarse de alguien** to take revenge on someone; **vengarse de algo** to avenge something
vengo vb see **venir**
venida nf arrival; **La venida la hicimos en autobús.** We came here by bus.
venir vb [56] ❶ to come ▷ **Vino en taxi.** He came by taxi. ❷ to be ▷ **La noticia venía en el periódico.** The news was in the paper.; **¡Venga, vámonos!** Come on, let's go!; **La casa se está viniendo abajo.** The house is falling apart.; **Mañana me viene mal.** Tomorrow isn't good for me.; **¿Te viene bien el sábado?** Is Saturday alright for you?; **el año que viene** next year; **¡Venga ya!** Come off it!
venta nf sale; **estar en venta** to be for sale
ventaja nf advantage
ventana nf window
ventanilla nf ❶ (of vehicle, at bank) window ❷ box office
ventilación nf ventilation
ventilar vb [25] to air
ventisca nf ❶ gale force wind ❷ blizzard
ver vb [57] ❶ to see ▷ **Te vi en el parque.** I saw you in the park. ▷ **¡Cuánto tiempo sin verte!** I haven't seen you for ages! ▷ **No he visto esa película.** I haven't seen that film. ▷ **El médico todavía no la ha visto.** The doctor hasn't seen her yet. ▷ **¿Ves? Ya te lo dije.** See? I told you so.; **Voy a ver si está en su**

a
b
c
d
e
f
g
h
i
j
k
l
m
n
ñ
o
p
q
r
s
t
u
v
w
x
y
z

despacho. I'll see if he's in his office.; **Quedamos en vernos en la estación.** We arranged to meet at the station.; **¡Luego nos vemos!** See you later!; **Eso no tiene nada que ver.** That has nothing to do with it.; **¡No la puede ver!** He can't stand her!; **A ver ...** Let's see ...; **Se ve que no tiene idea de informática.** It's clear he's got no idea about computers. ❷ to watch

veranear vb [**25**] to spend the summer holidays ▷ *Veraneamos en Calpe.* We spend our summer holidays in Calpe.

veraneo nm lugar de veraneo summer resort; **No pudimos ir de veraneo el año pasado.** We couldn't go on holiday last summer.

verano nm summer

veras nfpl de veras really

veraz (pl veraces) adj truthful

verbena nf open-air dance; **la verbena de San Roque** the festival of San Roque

verbo nm verb

verdad nf truth ▷ *Les dije la verdad.* I told them the truth.; **¡Es verdad!** It's true!; **La verdad es que no tengo ganas.** I don't really feel like it.; **¿De verdad?** Really?; **De verdad que yo no dije eso.** I didn't say that, honestly.; **No era un policía de verdad.** He wasn't a real police officer.; **Es bonito, ¿verdad?** It's pretty, isn't it?; **No te gusta, ¿verdad?** You don't like it, do you?

verdadero, -a adj real

verde adj, nm ❶ green ▷ *Tiene los ojos verdes.* She has green eyes. ❷ dirty ▷ *un chiste verde* a dirty joke; **los verdes** the Green Party

verdugo nm ❶ executioner ❷ hangman

verdulería nf greengrocer's

verdura nf vegetables pl ▷ *Comemos mucha verdura.* We eat a lot of vegetables.

vereda nf ❶ path ❷ (Chile, River Plate) pavement

vergonzoso, -a adj ❶ shy ❷ disgraceful

vergüenza nf ❶ embarrassment ▷ *Casi me muero de vergüenza.* I almost died of embarrassment. ❷ shame ▷ *No tienen vergüenza.* They have no shame.; **¡Qué vergüenza!** How embarrassing!; **Le da vergüenza pedírselo.** He's embarrassed to ask her.; **¡Es una vergüenza!** It's disgraceful!

verídico, -a adj true

verificar vb [**48**] to check

verja nf ❶ railings pl ❷ gate

vermut nm vermouth

verruga nf ❶ wart ❷ verruca

versión (pl versiones) nf version; **una película francesa en versión original** a French film in the original version

verso nm ❶ line ❷ verse

vértebra nf vertebra

vertedero nm rubbish tip

verter vb [**20**] ❶ to pour ❷ to dump

vertical adj vertical; **Ponlo vertical.** Put it upright.

vértigo nm vertigo; **Me da vértigo.** It makes me dizzy.

Vespa® nf scooter

vespertino, -a adj evening ▷ un diario vespertino an evening paper

vestíbulo nm ❶ hall ❷ foyer

vestido, -a adj **Iba vestida de negro.** She was dressed in black.; **Yo iba vestido de payaso.** I was dressed as a clown.; **un hombre bien vestido** a well-dressed man ▶ nm dress; **el vestido de novia** the bridal gown

vestir vb [38] to wear; **vestir a alguien** to dress someone; **vestir bien** to dress well; **vestirse** to get dressed; **Se vistió de princesa.** She dressed up as a princess.; **ropa de vestir** smart clothes pl

vestón (pl vestones) nm (Chile, River Plate) jacket

vestuario nm ❶ (at baths, gym) changing room ❷ (for film, play) wardrobe

veterinario, -a nm/f vet

vez (pl veces) nf time ▷ la próxima vez next time ▷ ¿Cuántas veces al año? How many times a year?; **a la vez** at the same time; **a veces** sometimes; **algunas veces** sometimes; **muchas veces** often; **cada vez más** more and more; **cada vez menos** less and less; **de una vez** once and for all; **de vez en cuando** from time to time; **en vez de** instead of; **¿La has visto alguna vez?** Have you ever seen her?; **otra vez** again; **tal vez** maybe; **una vez** once ▷ La veo una vez a la semana. I see her once a

week.; **dos veces** twice; **una y otra vez** again and again

vi vb see **ver**

vía nf ❶ track ❷ platform ▷ Nuestro tren sale por la vía dos. Our train leaves from platform two.; **por vía aérea** by airmail; **Madrid-Berlín vía París** Madrid-Berlin via Paris

viajar vb [25] to travel

viaje nm ❶ trip; **¡Buen viaje!** Have a good trip!; **un viaje de negocios** a business trip ❷ journey ▷ Es un viaje muy largo. It's a very long journey.; **estar de viaje** to be away; **salir de viaje** to go away; **una agencia de viajes** a travel agency; **el viaje de novios** honeymoon

viajero, -a nm/f passenger

víbora nf viper

vibración (pl vibraciones) nf vibration

vibrar vb [25] to vibrate

vicepresidenta nf ❶ vice president ❷ chairwoman

vicepresidente nm ❶ vice president ❷ chairman

viceversa adv vice versa

viciarse vb [25] to deteriorate; **viciarse con las drogas** to become addicted to drugs

vicio nm vice; **Tengo el vicio de morderme las uñas.** I bite my nails; I know it's a bad habit.

víctima nf victim

victoria nf victory; **su primera victoria fuera de casa** their first away win

vid nf vine

vida nf life ▷ *Llevan una vida muy tranquila.* They lead a very quiet life. ▷ *¡Esto sí que es vida!* This is the life!; **la media de vida de un televisor** the average life span of a television set; **vida nocturna** nightlife; **estar con vida** to be alive; **salir con vida** to escape alive; *Se gana la vida haciendo traducciones.* He earns his living by translating.; **¡Vida mía!** My darling!

video nm (LatAm) video

vídeo nm **①** video ▷ *Tengo la película en vídeo.* I've got the film on video.; **cinta de vídeo** videotape

videocámara nf video camera

videojuego nm video game

videollamada nf video call

videoteléfono nm videophone

vidriera nf **①** stained glass window **②** (LatAm) shop window

vidrio nm **①** glass **②** windowpane

vieja nf old woman

viejo, -a adj old ▷ *un viejo amigo mío* an old friend of mine ▷ *Estos zapatos ya están muy viejos.* These shoes are very old now.; **hacerse viejo** to get old

▶ nm old man; **los viejos** old people; **llegar a viejo** to reach old age

viene vb see **venir**

viento nm wind; *Hace mucho viento.* It's very windy.

vientre nm stomach; **hacer de vientre** to go to the toilet

viernes (pl **viernes**) nm Friday ▷ *el viernes pasado* last Friday ▷ *el*

viernes que viene next Friday; **Viernes Santo** Good Friday

■ Word for word, **Viernes Santo** means 'Holy Friday'.

vierta vb see **verter**

vietnamita adj, nmf Vietnamese; **los vietnamitas** the Vietnamese

viga nf **①** beam **②** girder

vigilancia nf **①** surveillance ▷ *bajo vigilancia policial* under police surveillance **②** vigilance; **patrulla de vigilancia** security patrol

vigilante nmf **①** security guard **②** store detective; **vigilante jurado** security guard; **vigilante nocturno** night watchman

vigilar vb [25] **①** to guard **②** to watch ▷ *Nos vigilan.* They're watching us. **③** to keep an eye on ▷ *¿Me vigilas el bolso un momento?* Can you keep an eye on my bag for a minute?

VIH abbr (= virus de inmunodeficiencia humana) HIV

villa nf **①** town **②** villa

villancico nm carol

vinagre nm vinegar

vínculo nm bond

vine vb see **venir**

viniendo vb see **venir**

vino nm wine; **vino blanco** white wine; **vino tinto** red wine; **vino de la casa** house wine

viña nf vineyard

viñedo nm vineyard

violación (pl **violaciones**) nf **①** rape **②** violation

violador, a nm/f rapist

violar vb [25] **①** to rape **②** to violate

violencia nf violence

violento, -a adj ❶ violent ❷ embarrassing ▷ *Era una situación violenta.* It was an embarrassing situation.; **Me resulta violento decírselo.** I'm embarrassed to tell him.

violeta adj, nm (colour) purple

When **violeta** is used as an adjective, it never changes its ending.

▷ *unas cortinas violeta* purple curtains

▶ nf (flower) violet

violín (pl violines) nm violin

violinista nmf violinist

violón (pl violones) nm double bass

violonchelista nmf cellist

violonchelo nm cello

virgen (pl vírgenes) adj ❶ virgin ❷ (tape) blank

▶ nf virgin; **la Virgen** the Virgin

Virgo nm (sign) Virgo; **Soy virgo.** I'm Virgo.

viril adj virile

virilidad nf virility

virtual adj virtual

virtud nf virtue

viruela nf smallpox

virus (pl virus) nm virus

visa nf (LatAm) visa

visado nm visa

visera nf ❶ (of cap) peak ❷ visor

visibilidad nf visibility

visible adj visible

visillo nm net curtain

visión (pl visiones) nf ❶ vision ❷ view; **Tú estás viendo visiones.** You're seeing things.

visita nf ❶ visit; **hacer una visita a alguien** to visit someone ❷ visitor ▷ *Tienes visita.* You've got visitors.; **horario de visita** visiting hours pl

visitante nmf visitor

visitar vb [25] to visit

visón (pl visones) nm mink; **un abrigo de visón** a mink coat

víspera nf the day before ▷ *la víspera de la boda* the day before the wedding; **la víspera de Navidad** Christmas Eve

vista nf ❶ (sense) sight ❷ view ▷ *una habitación con vistas al mar* a room with a sea view; **a primera vista** at first glance; **alzar la vista** to look up; **bajar la vista** to look down; **perder la vista** to lose one's sight; **volver la vista** to look back; **conocer a alguien de vista** to know someone by sight; **hacer la vista gorda** to turn a blind eye; **¡Hasta la vista!** See you!

vistazo nm echar un vistazo a algo to have a look at something

vistiendo vb see **vestir**

visto vb see **ver**

▶ adj **Está visto que ...** It's clear that ...; **Hurgarse la nariz está mal visto.** Picking your nose is frowned upon.; **por lo visto** apparently; **dar el visto bueno a algo** to give something's approval

vistoso, -a adj showy

vital adj vital

vitalidad nf vitality

vitamina nf vitamin

vitorear vb [25] to cheer

a b c d e f g h i j k l m n ñ o p q r s t u v w x y z

vitrina nf ❶ glass cabinet ❷ (LatAm) shop window

viuda adj Es viuda. She's a widow.
▶ nf widow

viudo adj Es viudo. He's a widower.; Se quedó viudo a los 50 años. He was widowed at 50.
▶ nm widower

vivaracho, -a adj lively

víveres nmpl provisions pl

vivero nm nursery

vivienda nf ❶ house ❷ flat ❸ housing ▷ la escasez de la vivienda the housing shortage

vivir vb [58] ❶ to live ▷ ¿Dónde vives? Where do you live? ❷ to be alive ▷ ¿Todavía vive? Is he still alive?; vivir de algo to live on something ▷ Viven de su pensión. They live on his pension.; ¡Viva! Hurray!

vivo, -a adj ❶ alive ▷ Estaba vivo. He was alive. ❷ (colour, eyes) bright; en vivo live ▷ una retransmisión en vivo a live broadcast

vocabulario nm vocabulary

vocación (pl vocaciones) nf vocation

vocal nf vowel

vodka nm vodka

volante nm ❶ steering wheel ❷ shuttlecock ❸ referral note; volantes flounce sg

volar vb [11] ❶ to fly ▷ El helicóptero volaba muy bajo. The helicopter was flying very low. ❷ to blow up ▷ Volaron el puente. They blew up the bridge.; Tuvimos que ir volando al hospital. We had to rush to the hospital.

volcán (pl volcanes) nm volcano

volcar vb [59, c → qu before e and i] ❶ (glass, container) to knock over ▷ El perro volcó el cubo de la basura. The dog knocked the dustbin over. ❷ (boat) to capsize ❸ (car, lorry) to overturn

voleibol nm volleyball

voltaje nm voltage

voltereta nf ❶ forward roll; dar una voltereta to do a forward roll ❷ somersault

voltio nm volt

volumen (pl volúmenes) nm volume; bajar el volumen to turn the volume down; subir el volumen to turn the volume up

voluntad nf ❶ will ▷ Lo hizo contra mi voluntad. He did it against my will. ❷ willpower

voluntaria nf volunteer

voluntario, -a adj voluntary; ofrecerse voluntario para algo to volunteer for something
▶ nm volunteer

volver vb [59] ❶ to come back ❷ to go back ❸ to turn ▷ Me volvió la espalda. He turned away from me.; Me volví para ver quién era. I turned round to see who it was. ❹ to become; Se ha vuelto muy cariñoso. He's become very affectionate.; volver a hacer algo to do something again; volver en sí to come round

vomitar vb [25] to be sick; Vomitó todo lo que había comido. He threw up everything he'd eaten.

vos pron (River Plate) you

vosotros, -as *pron pl* you
▷ *Vosotros vendréis conmigo.* You'll come with me.; **Hacedlo vosotros mismos.** Do it yourselves.

votación *(pl* votaciones*) nf*
Hicimos una votación. We took a vote.; **Salió elegida por votación.** She was voted in.

votar *vb* [25] to vote; **Votaron a los socialistas.** They voted for the Socialists.

voy *vb see* **ir**

voz *(pl* voces*) nf* voice; **hablar en voz alta** to speak loudly; **dar voces** to shout

vuelco *vb see* **volcar**
▶ *nm* **dar un vuelco (1)** *(car)* to overturn **(2)** *(boat)* to capsize; **Me dio un vuelco el corazón.** My heart missed a beat.

vuelo *vb see* **volar**
▶ *nm* flight; **vuelo chárter** charter flight; **vuelo regular** scheduled flight

vuelta *nf* ❶ return ▷ *un billete de ida y vuelta* a return ticket ❷ lap ▷ *Di tres vueltas a la pista.* I did three laps of the track. ❸ change ▷ *Quédese con la vuelta.* Keep the change.; **a vuelta de correo** by return of post; **Vive a la vuelta de la esquina.** He lives round the corner.; **El coche dio la vuelta.** The car turned round.; **dar la vuelta a la página** to turn the page; **dar la vuelta al mundo** to go round the world; **No le des más vueltas a lo que dijo.** Stop worrying about what he said.; **dar una vuelta (1)** to go for

a walk **(2)** to go for a drive; **dar media vuelta** to turn round; **estar de vuelta** to be back; **vuelta ciclista** cycle race

vuelto *vb see* **volver**
▶ *nm (LatAm)* change

vuelvo *vb see* **volver**

vuestro, -a *adj, pron* ❶ your ▷ *vuestra casa* your house ▷ *vuestros amigos* your friends; **un amigo vuestro** a friend of yours ❷ yours ▷ *¿Son vuestros?* Are they yours?; **¿Es esta la vuestra?** Is this one yours?; **¿Y los bocadillos? — Los vuestros están aquí.** Where are the sandwiches? — Yours are over here.

vulgar *adj* vulgar

W X

walkie-talkie (*pl* walkie-talkies) *nm* walkie-talkie
wáter *nm* loo
web *nf* ❶ website ❷ (World Wide) Web
western (*pl* westerns) *nm* western
whisky (*pl* whiskys) *nm* whisky
wifi *nm* Wi-Fi
windsurf *nm* ❶ windsurfing ❷ windsurf

xenófobo, -a *adj* xenophobic
xilófono *nm* xylophone

y

y conj and ▷ *Andrés y su novia.* Andrés and his girlfriend.; **Yo quiero una ensalada. ¿Y tú?** I'd like a salad. What about you?; **¡Y yo!** Me too!; **¿Y qué?** So what?; **Son las tres y cinco.** It's five past three.

ya adv already; **ya no** any more ▷ *Ya no salimos juntos.* We're not going out any more.; **Estos zapatos ya me están pequeños.** These shoes are too small for me now.; **ya que** since; **Ya lo sé.** I know.; **Ya veremos.** We'll see.; **Rellena el impreso y ya está.** Fill in the form and that's it.; **¡Ya voy!** I'm coming!

yacimiento nm site; **un yacimiento petrolífero** an oilfield

yanqui (pl **yanquis**) adj, nmf Yank

yate nm ❶ pleasure cruiser ❷ yacht

yedra nf ivy

yegua nf mare

yema nf ❶ yolk ❷ fingertip

yendo vb see **ir**

yerno nm son-in-law

yeso nm plaster

yo pron ❶ I ▷ *Carlos y yo no fuimos.* Carlos and I didn't go. ❷ me ▷ *¿Quién ha visto la película? —Ana y yo.* Who's seen the film? — Ana and me. ▷ *Es más alta que yo.* She's taller than me. ▷ *Soy yo, María.* It's me, María.; **¡Yo también!** Me too!; **yo mismo** myself ▷ *Lo hice yo misma.* I did it myself.; **yo que tú** if I were you

yoga nm yoga

yogur nm yoghurt

yudo nm judo

Yugoslavia nf Yugoslavia ▷ *en la antigua Yugoslavia* in the former Yugoslavia

Z

zafiro nm sapphire
zambullirse vb [**45**] to dive underwater
zamparse vb [**25**] to wolf down
zanahoria nf carrot
zancadilla nf poner la zancadilla a alguien to trip someone up
zancudo nm (LatAm) mosquito
zanja nf ditch
zanjar vb [**25**] to settle
zapatería nf ❶ shoe shop ❷ shoe repairer's
zapatero nm shoemaker
zapatilla nf slipper; zapatillas de ballet ballet shoes; zapatillas de deporte trainers
zapato nm shoe; zapatos de tacón high-heeled shoes; zapatos planos flat shoes
zarpa nf paw

zarpar vb [**25**] to set sail
zarza nf bramble
zarzamora nf blackberry bush
zigzag nm zigzag; una carretera en zigzag a winding road
Zimbabue nm Zimbabwe
zíper (pl zípers) nm (LatAm) zip
zócalo nm ❶ skirting board ❷ (LatAm) main square
zodíaco nm zodiac ▷ los signos del zodíaco the signs of the zodiac
zona nf area ▷ Viven en una zona muy tranquila. They live in a very quiet area.; Fue declarada zona neutral. It was declared a neutral zone.; una zona azul a pay-and-display area; una zona industrial an industrial park; una zona peatonal a pedestrian precinct; una zona verde a green space
zoo nm zoo
zoóloga nf zoologist
zoología nf zoology
zoológico nm zoo
zoólogo nm zoologist
zoom (pl zooms) nm zoom lens
zorro nm fox
zueco nm clog
zumbar vb [**25**] to buzz ▷ Me zumban los oídos. My ears are buzzing.
zumo nm juice ▷ zumo de naranja orange juice
zurcir vb [**58**, c → z before a and o] to darn
zurdo, -a adj ❶ left-handed ❷ left-footed
zurrar vb [**25**] to thrash

a

a *indef art*

Use **un** for masculine nouns, **una** for feminine nouns.

❶ **un** *m* ▷ *a book* un libro ❷ **una** *f* ▷ *an apple* una manzana

Sometimes 'a' is not translated, particularly if referring to professions.

▷ *He's a butcher.* Es carnicero. ▷ *I haven't got a car.* No tengo coche.; **70 kilometres an hour** 70 kilómetros por hora; **30 pence a kilo** 30 peniques el kilo

abandon *vb* abandonar **[25]**

abbey *n* abadía *f*

abbreviation *n* abreviatura *f*

ability *n* capacidad *f*; **to have the ability to do something** tener **[53]** la capacidad de hacer algo

able *adj* **to be able to do something** poder **[40]** hacer algo
▷ *Will you be able to come on Saturday?* ¿Puedes venir el sábado?

abolish *vb* abolir **[58]**

abortion *n* aborto *m*; **to have an abortion** abortar **[25]**

about *prep, adv* ❶ sobre ▷ *a book about London* un libro sobre Londres ▷ *I don't know anything about it.* No sé nada sobre eso.; **I'm phoning you about tomorrow's meeting.** Te llamo por lo de la reunión de mañana.; **What's it about?** ¿De qué trata? ❷ *(approximately)* unos *(f* unas*)* ▷ *It takes about 10 hours.* Se tarda unas 10 horas.; **at about 11 o'clock** sobre las 11 ❸ por ▷ *to walk about the town* caminar por la ciudad; **What about me?** ¿Y yo?; **to be about to do something** estar **[22]** a punto de hacer algo ▷ *I was about to go out.* Estaba a punto de salir.; **How about going to the cinema?** ¿Qué tal si vamos al cine?

above *prep, adv*

When something is located above something, use **encima de**. When there is movement involved, use **por encima de**.

❶ encima de ▷ *There was a picture above the fireplace.* Había un cuadro encima de la chimenea. ❷ por encima de ▷ *He put his hands above his head.* Puso las manos por encima de la cabeza.; **above all** sobre todo ❸ *(more than)* más de ▷ *above 40 degrees* más de 40 grados

abroad *adv* **to go abroad** ir [**27**] al extranjero; **to live abroad** vivir [**58**] en el extranjero

absence *n* ❶ (*of people*) ausencia *f* ❷ (*of things*) falta *f*; **absence from school** la falta de asistencia a clase

absent *adj* ausente

absent-minded *adj* distraído(-a)

absolutely *adv* totalmente ▷ I *absolutely refuse to do it.* Me niego totalmente a hacerlo.; **Jill's absolutely right.** Jill tiene toda la razón.; **It's absolutely delicious!** ¡Está riquísimo!; **They did absolutely nothing to help him.** No hicieron absolutamente nada para ayudarle.

abuse *n* (*of power*) abuso *m*; **to shout abuse at somebody** insultar [**25**] a alguien ▷ *vb* maltratar [**25**] ▷ *abused children* niños maltratados

academic *adj* académico(-a) ▷ *the academic year* el año académico

academy *n* academia *f*

accelerate *vb* acelerar [**25**]

accelerator *n* acelerador *m*

accent *n* acento *m* ▷ *He's got a Spanish accent.* Tiene acento español.

accept *vb* aceptar [**25**] ▷ *She accepted the offer.* Aceptó la oferta.; **to accept responsibility for something** asumir [**58**] la responsabilidad de algo

acceptable *adj* aceptable

access *n* acceso *m* ▷ *He has access to confidential information.* Tiene acceso a información reservada.; **Her ex-husband has access to**

the children. Su ex marido puede ver a los niños.

accessory *n* accesorio *m* ▷ *fashion accessories* los accesorios de moda

accident *n* accidente *m* ▷ *to have an accident* sufrir un accidente; **by accident (1)** (*by chance*) por casualidad ▷ *They made the discovery by accident.* Lo descubrieron por casualidad. **(2)** (*by mistake*) sin querer ▷ *The burglar killed him by accident.* El ladrón lo mató sin querer.

accidental *adj* **I didn't do it deliberately, it was accidental.** No lo hice adrede, fue sin querer.

accommodation *n* alojamiento *m*

accompany *vb* acompañar [**25**]

according to *prep* según ▷ *According to him, everyone had gone.* Según él, todos se habían ido.

account *n* ❶ cuenta *f*; **to do the accounts** llevar [**25**] la contabilidad ❷ (*report*) informe *m*; **to take something into account** tener [**53**] algo en cuenta; **by all accounts** a decir de todos; **on account of** (*because of*) a causa de algo

account for *vb* explicar [**48**]

accountancy *n* contabilidad *f*

accountant *n* contable *mf* (contador *m*, contadora *f LatAm*) ▷ *She's an accountant.* Es contable.

accuracy *n* exactitud *f*

accurate *adj* exacto(-a)

accurately *adv* con exactitud

accuse *vb* **to accuse somebody of something** acusar [**25**] a alguien de algo ▷ *The police are accusing her* *of murder.* La policía la acusa de asesinato.

ace n as m ▷ *the ace of hearts* el as de corazones

ache n dolor m ▷ *stomach ache* dolor de estómago
▷ vb **My leg's aching.** Me duele la pierna.

achieve vb conseguir [**50**]

achievement n logro m

acid n ácido m

acid rain n lluvia ácida f

acne n acné m

acrobat n acróbata mf

across prep, adv ❶ al otro lado de ▷ *He lives across the river.* Vive al otro lado del río. ❷ a través de ▷ *an expedition across the Sahara* una expedición a través del Sahara; **to run across the road** cruzar [**13**] la calle corriendo

act vb actuar [**1**] ▷ *The police acted quickly.* La policía actuó con rapidez. ▷ *He acts really well.* Actúa muy bien.
▷ n acto m ▷ *in the first act* en el primer acto; **It was all an act.** Era todo un cuento.

action n acción f (pl acciones)

active adj activo(-a) ▷ *He's a very active person.* Es una persona muy activa.

activity n actividad f

actor n actor m

actress n actriz f (pl actrices)

actual adj real ▷ *The film is based on actual events.* La película está basada en hechos reales.

> Be careful not to translate **actual** by the Spanish word **actual**.

actually adv ❶ realmente ▷ *Did it actually happen?* ¿Ocurrió realmente?; **You only pay for the electricity you actually use.** Solo pagas la electricidad que consumes. ❷ de hecho ▷ *I was so bored I actually fell asleep!* ¡Me aburría tanto que de hecho me quedé dormido!; **Fiona's awful, isn't she? — Actually, I quite like her.** Fiona es una antipática, ¿verdad? — Pues a mí me cae bien.; **Actually, I don't know him at all.** La verdad es que no lo conozco de nada.

AD abbr (= Anno Domini) d.C. (= después de Cristo) ▷ *in 800 AD* en el año 800 d.C.

ad n anuncio m

adapt vb adaptar [**25**] ▷ *His novel was adapted for television.* Su novela fue adaptada para la televisión.; **to adapt to something** adaptarse [**25**] a algo ▷ *He adapted to his new school very quickly.* Se adaptó a su nuevo colegio muy rápidamente.

adaptor n ❶ (for several plugs) ladrón m (pl ladrones) ❷ (for different types of plugs) adaptador m

add vb añadir [**58**] ▷ *Add more flour to the dough.* Añada más harina a la masa.

add up vb sumar [**25**] ▷ *Add up the figures.* Suma las cifras.

addict n adicto m, adicta f; **a drug addict** un drogadicto ▷ *She's a drug addict.* Es drogadicta.; **Martin's a football addict.** Martin es un fanático del fútbol.

addicted adj **to be addicted to drugs** ser [52] drogadicto; **She's addicted to heroin.** Es heroinómana.; **She's addicted to soaps.** Es una apasionada de las telenovelas.

addition n **in addition** además; **in addition to** además de

address n dirección f (pl direcciones)

adjective n adjetivo m

adjust vb ❶ (temperature, height) regular [25] ❷ (mechanism) ajustar [25]; **to adjust to something** adaptarse [25] a algo ▷ He adjusted to his new school very quickly. Se adaptó a su nuevo colegio muy rápidamente.

adjustable adj regulable

administration n administración f

admiral n almirante m

admire vb admirar [25]

admission n entrada f; **'admission free'** 'entrada gratuita'

admit vb reconocer [12] ▷ He admitted that he'd done it. Reconoció que lo había hecho.

adolescent n adolescente mf

adopt vb adoptar [25]

adopted adj adoptivo(-a)

adoption n adopción f (pl adopciones)

adore vb adorar [25]

adult n adulto m, adulta f; **adult education** la educación de adultos

advance vb avanzar [13]
▷ Technology has advanced a lot. La tecnología ha avanzado mucho.
▶ n **in advance** con antelación

▷ They bought the tickets a month in advance. Compraron los billetes con un mes de antelación.

advanced adj avanzado(-a)

advantage n ventaja f ▷ Going to university has many advantages. Ir a la universidad tiene muchas ventajas.; **to take advantage of something** aprovechar [25] algo ▷ He took advantage of his day off to have a rest. Aprovechó su día libre para descansar.; **to take advantage of somebody** aprovecharse [25] de alguien ▷ The company was taking advantage of its employees. La compañía se aprovechaba de sus empleados.

adventure n aventura f

adverb n adverbio m

advert n anuncio m

advertise vb anunciar [25] ▷ Jobs are advertised in the papers. Las ofertas de empleo se anuncian en los periódicos.

advertisement n anuncio m

advertising n publicidad f

advice n consejo m ▷ to ask for advice pedir consejo ▷ I'd like to ask your advice. Quería pedirle consejo.; **to give somebody advice** aconsejar [25] a alguien; **a piece of advice** un consejo

advise vb aconsejar [25]

aconsejar que has to be followed by a verb in the subjunctive.

▷ He advised me to wait. Me aconsejó que esperara. ▷ He advised me not to go there. Me aconsejó que no fuera.

aerial n antena f

aerobics n aerobic m ▷ I do aerobics. Hago aerobic.

aeroplane n avión m (pl aviones)

aerosol n aerosol m

affair n ❶ aventura f ▷ to have an affair with somebody tener una aventura con alguien ❷ asunto m ▷ The government has mishandled the affair. El gobierno ha llevado mal el asunto.

affect vb afectar [**25**]

affectionate adj cariñoso(-a)

afford vb permitirse [**58**] ▷ I can't afford a new pair of jeans. No puedo permitirme comprar otros vaqueros.; **We can't afford to go on holiday.** No podemos permitirnos el lujo de ir de vacaciones.

afraid adj **to be afraid of something** tener [**53**] miedo de algo ▷ I'm afraid of spiders. Tengo miedo de las arañas.; **I'm afraid I can't come.** Me temo que no puedo ir.; **I'm afraid so.** Me temo que sí.; **I'm afraid not.** Me temo que no.

Africa n África f

African adj africano(-a)
▶ n africano m, africana f

after prep, conj, adv ❶ después de ▷ after the match después del partido ▷ After watching television I went to bed. Después de ver la televisión me fui a la cama. ▷ After I'd had a rest I went for a walk. Después de descansar me fui a dar un paseo. ❷ después de que

When there's a change of subject in an 'after' clause, use **después de que** with a verb in an appropriate tense instead of **después de** + infinitive.

▷ I met her after she had left the company. La conocí después de que dejó la empresa.

después de que has to be followed by a verb in the subjunctive when referring to an event in the future.

▷ I'll help you after we've finished this. Te ayudaré después de que terminemos esto. ▷ She said she'd phone after her mother had gone out. Dijo que me llamaría después de que se marchara su madre.; **after dinner** después de cenar; **He ran after me.** Corrió detrás de mí.; **after all** después de todo; **soon after** poco después

afternoon n tarde f ▷ in the afternoon por la tarde ▷ at 3 o'clock in the afternoon a las 3 de la tarde ▷ on Saturday afternoon el sábado por la tarde

afters n postre m ▷ What's for afters? ¿Qué hay de postre?

aftershave n aftershave m

afterwards adv después ▷ She left not long afterwards. Se marchó poco después.

again adv otra vez ▷ I'd like to hear it again. Me gustaría escucharlo otra vez.

In Spanish you often use the verb **volver a** and an infinitive to talk about doing something 'again'.

a b c d e f g h i j k l m n o p q r s t u v w x y z

▷ I'd like to hear it again. Me gustaría volver a escucharlo. ▷ I won't tell you again! ¡No te lo vuelvo a repetir! **Can you tell me again?** ¿Me lo puedes repetir?; **Do it again!** ¡Vuelve a hacerlo!; **again and again** una y otra vez

against prep ❶ contra ▷ He leant against the wall. Se apoyó contra la pared. ❷ en contra de ▷ I'm against nuclear testing. Estoy en contra de las pruebas nucleares.

age n edad f ▷ an age limit un límite de edad; **at the age of sixteen** a los dieciséis años; **I haven't been to the cinema for ages.** Hace siglos que no voy al cine.

agenda n orden del día m

> Be careful not to translate **agenda** by the Spanish word **agenda**.

agent n agente mf

aggressive adj agresivo(-a)

ago adv **two days ago** hace dos días; **How long ago did it happen?** ¿Cuánto hace que ocurrió?

agony n **to be in agony** sufrir [58] mucho dolor

agree vb estar [22] de acuerdo ▷ I don't agree! ¡No estoy de acuerdo! ▷ I agree with Carol. Estoy de acuerdo con Carol.; **to agree to do something** (1) (when someone requests) aceptar [25] hacer algo ▷ He agreed to go with her. Aceptó acompañarla. (2) (arrange) acordar [11] hacer algo ▷ They agreed to meet again next week. Acordaron volver a reunirse la semana próxima.; **to**

agree that… reconocer [12] que… ▷ I agree it's difficult. Reconozco que es difícil.; **Garlic doesn't agree with me.** El ajo no me sienta bien.

agreement n acuerdo m; **to be in agreement** estar [22] de acuerdo

agricultural adj agrícola

agriculture n agricultura f

ahead adv delante ▷ She looked straight ahead. Miró hacia delante.; **to plan ahead** hacer [26] planes con antelación; **The Spanish are five points ahead.** Los españoles llevan cinco puntos de ventaja.; **Go ahead! Help yourself!** ¡Venga! ¡Sírvete!

aid n ayuda f; **in aid of sick children** a beneficio de los niños enfermos

AIDS n sida m

aim vb **to aim at** apuntar [25] a ▷ He aimed a gun at me. Me apuntó con una pistola.; **The film is aimed at children.** La película está dirigida a los niños.; **to aim to do something** pretender [8] hacer algo
▶ n propósito m

air n aire m ▷ to get some fresh air tomar un poco el aire; **by air** en avión

air-conditioned adj con aire acondicionado

air conditioning n aire acondicionado m

Air Force n ejército del aire m

air hostess n azafata f ▷ She's an air hostess. Es azafata.

airline n línea aérea f

airmail n **by airmail** por correo aéreo

airplane n (US) avión m (pl aviones)

airport n aeropuerto m

aisle n (in plane, cinema) pasillo m

alarm n alarma f; **a fire alarm** una alarma contra incendios

alarm clock n despertador m

album n álbum m

alcohol n alcohol m

alcoholic n alcohólico m, alcohólica f

　▸ adj alcohólico(-a) ▷ alcoholic drinks bebidas alcohólicas

alert adj ❶ despierto(-a) ▷ He's a very alert baby. Es un bebé muy despierto. ❷ atento(-a) ▷ We must stay alert. Hay que estar atentos.

A levels npl

　　Under the reformed Spanish
　　Educational System, if students
　　stay on at school after the age of
　　16, they can do a two-year
　　course – **bachillerato** – at the
　　end of which they sit an exam in
　　order to qualify for university.
　　The old university entrance
　　exam – the **selectividad** – is being
　　phased out, so that each
　　university has its own selection
　　process.

Algeria n Argelia f

alike adv **to look alike** parecerse [12] ▷ The two sisters look alike. Las dos hermanas se parecen.

alive adj vivo(-a)

all adj, pron, adv todo(-a) ▷ That's all I can remember. Eso es todo lo que recuerdo. ▷ I ate all of it. Me lo comí

todo. ▷ all day todo el día ▷ all the apples todas las manzanas; **All of us went.** Fuimos todos.; **all alone** completamente solo; **not at all** en absoluto ▷ I'm not at all tired. No estoy en absoluto cansado.; **Thank you. — Not at all.** Gracias. — De nada.; **She talks all the time.** No para de hablar.

allergic adj alérgico(-a) ▷ to be allergic to something ser alérgico a algo

allow vb **to allow somebody to do something** dejar [25] a alguien hacer algo ▷ His mum allowed him to go out. Su madre le dejó salir. ▷ He's not allowed to go out at night. No le dejan salir por la noche.; **Smoking is not allowed.** Está prohibido fumar.

all right adv, adj bien ▷ Everything turned out all right. Todo salió bien. ▷ Are you all right? ¿Estás bien?; **Is that all right with you?** ¿Te parece bien?; **The film was all right.** La película no estuvo mal.; **We'll talk about it later. — All right.** Lo hablamos después. —Vale.

almond n almendra f

almost adv casi ▷ I've almost finished. Ya casi he terminado.

alone adj, adv solo(-a) ▷ She lives alone. Vive sola.; **to leave somebody alone** dejar [25] en paz a alguien ▷ Leave her alone! ¡Déjala en paz!; **to leave something alone** no tocar [48] algo ▷ Leave my things alone! ¡No toques mis cosas!

along prep, adv por ▷ Chris was walking along the beach. Chris

paseaba por la playa.; **all along**
(1) a lo largo de (2) desde el
principio ▷ *He was lying to me all
along.* Me había mentido desde el
principio.

aloud *adv* en voz alta

alphabet *n* alfabeto *m*

Alps *npl* Alpes *mpl*

already *adv* ya ▷ *Liz had already
gone.* Liz ya se había ido.

also *adv* también

alter *vb* cambiar [25]

alternate *adj* **on alternate days**
en días alternos

alternative *n* alternativa *f* ▷ *You
have no alternative.* No tienes otra
alternativa.; **Fruit is a healthy
alternative to chocolate.** La fruta
es una opción más sana que el
chocolate.; **There are several
alternatives.** Hay varias
posibilidades.

alternatively *adv* **Alternatively,
we could just stay at home.** Si no,
podemos simplemente quedarnos
en casa.

although *conj* aunque ▷ *Although
she was tired, she stayed up late.*
Aunque estaba cansada, se quedó
levantada hasta tarde.

altogether *adv* ❶ (in total) en total
▷ *You owe me £20 altogether.* En total
me debes 20 libras. ❷ (completely)
del todo ▷ *I'm not altogether happy
with your work.* No estoy del todo
satisfecho con tu trabajo.

aluminium (US **aluminum**) *n*
aluminio *m*

always *adv* siempre ▷ *He's always
moaning.* Siempre está quejándose.

am *vb* see **be**

a.m. *abbr* de la mañana ▷ *at 4 a.m.*
a las 4 de la mañana

amateur *n* amateur *mf* (*pl*
amateurs)

amazed *adj* asombrado(-a) ▷ *I was
amazed that I managed to do it.*
Estaba asombrado de haberlo
conseguido.

amazing *adj* ❶ asombroso(-a)
▷ *That's amazing news!* ¡Es una
noticia asombrosa!
❷ extraordinario(-a) ▷ *Vivian's an
amazing cook.* Vivian es una
cocinera extraordinaria.

ambassador *n* embajador *m*,
embajadora *f*

ambition *n* ambición *f* (*pl*
ambiciones)

ambitious *adj* ambicioso(-a)

ambulance *n* ambulancia *f*

amenities *npl* **The town has
many amenities.** La ciudad ofrece
gran variedad de servicios.

America *n* ❶ (United States)
Estados Unidos *mpl* ❷ (continent)
América *f*

American *adj* norteamericano(-a)
▶ *n* norteamericano *m*,
norteamericana *f* ▷ *the Americans*
los norteamericanos

among *prep* entre

amount *n* cantidad *f* ▷ *a huge
amount of rice* una cantidad
enorme de arroz; **a large amount
of money** una alta suma de
dinero

amp *n* ❶ (amplifier) amplificador *m*
❷ (ampere) amperio *m*

amplifier *n* amplificador *m*

amuse vb (make laugh) divertir [**51**]
▷ The thought seemed to amuse him.
La idea parecía divertirle.

amusement arcade n salón de
juegos m

an indef art see **a**

analyse vb analizar [**13**]

analysis n análisis m (pl análisis)

analyze vb (US) analizar [**13**]

ancestor n antepasado m

anchor n ancla f

Although it's a feminine noun,
remember that you use **el** and
un with **ancla**.

ancient adj antiguo(-a) ▷ ancient
Greece la antigua Grecia; **an
ancient monument** un
monumento histórico

and conj y ▷ Mary and Jane Mary y
Jane

Use **e** to translate 'and' before
words beginning with **i** or **hi**
but not **hie**.
▷ Miguel and Ignacio Miguel e
Ignacio

'and' is not translated when
linking numbers.
▷ two hundred and fifty doscientos
cincuenta; **Please try and come!**
¡Procura venir!; **He talked and
talked.** No paraba de hablar.;
better and better cada vez mejor

angel n ángel m

anger n enfado m (enojo m LatAm)

angle n ángulo m

angry adj enfadado(-a) (enojado
LatAm) ▷ **to be angry with somebody**
estar enfadado con alguien ▷ Your
father looks very angry. Tu padre
parece estar muy enfadado.;

to get angry enfadarse [**25**]
(enojarse [**25**] LatAm)

animal n animal m

ankle n tobillo m ▷ I've twisted my
ankle. Me he torcido el tobillo.

anniversary n aniversario m
▷ wedding anniversary aniversario
de bodas

announce vb anunciar [**25**]

announcement n anuncio m

annoy vb molestar [**25**] ▷ Make a
note of the things that annoy you.
Haz una lista de las cosas que te
molestan.; **He's really annoying
me.** Me está fastidiando de
verdad.; **to be annoyed with
somebody** estar [**22**] molesto con
alguien; **to get annoyed** enfadarse
[**25**] (enojarse [**25**] LatAm) ▷ Don't
get annoyed! ¡No te enfades!

annoying adj molesto(-a) ▷ the
most annoying problem el problema
más molesto; **I find it very
annoying.** Me molesta mucho.

annual adj anual

anorak n anorak m (pl anoraks)

another adj, pron otro(-a) ▷ Have
you got another skirt? ¿Tienes otra
falda?; **another two kilometres**
dos kilómetros más

answer vb responder [**8**] ▷ Can you
answer my question? ¿Puedes
responder a mi pregunta?; **to
answer the phone** contestar [**25**]
al teléfono; **to answer the door**
abrir [**58**] la puerta ▷ Can you
answer the door please? ¿Puedes ir a
abrir la puerta?
▶ n ❶ (to question) respuesta f ❷ (to
problem) solución f (pl soluciones)

a
b
c
d
e
f
g
h
i
j
k
l
m
n
o
p
q
r
s
t
u
v
w
x
y
z

answering machine n
  contestador automático m

ant n hormiga f

Antarctic n **the Antarctic** el
Antártico

anthem n **the national anthem**
el himno nacional

antibiotic n antibiótico m

antique n antigüedad f

antique shop n tienda de
antigüedades f

antiseptic n antiséptico m

any adj, adv

In questions and negative
sentences 'any' is usually not
translated.

▷ Have you got any change?
¿Tienes cambio? ▷ Are there any
beans left? ¿Quedan alubias? ▷ He
hasn't got any friends. No tiene
amigos.

Use **algún/alguna** + singular
noun in questions and
ningún/ninguna + singular
noun in negatives where 'any'
is used with plural nouns and
the number of items is
important.

▷ Do you speak any foreign
languages? ¿Hablas algún idioma
extranjero? ▷ I haven't got any books
by Cervantes. No tengo ningún libro
de Cervantes.

Use **cualquier** in affirmative
sentences.

▷ Any teacher will tell you. Cualquier
profesor te lo dirá.; **Come any
time you like.** Ven cuando
quieras.; **Would you like any
more coffee?** ¿Quieres más café?;

I don't love him any more. Ya no
le quiero.

▶ pron ❶ (in questions) alguno(-a)
▷ I need a stamp. Have you got any
left? Necesito un sello. ¿Te queda
alguno?

Only use **alguno/alguna** if
'any' refers to a countable
noun. Otherwise don't
translate it.

▷ I fancy some soup. Have we got any?
Me apetece sopa. ¿Tenemos? ❷ (in
negatives) ninguno(-a) ▷ I don't like
any of them. No me gusta ninguno.

Only use **ninguno/ninguna** if
by 'not … any' you mean 'not a
single one'. Otherwise don't
translate it.

▷ Can I have some more milk? — No,
there isn't any left. ¿Me pones un
poco más de leche? — No, no
queda.

anybody pron ❶ alguien

Use **alguien** in questions.

▷ Has anybody got a pen? ¿Tiene
alguien un bolígrafo? ❷ nadie

Use **nadie** in negative
sentences.

▷ I can't see anybody. No veo a nadie.
❸ cualquiera

Use **cualquiera** in affirmative
sentences.

▷ Anybody can learn to swim.
Cualquiera puede aprender a
nadar.

anyhow adv de todas maneras

anyone pron ❶ alguien ❷ nadie
❸ cualquiera

anything pron ❶ algo

Use **algo** in questions.

▷ *Do you need anything?* ¿Necesitas algo? ▷ *Would you like anything to eat?* ¿Quieres algo de comer? ❷ **nada**

Use **nada** in negative sentences.

▷ *I can't hear anything.* No oigo nada. ❸ **cualquier cosa**

Use **cualquier cosa** in affirmative sentences.

▷ *Anything could happen.* Puede pasar cualquier cosa.

anyway adv de todas maneras

anywhere adv ❶ en algún sitio

Use **en** or **a algún sitio** in questions.

▷ *Have you seen my coat anywhere?* ¿Has visto mi abrigo en algún sitio? ▷ *Are we going anywhere?* ¿Vamos a algún sitio? ❷ **en ningún sitio**

Use **en a ningún sitio** in negative sentences.

▷ *I can't find it anywhere.* No lo encuentro en ningún sitio. ▷ *I can't go anywhere.* No puedo ir a ningún sitio. ❸ **en cualquier sitio**

Use **en cualquier sitio** in affirmative sentences.

▷ *You can buy stamps almost anywhere.* Se pueden comprar sellos casi en cualquier sitio.; **You can sit anywhere you like.** Siéntate donde quieras.

apart adv **The two towns are 10 kilometres apart.** Los dos pueblos están a 10 kilómetros el uno del otro.; **It was the first time we had been apart.** Era la primera vez que estábamos separados.; **apart from** aparte de ▷ *Apart from*

that, everything's fine. Aparte de eso, todo va bien.

apartment n piso m (apartamento m LatAm)

apologize vb disculparse [25] ▷ *He apologized for being late.* Se disculpó por llegar tarde.; **I apologize!** ¡Lo siento!

apology n disculpa f

apostrophe n apóstrofo m

app n (= application) aplicación f (pl aplicaciones)

apparent adj ❶ aparente ▷ *for no apparent reason* sin razón aparente ❷ **claro(-a)** ▷ *It was apparent that he disliked me.* Estaba claro que no le caigo bien.

apparently adv por lo visto (dizque LatAm) ▷ *Apparently he was abroad when it happened.* Por lo visto estaba en el extranjero cuando ocurrió.

appeal vb ❶ hacer [26] un llamamiento ▷ *They appealed for help.* Hicieron un llamamiento de ayuda. ❷ atraer [54] ▷ *Greece doesn't appeal to me.* Grecia no me atrae.

▷ n llamamiento m ▷ *They have launched an appeal for unity.* Han hecho un llamamiento a la unidad.

appear vb ❶ aparecer [12] ▷ *The bus appeared around the corner.* El autobús apareció por la esquina.; **to appear on TV** salir [49] en la tele ❷ parecer [12] ▷ *She appeared to be asleep.* Parecía estar dormida.

appendicitis n apendicitis f ▷ *She's got appendicitis.* Tiene apendicitis.

appetite n apetito m

a b c d e f g h i j k l m n o p q r s t u v w x y z

applaud vb aplaudir [**58**]

applause n aplausos mpl

apple n manzana f; **an apple tree** un manzano

applicant n candidato m, candidata f

application n **a job application** una solicitud de empleo

application form n impreso de solicitud m

apply vb **to apply for a job** solicitar [**25**] un empleo; **to apply to** afectar [**25**] a ▷ *This rule doesn't apply to us.* Esta norma no nos afecta.

appointment n cita f ▷ *to make an appointment* concertar una cita con alguien; **I've got a dental appointment.** Tengo hora con el dentista.

appreciate vb agradecer [**12**] ▷ *I really appreciate your help.* Agradezco de veras tu ayuda.

apprentice n aprendiz m (pl aprendices), aprendiza f

approach vb ① acercarse [**48**] a ▷ *He approached the house.* Se acercó a la casa. ② abordar [**25**] ▷ *to approach a problem* abordar un problema

appropriate adj apropiado(-a) ▷ *That dress isn't very appropriate for an interview.* Ese vestido no es muy apropiado para una entrevista.; **Tick the appropriate box.** Marque la casilla que corresponda.

approval n aprobación f

approve vb **I don't approve of his choice.** No me parece bien su elección.; **They didn't approve of**

his girlfriend. No veían con buenos ojos a su novia.

approximate adj aproximado(-a)

apricot n albaricoque m

April n abril m ▷ *in April* en abril ▷ *on 4 April* el 4 de abril; **April Fools' Day** el día de los Santos Inocentes

　● In Spanish-speaking countries **el día de los Santos Inocentes** falls on the 28th of December. People play practical jokes in the same way as they do on April Fools' Day.

apron n delantal m

Aquarius n (sign) Acuario m; **I'm Aquarius.** Soy acuario.

Arab adj árabe
　▶ n árabe mf ▷ *the Arabs* los árabes

Arabic adj árabe

arch n arco m

archaeologist n arqueólogo m, arqueóloga f ▷ *He's an archaeologist.* Es arqueólogo.

archaeology n arqueología f

archbishop n arzobispo m

archeologist n (US) arqueólogo m, arqueóloga f

archeology n (US) arqueología f

architect n arquitecto m, arquitecta f ▷ *She's an architect.* Es arquitecta.

architecture n arquitectura f

Arctic n **the Arctic** el Ártico

are vb see **be**

area n ① zona f ▷ *a mountainous area of Spain* una zona montañosa de España ② (surface area) superficie f ③ (in football) área f

　▍ Although it's a feminine noun, remember that you use **el** and **un** with **área**.

Argentina n Argentina f

Argentinian adj argentino(-a)
▸ n argentino m, argentina f

argue vb discutir [58] ▷ *They never stop arguing.* Siempre están discutiendo.

argument n discusión f (pl discusiones) ▷ *to have an argument* discutir

Aries n (sign) Aries m; **I'm Aries.** Soy aries.

arm n brazo m ▷ *I burnt my arm.* Me quemé el brazo.

armchair n sillón m (pl sillones)

army n ejército m

around prep, adv ❶ alrededor de ▷ *She wore a scarf around her neck.* Llevaba una bufanda alrededor del cuello. ▷ *It costs around £100.* Cuesta alrededor de 100 libras.; **She ignored the people around her.** Ignoró a la gente que estaba a su alrededor.; **Shall we meet at around 8 o'clock?** ¿Quedamos sobre las 8? ❷ por ▷ *I've been walking around the town.* He estado paseando por la ciudad.; **We walked around for a while.** Paseamos por ahí durante un rato.; **around here** por aquí ▷ *Is there a chemist's around here?* ¿Hay alguna farmacia por aquí?

arrange vb organizar [13] ▷ *to arrange a party* organizar una fiesta; **to arrange to do something** quedar [25] en hacer algo ▷ *They arranged to go out together on Friday.* Quedaron en salir juntos el viernes.

arrangement n to make an arrangement to do something

quedar [25] en hacer algo; **a flower arrangement** un arreglo floral; **arrangements** los preparativos ▷ *Pamela is in charge of the travel arrangements.* Pamela se encarga de los preparativos para el viaje.

arrest vb detener [53]
▸ n detención f (pl detenciones); **You're under arrest!** ¡Queda detenido!

arrival n llegada f ▷ *the airport arrivals hall* la sala de llegadas del aeropuerto

arrive vb llegar [37] ▷ *I arrived at 5 o'clock.* Llegué a las 5.

arrow n flecha f

art n arte m; **works of art** las obras de arte; **art school** la escuela de Bellas Artes

artery n arteria f

art gallery n ❶ (state-owned) museo m ❷ (private) galería de arte f

article n artículo m

artificial adj artificial

artist n artista mf ▷ *She's an artist.* Es artista.

artistic adj artístico(-a)

as conj, adv ❶ cuando ▷ *He came in as I was leaving.* Entró cuando yo me iba. ❷ mientras ▷ *Everyone looked at him as he stood up.* Todos lo miraron mientras se levantaba. ❸ como ▷ *As it's Sunday, you can have a lie-in.* Como es domingo, puedes quedarte en la cama hasta tarde. ❹ de ▷ *He works as a waiter in the holidays.* En vacaciones trabaja de camarero.; **as...as** tan...como

a
b
c
d
e
f
g
h
i
j
k
l
m
n
o
p
q
r
s
t
u
v
w
x
y
z

▷ *Peter's as tall as Michael.* Peter es tan alto como Michael.; **as much…as** tanto…como ▷ *I haven't got as much energy as you.* No tengo tanta energía como tú.; **Her coat cost twice as much as mine.** Su abrigo costó el doble que el mío.; **as soon as possible** cuanto antes; **as from tomorrow** a partir de mañana; **as if** como si

▌ **como si** has to be followed by a verb in the subjunctive.

▷ *She acted as if she hadn't seen me.* Hizo como si no me hubiese visto.; **as though** como si ▷ *She acted as though she hadn't seen me.* Hizo como si no me hubiese visto

ash n ❶ (*from fire, cigarette*) ceniza f ❷ (*tree, wood*) fresno m

ashamed adj **to be ashamed** estar [22] avergonzado ▷ *I'm ashamed of myself for shouting at you.* Estoy avergonzado de gritarte.; **You should be ashamed of yourself!** ¡Debería darte vergüenza!

ashtray n cenicero m

Asia n Asia f

Asian adj asiático(-a)
▶ n asiático m, asiática f

ask vb ❶ preguntar [25] ▷ *'Have you finished?' she asked.* '¿Has terminado?' preguntó.; **to ask somebody something** preguntar [25] algo a alguien; **to ask about something** preguntar [25] por algo ▷ *I asked about train times to Leeds.* Pregunté por el horario de trenes a Leeds.; **to ask somebody a question** hacer [26] una pregunta a alguien ❷ pedir [38]

▌ **pedir que** has to be followed by a verb in the subjunctive.

▷ *She asked him to do the shopping.* Le pidió que hiciera la compra.; **to ask for something** pedir [38] algo ▷ *He asked for a cup of tea.* Pidió una taza de té.; **Peter asked her out.** Peter le pidió que saliera con él. ❸ invitar [25] ▷ *Have you asked Matthew to the party?* ¿Has invitado a Matthew a la fiesta?

asleep adj **to be asleep** estar [22] dormido; **to fall asleep** quedarse [25] dormido

asparagus n espárragos mpl

aspirin n aspirina f

assignment n (*at school*) tarea f

assistance n ayuda f

assistant n ❶ (*in shop*) dependiente m, dependienta f ❷ (*helper*) ayudante mf

association n asociación f (pl asociaciones)

assortment n surtido m

assume vb suponer [41] ▷ *I assume she won't be coming.* Supongo que no vendrá.

assure vb asegurar [25] ▷ *He assured me he was coming.* Me aseguró que venía.

asthma n asma f ▷ *He's got asthma.* Tiene asma.

▌ Although it's a feminine noun, remember that you use **el** with **asma**.

astonish vb pasmar [25]

astrology n astrología f

astronaut n astronauta mf

astronomy n astronomía f

at prep ❶ en ▷ at home en casa ▷ at school en la escuela ▷ at the office en la oficina ▷ at work en el trabajo ❷ a ▷ at 50 km/h a 50 km/h; **two at a time** de dos en dos; **at 4 o'clock** a las 4; **at night** por la noche; **at Christmas** en Navidad; **What are you doing at the weekend?** ¿Qué haces este fin de semana?
▶ n (@ symbol) arroba f

ate vb see **eat**

Athens n Atenas f

athlete n atleta mf

athletic adj atlético(-a)

athletics n atletismo m ▷ I enjoy watching the athletics on television. Me gusta ver el atletismo en la televisión.

Atlantic n Atlántico m

atlas n atlas m (pl atlas)

atmosphere n atmósfera f

atom n átomo m

atomic adj atómico(-a)

attach vb atar [25] ▷ They attached a rope to the car. Ataron una cuerda al coche.

attached adj **to be attached to somebody** tener [53] cariño a alguien

attachment n (to email) documento adjunto m

attack vb atacar [48]
▶ n ataque m; **to be under attack** ser [52] atacado

attempt n intento m
▶ vb **to attempt to do something** intentar [25] hacer algo ▷ I attempted to write a song. Intenté escribir una canción.

attend vb asistir [58] a ▷ to attend a meeting asistir a una reunión

attention n atención f; **to pay attention to** prestar [25] atención a ▷ He didn't pay attention to what I was saying. No prestó atención a lo que estaba diciendo.; **Don't pay any attention to him!** ¡No le hagas caso!

attic n desván m (pl desvanes) (altillo m LatAm)

attitude n actitud f

attorney n (US) abogado m, abogada f

attract vb atraer [54] ▷ The Lake District attracts lots of tourists. La Región de los Lagos atrae a muchos turistas.

attraction n atracción f (pl atracciones) ▷ a tourist attraction una atracción turística

attractive adj atractivo(-a)

aubergine n berenjena f

auction n subasta f

audience n público m

August n agosto m ▷ in August en agosto ▷ on 13 August el 13 de agosto

aunt n tía f; **my aunt and uncle** mis tíos

aunty n tía f

au pair n au pair f (pl au pairs)

Australia n Australia f

Australian adj australiano(-a)
▶ n australiano m, australiana f
▷ the Australians los australianos

Austria n Austria f

Austrian adj austriaco(-a)
▶ n austríaco m, austríaca f ▷ the Austrians los austríacos

a b c d e f g h i j k l m n o p q r s t u v w x y z

author n autor m, autora f ▷ *the author of the book* el autor del libro; **a famous author** un escritor famoso

autobiography n autobiografía f

autograph n autógrafo m

automatic adj automático(-a)

automatically adv automáticamente

autumn n otoño m ▷ *in autumn* en el otoño

availability n disponibilidad f

available adj disponible ▷ *There is very little available information.* Hay muy poca información disponible.; **Free brochures are available on request.** Disponemos de folletos gratuitos para quien los solicite.; **Is Mr Cooke available today?** ¿Está libre el señor Cooke hoy?

avalanche n alud m

avenue n avenida f

average n media f ▷ *on average* de media
▶ adj medio(-a) ▷ *the average price* el precio medio

avocado n aguacate m

avoid vb evitar [25] ▷ *Avoid going out on your own at night.* Evite salir solo por la noche.

awake adj **to be awake** estar [22] despierto

award n premio m ▷ *the award for the best actor* el premio al mejor actor

aware adj **to be aware that** saber [47] que; **to be aware of something** ser [52] consciente de algo; **not that I am aware of** que yo sepa, no

away adj, adv **It's two kilometres away.** Está a dos kilómetros de distancia.; **The holiday was two weeks away.** Faltaban dos semanas para las vacaciones.; **to be away** estar [22] fuera ▷ *Jason was away on a business trip.* Jason estaba fuera en viaje de negocios.; **He's away for a week.** Se ha ido una semana.; **Go away!** ¡Vete!; **away from** lejos de ▷ *away from family and friends* lejos de la familia y los amigos; **It's 30 miles away from town.** Está a 30 millas de la ciudad.

away match n **It is their last away match.** Es el último partido que juegan fuera.

awful adj horrible ▷ *The weather's awful.* Hace un tiempo horrible.; **I feel awful.** Me siento fatal.; **We met and I thought he was awful.** Nos conocimos y me cayó fatal.; **an awful lot of work** un montón de trabajo

awkward adj **①** incómodo(-a); **Mike's being awkward about letting me have the car.** Mike no hace más que ponerme pegas para dejarme el coche. **②** torpe ▷ *an awkward gesture* un gesto torpe

axe n hacha f

> Although it's a feminine noun, remember that you use **el** and **un** with **hacha**.

b

baby n bebé m (pl bebés) (bebe m LatAm)
baby carriage n (US) cochecito de niño m
babysit vb hacer [26] de canguro
babysitter n canguro mf
babysitting n I don't like babysitting. No me gusta hacer de canguro.
bachelor n soltero m
back n ➊ (of person) espalda f ➋ (of animal) lomo m; **at the back of the house** en la parte de atrás de la casa; **in the back of the car** en la parte trasera del coche; **at the back of the class** al fondo de la clase
▶ adj, adv trasero(-a) ▷ the back seat el asiento trasero; **the back door** la puerta de atrás; **He's not back yet.** Todavía no ha vuelto.; **to get back** volver [59] ▷ What time did you get back? ¿A qué hora volviste?; **I'll call back later.** Volveré a llamar más tarde.
▶ vb respaldar [25] ▷ The union is backing his claim for compensation. El sindicato respalda su demanda de compensación.; **to back a horse** apostar [11] por un caballo; **She backed into the parking space.** Aparcó dando marcha atrás.
back out vb echarse [25] para atrás
back up vb respaldar [25] ▷ She complained, and her colleagues backed her up. Presentó una queja y sus colegas la respaldaron.
backache n dolor de espalda m ▷ to have backache tener dolor de espalda
backbone n columna vertebral f
backfire vb (go wrong) tener [53] el efecto contrario
background n (of picture) fondo m ▷ a house in the background una casa en el fondo; **background noise** ruido de fondo; **his family background** su historial familiar
backhand n revés m (pl reveses)
backing n apoyo m
backpack n mochila f
backpacker n mochilero m, mochilera f
backside n trasero m
backstroke n espalda f
backup n apoyo m ▷ We have extensive computer backup. Tenemos amplio apoyo informático.;

a backup file una copia de seguridad

backwards adv hacia atrás ▷ to take a step backwards dar un paso hacia atrás; **to fall backwards** caerse [5] de espaldas

bacon n bacon m (tocino m LatAm) ▷ bacon and eggs los huevos fritos con bacon

bad adj ❶ malo(-a) ▷ You bad boy! ¡Malo!

▌ Use **mal** before a masculine singular noun.

▷ bad weather mal tiempo; **to be in a bad mood** estar [22] de mal humor; **to be bad at something** ser [52] malo para algo ▷ I'm really bad at maths. Soy muy malo para las matemáticas. ❷ (serious) **grave** ▷ a bad accident un accidente grave; **to go bad** (food) echarse [25] a perder; **I feel bad about it.** (guilty) Me siento un poco culpable.; **How are you? — Not bad.** ¿Cómo estás? — Bien.; **That's not bad at all.** No está nada mal.; **bad language** las palabrotas

badge n ❶ (metal, plastic) **chapa** f ❷ (cloth) **escudo** m

badly adv mal ▷ badly paid mal pagado; **badly wounded** gravemente herido; **He badly needs a rest.** Le hace muchísima falta un descanso.

badminton n bádminton m ▷ to play badminton jugar al bádminton

bad-tempered adj **to be bad-tempered (1)** (by nature) tener [53] mal genio ▷ He's a really

bad-tempered person. Es una persona con muy mal genio. **(2)** (temporarily) estar [22] de mal humor ▷ He was really bad-tempered yesterday. Ayer estaba de muy mal humor.

bag n bolsa f

baggage n equipaje m

baggage reclaim n recogida de equipajes f

baggy adj (trousers) ancho(-a)

bagpipes npl gaita f

bake vb **to bake bread** hacer [26] pan; **She loves to bake.** Le gusta cocinar al horno.

baked beans npl alubias blancas en salsa de tomate fpl

baked potato n patata asada f

baker n panadero m, panadera f ▷ He's a baker. Es panadero.; **at the baker's** en la panadería

bakery n panadería f

balance n equilibrio m ▷ to lose one's balance perder el equilibrio

balanced adj equilibrado(-a)

balcony n balcón m (pl balcones)

bald adj calvo(-a)

ball n ❶ (for tennis, basketball, rugby) **pelota** f ❷ (for football) **balón** m (pl balones)

ballet n ballet m (pl ballets); **ballet lessons** las clases de ballet

ballet dancer n bailarín m (pl bailarines), bailarina f

ballet shoes npl zapatillas de ballet fpl

balloon n globo m; **a hot-air balloon** un globo aerostático

ballpoint pen n bolígrafo m

ballroom dancing n baile de salón m

ban n prohibición f (pl prohibiciones)
▶ vb prohibir [**42**]

banana n plátano m ▷ a banana skin una piel de plátano

band ❶ (pop, rock) grupo m ❷ (military) banda f ❸ (at a dance) orquesta f

bandage n venda f
▶ vb vendar [**25**] ▷ The nurse bandaged his arm. La enfermera le vendó el brazo.

Band-Aid® n (US) tirita f

bang n ❶ (noise) estallido m ▷ I heard a loud bang. Oí un fuerte estallido. ❷ (blow) golpe m ▷ a bang on the head un golpe en la cabeza
▶ vb golpear [**25**] ▷ I banged my head. Me golpeé la cabeza.; **to bang on the door** aporrear [**25**] la puerta; **to bang the door** dar [**14**] un portazo

bank n ❶ (financial) banco m ❷ (of river, lake) orilla f

bank account n cuenta bancaria f

banker n banquero m, banquera f
▷ He's a banker. Es banquero.

bank holiday n día festivo m

banknote n billete de banco m

bar n ❶ (pub) bar m ❷ (counter) barra f; **a bar of chocolate** (1) (large) una tableta de chocolate (2) (small) una chocolatina; **a bar of soap** una pastilla de jabón

barbecue n barbacoa f ▷ to have a barbecue hacer una barbacoa

bare adj desnudo(-a)

barefoot adj, adv descalzo(-a)
▷ The children go around barefoot. Los niños van descalzos.

barely adv apenas ▷ I could barely hear what she was saying. Apenas oía lo que estaba diciendo.

bargain n ganga f ▷ It was a bargain! ¡Era una ganga!

barge n barcaza f

bark vb ladrar [**25**]

barmaid n camarera f ▷ She's a barmaid. Es camarera.

barman n barman m (pl barmans)
▷ He's a barman. Es barman.

barn n granero m

barrel n ❶ (container) barril m ❷ (of gun) cañón m (pl cañones)

barrier n barrera f

bartender n (US) barman mf (pl barmans) ▷ He's a bartender. Es barman.

baseball n béisbol m ▷ to play baseball jugar al béisbol; **a baseball cap** una gorra de béisbol

based adj **based on** basado en

basement n sótano m ▷ a basement flat un apartamento en el sótano

bash vb golpear [**25**] con fuerza
▶ n I'll have a bash at it. Lo intentaré.

basic adj básico(-a) ▷ It's a basic model. Es un modelo básico.; **The accommodation was pretty basic.** El alojamiento tenía solo lo imprescindible.

basically adv básicamente ▷ They are basically the same thing. Son básicamente lo mismo.;

a
b
c
d
e
f
g
h
i
j
k
l
m
n
o
p
q
r
s
t
u
v
w
x
y
z

Basically, I just don't like him.
Simplemente, no me gusta.

basics npl principios básicos mpl

basin n ① (washbasin) lavabo m
② (for cooking, mixing food)
cuenco m

basis n base f ▷ On the basis of what
you've said. En base a lo que has
dicho.; **on a daily basis**
diariamente; **on a regular basis**
regularmente

basket n cesto m

basketball n baloncesto m ▷ to
play basketball jugar al baloncesto

bass n (voice) bajo m; **a bass guitar**
un bajo; **a double bass** un
contrabajo

bass drum n bombo m

bassoon n fagot m (pl fagots)

bat n ① (for baseball, cricket) bate m
② (for table tennis) raqueta f
③ (animal) murciélago m

bath n ① baño m ▷ a hot bath un
baño caliente; **to have a bath**
bañarse [25] ② (bathtub)
bañera f

bathe vb bañarse [25]

bathing suit n (US) traje de
baño m

bathroom n cuarto de baño m

bath towel n toalla de baño f

batter n masa para rebozar f

battery n ① (for torch, toy) pila f
② (for car) batería f

battle n batalla f ▷ the Battle of
Hastings la batalla de Hastings;
**It was a battle, but we managed
in the end.** Fue muy difícil, pero al
final lo conseguimos.

bay n bahía f

BC abbr (= before Christ) a.C. (= antes
de Cristo)

be vb

> There are two basic verbs to
> translate 'be' into Spanish:
> **estar** and **ser**. **estar** is used to
> form continuous tenses; to
> talk about where something
> is; and with adjectives
> describing a temporary state.
> It is also used with past
> participles used adjectivally
> even if these describe a
> permanent state.

① estar [22] ▷ What are you doing?
¿Qué estás haciendo? ▷ Edinburgh
is in Scotland. Edimburgo está en
Escocia. ▷ I've never been to Madrid.
No he estado nunca en Madrid.
▷ I'm very happy. Estoy muy
contento. ▷ He's dead. Está
muerto.

> **ser** is used to talk about the
> time and date; with adjectives
> describing permanent and
> inherent states such as
> nationality and colour; with
> nouns to say what somebody
> or something is; and to form
> the passive.

② ser [52] ▷ It's four o'clock. Son las
cuatro. ▷ It's the 28th of October
today. Hoy es 28 de octubre. ▷ She's
English. Es inglesa. ▷ He's a doctor.
Es médico. ▷ Paris is the capital of
France. París es la capital de
Francia. ▷ He's very tall. Es muy
alto. ▷ The house was destroyed by an
earthquake. La casa fue destruida
por un terremoto.

Passive constructions are not as common in Spanish as in English. Either the active or a reflexive construction is preferred.

▷ *He was killed by a terrorist.* Lo mató un terrorista. ▷ *These cars are produced in Spain.* Estos coches se fabrican en España.

When referring to the weather, use hacer.

▷ *It's a nice day, isn't it?* Hace buen día, ¿verdad? ▷ *It's cold.* Hace frío. ▷ *It's too hot.* Hace demasiado calor.

With certain adjectives, such as 'cold', 'hot', 'hungry', and 'thirsty', use tener with a noun.

▷ *I'm cold.* Tengo frío. ▷ *I'm hungry.* Tengo hambre.

When saying how old somebody is, use tener.

▷ *I'm fourteen.* Tengo catorce años. ▷ *How old are you?* ¿Cuántos años tienes?

beach n playa f
bead n cuenta f
beak n pico m
beam n (of light) rayo m
beans npl alubias fpl; **beans on toast** las alubias blancas en salsa de tomate sobre una tostada
bear n oso m
▶ vb aguantar [25] ▷ *I can't bear it!* ¡No lo aguanto!
beard n barba f ▷ *a man with a beard* un hombre con barba; **He's got a beard.** Lleva barba.
bearded adj con barba

beat n ritmo m
▶ vb ganar [25] ▷ *We beat them three-nil.* Les ganamos tres a cero.; **Beat it!** ¡Lárgate! (informal)
beat up vb dar [14] una paliza a
beautiful adj precioso(-a)
beauty n belleza f
beauty spot n (place) lugar pintoresco m
became vb see **become**
because conj porque; **because of** a causa de
become vb llegar [37] a ser
bed n cama f; **to go to bed** acostarse [11]; **to go to bed with somebody** irse [27] a la cama con alguien
bed and breakfast n pensión f (pl pensiones) ▷ *We stayed in a bed and breakfast.* Nos quedamos en una pensión.; **How much is it for bed and breakfast?** ¿Cuánto es la habitación con desayuno?
bedclothes npl ropa de cama f
bedding n ropa de cama f
bedroom n dormitorio m
bedsit n cuarto de alquiler m
bedspread n colcha f
bedtime n **Ten o'clock is my usual bedtime.** Normalmente me voy a la cama a las diez.; **Bedtime!** ¡A la cama!
bee n abeja f
beef n carne de vaca f; **roast beef** el rosbif
beefburger n hamburguesa f
been vb see **be**
beer n cerveza f
beetle n escarabajo m
beetroot n remolacha f

a
b
c
d
e
f
g
h
i
j
k
l
m
n
o
p
q
r
s
t
u
v
w
x
y
z

before *prep, conj, adv* **①** antes de
▷ *before Tuesday* antes del martes
▷ *Before opening the packet, read the instructions.* Antes de abrir el paquete, lea las instrucciones. ▷ *I'll phone before I leave.* Llamaré antes de salir. **②** antes de que

antes de que has to be followed by a verb in the subjunctive.

▷ *I'll call her before she leaves.* La llamaré antes de que se vaya.; **I've seen this film before.** Esta película ya la he visto.; **the week before** la semana anterior

beforehand *adv* con antelación

beg *vb* **①** (*for money, food*) mendigar [**37**] ▷ **②** suplicar [**48**]

suplicar que has to be followed by a verb in the subjunctive.

▷ *He begged me to stop.* Me suplicó que parara.

began *vb see* **begin**

beggar *n* mendigo *m*, mendiga *f*

begin *vb* empezar [**19**]; **to begin doing something** empezar [**19**] a hacer algo

beginner *n* principiante *mf*

beginning *n* comienzo *m*; **in the beginning** al principio

begun *vb see* **begin**

behalf *n* **on behalf of somebody** de parte de alguien

behave *vb* comportarse [**25**] ▷ *He behaved like an idiot.* Se comportó como un idiota.; **to behave oneself** portarse [**25**] bien ▷ *Did the children behave themselves?* ¿Se portaron bien los niños?; **Behave!** ¡Compórtate!

behaviour (*US* **behavior**) *n* comportamiento *m*

behind *prep, adv* detrás de ▷ *behind the television* detrás de la televisión; **to be behind** (*late*) ir [**27**] atrasado ▷ *I'm behind with my work.* Voy atrasado con mi trabajo.
▶ *n* trasero *m*

beige *adj* beige

Pronounce this word like the English word 'base'.

Belgian *adj* belga ▷ *He's Belgian.* Es belga.
▶ *n* belga *mf* ▷ *the Belgians* los belgas

Belgium *n* Bélgica *f*

believe *vb* creer [**30**] ▷ *I don't believe you.* No te creo.; **I don't believe it!** ¡No me lo creo!; **to believe in something** creer [**30**] en algo
▷ *Do you believe in ghosts?* ¿Crees en los fantasmas?

bell *n* **①** (*of door, in school*) timbre *m* ▷ *The bell goes at half past three.* El timbre suena a las tres y media. **②** (*of church*) campana *f* ▷ *the church bell* la campana de la iglesia **③** (*of toy, an animal*) cascabel *m* ▷ *Our cat has a bell on its collar.* Nuestro gato lleva un cascabel en el collar.

belong *vb* **to belong to somebody** pertenecer [**12**] a alguien ▷ *This ring belonged to my grandmother.* Este anillo perteneció a mi abuela.; **Who does it belong to?** ¿De quién es?; **That belongs to me.** Eso es mío.; **Do you belong to any clubs?** ¿Eres miembro de algún club?

belongings npl I collected my belongings. Recogí mis cosas.; **personal belongings** los efectos personales

below prep, adv ❶ debajo de ▷ the apartment directly below ours el apartamento que está justo debajo del nuestro ❷ abajo ▷ seen from below visto desde abajo ▷ on the floor below en el piso de abajo; **ten degrees below freezing** diez grados bajo cero

belt n cinturón m (pl cinturones)

bench n banco m

bend n curva f
▶ vb ❶ doblar [25] ▷ I can't bend my arm. No puedo doblar el brazo. ❷ torcerse [6] ▷ It bends easily. Se tuerce fácilmente.

bend down vb agacharse [25]

bend over vb inclinarse [25]

beneath prep bajo

benefit n beneficio m; **state benefits** los subsidios estatales
▶ vb beneficiar [25] ▷ This will benefit us all. Esto nos beneficiará a todos.; **He'll benefit from the change.** Se beneficiará con el cambio.

bent vb see **bend**
▶ adj torcido(-a) ▷ a bent fork un tenedor torcido; **to be bent on doing something** estar [22] empeñado en hacer algo

beret n boina f

berth n (bunk) litera f

beside prep al lado de ▷ beside the television al lado de la televisión; **He was beside himself.** Estaba fuera de sí.; **That's beside the point.** Eso no viene al caso.

besides adv además ▷ Besides, it's too expensive. Además, es demasiado caro.; **... and much more besides.** ... y mucho más todavía.

best adj, adv mejor ▷ He's the best player in the team. Es el mejor jugador del equipo. ▷ Janet's the best at maths. Janet es la mejor en matemáticas. ▷ Emma sings best. Emma es la que canta mejor.; **That's the best I can do.** No puedo hacer más.; **to do one's best** hacer [26] todo lo posible ▷ It's not perfect, but I did my best. No es perfecto, pero he hecho todo lo posible.; **You'll just have to make the best of it.** Tendrás que arreglártelas con lo que hay.

best man n padrino de boda m

bet n apuesta f
▶ vb apostar [11] ▷ I bet you he won't come. Te apuesto a que no viene.

better adj, adv mejor ▷ This one's better than that one. Este es mejor que aquel. ▷ Are you feeling better now? ¿Te sientes mejor ahora?; **That's better!** ¡Así está mejor!; **to get better (1) (improve)** mejorar [25] ▷ I hope the weather gets better soon. Espero que el tiempo mejore pronto. **(2) (from illness)** mejorarse [25] ▷ I hope you get better soon. Espero que te mejores pronto.; **You'd better do it straight away.** Más vale hacerlo enseguida.; **I'd better go home.** Tengo que irme a casa.

between prep entre ▷ between 15 and 20 minutes entre 15 y 20 minutos

beware vb **Beware of the dog!**
¡Cuidado con el perro!

beyond prep, adv al otro lado de
▷ *There is a lake beyond the mountains.*
Hay un lago al otro lado de las
montañas.; **We have no plans
beyond the year 2017.** No tenemos
planes para después del año 2017.;
**the wheat fields and the
mountains beyond** los campos de
trigo y las montañas al fondo; **It's
beyond me.** No lo entiendo.;
beyond belief increíble; **beyond
repair** irreparable

Bible n Biblia f

bicycle n bicicleta f

big adj grande ▷ *a big house* una casa
grande ▷ *a big car* un coche grande

▌ Use **gran** before a singular
▌ noun.

▷ *It's a big business.* Es un gran
negocio.; **my big brother** mi
hermano mayor; **He's a big guy.**
Es un tipo grandote.; **Big deal!**
¡Vaya cosa!

bigheaded adj **to be bigheaded**
ser [**52**] engreído

bike n ❶ (bicycle) bici f ▷ *by bike* en
bici ❷ (motorbike) moto f

▌ Although **moto** ends in **-o**,
▌ it is actually a feminine noun.

bikini n bikini m

bilingual adj bilingüe

bill n ❶ (in restaurant) cuenta f ▷ *Can
we have the bill, please?* ¿Nos trae la
cuenta, por favor? ❷ (for gas,
electricity, telephone) factura f ▷ *the
gas bill* la factura del gas ❸ (US)
billete m ▷ *a five-dollar bill* un billete
de cinco dólares

billiards n billar m ▷ *to play billiards*
jugar al billar

billion n mil millones mpl ▷ *two
billion dollars* dos mil millones de
dólares

bin n ❶ (in kitchen) cubo de la
basura m ❷ (for paper) papelera f

binoculars npl prismáticos mpl ▷ *a
pair of binoculars* unos prismáticos

biochemistry n bioquímica f

biography n biografía f

biology n biología f

bird n pájaro m

birdwatching n **He likes to go
birdwatching on Sundays.** Los
domingos le gusta ir a ver pájaros.

Biro® n bolígrafo m

birth n nacimiento m ▷ *date of birth*
la fecha de nacimiento

birth certificate n partida de
nacimiento f

birth control n control de
natalidad m

birthday n cumpleaños m (pl
cumpleaños) ▷ *a birthday cake* un
pastel de cumpleaños ▷ *a birthday
card* una tarjeta de cumpleaños
▷ *a birthday party* una fiesta de
cumpleaños ▷ *When's your
birthday?* ¿Cuándo es tu
cumpleaños?

biscuit n galleta f

bishop n obispo m

bit vb see **bite**
▶ n (piece) trozo m; **a bit** un poco
▷ *He's a bit mad.* Está un poco loco.;
a bit of (1) un trozo de ▷ *a bit of cake*
un trozo de pastel (2) un poco de
▷ *a bit of music* un poco de música.;
It's a bit of a nuisance. Es un poco

fastidioso.; **to fall to bits** caerse [5] a pedazos; **to take something to bits** desmontar [25] algo; **bit by bit** poco a poco

bite vb ① (person, dog) morder [33] ▷ My dog's never bitten anyone. Mi perro nunca ha mordido a nadie. ② (insect) picar [48] ▷ I got bitten by mosquitoes. Me picaron los mosquitos.; **to bite one's nails** morderse [33] las uñas
▶ ① (insect bite) picadura f ② (animal bite) mordisco m; **to have a bite to eat** comer [8] alguna cosa

bitter adj ① amargo(-a) ▷ It tastes bitter. Sabe amargo. ② glacial ▷ It's bitter today. Hoy hace un frío glacial.

black adj negro(-a) ▷ a black jacket una chaqueta negra ▷ She's black. Es negra.; **black and white** blanco y negro

blackberry n mora f
blackbird n mirlo m
blackboard n pizarra f
black coffee n café solo m
blackcurrant n grosella negra f
blackmail n chantaje m
▶ vb chantajear [25]

black pudding n morcilla f
blade n hoja f
blame vb echar [25] la culpa a ▷ Don't blame me! ¡No me eches la culpa a mí! ▷ He blamed it on his sister. Le echó la culpa a mi hermana.

blank adj (sheet of paper) en blanco; **My mind went blank.** Me quedé en blanco.

blanket n manta f
blast n **a bomb blast** una explosión
blaze n incendio m
blazer n blazer m (pl blazers)
bleach n lejía f
bleed vb sangrar [25]; **to bleed to death** morir [32] desangrado; **My nose is bleeding.** Me sangra la nariz.

blender n licuadora f
bless vb bendecir [15]; **Bless you!** (after sneezing) ¡Jesús! (¡Salud! LatAm)

blew vb see **blow**
blind adj ciego(-a)
▶ n (for window) persiana f
blindfold n venda f
blink vb parpadear [25]
blister n ampolla f
blizzard n ventisca de nieve f
block n bloque m ▷ a block of flats un bloque de apartamentos
▶ vb bloquear [25]

blog n blog m (pl blogs)
▶ vb (have a blog) tener [53] un blog
blogger n bloguero m, bloguera f
blonde adj rubio(-a) ▷ She's got blonde hair. Tiene el pelo rubio.
blood n sangre f
blood pressure n presión sanguínea f; **to have high blood pressure** tener [53] la tensión alta
blood test n análisis de sangre m (pl análisis de sangre)
blouse n blusa f
blow n golpe m
▶ vb soplar [25] ▷ A cold wind was blowing. Soplaba un viento frío.; **to blow one's nose** sonarse [11] la nariz

blow out vb apagar [**37**] ▷ *Blow out the candles!* ¡Apaga las velas!

blow up vb ❶ volar [**11**] ▷ *They blew up a plane.* Volaron un avión.
❷ inflar [**25**] ▷ *We've blown up the balloons.* Hemos inflado los globos.
❸ saltar [**25**] por los aires ▷ *The house blew up.* La casa saltó por los aires.

blow-dry n secado con secador de mano m; *A cut and blow-dry, please.* Un corte y un secado a mano, por favor.

blue adj azul ▷ *a blue dress* un vestido azul; *out of the blue* en el momento menos pensado

blues npl (music) blues m (pl blues)

blunder n metedura de pata f

blunt adj ❶ (person) directo(-a)
❷ (knife) desafilado(-a)

blush vb ruborizarse [**13**]

board n ❶ (plank) tabla f
❷ (blackboard) pizarra f
❸ (noticeboard) tablón de anuncios m (pl tablones de anuncios) ❹ (for diving) trampolín m (pl trampolines) ❺ (for games) tablero m; *on board* a bordo; *'full board'* 'pensión completa'

boarder n interno m, interna f

board game n juego de mesa m

boarding card n tarjeta de embarque f

boarding school n internado m

boast vb alardear [**25**] ▷ *to boast about something* alardear de algo; *Stop boasting!* ¡Deja ya de presumir!

boat n barco m

body n ❶ cuerpo m ▷ *the human body* el cuerpo humano ❷ (corpse) cadáver m

bodybuilding n culturismo m

bodyguard n guardaespaldas m (pl guardaespaldas) ▷ *He's a bodyguard.* Es guardaespaldas.

boil n furúnculo m
▶ vb hervir [**51**] ▷ *The water's boiling.* El agua está hirviendo.

boil over vb salirse [**49**]

boiled adj hervido(-a); *a boiled egg* un huevo pasado por agua

boiling adj *It's boiling in here!* ¡Aquí dentro se asa uno!

bolt n ❶ (on door, window) cerrojo m ❷ (type of screw) tornillo m

bomb n bomba f
▶ vb bombardear [**25**]

bomber n (plane) bombardero m

bombing n bombardeo m

bone n ❶ (of human, animal) hueso m ❷ (of fish) espina f

bonfire n hoguera f

bonnet n (of car) capó m

bonus n ❶ (extra payment) plus m ❷ (added advantage) ventaja f

book n libro m
▶ vb reservar [**25**]; *We haven't booked.* No hemos hecho reserva.

bookcase n librería f

booklet n folleto m

bookshelf n estantería f

bookshop n librería f

boot n ❶ (of car) maletero m ❷ (fashion boots) bota f ❸ (for hiking) borceguí m (pl borceguíes)

border n frontera f

bore vb see **bear**

bored adj aburrido(-a) ▷ *to be bored* estar aburrido; *to get bored* aburrirse [**58**]

boring adj aburrido(-a) ▷ It's boring. Es aburrido.

born adj to be born nacer [12] ▷ I was born in 2002. Nací en 2002.

borne vb see **bear**

borrow vb pedir [38] prestado; to borrow something from somebody pedir [38] algo prestado a alguien ▷ I borrowed some money from a friend. Le pedí dinero prestado a un amigo.; **Can I borrow your pen?** ¿Me prestas el bolígrafo?

Bosnia n Bosnia f

Bosnian adj bosnio(-a)

boss n jefe m, jefa f

boss around vb to boss somebody around mandonear [25] a alguien

bossy adj mandón (f mandona, pl mandones)

both adj, pron, adv los dos (f las dos) ▷ We both went. Fuimos los dos. ▷ Both of your answers are wrong. Tus respuestas están las dos mal. ▷ Both of them play the piano. Los dos tocan el piano.; **He has houses in both France and Spain.** Tiene casas tanto en Francia como en España.

bother vb **①** (worry) preocupar [25] ▷ What's bothering you? ¿Qué es lo que te preocupa? **②** (disturb) molestar [25] ▷ I'm sorry to bother you. Siento molestarle.; **Don't bother!** ¡No te preocupes!; to bother to do something tomarse [25] la molestia de hacer algo ▷ He didn't bother to tell me about it. Ni se tomó la molestia de decírmelo.

▶ n molestia f; **No bother!** No es ninguna molestia.

bottle n botella f

bottle bank n contenedor del vidrio m

bottle-opener n abrebotellas m (pl abrebotellas)

bottom n **①** (of container, bag, sea) fondo m; **at the bottom of the page** al final de la página; **He was always bottom of the class.** Siempre era el último de la clase. **②** (buttocks) trasero m

▶ adj de abajo ▷ the bottom shelf el estante de abajo

bought vb see **buy**

bounce vb rebotar [25]

bouncer n gorila m

> Although **gorila** ends in **-a**, it is actually a masculine noun.

bound adj **He's bound to fail.** Seguro que suspende.; **She's bound to come.** Es seguro que vendrá.

boundary n límite m

bow n **①** (knot) lazo m ▷ to tie a bow hacer un lazo **②** arco m ▷ a bow and arrow un arco y flecha

▶ vb hacer [26] una reverencia

bowl n **①** (for soup, cereals) tazón m (pl tazones) **②** (for cooking, mixing food) cuenco m

▶ vb lanzar [13] la pelota

bowling n bolos mpl; to go bowling jugar [28] a los bolos; **a bowling alley** una bolera

bowls npl bolos mpl

bow tie n pajarita f

box n **①** caja f ▷ a box of matches una caja de cerillas; **a cardboard box**

una caja de cartón ❷ *(on form)*
casilla *f*

boxer *n* boxeador *m*

boxer shorts *npl* bóxers *mpl* ▷ *a
pair of boxer shorts* unos bóxers

boxing *n* boxeo *m*

Boxing Day *n* 26 de diciembre *m*

boy *n* ❶ *(young man)* muchacho *m* ▷ *a
boy of fifteen* un muchacho de quince
años ❷ *(child)* niño *m* ▷ *a boy of seven*
un niño de siete años; **She has two
boys and a girl.** Tiene dos niños y
una niña.; **a baby boy** un niño

boyfriend *n* novio *m* ▷ *Have you got
a boyfriend?* ¿Tienes novio?

bra *n* sostén *m* (*pl* sostenes)

brace *n* *(on teeth)* aparato *m*
▷ *Richard wears a brace.* Richard
lleva un aparato.

bracelet *n* pulsera *f*

brackets *npl* **in brackets** entre
paréntesis

brain *n* cerebro *m*

brainy *adj* inteligente

brake *n* freno *m*
▶ *vb* frenar [**25**]

branch *n* ❶ *(of tree)* rama *f* ❷ *(of
bank)* sucursal *f*

brand *n* marca *f* ▷ *a well-known
brand of coffee* una marca de café
muy conocida

brand-new *adj* flamante

brandy *n* coñac *m* (*pl* coñacs)

brass *n* *(metal)* latón *m*; **the brass
section** los bronces

brass band *n* banda de música *f*

brave *adj* valiente

Brazil *n* Brasil *m*

bread *n* pan *m* ▷ *bread and butter* el
pan con mantequilla

break *n* ❶ *(rest)* pausa *f* ▷ *to take a
break* hacer una pausa ❷ *(at school)*
recreo *m*; **the Christmas break** las
vacaciones de Navidad; **Give me a
break!** ¡Déjame en paz!
▶ *vb* ❶ romper [**8**] ▷ *Careful, you'll
break something!* ¡Cuidado, que vas
a romper algo!; **I broke my leg.**
Me rompí la pierna. ❷ romperse
[**8**] ▷ *Careful, it'll break!* ¡Ten
cuidado, que se va a romper!; **to
break a promise** faltar [**25**] a una
promesa; **to break a record** batir
[**58**] un récord

break down *vb* averiarse [**21**]; **The
car broke down.** El coche se
averió.

break in *vb* **The thief had broken
in through a window.** El ladrón
había entrado por una ventana.

break into *vb* *(house)* entrar [**25**] en
▷ *Thieves broke into the house.* Los
ladrones entraron en la casa.

break off *vb* *(come free)*
desprenderse [**8**]

break out *vb* ❶ *(war)* estallar [**25**]
❷ *(fire, fighting)* desencadenarse
[**25**] ❸ *(prisoner)* escaparse [**25**];
He broke out in a rash. Le salió un
sarpullido.

break up *vb* ❶ disolver [**33**] ▷ *Police
broke up the demonstration.* La
policía disolvió la demostración.
❷ *(crowd)* dispersarse [**25**]
❸ *(marriage)* fracasar [**25**] ▷ *More
and more marriages break up.* Cada
día fracasan más matrimonios.
❹ *(two lovers)* romper [**8**] ▷ *Richard
and Marie have broken up.* Richard y
Marie han roto.; **to break up a**

fight poner [**41**] fin a una pelea; **We break up next Wednesday.** El miércoles que viene empezamos las vacaciones.; **You're breaking up.** (mobile phone) No hay cobertura.

breakdown n ❶ crisis nerviosa f (pl crisis nerviosas) ▷ He had a breakdown because of the stress. Sufrió una crisis nerviosa debida al estrés. ❷ (in vehicle) avería f ▷ to have a breakdown tener una avería

breakdown van n grúa f

breakfast n desayuno m; **to have breakfast** desayunar [**25**]

break-in n **There have been a lot of break-ins in my area.** Han entrado a robar en muchas casas de mi barrio.

breast n pecho m; **chicken breast** la pechuga de pollo

breaststroke n braza f

breath n aliento m ▷ He's got bad breath. Tiene mal aliento.; **I'm out of breath.** Estoy sin aliento.; **to get one's breath back** recobrar [**25**] el aliento

breathe vb respirar [**25**]

breathe in vb aspirar [**25**]

breathe out vb espirar [**25**]

breed vb (reproduce) reproducirse [**9**]; **to breed dogs** criar [**21**] perros ▷ n raza f

breeze n brisa f

brewery n fábrica de cerveza f

bribe n soborno m ▷ vb sobornar [**25**]

brick n ladrillo m

bride n novia f

bridegroom n novio m

bridesmaid n dama de honor f

bridge n ❶ puente m ❷ (card game) bridge m ▷ to play bridge jugar al bridge

brief adj breve

briefcase n maletín m (pl maletines)

briefly adv brevemente

briefs npl calzoncillos mpl ▷ a pair of briefs unos calzoncillos

bright adj ❶ vivo(-a) ▷ a bright colour un color vivo ▷ bright red rojo vivo ❷ (light) brillante ❸ listo(-a) ▷ He's not very bright. No es muy listo.

brilliant adj ❶ estupendo(-a); **We had a brilliant time!** ¡Lo pasamos estupendo! ❷ genial ▷ a brilliant scientist un científico genial

bring vb traer [**54**] ▷ Can I bring a friend? ¿Puedo traer a un amigo?

bring back vb (book) devolver [**59**]; **That song brings back memories.** Esa canción me trae recuerdos.

bring forward vb adelantar [**25**]

bring up vb criar [**21**] ▷ She brought up five children on her own. Crió a cinco hijos ella sola.

Britain n Gran Bretaña f

British adj británico(-a); **the British** los británicos; **the British Isles** las Islas Británicas; **She's British.** Es británica.

broad adj ancho(-a)

broadband n banda ancha f

broadcast n emisión f (pl emisiones) ▷ vb emitir [**58**] ▷ The interview was broadcast all over the world. La entrevista se emitió a todo el mundo.; **to broadcast live** emitir [58] en directo

broccoli n brécol m

brochure n folleto m

broil vb (US) ① (in cooker) hacer [26] al grill ② (barbecue) asar [25] a la parrilla

broke vb see **break**
▶ adj **to be broke** estar [22] sin blanca (informal)

broken vb see **break**
▶ adj roto(-a) ▷ It's broken. Está roto. ▷ He's got a broken arm. Tiene un brazo roto.

bronchitis n bronquitis f

bronze n bronce m ▷ the bronze medal la medalla de bronce

brooch n broche m

broom n escoba f

brother n hermano m

brother-in-law n cuñado m

brought vb see **bring**

brown adj ① (clothes) marrón (pl marrones) ② (hair, eyes) castaño(-a) ③ (tanned) moreno(-a); **brown bread** el pan integral

Brownie n guía f

bruise n moretón m (pl moretones)

brush n ① (for hair, teeth) cepillo m ② (paintbrush) pincel m
▶ vb cepillar [25]; **to brush one's hair** cepillarse [25] el pelo; **to brush one's teeth** cepillarse [25] los dientes ▷ I brush my teeth every night. Me cepillo los dientes todas las noches.

Brussels n Bruselas f

Brussels sprouts npl coles de Bruselas fpl

bubble n ① (of soap) pompa f ② (of air, gas) burbuja f

bubble bath n baño de espuma m

bubble gum n chicle m

bucket n cubo m

buckle n (on belt, watch, shoe) hebilla f

Buddhism n budismo m

Buddhist adj budista

buddy n (US) amiguete m, amigueta f

budget n presupuesto m

budgie n periquito m

buffet n bufet m

buffet car n coche restaurante m

bug n ① (insect) insecto m ② (illness, in computer) virus m (pl virus)
▷ There's a bug going round. Hay un virus en el ambiente.; **a stomach bug** una gastroenteritis

build vb construir [10] ▷ They're going to build houses here. Van a construir viviendas aquí.

build up vb ① acumular [25] ▷ He has built up a huge collection of stamps. Ha ido acumulando una gran colección de sellos. ② acumularse [25] ▷ Our debts are building up. Nuestras deudas se están acumulando.

builder n ① (contractor) contratista mf ② (worker) albañil m

building n edificio m

built vb see **build**

bulb n ① (electric) bombilla f ② (of flower) bulbo m

bull n toro m

bullet n bala f

bullfighting n **Do you like bullfighting?** ¿Te gustan los toros?

bullring n plaza de toros f

bully n matón m (pl matones) ▷ He's a bully. Es un matón.
▶ vb intimidar [25]

bum n culo m (informal)

bum bag n riñonera f

bump n ❶ (on head) chichón m (pl chichones) ❷ (on surface) bulto m ❸ (on road) bache m ❹ (minor accident) golpe m ▷ We had a bump. Nos dimos un golpe.
▶ vb ▷ I bumped my head on the wall. Me di con la cabeza en la pared.

bump into vb ❶ tropezarse [19] con ▷ I bumped into Paul yesterday. Me tropecé con Paul ayer. ❷ darse [14] contra ▷ We bumped into a tree. Nos dimos contra un árbol.

bumper n parachoques m (pl parachoques)

bumpy adj (road) lleno de baches (f llena de baches)

bun n (bread) bollo m

bunch n **a bunch of flowers** un ramo de flores

bunches npl coletas fpl ▷ She has her hair in bunches. Lleva coletas.

bungalow n bungalow m

bunk n litera f

burger n hamburguesa f

burglar n ladrón m (pl ladrones), ladrona f

burglarize vb (US) entrar [25] a robar en

burglary n robo m

burgle vb entrar [25] a robar en ▷ Her house was burgled. Le entraron a robar en casa.

burn n quemadura f
▶ vb (rubbish, documents) quemar

[25] ▷ I burned the rubbish. Quemé la basura.; **I burned the cake.** Se me quemó el pastel.; **to burn oneself** quemarse [25]; **I've burned my hand.** Me quemé la mano.

burn down vb quedar [25] reducido a cenizas ▷ The factory burned down. La fábrica quedó reducida a cenizas.

burst vb reventarse [39] ▷ The balloon burst. El globo se reventó.; **to burst a balloon** reventar [39] un globo; **to burst out laughing** echarse [25] a reír; **to burst into tears** romper [8] a llorar; **to burst into flames** incendiarse [25]

bury vb enterrar [39]

bus n autobús m (pl autobuses) ▶ by bus en autobús; **the school bus** el autocar escolar; **a bus ticket** un billete de autobús

bush n arbusto m

business n ❶ (firm) negocio m ▷ He's got his own business. Tiene su propio negocio. ❷ negocios mpl ▷ He's away on business. Está en un viaje de negocios.; **a business trip** un viaje de negocios; **It's none of my business.** No es asunto mío.

businessman n hombre de negocios m

businesswoman n mujer de negocios f

busker n músico callejero m, música callejera f

bus station n estación de autobuses f (pl estaciones de autobuses)

bus stop n parada de autobús f

a
b
c
d
e
f
g
h
i
j
k
l
m
n
o
p
q
r
s
t
u
v
w
x
y
z

bust n busto m

busy adj ❶ (person, telephone line) ocupado(-a) ▷ She's a very busy woman. Es una mujer muy ocupada. ❷ (day, week) ajetreado(-a) ▷ It's been a very busy day. Ha sido un día muy ajetreado. ❸ (street, shop) concurrido(-a)

but prep, conj ❶ pero ▷ I'd like to come, but I'm busy. Me gustaría venir, pero tengo trabajo. ❷ sino

> Use **sino** when you want to correct a previous negative statement.

▷ He's not English but French. No es inglés sino francés. ❸ menos ▷ They won all but two of their matches. Ganaron todos los partidos menos dos.; **the last but one** el penúltimo

butcher n carnicero m, carnicera f ▷ He's a butcher. Es carnicero.; **at the butcher's** en la carnicería

butter n mantequilla f

butterfly n (insect, swimming) mariposa f ▷ Her favourite stroke is the butterfly. Su estilo favorito es mariposa.

button n ❶ botón m (pl botones) ❷ (US: metal, plastic) chapa f

buy vb comprar [25] ▷ He bought me an ice cream. Me compró un helado.; **to buy something from somebody** comprar [25] algo a alguien ▷ I bought a watch from him. Le compré un reloj.

▶ n **It was a good buy.** Fue una buena compra.

by prep ❶ por ▷ The thieves were caught by the police. Los ladrones

fueron capturados por la policía. ❷ de ▷ a painting by Picasso un cuadro de Picasso ❸ en; **by car** en coche ▷ by train en tren ▷ by bus en autobús ❹ (next to) junto a ▷ Where's the bank? — It's by the post office. ¿Dónde está el banco? — Está junto a la oficina de correos. ❺ para ▷ We have to be there by four o'clock. Tenemos que estar allí para las cuatro.; **by the time...** cuando ▷ By the time I got there it was too late. Cuando llegué allí ya era demasiado tarde. ▷ It'll be ready by the time you get back. Estará listo para cuando regreses.; **That's fine by me.** Por mí no hay problema.; **all by himself** él solo; **I did it all by myself.** Lo hice yo solo.; **by the way** a propósito

bye excl ¡adiós!

bypass n (road) carretera de circunvalación f

C

cab n taxi m ▷ I'll go by cab. Iré en taxi.

cabbage n berza f

cabin n ❶ (on ship) camarote m ❷ (on aeroplane) cabina f

cable n cable m

cable car n teleférico m

cable television n televisión por cable f

café n cafetería f

cage n jaula f

cagoule n canguro m

cake n pastel m

calculate vb calcular [25]

calculation n cálculo m

calculator n calculadora f

calendar n calendario m

calf n ❶ (of cow) ternero m ❷ (of leg) pantorrilla f

call n llamada f ▷ Thanks for your call. Gracias por su llamada. ▷ a phone call una llamada telefónica; **to be on call** (doctor) estar [22] de guardia
▶ vb llamar [25] ▷ We called the police. Llamamos a la policía. ▷ I'll tell him you called. Le diré que has llamado.; **to be called** llamarse [25] ▷ He's called Fluffy. Se llama Fluffy. ▷ What's she called? ¿Cómo se llama?

call back vb volver [59] a llamar ▷ I'll call back later. Volveré a llamar más tarde.; **Can I call you back later?** ¿Puedo llamarte más tarde?

call for vb ❶ pasar [25] a recoger ▷ Shall I call for you at seven thirty? ¿Paso a recogerte a las siete y media? ❷ requerir [51] ▷ This calls for strong nerves. Esto requiere unos nervios de acero.; **This calls for a drink!** ¡Esto hay que celebrarlo!

call off vb suspender [8] ▷ The match was called off. El partido se suspendió.

call box n cabina telefónica f

call centre n centro de atención al cliente m

calm adj tranquilo(-a)

calm down vb calmarse [25] ▷ Calm down! ¡Cálmate!

calorie n caloría f

calves npl see **calf**

camcorder n videocámara f

came vb see **come**

camel n camello m

camera n cámara f

cameraman n cámara m

camera phone n teléfono con cámara m

camp vb acampar [**25**]
▶ n campamento m ▷ a summer camp un campamento de verano; **a refugee camp** un campo de refugiados

campaign n campaña f
▶ vb hacer [**26**] campaña ▷ They are campaigning for a change in the law. Están haciendo campaña a favor de un cambio legislativo.

camper n campista mf; **a camper van** una autocaravana

camping n **to go camping** ir [**27**] de camping

campsite n camping m (pl campings)

can vb ❶ (be able to, be allowed to) poder [**40**] ▷ Can I use your phone? ¿Puedo usar el teléfono? ▷ I can't do that. No puedo hacer eso. ▷ I'll do it as soon as I can. Lo haré tan pronto como pueda. ▷ That can't be true! ¡No puede ser cierto! ▷ You could hire a bike. Podrías alquilar una bici. ▷ He couldn't concentrate because of the noise. No se podía concentrar a causa del ruido. ❷ (know how to) saber [**47**] ▷ I can swim. Sé nadar. ▷ He can't drive. No sabe conducir.

▌'can' is sometimes not translated.

▷ I can't hear you. No te oigo. ▷ I can't remember. No me acuerdo. ▷ Can you speak French? ¿Hablas francés?; **You could be right.** Es posible que tengas razón.
▶ n lata f ▷ a can of beer una lata de cerveza; **a can of petrol** un bidón de gasolina

Canada n Canadá m

Canadian adj canadiense
▶ n canadiense mf

canal n canal m

Canaries n the Canaries las Canarias

canary n canario m; **the Canary Islands** las islas Canarias

cancel vb cancelar [**25**] ▷ Our flight was cancelled. Cancelaron nuestro vuelo.

Cancer n (sign) Cáncer m; **I'm Cancer.** Soy cáncer.

cancer n cáncer m ▷ He's got cancer. Tiene cáncer.

candidate n candidato m, candidata f

candle n ❶ vela f ❷ (in church) cirio m

candy n (US) dulces mpl ▷ I love candy. Me encantan los dulces.; **a candy** un caramelo

candyfloss n algodón de azúcar m

canned adj (food) en lata

cannot vb = **can not**

canoe n canoa f

canoeing n

can-opener n abrelatas m (pl abrelatas)

can't vb = **can not**

canteen n cantina f

canvas n lona f

cap n ❶ (of bottle, tube) tapón m (pl tapones) ❷ (hat) gorra f

capable adj capaz (pl capaces); **to be capable of doing something** ser [**52**] capaz de hacer algo ▷ She's capable of doing much more. Es capaz de hacer mucho más.

capacity n capacidad f

capital n ① capital f ▷ Cardiff is the capital of Wales. Cardiff es la capital del país de Gales. ② (letter) mayúscula f ▷ in capitals en mayúsculas

capitalism n capitalismo m

Capricorn n (sign) Capricornio m; **I'm Capricorn.** Soy capricornio.

captain n capitán m (pl capitanes), capitana f

capture vb capturar [25]

car n coche m; **to go by car** ir [27] en coche ▷ We went by car. Fuimos en coche.; **a car crash** un accidente de coche

caramel n caramelo m

caravan n caravana f ▷ a caravan site un camping de caravanas

card n ① tarjeta f ▷ I got lots of cards and presents on my birthday. Recibí muchas tarjetas y regalos para mi cumpleaños. ② (playing card) carta f; **a card game** un juego de cartas

cardboard n cartón m ▷ a cardboard box una caja de cartón

cardigan n rebeca f

cardphone n teléfono de tarjeta m

care n cuidado m ▷ with care con cuidado; **to take care of** cuidar [25] ▷ I take care of the children on Saturdays. Cuido a los niños los sábados.; **Take care!** (1) (be careful!) ¡Ten cuidado! (2) (look after yourself!) ¡Cuídate!

▶ vb **to care about** preocuparse [25] por ▷ They don't care about their image. No se preocupan por su imagen.; **I don't care!** ¡No me importa!; **Who cares?** ¿Y a quién le importa?

career n carrera f

careful adj **Be careful!** ¡Ten cuidado!

carefully adv (cautiously) con cuidado ▷ Drive carefully! ¡Conduce con cuidado!; **Think carefully!** ¡Piénsalo bien!; **She carefully avoided talking about it.** Tuvo mucho cuidado de no hablar del tema.

careless adj ① (work) poco cuidado(-a); **a careless mistake** un error de descuido ② (person) poco cuidadoso(-a) ▷ She's very careless. Es muy poco cuidadosa.; **a careless driver** un conductor imprudente

caretaker n conserje mf; **school caretaker** el bedel

cargo n cargamento m

car hire n alquiler de coches m

Caribbean adj caribeño(-a)
▶ n **We're going to the Caribbean.** Vamos al Caribe.; **the Caribbean** (sea) el mar Caribe

caring adj bondadoso(-a)

carnation n clavel m

carnival n carnaval m

carol n **a Christmas carol** un villancico

car park n aparcamiento m

carpenter n carpintero m, carpintera f ▷ He's a carpenter. Es carpintero.

carpet n ① (fitted) moqueta f ② alfombra f ▷ a Persian carpet una alfombra persa

car rental n (US) alquiler de coches m

carriage n (of train) vagón m (pl vagones)

a b c d e f g h i j k l m n o p q r s t u v w x y z

carrier bag n bolsa de plástico f

carrot n zanahoria f

carry vb ❶ llevar [**25**] ▷ I'll carry your bag. Te llevo la bolsa. ❷ transportar [**25**] ▷ a plane carrying 100 passengers un avión que transporta 100 pasajeros

carry on vb seguir [**50**] ▷ She carried on talking. Siguió hablando.; **Carry on!** ¡Sigue! ▷ Am I boring you? — No, carry on! ¿Te estoy aburriendo? — ¡No, sigue!

carry out vb ❶ (orders) cumplir [**58**] ❷ (threat, task, instructions) llevar [**25**] a cabo

carrycot n moisés m (pl moisés)

cart n carro m

carton n (of milk, fruit juice) cartón m (pl cartones)

cartoon n ❶ (film) dibujos animados mpl ❷ (in newspaper) chiste m

cartridge n cartucho m

carve vb trinchar [**25**] ▷ Dad carved the roast. Papá trinchó el asado.; **a carved oak chair** una silla de roble tallado

case n ❶ maleta f ▷ I've packed my case. He hecho mi maleta. ❷ caso m ▷ in some cases en algunos casos; **in case it rains** por si llueve; **just in case** por si acaso ▷ Take some money with you, just in case. Llévate algo de dinero por si acaso.

cash n dinero m ▷ I'm a bit short of cash. Ando un poco justo de dinero.; **in cash** en efectivo ▷ £200 in cash 200 libras esterlinas en efectivo; **to pay cash** pagar [**37**] al contado

cash desk n caja f

cashew nut n anacardo m

cashier n cajero m, cajera f

cashmere n cachemir m ▷ a cashmere sweater un suéter de cachemir

casino n casino m

cast n reparto m ▷ There is a very famous actor in the cast. Hay un actor muy famoso en el reparto.; **After the play, we met the cast.** Cuando terminó la obra charlamos con los actores.

castle n castillo m

casual adj ❶ informal ▷ I prefer casual clothes. Prefiero la ropa informal. ❷ despreocupado(-a) ▷ a casual attitude una actitud despreocupada ❸ eventual ▷ It's just a casual job. Es solo un trabajo eventual.

casualty n ❶ (hospital department) urgencias fpl ▷ He was taken to casualty after the accident. Lo llevaron a urgencias después del accidente. ❷ víctima f ▷ The casualties include a young boy. Entre las víctimas se encuentra un niño.

cat n gato m, gata f

catalogue n catálogo m

catastrophe n catástrofe f

catch vb ❶ coger [**7**] (agarrar [**25**] LatAm)

> Be very careful with the verb **coger**: in most of Latin America this is an extremely rude word that should be avoided. However, in Spain this verb is common and not rude at all.

▷ *They caught the thief.* Cogieron al ladrón. ▷ *We caught the last train.* Cogimos el último tren.; **My cat catches birds.** Mi gato caza pájaros. ❷ agarrar [**25**] ▷ *He caught her arm.* La agarró del brazo.; **to catch a cold** resfriarse [**21**]; **I didn't catch his name.** No me enteré de su nombre.; **He caught her stealing.** La pilló robando.; **If they catch you smoking you'll be in trouble.** Si te pillan fumando te la vas a cargar.

catch up vb ❶ ponerse [**41**] al día ▷ *I've got to catch up on my work.* Tengo que ponerme al día con el trabajo. ❷ alcanzar [**13**] ▷ *She caught me up.* Me alcanzó.

catering n The hotel did all the catering for the wedding. El hotel se encargó de organizar el banquete de bodas.

cathedral n catedral f

Catholic adj católico(-a)
▶ n católico m, católica f ▷ *I'm a Catholic.* Soy católico.

cattle npl ganado m

caught vb see **catch**

cauliflower n coliflor f

cause n causa f
▶ vb causar [**25**]

cautious adj prudente

cave n cueva f

CD n CD m (pl CDs)

CD player n reproductor de CD m

CD-ROM n CD-ROM m

ceiling n techo m

celebrate vb celebrar [**25**]

celebration n celebración f (pl celebraciones)

celebrity n famoso m, famosa f

celery n apio m

cell n ❶ (of prisoner) celda f ❷ (in biology) célula f

cellar n sótano m

cello n violonchelo m

cell phone n móvil m

cement n cemento m

cemetery n cementerio m

cent n ❶ (division of dollar) centavo m ❷ (division of euro) céntimo m

centenary n centenario m

center n (US) centro m

centigrade adj centígrado(-a)
▷ *20 degrees centigrade* 20 grados centígrados

centimetre (US **centimeter**) n centímetro m

central adj central

central heating n calefacción central f

centre n centro m

century n siglo m ▷ *the twentieth century* el siglo veinte

cereal n cereales mpl ▷ *I have cereal for breakfast.* Desayuno cereales.

ceremony n ceremonia f

certain adj ❶ (particular) cierto(-a) ▷ *a certain person* cierta persona ❷ (definite) seguro(-a) ▷ *I am certain he's not coming.* Estoy seguro de que no viene.; **for certain** con certeza; **to make certain** cerciorarse [**25**] ▷ *I made certain the door was locked.* Me cercioré de que la puerta estaba cerrada con llave.

certainly adv por supuesto ▷ *I shall certainly be there.* Por supuesto que estaré allí. ▷ *Certainly not!* ¡Por supuesto que no!; **So it was a**

surprise! — **It certainly was!** ¿Así que fue una sorpresa? — ¡Ya lo creo!

certificate n certificado m

chain n cadena f ⊳ a gold chain una cadena de oro

chair ❶ silla f ⊳ a table and four chairs una mesa y cuatro sillas ❷ (armchair) sillón m (pl sillones)

chairlift n telesilla m

　Although **telesilla** ends in -a, it is actually a masculine noun.

chairman n presidente m, presidenta f

chalet n chalet m (pl chalets)

chalk n tiza f; **a piece of chalk** una tiza

challenge n reto m
　▶ vb retar [25] ⊳ She challenged me to a race. Me retó a echar una carrera.

chambermaid n camarera f

champagne n champán m

champion n campeón m (pl campeones), campeona f

championship n campeonato m

chance n ❶ posibilidad f ⊳ The team's chances of winning are very good. El equipo tiene muchas posibilidades de ganar. ❷ oportunidad f ⊳ I had the chance of working in Brazil. Tuve la oportunidad de trabajar en Brasil.; **I'll write when I get the chance.** Te escribiré cuando tenga un momento.; **by chance** por casualidad; **No chance!** ¡Ni en bromal; **to take a chance** arriesgarse [37] ⊳ I'm taking no chances! ¡No me quiero arriesgar!

change vb ❶ cambiar [25] ⊳ The town has changed a lot. La ciudad ha

cambiado mucho. ⊳ I'd like to change £50. Quisiera cambiar 50 libras esterlinas. ❷ cambiar [25] de ⊳ He wants to change his job. Quiere cambiar de trabajo. ⊳ I'm going to change my shoes. Voy a cambiarme de zapatos.; **to get changed** cambiarse [25]; **to change one's mind** cambiar [25] de idea
　▶ n ❶ cambio m ⊳ There's been a change of plan. Ha habido un cambio de planes.; **a change of clothes** una muda; **for a change** para variar ❷ dinero suelto m ⊳ I haven't got any change. No tengo dinero suelto.; **Can you give me change for a pound?** ¿Me puede cambiar una libra?; **There's your change.** Aquí tiene el cambio.

changing room n ❶ (in shop) probador m ❷ (for sport) vestuario m

channel n (TV) canal m; **the English Channel** el Canal de la Mancha; **the Channel Islands** las islas del Canal de la Mancha; **the Channel Tunnel** el túnel del Canal de la Mancha

chaos n caos m

chapel n capilla f

chapter n capítulo m

character n ❶ carácter m (pl caracteres) ⊳ Can you describe his character? ¿Puede describirme cómo es su carácter? ❷ (in film, book) personaje m; **She's quite a character.** Es todo un personaje.

characteristic n característica f

charcoal n ① (for barbecue) carbón vegetal m ② (for drawing) carboncillo m

charge n **Is there a charge for delivery?** ¿Cobran por el envío?; **an extra charge** un suplemento; **free of charge** gratuito; **I'd like to reverse the charges.** Quisiera llamar a cobro revertido.; **to be in charge** ser [52] el responsable ▷ She was in charge of the group. Ella era la responsable del grupo.
▶ vb ① cobrar [25] ▷ How much did he charge you? ¿Cuánto te cobró? ② (with crime) acusar [25] ▷ The police have charged him with murder. La policía lo ha acusado de asesinato.

charity n (organization) organización benéfica f (pl organizaciones benéficas) ▷ He gave the money to charity. Donó el dinero a una organización benéfica.; **to collect for charity** recaudar [25] dinero para obras benéficas

charm n encanto m

charming adj encantador(a)

chart n gráfico m ▷ The chart shows the rise of unemployment. El gráfico muestra el aumento del desempleo.; **the charts** la lista de éxitos ▷ The album is still in the charts. El álbum está todavía en la lista de éxitos.

charter flight n vuelo chárter m

chase vb ① perseguir [50] ▷ The police officer chased the thief along the road. El policía persiguió al ladrón a lo largo de la calle. ② ir [27] detrás

de ▷ He's always chasing the girls. Siempre va detrás de las chicas.
▶ n persecución f (pl persecuciones) ▷ a car chase una persecución en coche

chat n charla f; **to have a chat** (talk) charlar [25]

chat up vb intentar [25] ligarse a ▷ Jake was chatting up one of the girls.

chatroom n chat m

chat show n programa de entrevistas m

> Although **programa** ends in -a, it is actually a masculine noun.

cheap adj barato(-a) ▷ a cheap T-shirt una camiseta barata ▷ It's cheaper by bus. Es más barato en autobús.; **a cheap flight** un vuelo económico

cheat vb ① (at cards) hacer [26] trampa ▷ You're cheating! ¡Estás haciendo trampa! ② (in exam) copiar [25]
▶ n tramposo m, tramposa f

check n ① control m ▷ a security check un control de seguridad ② (US) cheque m ▷ to write a check extender un cheque ③ (US) cuenta f ▷ The waiter brought us the check. El camarero nos trajo la cuenta.
▶ vb comprobar [11] ▷ Could you check the oil, please? ¿Podría comprobar el aceite, por favor?; **to check with somebody** preguntarle [25] a alguien ▷ I'll check with the driver what time the bus leaves. Le preguntaré al conductor a qué hora sale el autobús.

check in vb ❶ (at airport) facturar [25] ❷ (in hotel) registrarse [25]

check out vb dejar [25] el hotel

checked adj a cuadros

checkers n (US) damas fpl ▷ to play checkers jugar a las damas

check-in n facturación de equipajes f

checkout n caja f

check-up n reconocimiento m

cheek n mejilla f ▷ He kissed her on the cheek. La besó en la mejilla.; **What a cheek!** ¡Qué cara!

cheeky adj descarado(-a) ▷ Don't be cheeky! ¡No seas descarado!; **a cheeky smile** una sonrisilla maliciosa

cheer n **Three cheers for the winner!** ¡Viva el ganador!; **Cheers!** (1) (when drinking) ¡Salud! (2) (thank you) ¡Gracias!
▶ vb vitorear [25]; **to cheer somebody up** levantar [25] el ánimo a alguien ▷ I was trying to cheer him up. Estaba intentando levantarle el ánimo.; **Cheer up!** ¡Anímate!

cheerful adj alegre

cheese n queso m

chef n chef mf (pl chefs)

chemical n sustancia química f

chemist n ❶ (dispenser) farmacéutico m, farmacéutica f ❷ (shop) farmacia f ▷ You get it from the chemist. Se compra en la farmacia.
　Chemist's shops in Spain are commonly identified by a green cross outside the shop.
❸ (scientist) químico m, química f

chemistry n química f ▷ the chemistry lab el laboratorio de química

cheque n cheque m ▷ to write a cheque extender un cheque ▷ to pay by cheque pagar con cheque

chequebook n talonario de cheques m

cherry n cereza f

chess n ajedrez m ▷ He likes playing chess. Le gusta jugar al ajedrez.

chessboard n tablero de ajedrez m

chest n pecho m ▷ I've got a pain in my chest. Tengo un dolor en el pecho.

chestnut n castaña f

chest of drawers n cómoda f

chew vb masticar [48]

chewing gum n chicle m; **a piece of chewing gum** un chicle

chick n polluelo m

chicken n ❶ (animal) gallina f ❷ (food) pollo m

chickenpox n varicela f ▷ I've got chickenpox. Tengo la varicela.

chickpeas npl garbanzos mpl

chief n jefe m, jefa f ▷ the chief of security el jefe de seguridad
▶ adj principal

child n ❶ niño m, niña f ▷ a child of six un niño de seis años ❷ hijo m, hija f ▷ Susan is our eldest child. Susan es nuestra hija mayor.
▷ They've got three children. Tienen tres hijos.

childish adj infantil

child minder n niñera f

children npl see **child**

Chile n Chile m

chill vb (drink, food) poner [**41**] a enfriar; **Serve chilled.** Sírvase bien frío.

chilli n chile m; **chilli con carne** el chile con carne

chilly adj frío(-a)

chimney n chimenea f

chin n barbilla f; **Keep your chin up!** ¡No pierdas el ánimo!

China n China f

china n porcelana f ▷ a china plate un plato de porcelana

Chinese adj chino(-a); **a Chinese man** un chino; **a Chinese woman** una china
  ▶ n (language) chino m; **the Chinese** los chinos

chip n ❶ (food) patata frita f (papa frita f LatAm) ❷ (in computer) chip m (pl chips)

chiropodist n podólogo m, podóloga f ▷ He's a chiropodist. Es podólogo.

chives npl cebollinos mpl

chocolate n ❶ chocolate m ▷ a chocolate cake un pastel de chocolate ❷ bombón m (pl bombones) ▷ a box of chocolates una caja de bombones

choice n elección f (pl elecciones); **I had no choice.** No tenía otro remedio.

choir n coro m

choke vb (on food) atragantarse [**25**]

choose vb elegir [**18**]

chop vb ❶ (onion, herbs) picar [**48**] ❷ (meat) cortar [**25**] en trozos pequeños
  ▶ n chuleta f ▷ a pork chop una chuleta de cerdo

chopsticks npl palillos mpl

Christ n Cristo m

christening n bautismo m

Christian n cristiano m, cristiana f
  ▶ adj cristiano(-a)

Christian name n nombre de pila m

Christmas n Navidad f ▷ Happy Christmas! ¡Feliz Navidad!; **Christmas Day** el día de Navidad; **on Christmas Day** el día de Navidad; **Christmas Eve** Nochebuena; **a Christmas tree** un árbol de Navidad; **Christmas dinner** la comida de Navidad
  ○ As well as lunch on Christmas Day, Spaniards also have a special supper on Christmas Eve.

a Christmas present un regalo de Navidad
  ○ In Spain Christmas presents are traditionally given on 6th January although more and more people are exchanging gifts on Christmas Eve.

Christmas pudding el pudín de Navidad; **Christmas card** la tarjeta de Navidad; **at Christmas** en Navidad

chunk n pedazo m ▷ Cut the meat into chunks. Córtese la carne en pedazos.

church n iglesia f; **the Church of England** la Iglesia Anglicana

cider n sidra f

cigar n puro m

cigarette n cigarrillo m

cigarette lighter n mechero m

cinema n cine m

a b c d e f g h i j k l m n o p q r s t u v w x y z

cinnamon n canela f

circle n círculo m

circular adj circular

circumstances npl circunstancias fpl ▷ in the circumstances dadas las circunstancias; **under no circumstances** bajo ningún concepto

circus n circo m

citizen n ciudadano m, ciudadana f

city n ciudad f ▷ the city centre el centro de la ciudad

civilization n civilización f (pl civilizaciones)

civil servant n funcionario m, funcionaria f ▷ He's a civil servant. Es funcionario.

civil war n guerra civil f

claim vb ❶ asegurar [25] ▷ He claims he found the money. Asegura haber encontrado el dinero. ❷ reclamar [25] ▷ He's claiming compensation from the company. Reclama una indemnización por parte de la empresa. ❸ cobrar [25] ▷ She's claiming unemployment benefit. Cobra subsidio de desempleo.; **We claimed on our insurance.** Reclamamos al seguro.
▶ n ❶ (on insurance policy) reclamación f (pl reclamaciones); **to make a claim** reclamar [25] al seguro ❷ afirmación f (pl afirmaciones) ▷ The manufacturer's claims are obviously untrue. Las afirmaciones del fabricante son obviamente falsas.

clap vb aplaudir [58]; **to clap one's hands** dar [14] palmadas

clarinet n clarinete m

clash vb ❶ (colours) desentonar [25] ▷ Red clashes with orange. El rojo desentona con el naranja. ❷ (events) coincidir [58] ▷ The party clashes with the meeting. La fiesta coincide con la reunión.

clasp n (of necklace, handbag) cierre m

class n clase f ▷ We're in the same class. Estamos en la misma clase. ▷ I go to dancing classes. Voy a clases de baile.

classic adj clásico(-a) ▷ a classic example un ejemplo clásico
▶ n clásico m

classical adj clásico(-a) ▷ classical music la música clásica

classmate n compañero de clase m, compañera de clase f

classroom n clase f

claw n ❶ (of lion, eagle) garra f ❷ (of cat, parrot) uña f ❸ (of crab, lobster) pinza f

clean adj limpio(-a)
▶ vb limpiar [25]

cleaner n ❶ (person) hombre de la limpieza m, mujer de la limpieza f ❷ (substance) producto de limpieza m

cleaner's n tintorería f ▷ He took his coat to the cleaner's. Llevó el abrigo a la tintorería.

clear adj ❶ claro(-a) ▷ a clear explanation una explicación clara ▷ It's clear you don't believe me. Está claro que no me crees.; **Have I made myself clear?** ¿Me explico? ❷ despejado(-a) ▷ Wait till the road is clear. Espera hasta que la carretera esté despejada. ▷ *a clear day* un día despejado

❸ transparente ▷ *It comes in a clear plastic bottle.* Viene en una botella de plástico transparente.

▶ vb ❶ despejar [25] ▷ *They are clearing the road.* Están despejando la carretera.; **She was cleared of murder.** La absolvieron del cargo de asesinato.; **to clear the table** quitar [25] la mesa ❷ (*fog, mist*) despejarse [25]

clear off vb largarse [37] ▷ *Clear off and leave me alone!* ¡Lárgate y déjame en paz!

clear up vb ❶ ordenar [25] ▷ *Who's going to clear all this up?* ¿Quién va a ordenar todo esto? ❷ resolver [33] ▷ *Let's try to clear up this problem.* Intentemos resolver este problema.; **I think it's going to clear up.** (*weather*) Creo que va a despejar.

clearly *adv* claramente ▷ *to speak clearly* hablar claramente; **Clearly this project will cost money.** Evidentemente este proyecto costará dinero.

clementine *n* clementina *f*

clever *adj* ❶ listo(-a) ▷ *She's very clever.* Es muy lista.
❷ ingenioso(-a) ▷ *a clever system* un sistema ingenioso; **What a clever idea!** ¡Qué idea más genial!

click on vb (*computing*) hacer [26] clic en ▷ *to click on an icon* hacer clic en un icono; **to click on the mouse** hacer [26] clic con el ratón

client *n* cliente *m*, clienta *f*

cliff *n* acantilado *m*

climate *n* clima *m*

Although **clima** ends in **-a**, it is actually a masculine noun.

climate change *n* cambio climático *m*

climb vb ❶ escalar [25] ▷ *Her ambition is to climb Mount Everest.* Su ambición es escalar el Monte Everest. ❷ trepar [25] a ▷ *They climbed a tree.* Treparon a un árbol.; **to climb the stairs** subir [58] las escaleras

climber *n* escalador *m*, escaladora *f*

climbing *n* montañismo *m*; **to go climbing** hacer [26] montañismo ▷ *We're going climbing in Scotland.* Vamos a hacer montañismo en Escocia.

clinic *n* ❶ (*in NHS hospital*) consultorio *m* ❷ (*private hospital*) clínica *f*

clip *n* ❶ (*for hair*) horquilla *f*
❷ secuencia *f* ▷ *some clips from Scarlett Johansson's latest film* unas secuencias de la última película de Scarlett Johansson

cloakroom *n* ❶ (*for coats*) guardarropa *m*

Although **guardarropa** ends in **-a**, it is actually a masculine noun.

❷ (*toilet*) servicios *mpl*

clock *n* reloj *m*; **an alarm clock** un despertador; **a clock radio** un radio-despertador

clone *n* clon *m*
▶ vb clonar [25] ▷ *to clone a sheep* clonar una oveja; **a cloned sheep** una oveja clónica

close adj, adv ❶ cerca ▷ The shops are very close. Las tiendas están muy cerca. ▷ The hotel is close to the station. El hotel está cerca de la estación.; **Come closer.** Acércate más.; **She was close to tears.** Estaba a punto de llorar. ❷ cercano(-a) ▷ We have only invited close relations. Solo hemos invitado a parientes cercanos. ❸ íntimo(-a) ▷ She's a close friend of mine. Es amiga íntima mía.; **I'm very close to my sister.** Estoy muy unida a mi hermana. ❹ reñido(-a) ▷ It was a very close contest. Fue un concurso muy reñido.; **It's close this afternoon.** Hace bochorno esta tarde.

▶ vb ❶ cerrar [39] ▷ The shops close at five thirty. Las tiendas cierran a las cinco y media. ▷ Please close the door. Cierra la puerta, por favor. ❷ cerrarse [39] ▷ The doors close automatically. Las puertas se cierran automáticamente.

closed adj cerrado(-a)

closely adv (look, examine) de cerca; **This will be a closely fought race.** Será una carrera muy reñida.

cloth n (material) tela f; **a cloth** un trapo ▷ Wipe it with a damp cloth. Límpialo con un trapo húmedo.

clothes npl ropa f; **clothes line** la cuerda de tender; **clothes peg** la pinza para tender la ropa

cloud n nube f

▶ adj **cloud computing** la computación en la nube

cloudy adj nublado(-a)

clove n **a clove of garlic** un diente de ajo

clown n payaso m

club n ❶ (society) club m ▷ a golf club un club de golf ▷ the youth club el club juvenil ❷ (night club) discoteca f ▷ We had dinner and went on to a club. Cenamos y fuimos a una discoteca.; **clubs** (at cards) los tréboles ▷ the ace of clubs el as de tréboles

club together vb hacer [26] una colecta

clubbing n **to go clubbing** ir [27] de discotecas

clue n pista f ▷ an important clue una pista clave; **I haven't a clue.** No tengo ni idea.

clumsy adj torpe

clutch n (of car) embrague m

coach n ❶ autobús m (pl autobuses) ▷ by coach en autobús ▷ the coach station la estación de autobuses ▷ a coach trip una excursión en autobús ❷ (trainer) entrenador m, entrenadora f; **the Spanish coach** el entrenador del equipo español

coal n carbón m; **a coal mine** una mina de carbón; **a coal miner** un minero de carbón

coarse adj ❶ basto(-a) ▷ The bag was made of coarse black cloth. La bolsa estaba hecha de una tela basta de color negro. ❷ grueso(-a) ▷ The sand is very coarse on that beach. La arena es muy gruesa en esa playa.

coast n costa f ▷ It's on the west coast of Scotland. Está en la costa oeste de Escocia.

coastguard n guardacostas m (pl guardacostas)

coat n abrigo m ▷ a woollen coat un abrigo de lana; **a coat of paint** una mano de pintura

coat hanger n percha f

cobweb n telaraña f

cocaine n cocaína f

cockerel n gallo m

cocoa n cacao m; **a cup of cocoa** una taza de chocolate

coconut n coco m

cod n bacalao m

code n ❶ clave f ▷ It's written in code. Está escrito en clave. ❷ (for telephone) prefijo m ▷ What is the code for London? ¿Cuál es el prefijo de Londres?

coffee n café m (pl cafés) ▷ a cup of coffee una taza de café; **A cup of coffee, please.** Un café, por favor.

coffee table n mesa de centro f

coffin n ataúd m

coin n moneda f ▷ a 20p coin una moneda de 20 peniques

coincidence n coincidencia f

Coke® n Coca-Cola® f

colander n colador m

cold adj frío(-a) ▷ The water's cold. El agua está fría. ▷ It's cold. Hace frío.
▷ Are you cold? ¿Tienes frío?
▶ n ❶ frío m ▷ I can't stand the cold. No soporto el frío. ❷ (illness) resfriado m; **to catch a cold** resfriarse [21]; **to have a cold** estar [22] resfriado

coleslaw n ensalada de col f

collapse vb ❶ venirse [56] abajo ▷ The bridge collapsed during the storm. El puente se vino abajo en medio de la tormenta. ❷ sufrir [58] un colapso ▷ He collapsed while playing tennis. Sufrió un colapso mientras jugaba al tenis.

collar n ❶ (of coat, shirt) cuello m ❷ (for animal) collar m

collarbone n clavícula f

colleague n colega mf

collect vb ❶ recoger [7] ▷ The teacher collected the exercise books. El maestro recogió los cuadernos. ▷ Their mother collects them from school. Su madre los recoge del colegio. ❷ coleccionar [25] ▷ He collects stamps. Colecciona sellos. ❸ hacer [26] una colecta ▷ I'm collecting for UNICEF. Estoy haciendo una colecta para la UNICEF.

collection n ❶ colección f (pl colecciones) ▷ my CD collection mi colección de CDs ❷ colecta f ▷ a collection for charity una colecta para obras benéficas

collector n coleccionista mf

college n (university) universidad f

collide vb chocar [48]

collision n colisión f (pl colisiones)

colon n (punctuation mark) dos puntos

colonel n coronel mf

colour (US color) n color m ▷ What colour is it? ¿De qué color es?; **a colour TV** una televisión en color

colourful (US colorful) adj de colores muy vistosos

colouring (US coloring) n (for food) colorante m

comb n peine m
▶ vb **You haven't combed your hair.** No te has peinado.

combination n combinación f (pl combinaciones)

combine vb ❶ combinar [25] ▷ The film combines humour with suspense. La película combina el humor con el suspense. ❷ compaginar [25] ▷ It's difficult to combine a career with a family. Es difícil compaginar la profesión con la vida familiar.

come vb ❶ venir [56] ▷ Helen came with me. Helen vino conmigo. ▷ Come home. Ven a casa. ▷ Come and see us soon. Ven a vernos pronto.; **Where do you come from?** ¿De dónde eres? ❷ llegar [37] ▷ They came late. Llegaron tarde. ▷ The letter came this morning. La carta llegó esta mañana.; **I'm coming!** ¡Ya voy!

come back vb volver [59] ▷ My brother is coming back tomorrow. Mi hermano vuelve mañana.

come down vb bajar [25]

come in vb entrar [25] ▷ Come in! ¡Entra!

come on vb **Come on!** (1) (expressing encouragement, urging haste) ¡Venga! (2) (expressing disbelief) ¡Venga ya!

come out vb ❶ salir [49] ▷ We came out of the cinema at 10. Salimos del cine a las 10. ❷ irse [27] ▷ I don't think this stain will come out. No creo que esta mancha se vaya a quitar.

come round vb (after faint, operation) volver [59] en sí

come up vb ❶ subir [58] ▷ Come up here! ¡Sube aquí! ❷ surgir [16] ▷ Something's come up so I'll be late home. Ha surgido algo, así es que

llegaré tarde a casa.; **to come up to somebody** acercarse [48] a alguien ▷ She came up to me and kissed me. Se me acercó y me besó.

comedian n cómico m, cómica f

comedy n comedia f

comfortable adj ❶ cómodo(-a) ▷ comfortable shoes zapatos cómodos ▷ Make yourself comfortable! ¡Ponte cómodo! ❷ (house, room) confortable ▷ Their house is small but comfortable. Su casa es pequeña pero confortable.

comic n cómic m (pl cómics)

comic strip n tira cómica f

comma n coma f

command n orden f (pl órdenes)

comment n comentario m ▷ He made no comment. No hizo ningún comentario.; **No comment!** ¡Sin comentarios!
▶ vb hacer [26] comentarios ▷ The police have not commented on these rumours. La policía no ha hecho comentarios sobre estos rumores.

commentary n crónica f

commentator n comentarista mf

commercial adj comercial

commit vb **to commit a crime** cometer [8] un crimen; **to commit suicide** suicidarse [25]; **I don't want to commit myself.** No quiero comprometerme.

committee n comité m

common adj común (pl comunes) ▷ 'Smith' is a very common surname. 'Smith' es un apellido muy común.; **in common** en común ▷ We've got a lot in common. Tenemos mucho en común.

▶ *n* campo comunal *m* ▷ We went for a walk on the common. Dimos un paseo por el campo comunal.

Commons *npl* **the House of Commons** la Cámara de los Comunes

common sense *n* sentido común *m*

communicate *vb* comunicar [48]

communication *n* comunicación *f* (pl comunicaciones)

communion *n* comunión *f* (pl comuniones)

communism *n* comunismo *m*

communist *n* comunista *mf*
▶ *adj* comunista

community *n* comunidad *f*; **the local community** el vecindario; **community service** el trabajo comunitario

commute *vb* ▷ She commutes between Oxford and London. Para ir al trabajo se desplaza diariamente de Oxford a Londres.

compact disc *n* disco compacto *m*; **a compact disc player** un lector de discos compactos

company *n* ❶ empresa *f* ▷ He works for a big company. Trabaja para una empresa grande. ❷ compañía *f* ▷ an insurance company una compañía de seguros ▷ a theatre company una compañía de teatro; **to keep somebody company** hacerle [26] compañía a alguien

comparatively *adv* relativamente

compare *vb* comparar [25] ▷ People always compare him with his brother. La gente siempre lo compara con

su hermano.; **compared with** en comparación a ▷ Oxford is small compared with London. Oxford es pequeño en comparación a Londres.

comparison *n* comparación *f* (pl comparaciones)

compartment *n* compartimento *m*

compass *n* (showing direction) brújula *f*

compensation *n* indemnización *f* ▷ They got £2000 compensation. Recibieron 2.000 libras esterlinas de indemnización.

compete *vb* **to compete in** competir [38] en ▷ I'm competing in the marathon. Compito en el maratón.; **to compete for something** competir [38] por algo ▷ There are 50 students competing for 6 places. Hay 50 estudiantes compitiendo por 6 puestos.

competent *adj* competente

competition *n* ❶ concurso *m* ▷ a singing competition un concurso de canto ❷ competencia *f* ▷ Competition in the computer sector is fierce. La competencia en el sector de la informática es muy intensa.

competitive *adj* competitivo(-a)

competitor *n* ❶ (contestant) concursante *m* ❷ rival *mf*

complain *vb* reclamar [25] ▷ We're going to complain to the manager. Vamos a reclamar al director. ▷ quejarse [25] ▷ She's always complaining about her husband. Siempre se está quejando de su marido.

complaint n queja f
complete adj completo(-a)
completely adv completamente
complexion n cutis m (pl cutis)
complicated adj complicado(-a)
compliment n cumplido m ▷ to
pay somebody a compliment hacerle
un cumplido a alguien
   ▶ vb felicitar [**25**] ▷ They
complimented me on my Spanish.
Me felicitaron por mi español.
compose vb (music) componer
[**41**]; **to be composed of**
componerse [**41**] de
composer n compositor m,
compositora f
comprehension n (school
exercise) ejercicio de
comprensión m
comprehensive school n
instituto m
compulsory adj obligatorio(-a)
computer n ordenador m
(computador m, computadora f
LatAm)
computer game n juego de
ordenador m
computer programmer n
programador m, programadora f
computer science n
informática f
computing n informática f
concentrate vb concentrarse [**25**]
▷ I couldn't concentrate. No me
podía concentrar. ▷ I was
concentrating on my homework. Me
estaba concentrando en los
deberes.
concentration n
concentración f

concerned adj preocupado(-a)
▷ His mother is concerned about him.
Su madre está preocupada por él.;
**As far as the new project is
concerned** ... En lo que respecta al
nuevo proyecto ...; **As far as I'm
concerned, you can come any
time you like.** Por mí, puedes
venir cuando quieras.; **It's a
stressful situation for everyone
concerned.** Es una situación
estresante para todos los
involucrados.
concert n concierto m
concrete n hormigón m
condemn vb condenar [**25**]
condition n condición f (pl
condiciones) ▷ I'll do it, on one
condition. Lo haré, con una
condición.; **in good condition** en
buen estado
conditional n condicional m
conditioner n (for hair) suavizante
m (enjuague m LatAm)
condom n preservativo m
conduct vb (orchestra) dirigir [**16**]
conductor n ❶ (of orchestra)
director de orquesta m, directora
de orquesta f ❷ (on bus) cobrador
m, cobradora f
cone n ❶ cucurucho m ▷ an ice cream
cone un cucurucho ❷ (geometric
shape) cono m; **a traffic cone** un
cono para señalizar el tráfico
conference n conferencia f
confess vb confesar [**39**] ▷ He
confessed to the murder. Confesó
haber cometido el asesinato.
confession n confesión f (pl
confesiones)

confidence n ❶ confianza f ▷ I've got a lot of confidence in him. Tengo mucha confianza en él. ❷ confianza en sí mismo f ▷ She lacks confidence. Le falta confianza en sí misma.; **I told you that story in confidence.** Te conté esa historia de manera confidencial.

confident adj ❶ (sure of something) seguro(-a) ▷ I'm confident everything will be okay. Estoy seguro de que todo saldrá bien. ❷ (self-assured) seguro de sí mismo (f segura de sí misma) ▷ She seems quite confident. Parece muy segura de sí misma.

confidential adj confidencial

confirm vb confirmar [25]

confuse vb confundir [58]

confused adj (person) confuso(-a)

confusing adj poco claro(-a) ▷ The traffic signs are confusing. Las señales de tráfico están poco claras.

confusion n confusión f

congratulate vb felicitar [25] ▷ My friends congratulated me on passing my test. Mis amigos me felicitaron por aprobar el examen.

congratulations npl enhorabuena f ▷ Congratulations on your new job! ¡Enhorabuena por tu nuevo empleo!

conjunction n conjunción f (pl conjunciones)

conjurer n prestidigitador m, prestidigitadora f

connection n ❶ conexión f (pl conexiones) ▷ There's no connection between the two events. No hay ninguna conexión entre los dos

sucesos. ❷ enlace m ▷ We missed our connection. Perdimos el enlace.

conscience n conciencia f; **to have a guilty conscience** tener [53] remordimientos de conciencia

conscious adj consciente ▷ He was still conscious when the doctor arrived. Estaba todavía consciente cuando llegó el médico. ▷ She was conscious of Max looking at her. Era consciente de que Max la miraba.; **He made a conscious decision to tell nobody.** Tomó la firme decisión de no decírselo a nadie.

consciousness n conocimiento m ▷ I lost consciousness. Perdí el conocimiento.

consequence n consecuencia f

consequently adv por consiguiente

conservation n conservación f; **energy conservation** la conservación de la energía

Conservative n conservador m, conservadora f; **to vote Conservative** votar [25] a favor del partido Conservador

conservative adj conservador(a); **the Conservative Party** el partido Conservador

conservatory n invernadero m

consider vb ❶ considerar [25] ▷ He considers it a waste of time. Lo considera una pérdida de tiempo. ❷ pensar [39] en ▷ We considered cancelling our holiday. Pensamos en cancelar nuestras vacaciones.

considerate adj considerado(-a)

considering prep ❶ teniendo en cuenta ▷ Considering he was ill, he

ate well. Teniendo en cuenta que estaba enfermo, comió bien.
❷ **después de todo** ▷ I got a good mark, considering. Saqué buena nota, después de todo.

consist vb **to consist of** consistir [**58**] en

consonant n consonante f

constant adj constante

constantly adv constantemente

constipated adj estreñido(-a) ▷ I'm constipated. Estoy estreñido.
▌ Be careful not to translate **constipated** by **constipado**.

construct vb construir [**10**]

construction n construcción f (pl construcciones)

consult vb consultar [**25**]

consumer n consumidor m, consumidora f

contact n contacto m ▷ I'm in contact with her. Estoy en contacto con ella.
▶ vb ponerse [**41**] en contacto con ▷ Where can we contact you? ¿Dónde podemos ponernos en contacto contigo?

contact lenses npl lentillas fpl (lentes de contacto mpl LatAm)

contain vb contener [**53**]

container n recipiente m

contents npl contenido m

contest n competición f (pl competiciones) ▷ a fishing contest una competición de pesca; **a beauty contest** un concurso de belleza

contestant n concursante mf

context n contexto m

continent n continente m; **the Continent** el continente europeo

continental breakfast n desayuno continental m

continue vb continuar [**1**] ▷ She continued talking to her friend. Continuó hablando con su amiga.

continuous adj continuo(-a); **continuous assessment** la evaluación continua

contraceptive n anticonceptivo m

contract n contrato m

contradict vb contradecir [**15**]

contrary n on the contrary al contrario

contrast n contraste m

contribute vb **to contribute to** contribuir [**10**] a ▷ Everyone contributed to the success of the play. Todos contribuyeron al éxito de la obra. ▷ She contributed £10 to the collection. Contribuyó 10 libras esterlinas a la colecta.

contribution n contribución f (pl contribuciones)

control n control m; **to lose control** (of vehicle) perder [**20**] el control; **He always seems to be in control.** Parece que siempre está en control de la situación.; **She can't keep control of the class.** No sabe controlar a la clase.; **out of control** fuera de control ▷ That boy is out of control. Ese muchacho está fuera de control.
▶ vb controlar [**25**] ▷ He can't control the class. No sabe controlar a la clase. ▷ Please control yourself, everyone's looking at us. Por favor contrólate, todos nos están mirando.

controversial adj polémico(-a) ▷ Euthanasia is a controversial subject. La eutanasia es un tema polémico.

convenient adj (place) bien situado(-a) ▷ The hotel's convenient for the airport. El hotel está bien situado con respecto al aeropuerto.; **It's not a convenient time for me.** A esa hora no me va bien.; **Would Monday be convenient for you?** ¿Te iría bien el lunes?

conventional adj convencional

conversation n conversación f (pl conversaciones) ▷ We had a long conversation. Tuvimos una larga conversación.

convert vb convertir [51] ▷ We've converted the loft into a bedroom. Hemos convertido el desván en un dormitorio.

convict vb declarar [25] culpable ▷ He was convicted of the murder. Fue declarado culpable del asesinato.

convince vb convencer [12] ▷ I'm not convinced. No me convence.

cook vb ① cocinar [25] ▷ I can't cook. No sé cocinar.; **The chicken isn't cooked.** El pollo no está hecho. ② preparar [25] ▷ She's cooking lunch. Está preparando el almuerzo.
▶ n cocinero m, cocinera f ▷ She is a cook in a hotel. Es cocinera en un hotel. ▷ Mary's an excellent cook. Mary es una cocinera excelente.

cookbook n libro de cocina m

cooker n cocina f ▷ a gas cooker una cocina de gas

cookery n cocina f

cookie n (US) galleta f

cooking n cocina f ▷ French cooking la cocina francesa; **I like cooking.** Me gusta cocinar.

cool adj ① fresco(-a) ▷ a cool place un lugar fresco ② (very good) genial; **Cool!** ¡Genial!; **to stay cool** (keep calm) mantenerse [53] en calma ▷ He stayed cool throughout the crisis. Se mantuvo en calma durante toda la crisis.

cooperation n cooperación f

cop n poli mf (informal)

cope vb arreglárselas [25] ▷ It was hard, but we coped. Fue difícil, pero nos las arreglamos.; **She's got a lot of problems to cope with.** Tiene muchos problemas a los que hacer frente.

copper n ① cobre m ▷ a copper bracelet un brazalete de cobre ② (informal: police officer) poli mf

copy n ① (of letter, document) copia f ② (of book) ejemplar m
▶ vb copiar [25]; **to copy and paste** (computing) copiar [25] y pegar

core n (of fruit) corazón m (pl corazones)

cork n corcho m

corkscrew n sacacorchos m (pl sacacorchos)

corn n ① (wheat) trigo m ② (sweetcorn) maíz m; **corn on the cob** la mazorca de maíz

corner n ① esquina f ▷ the shop on the corner la tienda de la esquina ▷ He lives just round the corner. Vive a la vuelta de la esquina. ② rincón m (pl rincones) ▷ *in a corner of the room* en un rincón de la habitación ❸ (*in football*) saque de esquina m

cornflakes npl copos de maíz mpl

Cornwall n Cornualles m

corpse n cadáver m

correct adj correcto(-a) ▷ *That's correct!* ¡Correcto! ▷ *the correct answer* la respuesta correcta; **You're absolutely correct.** Tienes toda la razón.
▶ vb corregir [**18**]

correction n corrección f (pl correcciones)

correctly adv correctamente

corridor n pasillo m

corruption n corrupción f

cosmetics npl productos de belleza mpl

cost vb costar [**11**] ▷ *The meal cost £20.* La comida costó 20 libras esterlinas. ▷ *How much does it cost?* ¿Cuánto cuesta?
▶ n coste m (coste m LatAm) ▷ *the cost of living* el coste de vida; **at all costs** a toda costa

costume n traje m

cosy adj acogedor(a) ▷ *a cosy room* una habitación acogedora

cot n cuna f

cottage n chalet m (pl chalets)

cotton n algodón m ▷ *a cotton shirt* una camisa de algodón

cotton wool n algodón m

couch n sofá m (pl sofás)

cough vb toser [**8**]
▶ n tos f ▷ *I've got a cough.* Tengo tos.; **cough mixture** el jarabe para la tos

could vb see **can**

council n (in town) ayuntamiento m ▷ *He's on the council.* Es concejal del ayuntamiento.; **a council estate** un barrio de viviendas de protección oficial; **a council house** una casa de protección oficial

councillor n concejal m, concejala f

count vb contar [**11**]

count on vb contar [**11**] con ▷ *You can count on me.* Puedes contar conmigo.

counter n ❶ (in shop) mostrador m ❷ (in bank, post office) ventanilla f ❸ (in game) ficha f

country n ❶ país m ▷ *the border between the two countries* la frontera entre los dos países ❷ campo m ▷ *I live in the country.* Vivo en el campo.; **country dancing** la danza folklórica

countryside n campo m

county n condado m
   The nearest Spanish equivalent of a county would be a **provincia.**

couple n ❶ pareja f ▷ *the couple who live next door* la pareja que vive al lado ❷ par m ▷ *a couple of hours* un par de horas

courage n valor m

courgette n calabacín m (pl calabacines)

courier n ❶ (for tourists) guía mf ❷ (delivery service) servicio de mensajero m ▷ *They sent it by courier.* Lo enviaron por servicio de mensajero.

course n ❶ curso m ▷ *a Spanish course* un curso de español ▷ *to go* *on a course* hacer un curso ❷ *plato m* ▷ *the main course* el segundo plato ▷ *the first course* el primer plato ❸ *campo m* ▷ *a golf course* un campo de golf; *of course* por supuesto ▷ *Do you love me?* — *Of course I do!* ¿Me quieres? — ¡Por supuesto que te quiero!

court *n* (*of law*) tribunal *m*; **a tennis court** una pista de tenis (una cancha de tenis *LatAm*)

courtyard *n* patio *m*

cousin *n* primo *m*, prima *f*

cover *n* ❶ (*of book*) tapa *f* ❷ (*of duvet*) funda *f*
▶ *vb* cubrir [58] ▷ *My face was covered with mosquito bites.* Tenía la cara cubierta de picaduras de mosquito. ▷ *Our insurance didn't cover it.* Nuestro seguro no lo cubría.

cow *n* vaca *f*

coward *n* cobarde *mf*

cowboy *n* vaquero *m*

crab *n* cangrejo *m*

crack *n* ❶ (*in wall*) grieta *f* ❷ (*in cup, window*) raja *f* ❸ (*drug*) crack *m*; **He opened the door a crack.** Abrió la puerta un poquito.; **I'll have a crack at it.** Lo intentaré.
▶ *vb* (*nut, egg*) cascar [48]; **He cracked his head on the pavement.** Se dio con la cabeza en la acera.; **I think we've cracked it!** ¡Creo que lo hemos resuelto!; **to crack a joke** contar [11] un chiste

crack down on *vb* tomar [25] medidas severas contra

cracked *adj* ❶ (*cup, window*) rajado(-a) ❷ (*wall*) resquebrajado(-a)

cracker *n* (*biscuit*) galleta salada *f*; **Christmas cracker** el petardo sorpresa

craft *n* artesanía *f*; **a craft shop** una tienda de objetos de artesanía

crane *n* (*machine*) grúa *f*

crash *vb* chocar [48] ▷ *The two cars crashed.* Los dos coches chocaron.; **to crash into something** chocar [48] con algo; **He's crashed his car.** Ha tenido un accidente con el coche.; **The plane crashed.** El avión se estrelló.
▶ *n* accidente *m*; **a crash helmet** un casco protector; **a crash course** un curso intensivo

crawl *vb* (*baby*) gatear [25]
▶ *n* crol *m*; **to do the crawl** nadar [25] estilo crol

crazy *adj* loco(-a)

cream *adj* de color crema ▷ *a cream silk blouse* una blusa de seda de color crema
▶ *n* ❶ nata *f* (crema de leche *f LatAm*) ▷ *strawberries and cream* fresas con nata ▷ *a cream cake* un pastel de nata; **cream cheese** el queso cremoso ▷ (*for skin*) crema *f*

crease *n* ❶ (*in clothes, paper*) arruga *f* ❷ (*in trousers*) raya *f*

creased *adj* arrugado(-a)

create *vb* crear [25]

creative *adj* creativo(-a)

creature *n* criatura *f*

crèche *n* guardería infantil *f*

credit *n* crédito *m* ▷ *on credit* a crédito; **He's a credit to his family.** Hace honor a su familia.

credit card *n* tarjeta de crédito *f*

crew n (of plane, boat) tripulación f (pl tripulaciones); **a film crew** un equipo de rodaje

crew cut n pelo cortado al rape m

cricket n ❶ críquet m ▷ I play cricket. Juego al críquet. ❷ (insect) grillo m

crime n ❶ (offence) delito m ▷ He committed a crime. Cometió un delito. ❷ The scene of the crime el lugar del delito ❷ (very serious) crimen m (pl crímenes) ▷ a crime against humanity un crimen contra la humanidad ❸ (activity) delincuencia f ▷ Crime is rising. La delincuencia va en aumento.

criminal n delincuente mf
▶ adj **It's a criminal offence.** Constituye un delito.; **to have a criminal record** tener [53] antecedentes penales

crisis n crisis f (pl crisis)

crisp adj (food) crujiente

crisps npl patatas fritas fpl (papas fritas fpl LatAm) ▷ a bag of crisps una bolsa de patatas fritas

critical adj crítico(-a)

criticism n crítica f

criticize vb criticar [48]

Croatia n Croacia f

crochet vb hacer [26] ganchillo ▷ She enjoys crocheting. Le gusta hacer ganchillo.

crocodile n cocodrilo m

crook n sinvergüenza mf

crop n cosecha f ▷ a good crop of apples una buena cosecha de manzanas

cross n cruz f (pl cruces)
▶ adj enfadado(-a) (enojado

LatAm) ▷ He was cross about something. Estaba enfadado por algo.
▶ vb (road, river) cruzar [13]

cross out vb tachar [25]

cross-country n a cross-country race un cross; **cross-country skiing** el esquí de fondo

crossing n ❶ travesía f ▷ a 10-hour crossing una travesía de 10 horas ❷ (for pedestrians) paso de peatones m

crossroads n cruce m

crossword n crucigrama m

> Although **crucigrama** ends in -a, it is actually a masculine noun.

crouch down vb agacharse [25]

crow n cuervo m

crowd n ❶ muchedumbre f ❷ (at sports match) público m

crowded adj abarrotado de gente (f abarrotada de gente)

crown n corona f

crude adj vulgar ▷ crude language lenguaje vulgar; **crude oil** el petróleo en crudo

cruel adj cruel

cruise n crucero m

crumb n miga f

crush vb ❶ (box, fingers) aplastar [25] ❷ machacar [48] ▷ Crush two cloves of garlic. Machacar dos dientes de ajo.

crutch n muleta f

cry n grito m ▷ He gave a cry of pain. Dio un grito de dolor.; **She had a good cry.** Se dio una buena de llorar.
▶ vb ❶ llorar [25] ▷ The baby's

crying. El bebé está llorando.
② gritar **[25]** ▷ 'You're wrong,' he cried. 'No es cierto', gritó.

crystal n cristal m

cub n **①** (animal) cachorro m **②** (scout) lobato m

cube n **①** (geometric shape) cubo m **②** dado m ▷ Cut the meat into cubes. Cortar la carne en dados. **③** (of sugar) terrón m (pl terrones)

cubic adj **a cubic metre** un metro cúbico

cucumber n pepino m

cuddle vb abrazar **[13]**

cue n (for snooker, pool) taco m

culture n cultura f

cunning adj **①** (person) astuto(-a) **②** ingenioso(-a) ▷ a cunning plan un plan ingenioso

cup n **①** taza f ▷ a china cup una taza de porcelana; **a cup of coffee** un café **②** (trophy) copa f

cupboard n armario m

cure vb curar **[25]**
▶ n cura f ▷ There is no simple cure for the common cold. No hay una cura sencilla para el catarro común.

curious adj curioso(-a); **to be curious about something** sentir **[51]** curiosidad por algo

curl n rizo m

curly adj rizado(-a)

currant n pasa f

currency n moneda f ▷ foreign currency la moneda extranjera

current n corriente f ▷ The current is very strong. La corriente es muy fuerte.
▶ adj **①** actual ▷ the current situation la situación actual **②** presente

▷ the current financial year el presente año financiero

current affairs npl temas de actualidad mpl

curriculum n plan de estudios m

curriculum vitae n currículum vitae m

curry n curry m (pl curries)

curtain n cortina f

cushion n cojín m (pl cojines)

custard n natillas fpl

custody n custodia f ▷ The mother has custody of the children. La madre tiene la custodia de los hijos.; **to be remanded in custody** estar **[22]** detenido

custom n costumbre f ▷ It's an old custom. Es una vieja costumbre.

customer n cliente m, clienta f

customs npl aduana f; **to go through customs** pasar **[25]** por la aduana

customs officer n oficial de aduanas mf

cut n **①** corte m ▷ He's got a cut on his forehead. Tiene un corte en la frente. **②** (in price, spending) reducción f (pl reducciones)
▶ vb **①** cortar **[25]** ▷ I'll cut some bread. Voy a cortar pan. ▷ I cut my foot on a piece of glass. Me corté el pie con un cristal.; **to cut oneself** cortarse **[25]** **②** (price, spending) reducir **[9]**

cut down vb cortar **[25]** ▷ She cut down the elm tree. Cortó el olmo.

cut off vb cortar **[25]** ▷ The electricity has been cut off. Han cortado la electricidad. ▷ We've been cut off. Se ha cortado la comunicación.

cut up vb (vegetables, meat) picar [**48**]

cute adj (baby, pet) mono(-a) ▷ Isn't he cute! ¡Qué mono es!

cutlery n cubertería f

CV n currículum vitae m

cyberbullying n ciberacoso m

cycle vb ir [**27**] en bicicleta ▷ I cycle to school. Voy al colegio en bicicleta.
▶ n bicicleta f ▷ a cycle ride un paseo en bicicleta

cycle lane n carril-bici m

cycling n ciclismo m; **The roads round here are ideal for cycling.** Las carreteras de por aquí son ideales para ir en bicicleta.

cyclist n ciclista mf

cylinder n cilindro m

Cyprus n Chipre f

Czech n ❶ (person) checo m, checa f ▷ the Czechs los checos ❷ (language) checo m
▶ adj checo(-a); **the Czech Republic** la República Checa

d

dad n ❶ padre m ▷ my dad mi padre ❷ papá ▷ I'll ask Dad. Se lo preguntaré a papá.

daffodil n narciso m

daft adj estúpido(-a)

daily adj, adv ❶ diario(-a) ▷ daily life la vida diaria ▷ It's part of my daily routine. Forma parte de mi rutina diaria.; **a daily paper** un periódico ❷ todos los días ▷ The pool is open daily. La piscina abre todos los días.

dairy products npl productos lácteos mpl

daisy n margarita f

dam n presa f

damage n daños mpl ▷ The storm did a lot of damage. La tormenta provocó muchos daños.
▶ vb dañar [**25**]

damn n **I don't give a damn!** ¡Me importa un rábano! (informal); **Damn!** (informal) ¡Maldita sea!

damp adj húmedo(-a)

dance n baile m
▷ vb bailar [**25**]

dancer n ❶ bailador m, bailadora f; **He is not a very good dancer.** No baila muy bien. ❷ (professional) bailarín m (pl bailarines), bailarina f

dandruff n caspa f

Dane n ❶ (pl daneses), danesa f ▷ the Danes los daneses

danger n peligro m; **in danger** en peligro; **We were in danger of missing the plane.** Corríamos el riesgo de perder el avión.

dangerous adj peligroso(-a)

Danish adj danés (f danesa, pl daneses)
▷ n (language) danés m

dare vb atreverse [**8**] ▷ I didn't dare to tell my parents. No me atrevía a decírselo a mis padres.; **Don't you dare!** ¡Ni se te ocurra!; **I dare you!** ¡A que no te atreves!

daring adj atrevido(-a)

dark adj oscuro(-a) ▷ a dark green sweater un jersey verde oscuro ▷ It's dark in here. Está oscuro aquí dentro.; **She's got dark hair.** Tiene el pelo oscuro.; **He's got dark skin.** Tiene la piel morena.; **It's getting dark.** Está oscureciendo.
▷ n oscuridad f ▷ I'm afraid of the dark. Me da miedo la oscuridad.

darkness n oscuridad f ▷ in the darkness en la oscuridad; **The room was in darkness.** La habitación estaba a oscuras.

darling n cariño ▷ Thank you, darling. Gracias, cariño.

dart n dardo m ▷ to play darts jugar a los dardos

data npl datos mpl

database n base de datos f

date n ❶ fecha f ▷ my date of birth mi fecha de nacimiento; **What's the date today?** ¿A qué estamos hoy?; **He's got a date with his girlfriend.** Ha quedado con su novia.; **out of date** (1) (document) caducado ▷ My passport's out of date. Tengo el pasaporte caducado. (2) (idea) anticuado ❷ (fruit) dátil m

daughter n hija f

daughter-in-law n nuera f

dawn n amanecer m ▷ at dawn al amanecer

day n día m

> Although **día** ends in **-a**, it is actually a masculine noun.

▷ during the day por el día ▷ It's a lovely day. Hace un día precioso. ▷ every day todos los días; **the day after tomorrow** pasado mañana; **the day before yesterday** anteayer; **a day off** un día libre; **a day return** un billete de ida y vuelta para el día

dead adj muerto(-a) ▷ He was dead. Estaba muerto.; **He was shot dead.** Lo mataron de un tiro.
▷ adv **You're dead right!** ¡Tienes toda la razón!; **It was dead easy.** Fue facilísimo.; **dead on time** a la hora exacta

dead end n callejón sin salida m

deadline n **October is the deadline for applications.** El plazo para presentar las solicitudes se acaba en octubre.

deaf adj sordo(-a)

deafening adj ensordecedor(a)

deal n trato m ▷ *He made a deal with the kidnappers.* Hizo un trato con los secuestradores.; **It's a deal!** ¡Trato hecho!; **Big deal!** ¡Vaya cosa!; **It's no big deal.** No pasa nada.; **a great deal** mucho ▷ *a great deal of money* mucho dinero ▶ vb dar [**14**] cartas ▷ *It's your turn to deal.* Te toca dar cartas.

dealer n **a drug dealer** un traficante de drogas (f una traficante de drogas); **an antique dealer** un anticuario (f una anticuaria)

dealt vb see **deal**

dear adj ❶ querido(-a) ▷ *Dear Paul* Querido Paul; **Dear Mrs Smith** Estimada señora Smith; **Dear Sir** Muy señor mío; **Dear Madam** Estimada señora; **Dear Sir/ Madam** (*in a letter*) Estimados Sres.; **Oh dear! I've spilled my coffee.** ¡Oh, no! He derramado el café. ❷ (*expensive*) caro(-a) ▷ *These shoes are too dear.* Estos zapatos son demasiado caros.

death n muerte f ▷ *after his death* después de su muerte; **I was bored to death.** Estaba aburrido como una ostra.

debate n debate m ▶ vb discutir [**58**]

debt n deuda f ▷ *heavy debts* grandes deudas; **to be in debt** estar [**22**] endeudado

decade n década f

decaffeinated adj descafeinado(-a)

deceive vb engañar [**25**]

December n diciembre m; **in December** en diciembre; **on 22 December** el 22 de diciembre

decent adj decente

decide vb ❶ decidir [**58**] ▷ *I decided to write to her.* Decidí escribirle. ❷ decidirse [**58**] ▷ *Haven't you decided yet?* ¿Aún no te has decidido?

decimal adj decimal; **a decimal point** una coma decimal

decision n decisión f (pl decisiones); **to make a decision** tomar [**25**] una decisión

deck n ❶ (*of ship*) cubierta f; **on deck** en cubierta ❷ (*of bus*) piso m; **a deck of cards** una baraja

deckchair n tumbona f

declare vb declarar [**25**]

decorate vb ❶ decorar [**25**] ▷ *I decorated the cake with glacé cherries.* Decoré el pastel con guindas confitadas. ❷ (*paint*) pintar [**25**] ❸ (*wallpaper*) empapelar [**25**]

decrease n disminución f (pl disminuciones) ▷ *There has been a decrease in the school roll.* Ha habido una disminución en el número de alumnos. ▶ vb disminuir [**10**]

deduct vb descontar [**11**]

deep adj ❶ profundo(-a); **a hole four metres deep** un agujero de cuatro metros de profundidad;

How deep is the lake? ¿Qué profundidad tiene el lago? ❷ espeso(-a) ▷ *a deep layer of snow* una espesa capa de nieve ❸ grave ▷ He's got a deep voice. Tiene la voz grave.; **to take a deep breath** respirar [25] hondo; **to be deep in debt** estar [22] hasta el cuello de deudas

deeply *adv* profundamente ▷ *deeply grateful* profundamente agradecido

deer *n* ciervo *m*

defeat *n* derrota *f*
  ▶*vb* derrotar [25]

defect *n* defecto *m*

defence *n* defensa *f*

defend *vb* defender [20]

defender *n* ❶ (of person, ideas) defensor *m*, defensora *f* ❷ (in sports) defensa *mf*

define *vb* definir [58]

definite *adj* ❶ concreto(-a) ▷ *I haven't got any definite plans.* No tengo planes concretos. ❷ definitivo(-a) ▷ *It's too soon to give a definite answer.* Es pronto aún para dar una respuesta definitiva. ❸ seguro(-a) ▷ *Maybe we'll go to Spain, but it's not definite.* Quizá vayamos a España, pero no es seguro.; **He was definite about it.** Fue rotundo acerca de esto. ❹ claro(-a) ▷ *It's a definite improvement.* Es una clara mejoría.

definitely *adv* sin duda ▷ *He's definitely the best player.* Es sin duda el mejor jugador.; **He's the best player. — Definitely!** Es el mejor jugador. — ¡Desde luego!; **Are you**

going out with him? — Definitely not! ¿Vas a salir con él? — ¡En absoluto!

definition *n* definición *f* (*pl* definiciones)

degree *n* ❶ (measure of temperature) grado *m* ▷ *a temperature of 30 degrees* una temperatura de 30 grados ❷ (from university) licenciatura *f* ▷ *a degree in English* una licenciatura en filología inglesa; **She's got a degree in English.** Es licenciada en filología inglesa.

delay *vb* retrasar [25] ▷ *We decided to delay our departure.* Decidimos retrasar la salida.; **to be delayed** retrasarse [25] ▷ *Our flight was delayed.* Nuestro vuelo se retrasó.
  ▶*n* retraso *m* ▷ *The tests have caused some delay.* Las pruebas han ocasionado algún retraso.

delete *vb* suprimir [58]

deliberate *adj* intencionado(-a)

deliberately *adv* a propósito

delicate *adj* delicado(-a)

delicatessen *n* charcutería *f*

delicious *adj* delicioso(-a)

delight *n* placer *m*

delighted *adj* encantado(-a) ▷ *He'll be delighted to see you.* Estará encantado de verte.

deliver *vb* ❶ repartir [58] ▷ *I deliver newspapers.* Reparto periódicos. ❷ entregar [37] ▷ *The package was delivered in the morning.* Entregaron el paquete por la mañana.; **Doctor Hamilton delivered the twins.** El Doctor Hamilton asistió en el parto de los gemelos.

delivery n ❶ entrega f ▷ *Allow 28 days for delivery.* La entrega se realizará en un plazo de 28 días. ❷ *(of baby)* parto m

demand vb exigir [16] ▷ *I demand an explanation.* Exijo una explicación. ▶ n ❶ *(firm request)* petición f *(pl* peticiones) ▷ *His demand for compensation was rejected.* Rechazaron su petición de indemnización. ❷ *(of trade union)* reivindicación f *(pl* reivindicaciones) ● demanda f ▷ *Demand for coal is down.* Ha bajado la demanda de carbón.

democracy n democracia f

democratic adj democrático(-a)

demolish vb derribar [25]

demonstrate vb ❶ demostrar [11] ▷ *You have to demonstrate that you are reliable.* Tienes que demostrar que se puede confiar en ti.; **She demonstrated the technique.** Hizo una demostración de la técnica. ❷ manifestarse [39] ▷ *They demonstrated outside the court.* Se manifestaron a las puertas del tribunal.

demonstration n ❶ *(of method, product)* demostración f *(pl* demostraciones) ❷ *(protest)* manifestación f *(pl* manifestaciones)

demonstrator n manifestante mf

denim n a denim jacket una cazadora vaquera

Denmark n Dinamarca f

dense adj ❶ *(smoke, fog)* denso(-a) ❷ *(vegetation)* espeso(-a)

dent n abolladura f
▶ vb abollar [25]

dental adj dental ▷ *dental treatment* el tratamiento dental; **a dental appointment** una cita con el dentista; **dental floss** la seda dental

dentist n dentista mf ▷ *Catherine is a dentist.* Catherine es dentista. ▷ *at the dentist's* en el dentista

deny vb negar [34] ▷ *She denied everything.* Lo negó todo.

deodorant n desodorante m

depart vb ❶ *(person)* partir [58] ▷ *He departed at three o'clock precisely.* Partió a las tres en punto. ❷ salir [49] ▷ *Trains depart for the airport every hour.* Los trenes salen para el aeropuerto cada media hora.

department n ❶ sección f *(pl* secciones) ▷ *the toy department* la sección de juguetes ❷ *(in school)* departamento m ▷ *the English department* el departamento de inglés

department store n grandes almacenes mpl

departure n salida f ▷ *The departure of this flight has been delayed.* Se ha retrasado la salida de este vuelo.

departure lounge n sala de embarque f

depend vb to depend on depender [8] de ▷ *The price depends on the quality.* El precio depende de la calidad.; **You can depend on him.** Puedes confiar en él.; **depending on** según

▌ **según** has to be followed by a verb in the subjunctive.

▷ *depending on the weather* según el

tiempo que haga; **It depends.** Depende.

deposit n ❶ (on hired goods) depósito m ▷ You get the deposit back when you return the bike. Al devolver la bici te devuelven el depósito. ❷ (advance payment) señal f ▷ You have to pay a deposit when you book. Se paga una señal al hacer la reserva. ❸ (in house buying) entrada f ▷ He paid a £2000 deposit on the house. Dio una entrada de 2.000 libras para la casa.

depressed adj deprimido(-a) ▷ I'm feeling depressed. Estoy deprimido.

depressing adj deprimente

depth n profundidad f ▷ 14 feet in depth 14 pies de profundidad

deputy head n subdirector m, subdirectora f

descend vb descender [20]

describe vb describir [58]

description n descripción f (pl descripciones)

desert n desierto m

desert island n isla desierta f

deserve vb merecer [12]

design n ❶ (of aircraft, equipment) diseño m ▷ The design of the plane makes it safer. El diseño del avión lo hace más seguro. ▷ a design fault un fallo en el diseño ❷ (pattern) motivo m ▷ a geometric design un motivo geométrico; **fashion design** diseño de modas
▶ vb ❶ diseñar [25] ▷ She designed the dress herself. Ella misma diseñó el vestido. ❷ elaborar [25] ▷ We will

design an exercise plan specially for you. Elaboraremos un programa de ejercicios especial para ti.

designer n (of clothes) modista mf; **designer clothes** la ropa de diseño

desire n deseo m
▶ vb desear [25]

desk n ❶ (in office) escritorio m ❷ (for pupil) pupitre m ❸ (in hotel, at airport) mostrador m

desktop n (computer) ordenador de sobremesa m (computadora de escritorio f LatAm)

despair n desesperación f ▷ a feeling of despair un sentimiento de desesperación; **to be in despair** estar [22] desesperado

desperate adj desesperado(-a) ▷ a desperate situation una situación desesperada; **I was starting to get desperate.** Estaba empezando a desesperarme.

desperately adv ❶ tremendamente ▷ We're desperately worried. Estamos tremendamente preocupados. ❷ desesperadamente ▷ He was desperately trying to persuade her. Intentaba desesperadamente convencerla.

despise vb despreciar [25]

despite prep a pesar de

dessert n postre m ▷ for dessert de postre

destination n destino m

destroy vb destruir [10]

destruction n destrucción f

detached house n casa no adosada f

detail n detalle m ▷ I can't remember the details. No recuerdo los detalles.; **in detail** detalladamente

detailed adj detallado(-a)

detective n detective mf ▷ He's a detective. Es detective. ▷ a private detective un detective privado; **a detective story** una novela policíaca

detention n to get a detention quedarse [25] castigado después de clase

detergent n detergente m

determined adj decidido(-a) ▷ She's determined to succeed. Está decidida a triunfar.

detour n desvío m

devastated adj deshecho(-a) ▷ I was devastated when they told me. Cuando me lo dijeron me quedé deshecho.

develop vb ❶ (idea, quality) desarrollar [25] ▷ I developed his original idea. Yo desarrollé su idea original. ❷ desarrollarse [25] ▷ Girls develop faster than boys. Las chicas se desarrollan más rápido que los chicos. ❸ revelar [25] ▷ to get a film developed revelar un carrete; **to develop into** convertirse [52] en ▷ The argument developed into a fight. La discusión se convirtió en una pelea.

development n desarrollo m ▷ economic development in Pakistan el desarrollo económico de Pakistán; **the latest developments** los últimos acontecimientos

devil n diablo m

devoted adj (friend) leal; **a devoted wife** una abnegada esposa; **He's completely devoted to her.** Está totalmente entregado a ella.

diabetes n diabetes f

diabetic adj diabético(-a) ▷ I'm diabetic. Soy diabético.

diagonal adj diagonal

diagram n diagrama m

■ Although **diagrama** ends in **-a**, it is actually a masculine noun.

dial vb marcar [48] (discar [48] LatAm)

dialling tone n señal de marcar f

dialogue n diálogo m

diamond n diamante m ▷ a diamond ring un anillo de diamantes; **diamonds** (at cards) los diamantes ▷ the ace of diamonds el as de diamantes

diaper n (US) pañal m

diarrhoea n diarrea f ▷ to have diarrhoea tener diarrea

diary n ❶ agenda f ▷ I've got her phone number in my diary. Tengo su número de teléfono en la agenda. ❷ diario m ▷ I keep a diary. Estoy escribiendo un diario.

dice n dado m

dictation n dictado m

dictionary n diccionario m

did vb see do

die vb morir [32] ▷ He died last year. Murió el año pasado. ▷ She's dying. Se está muriendo.; **to be dying to do something** morirse [32] de ganas de hacer algo

diesel n ❶ (fuel) gasoil m ❷ (car) coche diesel m

diet n ❶ dieta f ▷ a healthy diet una dieta sana ❷ régimen m

(pl regímenes.) ▷ I'm on a diet. Estoy a régimen.; **a diet Coke®** una Coca-Cola light®
▶vb hacer [**26**] régimen

difference n diferencia f ▷ There's not much difference in age between us. No hay mucha diferencia de edad entre nosotros.; **Good weather makes all the difference.** Con buen tiempo la cosa cambia mucho.; **It makes no difference.** Da lo mismo.

different adj distinto(-a)

difficult adj difícil ▷ It was difficult to choose. Era difícil escoger.

difficulty n dificultad f ▷ What's the difficulty? ¿Cuál es la dificultad?; **to have difficulty doing something** tener [**53**] dificultades para hacer algo

dig vb ❶ cavar [**25**] ▷ They're digging a hole in the road. Están cavando un hoyo en la calle. ❷ escarbar [**25**] ▷ The dog dug a hole in the sand. El perro escarbó un agujero en la arena.

digestion n digestión f

digital camera n cámara digital f

digital television n televisión digital f

digital watch n reloj digital m (pl relojes digitales)

dim adj ❶ (light) tenue ❷ (person) lerdo(-a)

dimension n dimensión f (pl dimensiones)

din n ❶ (of traffic, machinery) estruendo m ❷ (of crowd, voices) jaleo m

diner n (US) restaurante barato m

dinghy n **a rubber dinghy** una lancha neumática

dining room n comedor m

dinner n ❶ (at midday) comida f ❷ (in the evening) cena f (comida f LatAm); **The children have dinner at school.** Los niños comen en la escuela.

dinner jacket n esmoquin m (pl esmóquines)

dinner party n cena f

dinner time n ❶ (at midday) hora de la comida f ❷ (in the evening) hora de la cena f

dinosaur n dinosaurio m

diploma n diploma m

Although diploma ends in **-a**, it is actually a masculine noun.

direct adj, adv directo(-a) ▷ the most direct route el camino más directo; **You can't fly to Manchester direct from Seville.** No hay vuelos directos a Manchester desde Sevilla.
▶vb dirigir [**16**]

direction n dirección f (pl direcciones) ▷ We're going in the wrong direction. Vamos en la dirección equivocada.; **to ask somebody for directions** preguntar [**25**] el camino a alguien

director n director m, directora f

directory n ❶ (telephone) guía telefónica f; **directory enquiries** información telefónica ❷ (in computing) directorio m

dirt n suciedad f

dirty adj sucio(-a) ▷ It's dirty. Está sucio.; **to get dirty** ensuciarse [**25**]; **to get something dirty**

a
b
c
d
e
f
g
h
i
j
k
l
m
n
o
p
q
r
s
t
u
v
w
x
y
z

ensuciarse [25] algo ▷ He got his hands dirty. Se ensució las manos.

disabled adj, n discapacitado(-a); **disabled people** los discapacitados

disadvantage n desventaja f; **to be at a disadvantage** estar [22] en desventaja

disagree vb He disagrees with me. No está de acuerdo conmigo.

disagreement n desacuerdo m

disappear vb desaparecer [12]

disappearance n desaparición f (pl desapariciones)

disappointed adj decepcionado(-a) ▷ I'm disappointed. Estoy decepcionado.

disappointment n decepción f (pl decepciones)

disaster n desastre m

disastrous adj desastroso(-a)

disc n disco m

discipline n disciplina f

disc jockey n discjockey mf (pl discjockeys) ▷ He's a disc jockey. Es discjockey.

disco n ❶ (place) discoteca f ❷ (occasion) baile m ▷ There's a disco at school tonight. Esta noche hay baile en la escuela.

disconnect vb (appliance) desconectar [25]; **to disconnect the water supply** cortar [25] el agua

discount n descuento m ▷ a 20% discount un descuento del 20 por ciento

discourage vb (dishearten) desanimar [25]; **to get discouraged** desanimarse [25]

discover vb descubrir [58]

discrimination n discriminación f ▷ racial discrimination la discriminación racial

discuss vb ❶ discutir [58] ▷ I'll discuss it with my parents. Lo discutiré con mis padres. ❷ (topic) discutir [58] sobre ▷ We discussed the topic at length. Discutimos sobre el tema largo y tendido.

discussion n discusión f (pl discusiones)

disease n enfermedad f

disgraceful adj vergonzoso(-a)

disgusted adj indignado(-a) ▷ I was completely disgusted. Estaba totalmente indignado.

◼ Be careful not to translate **disgusted** by disgustado.

disgusting adj ❶ (food, smell) asqueroso(-a) ▷ It looks disgusting. Tiene un aspecto asqueroso. ❷ (disgraceful) indignante ▷ That's disgusting! ¡Es indignante!

dish n plato m ▷ a china dish un plato de porcelana ▷ a vegetarian dish un plato vegetariano; **to do the dishes** fregar [34] los platos; **a satellite dish** una antena parabólica

dishonest adj poco honrado(-a)

dish soap n (US) lavavajillas m (pl lavavajillas)

dishwasher n lavaplatos m (pl lavaplatos)

disinfectant n desinfectante m

disk n disco m; **the hard disk** el disco duro

dislike vb I dislike it. No me gusta.

dismiss vb (employee) despedir [38]

disobedient adj desobediente

display n **The assistant took the watch out of the display.** El dependiente sacó el reloj de la vitrina.; **There was a lovely display of fruit in the window.** Había un estupendo surtido de fruta en el escaparate.; **to be on display** estar [**22**] expuesto; **a firework display** fuegos artificiales
▸ vb ❶ mostrar [**11**] ▷ She proudly displayed her medal. Mostró con orgullo su medalla. ❷ (in shop window) exponer [**41**]

disposable adj desechable ▷ a disposable razor una maquinilla desechable

disqualify vb descalificar [**48**]; **to be disqualified** ser [**52**] descalificado ▷ They were disqualified from the competition. Fueron descalificados del campeonato.

disrupt vb interrumpir [**58**]

dissolve vb disolver [**33**]

distance n distancia f ▷ a distance of forty kilometres una distancia de cuarenta kilómetros.; **It's within walking distance.** Se puede ir andando.; **in the distance** a lo lejos

distant adj lejano(-a) ▷ in the distant future en un futuro lejano

distract vb distraer [**54**]

distribute vb distribuir [**10**]

district n ❶ (of town) barrio m ❷ (of country) región f (pl regiones)

disturb vb molestar [**25**] ▷ I'm sorry to disturb you. Siento molestarte.

ditch n zanja f
▸ vb dejar [**25**] ▷ She's just ditched her boyfriend. Acaba de dejar al novio.

dive n ❶ (into water) salto de cabeza m ❷ (under water) buceo m
▸ vb ❶ (into water) tirarse [**25**] de cabeza ❷ (under water) bucear [**25**]

diver n buzo mf

diversion n (for traffic) desvío m

Be careful not to translate **diversion** by **diversión**.

divide vb ❶ dividir [**58**] ▷ Divide the pastry in half. Divide la masa en dos.; **12 divided by 3 is 4.** 12 dividido entre 3 es 4. ❷ dividirse [**58**] ▷ We divided into two groups. Nos dividimos en dos grupos.

diving n ❶ (under water) buceo m ▷ diving equipment equipo de buceo ❷ (into water) salto de trampolín m ▷ a diving competition una competición de saltos de trampolín

division n división f (pl divisiones)

divorce n divorcio m

divorced adj divorciado(-a) ▷ My parents are divorced. Mis padres están divorciados.; **to get divorced** divorciarse [**25**]

DIY n bricolaje m ▷ a DIY shop una tienda de bricolaje

dizzy adj **I feel dizzy.** Estoy mareado.

DJ n discjockey mf (pl discjockeys) ▷ He's a DJ. Es discjockey.

do vb ❶ hacer [**26**] ▷ What are you doing this evening? ¿Qué vas a hacer esta noche? ▷ She did it by herself. Lo hizo ella sola. ▷ I'll do my best. Haré todo lo que pueda. ▷ *I want to do physics at university.* Quiero hacer física en la universidad.; **What does your father do?** ¿A qué se dedica tu padre? ❷ **ir [27]** ▷ *She's doing well at school.* Va bien en el colegio.; **How are you doing?** ¿Qué tal?; **How do you do?** Mucho gusto. ❸ **valer [55]** ▷ *It's not very good, but it'll do.* No es muy bueno, pero valdrá. ▷ *Will £10 do?* ¿Valdrá con diez libras?; **That'll do, thanks.** Así está bien, gracias.

▌ 'do' is not translated when used to form questions. ▷ *Do you speak English?* ¿Hablas inglés? ▷ *Do you like reading?* ¿Te gusta leer? ▷ *Where does he live?* ¿Dónde vive? ▷ *Where did you go for your holidays?* ¿Dónde te fuiste de vacaciones?

▌ Use 'no' in negative sentences for 'don't'.
▷ *I don't understand.* No entiendo. ▷ *You didn't tell me anything.* No me dijiste nada. ▷ *He didn't come.* No vino. ▷ *Why didn't you come?* ¿Por qué no viniste?

▌ 'do' is not translated when it is used in place of another verb.
▷ *I hate maths.* — *So do I.* Odio las matemáticas. — Yo también. ▷ *I didn't like the film.* — *Neither did I.* No me gustó la película. — A mí tampoco. ▷ *Do you speak English?* — *Yes, I do.* ¿Hablas inglés? — Sí. ▷ *Do you like horses?* — *No, I don't.* ¿Te gustan los caballos? — No.

▌ Use **¿no?** or **¿verdad?** to check information.

▷ *You go swimming on Fridays, don't you?* Los viernes vas a nadar, ¿no? ▷ *It doesn't matter, does it?* No importa, ¿verdad?

do up vb ❶ (shoes) atarse **[25]** ▷ *Do up your shoes!* ¡Átate los zapatos! ❷ (shirt, cardigan, coat) abrocharse **[25]** ▷ *Do up your coat.* Abróchate el abrigo.; **Do up your zip!** ¡Súbete la cremallera! ❸ (house, room) reformar **[25]**

do without vb pasar **[25]** sin ▷ *I can't do without my computer.* Yo no puedo pasar sin el ordenador.

doctor n médico m, médica f ▷ *He's a doctor.* Es médico. ▷ *at the doctor's* en el médico

document n documento m

documentary n documental m

dodge vb (attacker, blow) esquivar **[25]**

dodgems npl coches de choque mpl

does vb see **do**

doesn't = **does not**

dog n perro m ▷ *Have you got a dog?* ¿Tienes perro?

do-it-yourself n bricolaje m

dole n subsidio de paro m; **He's on the dole.** Está parado.; **to go on the dole** quedarse **[25]** parado

doll n muñeca f

dollar n dólar m

dolphin n delfín m (pl delfines)

dominoes npl **to have a game of dominoes** echar **[25]** una partida al dominó

donate vb donar **[25]**

done adj listo(-a) ▷ *Is the pasta done?* ¿Está lista la pasta?; **How do you**

like your steak? — Well done. ¿Cómo quieres el filete? — Muy hecho.

donkey n burro m

don't = **do not**

door n puerta f

doorbell n timbre m

doorstep n peldaño de la puerta m; **on my doorstep** en mi puerta

dormitory n dormitorio m

dot n punto m; **on the dot** en punto ▷ He arrived at nine on the dot. Llegó a las nueve en punto.

double vb ❶ doblar [**25**] ▷ They doubled their prices. Doblaron los precios. ❷ doblarse [**25**] ▷ The number of attacks has doubled. El número de agresiones se ha doblado.

▶ adj, adv doble ▷ a double helping una ración doble ▷ to cost the double costar el doble; **double bed** la cama de matrimonio; **a double room** una habitación doble

double bass n contrabajo m

double-click vb hacer [**26**] doble clic ▷ to double-click on an icon hacer doble clic en un icono

double-decker bus n autobús de dos pisos m

double glazing n doble acristalamiento m

doubles npl (in tennis) dobles mpl ▷ to play mixed doubles jugar un partido de dobles mixtos

doubt n duda f ▷ I have my doubts. Tengo mis dudas.; **no doubt** sin duda ▷ as you no doubt know como sin duda sabrá

▶ vb dudar [**25**] ▷ I doubt it. Lo dudo.

Use the subjunctive after **dudar que**.

▷ I doubt that he'll agree. Dudo que vaya a estar de acuerdo.

doubtful adj dudoso(-a) ▷ It's doubtful. Es dudoso.; **to be doubtful about doing something** no estar [**22**] seguro de hacer algo ▷ I'm doubtful about going by myself. No estoy seguro de ir solo.; **You sound doubtful.** No pareces muy convencido.

dough n masa f

doughnut n buñuelo m ▷ a jam doughnut un buñuelo de mermelada

down adj, adv, prep ❶ abajo ▷ His office is down on the first floor. Su despacho está abajo en el primer piso. ▷ It's down there. Está allí abajo. ❷ al suelo ▷ He threw down his racket. Tiró la raqueta al suelo.; **They live just down the road.** Viven más adelante en esta calle.; **to feel down** estar [**22**] desanimado; **The computer's down.** El ordenador no funciona.

download vb bajarse [**25**] ▷ to download something from the internet bajarse algo de Internet

downstairs adv, adj ❶ abajo ▷ The bathroom's downstairs. El baño está abajo.; **to go downstairs** bajar [**25**] ❷ de abajo ▷ the downstairs bathroom el baño de abajo; **the neighbours downstairs** los vecinos de abajo

downtown adv (US) ❶ (go, come) al centro de la ciudad ❷ (live, be) en el centro de la ciudad

a b c d e f g h i j k l m n o p q r s t u v w x y z

doze vb dormitar [25]

doze off vb quedarse [25] dormido

dozen n docena f ▷ a dozen eggs una docena de huevos ▷ two dozen dos docenas; **I've told you that dozens of times.** Te lo he dicho cientos de veces.

draft n (US) corriente de aire f

drag vb (thing, person) arrastrar [25] ▷ n **It's a real drag!** ¡Es una verdadera lata! (informal)

dragon n dragón m (pl dragones)

drain n ❶ (of house) desagüe m ❷ (in street) alcantarilla f ▷ vb (vegetables, pasta) escurrir [58]

drama n ❶ (play) drama m

> Although **drama** ends in -a, it is actually a masculine noun.

▷ a TV drama un drama para televisión ❷ teatro m ▷ Drama is my favourite subject. Mi asignatura favorita es teatro.; **drama school** la escuela de arte dramático

dramatic adj espectacular ▷ a dramatic improvement una espectacular mejoría

drank vb see **drink**

drapes npl (US) cortinas fpl

draught n corriente de aire f ▷ There's a draught from the window. Entra corriente por la ventana.

draughts n damas fpl ▷ to play draughts jugar a las damas

draw n ❶ empate m ▷ The game ended in a draw. El partido terminó en empate. ❷ (of lottery) sorteo m ▷ vb ❶ (a scene, a person) dibujar [25]; **to draw a picture** hacer [26] un dibujo; **to draw a picture of somebody** hacer [26] un retrato

de alguien; **to draw a line** trazar [13] una línea ❷ empatar [25] ▷ We drew two all. Empatamos a dos.; **to draw the curtains (1)** (open) descorrer [8] las cortinas **(2)** (close) correr [8] las cortinas

drawback n inconveniente m

drawer n cajón m (pl cajones)

drawing n dibujo m; **He's good at drawing.** Se le da bien dibujar.

drawing pin n chincheta f

drawn vb see **draw**

dreadful adj ❶ terrible ▷ a dreadful mistake un terrible error ❷ horrible ▷ The weather was dreadful. Hizo un tiempo horrible.; **You look dreadful.** Tienes muy mal aspecto.; **I feel dreadful about not having phoned.** Me siento muy mal por no haber llamado.

dream vb soñar [11] ▷ Do you dream every night? ¿Sueñas todas las noches? ▷ She dreamt about her baby. Soñó con su bebé. ▷ n sueño m

drench vb **I got drenched.** Me puse empapado.

dress n vestido m ▷ vb vestirse [38] ▷ I got up, dressed, and went downstairs. Me levanté, me vestí y bajé.; **to get dressed** vestirse [38]

dress up vb disfrazarse [13] ▷ I dressed up as a ghost. Me disfracé de fantasma.

dressed adj vestido(-a) ▷ I'm not dressed yet. Aún no estoy vestido. ▷ She was dressed in white. Iba vestida de blanco.

dresser n (furniture) aparador m

dressing gown n bata f

dressing table n tocador m

drew vb see **draw**

dried adj seco(-a); **dried milk** la leche en polvo; **dried fruits** las frutas pasas

drier = **dryer**

drift n a snow drift el ventisquero
▶ vb ❶ (boat) ir [27] a la deriva ❷ (snow) amontonarse [25]

drill n taladradora f
▶ vb taladrar [25]; **He drilled a hole in the wall.** Hizo un agujero en la pared.

drink n beber [8] (tomar [25] LatAm) ▷ What would you like to drink? ¿Qué te apetece beber? ▷ She drank three cups of tea. Se bebió tres tazas de té.
▶ n ❶ bebida f ▷ a cold drink una bebida fría ❷ (alcoholic) copa f ▷ They've gone out for a drink. Han salido a tomar una copa.; **to have a drink** tomar [25] algo ▷ Would you like a drink? ¿Quieres tomar algo?

drive n ❶ paseo en coche m ▷ to go for a drive ir a dar un paseo en coche; **We've got a long drive tomorrow.** Mañana nos espera un largo viaje en coche. ❷ camino de entrada a la casa m ▷ He parked his car in the drive. Aparcó el coche en el camino de entrada a la casa.
▶ vb ❶ (a car) conducir [9] (manejar [25] LatAm) ▷ Can you drive? ¿Sabes conducir? ❷ (go by car) ir [27] en coche ▷ We never drive into the town centre. Nunca vamos en coche al centro. ❸ (transport) llevar [25] en

coche ▷ My mother drives me to school. Mi madre me lleva al colegio en coche.; **to drive somebody home** acercar [48] a alguien a su casa en coche; **to drive somebody mad** volver [59] loco a alguien ▷ He drives her mad. La vuelve loca.

driver n conductor m, conductora f ▷ He's a bus driver. Es conductor de autobús.; **She's an excellent driver.** Conduce muy bien.

driver's license n (US) permiso de conducir m

driving instructor n profesor de autoescuela m, profesora de autoescuela f ▷ He's a driving instructor. Es profesor de autoescuela.

driving lesson n clase de conducir f

driving licence n permiso de conducir m

driving test n to take one's driving test hacer [26] el examen de conducir; **She's just passed her driving test.** Acaba de sacarse el carnet de conducir.

drop n ❶ (of liquid) gota f ▷ Would you like some milk? — Just a drop. ¿Quieres leche? — Una gota nada más. ❷ (fall) bajada f ▷ a drop in temperature una bajada de las temperaturas
▶ vb ❶ bajar [25] ▷ The temperature will drop tonight. La temperatura bajará esta noche. ❷ soltar [11] ▷ The cat dropped the mouse at my feet. El gato soltó al ratón junto a mis pies.; **I dropped the glass.**

Se me cayó el vaso. ❸ **dejar [25]**
▷ *Could you drop me at the station?*
¿Me puedes dejar en la estación?;
I'm going to drop chemistry. No
voy a dar más química.

drought n sequía f

drove vb see **drive**

drown vb ahogarse **[37]** ▷ *A boy
drowned here yesterday.* Un chico se
ahogó ayer aquí.

drug n ❶ medicamento m ▷ *They
need food and drugs.* Necesitan
comida y medicamentos. ❷ **droga**
f ▷ *hard drugs* drogas duras; **to
take drugs** drogarse **[37]**; **a drug
addict** un drogadicto

drugstore n (US) farmacia f

drum n ❶ tambor m ▷ *an African drum*
un tambor africano; **a drum kit**
una batería; **to play the drums**
tocar **[48]** la batería

drummer n (in rock group)
batería mf

drunk vb see **drink**
▶ adj borracho(-a) ▷ *He was drunk.*
Estaba borracho.; **to get drunk**
emborracharse **[25]**
▶ n borracho m, borracha f

dry adj seco(-a) ▷ *The paint isn't dry
yet.* Aún no está seca la pintura.
▶ vb ❶ secar **[48]** ▷ *to dry the dishes*
secar los platos ❷ secarse **[48]**
▷ *The washing will dry quickly in the
sun.* La colada se secará rápido al
sol.; **to dry one's hair** secarse **[48]**
el pelo

dry-cleaner's n tintorería f

dryer n a **tumble dryer** una
secadora; **a hair dryer** un
secador

dubbed adj doblado(-a) ▷ *The film
was dubbed into Spanish.* La película
estaba doblada al español.

duck n pato m

due adj, adv **He's due to arrive
tomorrow.** Debe llegar mañana.;
The plane's due in half an hour.
El avión llegará en media hora.;
When's the baby due? ¿Para
cuándo nacerá el niño?; **due to**
debido a ▷ *The trip was cancelled due
to bad weather.* El viaje se suspendió
debido al mal tiempo.

dug vb see **dig**

dull adj ❶ soso(-a) ▷ *He's nice, but a
bit dull.* Es simpático, pero un poco
soso. ❷ gris ▷ *It's always dull and
wet.* El tiempo está siempre gris y
lluvioso.

dumb adj ❶ (not speaking) mudo(-a).
❷ bobo(-a)

dummy n (for baby) chupete m

dump n **It's a real dump!** ¡Es una
auténtica pocilga!; **a rubbish
dump** un vertedero
▶ vb (waste) verter **[20]**

dungarees npl mono m (overol m
LatAm)

dungeon n mazmorra f

during prep durante

dusk n anochecer m; **at dusk** al
anochecer

dust n polvo m
▶ vb limpiar **[25]** el polvo de ▷ *I
dusted the shelves.* Limpié el polvo
de las estanterías.

dustbin n cubo de la basura m
(balde m LatAm)

dustman n basurero m

dusty adj polvoriento(-a)

Dutch adj holandés (f holandesa, pl holandeses) ▷ *She's Dutch.* Es holandesa.
▶ n *(language)* holandés m; **the Dutch** los holandeses

Dutchman n holandés m (pl holandeses)

Dutchwoman n holandesa f

duty n deber m ▷ *It was his duty to tell the police.* Su deber era decírselo a la policía.; **to be on duty (1)** *(police officer)* estar [22] de servicio **(2)** *(doctor, nurse)* estar [22] de guardia

duty-free adj libre de impuestos

duvet n edredón m (pl edredones)

DVD n DVD m; **a DVD player** un lector de DVD

dying vb see **die**

dynamic adj dinámico(-a)

dyslexia n dislexia f

e

each adj, pron ❶ cada ▷ *each day* cada día; **Each house has its own garden.** Todas las casas tienen jardín. ❷ cada uno(-a) ▷ *The plates cost £5 each.* Los platos cuestan 5 libras cada uno. ▷ *He gave each of us £10.* Nos dio 10 libras a cada uno.

> Use a reflexive verb to translate 'each other'.

▷ *They hate each other.* Se odian.
▷ *They don't know each other.* No se conocen.

eagle n águila f

> Although it's a feminine noun, remember that you use **el** and **un** with **águila**.

ear n oreja f

earache n **to have earache** tener [53] dolor de oídos

earlier adv ❶ antes ▷ I saw him earlier. Lo vi antes. ❷ (in the morning) más temprano ▷ I ought to get up earlier. Debería levantarme más temprano.

early adv, adj ❶ temprano ▷ I have to get up early. Tengo que levantarme temprano.; **to have an early night** irse [27] a la cama temprano ❷ (ahead of time) pronto ▷ I came early to avoid the heavy traffic. Vine pronto para evitar el tráfico denso.

earn vb ganar [25] ▷ She earns £10 an hour. Gana 10 libras esterlinas a la hora.

earnings npl (income) ingresos mpl

earring n pendiente m (arete m LatAm)

earth n tierra f; **What on earth are you doing here?** ¿Qué diablos haces aquí?

earthquake n terremoto m

easily adv fácilmente

east adj, adv hacia el este ▷ We were travelling east. Viajábamos hacia el este.; **an east wind** un viento del este; **the east coast** la costa oriental; **east of** al este de ▷ It's east of London. Está al este de Londres.
▶ n (direction, region) este m ▷ in the east of the country al este del país

Easter n Pascua f; **Easter egg** el huevo de Pascua; **the Easter holidays** las vacaciones de Semana Santa

eastern adj oriental ▷ the eastern part of the island la parte oriental de

la isla; **Eastern Europe** la Europa del Este

easy adj fácil

eat vb comer [8] ▷ Would you like something to eat? ¿Quieres comer algo?

e-book n libro electrónico m

echo n eco m

ecology n ecología f

economic adj ❶ (growth, development, policy) económico(-a) ❷ (profitable) rentable

economical adj económico(-a) ▷ My car is very economical to run. Mi coche me sale muy económico.

economics n economía f ▷ the economics of the third world countries la economía de los países tercermundistas; **He's doing economics at university.** Estudia económicas en la universidad.

economy n economía f

ecstasy n (drug) éxtasis m; **to be in ecstasy** estar [22] en éxtasis

eczema n eczema m

　　Although **eczema** ends in -a, it is actually a masculine noun.
　　▷ She's got eczema. Tiene eczema.

edge n ❶ borde m ▷ on the edge of the desk en el borde del escritorio; **They live on the edge of the town.** Viven en los límites de la ciudad. ❷ (of lake) orilla f

Edinburgh n Edimburgo m

editor n ❶ (of newspaper, magazine) director m, directora f ❷ redactor m, redactora f ▷ the sports editor el redactor de la sección de deportes

education n ❶ educación f ▷ There should be more investment in

education. Debería invertirse más dinero en educación. ❷ (teaching) enseñanza f ▷ She works in education. Trabaja en la enseñanza.

educational adj ❶ (toy) educativo(-a) ❷ (experience, film) instructivo(-a)

effect n efecto m ▷ special effects los efectos especiales

effective adj eficaz (pl eficaces)

efficient adj ❶ eficiente ▷ His secretary is very efficient. Su secretaria es muy eficiente. ❷ eficaz (pl eficaces) ▷ It's a very efficient system. Es un sistema muy eficaz.

effort n esfuerzo m; **to make an effort to do something** esforzarse [3] en hacer algo

e.g. abbr p.ej.

egg n huevo m ▷ a hard-boiled egg un huevo duro ▷ a soft-boiled egg un huevo pasado por agua ▷ a fried egg un huevo frito ▷ scrambled eggs los huevos revueltos

egg cup n huevera f

eggplant n (US) berenjena f

Egypt n Egipto m

eight num ocho ▷ She's eight. Tiene ocho años.

eighteen num dieciocho ▷ She's eighteen. Tiene dieciocho años.

eighteenth adj decimoctavo(-a); **the eighteenth floor** la planta dieciocho; **the eighteenth of August** el dieciocho de agosto

eighth adj octavo(-a) ▷ the eighth floor el octavo piso; **the eighth of August** el ocho de agosto

eighty num ochenta ▷ He's eighty. Tiene ochenta años.

Eire n Eire m

either adj, conj, pron, adv tampoco ▷ I don't like milk, and I don't like eggs either. No me gusta la leche, y tampoco me gustan los huevos.; **either...or...** o...o... ▷ You can have either ice cream or yoghurt. Puedes tomar o helado o yogur.; **I don't like either of them.** No me gusta ninguno de los dos.; **on either side of the road** a ambos lados de la carretera

elastic n elástico m

elastic band n goma elástica f

elbow n codo m

elder adj mayor ▷ my elder sister mi hermana mayor

elderly adj anciano(-a); **an elderly man** un anciano

eldest adj, n mayor ▷ my eldest sister mi hermana mayor; **He's the eldest.** Él es el mayor.

elect vb elegir [18]

election n elección f (pl elecciones)

electric adj eléctrico(-a) ▷ an electric fire una estufa eléctrica ▷ an electric guitar una guitarra eléctrica

electrical adj eléctrico(-a) ▷ electrical engineering la ingeniería eléctrica

electrician n electricista mf ▷ He's an electrician. Es electricista.

electricity n electricidad f

electronic adj electrónico(-a)

electronics n electrónica f

elegant adj elegante

elementary school n (US) escuela primaria f

elephant n elefante m

elevator n (US) ascensor m

eleven num once ▷ She's eleven.
Tiene once años.

eleventh adj undécimo(-a); **the
eleventh floor** el piso once; **the
eleventh of August** el once de
agosto

else adv **somebody else** otra
persona; **nobody else** nadie más;
something else otra cosa;
nothing else nada más;
somewhere else en algún otro
sitio; **Did you look anywhere
else?** ¿Miraste en otro sitio?;
I didn't look anywhere else.
No miré en ningún otro sitio.;
Would you like anything else?
¿Desea alguna otra cosa?; **I don't
want anything else.** No quiero
nada más.

email n e-mail m
  ▶ vb **to email somebody** enviar
  [21] un e-mail a alguien; **I'll email
  you the details.** Te mandaré la
  información por e-mail.

email address n dirección de
e-mail f ▷ My email address is jones
at collins dot uk. Mi dirección de
e-mail es jones arroba collins
punto uk.

embankment n (of railway)
terraplén m (pl terraplenes)

embarrassed adj **I was really
embarrassed.** Me dio mucha
vergüenza.

> Be careful not to translate
embarrassed by embarazada.

embarrassing adj (mistake,
situation) embarazoso(-a); **It was**

so embarrassing. Fue una
situación muy violenta.; **How
embarrassing!** ¡Qué vergüenza!

embassy n embajada f

embroider vb bordar [25]

embroidery n bordado m; **I do
embroidery in the afternoon.**
Bordo por las tardes.

emergency n emergencia f ▷ This
is an emergency! ¡Es una
emergencia!; **in an emergency** en
caso de emergencia; **an
emergency exit** una salida de
emergencia; **an emergency
landing** un aterrizaje forzoso; **the
emergency services** los servicios
de urgencia

emigrate vb emigrar [25]

emotion n emoción f (pl
emociones)

emotional adj emotivo(-a) ▷ She's
very emotional. Es una persona muy
emotiva.; **He got very emotional
at the farewell party.** Se
emocionó mucho en la fiesta de
despedida.

emperor n emperador m

emphasize vb recalcar [48] ▷ He
emphasized the importance of the
issue. Recalcó la importancia de la
cuestión.; **to emphasize that**
subrayar [25] que

empire n imperio m

employ vb emplear [25] ▷ The
factory employs 600 people. La
fábrica emplea a 600
trabajadores.; **Thousands of
people are employed in tourism.**
Miles de personas trabajan en el
sector de turismo.

employee n empleado m, empleada f

employer n empresario m, empresaria f

employment n empleo m

empty adj vacío(-a)
▶ vb vaciar [21]; **to empty something out** vaciar [21] algo

encourage vb animar [25] ▷ to encourage somebody to do something animar a alguien a hacer algo

encouragement n estímulo m

encyclopedia n enciclopedia f

end n ❶ final m ▷ the end of the film el final de la película; **in the end** al final ▷ In the end I decided to stay at home. Al final decidí quedarme en casa. ❷ extremo m ▷ at the other end of the table al otro extremo de la mesa; **at the end of the street** al final de la calle; **for hours on end** durante horas enteras
▶ vb terminar [25] ▷ What time does the film end? ¿A qué hora termina la película?; **to end up doing something** terminar [25] haciendo algo ▷ I ended up walking home. Terminé yendo a casa andando.

ending n final m ▷ a happy ending un final feliz

endless adj interminable ▷ The journey seemed endless. El viaje parecía interminable.

enemy n enemigo m, enemiga f

energetic adj activo(-a) ▷ She's very energetic. Es muy activa.

energy n energía f

engaged adj ❶ (telephone, toilet) ocupado(-a) ❷ prometido(-a)

▷ Brian and Mary are engaged. Brian y Mary están prometidos.; **to get engaged** prometerse [8]

engagement n compromiso m ▷ They announced their engagement yesterday. Anunciaron su compromiso ayer.; **The engagement lasted 10 months.** El noviazgo duró 10 meses.; **engagement ring** el anillo de compromiso

engine n ❶ (of vehicle) motor m ❷ (of train) locomotora f

engineer n ingeniero m, ingeniera f ▷ He's an engineer. Es ingeniero.

engineering n ingeniería f

England n Inglaterra f

English adj inglés (f inglesa, pl ingleses)
▶ n (language) inglés m ▷ the English teacher el profesor de inglés; **the English** (people) los ingleses

Englishman n inglés m (pl ingleses)

Englishwoman n inglesa f

enjoy vb Did you enjoy the film? ¿Te gustó la película?; **to enjoy oneself** divertirse [51] ▷ Did you enjoy yourselves at the party? ¿Os divertisteis en la fiesta?

enjoyable adj agradable

enlargement n (of photo) ampliación f (pl ampliaciones)

enormous adj enorme

enough adj, pron, adv bastante ▷ I didn't have enough money. No tenía bastante dinero.; **big enough** suficientemente grande; **I've had enough!** ¡Ya estoy harto!; **That's enough!** ¡Ya basta!

enquire vb to enquire about something informarse **[25]** acerca de algo

enquiry n (official investigation) investigación f (pl investigaciones)

enter vb entrar **[25]** en ▷ He entered the room and sat down. Entró en la habitación y se sentó.; **to enter a competition** presentarse **[25]** a un concurso

entertain vb (guests) recibir **[58]**

entertaining adj (book, movie) entretenido(-a)

enthusiasm n entusiasmo m

enthusiast n entusiasta mf ▷ She's a DIY enthusiast. Es una entusiasta del bricolaje.

enthusiastic adj (response, welcome) entusiasta; **She didn't seem very enthusiastic about your idea.** No pareció muy entusiasmada con tu idea.

entire adj entero(-a) ▷ the entire world el mundo entero

entirely adv completamente ▷ an entirely new approach un enfoque completamente nuevo; **I agree entirely.** Estoy totalmente de acuerdo.

entrance n entrada f; **an entrance exam** un examen de ingreso; **entrance fee** la cuota de entrada

entry n entrada f; **'no entry' (1)** (on door) 'prohibido el paso' **(2)** (on road sign) 'dirección prohibida'; **an entry form** un impreso de inscripción

entry phone n portero automático m

envelope n sobre m

envious adj envidioso(-a)

environment n (surroundings) entorno m; **the environment** el medio ambiente

environmental adj medioambiental ▷ environmental pollution contaminación ambiental; **environmental groups** grupos ecologistas

environment-friendly adj ecológico(-a)

envy n envidia f
  ▶ vb envidiar **[25]**

epileptic n epiléptico m, epiléptica f

episode n episodio m

equal adj igual ▷ The cake was divided into 12 equal parts. El pastel se dividió en 12 partes iguales.; **Women demand equal rights at work.** Las mujeres exigen igualdad de derechos en el trabajo.

equality n igualdad f

equalize vb (in sport) empatar **[25]**

equator n ecuador m

equipment n equipo m ▷ skiing equipment el equipo de esquí

equipped adj equipado(-a) ▷ This caravan is equipped for four people. Esta caravana está equipada para cuatro personas.; **equipped with** provisto de ▷ All rooms are equipped with phones, computers and faxes. Todas las habitaciones están provistas de teléfonos, ordenadores y fax.; **He was well equipped for the job.** Estaba bien preparado para el puesto.

equivalent equivalente m

error n error m

escalator n escalera mecánica f

escape n (from prison) fuga f; **We had a narrow escape.** Nos salvamos por muy poco.
▶ vb escaparse [**25**] ▷ A lion has escaped. Se ha escapado un león.; **The passengers escaped unhurt.** Los pasajeros salieron ilesos.; **to escape from prison** fugarse [**25**] de la cárcel

escort n escolta f ▷ a police escort una escolta policial

especially adv especialmente ▷ It's very hot there, especially in the summer. Allí hace mucho calor, especialmente en verano.

essay n trabajo m ▷ a history essay un trabajo de historia

essential adj esencial ▷ It's essential to bring warm clothes. Es esencial traer ropa de abrigo.

estate n ❶ urbanización f (pl urbanizaciones) ❷ (country estate) finca f

estate agent n agente inmobiliario m, agente inmobiliaria f ▷ She's an estate agent. Es agente inmobiliaria.

estate agent's n agencia inmobiliaria f

estate car n ranchera f

estimate vb calcular [**25**] ▷ They estimated it would take three weeks. Calcularon que llevaría tres semanas.

etc abbr (= et cetera) etc.

Ethiopia n Etiopía f

ethnic adj ❶ étnico(-a) ▷ an ethnic minority una minoría étnica; **ethnic cleansing** la limpieza

étnica ❷ (restaurant, food) exótico(-a)

EU n (= European Union) UE f

euro n euro m

Europe n Europa f

European adj europeo(-a)
▶ n europeo m, europea f

eve n **Christmas Eve** la Nochebuena; **New Year's Eve** la Nochevieja

even adv incluso ▷ I like all animals, even snakes. Me gustan todos los animales, incluso las serpientes.; **not even** ni siquiera ▷ He didn't even say hello. Ni siquiera saludó.; **even if** aunque

> Use the subjunctive after aunque when translating 'even if'.

▷ I'd never do that, even if you asked me. Nunca haría eso, aunque me lo pidieras.; **even though** aunque ▷ She's a successful writer, even though she's still only 25. Es una escritora de éxito, aunque todavía tiene solo 25 años.; **even more** aún más ▷ I liked Granada even more than Seville. Me gustó Granada aún más que Sevilla.
▶ adj uniforme ▷ an even layer of snow una capa de nieve uniforme; **an even surface** una superficie lisa; **an even number** un número par; **to get even with somebody** vengarse [**37**] en alguien

evening n ❶ (before dark) tarde f ❷ (after dark) noche f ▷ in the evening por la tarde/noche; **Good evening!** ¡Buenas tardes/noches!; **evening class** la clase nocturna

a b c d e f g h i j k l m n o p q r s t u v w x y z

event n ❶ acontecimiento m ▷ It was one of the most important events in his life. Fue uno de los acontecimientos más importantes de su vida. ❷ (in sport) prueba f; **in the event of** en caso de ▷ in the event of an accident en caso de accidente

eventful adj (race, journey) lleno de incidentes (f llena de incidentes)

eventually adv finalmente

ever adv **Have you ever been to Portugal?** ¿Has estado alguna vez en Portugal?; **Have you ever seen her?** ¿La has visto alguna vez?; **the best I've ever seen** el mejor que he visto; **I haven't ever done that.** Jamás he hecho eso.; **It will become ever more complex.** Irá siendo cada vez más complicado.; **for the first time ever** por primera vez; **ever since** desde que ▷ ever since I met him desde que lo conozco; **ever since then** desde entonces; **It's ever so kind of you.** Es muy amable de su parte.

every adj cada ▷ every time cada vez; **every day** todos los días; **every now and then** de vez en cuando

everybody pron todo el mundo ▷ Everybody makes mistakes. Todo el mundo se equivoca.; **Everybody had a good time.** Todos se lo pasaron bien.

everyone pron todo el mundo

everything pron todo ▷ You've thought of everything! ¡Has pensado en todo!

everywhere adv en todas partes ▷ I looked everywhere, but I couldn't find it. Miré en todas partes, pero no lo encontré.

▌ **dondequiera** has to be followed by a verb in the subjunctive.

I see him everywhere I go. Lo veo dondequiera que vaya.

evil adj ❶ (person) malvado(-a) ❷ (plan, spirit) maligno(-a)

ex- prefix ex- ▷ his ex-wife su ex-esposa

exact adj exacto(-a)

exactly adv exactamente ▷ exactly the same exactamente igual; **It's exactly 10 o'clock.** Son las 10 en punto.

exaggerate vb exagerar **[25]**

exaggeration n exageración f (pl exageraciones)

exam n examen m (pl exámenes) ▷ a French exam un examen de francés

examination n examen m (pl exámenes)

examine vb examinar **[25]** ▷ The doctor examined him. El médico lo examinó.

examiner n examinador m, examinadora f

example n ejemplo m ▷ for example por ejemplo

excellent adj excelente

except prep excepto ▷ everyone except me todos excepto yo; **except for** excepto; **except that** salvo que

▌ **salvo que** may be followed by a verb in the subjunctive.

▷ *The weather was great, except that it was a bit cold.* El tiempo fue estupendo, salvo que hizo un poco de frío.

exception n excepción f (pl excepciones) ▷ **to make an exception** hacer una excepción

exchange vb cambiar [25] ▷ *I exchanged the book for a CD.* Cambié el libro por un CD. ▶ n intercambio m ▷ *I'd like to do an exchange with an English student.* Me gustaría hacer un intercambio con un estudiante inglés.; **in exchange for** a cambio de

exchange rate n tipo de cambio m

excited adj entusiasmado(-a)

exciting adj emocionante

exclamation mark n signo de admiración m

excuse n excusa f
▶ vb **Excuse me!** (1) *(to attract attention, apologize)* ¡Perdón! (2) *(when you want to get past)* ¡Con permiso!

exercise n ejercicio m ▷ *page ten, exercise three* página diez, ejercicio tres ▷ *to take some exercise* hacer un poco de ejercicio; **exercise book** el cuaderno

exhaust n tubo de escape m

exhausted adj agotado(-a)

exhaust fumes npl gases de escape mpl

exhaust pipe n tubo de escape m

exhibition n exposición f (pl exposiciones)

exist vb existir [58]

exit n salida f
Be careful not to translate **exit** by **éxito**.

expect vb ① esperar [25] ▷ *I'm expecting him for dinner.* Lo espero para cenar. ▷ *She's expecting a baby.* Está esperando un bebé. ② imaginarse [25] ▷ *I expect he'll be late.* Me imagino que llegará tarde.; **I expect so.** Me imagino que sí.

expedition n expedición f (pl expediciones)

expel vb **to get expelled** *(from school)* ser [52] expulsado

expenses npl gastos mpl

expensive adj caro(-a)

experience n experiencia f

experienced adj **an experienced teacher** un maestro con experiencia; **She's very experienced in looking after children.** Tiene mucha experiencia en cuidar niños.

experiment n experimento m

expert adj experto(-a); **He's an expert cook.** Es un experto cocinero.

expire vb caducar [48] ▷ *My passport has expired.* Mi pasaporte ha caducado.

explain vb explicar [48]

explanation n explicación f (pl explicaciones)

explode vb estallar [25]

explore vb *(place)* explorar [25]

explosion n explosión f (pl explosiones)

express vb expresar [25]; **to express oneself** expresarse [25]

▷ *It's not easy to express oneself in a foreign language.* No es fácil expresarse en un idioma extranjero.

expression n expresión f (pl expresiones) ▷ *It's an English expression.* Es una expresión inglesa.

expressway n (US) autopista f

extension n ❶ (of building) ampliación f (pl ampliaciones) ❷ (telephone) extensión f (pl extensiones) ▷ *Extension three one three seven, please.* Con la extensión tres uno tres siete, por favor.

extent n to some extent hasta cierto punto

extinct adj extinto(-a) ▷ *Dinosaurs are extinct.* Los dinosaurios están extintos.; **to become extinct** extinguirse [**58**]

extinguisher n extintor m (extinguidor m LatAm)

extra adj, adv **He gave me an extra blanket.** Me dio una manta más.; **to pay extra** pagar [**37**] un suplemento; **Breakfast is extra.** El desayuno no está incluido.; **Be extra careful!** ¡Ten muchísimo cuidado!

extraordinary adj extraordinario(-a)

extravagant adj (person) derrochador(a)

extreme adj extremo(-a); **with extreme caution** con sumo cuidado

extremely adv sumamente

extremist n extremista mf

eye n ojo m ▷ *I've got green eyes.* Tengo los ojos verdes.; **to keep an eye on something** vigilar [**25**] algo

eyebrow n ceja f

eyelash n pestaña f

eyelid n párpado m

eyeliner n lápiz de ojos m (pl lápices de ojos)

eye shadow n sombra de ojos f

eyesight n vista f ▷ *to have good eyesight* tener buena vista

f

fabric n tela f

| Be careful not to translate **fabric** by **fábrica**.

fabulous adj fabuloso(-a)

face n ❶ cara f; **face to face** cara a cara ❷ (of clock) esfera f; **in the face of these difficulties** en vista de estas dificultades
▷ vb ❶ estar [22] frente a ▷ They stood facing each other. Estaban de pie el uno frente al otro.; **The garden faces south.** El jardín da al sur. ❷ enfrentarse [25] a ▷ They face serious problems. Se enfrentan a graves problemas.; **Let's face it, we're lost.** Tenemos que admitirlo, estamos perdidos.

Facebook® n Facebook® m
▷ vb enviar [21] un mensaje por Facebook

face cloth n toallita para lavarse f

facilities npl instalaciones fpl
▷ This school has excellent facilities. Esta escuela tiene unas instalaciones magníficas.; **The youth hostel has cooking facilities.** El albergue juvenil dispone de cocina.

fact n

| Use the subjunctive after **el hecho de que**.

the fact that ... el hecho de que ...
▷ The fact that you are very busy is of no interest to me. El hecho de que estés muy ocupado no me interesa.; **facts and figures** datos y cifras; **in fact** de hecho

factory n fábrica f

fail vb ❶ suspender [8] ▷ He failed his driving test. Suspendió el examen de conducir. ❷ fallar [25] ▷ The lorry's brakes failed. Al camión le fallaron los frenos. ❸ fracasar [25] ▷ The plan failed. El plan fracasó.; **to fail to do something** no lograr [25] hacer algo ▷ They failed to reach the quarter finals. No lograron llegar a los cuartos de final.; **The bomb failed to explode.** La bomba no llegó a estallar.
▷ n suspenso m ▷ D is a pass, E is a fail. D es un aprobado, E es un suspenso.

failure n ❶ fracaso m ▷ The attempt was a complete failure. El intento fue un completo fracaso. ❷ fallo m ▷ a mechanical failure un fallo mecánico

faint adj débil ▷ His voice was very faint. Tenía la voz muy débil.;

to feel faint sentirse [**51**] mareado
▸ vb **desmayarse** [**25**]

fair adj ❶ **justo(-a)** ▷ *That's not fair.*
Eso no es justo.; **I paid more than
my fair share.** Pagué más de lo
que me correspondía. ❷ **rubio(-a)**
▷ *He's got fair hair.* Tiene el pelo
rubio. ❸ **blanco(-a)** ▷ *people with
fair skin* la gente con la piel blanca
❹ **considerable** ▷ *That's a fair
distance.* Esa es una distancia
considerable.; **I have a fair
chance of winning.** Tengo
bastantes posibilidades de ganar.
❺ (weather) **bueno(-a)**
▸ n ❶ (travelling funfair) **feria** f
❷ (on permanent site) **parque de
atracciones** m; **a trade fair** una
feria de muestras

fair-haired adj **rubio(-a)**

fairly adv ❶ **equitativamente** ▷ *The
cake was divided fairly.* La tarta se
repartió equitativamente.
❷ **bastante** ▷ *My car is fairly new.*
Mi coche es bastante nuevo. ▷ *The
weather was fairly good.* El tiempo
fue bastante bueno.

fairy n **hada** f
▣ Although it's a feminine noun,
remember that you use **el** and
un with **hada**.

fairy tale n **cuento de hadas** m

faith n ❶ **confianza** f ▷ *People have
lost faith in the government.* La gente
ha perdido la confianza en el
gobierno. ❷ (religion) **fe** f

faithful adj **fiel**

faithfully adv **Yours faithfully...**
(in letter) Le saluda
atentamente...

fake n **falsificación** f (pl
falsificaciones) ▷ *The painting was a
fake.* El cuadro era una falsificación.
▸ adj **falso(-a)** ▷ *a fake banknote* un
billete falso; **a fake fur coat** un
abrigo de piel sintética

fall n ❶ **caída** f ▷ *She had a nasty fall.*
Tuvo una mala caída.; **a fall of
snow** una nevada ❷ (US: autumn)
otoño m
▸ vb ❶ **caer** [**5**] ▷ *Bombs fell on the
town.* Las bombas caían sobre la
ciudad.
▣ When the action of falling is
not deliberate, use **caerse**.
▷ *He tripped and fell.* Tropezó y se
cayó. ▷ *The book fell off the shelf.*
El libro se cayó de la estantería.;
to fall in love with someone
enamorarse [**25**] de alguien
❷ (price, temperature) **bajar** [**25**]

fall down vb **caerse** [**5**] ▷ *She's fallen
down.* Se ha caído.

fall for vb ❶ **tragarse** [**37**] ▷ *They fell
for it!* ¡Se lo tragaron!
❷ **enamorarse** [**25**] de ▷ *She fell for
him immediately.* Se enamoró de él
en el acto.

fall out vb **reñir** [**45**] ▷ *Sarah's fallen
out with her boyfriend.* Sarah ha
reñido con su novio.

fall through vb **fracasar** [**25**]

false adj **falso(-a)**; **a false alarm**
una falsa alarma; **false teeth** la
dentadura postiza

fame n **fama** f

familiar adj **familiar** ▷ *The name
sounded familiar to me.* El nombre
me sonaba familiar.; **a familiar
face** un rostro conocido; **to be**

familiar with something conocer [12] bien algo ▷ *I'm familiar with his work.* Conozco bien su obra.

family n familia f ▷ *the Cooke family* la familia Cooke

famine n hambruna f

famous adj famoso(-a)

fan n ❶ (of sport) hincha mf ❷ **fan** mf (pl **fans**) ▷ *the Adele fan club* el club de fans de Adele; **I'm one of his greatest fans.** Soy uno de sus mayores admiradores. ❸ aficionado m, aficionada f ▷ *a rap music fan* un aficionado al rap ❹ (to keep cool) abanico m; **an electric fan** un ventilador

fanatic n fanático m, fanática f

fancy vb apetecer [12] ▷ *I fancy an ice cream.* Me apetece un helado. ▷ *What do you fancy doing?* ¿Qué te apetece hacer?

> **apetecer que** has to be followed by a verb in the subjunctive.
>
> ▷ *Do you fancy going to the cinema sometime?* ¿Te apetece que vayamos al cine algún día? ▷ **He fancies her.** Le gusta ella.

fancy dress n disfraz m (pl disfraces); **a fancy dress ball** un baile de disfraces

fantastic adj fantástico(-a)

far adj, adv lejos ▷ *Is it far?* ¿Está lejos? ▷ *It's not far from London.* No está lejos de Londres.; **How far is it to Madrid?** ¿A qué distancia está Madrid?; **at the far end of the swimming pool** al otro extremo de la piscina; **as far as I know** por lo que yo sé; **so far** hasta ahora

fare n tarifa f ▷ *Rail fares are very high in Britain.* Las tarifas de tren son muy altas en Gran Bretaña. ▷ *The air fare was very reasonable.* La tarifa del vuelo fue bastante razonable.; **He didn't have the bus fare, so he had to walk.** No tenía dinero para el autobús, así que tuvo que ir andando.; **full fare** el precio del billete completo; **Children pay half fare on the bus.** Los niños pagan la mitad en el autobús.

Far East n **the Far East** el Extremo Oriente

farm n granja f (estancia f LatAm)

farmer n granjero m, granjera f (estanciero m, estanciera f LatAm) ▷ *He's a farmer.* Es granjero.

farmhouse n caserío m

farming n agricultura f ▷ *organic farming* agricultura biológica

fascinating adj fascinante

fashion n moda f; **to be in fashion** estar [22] de moda; **to go out of fashion** pasar [25] de moda

fashionable adj de moda ▷ *That colour is very fashionable.* Ese color está muy de moda.; **Jane wears fashionable clothes.** Jane viste a la moda.

fast adj, adv rápido(-a) ▷ *a fast car* un coche rápido ▷ *They work very fast.* Trabajan muy rápido.; **That clock's fast.** Ese reloj va adelantado.; **He's fast asleep.** Está profundamente dormido.

fat adj gordo(-a) ▷ *She thinks she's too fat.* Piensa que está demasiado gorda.

▶ n ① (on meat, in food) grasa f ▷ It's
very high in fat. Es muy rico en
grasas. ② (used for cooking)
manteca f

fatal adj ① mortal ▷ a fatal accident
un accidente mortal ② fatal ▷ a
fatal mistake un error fatal

father n padre m; **Father
Christmas** Papá Noel

father-in-law n suegro m

faucet n (US) grifo m

fault n ① culpa f ▷ It wasn't my fault.
No fue culpa mía. ② defecto m
▷ He has his faults, but I still like him.
Tiene sus defectos, pero aun así
me gusta.; **a mechanical fault** un
fallo mecánico

favour (US favor) n favor m (pl
favores) ▷ Could you do me a favour?
¿Me harías un favor?; **to be in
favour of something** estar [22] a
favor de algo

favourite (US favorite) adj
favorito(-a) ▷ Blue's my favourite
colour. El azul es mi color favorito.
▶ n favorito m, favorita f

fax n fax m (pl faxes)
▶ vb mandar [25] por fax ▷ I'll fax
you the details. Te mandaré la
información por fax.

fear n miedo m
▶ vb temer [8] ▷ You have nothing to
fear. No tienes nada que temer.

feather n pluma f

feature n característica f ▷ an
important feature una
característica importante

February n febrero m ▷ in February
en febrero ▷ on 18 February el 18 de
febrero

fed vb see **feed**

fed up adj **to be fed up with
something** estar [22] harto de
algo

feed vb dar [14] de comer a ▷ Have
you fed the cat? ¿Le has dado de
comer al gato? ▷ He worked hard to
feed his family. Trabajaba mucho
para dar de comer a su familia.

feel vb ① (pain, heat) sentir [51]
▷ I didn't feel much pain. No sentí
mucho dolor. ② sentirse [51]
▷ I don't feel well. No me siento
bien. ▷ I felt lonely. Me sentía solo.;
I was feeling hungry. Tenía
hambre.; **I was feeling cold, so I
went inside.** Tenía frío, así que
entré. ③ (touch) tocar [48] ▷ The
doctor felt his forehead. El médico le
tocó la frente.; **to feel like doing
something** tener [53] ganas de
hacer algo ▷ I don't feel like going
out tonight. No tengo ganas de
salir esta noche.; **Do you feel like
an ice cream?** ¿Te apetece un
helado?

feeling n ① sensación f (pl
sensaciones) ▷ a burning feeling una
sensación de escozor
② sentimiento m ▷ He was afraid of
hurting my feelings. Tenía miedo de
herir mis sentimientos.; **What are
your feelings about it?** ¿Tú qué
opinas de ello?

feet npl see **foot**

fell vb see **fall**

felt vb see **feel**

felt-tip pen n rotulador m

female adj ① hembra ▷ a female bat
un murciélago hembra

❷ femenino(-a) ▷ *the female sex* el sexo femenino

▶ n *(animal)* hembra f

feminine adj femenino(-a)

feminist n feminista mf

fence n valla f

fern n helecho m

ferry n ferry m

festival n festival m ▷ *a jazz festival* un festival de jazz

fetch vb ❶ ir [27] a por ▷ *Fetch the bucket.* Ve a por el cubo.; **to fetch something for someone** traer [54] algo a alguien ▷ *Fetch me a glass of water.* Tráeme un vaso de agua. ❷ venderse [8] por ▷ *His painting fetched £5000.* Su cuadro se vendió por 5.000 libras esterlinas.

fever n fiebre f

few adj, pron ❶ pocos (f pocas) ▷ *He has few friends.* Tiene pocos amigos.; **a few** unos ▷ *She was silent for a few seconds.* Se quedó callada unos segundos. ❷ algunos (f algunas) ▷ *a few of them* algunos de ellos; **quite a few people** bastante gente

fewer adj menos ▷ *There were fewer people than yesterday.* Había menos gente que ayer.

fiancé n novio m

fiancée n novia f

fiction n *(novels)* narrativa f

field n campo m ▷ *He's an expert in his field.* Es un experto en su campo.

fierce adj ❶ feroz (pl feroces) ▷ *a fierce Alsatian* un pastor alemán feroz ❷ encarnizado(-a) ▷ *There's fierce competition between the*

companies. Existe una encarnizada competencia entre las empresas. ❸ violento(-a) ▷ *a fierce attack* un violento ataque

fifteen num quince ▷ *I'm fifteen.* Tengo quince años.

fifteenth adj decimoquinto(-a); **the fifteenth of August** el quince de agosto

fifth adj quinto(-a) ▷ *the fifth floor* el quinto piso; **the fifth of August** el cinco de agosto

fifty num cincuenta ▷ *He's fifty.* Tiene cincuenta años.

fight n ❶ pelea f ▷ *There was a fight in the pub.* Hubo una pelea en el pub.; **She had a fight with her best friend.** Se peleó con su mejor amiga. ❷ lucha f ▷ *the fight against cancer* la lucha contra el cáncer

▶ vb ❶ pelearse [25] ▷ *The fans started fighting.* Los hinchas empezaron a pelearse. ❷ luchar [25] ▷ *She has fought against racism all her life.* Ha luchado toda su vida contra el racismo.; **The doctors tried to fight the disease.** Los médicos intentaron combatir la enfermedad.

figure n ❶ cifra f ▷ *Can you give me the exact figures?* ¿Me puedes dar las cifras exactas? ❷ silueta f ▷ *Helen saw the figure of a man on the bridge.* Helen vio la silueta de un hombre en el puente.; **She's got a good figure.** Tiene buen tipo.; **I have to watch my figure.** Tengo que mantener la línea. ❸ figura f ▷ *She's an important political figure.* Es una importante figura política.

figure out vb ❶ calcular [25] ▷ I'll try to figure out how much it'll cost. Intentaré calcular lo que va a costar. ❷ llegar [37] a comprender ▷ I couldn't figure out what it meant. No llegué a comprender lo que significaba.

file n ❶ expediente m ▷ There was stuff in that file that was private. Había cosas privadas en ese expediente.; **The police have a file on him.** Está fichado por la policía. ❷ carpeta f ▷ She put the photocopy into her file. Metió la fotocopia en su carpeta. ❸ lima f ▷ a nail file una lima de uñas ❹ (on computer) fichero m
▶ vb ❶ archivar [25] ▷ You have to file all these documents. Tienes que archivar todos estos documentos. ❷ limarse [25] ▷ She was filing her nails. Se estaba limando las uñas.

fill vb llenar [25] ▷ She filled the glass with water. Llenó el vaso de agua.

fill in vb ❶ rellenar [25] ▷ Can you fill in this form, please? Rellene este impreso, por favor. ❷ llenar [25] ▷ He filled the hole in with soil. Llenó el agujero de tierra.

fill up vb llenar [25]

film n ❶ (movie) película f ❷ carrete m ▷ I need a 36-exposure film. Quería un carrete de 36.

film star n estrella de cine f

filthy adj mugriento(-a)

final adj ❶ último(-a) ▷ a final attempt un último intento ❷ definitivo(-a) ▷ a final decision una decisión definitiva; **I'm not**

going and that's final. He dicho que no voy y se acabó.
▶ n final f ▷ Andy Murray is in the final. Andy Murray ha llegado a la final.

finally adv ❶ por último ▷ Finally, I would like to say thank you to all of you. Por último me gustaría darles las gracias a todos. ❷ al final ▷ They finally decided to leave on Saturday. Al final decidieron salir el sábado.

find vb encontrar [11] ▷ I can't find the exit. No encuentro la salida.

find out vb averiguar [25] ▷ I found out what happened. Averigüé lo que ocurrió.; **to find out about** enterarse [25] de ▷ Find out as much as possible about the town. Entérate de todo lo que puedas sobre la ciudad.

fine adj, adv ❶ estupendo(-a) ▷ He's a fine musician. Es un músico estupendo.; **How are you? — I'm fine.** ¿Qué tal estás? — Bien.; **I feel fine.** Me siento bien.; **It'll be ready tomorrow. — That's fine, thanks.** Mañana estará listo. — Muy bien, gracias.; **The weather is fine today.** Hoy hace muy buen tiempo. ❷ fino(-a) ▷ She's got very fine hair. Tiene el pelo muy fino.
▶ n multa f ▷ I got a fine for driving through a red light. Me pusieron una multa por saltarme un semáforo en rojo.

finger n dedo m; **my little finger** el meñique

fingernail n uña f

finish n **❶** fin m ▷ *from start to finish* de principio a fin **❷** *(of race)* llegada f
▶ vb terminar [25] ▷ *I've finished!* ¡Ya he terminado!; **to finish doing something** terminar [25] de hacer algo ▷ *Have you finished eating?* ¿Has terminado de comer?

Finland n Finlandia f

Finn n finlandés m (pl finlandeses), finlandesa f ▷ *the Finns* los finlandeses

Finnish adj finlandés (f finlandesa, pl finlandeses)
▶ n *(language)* finlandés m

fire n **❶** *(flames)* fuego m ▷ *The fire spread quickly.* El fuego se extendió rápidamente. **❷** *(blaze)* incendio m ▷ *The house was destroyed by a fire.* La casa fue destruida por un incendio. **❸** *(bonfire)* hoguera f ▷ *He made a fire to warm himself up.* Encendió una hoguera para calentarse. **❹** *(heater)* estufa f ▷ *an electric fire* una estufa eléctrica; **to be on fire** estar [22] ardiendo
▶ vb *(shoot)* disparar [25] ▷ *She fired at him.* Le disparó.; **to fire a gun** disparar [25]; **to fire somebody** despedir [38] a alguien ▷ *He was fired from his job.* Le despidieron del trabajo.

fire alarm n alarma contra incendios f

fire brigade n cuerpo de bomberos m

fire engine n coche de bomberos m

fire escape n escalera de incendios f

fire extinguisher n extintor m

firefighter n bombero m, bombera f ▷ *She's a firefighter.* Es bombera.

fireplace n chimenea f

fire station n parque de bomberos m

fireworks npl fuegos artificiales mpl

firm adj **❶** firme ▷ *to be firm with somebody* mostrarse firme con alguien **❷** duro(-a) ▷ *a firm mattress* un colchón duro
▶ n empresa f

first adj, n, adv **❶** primero(-a) ▷ *for the first time* por primera vez ▷ *Rachel came first in the race.* Rachel quedó primera en la carrera. ▷ *She was the first to arrive.* Fue la primera en llegar.

> Use **primer** before a masculine singular noun.

▶ my first job mi primer trabajo; **the first of September** el uno de septiembre; **at first** al principio **❷** antes ▷ *I want to get a job, but first I have to graduate.* Quiero encontrar un trabajo, pero antes tengo que acabar la carrera.; **first of all** ante todo

first aid n primeros auxilios mpl; **a first aid kit** un botiquín

first-class adj, adv **❶** de primera clase ▷ *a first-class ticket* un billete de primera clase **❷** de primera ▷ *a first-class meal* una comida de primera; **a first-class stamp** un sello para correo urgente

> In Spain there is no first-class or second-class postage. If you want your mail to arrive fast, you must have it sent express – **urgente** – from a post office.

firstly adv en primer lugar
fish n ❶ (animal) pez m (pl peces)
▷ I caught three fish. Pesqué tres peces. ❷ (food) pescado m ▷ fish and chips pescado rebozado con patatas fritas
▶ vb pescar [48]; **to go fishing** ir [27] a pescar
fisherman n pescador m ▷ He's a fisherman. Es pescador.
fishing n pesca f ▷ I enjoy fishing. Me gusta la pesca.; **a fishing boat** un barco pesquero; **fishing rod** la caña de pescar
fishing tackle n aparejos de pesca mpl
fishmonger's n pescadería f
fist n puño m
fit adj en forma ▷ He felt relaxed and fit after his holiday. Se sentía relajado y en forma tras las vacaciones.; **Will he be fit to play next Saturday?** ¿Estará en condiciones de jugar el próximo sábado?
▶ n **to have a fit (1)** (epileptic) sufrir [58] un ataque de epilepsia **(2)** (be angry) ponerse [41] hecho una furia ▷ My Mum will have a fit when she sees the carpet! ¡Mi madre se va a poner hecha una furia cuando vea la moqueta!
▶ vb ❶ (go into a space) caber [47] ▷ It's small enough to fit into your pocket. Es lo bastante pequeño como para caber en el bolsillo. ❷ encajar [25] ▷ Make sure the cork fits well into the bottle. Asegúrese de que el corcho encaja bien en la botella. ❸ (install) instalar [25] ▷ He fitted an alarm in his car. Instaló

una alarma en el coche. ❹ (attach) poner [41] ▷ She fitted a plug to the hair dryer. Le puso un enchufe al secador.; **to fit somebody** estar [22] bien a alguien ▷ These trousers don't fit me. Estos pantalones no me están bien.; **Does it fit?** ¿Te está bien?
fit in vb ❶ encajar [25] ▷ That story doesn't fit in with what he told us. Esa historia no encaja con lo que él nos contó. ❷ adaptarse [25] ▷ She fitted in well at her new school. Se adaptó bien al nuevo colegio.
five num cinco ▷ He's five. Tiene cinco años.
fix vb ❶ arreglar [25] ▷ Can you fix my bike? ¿Me puedes arreglar la bici? ❷ fijar [25] ▷ Let's fix a date for the party. Vamos a fijar una fecha para la fiesta.
fizzy adj gaseoso(-a)
flag n bandera f
flame n llama f
flan n ❶ (sweet) tarta f ▷ a raspberry flan una tarta de frambuesa ❷ (savoury) pastel m ▷ a cheese and onion flan un pastel de queso y cebolla
flap vb The bird flapped its wings. El pájaro batió las alas.
flash n (of camera) flash m; **a flash of lightning** un relámpago; **in a flash** en un abrir y cerrar de ojos
▶ vb They flashed a torch in his face. Le enfocaron con una linterna en la cara.
flask n (vacuum flask) termo m
flat adj llano(-a) ▷ a flat surface una superficie llana; **flat shoes**

los zapatos bajos; **I've got a flat tyre.** Tengo una rueda desinflada.
▶ *n* piso *m* (apartamento *m LatAm*)

flavour (*US* flavor) *n* sabor *m* (pl sabores) ▷ *Which flavour of ice cream would you like?* ¿De qué sabor quieres el helado?

flea *n* pulga *f*

flew *vb see* **fly**

flexible *adj* flexible ▷ *flexible working hours* un horario de trabajo flexible

flick *vb* **to flick through a book** hojear [25] un libro

flight *n* vuelo *m* ▷ *What time is the flight to Paris?* ¿A qué hora es el vuelo para París?; **a flight of stairs** un tramo de escaleras

flight attendant *n* auxiliar de vuelo *mf*

fling *vb* arrojar [25] ▷ *He flung the dictionary onto the floor.* Arrojó el diccionario al suelo.

float *vb* flotar [25]

flood *n* inundación *f* (pl inundaciones) ▷ *The rain has caused many floods.* La lluvia ha provocado muchas inundaciones.; **He received a flood of letters.** Recibió un aluvión de cartas.
▶ *vb* inundar [25] ▷ *The river was flooded the village.* El río ha inundado el pueblo.

floor *n* **①** suelo *m* (piso *m LatAm*); **the dance floor** la pista de baile **②** piso *m* ▷ *on the first floor* en el primer piso

florist *n* florista *mf*

flour *n* harina *f*

flower *n* flor *f* (pl flores)
▶ *vb* florecer [12]

flown *vb see* **fly**

flu *n* gripe *f* ▷ *I've got flu.* Tengo gripe.

fluent *adj* **He speaks fluent Spanish.** Habla español con fluidez.

flung *vb see* **fling**

flush *vb* **to flush the toilet** tirar [25] de la cadena

flute *n* flauta *f*

fly *n* mosca *f*
▶ *vb* volar [11] ▷ *He flew from London to Glasgow.* Voló de Londres a Glasgow. ▷ *The bird flew away.* El pájaro salió volando.

focus *n* centro *m* ▷ *He was the focus of attention.* Era el centro de atención.; **to be out of focus** estar [22] desenfocado
▶ *vb* enfocar [48] ▷ *Try to focus the binoculars.* Intenta enfocar los prismáticos.; **to focus on something** (1) (*with camera, telescope*) enfocar [48] algo ▷ *The cameraman focused on the bird.* El cámara enfocó al pájaro. (2) (*concentrate on*) centrarse [25] en algo

fog *n* niebla *f*

foggy *adj* **It's foggy.** Hay niebla.; **a foggy day** un día de niebla

foil *n* (*kitchen foil*) papel de aluminio *m*

fold *n* pliegue *m*
▶ *vb* doblar [25] ▷ *He folded the newspaper in half.* Dobló el periódico por la mitad.; **to fold one's arms** cruzarse [13] de brazos

folder *n* carpeta *f*

follow vb seguir [**50**] ▷ You go first and I'll follow. Ve tú primero y yo te sigo.

following adj siguiente ▷ the following day al día siguiente

fond adj **to be fond of somebody** tener [**53**] cariño a alguien ▷ I'm very fond of her. Le tengo mucho cariño.

food n comida f ▷ cat food comida para gatos ▷ We need to buy some food. Hay que comprar comida.

fool n idiota mf

foot n ❶ (of person) pie m ▷ My feet are aching. Me duelen los pies.; **on foot** a pie

- In Spain measurements are in metres and centimetres rather than feet and inches. A foot is about 30 centimetres.

▷ Dave is six foot tall. Dave mide un metro ochenta. ❷ (of animal) pata f

football n ❶ fútbol m ▷ I like playing football. Me gusta jugar al fútbol. ❷ balón m (pl balones) ▷ Paul threw the football over the fence. Paul lanzó el balón por encima de la valla.

footballer n futbolista mf

footpath n sendero m

for prep

> There are three basic ways of translating 'for' into Spanish: **para**, **por** and **durante**. Check the tips and examples that follow each translation to find the meaning or example you need. If you can't find it look at the phrases at the end of the entry.

❶ **para**

> **para** is used to indicate destination, employment, intention and purpose.

▷ a present for me un regalo para mí
▷ He works for the government. Trabaja para el gobierno. ▷ What for? ¿Para qué? ▷ What's it for? ¿Para qué es? ❷ **por**

> **por** is used to indicate reason or cause. Use it also when talking about amounts of money.

▷ I'll do it for you. Lo haré por ti.
▷ I sold it for £5. Lo vendí por 5 libras.
▷ What did he do that for? ¿Por qué ha hecho eso? ❸ **durante**

> When referring to periods of time, use **durante** to refer to the future and completed actions in the past. Note that it can often be omitted, as in the next two examples.

▷ She will be away for a month. Estará fuera (durante) un mes.
▷ He worked in Spain for two years. Trabajó (durante) dos años en España.

> Use **hace...que** and the present to describe actions and states that started in the past and are still going on. Alternatively use the present and **desde hace**. Another option is **llevar** and an **-ando/-iendo** form.

▷ He has been learning French for two years. Hace dos años que estudia francés. ▷ I haven't seen her for two years. No la veo desde hace dos

367 | **formal**

años. ▷ *She's been learning German for four years.* Lleva cuatro años estudiando alemán.

See how the tenses change when talking about something that 'had' happened or 'had been' happening 'for' a time. ▷ *He had been learning French for two years.* Hacía dos años que estudiaba francés. ▷ *I hadn't seen her for two years.* No la veía desde hacía dos años. ▷ *She had been learning German for four years.* Llevaba cuatro años estudiando alemán.; **There are road works for three kilometres.** Hay obras en tres kilómetros.; **What's the English for 'león'?** ¿Cómo se dice 'león' en inglés?; **It's time for lunch.** Es la hora de comer.; **Can you do it for tomorrow?** ¿Puedes hacerlo para mañana?; **Are you for or against the idea?** ¿Estás a favor o en contra de la idea?

forbid *vb* prohibir [42]; **to forbid somebody to do something** prohibir [42] a alguien que haga algo

force *n* fuerza *f* ▷ *the force of the explosion* la fuerza de la explosión; **UN forces** las fuerzas de la ONU; **in force** *(law, rules)* en vigor ▸ *vb* obligar [37] ▷ *They forced him to open the safe.* Le obligaron a abrir la caja fuerte.

forecast *n* **the weather forecast** el pronóstico del tiempo

forehead *n* frente *f*

foreign *adj* **❶** extranjero(-a) ▷ *a foreign language* una lengua

extranjera **❷** exterior ▷ *US foreign policy* la política exterior estadounidense

foreigner *n* extranjero *m*, extranjera *f*

forest *n* bosque *m*

forever *adv* **❶** para siempre ▷ *He's gone forever.* Se ha ido para siempre. **❷** siempre ▷ *She's forever complaining.* Siempre se está quejando.

forgave *vb see* **forgive**

forge *vb* falsificar [48] ▷ *She forged his signature.* Falsificó su firma.

forget *vb* olvidar [25] ▷ *I've forgotten his name.* He olvidado su nombre.; **to forget to do something** olvidarse [25] de hacer algo ▷ *I forgot to close the window.* Me olvidé de cerrar la ventana.; **I'm sorry, I had completely forgotten!** ¡Lo siento, se me había olvidado por completo!; **Forget it!** ¡No importa!

forgive *vb* perdonar [25] ▷ *I forgive you.* Te perdono.; **to forgive somebody for doing something** perdonar [25] a alguien que haya hecho algo

fork *n* **❶** *(for eating)* tenedor *m* **❷** horca *f* **❸** *(in road)* bifurcación *f* *(pl* bifurcaciones)

form *n* **❶** impreso *m* (planilla *f* LatAm); **to fill in a form** rellenar [25] un impreso **❷** forma *f* ▷ *I'm against hunting in any form.* Estoy en contra de cualquier forma de caza.

formal *adj* **❶** oficial ▷ *a formal occasion* un acto oficial **❷** formal ▷ *In English, 'residence' is a formal*

a
b
c
d
e
f
g
h
i
j
k
l
m
n
o
p
q
r
s
t
u
v
w
x
y
z

term. En inglés, 'residence' es un término formal.

former *adj* antiguo(-a)
> ▌Put **antiguo** before the noun when translating 'former'.
▷ *a former pupil* un antiguo alumno

fort *n* fuerte *m*

fortnight *n* a **fortnight** quince días ▷ *I'm going on holiday for a fortnight*. Me voy quince días de vacaciones.

fortunate *adj* He was extremely **fortunate to survive**. Tuvo la gran suerte de salir vivo.; **It's fortunate that I remembered the map.** Menos mal que me acordé de traer el mapa.

fortunately *adv* afortunadamente

fortune *n* fortuna *f* ▷ *He made his fortune in car sales*. Consiguió su fortuna con la venta de coches.; **Kate earns a fortune!** ¡Kate gana un dineral!; **to tell somebody's fortune** decir [15] la buenaventura a alguien

forty *num* cuarenta ▷ *He's forty*. Tiene cuarenta años.

forward *adv* hacia delante ▷ *to look forward* mirar hacia delante; **to move forward** avanzar [13]
▶ *vb* (letter) remitir [58]

foster child *n* niño acogido en una familia *m*

fought *vb* see **fight**

foul *adj* ❶ horrible ▷ *The weather was foul*. El tiempo era horrible.
❷ asqueroso(-a) ▷ *It smells foul*. Huele asqueroso.; **Brenda is in**

a foul mood. Brenda está de muy mal humor.
▶ *n* (in sports) falta *f*

found *vb* see **find**
▶ *vb* fundar [25]

fountain *n* fuente *f*

fountain pen *n* pluma estilográfica *f* (plumafuente *f* LatAm)

four *num* cuatro ▷ *She's four*. Tiene cuatro años.

fourteen *num* catorce ▷ *I'm fourteen*. Tengo catorce años.

fourteenth *adj* decimocuarto(-a); **the fourteenth of July** el catorce de julio

fourth *adj* cuarto(-a) ▷ *the fourth floor* el cuarto piso; **the fourth of July** el cuatro de julio

fox *n* zorro *m*

fragile *adj* frágil

frame *n* marco *m* ▷ *a silver frame* un marco de plata; **glasses with plastic frames** gafas con montura de plástico

France *n* Francia *f*

frantic *adj* frenético(-a) ▷ *I was going frantic*. Me estaba poniendo frenético.; **to be frantic with worry** estar [22] muerto de preocupación

fraud *n* ❶ fraude *m* ▷ *He was jailed for fraud*. Lo encarcelaron por fraude. ❷ impostor *m*, impostora *f* ▷ *You're a fraud!* ¡Eres un impostor!

freckles *npl* pecas *fpl*

free *adj* ❶ gratuito(-a) ▷ *a free brochure* un folleto gratuito; **You can get it for free.** Se puede conseguir gratis. ❷ libre ▷ *Is this*

seat free? ¿Está libre este asiento?
▷ *Are you free after school?* ¿Estás libre después de clase?
▶ *vb* liberar **[25]**

freedom n libertad f

freeway n (US) autopista f

freeze vb ❶ congelar **[25]** ▷ *She froze the rest of the raspberries.* Congeló el resto de las frambuesas. ❷ helarse **[39]** ▷ *The water had frozen.* El agua se había helado.

freezer n congelador m

freezing adj **It's freezing!** ¡Hace un frío que pela! (informal); **I'm freezing!** ¡Me estoy congelando!

French adj francés (f francesa, pl franceses)
▶ n (language) francés m ▷ *the French teacher* el profesor de francés; **the French** los franceses

French beans npl judías verdes fpl

French fries npl patatas fritas fpl (papas fritas fpl LatAm)

French horn n trompa de llaves f

French loaf n barra de pan f

Frenchman n francés m (pl franceses)

French windows npl puerta ventana f

Frenchwoman n francesa f

frequent adj frecuente

fresh adj fresco(-a) ▷ *I always buy fresh fish.* Siempre compro pescado fresco.; **I need some fresh air.** Necesito tomar el aire.

Friday n viernes m (pl viernes)
▷ *I saw her on Friday.* La vi el viernes.
▷ *every Friday* todos los viernes
▷ *last Friday* el viernes pasado

▷ *next Friday* el viernes que viene
▷ *on Fridays* los viernes

fridge n nevera f (refrigeradora f LatAm)

fried adj frito(-a) ▷ *a fried egg* un huevo frito

friend n amigo m, amiga f
▶ *vb* añadir **[58]** como amigo a
▷ *I've friended her on Facebook.* La he añadido como amiga en Facebook.

friendly adj simpático(-a) ▷ *She's really friendly.* Es muy simpática.; **Liverpool is a friendly city.** Liverpool es una ciudad acogedora.; **a friendly match** un partido amistoso

friendship n amistad f

fright n susto m ▷ *She gave us a fright.* Nos dio un susto. ▷ *to get a fright* llevarse un susto

frighten vb asustar **[25]** ▷ *She was trying to frighten him.* Intentaba asustarlo.; **Horror films frighten him.** Le dan miedo las películas de terror.

frightened adj **to be frightened** tener **[53]** miedo ▷ *I'm frightened!* ¡Tengo miedo!; **Anna's frightened of spiders.** A Anna le dan miedo las arañas.

frightening adj aterrador(a)

fringe n flequillo m ▷ *She's got a fringe.* Lleva flequillo.

frog n rana f

from prep ❶ de ▷ *Where do you come from?* ¿De dónde eres? ▷ *a letter from my sister* una carta de mi hermana ▷ *The hotel is one kilometre from the beach.* El hotel está a un kilómetro de la playa. ▷ *The price was reduced from £10 to £5.* Rebajaron el precio de 10 a 5 libras esterlinas. ❷ **desde** ▷ *Breakfast is available from 6 a.m.* Se puede desayunar desde las 6 de la mañana. ▷ *I can't see anything from here.* Desde aquí no veo nada.

> In the following three phrases **de** and **desde** are interchangeable. Use **a** to translate 'to' if you have chosen **de** and **hasta** if you have opted for **desde**.

He flew from London to Bilbao. Voló de Londres a Bilbao.; **from one o'clock to three** desde la una hasta las tres; **from...onwards** a partir de... ▷ *We'll be at home from seven o'clock onwards.* Estaremos en casa a partir de las siete.

front *n* parte delantera *f* ▷ *The switch is at the front of the vacuum cleaner.* El interruptor está en la parte delantera de la aspiradora.; **the front of the dress** el delantero del vestido; **the front of the house** la fachada de la casa; **I was sitting in the front.** *(of car)* Yo iba sentado delante.; **at the front of the train** al principio del tren; **in front** delante ▷ *the car in front* el coche de delante; **in front of** delante de ▷ *Irene sits in front of me in class.* Irene se sienta delante de mí en clase.

▷ *adj* ❶ primero(-a) ▷ *the front row* la primera fila

> Use **primer** before a masculine singular noun.

▷ *the front seat* el primer asiento ❷ delantero(-a) ▷ *the front seats of the car* los asientos delanteros del coche; **the front door** la puerta principal

frontier *n* frontera *f*

frost *n* helada *f* ▷ *There was a frost last night.* Anoche cayó una helada.

frosting *n* (US: on cake) glaseado *m*

frosty *adj* **It's frosty today.** Hoy ha helado.

frown *vb* fruncir [58] el ceño

frozen *adj* congelado(-a)

fruit *n* fruta *f*; **fruit juice** el zumo de fruta (el jugo de fruta *LatAm*); **fruit salad** la macedonia (la ensalada de frutas *LatAm*)

frustrated *adj* frustrado(-a)

fry *vb* freír [23]

frying pan *n* sartén *f* (pl sartenes)

fuel *n* combustible *m* ▷ *We've run out of fuel.* Nos hemos quedado sin combustible.

full *adj* ❶ lleno(-a) ▷ *The tank's full.* El depósito está lleno.; **I'm full.** Estoy lleno.; **There was a full moon.** Había luna llena. ❷ completo(-a) ▷ *He asked for full information on the job.* Solicitó información completa sobre el trabajo. ▷ *My full name is Ian John Marr.* Mi nombre completo es Ian John Marr.; **full board** la pensión completa; **at full speed** a toda velocidad

full stop *n* (punctuation mark) punto *m*

full-time *adj, adv* **She's got a full-time job.** Tiene un trabajo de jornada completa.; **She works full-time.** Trabaja la jornada completa.

fully adv (completely) completamente

fumes npl humo m

fun adj divertido(-a) ▷ She's a fun person. Es una persona divertida. ▶ n to have fun divertirse [**51**]; **It's fun!** ¡Es divertido!; **Have fun!** ¡Que te diviertas!; **for fun** por gusto; **to make fun of somebody** reírse [**44**] de alguien

funds npl fondos mpl ▷ to raise funds recaudar fondos

funeral n funeral m

funfair n ❶ (travelling fair) feria f ❷ (fair on permanent site) parque de atracciones m

funny adj ❶ gracioso(-a) ▷ a funny joke un chiste gracioso ❷ raro(-a) ▷ There's something funny about him. Hay algo raro en él.

fur n ❶ piel f; **a fur coat** un abrigo de pieles ❷ pelaje m ▷ the cat's fur el pelaje del gato

furious adj furioso(-a)

furniture n muebles mpl; **a piece of furniture** un mueble

further adv, adj ❶ más lejos ▷ London is further from here than Paris. Londres está más lejos de aquí que París.; **I can't walk any further.** No puedo andar más.; **How much further is it?** ¿Cuánto queda todavía? ❷ más ▷ Please write to us if you need any further information. No dude en escribirnos si necesita más información.

further education n educación superior f

fuse n fusible m ▷ The fuse has blown. Se ha fundido el fusible.

fuss n jaleo m ▷ What's all the fuss about? ¿A qué viene tanto jaleo?; **He's always making a fuss about nothing.** (informal) Siempre monta el número por cualquier tontería.

fussy adj quisquilloso(-a) ▷ She is very fussy about her food. Es muy quisquillosa con la comida.

future n futuro m ▷ What are your plans for the future? ¿Qué planes tienes para el futuro?; **in future** de ahora en adelante ▷ Be more careful in future. De ahora en adelante ten más cuidado.

g

gain vb ganar [25] ▷ *What do you hope to gain from this?* ¿Qué esperas ganar con esto?; **to gain speed** adquirir [2] velocidad; **to gain weight** engordar [25]

gallery n ❶ (state-owned) museo de arte m ❷ (private) galería de arte

gamble vb jugarse [28] ▷ *He gambled £100 at the casino.* Se jugó 100 libras en el casino.

gambling n juego m

game n ❶ juego m ▷ *The children were playing a game.* Los niños jugaban a un juego. ❷ partido m ▷ *a game of football* un partido de fútbol; **a game of cards** una partida de cartas; **We have games on Thursdays.** Tenemos deporte los jueves.

gamer n (on computer) gamer mf

gang n ❶ (of thieves, troublemakers) banda f ❷ (of friends) pandilla f

gangster n gángster m

gap n ❶ hueco m ▷ *There's a gap in the hedge.* Hay un hueco en el seto. ❷ intervalo m ▷ *a gap of four years* un intervalo de cuatro años

garage n ❶ (for keeping the car) garaje m ❷ (for car repairs) taller m

garbage n basura f ▷ *the garbage can* el cubo de la basura; **That's garbage!** ¡Eso son tonterías!

garden n jardín m (pl jardines)

gardener n jardinero m, jardinera f ▷ *He's a gardener.* Es jardinero.

gardening n jardinería f ▷ *Margaret loves gardening.* A Margaret le encanta la jardinería.

garlic n ajo m

garment n prenda de vestir f

gas n ❶ gas m ▷ **a gas cooker** una cocina de gas; **a gas fire** una estufa de gas; **a gas leak** un escape de gas ❷ (US: petrol) gasolina f

gasoline n (US) gasolina f

gate n ❶ (made of wood) puerta f ❷ (made of metal) verja f; **Please go to gate seven.** Diríjanse a la puerta siete.

gather vb ❶ reunirse [46] ▷ *We gathered around the fireplace.* Nos reunimos en torno a la chimenea. ❷ reunir [46] ▷ *We gathered enough firewood to last the night.* Reunimos leña suficiente para toda la noche.; **to gather speed** adquirir [2] velocidad ▷ *The train gathered speed.* El tren adquirió velocidad.

gave vb see **give**

gay adj gay

GCSE n (= General Certificate of Secondary Education)
  In Spain, under the reformed educational system, if you leave school at the age of 16, you get a **Título de Graduado en Educación Secundaria**.

gear n ❶ marcha f ▷ to change gear cambiar de marcha; **in first gear** en primera ❷ equipo m ▷ camping gear el equipo de acampada; **sports gear** la ropa de deporte

gear lever n palanca de cambio f

gearshift n (US) palanca de cambio f

geese npl see **goose**

gel n gel m; **hair gel** el fijador

Gemini n (sign) Géminis m; **I'm Gemini.** Soy géminis.

gender n (of noun) género m

general n general m
  ▶adj general; **in general** en general

general election n elecciones generales fpl

general knowledge n cultura general f

generally adv generalmente ▷ I generally go shopping on Saturdays. Generalmente voy de compras los sábados.

generation n generación f (pl generaciones) ▷ the younger generation la nueva generación

generous adj generoso(-a) ▷ That's very generous of you. Es muy generoso de tu parte.

Geneva n Ginebra f

genius n genio m ▷ She's a genius. Es un genio.

gentle adj ❶ (person, voice) dulce ❷ (wind, touch) suave

gentleman n caballero m

gently adv ❶ (to say, smile) dulcemente ❷ (to touch) suavemente

gents n servicio de caballeros m ▷ Can you tell me where the gents is, please? ¿El servicio de caballeros, por favor?; **'gents'** (on sign) 'caballeros'

genuine adj ❶ auténtico(-a) ▷ These are genuine diamonds. Estos son diamantes auténticos. ❷ sincero(-a) ▷ She's a very genuine person. Es una persona muy sincera.

geography n geografía f

gerbil n gerbo m

germ n microbio m

German adj alemán (f alemana, pl alemanes)
  ▶n ❶ (person) alemán m (pl alemanes), alemana f ▷ the Germans los alemanes ❷ (language) alemán m ▷ our German teacher nuestro profesor de alemán

German measles n rubéola f ▷ to have German measles tener rubéola

Germany n Alemania f

get vb
  There are several ways of translating 'get'. Scan the examples to find one that is similar to what you want to say.
  ❶ (have, receive) recibir [58] ▷ I got a letter from him. Recibí una carta de él.; **I got lots of presents.** Me hicieron muchos regalos.

❷ (obtain) conseguir [**50**] ▷ He had trouble getting a hotel room. Tuvo dificultades para conseguir una habitación de hotel.; **to get something for somebody** conseguir [**50**] algo a alguien ▷ The librarian got the book for me. El bibliotecario me consiguió el libro.; **Jackie got good exam results.** Jackie sacó buenas notas en los exámenes. **❸** (fetch) ir [**27**] a buscar ▷ Quick, get help! ¡Rápido, ve a buscar ayuda! **❹** (catch, take) coger [**7**]

Be very careful with the verb **coger**: in most of Latin America this is an extremely rude word that should be avoided. However, in Spain this verb is common and not rude at all.

▷ They've got the thief. Han cogido al ladrón. (Han atrapado al ladrón. LatAm) ▷ I'm getting the bus into town. Voy a coger el autobús al centro. (Voy a tomar el autobús al centro. LatAm) **❺** (understand) entender [**20**] ▷ I don't get the joke. No entiendo el chiste. **❻** (arrive) llegar [**37**] ▷ He should get here soon. Debería llegar pronto.; **to get angry** enfadarse [**25**] (enojarse [**25**] LatAm); **to get tired** cansarse [**25**]

For other phrases with 'get' and an adjective, such as 'to get old', 'to get drunk', you should look under the word 'old', 'drunk', etc.

to get something done mandar

[**25**] hacer algo ▷ I'm getting my car fixed. He mandado arreglar el coche.; **I got my hair cut.** Me corté el pelo.; **I'll get it!** (1) (telephone) ¡Yo contesto! (2) (door) ¡Ya voy yo!

get away vb escapar [**25**] ▷ One of the burglars got away. Uno de los ladrones escapó.

get back vb **❶** volver [**59**] ▷ What time did you get back? ¿A qué hora volvisteis? **❷** recuperar [**25**] ▷ He got his money back. Recuperó el dinero.

get in vb llegar [**37**] ▷ What time did you get in last night? ¿A qué hora llegaste anoche?

get into vb entrar [**25**] en ▷ How did you get into the house? ¿Cómo entraste en la casa?; **Sharon got into the car.** Sharon subió al coche.; **Get into bed!** ¡Métete en la cama!

get off vb **❶** bajarse [**25**] de ▷ Isobel got off the train. Isobel se bajó del tren. **❷** salir [**49**] ▷ He managed to get off early from work yesterday. Logró salir de trabajar pronto ayer.

get on vb **❶** subirse [**58**] a ▷ Phyllis got on the bus. Phyllis se subió al autobús. **❷** llevarse [**25**] bien ▷ We got on really well. Nos llevábamos muy bien. ▷ He doesn't get on with his parents. No se lleva bien con sus padres.; **How are you getting on?** ¿Cómo te va?

get out vb **❶** salir [**49**] ▷ Get out! ¡Sal!; **She got out of the car.** Se bajó del coche. **❷** sacar [**48**] ▷ She got the map out. Sacó el mapa.

get over vb ❶ recuperarse [25] de
▷ It took her a long time to get over the
illness. Tardó mucho tiempo en
recuperarse de la enfermedad.
❷ superar [25] ▷ He managed to get
over the problem. Logró superar el
problema.

get together vb reunirse [46]
▷ Could we get together this evening?
¿Podemos reunirnos esta tarde?

get up vb levantarse [25] ▷ What
time do you get up? ¿A qué hora te
levantas?

ghost n fantasma m

Although **fantasma** ends in -a,
it is actually a masculine noun.

giant adj enorme

gift n ❶ regalo m; **to have a gift for
something** tener [53] dotes para
algo ▷ Dave's got a gift for painting.
Dave tiene dotes para la pintura.

gin n ginebra f

ginger n jengibre m
▶ adj **She's got ginger hair.** Es
pelirroja.

giraffe n jirafa f

girl n ❶ (young) niña f ▷ a five-year
old girl una niña de cinco años
❷ (older) chica f ▷ a sixteen-year old
girl una chica de dieciséis años

girlfriend n ❶ novia f ▷ Paul's
girlfriend is called Janice. La novia de
Paul se llama Janice. ❷ amiga f
▷ She often went out with her girlfriends.
Solía salir con sus amigas.

give vb dar [14]; **to give
something to somebody** dar [14]
algo a alguien ▷ He gave me £10. Me
dio 10 libras.; **to give somebody a
present** hacer [26] un regalo a

alguien; **to give way** (in car) ceder
[8] el paso

give in vb rendirse [38] ▷ I give in!
¡Me rindo!

give out vb repartir [58]

give up vb darse [14] por vencido
▷ I couldn't do it, so I gave up. No
podía hacerlo, así que me di por
vencido.; **to give oneself up**
entregarse [37] ▷ She gave herself
up. Se entregó.; **to give up doing
something** dejar [25] de hacer
algo ▷ He gave up smoking. Dejó de
fumar.

glad adj contento(-a) ▷ She's glad
she's done it. Está contenta de
haberlo hecho.

alegrarse de que has to be
followed by a verb in the
subjunctive.

I'm glad you're here. Me alegro de
que estés aquí.

glamorous adj atractivo(-a)

glance vb to glance at something
echar [25] una mirada a algo
▷ Peter glanced at his watch. Peter
echó una mirada al reloj.
▶ n mirada f

glass n ❶ (without stem) vaso m ▷ a
glass of milk un vaso de leche
❷ (with stem) copa f ▷ a glass of
champagne una copa de champán
❸ (substance) vidrio m ▷ a glass door
una puerta de vidrio

glasses npl gafas fpl (anteojos mpl
LatAm)

glider n planeador m

global adj mundial ▷ on a global
scale a escala mundial; **a global
view** una visión global

global warming n calentamiento global m

globe n globo terráqueo m

gloomy adj oscuro(-a) ▷ He lives in a small gloomy flat. Vive en un piso pequeño y oscuro.; **She's been feeling very gloomy recently.** Últimamente está muy desanimada.

glorious adj espléndido(-a)

glove n guante m

glue n pegamento m
▶ vb pegar [37]; **to glue something together** pegar [37] algo

GM adj (= genetically-modified); **GM foods** los alimentos transgénicos

go n to have a go at doing something probar [11] a hacer algo ▷ He had a go at making a cake. Probó a hacer una tarta.; **Whose go is it?** ¿A quién le toca?; **It's your go.** Te toca a ti.
▶ vb ❶ ir [27] ▷ Where are you going? ¿Adónde vas? ▷ I'm going to the cinema tonight. Voy al cine esta noche. ❷ (leave, go away) irse [27] ▷ Where's Judy? — She's gone. ¿Dónde está Judy? — Se ha ido. ▷ I'm going now. Yo me voy ya. ▷ We went home. Nos fuimos a casa. ❸ (work) funcionar [25] ▷ My car won't go. El coche no funciona.; **to go home** irse [27] a casa; **to go into** entrar [25] en ▷ She went into the kitchen. Entró en la cocina.; **to go for a walk** ir [27] a dar un paseo; **How did the exam go?** ¿Cómo te fue en el examen?; **I'm going to do it tomorrow.** Lo voy a hacer mañana.; **It's going to be**

difficult. Va a ser difícil.

go after vb perseguir [50] ▷ Quick, go after them! ¡Rápido, persíguelos!

go ahead vb seguir [50] adelante ▷ We'll go ahead with your suggestion. Seguiremos adelante con su propuesta.

go away vb irse [27] ▷ Go away! ¡Vete!

go back vb volver [59] ▷ We went back to the same place. Volvimos al mismo sitio. ▷ He's gone back home. Ha vuelto a casa.

go by vb pasar [25] ▷ Two police officers went by. Pasaron dos policías.

go down vb ❶ bajar [25] ▷ He went down the stairs. Bajó las escaleras. ▷ The price of computers has gone down. Ha bajado el precio de los ordenadores. ❷ (deflate) desinflarse [25] ▷ My airbed's gone down. Mi colchoneta se ha desinflado.; **My brother's gone down with flu.** Mi hermano ha pillado la gripe.

go for vb ir [27] a por ▷ Suddenly the dog went for me. De pronto el perro fue a por mí.; **Go for it!** ¡Adelante!

go in vb entrar [25] ▷ He knocked on the door and went in. Llamó a la puerta y entró.

go off vb ❶ (leave) marcharse [25] ▷ They went off after lunch. Se marcharon después de comer. ❷ (explode) estallar [25] ▷ The bomb went off at 10 o'clock. La bomba estalló a las 10.; **The gun went off by accident.** El arma se disparó accidentalmente. ❸ (sound) sonar

[11] ▷ *My alarm goes off at seven.* Mi despertador suena a las siete. ❹ *(go bad)* echarse **[25]** ▷ *This milk has gone off.* Esta leche se ha echado a perder. ❺ *(go out)* apagarse **[37]** ▷ *All the lights went off.* Se apagaron todas las luces.; **I've gone off that idea.** Ya no me gusta la idea.

go on *vb* ❶ pasar **[25]** ▷ *What's going on?* ¿Qué pasa? ❷ *(continue)* seguir **[50]**; **to go on doing** seguir **[50]** haciendo ▷ *He went on reading.* Siguió leyendo. ❸ durar **[25]** ▷ *The concert went on until* 11 *o'clock at night.* El concierto duró hasta las 11 de la noche.; **to go on at somebody** dar **[14]** la lata a alguien ▷ *They're always going on at me.* Están siempre dándome la lata.; **Go on!** ¡Venga! ▷ *Go on, tell me what the problem is!* ¡Venga, dime cuál es el problema!

go out *vb* ❶ salir **[49]** ▷ *Are you going out tonight?* ¿Vas a salir esta noche? ▷ *I went out with Steven last night.* Ayer por la noche salí con Steven. ▷ *They went out for a meal.* Salieron a comer.; **Are you going out with him?** ¿Estás saliendo con él? ❷ apagarse **[37]** ▷ *Suddenly the lights went out.* De pronto se apagaron las luces.

go past *vb* **to go past something** pasar **[25]** por delante de algo ▷ *He went past the shop.* Pasó por delante de la tienda.

go round *vb* visitar **[25]** ▷ *We want to go round the museum today.* Hoy queremos visitar el museo.; **I love**

going round the shops. Me encanta ir de tiendas.; **to go round to somebody's house** **[27]** a casa de alguien ▷ *We're all going round to Linda's house tonight.* Esta noche vamos todos a casa de Linda.; **There's a bug going round.** Hay un virus por ahí rondando.; **Is there enough food to go round?** ¿Hay comida suficiente para todos?

go through *vb* ❶ atravesar **[39]** ▷ *We went through London to get to Brighton.* Atravesamos Londres para llegar a Brighton. ❷ pasar **[25]** por ▷ *I know what you're going through.* Sé por lo que estás pasando. ❸ repasar **[25]** ▷ *They went through the plan again.* Repasaron de nuevo el plan. ❹ registrar **[25]** ▷ *Someone had gone through her things.* Alguien había registrado sus cosas.

go up *vb* subir **[58]** ▷ *She went up the stairs.* Subió las escaleras. ▷ *The price has gone up.* El precio ha subido.; **to go up in flames** arder **[8]** en llamas

go with *vb* pegar **[37]** con ▷ *Does this blouse go with that skirt?* ¿Pega esta blusa con la falda?

goal *n* ❶ gol *m* ▷ *He scored the first goal.* Él metió el primer gol. ❷ objetivo *m* ▷ *His goal is to become the world champion.* Su objetivo es ser campeón del mundo.

goalkeeper *n* portero *m*

goat *n* cabra *f*; **goat's cheese** el queso de cabra

god n dios m ▷ I believe in God. Creo en Dios.

goddaughter n ahijada f

godfather n padrino m

godmother n madrina f

godson n ahijado m

goggles npl gafas protectoras fpl (anteojos protectores mpl LatAm)

gold n oro m ▷ a gold necklace un collar de oro

goldfish n pez de colores m (pl peces de colores)

golf n golf m; **a golf club (1)** (stick) un palo de golf **(2)** (place) un club de golf; **a golf course** un campo de golf

gone vb see **go**

good adj ❶ bueno(-a)

    Use **buen** before a masculine singular noun.

▷ a good day un buen día ▷ It's a very good film. Es una película muy buena. ❷ (kind) amable ▷ That's very good of you. Es muy amable de tu parte.; **They were very good to me.** Se portaron muy bien conmigo.; **Have a good journey!** ¡Buen viaje!; **Good!** ¡Bien!; **Good morning!** ¡Buenos días!; **Good afternoon!** ¡Buenas tardes!; **Good evening!** ¡Buenas noches!; **Good night!** ¡Buenas noches!; **I'm feeling really good today.** Hoy me siento realmente bien.; **to be good for somebody** hacer [26] bien a alguien ▷ Vegetables are good for you. La verdura te hace bien.; **Jane's very good at maths.** A Jane se le dan muy bien las matemáticas.; **for good**

definitivamente ▷ One day he left for good. Un día se marchó definitivamente.; **It's no good complaining.** De nada sirve quejarse.

goodbye excl ¡adiós!

Good Friday n Viernes Santo m

good-looking adj guapo(-a)

goods npl productos mpl ▷ They sell a wide range of goods. Venden una amplia gama de productos.

google vb buscar [48] en Google

goose n oca f

gorgeous adj ❶ guapísimo(-a) ▷ She's gorgeous! ¡Es guapísima! ❷ estupendo(-a) ▷ The weather was gorgeous. El tiempo fue estupendo.

gorilla n gorila m

    Although **gorila** ends in **-a**, it is actually a masculine noun.

gospel n evangelio m

gossip n ❶ (rumours) cotilleo m ❷ (person) cotilla mf
▶ vb cotillear [25] (comadrear [25] LatAm) ▷ They were always gossiping. Siempre estaban cotilleando.

got vb **to have got** (own) tener [53] ▷ How many have you got? ¿Cuántos tienes?; **to have got to do something** tener [53] que hacer algo ▷ I've got to tell him. Tengo que decírselo.

government n gobierno m

GP n (= General Practitioner) médico de cabecera m, médica de cabecera f

grab vb agarrar [25] ▷ He grabbed my arm. Me agarró el brazo.

graceful adj elegante

grade n nota f ▷ He got good grades in his exams. Sacó buenas notas en los exámenes.

grade school n (US) escuela primaria f

gradual adj gradual

gradually adv gradualmente

graduate n ❶ (from university) licenciado m, licenciada f (egresado m, egresada f LatAm) ❷ (from US high school) bachiller mf

graffiti npl pintadas fpl

grain n ❶ grano m ▷ a grain of rice un grano de arroz ❷ (wheat, corn etc) cereales mpl

gram n gramo m

grammar n gramática f

grammar school n

The equivalent to a grammar school in Spain is **el instituto de segunda enseñanza**.

grammatical adj gramatical

gramme n gramo m

grand adj grandioso(-a) ▷ Her house is very grand. Su casa es grandiosa.

grandchildren npl nietos mpl

granddad n abuelo m

granddaughter n nieta f

grandfather n abuelo m

grandma n abuela f

grandmother n abuela f

grandpa n abuelo m

grandparents npl abuelos mpl

grandson n nieto m

granny n abuelita f

grape n uva f

grapefruit n pomelo m

graph n gráfico m

grass n ❶ hierba f ▷ The grass is long. La hierba está alta. ❷ (lawn)

césped m; **'Keep off the grass'** 'Prohibido pisar el césped'; **to cut the grass** cortar [25] el césped

grasshopper n saltamontes m (pl saltamontes)

grate vb rallar [25] ▷ grated cheese el queso rallado

grateful adj agradecido(-a)

grave n tumba f

gravel n grava f

graveyard n cementerio m

gravy n jugo de carne m

grease n ❶ (in hair, on skin) grasa f ❷ (for cars, machines) aceite m

greasy adj ❶ aceitoso(-a) ▷ The food was very greasy. La comida estaba muy aceitosa. ❷ graso(-a) ▷ He has greasy hair. Tiene el pelo graso.

great adj ❶ estupendo(-a) (chévere LatAm) ▷ That's great! ¡Estupendo! ❷ grande

Use **gran** before a singular noun.

▷ a great oak tree un gran roble

Great Britain n Gran Bretaña f

great-grandfather n bisabuelo m

great-grandmother n bisabuela f

Greece n Grecia f

greedy adj ❶ glotón (f glotona, pl glotones) ▷ Don't be greedy, you've already had three doughnuts. No seas glotón, ya te has comido tres donuts. ❷ codicioso(-a) ▷ She is greedy and selfish. Es codiciosa y egoísta.

Greek adj griego(-a)

▶ n ❶ (person) griego m, griega f ▷ the Greeks los griegos ❷ (language) griego m

a
b
c
d
e
f
g
h
i
j
k
l
m
n
o
p
q
r
s
t
u
v
w
x
y
z

green adj verde ▷ a green car un coche verde ▷ a green light (at traffic lights) un semáforo en verde; **the Green Party** el Partido Verde
▶ **n** verde m ▷ a dark green un verde oscuro; **greens** (vegetables) la verdura; **the Greens** (party) los verdes

greengrocer's n verdulería f

greenhouse n invernadero m; **the greenhouse effect** el efecto invernadero

greetings card n tarjeta de felicitación f

grew vb see **grow**

grey adj gris ▷ They wore grey suits. Llevaban trajes grises.; **He's going grey.** Se está saliendo canas.; **grey hair** las canas

grid n ❶ (in road, on map) cuadrícula f ❷ (of electricity) red f

grief n pena f

grill n ❶ (of cooker) grill m ❷ (for barbecue) parrilla f; **a mixed grill** una parrillada mixta
▶ **vb** ❶ (in cooker) hacer [**26**] al grill ❷ (barbecue) asar [**25**] a la parrilla

grin vb sonreír [**44**] ampliamente
▷ Dave grinned at me. Dave me sonrió ampliamente.
▶ **n** amplia sonrisa f

grip vb agarrar [**25**]

grit n gravilla f

groan vb gemir [**38**] ▷ He groaned with pain. Gimió de dolor.
▶ **n** gemido m

grocer n tendero m, tendera f

groceries npl (food) comestibles mpl; **I'll get some groceries.** Traeré algunas provisiones.

grocer's n tienda de ultramarinos f

grocery store n (US) tienda de ultramarinos f

groom n novio m ▷ the groom and his best man el novio y su padrino de boda

gross adj ❶ (revolting) horrible; **That's gross!** ¡Qué asco! ❷ bruto(-a) ▷ gross income ingresos brutos

ground n ❶ suelo m ▷ The ground's wet. El suelo está húmedo. ❷ campo m (cancha f LatAm) ▷ a football ground un campo de fútbol ❸ motivo m ▷ We've got grounds for complaint. Tenemos motivos para quejarnos.; **on the ground** en el suelo ▷ We sat on the ground. Nos sentamos en el suelo.

ground coffee n café molido m

ground floor n planta baja f

group n grupo m

grow vb ❶ crecer [**12**] ▷ Haven't you grown! ¡Cómo has crecido! ❷ aumentar [**25**] ▷ The number of unemployed has grown. Ha aumentado el número de desempleados. ❸ cultivar [**25**] ▷ He grew vegetables in his garden. Cultiva hortalizas en su jardín.; **He's grown out of his jacket.** La chaqueta se le ha quedado pequeña.; **to grow a beard** dejarse [**25**] barba ▷ I'm growing a beard. Me estoy dejando barba.; **He grew a moustache.** Se dejó bigote.

grow up vb criarse [**21**] ▷ I grew up in Rome. Me crie en Roma.; **Oh, grow up!** ¡No seas crío!

growl vb gruñir [45]

grown vb see **grow**

growth n crecimiento m ▷ economic growth crecimiento económico

grudge n to have a grudge against somebody guardar [25] rencor a alguien ▷ He's always had a grudge against me. Siempre me ha guardado rencor.

gruesome adj horroroso(-a)

guarantee n garantía f ▷ a five-year guarantee una garantía de cinco años ▷ It's still under guarantee. Todavía tiene garantía.
  ▶vb garantizar [13] ▷ I can't guarantee he'll come. No puedo garantizar que venga.

guard vb vigilar [25] ▷ The police were guarding the entrance. La policía vigilaba la entrada.
  ▶n ❶ (person) guardia mf ❷ (on train) jefe de tren m; **a security guard** un guarda jurado

guess vb adivinar [25] ▷ Can you guess what it is? A ver si adivinas qué es.; **to guess wrong** equivocarse [48]; **Guess what!** ¿Sabes qué?
  ▶n suposición f (pl suposiciones) ▷ It's just a guess. Solo es una suposición.; **Have a guess!** ¡Adivina!

guest n ❶ invitado m, invitada f ▷ We have guests staying with us. Tenemos invitados en casa. ❷ (in hotel) huésped mf

guide n ❶ (book) guía f ❷ (person) guía mf ❸ (girl guide) exploradora f

guidebook n guía f

guide dog n perro lazarillo m

guilty adj culpable ▷ He felt guilty about lying to her. Se sentía culpable por haberle mentido.; **He has a guilty conscience.** Tiene remordimientos de conciencia.

guinea pig n cobayo m ▷ She's got a guinea pig. Tiene un cobayo.

guitar n guitarra f

gum n (chewing gum) chicle m; **a piece of gum** un chicle; **gums** (in mouth) las encías

gun n ❶ (small) pistola f ❷ (rifle) fusil m

gunpoint n at gunpoint a punta de pistola

guy n tío m (informal)

> The word **tío** in this sense is confined to Spain. In Latin America, the equivalent is **tipo**.

▷ Who's that guy? ¿Quién es ese tío? ▷ He's a nice guy. Es un tío simpático.

gym n gimnasio m ▷ I go to the gym every day. Voy al gimnasio todos los días.; **gym classes** las clases de gimnasia

gymnast n gimnasta mf

gymnastics n gimnasia f

gypsy n gitano m, gitana f

h

habit n costumbre f

had vb see **have**

hadn't = had not

hail n granizo m
▷ vb granizar [13]

hair n pelo m ▷ She's got long hair. Tiene el pelo largo.; **to have one's hair cut** cortarse [25] el pelo; **to brush one's hair** cepillarse [25] el pelo; **to wash one's hair** lavarse [25] la cabeza

hairbrush n cepillo m

haircut n corte de pelo m ▷ You need a haircut. Necesitas un corte de pelo.; **to have a haircut** cortarse [25] el pelo

hairdresser n peluquero m, peluquera f ▷ He's a hairdresser. Es peluquero.; **at the hairdresser's** en la peluquería

hair dryer n secador de pelo m

hair gel n fijador m

hairgrip n horquilla f

hair spray n laca f

hairstyle n peinado m

half n ❶ mitad f ▷ half of the cake la mitad de la tarta; **to cut something in half** cortar [25] algo por la mitad ❷ (ticket) billete para niños m ▷ One and two halves, please. Un billete normal y dos para niños, por favor.; **two and a half** dos y medio; **half a kilo** medio kilo; **half an hour** media hora; **half past ten** las diez y media
▶ adj, adv medio(-a) ▷ a half chicken medio pollo

> When you use **medio** before an adjective, it does not change.

▷ She was half asleep. Estaba medio dormida. ▷ They were half drunk. Estaban medio borrachos.

half-price adj, adv a mitad de precio ▷ I bought it half-price. Lo compré a mitad de precio.

half-term n vacaciones de mitad de trimestre fpl

half-time n descanso m

halfway adv ❶ a medio camino ▷ Reading is halfway between Oxford and London. Reading está a medio camino entre Oxford y Londres. ❷ a la mitad ▷ halfway through the film a la mitad de la película

hall n ❶ (in house) vestíbulo m ❷ sala f ▷ a lecture hall una sala de conferencias; **a concert hall** un auditorio; **a sports hall** un gimnasio; **village hall** el salón de actos municipal

Hallowe'en n víspera de Todos los Santos f

hallway n vestíbulo m

ham n jamón m (pl jamones)

In Spain there are two basic kinds of ham in the shops: **jamón serrano**, which is cured and similar to Parma ham, and **jamón de York** or **jamón dulce**, which is boiled and similar to British ham.

hamburger n hamburguesa f

hammer n martillo m

hamster n hámster m

hand n ❶ (of person) mano f

Although **mano** ends in -o it is actually a feminine noun.

❷ (of clock) manecilla f; **to give someone a hand** echar [25] una mano a alguien ▷ Can you give me a hand? ¿Me echas una mano?; **on the one hand ..., on the other hand ...** por un lado ..., por otro ...

▶ vb pasar [25] ▷ He handed me the book. Me pasó el libro.

hand in vb entregar [37] ▷ Martin handed in his exam paper. Martin entregó su examen.

hand out vb repartir [58] ▷ The teacher handed out the books. El profesor repartió los libros.

handbag n bolso m (cartera f LatAm)

handcuffs npl esposas fpl

handkerchief n pañuelo m

handle n ❶ (of door) picaporte m ❷ (of cup, briefcase) asa f ❸ (of knife, saucepan) mango m

▶ vb ❶ encargarse [37] de ▷ Kath handled the travel arrangements. Kath se encargó de organizar el viaje. ❷ manejar [25] ▷ It was a difficult situation, but he handled it well. Era una situación difícil, pero él supo manejarla bien. ❸ tratar [25] ▷ She's good at handling children. Sabe tratar a los niños.; **'handle with care'** 'frágil'

handlebars npl manillar m

handmade adj hecho a mano (f hecha a mano)

handsome adj guapo(-a) ▷ My father's very handsome. Mi padre es muy guapo.

handwriting n letra f ▷ His handwriting is terrible. Tiene una letra horrible.

handy adj ❶ práctico(-a) ▷ This knife's very handy. Este cuchillo es muy práctico. ❷ a mano ▷ Have you got a pen handy? ¿Tienes un bolígrafo a mano?

hang vb ❶ colgar [28] ▷ Mike hung the painting on the wall. Mike colgó el cuadro en la pared. ▷ There was a bulb hanging from the ceiling. Una bombilla colgaba del techo. ❷ (execute) ahorcar [48]

hang around vb pasar [25] el rato ▷ On Saturdays we hang around in the park. Los sábados pasamos el rato en el parque.

hang on vb esperar [25] ▷ Hang on a minute please. Espera un momento, por favor.

hang up vb (clothes, phone) colgar [28] ▷ Don't hang up! ¡No cuelgues! ▷ He hung up on me. Me colgó.

hanger n percha f

a b c d e f g h i j k l m n o p q r s t u v w x y z

hangover n resaca f ▷ I woke up with a hangover. Me desperté con resaca.

happen vb pasar [25] ▷ What happened? ¿Qué pasó?; **As it happens, I do know him.** Da la casualidad de que lo conozco.; **Do you happen to know if she's at home?** ¿Por casualidad sabes si está en casa?

happily adv ❶ alegremente ▷ 'Don't worry!' he said happily. '¡No te preocupes!' dijo alegremente. ❷ felizmente ▷ He's happily married. Está felizmente casado.; **And they lived happily ever after.** Y vivieron felices y comieron perdices. ❸ afortunadamente ▷ Happily, everything went well. Afortunadamente todo fue bien.

happiness n felicidad f

happy adj feliz (pl felices) ▷ Janet looks happy. Janet parece feliz.; **to be happy with something** estar [22] contento con algo ▷ I'm very happy with your work. Estoy muy contento con tu trabajo.; **Happy birthday!** ¡Feliz cumpleaños!; **a happy ending** un final feliz

harbour (US harbor) n puerto m

hard adj, adv ❶ (not soft) duro(-a) ▷ to work hard trabajar duro ❷ (difficult) difícil

hard disk n disco duro m

hardly adv apenas ▷ I hardly know you. Apenas te conozco.; **I've got hardly any money.** Casi no tengo dinero.; **hardly ever** casi nunca; **hardly anything** casi nada

hard up adj **to be hard up** (informal) estar [22] sin un duro (estar sin plata LatAm)

harm vb **to harm somebody** hacer [26] daño a alguien ▷ I didn't mean to harm you. No quería hacerte daño.; **to harm something** dañar [25] algo ▷ Chemicals harm the environment. Los productos químicos dañan el medio ambiente.

harmful adj perjudicial ▷ harmful to the environment perjudicial para el medio ambiente

harmless adj inofensivo(-a)

has vb see **have**

hasn't = **has not**

hat n sombrero m

hate vb odiar [25]

hatred n odio m

haunted adj **a haunted house** una casa embrujada

have vb

> Use the verb **haber** to form the perfect tenses.

❶ haber [24] ▷ I've already seen that film. Ya he visto esa película. ▷ Has he gone? ¿Se ha ido? ▷ If you had phoned me I would have come around. Si me hubieras llamado habría venido.

> If you are using 'have' in question tags to confirm a statement use **¿no?** or **¿verdad?**

▷ You've done it, haven't you? Lo has hecho, ¿verdad? ▷ They've arrived, haven't they? Ya han llegado, ¿no?

> 'have' is not translated when giving simple negative or positive answers to questions.

▷ Have you read that book? — Yes, I have. ¿Has leído el libro? — Sí. ▷ Has he told you? — No, he hasn't. ¿Te lo ha dicho? — No. **②** tener [**53**] ▷ I have a terrible cold. Tengo un resfriado horrible. ▷ She had a baby last year. Tuvo un niño el año pasado. ▷ Do you have any brothers or sisters? ¿Tienes hermanos?; **to have to do something** tener [**53**] que hacer algo **③** tomar [**25**] ▷ I'll have a coffee. Tomaré un café. ▷ Shall we have a drink? ¿Tomamos algo de beber?; **to have a shower** ducharse [**25**]; **to have one's hair cut** cortarse [**25**] el pelo

haven't = have not

hay n heno m

hay fever n alergia al polen f

hazelnut n avellana f

he pron él

  he generally isn't translated unless it is emphatic. ▷ He is very tall. Es muy alto.
  Use **él** for emphasis. ▷ He did it but she didn't. Él lo hizo, pero ella no.

head n **①** cabeza f ▷ Mind your head! ¡Cuidado con la cabeza! ▷ The wine went to my head. El vino se me subió a la cabeza. ▷ He lost his head and started screaming. Perdió la cabeza y empezó a gritar. **②** (of school) director m, directora f **③** (leader) jefe m, jefa f ▷ a head of state un jefe de Estado; **I've got no head for figures.** No se me dan bien los números.; **Heads or tails? — Heads.** ¿Cara o cruz? — Cara.
▷ vb **to head for** dirigirse [**16**] a

▷ They headed for the church. Se dirigieron a la iglesia.

headache n dolor de cabeza m
▷ I've got a headache. Tengo dolor de cabeza.

headlight n faro m

headline n titular m

headmaster n director m

headmistress n directora f

headphones npl auriculares mpl

headquarters npl (of army) cuartel general m

headteacher n director m, directora f

heal vb curar [**25**]

health n salud f ▷ She's in good health. Tiene buena salud.

healthy adj sano(-a) ▷ a healthy diet una dieta sana

heap n montón m (pl montones)

hear vb oír [**35**] ▷ We heard the dog bark. Oímos ladrar al perro. ▷ She can't hear very well. No oye bien.; **I heard she was ill.** Me han dicho que estaba enferma.; **to hear about something** enterarse [**25**] de algo ▷ I've heard about your new job. Me he enterado de que tienes un nuevo trabajo. ▷ Did you hear the good news? ¿Te has enterado de la buena noticia?; **to hear from somebody** tener [**53**] noticias de alguien ▷ I haven't heard from him recently. Últimamente no tengo noticias de él.

heart n corazón m (pl corazones); **hearts** (at cards) los corazones ▷ the ace of hearts el as de corazones; **to learn something by heart** aprender [**8**] algo de memoria

a
b
c
d
e
f
g
h
i
j
k
l
m
n
o
p
q
r
s
t
u
v
w
x
y
z

heart attack n infarto m

heartbroken adj **to be heartbroken** tener [53] el corazón partido

heat n calor m
  ▶ vb calentar [39] ▷ Heat gently for five minutes. Caliente a fuego lento durante cinco minutos.

heat up vb ❶ calentar [39]
  ❷ (water, oven) calentarse [39]

heater n calentador m ▷ a water heater un calentador de agua; **an electric heater** una estufa eléctrica; **Could you put on the heater?** (in car) ¿Puedes poner la calefacción?

heather n brezo m

heating n calefacción f

heaven n cielo m; **to go to heaven** ir [27] al cielo

heavy adj pesado(-a) ▷ a heavy load una carga pesada; **This bag's very heavy.** Esta bolsa pesa mucho.; **heavy rain** fuerte lluvia; **He's a heavy drinker.** Es un bebedor empedernido.

he'd = he would; he had

hedge n seto m

hedgehog n erizo m

heel n ❶ (of shoe) tacón m (pl tacones) ❷ (of foot) talón m (pl talones)

height n ❶ (of person) estatura f ❷ (of object, mountain) altura f

held vb see **hold**

helicopter n helicóptero m

hell n infierno m; **Hell!** ¡Maldita sea!

he'll = he will; he shall

hello excl ❶ (when you see somebody) ¡hola! ❷ (on the phone) ¡dígame! (¡aló! LatAm)

helmet n casco m

help vb ayudar [25] ▷ Can you help me? ¿Puedes ayudarme?; **Help!** ¡Socorro!; **Help yourself!** ¡Sírvete! **I couldn't help laughing.** No pude evitar reírme.
  ▶ n ayuda f ▷ Do you need any help? ¿Necesitas ayuda?

helpful adj útil; **You've been very helpful!** ¡Muchas gracias por su ayuda!

hen n gallina f

her adj su (pl sus) ▷ her house su casa ▷ her sisters sus hermanas
  ▷ 'her' is usually translated by the definite article **el/los** or **la/las** when it's clear from the sentence who the possessor is or when referring to clothing or parts of the body.
  ▷ They stole her car. Le robaron el coche. ▷ She took off her coat. Se quitó el abrigo. ▷ She's washing her hair. Se está lavando la cabeza.
  ▶ pron ❶ la
    Use **la** when 'her' is the direct object of the verb in the sentence.
  ▷ I saw her. La vi. ▷ Look at her! ¡Mírala! ❷ le
    Use **le** when 'her' means 'to her'.
  ▷ I gave her a book. Le di un libro. ▷ You have to tell her the truth. Tienes que decirle la verdad.
  ❸ se
    Use **se** not **le** when 'her' is used in combination with a direct-object pronoun.

▷ *Give it to her.* Dáselo. ❹ ella
Use **ella** after prepositions,
in comparisons, and with the
verb 'to be'.
▷ *I'm going with her.* Voy con ella.
▷ *I'm older than her.* Soy mayor que
ella. ▷ *It must be her.* Debe de ser
ella.

herb n hierba f

here adv aquí ▷ *I live here.* Vivo aquí.
▷ *Here he is!* ¡Aquí está! ▷ *Here are
the books.* Aquí están los libros.;
Here's your coffee. Aquí tienes el
café.; **Have you got my pen?
— Here you are.** ¿Tienes mi boli?
— Aquí tienes.; **Here are the
papers you asked for.** Aquí tienes
los papeles que pediste.

hero n héroe m

heroin n heroína f; **a heroin addict**
un heroinómano

heroine n heroína f

hers pron ❶ el suyo m (pl los suyos)
▷ *Is this her coat? — No, hers is black.*
¿Es este su abrigo? — No, el suyo
es negro. ❷ la suya f
▷ *my parents and hers* mis
padres y los suyos ❷ la suya f
(pl las suyas) ▷ *Is this her scarf?* —
No, hers is red. ¿Es esta su bufanda?
— No, la suya es roja. ▷ *my sisters
and hers* mis hermanas y las suyas
❸ suyo m (pl suyos) ▷ *Is that car
hers?* ¿Es suyo ese coche? ❹ suya f
(pl las suyas) ▷ *Is that wallet hers?*
¿Es suya esa cartera?; **Isobel is a
friend of hers.** Isobel es amiga
suya.

Use **de ella** instead of **suyo** if
you want to avoid confusion
with 'his', 'theirs', etc.

▷ *Whose is this? — It's hers.* ¿De
quién es esto? — Es de ella.

herself pron ❶ (reflexive) se ▷ *She's
hurt herself.* Se ha hecho daño.
❷ (after preposition) sí misma ▷ *She
talked mainly about herself.* Habló
principalmente de sí misma.;
❸ (for emphasis) ella misma ▷ *She
did it herself.* Lo hizo ella misma.;
by herself (alone) sola ▷ *She came
by herself.* Vino sola.

he's = **he is**; **he has**

hesitate vb dudar [25] ▷ *Don't
hesitate to ask.* No dudes en
preguntar.

heterosexual adj heterosexual

hi excl ¡hola!

hiccup n hipo m ▷ *The baby's got
hiccups.* El bebé tiene hipo.

hide vb ❶ esconder [8] ▷ *Paula hid
the present.* Paula escondió el
regalo. ❷ esconderse [8] ▷ *He hid
behind a bush.* Se escondió detrás
de un arbusto.

hide-and-seek n to play
hide-and-seek jugar [28] al
escondite

hi-fi n equipo de alta fidelidad m

high adj, adv alto(-a) ▷ *Prices are
higher in Germany.* Los precios están
más altos en Alemania.; **How high
is the wall?** ¿Cómo es de alto el
muro?; **The wall's two metres
high.** El muro tiene dos metros de
altura. ❷ agudo(-a) ▷ *She's got a very
high voice.* Tiene la voz muy aguda.;
at high speed a gran velocidad;
to be high (on drugs) estar [22]
colocado (informal); **to get high**
(on drugs) colocarse [48] (informal)

higher education n enseñanza
superior f

high-heeled adj **high-heeled
shoes** los zapatos de tacón alto

high jump n salto de altura m

high-rise n torre de pisos f

high school n instituto m (liceo m
LatAm)

hijack vb secuestrar [25]

hijacker n secuestrador m,
secuestradora f

hiking n **to go hiking** ir [27] de
excursión al campo

hilarious adj graciosísimo(-a)

hill n ❶ colina f ▷ a house at the top of
a hill una casa en lo alto de una
colina ❷ cuesta f ▷ I climbed the hill
up to the office. Subí la cuesta hasta
la oficina.

hill-walking n senderismo m
▷ to go hill-walking hacer
senderismo

him pron ❶ lo

Use **lo** when 'him' is the direct
object of the verb in the
sentence.

▷ I saw him. Lo vi. ▷ Look at him!
¡Míralo! ❷ le

Use **le** when 'him' means 'to
him'.

▷ I gave him a book. Le di un libro.
▷ You have to tell him the truth.
Tienes que decirle la verdad. ❸ se

Use **se** not **le** when 'him' is used
in combination with a
direct-object pronoun.

▷ Give it to him. Dáselo. ❹ él

Use **él** after prepositions, in
comparisons and with the verb
'to be'.

▷ I'm going with him. Voy con él.
▷ I'm older than him. Soy mayor que
él. ▷ It must be him. Debe de ser él.

himself pron ❶ (reflexive) se ▷ He's
hurt himself. Se ha hecho daño.
❷ (after preposition) sí mismo ▷ He
talked mainly about himself. Habló
principalmente de sí mismo.
❸ (for emphasis) él mismo ▷ He did
it himself. Lo hizo él mismo.; **by
himself** (alone) solo ▷ He came by
himself. Vino solo.

Hindu adj hindú (pl hindúes)

hint n indirecta f; **to drop a hint**
soltar [11] una indirecta; **to take a
hint** captar [25] una indirecta
▶ vb insinuar [1] ▷ He hinted that
something was going on. Insinuó
que estaba pasando algo.

hip n cadera f ▷ She put her hands on
her hips. Se puso las manos en las
caderas.

hippo n hipopótamo m

hire vb ❶ alquilar [25] ▷ We hired a
car. Alquilamos un coche.
❷ contratar [25] ▷ They hired a
lawyer. Contrataron a un
abogado.
▶ n alquiler m ▷ car hire el alquiler
de coches; **'for hire'** 'se alquila'

his adj su (pl sus) ▷ his father su
padre ▷ his house su casa ▷ his two
best friends sus dos mejores amigos
▷ his sisters sus hermanas

'his' is usually translated by the
definite article **el/los** or **la/las**
when it's clear from the
sentence who the possessor is
or when referring to clothing
or parts of the body.

▷ They stole his car. Le robaron el coche. ▷ He took off his coat. Se quitó el abrigo. ▷ He's washing his hair. Se está lavando la cabeza.
▶ **pron** ❶ el suyo m (pl los suyos) ▷ Is this his coat? — No, his is black. ¿Es este su abrigo? — No, el suyo es negro. ▷ my parents and his mis padres y los suyos ❷ la suya f (pl las suyas) ▷ Is this his scarf? — No, his is red. ¿Es esta su bufanda? — No, la suya es roja. ▷ my sisters and his mis hermanas y las suyas ❸ suyo m (pl suyos) ▷ Is that car his? ¿Es suyo ese coche? ❹ suya f (pl suyas) ▷ Is that wallet his? ¿Es suya esa cartera? ; **Isobel is a friend of his.** Isobel es amiga suya.

> Use **de él** instead of **suyo** if you want to avoid confusion with 'hers', 'theirs', etc.

▷ Whose is this? — It's his. ¿De quién es esto? — Es de él.

history n historia f

hit vb ❶ pegar [37] ▷ He hit the ball. Le pegó a la bola. ▷ Andrew hit him. Andrew le pegó. ❷ chocar [48] con ▷ The car hit a road sign. El coche chocó con una señal de tráfico.; **She was hit by a car.** La pilló un coche.; **to hit the target** dar [14] en el blanco; **to hit it off with somebody** hacer [26] buenas migas con alguien
▶ n éxito m ▷ Coldplay's latest hit el último éxito de Coldplay ▷ The film was a massive hit. La película fue un éxito enorme.

hitch n contratiempo m ▷ There's been a slight hitch. Ha habido un pequeño contratiempo.

hitchhike vb hacer [26] autoestop
hitchhiker n autoestopista mf
hitchhiking n autoestop m
HIV-positive adj seropositivo(-a)
hobby n afición f (pl aficiones)
hockey n hockey m ▷ I like playing hockey. Me gusta jugar al hockey.
hold vb ❶ tener [53] ▷ He was holding her in his arms. La tenía entre sus brazos. ❷ sujetar [25] ▷ Hold the ladder. Sujeta la escalera. ❸ contener [53] ▷ This bottle holds one litre. Esta botella contiene un litro.; **to hold a meeting** [25] una reunión; **Hold the line!** (on telephone) ¡No cuelgue!; **Hold it!** ¡Espera!; **to get hold of something** hacerse [26] con algo

hold on ❶ (keep hold) agarrarse [25] ▷ The cliff was slippery but he managed to hold on. El acantilado se escurría, pero logró agarrarse.; **to hold on to something** agarrarse [25] a algo ❷ (wait) esperar [25] ▷ Hold on, I'm coming! ¡Espera que ya voy!; **Hold on!** (on telephone) ¡No cuelgue!

hold up vb ❶ levantar [25] ▷ Peter held up his hand. Peter levantó la mano. ❷ retrasar [25] ▷ We were held up by the traffic. Nos retrasamos por culpa del tráfico. ❸ atracar [48] ▷ to hold up a bank atracar un banco; **I was held up at the office.** Me entretuvieron en la oficina.

hold-up n ❶ (at gunpoint) atraco m ▷ A bank clerk was injured in the hold-up. Un empleado del banco resultó herido en el atraco. ❷ (delay) retraso m ▷ No one

explained the reason for the hold-up.
Nadie explicó el motivo del
retraso. ❸ (traffic)
embotellamiento m ▷ a hold-up on
the motorway un embotellamiento
en la autopista

hole n ❶ (in general) agujero m ▷ a
hole in the wall un agujero en la
pared ❷ (in the ground, in golf) hoyo
m ▷ to dig a hole cavar un hoyo

holiday n ❶ vacaciones fpl ▷ the
school holidays las vacaciones
escolares ▷ to go on holiday irse de
vacaciones ▷ to be on holiday estar
de vacaciones ❷ día festivo m (día
feriado m LatAm) ▷ Next Monday is a
holiday. El lunes que viene es día
festivo.

Holland n Holanda f

hollow adj hueco(-a)

holly n acebo m

holy adj ❶ santo(-a) ▷ the Holy Spirit
el Espíritu Santo ❷ sagrado(-a) ▷ a
holy place un lugar sagrado

home n casa f ▷ at home en casa;
Make yourself at home. Estás en
tu casa.; **an old people's home**
una residencia de ancianos
▶ adv ❶ en casa ▷ I'll be home at five
o'clock. Estaré en casa a las cinco.
❷ a casa ▷ to get home llegar a casa

homeless adj sin hogar; **homeless
people** los sin techo

home match n partido en casa m

home page n página principal f

homesick adj to be homesick
tener [53] morriña

homework n deberes mpl ▷ Have
you done your homework? ¿Has
hecho los deberes?

homosexual adj homosexual

honest adj ❶ honrado(-a) ▷ She's a
very honest person. Es una persona
muy honrada. ❷ sincero(-a) ▷ Tell
me your honest opinion. Dame tu
sincera opinión.; **To be honest,
I don't like the idea.** La verdad es
que no me gusta la idea.

honestly adv francamente ▷ I
honestly don't know. Francamente
no lo sé.

honesty n honradez f

honey n miel f

honeymoon n luna de miel f; **to
go on honeymoon** irse de [**27**] de
luna de miel

honour (US honor) n honor m

hood n ❶ (on coat) capucha f
❷ (US: bonnet of car) capó m

hook n ❶ (for hanging clothes)
gancho m ❷ (for hanging
paintings) alcayata f ❸ (for fishing)
anzuelo m; **to take the phone off
the hook** descolgar [**28**] el
teléfono

hooligan n gamberro m,
gamberra f

hooray excl ¡hurra!

Hoover® n aspiradora f

hoover vb pasar [**25**] la aspiradora
por ▷ He hoovered the lounge. Pasó
la aspiradora por el salón.

hope vb esperar [**25**]
▌ Use the subjunctive after
esperar que.

▷ I hope he comes. Espero que
venga.; I hope so. Espero que sí.;
I hope not. Espero que no.
▶ n esperanza f ▷ to give up hope
perder la esperanza

hopefully adv

Use the subjunctive after **esperar que**.

Hopefully, he'll make it in time. Esperemos que llegue a tiempo.

hopeless adj She's hopeless at maths. Es una negada para las matemáticas.

horizon n horizonte m

horizontal adj horizontal

horn ❶ claxon m ▷ He sounded the horn. Tocó el claxon. ❷ (instrument) trompa f ❸ (of bull) cuerno m (cacho m LatAm)

horoscope n horóscopo m

horrible adj horrible ▷ What a horrible dress! ¡Qué vestido tan horrible!

horror n horror m ▷ To my horror I discovered I was locked out. Descubrí con horror que me había dejado las llaves dentro.

horror film n película de terror f

horse n caballo m

horse-racing n carreras de caballos fpl

hose n manguera f

hospital n hospital m ▷ to go into hospital ingresar en el hospital

hospitality n hospitalidad f

host n anfitrión m (pl anfitriones), anfitriona f

hostage n rehén m (pl rehenes); to take somebody hostage tomar [25] como rehén a alguien

hot adj ❶ caliente ▷ a hot bath un baño caliente ❷ caluroso(-a) ▷ a hot country un país caluroso

When you are talking about a person being hot, you use **tener calor**.

▷ I'm hot. Tengo calor.

When you talk about the weather being hot, you use **hacer calor**.

▷ It's hot today. Hoy hace calor. ❸ picante ▷ Mexican food's too hot. La comida mexicana es demasiado picante.

hot dog n perrito caliente m

hotel n hotel m

hour n hora f ▷ She always takes hours to get ready. Siempre se tira horas para arreglarse.; a quarter of an hour un cuarto de hora; two and a half hours dos horas y media; half an hour media hora

hourly adj, adv There are hourly buses. Hay autobuses cada hora.; She's paid hourly. Le pagan por horas.

house n casa f ▷ at his house en su casa

housewife n ama de casa f (pl amas de casa) ▷ She's a housewife. Es ama de casa.

housework n tareas de la casa fpl

hovercraft n aerodeslizador m

how adv ❶ cómo ▷ How are you? ¿Cómo estás? ❷ qué ▷ How strange! ¡Qué raro!; He told them how happy he was. Les dijo lo feliz que era.; How many? ¿Cuántos?; How much? ¿Cuánto? ▷ How much is it? ¿Cuánto es? ▷ How much sugar do you want? ¿Cuánto azúcar quieres?; How old are you? ¿Cuántos años tienes?; How far is it to Edinburgh? ¿Qué distancia hay de aquí a Edimburgo?; How long have you been here? ¿Cuánto

a
b
c
d
e
f
g
h
i
j
k
l
m
n
o
p
q
r
s
t
u
v
w
x
y
z

tiempo llevas aquí?; **How long does it take?** ¿Cuánto se tarda?
> Remember the accents on question and exclamation words **cómo**, **qué** and **cuánto**.

however conj sin embargo ▷ This, however, isn't true. Esto, sin embargo, no es cierto.

hug vb abrazar [13] ▷ They hugged each other. Se abrazaron.
▶ n abrazo m ▷ to give somebody a hug dar un abrazo a alguien

huge adj enorme

hum vb tararear [25]

human adj humano(-a) ▷ the human body el cuerpo humano

human being n ser humano m

humour (US humor) n humor m; **to have a sense of humour** tener [53] sentido del humor

hundred num
> Use **cien** before nouns or before another number that is being multiplied by a hundred.
a hundred cien b ▷ a hundred people cien personas ▷ a hundred thousand cien mil
> Use **ciento** before a number that is not multiplied but simply added to a hundred.
> ▷ a hundred and one ciento uno
> When 'hundred' follows another number, use the compound forms, which must agree with the noun.
> ▷ three hundred trescientos ▷ five hundred quinientos ▷ five hundred people quinientas personas ▷ five hundred and one quinientos uno; **hundreds of people** cientos de personas

hung vb see **hang**

Hungary n Hungría f

hunger n hambre f
> Although it's a feminine noun, remember that you use **el** and **un** with **hambre**.

hungry adj to be hungry tener [53] hambre ▷ I'm very hungry. Tengo mucha hambre.

hunt vb ① cazar [13] ▷ They hunt foxes. Cazan zorros. ② (look for) buscar [48] ▷ The police are hunting the killer. La policía está buscando al asesino.; **to go hunting** ir [27] de caza; **to hunt for something** buscar [48] algo ▷ I've hunted everywhere for that book. He buscado ese libro por todas partes.

hunting n caza f ▷ fox-hunting la caza del zorro

hurricane n huracán m (pl huracanes)

hurry vb darse [14] prisa (apurarse [25] LatAm) ▷ Hurry up! ¡Date prisa!; Sharon hurried back home. Sharon volvió a casa a toda prisa.
▶ n to be in a hurry tener [53] prisa (tener apuro LatAm); **to do something in a hurry** hacer [26] algo a toda prisa; **There's no hurry.** No hay prisa.

hurt vb ① hacer [26] daño a ▷ You're hurting me! ¡Me haces daño! ▷ Have you hurt yourself? ¿Te has hecho daño? ② doler [33] ▷ My leg hurts. Me duele la pierna.; **Hey! That hurts!** ¡Hey! ¡Que me haces daño! ③ (upset) herir [51]
▶ adj herido(-a) ▷ Is he badly hurt?

¿Está herido de gravedad? ▷ *Luckily, nobody got hurt.* Por suerte, nadie salió herido.; **I was hurt by what he said.** Me hirió lo que dijo.

husband *n* marido *m*

hut *n* cabaña *f*

hymn *n* himno *m*

hypermarket *n* hipermercado *m*

hyphen *n* guion *m* (*pl* guiones)

I *pron* yo ▷ *Ann and I* Ann y yo

▪ 'I' generally isn't translated unless it is emphatic.

▷ *I speak Spanish.* Hablo español.

▪ Use **yo** for emphasis.

▷ *He was frightened but I wasn't.* Él estaba asustado, pero yo no.

ice *n* hielo *m*

iceberg *n* iceberg *m* (*pl* icebergs)

ice cream *n* helado *m* ▷ *vanilla ice cream* el helado de vainilla

ice cube *n* cubito de hielo *m*

ice hockey *n* hockey sobre hielo *m*

Iceland *n* Islandia *f*

ice rink *n* pista de patinaje sobre hielo *f*

ice-skating *n* patinaje sobre hielo *m*; **Yesterday we went ice-skating.** Ayer fuimos a patinar sobre hielo.

icing n (on cake) glaseado m; **icing sugar** el azúcar glas

icon n icono m

ICT n (= Information and Communications Technology) informática f

icy adj helado(-a) ▷ an icy wind un viento helado ▷ The roads are icy. Las carreteras están heladas.

I'd = **I had**; **I would**

idea n idea f ▷ Good idea! ¡Buena idea!

ideal adj ideal

identical adj idéntico(-a)

identification n identificación f (pl identificaciones)

identify vb identificar [48]

identity card n carnet de identidad m

idiot n idiota mf

idiotic adj idiota

i.e. abbr es decir

if conj si ▷ If it's fine we'll go swimming. Si hace bueno, iremos a nadar.

Use **si** with a past subjunctive to translate 'if' followed by a past tense when talking about conditions.
▷ If you studied harder you would pass your exams. Si estudiaras más aprobarías los exámenes.; **if only** ojalá

ojalá has to be followed by a verb in the subjunctive.
▷ If only I had more money! ¡Ojalá tuviera más dinero!; **if not** si no ▷ Are you coming? If not, I'll go with Mark. ¿Vienes? Si no, iré con Mark.; **if so** si es así ▷ Are you

coming? If so, I'll wait. ¿Vienes? Si es así te espero.; **If I were you I would go to Spain.** Yo que tú iría a España.

ignore vb **to ignore something** hacer [26] caso omiso de algo ▷ She ignored my advice. Hizo caso omiso de mi consejo.; **to ignore somebody** ignorar [25] a alguien ▷ She saw me, but she ignored me. Me vio, pero me ignoró completamente.; **Just ignore him!** ¡No le hagas caso!

ill adj enfermo(-a) ▷ She was taken ill. Se puso enferma.

I'll = **I will**

illegal adj ilegal

illness n enfermedad f

illusion n ilusión f (pl ilusiones) ▷ an optical illusion una ilusión óptica; **He was under the illusion that he would win.** Se creía que iba a ganar.

illustration n ilustración f (pl ilustraciones)

image n imagen f (pl imágenes) ▷ The company has changed its image. La empresa ha cambiado de imagen.

imagination n imaginación f (pl imaginaciones) ▷ She lets her imagination run away with her. Se deja llevar por su imaginación. ▷ It's only your imagination. Son imaginaciones tuyas.

imagine vb imaginarse [25] ▷ You can imagine how I felt! ¡Imagínate cómo me sentí! ▷ Is he angry? — I imagine so! ¿Está enfadado? — ¡Me imagino que sí!

imitate vb imitar [**25**]

imitation n imitación f (pl imitaciones); **imitation leather** el cuero de imitación

immediate adj inmediato(-a)

immediately adv inmediatamente

immigrant n inmigrante mf

immigration n inmigración f (pl inmigraciones)

impatience n impaciencia f

impatient adj impaciente; **to get impatient** impacientarse [**25**] ▷ People are getting impatient. La gente se está impacientando.

impatiently adv con impaciencia

importance n importancia f

important adj importante

impossible adj imposible

impress vb impresionar [**25**] ▷ She's trying to impress you. Está tratando de impresionarte.

impressed adj impresionado(-a); **I'm very impressed!** ¡Estoy impresionado!

impression n impresión f (pl impresiones) ▷ I was under the impression that you were going out. Tenía la impresión de que te ibas.

impressive adj impresionante

improve vb mejorar [**25**] ▷ The weather is improving. El tiempo está mejorando.

improvement n ① (in situation, design) mejora f ▷ I've been an improvement in his French. Su francés ha mejorado. ② (in health) mejoría f

in prep, adv

> There are several ways of translating 'in'. Scan the examples to find one that is similar to what you want to say. For other expressions with 'in', see the verbs 'go', 'come', 'get', 'give', etc.

① en ▷ in Spain en España ▷ in hospital en el hospital ▷ in London en Londres ▷ in spring en primavera ▷ in May en Mayo ▷ in 1996 en mil novecientos noventa y seis ▷ I did it in three hours. Lo hice en tres horas. ▷ in French en francés ▷ in a loud voice en voz alta ② de ▷ the best pupil in the class el mejor alumno de la clase ▷ at two o'clock in the afternoon a las dos de la tarde ▷ the boy in the blue shirt el muchacho de la camisa azul ③ dentro de ▷ I'll see you in three weeks. Te veré dentro de tres semanas. ④ por ▷ I always feel sleepy in the afternoon. Siempre tengo sueño por la tarde.; **in the sun** al sol; **in the rain** bajo la lluvia; **It was written in pencil.** Estaba escrito a lápiz.; **in here** aquí dentro ▷ It's hot in here. Aquí dentro hace calor.; **one person in ten** una persona de cada diez; **to be in** (at home, work) estar [**22**] ▷ He wasn't in. No estaba.; **in writing** por escrito

including prep **It will be two hundred pounds, including tax.** Son doscientas libras esterlinas con impuestos incluidos.

include vb incluir [**10**] ▷ Service is not included. El servicio no está incluido.

income n ingresos mpl ▷ his main source of income su principal fuente de ingresos

income tax n impuesto sobre la renta m

inconvenient adj It's a bit inconvenient at the moment. Me viene un poco mal en este momento.

incorrect adj incorrecto(-a)

increase n aumento m ▷ an increase in road accidents un aumento de accidentes de tráfico
  ▶ vb aumentar [25] ▷ They have increased his salary. Le han aumentado el sueldo.; to increase in size aumentar [25] de tamaño

incredible adj increíble

indeed adv realmente ▷ It's very hard indeed. Es realmente difícil.; Know what I mean? — Indeed I do. ¿Me comprendes? — Por supuesto que sí.; Thank you very much indeed! ¡Muchísimas gracias!

independence n independencia f

independent adj independiente; an independent school un colegio privado

index n (in book) índice alfabético m

index finger n dedo índice m

India n India f

Indian adj indio(-a)
  ▶ indio m, india f ▷ the Indians los indios; **American Indian** el indio americano (india f americana)

indicate vb ❶ indicar [48] ▷ The report indicates that changes are needed. El informe indica que se

necesitan cambios. ❷ (when driving) señalizar [13] ▷ He indicated right and turned into the Gran Vía. Señalizó hacia la derecha y torció a la Gran Vía.

indicator n (in car) intermitente m

indigestion n indigestión f (pl indigestiones) ▷ I've got indigestion. Tengo indigestión.

individual n individuo m

indoor adj an indoor swimming pool una piscina cubierta

indoors adv dentro ▷ They're indoors. Están dentro.; We'd better go indoors. Es mejor que entremos.

industrial adj industrial

industrial estate n zona industrial f

industry n industria f ▷ the oil industry la industria petrolífera
  ▷ I'd like to work in industry. Me gustaría trabajar en la industria.; the tourist industry el turismo

inevitable adj inevitable

inexperienced adj inexperto(-a)

infant school n colegio m

infection n infección f (pl infecciones) ▷ an ear infection una infección de oído

infectious adj contagioso(-a)

infinitive n infinitivo m

inflation n inflación f (pl inflaciones)

influence n influencia f ▷ He's a bad influence on her. Ejerce mala influencia sobre ella.
  ▶ vb influenciar [25]

inform vb informar [25] ▷ Nobody informed me of the change of plan. Nadie me informó del cambio de planes.

informal *adj* 'informal dress' 'no se requiere traje de etiqueta'

information *n* información *f* (*pl* informaciones) ▷ *Could you give me some information about trains to Barcelona?* ¿Podría darme información sobre trenes a Barcelona?; **a piece of information** un dato

information office *n* oficina de información *f*

information technology *n* informática *f*

infuriating *adj* exasperante

ingredient *n* ingrediente *m*

inherit *vb* heredar [**25**] ▷ *She inherited her father's house.* Heredó la casa de su padre.

initials *npl* iniciales *fpl*

injection *n* inyección *f* (*pl* inyecciones) ▷ *The doctor gave me an injection.* El médico me puso una inyección.

injure *vb* herir [**51**] ▷ *He injured his leg.* Se hirió la pierna.

injured *adj* herido(-a)

injury *n* lesión *f* (*pl* lesiones)

ink *n* tinta *f*

in-laws *npl* suegros *mpl*

innocent *adj* inocente

insane *adj* loco(-a)

inscription *n* inscripción *f* (*pl* inscripciones)

insect *n* insecto *m*

insect repellent *n* loción anti-insectos *f* (*pl* lociones anti-insectos)

inside *n* interior *m*
▶ *prep, adv* dentro ▷ *inside the house* dentro de la casa; **Come inside!**

¡Entra!; **Let's go inside, it's starting to rain.** Entremos, está empezando a llover.; **inside out** al revés ▷ *He put his jumper on inside out.* Se puso el jersey al revés.

insist *vb* insistir [**58**] ▷ *I didn't want to, but he insisted.* Yo no quería, pero él insistió. ▷ *He insisted he was innocent.* Insistía en que era inocente.; **to insist on doing something** insistir [**58**] en hacer algo ▷ *She insisted on paying.* Insistió en pagar.

inspector *n* inspector *m*, inspectora *f*

instalment *n* ❶ (*of payment*) plazo *m* ▷ *to pay in instalments* pagar a plazos ❷ (*of TV, radio serial*) episodio *m* ❸ (*of publication*) fascículo *m*

instance *n* **for instance** por ejemplo

instant *adj* inmediato(-a) ▷ *It was an instant success.* Fue un éxito inmediato.; **instant coffee** el café instantáneo
▶ *n* instante *m*

instantly *adv* al instante

instead *prep, adv* **instead of** en lugar de ▷ *We played tennis instead of going swimming.* Jugamos al tenis en lugar de ir a nadar. ▷ *She went instead of Peter.* En lugar de ir Peter, fue ella.; **The pool was closed, so we played tennis instead.** La piscina estaba cerrada, así que jugamos al tenis.

instinct *n* instinto *m*

instruct *vb* **to instruct somebody to do something** ordenar [**25**] a

alguien que haga algo
> **ordenar que** has to be
followed by a verb in the
subjunctive.
▷ *She instructed us to wait outside.*
*Nos ordenó que esperáramos
fuera.*

instructions npl instrucciones fpl

instructor n instructor m,
instructora f ▷ *skiing instructor* el
instructor de esquí ▷ *driving
instructor* el instructor de
autoescuela

instrument n instrumento m ▷ *Do
you play an instrument?* ¿Tocas
algún instrumento?

insulin n insulina f

insult n insulto m
▶ vb insultar [25]

insurance n seguro m ▷ *his car
insurance* su seguro de automóvil;
an insurance policy una póliza de
seguros

intelligent adj inteligente

intend vb to **intend to
something** tener [53] la intención
de hacer algo ▷ *I intend to do
languages at university.* Tengo la
intención de estudiar idiomas en
la universidad.

intensive adj intensivo(-a)

intention n intención f (pl
intenciones)

interest n ❶ interés m (pl
intereses) ▷ *to show an interest in
something* mostrar interés en algo
❷ afición f (pl aficiones) ▷ *My main
interest is music.* Mi mayor afición
es la música.; **It's in your own
interest to study hard.** Te

conviene estudiar mucho.
▶ vb interesar [25] ▷ *It doesn't
interest me.* No me interesa.; **to be
interested in something** estar
[22] interesado en algo ▷ *I'm very
interested in what you're telling me.*
Estoy muy interesado en lo que me
dices.; **Are you interested in
politics?** ¿Te interesa la política?

interesting adj interesante

interior n interior m

interior designer n diseñador de
interiores m, diseñadora de
interiores f

international adj internacional

internet n Internet mf ▷ *on the
internet* en internet

internet café n cibercafé m

internet user n internauta mf

interpreter n intérprete mf

interrupt vb interrumpir [58]

interruption n interrupción f
(pl interrupciones)

interval n intervalo m

interview n entrevista f
▶ vb entrevistar [25] ▷ *I was
interviewed on the radio.* Me
entrevistaron en la radio.

interviewer n entrevistador m,
entrevistadora f

into prep ❶ a b *I'm going into town.*
Voy a la ciudad. ▷ *Translate it into
Spanish.* Tradúcelo al español. ❷ en
▷ *I poured the milk into a cup.* Vertí la
leche en una taza.; **to walk into a
lamppost** tropezar [19] con una
farola

introduce vb presentar [25] ▷ *He
introduced me to his parents.* Me
presentó a sus padres.

introduction n (in book)
  introducción f (pl introducciones)
invade vb invadir **[58]**
invalid adj inválido m, inválida f
invent vb inventar **[25]**
invention n invento m
investigation n investigación f (pl
  investigaciones)
invisible adj invisible
invitation n invitación f (pl
  invitaciones)
invite vb invitar **[25]** ▷ You're invited
  to a party at Claire's house. Estás
  invitado a una fiesta en casa de
  Claire.
involve vb suponer **[41]** ▷ It involves
  a lot of work. Supone mucho
  trabajo.; **He wasn't involved in
  the robbery.** No estuvo implicado
  en el robo.; **She was involved in
  politics.** Estaba metida en
  política.; **to be involved with
  somebody** tener **[53]** una relación
  con alguien ▷ She was involved with
  a married man. Tenía una relación
  con un hombre casado.; **I don't
  want to get involved in the
  argument.** No quiero meterme en
  la discusión.
iPad® n iPad® m
iPhone® n iPhone® m
Iran n Irán m
Iraq n Iraq m
Ireland n Irlanda f
Irish n (language) irlandés m; **the
  Irish** (people) los irlandeses
  ▶ adj irlandés (firlandesa, pl
  irlandeses)
Irishman n irlandés m (pl
  irlandeses)

Irishwoman n irlandesa f
iron n ❶ (for clothes) plancha f
  ❷ (metal) hierro m
  ▶ vb planchar **[25]**
ironing n to do the ironing
  planchar **[25]**; **I hate ironing.** No
  me gusta nada planchar.
ironing board n tabla de
  planchar f
irresponsible adj irresponsable
  ▷ That was irresponsible of him. Eso
  fue irresponsable por su parte.
irritating adj irritante
is vb see be
Islam n Islam m
Islamic adj islámico(-a) ▷ Islamic
  law la ley islámica
island n isla f
isle n the Isle of Wight la Isla de
  Wight
isolated adj aislado(-a)
Israel n Israel m
issue n ❶ tema m

  Although **tema** ends in **-a**, it is
  actually a masculine noun.

  ▷ a controversial issue un tema
  polémico ❷ (magazine) número m
  ▷ a back issue un número atrasado
  ▶ vb ❶ hacer **[26]** público ▷ The
  minister issued a statement yesterday.
  El ministro hizo pública una
  declaración ayer. ❷ (equipment,
  supplies) proporcionar **[25]**
it pron

  When 'it' is the subject of a
  sentence it is practically never
  translated.

  ▷ Where's my book? — It's on the
  table. ¿Dónde está mi libro? — Está
  sobre la mesa. ▷ It's raining. Está

lloviendo. ▷ *It's six o'clock.* Son las seis. ▷ *It's Friday tomorrow.* Mañana es viernes. ▷ *It's expensive.* Es caro. ▷ *Who is it? — It's me.* ¿Quién es? — Soy yo.

| When 'it' is the direct object of the verb in a sentence, use **lo** if it stands for a masculine noun or **la** if it stands for a feminine noun.

▷ *There's a croissant left. Do you want it?* Queda un croissant. ¿Lo quieres? ▷ *I doubt it.* Lo dudo. ▷ *It's a good film. Have you seen it?* Es una buena película. ¿La has visto?

| Use **le** when 'it' is the indirect object of the verb in the sentence.

▷ *Give it another coat of paint.* Dale otra mano de pintura.

| For general concepts use the word **ello**.

▷ *I spoke to him about it.* Hablé con él sobre ello. ▷ *I'm against it.* Estoy en contra de ello.

Italian *adj* italiano(-a)
  ▶ *n* ❶ (*person*) italiano *m*, italiana *f*
  ▶ *the Italians* los italianos
  ❷ (*language*) italiano *m*

Italy *n* Italia *f*

itch *vb* picar [48] ▷ *It itches.* Me pica. ▷ *My head is itching.* Me pica la cabeza.

itchy *adj* I've got an itchy nose. Me pica la nariz.

it'd = **it had**; **it would**

item *n* ❶ pieza *f* ▷ *a collector's item* una pieza de colección ❷ (*on list*) artículo *m* ▷ *The first item he bought was an alarm clock.* El primer

artículo que compró fue un despertador. ❸ (*on bill*) partida *f* ▷ *He checked the items on his bill.* Comprobó las partidas de su factura. ❹ **punto** *m* ▷ *The next item on the agenda is...* El siguiente punto del orden del día es...; **an item of news** una noticia

it'll = **it will**

its *adj* su (*pl* sus) ▷ *Everything in its place.* Cada cosa en su sitio. ▷ *It has its advantages.* Tiene sus ventajas.

| 'its' is usually translated by the definite article **el/los** or **la/las** when it's clear from the sentence who the possessor is or when referring to clothing or parts of the body.

▷ *The dog is losing its hair.* El perro está perdiendo el pelo. ▷ *The bird was in its cage.* El pájaro estaba en la jaula.

it's = **it is**; **it has**

itself *pron* (*reflexive*) se ▷ *The heating switches itself off.* La calefacción se apaga sola. ▷ *The dog scratched itself.* El perro se rascó.; **The meal itself was tasty, though expensive.** La comida en sí estaba rica, aunque era cara.

I've = **I have**

j

jack n **①** gato m **②** (in ordinary pack of cards) jota f **③** (in Spanish pack of cards) sota f

jacket n chaqueta f; **jacket potatoes** las patatas asadas con piel (las papas asadas con cáscara LatAm)

jail n cárcel f ▷ to go to jail ir a la cárcel
▶ vb **He was jailed for ten years.** Lo condenaron a diez años de cárcel.

jam n mermelada f ▷ strawberry jam la mermelada de fresas; **a traffic jam** un atasco

jammed adj atascado(-a) ▷ The window's jammed. La ventana está atascada.

janitor n conserje mf ▷ He's a janitor. Es conserje.

January n enero m ▷ in January en enero ▷ the January sales las rebajas de enero

Japan n Japón m

Japanese adj japonés (f japonesa)
▶ n **①** (person) japonés m, japonesa f; **the Japanese** los japoneses **②** (language) japonés m

jar n tarro m ▷ a jar of honey un tarro de miel

javelin n jabalina f

jaw n mandíbula f

jazz n jazz m

jealous adj celoso(-a) ▷ to be jealous estar celoso

jeans npl vaqueros mpl ▷ a pair of jeans unos vaqueros

Jello® n (US) gelatina f

jelly n gelatina f

jellyfish n medusa f

jersey n jersey m (pl jerseys)

Jesus n Jesús m

Jew n judío m, judía f

jewel n joya f

jeweller (US jeweler) n joyero m, joyera f ▷ She's a jeweller. Es joyera.

jeweller's shop (US jeweler's shop) n joyería f

jewellery (US jewelry) n joyas fpl

Jewish adj judío(-a)

jigsaw n rompecabezas m (pl rompecabezas)

job n trabajo m ▷ a part-time job un trabajo de media jornada; **You've done a good job.** Lo has hecho muy bien.

job centre n oficina de empleo f

jobless adj desempleado(-a)

jockey n jockey mf (pl jockeys)

jog vb hacer [26] footing

jogging n footing m ▷ **to go jogging** hacer footing

join vb hacerse [26] socio de ▷ **I'm going to join the ski club.** Voy a hacerme socio del club de esquí.; **I'll join you later if I can.** Yo iré luego si puedo.; **If you're going for a walk, do you mind if I join you?** Si vais a dar un paseo, ¿os importa que os acompañe?

join in vb **He doesn't join in with what we do.** No participa en lo que hacemos.; **She started singing, and the audience joined in.** Empezó a cantar, y el público se unió a ella.

joiner n carpintero m, carpintera f ▷ **He's a joiner.** Es carpintero.

joint n ❶ articulación f (pl articulaciones) ▷ **I've got pains in my joints.** Me duelen las articulaciones. ❷ (drugs: informal) porro m; **We had a joint of lamb for dinner.** Comimos asado de cordero.

joke n ❶ broma f ▷ **Don't get upset, it was only a joke.** No te enfades, era solo una broma.; **to play a joke on somebody** gastarle [25] una broma a alguien ▷ ❷ chiste m ▷ **to tell a joke** contar un chiste ▶ vb bromear [25]; **You must be joking!** ¡Estás de broma!

jolly adj alegre

Jordan n Jordania f

jotter n bloc m (pl blocs)

journalism n periodismo m

journalist n periodista mf ▷ **I'm a journalist.** Soy periodista.

journey n viaje m ▷ **to go on a journey** hacer un viaje; **The**

journey to school takes about half an hour. Se tarda una media hora en ir al colegio.

joy n alegría f

joystick n (for computer games) mando m

judge n juez mf (pl jueces) ▶ vb juzgar [37]

judo n judo m ▷ **My favourite sport is judo.** Mi deporte favorito es el judo.

jug n jarra f

juice n zumo m ▷ **orange juice** el zumo de naranja

July n julio m ▷ **in July** en julio

jumble sale n venta de objetos usados f

jump vb saltar [25] ▷ **They jumped over the wall.** Saltaron el muro. ▷ **He jumped out of the window.** Saltó por la ventana. ▷ **He jumped off the roof.** Saltó del tejado.; **You made me jump!** ¡Qué susto me has dado!

jumper n jersey m (pl jerseys)

junction n (of roads) cruce m

June n junio m ▷ **in June** en junio

jungle n selva f

junior school n colegio m

junk n trastos viejos mpl ▷ **The attic's full of junk.** El desván está lleno de trastos viejos.; **to eat junk food** comer [8] porquerías; **junk shop** la tienda de objetos usados

jury n jurado m

just adv ❶ justo ▷ **just in time** justo a tiempo ▷ **just after Christmas** justo después de Navidad ▷ **We had just enough money.** Teníamos el dinero justo.; **He's just arrived.** Acaba de llegar.; **I did it just now.** Lo acabo de hacer.; **I'm rather busy just**

now. Ahora mismo estoy bastante ocupada.; **I'm just coming!** ¡Ya voy!; **just here** aquí mismo ❷ solo ▷ *It's just a suggestion.* Es solo una sugerencia.; **Just a minute!** ¡Un momento!; **just about** casi ▷ *It's just about finished.* Está casi terminado.

justice n justicia f

k

kangaroo n canguro m
karate n kárate m
kebab n pincho moruno m
keen adj entusiasta ▷ *a keen supporter* un hincha entusiasta; **He doesn't seem very keen.** No parece muy entusiasmado.; **She's a keen student.** Es una alumna aplicada.; **I'm not very keen on maths.** No me gustan mucho las matemáticas.; **He's keen on her.** Ella le gusta.; **to be keen on doing something** tener [53] ganas de hacer algo ▷ *I'm not very keen on going.* No tengo muchas ganas de ir.

keep vb ❶ quedarse [25] con ▷ *You can keep the watch.* Puedes quedarte con el reloj.; **You can keep it.** Puedes quedártelo. ❷ (remain) mantenerse [53] ▷ *to*

keep fit mantenerse en forma; **Keep still!** ¡Estáte quieto!; **Keep quiet!** ¡Cállate! ➌ seguir **[50]** ▷ *Keep straight on.* Siga recto.; **I keep forgetting my keys.** Siempre me olvido las llaves.; **'keep out'** 'prohibida la entrada'; **'keep off the grass'** 'prohibido pisar el césped'

keep on vb continuar **[1]** ▷ *He kept on reading.* Continuó leyendo.; **The car keeps on breaking down.** El coche no deja de averiarse.

keep up vb **Matthew walks so fast I can't keep up.** Matthew camina tan rápido que no puedo seguirle el ritmo.

keep-fit n gimnasia f ▷ *I go to keep-fit classes.* Voy a clases de gimnasia.

kept vb see **keep**

kettle n hervidor m

key n llave f

keyboard n teclado m

kick n patada f
▶ vb **to kick somebody** dar **[14]** una patada a alguien ▷ *He kicked me.* Me dio una patada.; **He kicked the ball hard.** Le dio un puntapié fuerte al balón.; **to kick off** (in football) hacer **[26]** el saque inicial

kick-off n saque inicial m; **The kick-off is at 10 o'clock.** El partido empieza a las diez.

kid n (informal) crío m, cría f ▷ *the kids* los críos
▶ vb bromear **[25]** ▷ *I'm not kidding, it's snowing.* No estoy bromeando, está nevando.; **I'm just kidding.** Es una broma.

kidnap vb secuestrar **[25]**

kidney n riñón m (pl riñones)

kill vb matar **[25]** ▷ *She killed her husband.* Mató a su marido.; **to be killed** morir **[32]** ▷ *He was killed in a car accident.* Murió en un accidente de coche.; **to kill oneself** suicidarse **[25]** ▷ *He killed himself.* Se suicidó.

killer n ❶ (murderer) asesino m, asesina f ❷ (hired killer) asesino a sueldo m, asesina a sueldo f

kilo n kilo m ▷ *at £5 a kilo* a 5 libras esterlinas el kilo

kilometre (US kilometer) n kilómetro m

kilt n falda escocesa f

kind adj amable ▷ *to be kind to somebody* ser amable con alguien; **Thank you for being so kind.** Gracias por su amabilidad.
▶ n tipo m ▷ *It's a kind of sausage.* Es un tipo de salchicha.

kindness n amabilidad f

king n rey m; **the King and Queen** los reyes

kingdom n reino m

kiosk n (stall) quiosco m; **a telephone kiosk** una cabina telefónica

kiss n beso m
▶ vb ❶ besar **[25]** ▷ *He kissed her passionately.* La besó apasionadamente. ❷ besarse **[25]** ▷ *They kissed.* Se besaron.

kit n equipo m ▷ *I've forgotten my gym kit.* Me he olvidado el equipo de gimnasia.; **a tool kit** un juego de herramientas; **a sewing kit** un costurero; **a first-aid kit** un botiquín; **a puncture repair kit** un juego de reparación de pinchazos; **a drum kit** una batería

kitchen n cocina f ⊳ a kitchen knife un cuchillo de cocina

kite n cometa f

kitten n gatito m, gatita f

knee n rodilla f ⊳ to be on one's knees estar de rodillas

kneel vb arrodillarse [25]

kneel down vb arrodillarse [25]

knew vb see **know**

knickers npl bragas fpl (calzones mpl LatAm) ⊳ a pair of knickers unas bragas

knife n cuchillo m

knit vb hacer [26] punto (tejer [8] LatAm) ⊳ I like knitting. Me gusta hacer punto.; **She is knitting a jumper.** Está haciendo un jersey a punto.

knives npl see **knife**

knob n ❶ (on door) pomo m ❷ (on radio, TV) dial m

knock vb llamar [25] ⊳ Someone's knocking at the door. Alguien llama a la puerta.; **to knock somebody down** atropellar [25] a alguien ⊳ She was knocked down by a car. La atropelló un coche.; **to knock somebody out** (1) (defeat) eliminar [25] a alguien ⊳ They were knocked out early in the tournament. Fueron eliminados al poco de iniciarse el torneo. (2) (stun) dejar [25] sin sentido a alguien ⊳ They knocked out the watchman. Dejaron al vigilante sin sentido.
▶ n golpe m

knot n nudo m ⊳ to tie a knot in something hacer un nudo en algo

know vb

Use **saber** for knowing facts, **conocer** for knowing people and places.

❶ saber [47] ⊳ Yes, I know. Sí, ya lo sé. ⊳ I don't know. No sé. ⊳ I don't know any German. No sé nada de alemán.; **to know that** saber [47] que ⊳ I didn't know that your Dad was a police officer. No sabía que tu padre era policía. ❷ conocer [12] ⊳ I know her. La conozco.; **to know about something** (1) (be aware of) estar [22] enterado de algo ⊳ Do you know about the meeting this afternoon? ¿Estás enterado de la reunión de esta tarde? (2) (be knowledgeable about) saber [47] de algo ⊳ He knows a lot about cars. Sabe mucho de coches. ⊳ I don't know much about computers. No sé mucho de ordenadores.; **to get to know somebody** llegar [37] a conocer a alguien; **How should I know?** ¿Y yo qué sé?; **You never know!** ¡Nunca se sabe!

knowledge n conocimiento m ⊳ scientific knowledge el conocimiento científico; **my knowledge of French** mis conocimientos de francés

known vb see **know**

Koran n Corán m

Korea n Corea f

kosher adj kosher

a
b
c
d
e
f
g
h
i
j
k
l
m
n
o
p
q
r
s
t
u
v
w
x
y
z

lab n laboratorio m ▷ a lab technician un técnico de laboratorio

label n etiqueta f

labor n (US) **to be in labor** estar [22] de parto; **the labor market** el mercado de trabajo; **labor union** el sindicato

laboratory n laboratorio m

Labour n laboristas mpl ▷ My parents vote Labour. Mis padres votan a los laboristas.; **the Labour Party** el Partido Laborista

labour n **to be in labour** estar [22] de parto

lace n ❶ (of shoe) cordón m (pl cordones) ❷ encaje m ▷ a lace collar un cuello de encaje

lad n muchacho m

ladder n escalera f

lady n señora f; **Ladies and gentlemen...** Damas y caballeros...; **the ladies** los servicios de señoras; **a young lady** una señorita

ladybird n mariquita f

lager n cerveza rubia f

laid vb see **lay**

laid-back adj relajado(-a) (informal)

lain vb see **lie**

lake n lago m ▷ Lake Michigan el Lago Michigan

lamb n cordero m ▷ a lamb chop una chuleta de cordero

lamp n lámpara f

lamppost n farola f

lampshade n pantalla f

land n tierra f ▷ We have a lot of land. Tenemos mucha tierra.; **a piece of land** un terreno
▷ vb aterrizar [13] ▷ The plane landed at five o'clock. El avión aterrizó a las cinco.

landing n ❶ (of plane) aterrizaje m ❷ (of staircase) rellano m

landlady n ❶ (of rented property) casera f ❷ (of pub) patrona f

landlord n ❶ (of rented property) casero m ❷ (of pub) patrón m (pl patrones)

landscape n paisaje m

lane n ❶ camino m ▷ a country lane un camino rural ❷ carril m ▷ the outside lane (in the UK) el carril de la derecha ▷ the outside lane (on the Continent) el carril de la izquierda

language n idioma m

Although **idioma** ends in **-a**, it is actually a masculine noun.

▷ *Greek is a difficult language.* El griego es un idioma difícil.; **to use bad language** decir [**15**] palabrotas

language laboratory n laboratorio de idiomas m

lap n vuelta f ▷ *I ran 10 laps.* Corrí 10 vueltas.; **Andrew was sitting on his mother's lap.** Andrew estaba sentado en el regazo de su madre.

laptop n (ordenador) portátil m

large adj grande ▷ *a large house* una casa grande

　　Use **gran** before a singular noun.

▷ *a large number of people* un gran número de personas

　　Be careful not to translate **large** by *largo*.

laser n láser m

last adj, adv ❶ pasado(-a) ▷ *last Friday* el viernes pasado ❷ último(-a) ▷ *the last time* la última vez ❸ por última vez ▷ *I've lost my bag. —When did you last see it?* He perdido el bolso. — ¿Cuándo lo viste por última vez? ❹ en último lugar ▷ *the team which finished last* el equipo que quedó en último lugar; **He arrived last.** Llegó el último.; **last night** anoche ▷ *I got home at midnight last night.* Anoche llegué a casa a medianoche. ▷ *I couldn't sleep last night.* Anoche no pude dormir.; **at last** por fin

▶ vb durar [**25**] ▷ *The concert lasts two hours.* El concierto dura dos horas.

lastly adv por último

late adj, adv tarde ▷ *I'm often late for school.* A menudo llego tarde al colegio. ▷ *I went to bed late.* Me fui a la cama tarde.; **The flight will be one hour late.** El vuelo llegará con una hora de retraso.; **in the late afternoon** al final de la tarde; **in late May** a finales de mayo; **the late Mr Philips** el difunto Sr. Philips

lately adv últimamente ▷ *I haven't seen him lately.* No lo he visto últimamente.

later adv más tarde ▷ *I'll do it later.* Lo haré más tarde.; **See you later!** ¡Hasta luego!

latest adv último(-a) ▷ *their latest album* su último álbum; **at the latest** como muy tarde ▷ *by 10 o'clock at the latest* a las 10 como muy tarde

Latin n latín m ▷ *I do Latin.* Estudio latín.

Latin America n América Latina f

Latin American adj latinoamericano(-a)

　　▶ n latinoamericano m, latinoamericana f

laugh n risa f; **It was a good laugh.** Fue muy divertido.

　　▶ vb reírse [**44**]; **to laugh at something** reírse [**44**] de algo ▷ *He laughed at my accent.* Se río de mi acento.; **to laugh at somebody** reírse [**44**] de alguien ▷ *They laughed at her.* Se rieron de ella.

launch vb (product, rocket) lanzar [**13**]

Launderette® n lavandería automática f

Laundromat® n (US) lavandería automática f

laundry n colada f ▷ She does my laundry. Me hace la colada.

lavatory n servicio m

lavender n lavanda f

law n ❶ ley f ▷ strict laws leyes severas; **It's against the law.** Es ilegal. ❷ derecho m ▷ My sister's studying law. Mi hermana estudia derecho.

lawn n césped m

lawnmower n cortacésped m

lawyer n abogado m, abogada f ▷ My mother's a lawyer. Mi madre es abogada.

lay vb poner [41] ▷ She laid the baby in his cot. Puso al bebé en la cuna. ▷ to lay the table poner la mesa

lay off vb despedir [38]

lay-by n área de descanso f

> Although it's a feminine noun, remember that you use **el** and **un** with **área**.

layer n capa f

lazy adj perezoso(-a)

lead (1) n (metal) plomo m ▷ a lead pipe una tubería de plomo

lead (2) n ❶ (cable) cable m ❷ (dog) correa f ▷ Dogs must be kept on a lead. Los perros deben llevarse siempre sujetos con una correa.; **to be in the lead** ir [27] en cabeza

lead vb llevar [25] ▷ the street that leads to the station la calle que lleva a la estación ▷ It could lead to a civil war. Podría llevar a una guerra

civil.; **to lead the way** ir [27] delante

leader n líder mf

lead singer n cantante principal mf

leaf n hoja f

leaflet n folleto m

league n liga f ▷ They are at the top of the league. Están a la cabeza de la liga.; **the Premier League** la primera división

leak n ❶ escape m ▷ a gas leak un escape de gas ❷ (in roof) gotera f ▶ vb ❶ (bucket, pipe) tener [53] un agujero ❷ (roof) tener [53] goteras ❸ (water, gas) salirse [49]

lean vb apoyar [25] ▷ to lean something against the wall apoyar algo contra la pared; **to lean on something** apoyarse [25] en algo ▷ He leant on the table. Se apoyó en la mesa.; **to be leaning against something** estar [22] apoyado contra algo ▷ The ladder was leaning against the wall. La escalera estaba apoyada contra la pared.

lean forward vb inclinarse [25] hacia adelante

lean out vb asomarse [25] ▷ She leant out of the window. Se asomó a la ventana.

lean over vb inclinarse [25]

leap year n año bisiesto m

learn vb aprender [8] ▷ I'm learning to ski. Estoy aprendiendo a esquiar.

learner n She's a quick learner. Aprende con mucha rapidez.

learner driver n conductor en prácticas m, conductora en prácticas f

learnt vb see **learn**

least adj, pron, adv ❶ menor ▷ I haven't the least idea. No tengo la menor idea. ❷ menos ▷ the least expensive hotel el hotel menos caro ▷ It's the least I can do. Es lo menos que puedo hacer. ▷ Maths is the subject I like the least. Las matemáticas es la asignatura que menos me gusta. ▷ That's the least of my worries. Eso es lo que menos me preocupa.; **at least (1)** por lo menos ▷ It'll cost at least £200. Costará por lo menos 200 libras esterlinas. **(2)** al menos ▷ There was a lot of damage but at least nobody was hurt. Hubo muchos daños pero al menos nadie resultó herido.

leather n cuero m ▷ a black leather jacket una chaqueta de cuero negra

leave n (from job, army) permiso m ▷ My brother's on leave for a week. Mi hermano está de permiso durante una semana.
▶ vb ❶ dejar [25] ▷ Don't leave your camera in the car. No dejes la cámara en el coche. ❷ salir [49] ▷ The bus leaves at eight. El autobús sale a las ocho. ❸ salir [49] de ▷ We leave London at six o'clock. Salimos de Londres a las seis. ❹ irse [27] ▷ They left yesterday. Se fueron ayer. ▷ She left home when she was sixteen. Se fue de casa a los dieciséis años.; **to leave somebody alone** dejar [25] a alguien en paz ▷ Leave me alone! ¡Déjame en paz!

leave out vb excluir [10] ▷ Not knowing the language I felt really left out. Al no saber el idioma me sentía muy excluido.

leaves npl see **leaf**

Lebanon n Líbano m

lecture n ❶ (at university) clase f ❷ (public) conferencia f
▶ vb ❶ dar [14] clases ▷ She lectures at the technical college. Da clases en la escuela politécnica. ❷ sermonear [25] ▷ He's always lecturing us. Siempre nos está sermoneando.

lecturer n profesor universitario m, profesora universitaria f; **She's a lecturer in German.** Es profesora de alemán en la universidad.

led vb see **lead**

leek n puerro m

left vb see **leave**
▶ adj, adv ❶ izquierdo(-a) ▷ my left hand mi mano izquierda ❷ a la izquierda ▷ Turn left at the traffic lights. Doble a la izquierda al llegar al semáforo.; **I haven't got any money left.** No me queda nada de dinero.; **Is there any ice cream left?** ¿Queda algo de helado?
▶ n izquierda f ▷ on the left a la izquierda

left-hand adj **It's on the left-hand side.** Está a la izquierda.

left-handed adj zurdo(-a)

left-luggage office n consigna f

leg n pierna f ▷ She's broken her leg. Se ha roto la pierna.; **a chicken leg** un muslo de pollo; **a leg of lamb** una pierna de cordero

legal adj legal

leggings n leggings mpl

leisure n tiempo libre m ▷ What do you do in your leisure time? ¿Qué haces en tu tiempo libre?

leisure centre n centro recreativo m

lemon n limón m (pl limones)

lemonade n gaseosa f

lend vb prestar [25] ▷ I can lend you some money. Te puedo prestar algo de dinero.

length n longitud f; **It's about a metre in length.** Mide aproximadamente un metro de largo.

lens n ❶ (contact lens) lentilla f (lente de contacto f LatAm) ❷ (of spectacles) cristal m ❸ (of camera) objetivo m

Lent n Cuaresma f

lent vb see **lend**

lentil n lenteja f

Leo n (sign) Leo m; **I'm Leo.** Soy leo.

leotard n leotardo m

lesbian n lesbiana f

less adj, pron, adv menos ▷ It's less than a kilometre from here. Está a menos de un kilómetro de aquí. ▷ I've got less than you. Tengo menos que tú. ▷ It cost less than we thought. Costó menos de lo que pensábamos.; **less and less** cada vez menos

lesson n ❶ clase f ▷ an English lesson una clase de inglés ❷ (in textbook) lección f (pl lecciones)

let vb ❶ dejar [25]; **to let somebody do something** dejar [25] a alguien hacer algo ▷ Let me

have a look. Déjame ver.; **Let me go!** ¡Suéltame!; **to let somebody know something** informar [25] a alguien de algo ▷ We must let him know that we are coming to stay. Tenemos que informarle de que venimos a quedarnos.; **When can you come to dinner? — I'll let you know.** ¿Cuándo puedes venir a cenar? — Ya te lo diré.; **to let in** dejar [25] entrar ▷ They wouldn't let me in because I was under 18. No me dejaron entrar porque tenía menos de 18 años.

> To make suggestions using 'let's', you can ask questions using **por qué no**.

▷ Let's go to the cinema! ¡Por qué no vamos al cine? ▷ Let's have a **break! — Yes, let's.** Vamos a descansar un poco. — ¡Buena idea!

❷ alquilar [25] ▷ 'to let' 'se alquila'

let down vb defraudar [25] ▷ I won't let you down. No te defraudaré.

letter n ❶ carta f ▷ She wrote me a long letter. Me escribió una carta larga. ❷ letra f ▷ 'A' is the first letter of the alphabet. La 'a' es la primera letra del alfabeto.

letterbox n buzón m (pl buzones)

lettuce n lechuga f

leukaemia n leucemia f ▷ He suffers from leukaemia. Tiene leucemia.

level adj llano(-a) ▷ a level surface una superficie llana
▶ n nivel m ▷ The level of the river is rising. El nivel del río está subiendo.

level crossing n paso a nivel m

lever n palanca f

liar n mentiroso m, mentirosa f

liberal adj (view, system) liberal; **the Liberal Democrats** los demócratas liberales

Libra n (sign) Libra f; **I'm Libra.** Soy libra.

librarian n bibliotecario m, bibliotecaria f ▷ I'm a librarian. Soy bibliotecaria.

library n biblioteca f

> Be careful not to translate library by librería.

Libya n Libia f

licence (US license) n permiso m; **a driving licence** un carnet de conducir

lick vb lamer [8]

lid n tapa f

lie n mentira f; **to tell a lie** mentir [51]

▶ vb ❶ mentir [51] ▷ I know she's lying. Sé que está mintiendo. ▷ You lied to me! ¡Me mentiste!

❷ tumbarse [25]; **He was lying on the sofa.** Estaba tumbado en el sofá.

lie-in n to have a lie-in quedarse [25] en la cama hasta tarde

lieutenant n teniente mf

life n vida f

lifebelt n salvavidas m (pl salvavidas)

lifeboat n bote salvavidas m (pl botes salvavidas)

lifeguard n socorrista mf

life jacket n chaleco salvavidas m (pl chalecos salvavidas)

lifestyle n estilo de vida m

lift vb levantar [25] ▷ It's too heavy, I can't lift it. Pesa mucho, no lo puedo levantar.

▶ n ascensor m ▷ The lift isn't working. El ascensor no funciona.; **He gave me a lift to the cinema.** Me acercó al cine en coche.; **Would you like a lift?** ¿Quieres que te lleve en coche?

light adj ❶ (not heavy) ligero(-a) ▷ a light jacket una chaqueta ligera ❷ (colour) claro(-a) ▷ a light blue sweater un jersey azul claro

▶ n luz f (pl luces) ▷ He switched on the light. Encendió la luz.; **the traffic lights** el semáforo; **Have you got a light?** ¿Tienes fuego?

▶ vb encender [20]

light bulb n bombilla f

lighter n mechero m

lighthouse n faro m

lightning n relámpago m
▷ thunder and lightning truenos y relámpagos ▷ a flash of lightning un relámpago

like vb

> The most common translation for 'to like' when talking about things and activities is gustar. Remember that the construction is the opposite of English, with the thing you like being the subject of the sentence.

▷ I don't like mustard. No me gusta la mostaza. ▷ Do you like apples? ¿Te gustan las manzanas? ▷ I like riding. Me gusta montar a caballo.; **I like him.** Me cae bien.; **I'd like...** Quería... ▷ I'd like this blouse in

a
b
c
d
e
f
g
h
i
j
k
l
m
n
o
p
q
r
s
t
u
v
w
x
y
z

size 10, please. Quería esta blusa en la talla 10, por favor.; **I'd like an orange juice, please.** Un zumo de naranja, por favor.; **I'd like to...** Me gustaría... ▷ *I'd like to go to China.* Me gustaría ir a China.

> To ask someone if they would like something, or like to do something, use **querer**.

▷ *Would you like some coffee?* ¿Quieres café? ▷ *Would you like to go for a walk?* ¿Quieres ir a dar un paseo?; ... **if you like** ... si quieres
▶ **prep** como ▷ *a city like Paris* una ciudad como París

> When asking questions, use **cómo** instead of **como**.

▷ *What was his house like?* ¿Cómo era su casa?; **What's the weather like?** ¿Qué tiempo hace?; **It's a bit like salmon.** Se parece un poco al salmón.; **It's fine like that.** Así está bien.; **Do it like this.** Hazlo así.; **something like that** algo así

likely *adj* probable ▷ *That's not very likely.* Es poco probable.

> **es probable** has to be followed by a verb in the subjunctive.

▷ *She's likely to come.* Es probable que venga. ▷ *She's not likely to come.* Es probable que no venga.

lime *n (fruit)* lima *f*
limit *n* límite *m* ▷ *the speed limit* el límite de velocidad
limp *vb* cojear **[25]**
line *n* ① línea *f* ▷ *a straight line* una línea recta ② *(of people)* fila *f*; **railway line** la vía férrea; **Hold the**

line, please. No cuelgue, por favor.; **It's a very bad line.** Se oye muy mal.

linen *n* lino *m* ▷ *a linen jacket* una chaqueta de lino
link *n* ① relación *f (pl* relaciones*)* ▷ *the link between smoking and cancer* la relación entre el tabaco y el cáncer; **cultural links** los lazos culturales ▷ *vb* ① *(facts)* asociar **[25]** ② *(towns, terminals)* conectar **[25]**
lion *n* león *m (pl* leones*)*
lip *n* labio *m*
lip-read *vb* leer **[30]** los labios
lipstick *n* lápiz de labios *m (pl* lápices de labios*)*
liquid *n* líquido *m*
liquidizer *n* licuadora *f*
list *n* lista *f*
▶ *vb* ① *(in writing)* hacer **[26]** una lista de ② *(verbally)* enumerar **[25]**
listen *vb* escuchar **[25]** ▷ *Listen to this!* ¡Escucha esto! ▷ *Listen to me!* ¡Escúchame!
lit *vb see* **light**
liter *n (US)* litro *m*
literature *n* literatura *f*
litre *n* litro *m*
litter *n* basura *f*
litter bin *n* cubo de la basura *m*
little *adj, pron* pequeño(-a) ▷ *a little girl* una niña pequeña; **a little** un poco ▷ *How much would you like?* — *Just a little.* ¿Cuánto quiere? — Solo un poco.; **very little** muy poco ▷ *We've got very little time.* Tenemos muy poco tiempo.; **little by little** poco a poco

live adj vivo(-a) ▷ *I'm against tests on live animals.* Estoy en contra de los experimentos en animales vivos.; **a live broadcast** una emisión en directo; **a live concert** un concierto en vivo
  ▶ vb vivir **[58]** ▷ *Where do you live?* ¿Dónde vives? ▷ *I live in Edinburgh.* Vivo en Edimburgo.

live together vb vivir **[58]** juntos

lively adj *She's got a lively personality.* Tiene un carácter muy alegre.

liver n hígado m

lives npl see **life**

living n to make a living ganarse **[25]** la vida; **What does she do for a living?** ¿A qué se dedica?

living room n sala de estar f

lizard n ❶ *(small)* lagartija f ❷ *(big)* lagarto m

load n **loads of** un montón de *(informal)* ▷ *They've got loads of money.* Tienen un montón de dinero.; **You're talking a load of rubbish!** ¡Lo que dices es una estupidez!
  ▶ vb cargar **[37]** ▷ *a trolley loaded with luggage* un carrito cargado de equipaje

loaf n pan m; **a loaf of bread** **(1)** *(French bread)* una barra de pan **(2)** *(baked in tin)* un pan de molde

loan n préstamo m
  ▶ vb prestar **[25]**

loaves npl see **loaf**

lobster n langosta f

local adj local ▷ *the local paper* el periódico local; **a local call** una llamada urbana

loch n lago m

lock n cerradura f
  ▶ vb cerrar **[39]** con llave ▷ *Make sure you lock your door.* No te olvides de cerrar tu puerta con llave.

lock out vb **The door slammed and I was locked out.** La puerta se cerró de golpe y me quedé fuera sin llaves.

locker n taquilla f ▷ *left-luggage lockers* las taquillas de consigna; **locker room** el vestuario

lodger n inquilino m, inquilina f

loft n desván m *(pl* desvanes*)*

log n leño m

log in vb entrar **[25]** en el sistema

log off vb salir **[49]** del sistema

log on vb entrar **[25]** en el sistema

log out vb salir **[49]** del sistema

logical adj lógico(-a)

lollipop n pirulí m *(pl* pirulís*)*

London n Londres m

Londoner n londinense mf

loneliness n soledad f

lonely adj solo(-a) ▷ *I sometimes feel lonely.* A veces me siento solo.; **a lonely cottage** una casita aislada

long adj, adv largo(-a) ▷ *She's got long hair.* Tiene el pelo largo. ▷ *The room is six metres long.* La habitación tiene seis metros de largo.; **a long time** mucho tiempo ▷ *It takes a long time.* Lleva mucho tiempo.; **How long?** *(time)* ¿Cuánto tiempo? ▷ *How long have you been here?* ¿Cuánto tiempo llevas aquí? ▷ *How long will it take?* ¿Cuánto tiempo llevará?;

How long is the flight? ¿Cuánto dura el vuelo?; **as long as** siempre que

> ▎ **siempre que** has to be followed by a verb in the subjunctive.

▷ *I'll come as long as it's not too expensive.* Iré siempre que no sea demasiado caro.

▶ *vb* **to long to do something** estar **[22]** deseando hacer algo

longer *adv* **They're no longer going out together.** Ya no salen juntos.; **I can't stand it any longer.** Ya no lo aguanto más.

long jump *n* salto de longitud *m*

loo *n* wáter *m* (baño *m* LatAm)

look *n* **Have a look at this!** ¡Échale una ojeada a esto!; **I don't like the look of it.** No me gusta nada.

▶ *vb* ❶ mirar **[25]** ▷ *Look!* ¡Mira!; **to look at something** mirar **[25]** algo ▷ *Look at the picture.* Mira la foto.; **Look out!** ¡Cuidado! ❷ parecer **[12]** ▷ *She looks surprised.* Parece sorprendida.; **That cake looks nice.** Ese pastel tiene buena pinta.; **to look like somebody** parecerse **[12]** a alguien ▷ *He looks like his brother.* Se parece a su hermano.; **What does she look like?** ¿Cómo es físicamente?

look after *vb* cuidar **[25]** ▷ *I look after my little sister.* Cuido a mi hermana pequeña.

look for *vb* buscar **[48]** ▷ *I'm looking for my passport.* Estoy buscando mi pasaporte.

look forward to *vb* tener **[53]** muchas ganas de ▷ *I'm looking*

forward to meeting you. Tengo muchas ganas de conocerte.; **I'm really looking forward to the holidays.** Estoy deseando que lleguen las vacaciones.; **Looking forward to hearing from you...** A la espera de sus noticias...

look round *vb* ❶ volverse **[59]** ▷ *I called him and he looked round.* Lo llamé y se volvió. ❷ mirar **[25]** ▷ *I'm just looking round.* Solo estoy mirando.; **to look round an exhibition** visitar **[25]** una exposición; **I like looking round the shops.** Me gusta ir a ver tiendas.

look up *vb* buscar **[48]** ▷ *If you don't know a word, look it up in the dictionary.* Si no conoces una palabra, búscala en el diccionario.

loose *adj* holgado(-a) ▷ *a loose shirt* una camisa holgada; **a loose screw** un tornillo flojo; **loose change** dinero suelto

lord *n* (feudal) señor *m*; **the House of Lords** la Cámara de los Lores; **the Lord** (God) el Señor; **Good Lord!** ¡Dios mío!

lorry *n* camión *m* (pl camiones)

lorry driver *n* camionero *m*, camionera *f* ▷ *He's a lorry driver.* Es camionero.

lose *vb* perder **[20]** ▷ *I've lost my purse.* He perdido el monedero.; **to get lost** perderse **[20]** ▷ *I was afraid of getting lost.* Tenía miedo de perderme.

loss *n* pérdida *f*

lost *vb* see **lose**

▶ *adj* perdido(-a)

lost-and-found n (US) oficina de objetos perdidos f

lost property office n oficina de objetos perdidos f

lot n **a lot** mucho ▷ She talks a lot. Habla mucho. ▷ Do you like football? — Not a lot. ¿Te gusta el fútbol? — No mucho.; **a lot of** mucho ▷ I drink a lot of coffee. Bebo mucho café. ▷ We saw a lot of interesting things. Vimos muchas cosas interesantes. ▷ He's got lots of friends. Tiene muchos amigos. ▷ She's got lots of self-confidence. Tiene mucha confianza en sí misma.; **That's the lot.** Eso es todo.

lottery n lotería f ▷ to win the lottery ganar la lotería

loud adj fuerte ▷ The television is too loud. La televisión está muy fuerte.

loudspeaker n altavoz m (pl altavoces)

lounge n sala de estar f

love n amor m; **to be in love** estar **[22]** enamorado ▷ She's in love with Paul. Está enamorada de Paul.; **to make love** hacer **[26]** el amor; **Give Gloria my love.** Dale recuerdos a Gloria de mi parte.; **Love, Rosemary.** Un abrazo, Rosemary.
▶ vb querer **[43]** ▷ Everybody loves her. Todos la quieren. ▷ I love you. Te quiero. ▷ **I love chocolate.** Me encanta el chocolate.; **Would you like to come? — Yes, I'd love to.** ¿Te gustaría venir? — Sí, me encantaría.

lovely adj ❶ (person) encantador(a) ▷ She's a lovely person. Es una persona encantadora.
❷ precioso(-a) ▷ They've got a lovely house. Tienen una casa preciosa.; **What a lovely surprise!** ¡Qué sorpresa tan agradable!; **It's a lovely day.** Hace un tiempo estupendo.; **Is your meal okay?** **— Yes, it's lovely.** ¿Está bueno? — Sí, buenísimo.; **Have a lovely time!** ¡Que lo pasáis bien!

lover n amante mf

low adj, adv bajo(-a) ▷ low prices los bajos precios ▷ That plane is flying very low. Ese avión vuela muy bajo.

lower vb bajar **[25]**
▶ adj inferior

loyalty n lealtad f

loyalty card n tarjeta de cliente f

luck n suerte f ▷ She hasn't had much luck. No ha tenido mucha suerte.; **Bad luck!** ¡Mala suerte!; **Good luck!** ¡Suerte!

luckily adv afortunadamente

lucky adj afortunado(-a) ▷ I consider myself lucky. Me considero afortunado.; **to be lucky** (fortunate) tener **[53]** suerte ▷ He's lucky, he's got a job. Tiene suerte de tener trabajo.; **That was lucky!** ¡Qué suerte!; **Black cats are lucky in Britain.** En Gran Bretaña los gatos negros traen buena suerte.; **a lucky horseshoe** una herradura de la suerte

luggage n equipaje m

lump n ❶ trozo m ▷ a lump of butter un trozo de mantequilla ❷ (swelling) chichón m (pl chichones) ▷ He's got a lump on his forehead. Tiene un chichón en la frente.

lunch n almuerzo m; **to have lunch** almorzar [3] ▷ We have lunch at half past twelve. Almorzamos a las doce y media.

lung n pulmón m (pl pulmones) ▷ lung cancer el cáncer de pulmón

Luxembourg n Luxemburgo m

luxurious adj lujoso(-a)

luxury n lujo m ▷ It was luxury! ¡Era un lujo! ▷ a luxury hotel un hotel de lujo

lying vb see **lie**

lyrics npl letra f

macaroni n macarrones mpl

machine n máquina f ▷ It's a complicated machine. Es una máquina complicada.

machine gun n ametralladora f

machinery n maquinaria f

mad adj ❶ loco(-a) ▷ You're mad! ¡Estás loco! ❷ furioso(-a) ▷ She'll be mad when she finds out. Se pondrá furiosa cuando se entere.; **He's mad about football.** Está loco por el fútbol.; **She's mad about horses.** Le encantan los caballos.

madam n señora f

made vb see **make**

madness n locura f ▷ It's absolute madness. Es una locura.

magazine n revista f

maggot n gusano m

magic n magia f
▶ adj mágico(-a) ▷ a magic wand
una varita mágica; **It was magic!**
(brilliant) ¡Fue fantástico!

magician n mago m, maga f

magnet n imán m (pl imanes)

magnifying glass n lupa f

maid n ❶ (servant) sirvienta f
❷ (in hotel) camarera f; **an old
maid** (spinster) una solterona

maiden name n apellido de
soltera m
  When women marry in Spain
  they don't usually take the
  name of their husband but keep
  their own instead. If the couple
  have children they take both
  their father's and mother's
  surnames.

mail n ❶ correo m; **by mail** por
correo ❷ (letters) correspondencia
f ▷ We receive a lot of mail.
Recibimos mucha
correspondencia.

mailbox n (US) buzón m (pl
buzones)

mailman n (US) cartero m

main adj ❶ principal ▷ the main
suspect el principal sospechoso;
**The main thing is to get it
finished.** Lo principal es
terminarlo.

mainly adv principalmente

main road n carretera principal f

majesty n majestad f; **Your
Majesty** su Majestad

major adj muy importante ▷ a
major factor un factor muy
importante; **Drugs are a major
problem.** La droga es un grave

problema.; **in C major** en do
mayor

Majorca n Mallorca f

majority n mayoría f

make n marca f ▷ What make is it?
¿De qué marca es?
▶ vb ❶ hacer [26] ▷ I'm going to
make a cake. Voy a hacer un pastel.
▷ I make my bed every morning. Me
hago la cama cada mañana. ▷ It's
well made. Está bien hecho.; **She's
making lunch.** Está preparando el
almuerzo.; **Two and two make
four.** Dos y dos son cuatro.
❷ fabricar [48] ▷ 'made in Spain'
'fabricado en España' ❸ ganar [25]
▷ He makes a lot of money. Gana
mucho dinero.; **to make
somebody do something** hacer
[26] a alguien hacer algo ▷ My
mother makes me eat vegetables.
Mi madre me hace comer
verduras.; **You'll have to make
do with a cheaper car.** Tendrás
que conformarte con un coche
más barato.; **What time do you
make it?** ¿Qué hora tienes?

make out vb ❶ descifrar [25]
▷ I can't make out the address on the
label. No consigo descifrar la
dirección que viene en la etiqueta.
❷ comprender [8] ▷ I can't make her
out at all. No la comprendo en
absoluto. ❸ dar [14] a entender
▷ They're making out it was my fault.
Están dando a entender que fue
culpa mía.

make up vb ❶ componer [41]
▷ Women make up thirty per cent of
the police force. Las mujeres

componen el treinta por ciento
del cuerpo de policía. ❷ **inventarse**
[25] ▷ *He made up the whole story.*
Se inventó toda la historia.
❸ **hacer [26] las paces** ▷ *They had a*
quarrel, but soon made up. Riñeron,
pero poco después hicieron las
paces. ❹ **maquillarse [25]** ▷ *She*
spends hours making herself up. Pasa
horas maquillándose.

make-up n maquillaje m; **She put**
on her make-up. Se maquilló.

male adj ❶ (animal, plant)
macho(-a) ▷ *a male kitten* un gatito
macho ❷ (person) varón (pl
varones) ▷ *Sex: Male* Sexo: Varón;
Most football players are male.
La mayoría de los futbolistas son
hombres.; **a male nurse** un
enfermero; **a male chauvinist** un
machista
 ▶ n (animal) macho m

mall n centro comercial m

Malta n Malta f

man n hombre m

manage vb ❶ (get by) arreglárselas
[25] ▷ *We haven't got much money,*
but we manage. No tenemos
mucho dinero, pero nos las
arreglamos. ❷ (be manager of)
dirigir **[16]** ▷ *She manages a big store.*
Dirige una tienda grande. ▷ *He*
manages our football team. Dirige
nuestro equipo de fútbol.; **to**
manage to do something
conseguir **[50]** hacer algo ▷ *Luckily*
I managed to pass the exam. Por
suerte, conseguí aprobar el
examen.; **Can you manage a bit**
more? *(food)* ¿Te pongo un poco

más?; **Can you manage with that**
suitcase? ¿Puedes con la maleta?

management n dirección f

manager n ❶ (of company,
department, performer) director m,
directora f ▷ *I complained to the*
manager. Fui a reclamar al director.
❷ (of restaurant, store) gerente mf
❸ (of team) entrenador m,
entrenadora f ▷ *the England*
manager el entrenador de la
selección inglesa

manageress n (of restaurant, store)
gerente f

mango n mango m

maniac n maníaco m, maníaca f;
He drives like a maniac. Conduce
como un loco.

manner n manera f ▷ *She was*
behaving in an odd manner. Se
comportaba de una manera
extraña.; **He has a confident**
manner. Se muestra seguro de sí
mismo.

manners npl modales mpl ▷ *Her*
manners are appalling. Tiene muy
malos modales.; **good manners**
la buena educación; **It's bad**
manners to speak with your
mouth full. Es de mala educación
hablar con la boca llena.

mansion n mansión f (pl
mansiones)

mantelpiece n repisa de la
chimenea f

manual n manual m

manufacture vb fabricar **[48]**

manufacturer n fabricante mf

many adj, pron muchos (f muchas)
▷ *He hasn't got many friends.* No

tiene muchos amigos.; **how many?** ¿cuántos? (f ¿cuántas?) ▷ *How many hours a week do you work?* ¿Cuántas horas trabajas a la semana?; **too many** demasiados (f demasiadas) ▷ *Sixteen people? That's too many.* ¿Dieciséis personas? Son demasiadas.; **so many** tantos (f tantas) ▷ *He told so many lies!* ¡Dijo tantas mentiras!

map n ❶ (of country, region) mapa m
Although **mapa** ends in -a, it is actually a masculine noun.
❷ (of town, city) plano m

marathon n maratón m (pl maratones)

marble n mármol m ▷ *a marble statue* una estatua de mármol; **a marble** una canica

March n marzo m ▷ *in March* en marzo ▷ *on 9 March* el 9 de marzo

march vb desfilar [**25**] ▷ *The troops marched past the King.* Las tropas desfilaron delante del Rey.
▶ n marcha f ▷ *a peace march* una marcha por la paz

mare n yegua f

margarine n margarina f

margin n margen m (pl márgenes) ▷ *She wrote a note in the margin.* Escribió una nota al margen.

marijuana n marihuana f

mark n ❶ nota f ▷ *I get good marks for French.* Saco buenas notas en francés. ❷ mancha f ▷ *You've got a mark on your shirt.* Tienes una mancha en la camisa. ❸ (former German currency) marco m
▶ vb ❶ corregir [**18**] ▷ *The teacher hasn't marked my homework yet.*

El maestro no me ha corregido los deberes todavía. ❷ señalar [**25**] ▷ *Mark its position on the map.* Señala su posición en el mapa.

market n mercado m

marketing n márketing m

marmalade n mermelada de naranja f

marriage n matrimonio m

married adj casado(-a) ▷ *They are not married.* No están casados.; **a married couple** un matrimonio; **to get married** casarse [**25**]

marry vb ❶ casarse [**25**] ▷ *They married in June.* Se casaron en junio. ❷ casarse [**25**] con ▷ *He wants to marry her.* Quiere casarse con ella.; **to get married** casarse [**25**] ▷ *My brother's getting married in March.* Mi hermano se casa en marzo.

marvellous (US **marvelous**) adj estupendo(-a) ▷ *That's a marvellous idea!* ¡Es una idea estupenda!

marzipan n mazapán m

mascara n rímel m

masculine adj masculino(-a)

mashed potatoes npl puré de patatas m (puré de papas m LatAm)

mask n máscara f

mass n ❶ montón m (pl montones) ▷ *a mass of books and papers* un montón de libros y papeles ❷ misa f ▷ *We go to mass on Sunday.* Vamos a misa los domingos.; **the mass media** los medios de comunicación de masas

massage n masaje m

massive adj enorme

master vb dominar [**25**] ▷ *Students need to master a second language.*

a b c d e f g h i j k l m n o p q r s t u v w x y z

Los estudiantes tienen que dominar un segundo idioma.

masterpiece n obra maestra f (pl obras maestras)

mat n (doormat) felpudo m; **a table mat** un mantel individual

match n ❶ partido m ▷ a football match un partido de fútbol ❷ cerilla f ▷ a box of matches una caja de cerillas
▶ vb ❶ hacer [26] juego con ▷ The jacket matches the trousers. La chaqueta hace juego con los pantalones. ❷ hacer [26] juego ▷ These colours don't match. Estos colores no hacen juego.

mate n amigo m, amiga f ▷ He always goes on holiday with his mates. Siempre va de vacaciones con sus amigos.

material n ❶ (cloth) tejido m ❷ material m ▷ I'm collecting material for my project. Estoy recogiendo material para mi proyecto.

mathematics n matemáticas fpl

maths n matemáticas fpl

matter n asunto m ▷ It's a matter of life and death. Es un asunto de vida o muerte.; **What's the matter?** ¿Qué pasa?; **as a matter of fact** de hecho
▶ vb importar [25] ▷ I can't give you the money today. — It doesn't matter. No te puedo dar el dinero hoy. — No importa.; **Shall I phone today or tomorrow? — Whenever, it doesn't matter.** ¿Telefoneo hoy o mañana? — Cuando quieras, da igual.; **It**

matters a lot to me. Significa mucho para mí.

mattress n colchón m (pl colchones)

mature adj maduro(-a)

maximum n máximo m ▷ a maximum of two years in prison un máximo de dos años de cárcel
▶ adj máximo(-a) ▷ The maximum speed is 100 km/h. La velocidad máxima permitida es 100km/h.

May n mayo m ▷ in May en mayo ▷ on 7 May el 7 de mayo; **May Day** el Primero de Mayo

may vb poder [40] ▷ The police may come and catch us here. La policía puede venir y pillarnos aquí. ▷ May I smoke? ¿Puedo fumar?

> **Puede que** has to be followed by a verb in the subjunctive.

▷ I may go. Puede que vaya. ▷ It may rain. Puede que llueva.

> **A lo mejor** can also be used but it is a more colloquial alternative.

▷ Are you going to the party? — I don't know, I may. ¿Vas a ir a la fiesta? — No sé, a lo mejor.

maybe adv a lo mejor ▷ Maybe she's at home. A lo mejor está en casa. ▷ Maybe he'll change his mind. A lo mejor cambia de idea.

mayonnaise n mayonesa f

mayor n alcalde m, alcaldesa f

me pron

> Use **me** to translate 'me' when it is the direct object of the verb in the sentence, or when it means 'to me'.

<u>me</u> ▷ Look at me! ¡Mírame! ▷ Could you lend me your pen? ¿Me prestas tu bolígrafo?

▪ Use **yo** after the verb 'to be' and in comparisons.

▷ It's me. Soy yo. ▷ He's older than me. Es mayor que yo.

▪ Use **mí** after prepositions.

▷ without me sin mí

▪ Remember that 'with me' translates as **conmigo**.

▷ He was with me. Estaba conmigo.

meal n comida f; **Enjoy your meal!** ¡Que aproveche!

mean vb ① significar [**48**] ▷ What does 'alcalde' mean? ¿Qué significa 'alcalde'? ▷ I don't know what it means. No sé lo que significa. ② querer [**43**] decir ▷ That's not what I meant. Eso no es lo que quería decir. ③ referirse [**51**] a ▷ Which one did he mean? ¿A cuál se refería? ▷ Do you mean me? ¿Te refieres a mí?; **to mean to do something** querer [**43**] hacer algo ▷ I didn't mean to hurt you. No quería hacerte daño.; **Do you really mean it?** ¿Lo dices en serio? ▶ adj ① (tight-fisted) tacaño(-a) ② (unkind) mezquino(-a) ▷ You're being mean to me. Estás siendo mezquino conmigo.

meaning n significado m

meant vb see **mean**

meanwhile adv mientras tanto

measles n sarampión m ▷ I've got measles. Tengo el sarampión.

measure vb medir [**38**]

meat n carne f

Mecca n La Meca

mechanic n mecánico m, mecánica f ▷ He's a mechanic. Es mecánico.

medal n medalla f

media npl **the media** los medios de comunicación

medical adj médico(-a) ▷ medical treatment el tratamiento médico; **medical insurance** el seguro médico; **to have medical problems** tener [**53**] problemas de salud; **She's a medical student.** Es una estudiante de medicina. ▶ n **He had a medical last week.** Se hizo un chequeo la semana pasada.

medicine n ① (science) medicina f ▷ I want to study medicine. Quiero estudiar medicina. ② (medication) medicamento m ▷ I need some medicine. Necesito un medicamento.

Mediterranean adj mediterráneo(-a) ▶ n **the Mediterranean** el Mediterráneo

medium adj mediano(-a) ▷ a man of medium height un hombre de estatura mediana

medium-sized adj a **medium-sized town** una ciudad de tamaño mediano

meet vb ① (by chance) encontrarse [**11**] con ▷ I met Paul in town. Me encontré con Paul en el centro.; **We met by chance in the supermarket.** Nos encontramos por casualidad en el supermercado. ② (by arrangement) reunirse [**46**] ▷ The committee met *at two o'clock.* El comité se reunió a las dos.; **Where shall we meet?** ¿Dónde quedamos?; **I'm going to meet my friends at the swimming pool.** He quedado con mis amigos en la piscina.; **I'll meet you at the station.** Te voy a buscar a la estación. ❸ *(get to know)* conocer **[12]** ▷ *He met Tim at a party.* Conoció a Tim en una fiesta.; **Have you met her before?** ¿La conoces?

meeting n ❶ *(socially)* encuentro m ▷ *their first meeting* su primer encuentro ❷ *(for work)* reunión f *(pl* reuniones*)* ▷ *a business meeting* una reunión de trabajo

melon n melón m *(pl* melones*)*

melt vb ❶ derretir **[38]** ▷ *Melt 100 grams of butter in a saucepan.* Derrita 100 gramos de mantequilla en una sartén. ❷ derretirse **[38]** ▷ *The snow is melting.* La nieve se está derritiendo.

member n miembro mf; **'members only'** 'reservado para los socios'; **a Member of Parliament** un diputado (f una diputada)

memorial n monumento conmemorativo m

memorize vb memorizar **[13]**

memory n ❶ *(also for computer)* memoria f ▷ *I've got a terrible memory.* Tengo una memoria espantosa. ❷ recuerdo m ▷ *happy memories* los recuerdos felices

men npl see **man**

mend vb arreglar **[25]**

mental adj mental ▷ *mental illness* la enfermedad mental

mention vb mencionar **[25]** ▷ *He didn't mention it to me.* No me lo mencionó.; **I mentioned she might come later.** Dije que a lo mejor vendría más tarde.; **Thank you! — Don't mention it!** ¡Gracias! — ¡No hay de qué!

menu n ❶ carta f ▷ *Could I have the menu please?* ¿Me trae la carta por favor? ❷ *(on computer)* menú m *(pl* menús*)*

meringue n merengue m

merry adj **Merry Christmas!** ¡Feliz Navidad!

merry-go-round n tiovivo m

mess n desorden m; **My hair's a mess today.** Hoy tengo el pelo hecho un desastre.; **I'll be in a mess if I fail the exam.** Voy a tener problemas si suspendo el examen.

mess about vb **Yesterday I just messed about with some friends.** Ayer estuve sin hacer nada con unos amigos.; **Stop messing about with my computer!** ¡Deja de toquetear mi ordenador!

mess up vb estropear **[25]** ▷ *You've messed up my CDs!* ¡Me has estropeado los CDs!; **I messed up my chemistry exam.** Metí la pata en el examen de química.

message n mensaje m ▷ *a secret message* un mensaje secreto; **Would you like to leave him a message?** ¿Quiere dejarle un recado?

▶ vb enviar [21] un mensaje ▷ She messaged me on Facebook.

messenger n mensajero m, mensajera f

messy adj desordenado(-a) ▷ Your room is really messy. Tu habitación está muy desordenada.; **Her writing is really messy.** Tiene muy mala letra.

met vb see **meet**

metal n metal m

meter n ① (for gas, electricity) contador m ② (for taxi) taxímetro m ③ (parking meter) parquímetro m ④ (US: unit of measurement) metro m

method n método m

Methodist n metodista mf ▷ He's a Methodist. Es metodista.

metre n metro m

metric adj métrico(-a)

Mexico n México m

mice npl see **mouse**

microchip n microchip m (pl microchips)

microphone n micrófono m

microscope n microscopio m

microwave n microondas m (pl microondas)

midday n mediodía m ▷ at midday al mediodía

middle n medio m ▷ The car was in the middle of the road. El coche estaba en medio de la carretera.; **in the middle of May** a mediados de mayo; **She was in the middle of her exams.** Estaba en plenos exámenes.

▶ adj del medio ▷ the middle seat el asiento del medio

middle-aged adj de mediana edad

middle-class adj de clase media

Middle East n the Middle East el Oriente Medio

middle name n segundo nombre m

midge n mosquito m

midnight n medianoche f ▷ at midnight a medianoche

midwife n comadrona f ▷ She's a midwife. Es comadrona.

might vb modal [40] ▷ The teacher might come at any moment. El profesor podría venir en cualquier momento.

> **Puede que** has to be followed by a verb in the subjunctive. ▷ He might come later. Puede que venga más tarde. ▷ She might not have understood. Puede que no haya entendido.

> **A lo mejor** can also be used but it is a more colloquial alternative. ▷ We might go to Spain next year. A lo mejor vamos a España el año que viene.

migraine n jaqueca f ▷ I've got a migraine. Tengo jaqueca.

mike n micro m

mild adj suave ▷ The winters are quite mild. Los inviernos son bastante suaves.

mile n milla f

> In Spain distances are expressed in kilometres. A mile is about 1.6 kilometres.

▷ It's five miles from here. Está a unas cinco millas de aquí. ▷ at 50 miles per hour a 50 millas por

hora; **We walked for miles!**
¡Caminamos kilómetros y
kilómetros!

military adj militar

milk n leche f
▶ vb ordeñar [25]

milk chocolate n chocolate con
leche m

milkman n lechero m
● In Spain milk is not delivered to
people's homes.

milk shake n batido m

millennium n milenio m

millimetre (US **millimeter**) n
milímetro m

million n millón m (pl millones)
▷ two million pounds dos millones
de libras esterlinas

millionaire n millonario m,
millonaria f

mince n carne picada f (carne
molida f LatAm)

mind vb ❶ (look after) cuidar [25]
▷ Could you mind the baby this
afternoon? ¿Podrías cuidar al niño
esta tarde? ▷ Could you mind my
bags for a few minutes? ¿Me cuidas
las bolsas un momento?
❷ (matter) importar [25] ▷ Do you
mind if I open the window? — No,
I don't mind. ¿Le importa que abra
la ventana? — No, no me importa.;
I don't mind the noise. No me
molesta el ruido.; **Never mind!**
(1) (don't worry) ¡No te preocupes!
(2) (it's not important) ¡No importa!;
Mind you don't fall. Ten cuidado,
no te vayas a caer.; **Mind the step!**
¡Cuidado con el escalón!
▶ n mente f ▷ What have you got

in mind? ¿Qué tienes en mente?;
I haven't made up my mind yet.
No me he decidido todavía.; **He's
changed my mind.** Me ha cambiado
de idea.; **Are you out of your
mind?** ¿Estás loco?

mine pron ❶ el mío m (pl los míos)
▷ Is this your coat? — No, mine is
black. ¿Es este tu abrigo? — No, el
mío es negro. ▷ your parents and
mine tus padres y los míos ❷ la mía
f (pl las mías) ▷ Is this your scarf?
— No, mine is red. ¿Es esta tu bufanda?
— No, la mía es roja. ▷ her sisters
and mine sus hermanas y las mías
❸ mío m (pl míos) ▷ That car is
mine. Ese coche es mío. ❹ mía f
(pl mías) ▷ Sorry, that beer is mine.
Disculpa, esa cerveza es mía.
▷ Isabel is a friend of mine. Isabel es
amiga mía.
▶ n mina f ▷ a coal mine una mina
de carbón ▷ a land mine una mina

miner n minero m, minera f ▷ My
father was a miner. Mi padre era
minero.

mineral water n agua mineral f
▌ Although it's a feminine noun,
remember that you use **el** and
un with **agua mineral**.

miniature adj en miniatura

minibus n microbús m (pl
microbuses)

minimum n mínimo m
▶ adj mínimo(-a) ▷ The minimum
age for driving is 17. La edad mínima
para poder conducir es 17 años.

miniskirt n minifalda f

minister n ❶ ministro m, ministra f
▷ the Minister for Education el

Ministro de Educación **2** (of church) pastor m, pastora f

minor adj secundario(-a) ▷ a minor problem un problema secundario; **a minor operation** una operación de poca importancia; **in D minor** en re menor

minority n minoría f

mint n **1** (sweet) caramelo de menta m **2** (plant) menta f ▷ mint sauce salsa de menta

minus prep menos ▷ sixteen minus three dieciséis menos tres; **I got a B minus for my French.** Me pusieron un notable bajo en francés.; **minus two degrees** dos grados bajo cero

minute n minuto m ▷ Wait a minute! ¡Espera un minuto!
▶ adj minúsculo(-a)

miracle n milagro m

mirror n **1** espejo m ▷ She looked at herself in the mirror. Se miró en el espejo. **2** (in car) retrovisor m

misbehave vb portarse **[25]** mal

mischief n She's always up to mischief. Siempre está haciendo travesuras.; **full of mischief** travieso

mischievous adj travieso(-a)

miser n avaro m, avara f

miserable adj infeliz (pl infelices) ▷ a miserable life una vida infeliz; **I'm feeling miserable.** Me siento deprimido.; **miserable weather** un tiempo deprimente

Miss n **1** señorita f ▷ Miss Peters wants to see you. La señorita Peters quiere verte. **2** (in address) Srta.

miss vb perder **[20]** ▷ Hurry or you'll miss the bus. Date prisa o perderás el autobús.; **It's too good an opportunity to miss.** Es una oportunidad demasiado buena para dejarla pasar.; **He missed the target.** No dio en el blanco.; **I miss my family.** Echo de menos a mi familia.; **You've missed a page.** Te has saltado una página.

missing adj perdido(-a) ▷ the missing link el eslabón perdido; **to be missing** faltar **[25]** ▷ Two members of the group are missing. Faltan dos miembros del grupo.; **a missing person** una persona desaparecida

mist n neblina f

mistake n error m ▷ There must be some mistake. Debe de haber algún error.; **a spelling mistake** una falta de ortografía; **to make a mistake (1)** (in speaking) cometer **[8]** un error ▷ He makes a lot of mistakes when he speaks English. Comete muchos errores cuando habla inglés. **(2)** (get mixed up) equivocarse **[48]** ▷ I'm sorry, I made a mistake. Lo siento, me equivoqué.; **by mistake** por error
▶ vb confundir **[58]** ▷ He mistook me for my sister. Me confundió con mi hermana.

mistaken adj to be mistaken estar **[22]** equivocado

mistletoe n muérdago m

mistook vb see **mistake**

misty adj neblinoso(-a) ▷ a misty morning una mañana neblinosa

misunderstand vb entender [20] mal ▷ Sorry, I misunderstood you. Lo siento, te entendí mal.

misunderstanding n malentendido m

misunderstood vb see **misunderstand**

mix n mezcla f ▷ The film is a mix of science fiction and comedy. La película es una mezcla de ciencia ficción y comedia.; a cake mix un preparado para pastel
▶ vb mezclar [25] ▷ Mix the flour with the sugar. Mezcle la harina con el azúcar.; I like mixing with all sorts of people. Me gusta tratar con todo tipo de gente.; He doesn't mix much. No se relaciona mucho.

mix up vb confundir [58] ▷ He mixed up their names. Confundió sus nombres.; I'm getting mixed up. Me estoy confundiendo.

mixed adj mixto(-a) ▷ a mixed salad una ensalada mixta ▷ a mixed school un colegio mixto; I've got mixed feelings about it. No sé qué pensar de ello.

mixer n (for food) batidora f

mixture n mezcla f ▷ a mixture of spices una mezcla de especias

mix-up n confusión f (pl confusiones)

moan vb quejarse [25] ▷ She's always moaning about something. Siempre se está quejando de algo.

mobile n (phone) móvil m

mobile home n caravana fija f (trailer m LatAm)

mobile phone n móvil m

mock vb ridiculizar [13]
▶ adj a mock exam un examen de práctica

model n ❶ modelo m ▷ His car is the latest model. Su coche es el último modelo. ❷ maqueta f ▷ a model of the castle una maqueta del castillo ❸ modelo mf ▷ She's a famous model. Es una modelo famosa.
▶ adj a model railway una vía férrea en miniatura; a model plane una maqueta de avión; He's a model pupil. Es un alumno modelo.

modem n módem m (pl módems)

moderate adj moderado(-a) ▷ His views are quite moderate. Tiene opiniones bastante moderadas.; I do a moderate amount of exercise. Hago un poco de gimnasia.

modern adj moderno(-a)

modernize vb modernizar [13]

moisturizer n crema hidratante f

moldy adj (US) mohoso(-a)

mole n ❶ lunar m ▷ I've got a mole on my back. Tengo un lunar en la espalda. ❷ (animal) topo m

moment n momento m ▷ Just a moment! ¡Un momento! ▷ at the moment en este momento ▷ any moment now de un momento a otro

monarchy n monarquía f

Monday n lunes m (pl lunes) ▷ I saw her on Monday. La vi el lunes. ▷ every Monday todos los lunes ▷ last Monday el lunes pasado ▷ next Monday el lunes que viene ▷ on Mondays los lunes

money n dinero m ▷ I need to change some money. Tengo que cambiar dinero.

mongrel n perro mestizo m; **My dog's a mongrel.** Mi perro es mestizo.

monitor n (on computer) monitor m

monkey n mono m, mona f

monster n monstruo m

month n mes m ▷ this month este mes ▷ next month el mes que viene ▷ last month el mes pasado

monthly adj mensual

monument n monumento conmemorativo m

mood n humor m ▷ to be in a good mood estar de buen humor ▷ to be in a bad mood estar de mal humor

moody adj (in a bad mood) malhumorado(-a); **to be moody** (temperamental) tener [53] un humor cambiante

moon n luna f ▷ There's a full moon tonight. Esta noche hay luna llena.; **She's over the moon about it.** Está en el séptimo cielo de contenta.

moped n ciclomotor m

moral adj moral ▷ The moral of the story is... La moraleja de la historia es...; **morals** la moral

more adj, pron, adv más ▷ It costs a lot more. Cuesta mucho más. ▷ There isn't any more. Ya no hay más. ▷ A bit more? ¿Un poco más? ▷ Is there any more? ¿Hay más? ▷ It'll take a few more days. Llevará unos cuantos días más.; **more than** más que

Use **más que** when comparing two things or people and **más de** when talking about quantities.

▷ He's more intelligent than me. Es más inteligente que yo. ▷ more than 20 people más de 20 personas; **more or less** más o menos; **more than ever** más que nunca; **more and more** cada vez más

morning n mañana f ▷ in the morning por la mañana ▷ at 7 o'clock in the morning a las 7 de la mañana ▷ on Saturday morning el sábado por la mañana ▷ tomorrow morning mañana por la mañana; **the morning papers** los periódicos de la mañana

Morocco n Marruecos m

mortgage n hipoteca f

Moscow n Moscú m

Moslem n musulmán m (pl musulmanes), musulmana f ▷ He's a Moslem. Es musulmán.

mosque n mezquita f

mosquito n mosquito m; **a mosquito bite** una picadura de mosquito

most adj, pron, adv más ▷ He's the one who talks the most. Es el que más habla. ▷ the most expensive restaurant el restaurante más caro; **most of** la mayor parte de ▷ most of the time la mayor parte del tiempo; **most of them** la mayoría ▷ Most of them have cars. La mayoría tienen coches. ▷ Most people go out on Friday nights. La mayoría de la gente sale los viernes por la noche.; **at the most** como mucho

▷ *two hours at the most* dos horas como mucho; **to make the most of something** aprovechar **[25]** algo al máximo ▷ *He made the most of his holiday.* Aprovechó sus vacaciones al máximo.

moth n ❶ mariposa nocturna f ❷ *(clothes moth)* polilla f

mother n madre f; **my mother and father** mis padres; **mother tongue** la lengua materna

mother-in-law n suegra f

Mother's Day n Día de la Madre m

motivated adj **He is highly motivated.** Está muy motivado.

motivation n motivación f *(pl* motivaciones)

motor n motor m

motorbike n moto f

> Although **moto** ends in *-o*, it is actually a feminine noun.

motorboat n lancha motora f

motorcycle n motocicleta f

motorcyclist n motociclista mf

motorist n conductor m, conductora f

motor racing n carreras de coches fpl

motorway n autopista f

mouldy adj mohoso(-a)

mountain n montaña f ▷ *in the mountains* en la montaña; **a mountain bike** una bicicleta de montaña

mountaineer n alpinista mf

mountaineering n alpinismo m ▷ *I go mountaineering.* Hago alpinismo.

mountainous adj montañoso(-a)

mouse n *(also for computer)* ratón m *(pl* ratones)

mouse mat n alfombrilla del ratón f

mousse n ❶ mousse f ▷ *chocolate mousse* la mousse de chocolate ❷ *(for hair)* espuma f

moustache n bigote m ▷ *He's got a moustache.* Tiene bigote.

mouth n boca f

mouthful n ❶ *(of food)* bocado m ❷ *(of drink)* trago m

mouth organ n armónica f

move n ❶ paso m ▷ *That was a good move!* ¡Ese fue un paso bien dado!; **It's your move.** Te toca jugar. ❷ mudanza f ▷ *our move from Oxford to Luton* nuestra mudanza de Oxford a Luton; **Get a move on!** ¡Date prisa!
▷ vb ❶ moverse **[33]** ▷ *Don't move!* ¡No te muevas! ❷ mover **[33]** ▷ *He can't move his arm.* No puede mover el brazo.; **Could you move your stuff please?** ¿Podrías quitar tus cosas de aquí, por favor? ❸ avanzar **[13]** ▷ *The car was moving very slowly.* El coche avanzaba muy lentamente. ❹ conmover **[33]** ▷ *I was very moved by the film.* La película me conmovió mucho.; **to move house** mudarse **[25]** de casa ▷ *We're moving in July.* Nos mudamos en julio.

move in vb **When are the new tenants moving in?** ¿Cuándo vienen los nuevos inquilinos?

move over vb correrse **[8]** ▷ *Could you move over a bit, please?* ¿Te podrías correr un poco, por favor?

movement n movimiento m

movie n película f; **the movies** el cine

moving adj ❶ en movimiento ▷ a moving bus un autobús en movimiento ❷ conmovedor(a) ▷ a moving story una historia conmovedora

MP abbr diputado m, diputada f

MP3 player n reproductor de MP3 m

Mr abbr ❶ señor m ▷ Mr Jones wants to see you. El señor Jones quiere verte. ❷ (in address) Sr.

Mrs abbr ❶ señora f ▷ Mrs Philips wants to see you. La señora Philips quiere verte. ❷ (in address) Sra.

Ms abbr ❶ señora f ▷ Ms Brown wants to see you. La señora Brown quiere verte. ❷ (in address) Sra.
   There isn't a direct equivalent of Ms in Spanish. If you are writing to a woman and you don't know whether she is married, use **Señora**.

much adj, pron, adv mucho(-a) ▷ I feel much better now. Ahora me siento mucho mejor. ▷ I haven't got much money. No tengo mucho dinero. ▷ Have you got a lot of luggage? — No, not much. ¿Tienes mucho equipaje? — No, no mucho.; **very much** mucho ▷ I enjoyed myself very much. Me divertí mucho.; **Thank you very much.** Muchas gracias.; **how much?** ¿cuánto? ▷ How much time have you got? ¿Cuánto tiempo tienes? ▷ How much is it? ¿Cuánto es?; **too much** demasiado ▷ That's too much! ¡Eso

es demasiado! ▷ They give us too much homework. Nos ponen demasiados deberes.; **so much** tanto ▷ I didn't think it would cost so much. No pensé que costaría tanto. ▷ I've never seen so much rain. Nunca había visto tanta lluvia.; **What's on TV? — Not much.** ¿Qué ponen en la tele? — Nada especial.

mud n barro m

muddle n to be in a muddle (books, photos) estar [22] todo revuelto

muddle up vb confundir [58] ▷ He muddles me up with my sister. Me confunde con mi hermana.; **to get muddled up** hacerse [26] un lío (informal) ▷ I'm getting muddled up. Me estoy haciendo un lío.

muddy adj lleno de barro (f llena de barro)

muesli n muesli m

mug n taza alta f ▷ Do you want a cup or a mug? ¿Quieres una taza normal o una taza alta?; **a beer mug** una jarra de cerveza
   ▷ vb atracar [48] ▷ He was mugged in the city centre. Lo atracaron en el centro de la ciudad.

mugging n atraco m

multiple choice test n examen tipo test m

multiplication n multiplicación f

multiply vb multiplicar [48] ▷ to multiply six by three multiplicar seis por tres

mum n mamá f ▷ my mum mi mamá

mummy n ❶ mamá f ▷ Mummy says I can go. Mamá dice que puedo ir. ❷ (Egyptian) momia f

mumps n paperas fpl ▷ *My brother's got mumps.* Mi hermano tiene paperas.

murder n asesinato m
  ▶ vb asesinar [**25**] ▷ *He was murdered.* Fue asesinado.

murderer n asesino m, asesina f

muscle n músculo m

museum n museo m

mushroom n champiñón m (pl champiñones)

music n música f

musical adj musical; **I'm not musical.** No tengo aptitudes para la música.
  ▶ n musical m

musician n músico m, música f ▷ *He's a musician.* Es músico.

Muslim n musulmán m (pl musulmanes), musulmana f ▷ *She's a Muslim.* Es musulmana.

mussel n mejillón m (pl mejillones)

must vb ❶ *(it's necessary)* tener [**53**] que ▷ *I must buy some presents.* Tengo que comprar unos regalos.; **You mustn't forget to send her a card.** No te vayas a olvidar de mandarle una tarjeta. ❷ *(I suppose)* deber [**8**] de ▷ *You must be tired.* Debes de estar cansada.

mustard n mostaza f

mustn't vb = must not

my adj mi (pl mis) ▷ *my father* mi padre ▷ *my house* mi casa ▷ *my two best friends* mis dos mejores amigos ▷ *my sisters* mis hermanas

  'my' is usually translated by the definite article **el/los** or **la/las** when it's clear from the sentence who the possessor is or when referring to clothing or parts of the body.
  ▷ *They stole my car.* Me robaron el coche. ▷ *I took off my coat.* Me quité el abrigo. ▷ *I'm washing my hair.* Me estoy lavando la cabeza.

myself pron ❶ *(reflexive)* me ▷ *I've hurt myself.* Me he hecho daño. ❷ *(after preposition)* mí mismo(-a) ▷ *I talked mainly about myself.* Hablé principalmente de mí mismo.; **a beginner like myself** un principiante como yo ❸ *(for emphasis)* yo mismo(-a) ▷ *I made it myself.* Lo hice yo misma.; **by myself** solo(-a) ▷ *I don't like travelling by myself.* No me gusta viajar solo.

mysterious adj misterioso(-a)

mystery n misterio m; **a murder mystery** una novela policíaca

myth n mito m

n

nag *vb* dar [**14**] la lata ▷ *She's always nagging me.* Siempre me está dando la lata.

nail *n* ❶ uña *f* ▷ *She bites her nails.* Se muerde las uñas. ❷ *(made of metal)* clavo *m*

nailbrush *n* cepillo de uñas *m*

nailfile *n* lima para las uñas *f*

nail scissors *npl* tijeras para las uñas *fpl*

nail varnish *n* esmalte de uñas *m*; **nail varnish remover** el quitaesmaltes

naked *adj* desnudo(-a)

name *n* nombre *m*; **What's your name?** ¿Cómo te llamas?

nanny *n (nursemaid)* niñera *f*

napkin *n* servilleta *f*

nappy *n* pañal *m*

narrow *adj* estrecho(-a)

nasty *adj* ❶ malo(-a) ▷ *Don't be nasty. No seas malo.*

　Use **mal** before a masculine singular noun.

❷ desagradable ▷ *a nasty smell* un olor desagradable

nation *n* nación *f* (*pl* naciones)

national *adj* nacional

national anthem *n* himno nacional *m*

nationality *n* nacionalidad *f*

national park *n* parque nacional *m*

natural *adj* natural

naturally *adv* naturalmente ▷ *Naturally, we were very disappointed.* Naturalmente, estábamos muy decepcionados.

nature *n* naturaleza *f* ▷ *the wonders of nature* las maravillas de la naturaleza; **It's not in his nature to behave like that.** Comportarse así no es propio de él.

naughty *adj* travieso(-a) ▷ *Naughty girl!* ¡Qué traviesa!

navy *n* armada *f* ▷ *He's in the navy.* Está en la armada.

navy-blue *adj* azul marino ▷ *a navy-blue skirt* una falda azul marino

near *adj* ❶ cerca ▷ *It's fairly near.* Está bastante cerca. ❷ cercano(-a) ▷ *Where's the nearest service station?* ¿Dónde está la gasolinera más cercana?; **in the near future** en un futuro cercano

▶ *prep, adv* ❶ cerca ▷ *Is there a bank near here?* ¿Hay algún banco por aquí cerca? ❷ cerca de ▷ *I live near Liverpool.* Vivo cerca de Liverpool.;

near to cerca de ▷ *It's very near to the school.* Está muy cerca del colegio.

nearby adj cercano(-a) ▷ *a nearby village* un pueblo cercano
▶ adv cerca ▷ *There's a supermarket nearby.* Hay un supermercado cerca.

nearly adv casi ▷ *Dinner's nearly ready.* La cena está casi lista.; **I nearly missed the train.** Por poco pierdo el tren.

neat adj ordenado(-a) ▷ *My brother's not very neat.* Mi hermano no es muy ordenado.; **He always looks very neat.** Siempre está muy pulcro.

necessarily adv not necessarily no necesariamente

necessary adj necesario(-a)

neck n cuello m ▷ *a V-neck sweater* un jersey de cuello en pico; **She had a stiff neck.** Tenía tortícolis.; **the back of your neck** la nuca

necklace n collar m

need vb necesitar **[25]** ▷ *I need to change some money.* Necesito cambiar dinero.; **You don't need to go.** No tienes por qué ir.
▶ n **There's no need to book.** No hace falta hacer reserva.

> **hace falta que** has to be followed by a verb in the subjunctive.

▷ *There's no need for you to do that.* No hace falta que hagas eso.

needle n aguja f

negative n (photo) negativo m
▶ adj negativo(-a) ▷ *He's got a negative attitude.* Tiene una actitud muy negativa.

neglected adj abandonado(-a)
▷ *The garden is neglected.* El jardín está abandonado.

negotiate vb negociar **[25]**

neighbour (US **neighbor**) n vecino m, vecina f

neighbourhood (US **neighborhood**) n barrio m

neither adj, conj, pron ❶ ninguno de los dos (f ninguna de las dos) ▷ *Carrots or peas?* — *Neither, thanks.* ¿Zanahorias o guisantes? — Ninguno de los dos, gracias. ▷ *Neither of them is coming.* No viene ninguno de los dos. ▷ *Neither woman looked happy.* Ninguna de las dos parecía contenta.
❷ tampoco ▷ *I don't like him.* — *Neither do I!* No me cae bien. — ¡A mí tampoco! ▷ *I've never been to Spain.* — *Neither have we.* No he estado nunca en España. — Nosotros tampoco.; **neither... nor...** ni... ni... ▷ *Neither Sarah nor Tamsin is coming to the party.* No vienen ni Sarah ni Tamsin a la fiesta.

nephew n sobrino m

nerve n nervio m ▷ *That noise really gets on my nerves.* Ese ruido me pone los nervios de punta.; **He's got a nerve!** ¡Qué cara tiene!; **I wouldn't have the nerve to do that!** ¡Yo no me atrevería a hacer eso!

nervous adj nervioso(-a) ▷ *I bite my nails when I'm nervous.* Cuando estoy nervioso me muerdo las uñas. ▷ *I'm a bit nervous about the exams.* Estoy un poco nervioso por los exámenes.

nest n nido m

Net n Red f; **to surf the Net** navegar [**37**] por la Red

net n red f ▷ *a fishing net* una red de pesca

netball n netball m

● Netball is not played in Spain.

Netherlands npl **the Netherlands** los Países Bajos

network n red f

never adv nunca ▷ *Never leave valuables in your car.* No dejen nunca objetos de valor en el coche.

When **nunca** comes before the verb in Spanish it is not necessary to use **no** as well. ▷ *I never believed him.* Yo nunca le creí.; **Never again!** ¡Nunca más!; **Never, ever do that again!** ¡No vuelvas a hacer eso nunca jamás!; **Never mind.** No importa.

new adj nuevo(-a) ▷ *her new boyfriend* su nuevo novio

news n ❶ noticias fpl ▷ *good news* buenas noticias ▷ *I watch the news every evening.* Veo las noticias todas las noches.; **It was nice to have your news.** Me dio alegría saber de ti. ❷ noticia f ▷ *That's wonderful news!* ¡Qué buena noticia!; **an interesting piece of news** una noticia interesante

newsagent n tienda de periódicos f

newspaper n periódico m

newsreader n ❶ (on TV) presentador m, presentadora f ❷ (on radio) locutor m, locutora f

New Year n Año Nuevo m ▷ *to celebrate New Year* celebrar el Año

Nuevo; **Happy New Year!** ¡Feliz Año Nuevo!; **New Year's Day** el día de Año Nuevo; **New Year's Eve** Nochevieja (la noche de Fin de Año LatAm); **a New Year's Eve party** una fiesta de Fin de Año

New Zealand n Nueva Zelanda f

New Zealander n neozelandés m (pl neozelandeses), neozelandesa f

next adj, adv, prep ❶ próximo(-a) ▷ *next Saturday* el próximo sábado ❷ siguiente ▷ *The next day we visited Gerona.* Al día siguiente visitamos Gerona. ❸ luego ▷ *What did you do next?* ¿Qué hiciste luego?; **next to** al lado de ▷ *next to the bank* al lado del banco; **next door** al lado ▷ *They live next door.* Viven al lado.; **the next-door neighbours** los vecinos de al lado; **the next room** la habitación de al lado

NHS abbr (= National Health Service) servicio sanitario de la Seguridad Social m

nice adj ❶ (friendly) simpático(-a) ▷ *Your parents are very nice.* Tus padres son muy simpáticos. ❷ (kind) amable ▷ *She was always very nice to me.* Siempre fue muy amable conmigo. ▷ *It was nice of you to remember my birthday.* Fue muy amable de tu parte que te acordaras de mi cumpleaños. ❸ (pretty) bonito(-a) ▷ *That's a nice dress!* ¡Qué vestido más bonito! ❹ (good) bueno(-a) ▷ *This paella is very nice.* Esta paella está muy buena.

Use **buen** before a masculine singular noun.

▷ *It's a nice day.* Hace buen día.; **Have a nice time!** ¡Que te diviertas!

nickname n apodo m

niece n sobrina f

night n <u>noche</u> f ▷ *I want a single room for two nights.* Quiero una habitación individual para dos noches.; **at night** por la noche; **Good night!** ¡Buenas noches!; **last night** anoche ▷ *We went to a party last night.* Anoche fuimos a una fiesta.

night club n sala de fiestas f

nightie n camisón m (pl camisones)

nightmare n pesadilla f ▷ *to have nightmares* tener pesadillas

nil n cero m ▷ *We won one-nil.* Ganamos uno a cero.

nine num nueve; **She's nine.** Tiene nueve años.

nineteen num diecinueve; **She's nineteen.** Tiene diecinueve años.

nineteenth adj decimonoveno(-a)

ninety num noventa ▷ *He's ninety.* Tiene noventa años.

ninth adj noveno(-a) ▷ *on the ninth floor* en el noveno piso; **on 9th August** el 9 de agosto

no adv, adj no ▷ *Are you coming? — No.* ¿Vienes? — No. ▷ *Would you like some more? — No thank you.* ¿Quieres un poco más? — No, gracias. ▷ *There's no hot water.* No hay agua caliente.; **I've got no idea.** No tengo ni idea.; **I have no questions.** No tengo ninguna pregunta.; **No way!** ¡Ni hablar!; **'no smoking'** 'prohibido fumar'

nobody pron nadie ▷ *There was nobody in the office.* No había nadie en la oficina.

> When 'nobody' goes before a verb in English it can be translated by either **nadie ...** or **no ... nadie**.

▷ *Nobody saw me.* Nadie me vio. ▷ *Nobody likes him.* No le cae bien a nadie.

nod vb ❶ (in agreement) asentir [51] con la cabeza ❷ (as greeting) saludar [25] con la cabeza

noise n ruido m; **to make a noise** hacer [26] ruido

noisy adj ruidoso(-a) ▷ *the noisiest city in the world* la ciudad más ruidosa del mundo; **It's very noisy here.** Hay mucho ruido aquí.

nominate vb nombrar [25] ▷ *She was nominated for the post.* La nombraron para el cargo.; **He was nominated for an Oscar.** Le nominaron para un Oscar.

none pron

> When 'none' refers to something you can count, such as sisters or friends, Spanish uses **ninguno** with a singular verb. When it refers to something you cannot count, such as wine, Spanish uses **nada**.

❶ ninguno(-a) ▷ *None of my friends wanted to come.* Ninguno de mis amigos quiso venir. ▷ *There are none left.* No queda ninguno. ❷ nada ▷ *There's none left.* No queda nada.

nonsense n tonterías fpl ▷ *She talks a lot of nonsense.* Dice muchas tonterías.; **Nonsense!** ¡Tonterías!

non-smoking adj a non-smoking area un área reservada para no fumadores

> Although it's a feminine noun, remember that you use **el** and **un** with **área**.

a non-smoking carriage un vagón para no fumadores

non-stop adj, adv ❶ directo(-a) ▷ a non-stop flight un vuelo directo; We flew non-stop. Tomamos un vuelo directo. ❷ sin parar ▷ He talks non-stop. Habla sin parar.

noodles npl fideos mpl

noon n doce del mediodía fpl; at noon a las doce del mediodía

no one pron nadie

nor conj tampoco ▷ I didn't like the film. — Nor did I. No me gustó la película. — A mí tampoco. ▷ We haven't seen him. — Nor have we. No lo hemos visto. — Nosotros tampoco.; **neither...nor** ni...ni ▷ neither the cinema nor the swimming pool ni el cine ni la piscina

normal adj normal

normally adv ❶ (usually) normalmente ▷ I normally arrive at nine o'clock. Normalmente llego a las nueve. ❷ (as normal) con normalidad ▷ Airports are working normally over Christmas. Durante las Navidades los aeropuertos funcionan con normalidad.

north n norte m ▷ in the north of Spain en el norte de España
▶ adj, adv hacia el norte ▷ We were travelling north. Viajábamos hacia el norte.; **North London** el norte

de Londres; **north of** al norte de ▷ It's north of London. Está al norte de Londres.; **the north coast** la costa septentrional

North America n América del Norte f

northeast n noreste m; in the northeast al noreste.

northern adj del norte ▷ Northern Europe Europa del Norte; **the northern part of the island** la zona norte de la isla

Northern Ireland n Irlanda del Norte f

North Pole n the North Pole el Polo Norte

North Sea n the North Sea el Mar del Norte

northwest n noroeste m; in the northwest al noroeste

Norway n Noruega f

Norwegian adj noruego(-a)
▶ n ❶ (person) noruego m, noruega f ▷ the Norwegians los noruegos ❷ (language) noruego m

nose n nariz f (pl narices)

nosebleed n I often get nosebleeds. Me sangra la nariz a menudo.

nosy adj fisgón (f fisgona)

not adv no ▷ I'm not sure. No estoy seguro. ▷ Are you coming or not? ¿Vienes o no? ▷ Did you like it? — Not really. ¿Te gustó? — No mucho.; **Thank you very much. — Not at all.** Muchas gracias. — De nada.; **not yet** todavía no ▷ They haven't arrived yet. Todavía no han llegado.

note n ❶ nota f ▷ I'll drop her a note. Le dejaré una nota.; **Remember**

to take notes. Acuérdate de tomar apuntes.; **to make a note of something** tomar [25] nota de algo ❷ billete m ▷ *a five pound note* un billete de cinco libras

note down vb anotar [25]

notebook n cuaderno m

notepad n bloc de notas m (pl blocs de notas)

nothing n nada ▷ *He does nothing.* No hace nada.; **He does nothing but sleep.** No hace nada más que dormir.; **There's nothing to do.** No hay nada que hacer.

> When 'nothing' goes before a verb in English it can be translated by either **nada ...** or **no ... nada.**
> ▷ *Nothing frightens him.* Nada lo asusta. ▷ *Nothing will happen.* No pasará nada.

notice n ❶ (physical object) letrero m ▷ *There was a notice outside the house.* Había un letrero fuera de la casa. ❷ (information) aviso m ▷ *There's a notice on the board about the trip.* Hay un aviso en el tablón sobre el viaje.; **a warning notice** un aviso; **He was transferred without notice.** Lo trasladaron sin previo aviso.; **until further notice** hasta nuevo aviso; **Don't take any notice of him!** ¡No le hagas caso!

> Be careful not to translate **notice** by noticia.

▶ vb **to notice something** darse [14] cuenta de algo ▷ *Don't worry. He won't notice the mistake.* No te preocupes. No se dará cuenta del error.

notice board n tablón de anuncios m (pl tablones de anuncios)

nought n cero m

noun n nombre m

novel n novela f

novelist n novelista mf

November n noviembre m ▷ *in November* en noviembre ▷ *on 7th November* el 7 de noviembre

now adv ahora ▷ *What are you doing now?* ¿Qué haces ahora?; **just now** en este momento ▷ *I'm rather busy just now.* En este momento estoy muy ocupado.; **I did it just now.** Lo acabo de hacer.; **It should be ready by now.** Ya debería estar listo.; **from now on** de ahora en adelante; **now and then** de vez en cuando

nowhere adv a ninguna parte ▷ *Where are you going for your holidays? — Nowhere.* ¿Adónde vas en vacaciones? — A ninguna parte.; **nowhere else** a ninguna otra parte ▷ *You can go to the shops but nowhere else.* Puedes ir a las tiendas pero a ninguna otra parte.; **The children were nowhere to be seen.** No se podía ver a los niños por ninguna parte.; **There was nowhere to play.** No se podía jugar en ninguna parte.

nuclear adj nuclear ▷ *nuclear power* la energía nuclear

nuisance n fastidio m ▷ *It's a nuisance having to clean the car.* Es un fastidio tener que limpiar el coche.; **Sorry to be a nuisance.** Siento molestarle.; **You're a nuisance!** ¡Eres un pesado!

numb adj **numb with cold** helado de frío

number n número m ▷ *They live at number five.* Viven en el número cinco. ▷ *a large number of people* un gran número de gente; **What's your number?** (telephone) ¿Cuál es tu teléfono?

number plate n matrícula f (placa f LatAm)

nun n monja f

nurse n enfermero m, enfermera f ▷ *She's a nurse.* Es enfermera.

nursery n ❶ (for children) guardería infantil f ❷ (for plants) vivero m

nursery school n preescolar m (la guardería f LatAm)

nut n ❶ (almond) almendra f ❷ (peanut) cacahuete m ❸ (hazelnut) avellana f ❹ (walnut) nuez f (pl nueces); **I don't like nuts.** No me gustan los frutos secos. ❺ (made of metal) tuerca f

nuts adj **He's nuts.** Está chiflado. (informal)

nylon n nylon m

O

oak n roble m ▷ *an oak barrel* un barril de roble

oar n remo m

oats npl avena f

obedient adj obediente

obey vb obedecer [12]; **to obey the rules** (in game) atenerse [53] a las reglas del juego

object n objeto m

objection n objeción f (pl objeciones) ▷ *There were no objections to the plan.* No hubo objeciones al plan.

oboe n oboe m

obsessed adj obsesionado(-a) ▷ *He's obsessed with trains.* Está obsesionado con los trenes.

obsession n obsesión f (pl obsesiones) ▷ *Football's an obsession of mine.* El fútbol es una obsesión mía.

obvious adj obvio(-a)
obviously adv claro ▷ It was obviously impossible. Estaba claro que era imposible.; **Obviously not!** ¡Claro que no!
occasion n ocasión f (pl ocasiones) ▷ a special occasion una ocasión especial; **on several occasions** en varias ocasiones
occasionally adv de vez en cuando
occupation n empleo m
occupy vb ocupar [25] ▷ The toilet was occupied. El lavabo estaba ocupado.
occur vb ocurrir [58] ▷ The accident occurred yesterday. El accidente ocurrió ayer.; **It suddenly occurred to me that...** De repente se me ocurrió que...
ocean n océano m
o'clock adv at four o'clock a las cuatro; **It's one o'clock.** Es la una.; **It's five o'clock.** Son las cinco.
October n octubre m ▷ in October en octubre ▷ on 12 October el 12 de octubre
octopus n pulpo m
odd adj ① raro(-a) ▷ That's odd! ¡Qué raro! ② impar(a) ▷ an odd number un número impar; **odd socks** calcetines desparejados
of prep de ▷ a boy of 10 un niño de 10 años ▷ a kilo of oranges un kilo de naranjas ▷ It's made of wood. Es de madera.

    de + el changes to **del**.

▷ the wheels of the car las ruedas del coche; **There were three of us.** Éramos tres.; **a friend of mine** un amigo mío; **That's very kind of you.** Es muy amable de su parte.
off adj, adv, prep

    For other expressions with 'off', see the verbs 'get', 'take', 'turn' etc.

① (heater, light, TV) apagado(-a) ▷ All the lights are off. Todas las luces están apagadas. ② (tap, gas) cerrado(-a) ▷ Are you sure the tap is off? ¿Seguro que el grifo está cerrado? ③ (milk) cortado(-a) ④ (meat) estropeado(-a); **to be off sick** estar [22] ausente por enfermedad; **a day off** un día libre ▷ She took a day off work to go to the wedding. Se tomó un día libre para ir a la boda.; **I've got tomorrow off.** Mañana tengo el día libre.; **She's off school today.** Hoy no ha ido al colegio.; **I must be off now.** Me tengo que ir ahora.; **I'm off.** Me voy.; **The match is off.** El partido se ha suspendido.
offence (US **offense**) n (crime) delito m
offer n ① (of money, job) oferta f ② (of help) ofrecimiento m; **There was a special offer on CDs.** Los CDs estaban de oferta.
    ▷ vb ofrecer [12] ▷ He offered me a cigarette. Me ofreció un cigarrillo.; **He offered to help me.** Se ofreció a ayudarme.
office n oficina f; **during office hours** en horas de oficina
officer n (in the army) oficial mf
official adj oficial
off-licence n tienda de bebidas alcohólicas f

offside adj fuera de juego

often adv a menudo ▷ It often rains.
Llueve a menudo.; **How often do
you go to the gym?** ¿Cada cuánto
vas al gimnasio?

oil n ❶ (for lubrication, cooking)
aceite m ❷ (crude oil) petróleo m;
an oil painting una pintura al
óleo
▶ vb engrasar [**25**]

oil rig n plataforma petrolífera f

ointment n pomada f

okay excl, adj ❶ (more formally) de
acuerdo ▷ Your appointment's at six
o'clock. — Okay. Su cita es a las seis.
— De acuerdo. ❷ (less formally) vale
▷ I'll meet you at six o'clock, okay? Te
veré a las seis, ¿vale?; **Are you
okay?** ¿Estás bien?; **I'll do it
tomorrow, if that's okay with
you.** Lo haré mañana, si te parece
bien.; **The film was okay.** La
película no estuvo mal.

old adj ❶ viejo(-a) ▷ an old house una
casa vieja; **an old man** un viejo

> When talking about people it is
> more polite to use **anciano**
> instead of **viejo**.

old people los ancianos ❷ (former)
antiguo(-a) ▷ my old English teacher
mi antiguo profesor de inglés;
How old are you? ¿Cuántos años
tienes?; **How old is the baby?**
¿Cuánto tiempo tiene el bebé?; **a
twenty-year-old woman** una
mujer de veinte años; **He's ten
years old.** Tiene diez años.; **older**
mayor ▷ my older sister mi hermana
mayor ▷ She's two years older than
me. Es dos años mayor que yo.; **I'm

the oldest in the family.** Soy el
mayor de la familia.

old age pensioner n
pensionista mf

old-fashioned adj anticuado(-a)
▷ My parents are rather
old-fashioned. Mis padres son
bastante anticuados.

olive n aceituna f

olive oil n aceite de oliva m

Olympic adj olímpico(-a); **the
Olympics** las Olimpiadas

omelette n tortilla francesa f

on prep, adv

> There are several ways of
> translating 'on'. Scan the
> examples to find one that is
> similar to what you want to
> say. For other expressions with
> 'on', see the verbs 'go', 'put',
> 'turn' etc.

❶ en ▷ on an island en una isla ▷ on
the wall en la pared ▷ It's on Channel
4. Lo dan en el Canal cuatro. ▷ on
TV en la tele ▷ on the 2nd floor en el
segundo piso ▷ I go to school on my
bike. Voy al colegio en bicicleta.
▷ We went on the train. Fuimos en
tren. ❷ (on top of, about) sobre ▷ on
the table sobre la mesa ▷ a book on
Gandhi un libro sobre Gandhi

> With days and dates, the
> definite article – **el, los** – is
> used in Spanish instead of a
> preposition.

▷ on Friday el viernes ▷ on Fridays los
viernes ▷ on 20 June el 20 de junio;
on the left a la izquierda; **on
holiday** de vacaciones; **It's about
10 minutes on foot.** Está a unos

10 minutos andando.; **She was on antibiotics for a week.** Estuvo una semana tomando antibióticos.; **The coffee is on the house.** Al café invita la casa.; **The drinks are on me.** Invito yo.; **What is he on about?** ¿De qué está hablando?

▶ adj ❶ (heater, light, TV) encendido(-a) ▷ I think I left the light on. Me parece que he dejado la luz encendida. ❷ (tap, gas) abierto(-a) ▷ Leave the tap on. Deja el grifo abierto. ❸ en marcha ▷ Is the dishwasher on? ¿Está en marcha el lavavajillas? ▷ What's on at the cinema? ¿Qué echan en el cine?; **Is the party still on?** ¿Todavía se va a hacer la fiesta?; **I've got a lot on this weekend.** Tengo mucho que hacer este fin de semana.

once adv una vez ▷ once a week una vez a la semana ▷ once more una vez más; **Once upon a time...** Érase una vez...; **once in a while** de vez en cuando; **once and for all** de una vez por todas; **at once** enseguida

one num, pron uno(-a); **one by one** uno a uno

❙ Use **un** before a masculine noun.

▷ I've got one brother and one sister. Tengo un hermano y una hermana.; **one another** unos a otros ▷ They all looked at one another. Se miraron todos unos a otros.

oneself pron ❶ (reflexive) se ▷ to wash oneself lavarse ❷ (after preposition,

for emphasis) uno mismo (f una misma) ▷ It's quicker to do it oneself. Es más rápido si lo hace uno mismo.

one-way adj a one-way street una calle de sentido único; **a one-way ticket** un billete de ida

onion n cebolla f

online adj en línea

only adv solo ▷ We only want to stay for one night. Solo queremos quedarnos una noche.

▶ adj único(-a) ▷ She's an only child. Es hija única. ▷ Monday is the only day I'm free. El lunes es el único día que tengo libre.

▶ conj pero ▷ I'd like the same sweater, only in black. Quería el mismo jersey, pero en negro.

onwards adv en adelante ▷ from July onwards de julio en adelante

open adj abierto(-a) ▷ The shop's open on Sunday mornings. La tienda está abierta los domingos por la mañana.; **Are you open tomorrow?** ¿Abre mañana?; **in the open air** al aire libre

▶ vb ❶ abrir [58] ▷ What time do the shops open? ¿A qué hora abren las tiendas? ▷ Can I open the window? ¿Puedo abrir la ventana? ❷ abrirse [58] ▷ The door opens automatically. La puerta se abre automáticamente.

opening hours npl horario de apertura m

opera n ópera f

operate vb (machine) operar [25]; **to operate on someone** operar [25] a alguien

operation n operación f (pl operaciones); **I've never had an operation.** Nunca me han operado.

opinion n opinión f (pl opiniones) ▷ **in my opinion** en mi opinión; **What's your opinion?** ¿Tú qué opinas?

opinion poll n sondeo de opinión m

opponent n adversario m, adversaria f

opportunity n oportunidad f ▷ **I've never had the opportunity to go to Spain.** No he tenido nunca la oportunidad de ir a España.

opposed adj **to be opposed to something** oponerse **[41]** a algo

opposite adj, adv, prep ❶ contrario(-a) ▷ **It's in the opposite direction.** Está en dirección contraria. ❷ opuesto(-a) ▷ **the opposite sex** el sexo opuesto ❸ enfrente ▷ **They live opposite.** Viven enfrente. ❹ frente a ▷ **the girl sitting opposite me** la chica sentada frente a mí

opposition n oposición f ▷ **There is a lot of opposition to the new law.** Hay una fuerte oposición a la nueva ley.

optician n óptico m, óptica f; **He's gone to the optician's.** Ha ido a la óptica.

optimistic adj optimista

option n ❶ opción f (pl opciones) ▷ **I've got no option.** No tengo otra opción. ❷ (at school) asignatura optativa f ▷ **I'm doing geology as my option.** Tengo geología como asignatura optativa.

or conj ❶ o ▷ **Would you like tea or coffee?** ¿Quieres té o café?

▮ Use **u** before words beginning with **o** or **ho.**

▷ **six or eight** seis u ocho ▷ **women or men** mujeres u hombres; **Hurry up or you'll miss the bus.** Date prisa, que vas a perder el autobús. ❷ ni ▷ **I don't eat meat or fish.** No como carne ni pescado. ▷ **She can't dance or sing.** No sabe bailar ni cantar.

oral adj oral ▷ **an oral exam** un examen oral

▸ n examen oral m (pl exámenes orales) ▷ **I've got my Spanish oral soon.** Tengo el examen oral de español pronto.

orange n naranja f; **orange juice** el zumo de naranja (el jugo de naranja LatAm)

▸ adj naranja

orchard n huerto m

orchestra n orquesta f

order n ❶ (arrangement) orden m ▷ **in alphabetical order** por orden alfabético ❷ (command) orden f (pl órdenes) ▷ **to obey an order** obedecer una orden; **The waiter took our order.** El camarero tomó nota de lo que íbamos a comer.; **in order to** para ▷ **He does it in order to earn money.** Lo hace para ganar dinero.; **'out of order'** "averiado"

▸ vb pedir **[38]** ▷ **We ordered steak and chips.** Pedimos un filete con patatas fritas.

ordinary adj normal y corriente ▷ **an ordinary day** un día normal y corriente

organ n (instrument) órgano m

organic adj (fruit, vegetables) ecológico(-a)

organization n organización f (pl organizaciones)

organize vb organizar [**13**]

original adj original

originally adv al principio

Orkneys npl **the Orkneys** las Islas Órcadas

ornament n adorno m

orphan n huérfano m, huérfana f

other adj, pron otro(-a) ▷ Have you got these jeans in other colours? ¿Tienen estos vaqueros en otros colores? ▷ on the other side of the street al otro lado de la calle; **the other one** el otro (f la otra) ▷ This one? — No, the other one. ¿Este? — No, el otro.; **the others** los demás (f las demás) ▷ The others are going but I'm not. Los demás van, pero yo no.

otherwise adv, conj ❶ (if not) si no ▷ Note down the number, otherwise you'll forget it. Apúntate el número, si no se te olvidará. ❷ (in other ways) por lo demás ▷ I'm tired, but otherwise I'm fine. Estoy cansado, pero por lo demás estoy bien.

ought vb

To translate 'ought to' use the conditional of **deber**.
▷ I ought to phone my parents. Debería llamar a mis padres. ▷ You ought not to do that. No deberías hacer eso. ▷ He ought to win. Debería ganar.

For 'ought to have' use the conditional of **deber** plus **haber** or the imperfect of **deber**.

▷ You ought to have warned me. Me deberías haber avisado. ▷ He ought to have known. Debía saberlo.

our adj nuestro(-a) ▷ our house nuestra casa

'Our' is usually translated by the definite article **el/los** or **la/las** when it's clear from the sentence who the possessor is or when referring to clothing or parts of the body.

▷ We took off our coats. Nos quitamos los abrigos. ▷ They stole our car. Nos robaron el coche.

ours pron ❶ el nuestro m (pl los nuestros) ▷ Your car is much bigger than ours. Vuestro coche es mucho más grande que el nuestro. ❷ la nuestra f (pl las nuestras) ▷ Your house is very different from ours. Vuestra casa es muy distinta a la nuestra. ❸ nuestro m (pl nuestros) ▷ Is this ours? ¿Esto es nuestro? ▷ a friend of ours un amigo nuestro ❹ nuestra f (pl nuestras) ▷ Sorry, that table is ours. Disculpen, esa mesa es nuestra. ▷ Isabel is a close friend of ours. Isabel es muy amiga nuestra.

ourselves pron ❶ (reflexive) nos ▷ We really enjoyed ourselves. Nos divertimos mucho. ❷ (after preposition, for emphasis) nosotros mismos (f nosotras mismas) ▷ Let's not talk about ourselves any more. No hablemos más de nosotros mismos. ▷ We built our garage ourselves. Nos construimos el garaje nosotros mismos.; **by ourselves** solos (f solas) ▷ We prefer *to be by ourselves.* Preferimos estar solos.

out *prep, adv*

There are several ways of translating 'out'. Scan the examples to find one that is similar to what you want to say. For other expressions with 'out', see the verbs 'go', 'put', 'turn' etc.

fuera ▷ *It's cold out.* Fuera hace frío. ▷ *It's dark out there.* Está oscuro ahí fuera.; **She's out.** Ha salido.; **She's out for the afternoon.** No estará en toda la tarde.; **to go out** salir **[49]** ▷ *I'm going out tonight.* Voy a salir esta noche.; **to go out with somebody** salir **[49]** con alguien ▷ *I've been going out with him for two months.* Llevo dos meses saliendo con él.; **a night out with my friends** una noche por ahí con mis amigos; **'way out'** 'salida'; **out of town** fuera de la ciudad ▷ *He lives out of town.* Vive fuera de la ciudad.; **three kilometres out of town** a tres kilómetros de la ciudad; **to take something out of your pocket** sacar **[48]** algo del bolsillo; **out of curiosity** por curiosidad; **We're out of milk.** Se nos ha acabado la leche.; **in nine cases out of ten** en nueve de cada diez casos

▶ *adj* ❶ (*lights, fire*) apagado(-a) ▷ *All the lights are out.* Todas las luces están apagadas.
❷ (*eliminated*) eliminado(-a); **That's it, Liverpool are out.** Ya está, Liverpool queda eliminado.;

The film is now out on DVD. La película ya ha salido en DVD.

outdoor *adj* al aire libre ▷ *an outdoor swimming pool* una piscina al aire libre

outdoors *adv* al aire libre

outfit *n* traje *m* ▷ *a cowboy outfit* un traje de vaquero

outing *n* excursión *f* (*pl* excursiones) ▷ *to go on an outing* ir de excursión

outline *n* ❶ (*summary*) esquema *m*

Although **esquema** ends in **-a**, it is actually a masculine noun.

▷ *This is an outline of the plan.* Aquí tienen un esquema del plan.
❷ (*shape*) contorno *m* ▷ *We could see the outline of the mountain.* Veíamos el contorno de la montaña.

outside *n, adj* ❶ exterior *m* ▷ *the outside of the house* el exterior de la casa ❷ exterior ▷ *the outside walls* las paredes exteriores

▶ *prep, adv* ❶ fuera ▷ *It's very cold outside.* Hace mucho frío fuera.
❷ fuera de ▷ *outside the school* fuera del colegio ▷ *outside school hours* fuera del horario escolar

outskirts *npl* afueras *fpl* ▷ *on the outskirts of town* en las afueras de la ciudad

outstanding *adj* excepcional

oval *adj* ovalado(-a)

oven *n* horno *m*

over *adj, adv, prep*

When something is located over something, use **encima de**. When there is movement over something, use **por encima de**.

a
b
c
d
e
f
g
h
i
j
k
l
m
n
o
p
q
r
s
t
u
v
w
x
y
z

❶ encima de ▷ *There's a mirror over the washbasin.* Encima del lavabo hay un espejo. ❷ por encima de ▷ *The ball went over the wall.* La pelota pasó por encima de la pared.; **a bridge over the Thames** un puente sobre el Támesis ❸ más de ▷ *It's over 20 kilos.* Pesa más de 20 kilos.; **The temperature was over 30 degrees.** La temperatura superaba los 30 grados. ❹ durante ▷ *over the holidays* durante las vacaciones ❺ terminado(-a); **I'll be happy when the exams are over.** Estaré feliz cuando se hayan terminado los exámenes.; **over here** aquí; **It's over there.** Está por allí.; **all over Scotland** en toda Escocia; **The shop is over the road.** La tienda está al otro lado de la calle.; **I spilled coffee over my shirt.** Me manché la camisa de café.

overcast *adj* cubierto(-a) ▷ *The sky was overcast.* El cielo estaba cubierto.

overdose *n* sobredosis *f* (*pl* sobredosis)

overdraft *n* descubierto *m*

overseas *adv* (live, work) en el extranjero ▷ *I'd like to work overseas.* Me gustaría trabajar en el extranjero.

overtake *vb* adelantar [**25**] (rebasar [**25**] LatAm)

overtime *n* horas extras *fpl*; **to work overtime** trabajar [**25**] horas extras

overweight *adj* **to be overweight** tener [**53**] exceso de peso

owe *vb* deber [**8**] ▷ *How much do I owe you?* ¿Cuánto te debo?

owing to *prep* debido a ▷ *owing to bad weather* debido al mal tiempo

owl *n* búho *m*

own *adj, pron* propio(-a) ▷ *This is my own recipe.* Esta es mi propia receta. ▷ *I wish I had a room of my own.* Me gustaría tener mi propia habitación.; **on his own** él solo; **on our own** nosotros solos
▶ *vb* tener [**53**]

own up *vb* confesarse [**39**] culpable; **to own up to something** confesar [**39**] algo

owner *n* propietario *m*, propietaria *f*

oxygen *n* oxígeno *m*

oyster *n* ostra *f*

ozone layer *n* capa de ozono *f*

p

Pacific n **the Pacific** el Pacífico

pacifier n (US) chupete m

pack vb hacer [26] las maletas (empacar [48] LatAm) ▷ I'll help you pack. Te ayudaré a hacer las maletas.; **I've already packed my case.** Ya he hecho mi maleta.; **Pack it in!** ¡Vale ya!
▶ n paquete m ▷ a pack of cigarettes un paquete de tabaco; **a pack of cards** una baraja

package n paquete m; **a package holiday** unas vacaciones organizadas

packed adj abarrotado(-a) ▷ The cinema was packed. El cine estaba abarrotado.

packed lunch n **I take a packed lunch to school.** Me llevo la comida al colegio.

packet n paquete m ▷ a packet of cigarettes un paquete de tabaco; **a packet of crisps** una bolsa de patatas fritas

pad n bloc m (pl blocs)

paddle vb ❶ (swim) chapotear [25]
❷ remar [25] ▷ to paddle a canoe remar en canoa
▶ n pala f; **to go for a paddle** mojarse [25] los pies

padlock n candado m

page n página f ▷ on page 13 en la página 13
▶ vb **to page somebody** llamar [25] a alguien al busca

paid vb see **pay**
▶ adj ❶ remunerado(-a)
❷ pagado(-a)

pain n dolor m ▷ a terrible pain un dolor tremendo; **I've got a pain in my stomach.** Me duele el estómago.; **She's in a lot of pain.** Tiene muchos dolores.; **He's a real pain.** Es un auténtico pelmazo. (informal)

painful adj

doloroso is used when talking about what causes pain, and dolorido for the person or thing that feels pain.

❶ doloroso(-a) ▷ a painful injury una herida dolorosa
❷ dolorido(-a) ▷ Her feet were swollen and painful. Tenía los pies hinchados y doloridos.; **Is it painful?** ¿Te duele?

painkiller n analgésico m

paint n pintura f
▶ vb pintar [25] ▷ to paint something green pintar algo de verde

paintbrush n ❶ (for an artist) pincel m ❷ (for decorating) brocha f

painter n pintor m, pintora f

painting n ❶ cuadro m ▷ a painting by Picasso un cuadro de Picasso ❷ (activity) pintura f

pair n par m ▷ a pair of shoes un par de zapatos; **a pair of scissors** unas tijeras; **a pair of trousers** unos pantalones; **in pairs** por parejas

Pakistan n Paquistán m

Pakistani adj paquistaní (pl paquistaníes)
▶ n paquistaní mf (pl paquistaníes)

palace n palacio m

pale adj ❶ pálido(-a) ▷ She still looks very pale. Está todavía muy pálida.; **to turn pale** ponerse [41] pálido ❷ claro(-a) ▷ pale green verde claro; **pale pink** rosa pálido; **pale blue** azul celeste

Palestine n Palestina f

Palestinian adj palestino(-a)
▶ n palestino m, palestina f

palm n (of hand) palma f; **a palm tree** una palmera

pan n ❶ (saucepan) cacerola f ❷ (frying pan) sartén f (pl sartenes)

pancake n crepe f (panqueque m LatAm)

panic n pánico m
▶ vb He panicked as soon as he saw the blood. Le entró pánico en cuanto vio la sangre.; **Don't panic!** ¡Tranquilo!

panther n pantera f

pantomime n revista musical representada en Navidad f

pants npl ❶ (for women) bragas fpl ❷ (for men) calzoncillos mpl ❸ (US: trousers) pantalones mpl

pantyhose npl (US) medias fpl

paper n ❶ papel m ▷ a paper bag una bolsa de papel; **a piece of paper** un papel (una hoja LatAm); **an exam paper** un examen ❷ (newspaper) periódico m

paperback n libro de bolsillo m

paper clip n clip m (pl clips)

paper round n **to do a paper round** repartir [58] los periódicos a domicilio

parachute n paracaídas m (pl paracaídas)

parade n desfile m

paradise n paraíso m

paragraph n párrafo m

parallel adj paralelo(-a)

paralysed adj paralizado(-a)

paramedic n auxiliar sanitario m, auxiliar sanitaria f

parcel n paquete m

pardon n **Pardon?** ¿Cómo?

parents npl padres mpl (papás mpl LatAm)

▮ Be careful not to translate **parents** by **parientes**.

Paris n París m

park n parque m; **a national park** un parque nacional; **a theme park** un parque temático; **a car park** un aparcamiento (un estacionamiento LatAm)
▶ vb aparcar [48] ▷ Where can I park my car? ¿Dónde puedo aparcar el coche?; **'no parking'** 'prohibido aparcar'

parking lot n (US) aparcamiento m

parking meter n parquímetro m

parking ticket n multa de aparcamiento f

parliament n parlamento m; **the Spanish Parliament** las Cortes

parole n **on parole** en libertad condicional

parrot n loro m

parsley n perejil m

part n ❶ parte f ▷ The first part of the play was boring. La primera parte de la obra fue aburrida. ❷ papel m ▷ She had a small part in the film. Tenía un pequeño papel en la película. ❸ pieza f ▷ spare parts piezas de repuesto; **to take part in something** participar [25] en algo ▷ Thousands of people took part in the demonstration. Miles de personas participaron en la manifestación.

particular adj ❶ (definite) concreto(-a) ▷ I can't remember that particular film. No recuerdo esa película concreta. ❷ (special) especial ▷ He showed a particular interest in the subject. Mostró un interés especial en el tema.; **in particular** en concreto ▷ Are you looking for anything in particular? ¿Busca algo en concreto? ▷ nothing in particular nada en concreto

particularly adv especialmente ▷ a particularly boring lecture una clase especialmente aburrida

partly adv en parte ▷ It was partly my own fault. En parte fue culpa mía.

partner n ❶ (in business) socio m, socia f ❷ (in relationship) pareja f

part-time adj, adv a tiempo parcial ▷ a part-time job un trabajo a tiempo parcial ▷ She works part-time. Trabaja a tiempo parcial.

party n ❶ fiesta f ▷ a birthday party una fiesta de cumpleaños ❷ partido m ▷ the Conservative Party el partido conservador ❸ grupo m ▷ a party of tourists un grupo de turistas

pass n ❶ (in football) pase m ❷ (in mountains) puerto m ❸ (in exam) aprobado m; **a bus pass** un abono para el autobús
▶ vb ❶ pasar [25] ▷ Could you pass me the salt, please? ¿Me pasas la sal, por favor? ▷ The time has passed quickly. El tiempo ha pasado rápido. ❷ adelantar [25] ▷ We were passed by a huge lorry. Nos adelantó un camión enorme. ❸ pasar [25] por delante de ▷ I pass his house on my way to school. Paso por delante de su casa de camino al colegio. ❹ aprobar [11] ▷ to pass an exam aprobar un examen

pass out vb desmayarse [25]

passage n ❶ pasaje m ▷ Read the passage carefully. Lea el pasaje con atención. ❷ pasillo m ▷ a narrow passage un estrecho pasillo

passenger n pasajero m, pasajera f

passion n pasión f (pl pasiones)

passive adj pasivo(-a) ▷ a passive smoker un fumador pasivo

Passover n Pascua judía f

passport n pasaporte m ▷ passport control el control de pasaportes

password n contraseña f

past adj, adv, prep pasado(-a) ▷ This past year has been very difficult. Este año pasado ha sido muy difícil.; **The school is 100 metres past the traffic lights.** El colegio está a unos 100 metros pasado el semáforo.; **to go past** pasar [25] ▷ The bus went past without stopping. El autobús pasó sin parar.; **It's half past ten.** Son las diez y media.; **It's a quarter past nine.** Son las nueve y cuarto.; **It's ten past eight.** Son las ocho y diez.; **It's past midnight.** Es pasada la medianoche.
▶ n pasado m ▷ I try not to think of the past. Intento no pensar en el pasado.; **This was common in the past.** Antiguamente esto era normal.

pasta n pasta f

pasteurized adj pasteurizado(-a)

pastry n ❶ (dough) masa f ❷ (cake) pastel m

patch n parche m ▷ a patch of material un parche de tela; **He's got a bald patch.** Tiene una calva incipiente.; **They're going through a bad patch.** Están pasando una mala racha.

pâté n paté m

path n sendero m

pathetic adj penoso(-a) ▷ That was a pathetic excuse. Fue una excusa penosa.

patience n ❶ paciencia f ▷ He hasn't got much patience. No tiene mucha paciencia. ❷ (game) solitario m

patient n paciente m, paciente f
▶ adj paciente

patio n patio m

patrol n patrulla f; **to be on patrol** estar [22] de patrulla

patrol car n coche patrulla m (pl coches patrulla)

pattern n ❶ (design) motivo m ❷ (for sewing) patrón m

pause n pausa f

pavement n acera f

paw n pata f

pay n sueldo m ▷ a pay rise un aumento de sueldo
▶ vb pagar [37] ▷ Can I pay by cheque? ¿Puedo pagar con cheque?; **to pay money into an account** ingresar [25] dinero a una cuenta; **I'll pay you back tomorrow.** Mañana te devuelvo el dinero.; **to pay for something** pagar [37] algo ▷ I paid for my ticket. Pagué el billete.; **I paid £50 for it.** Me costó 50 libras.; **to pay somebody a visit** ir [27] a ver a alguien ▷ Paul paid us a visit last night. Paul vino a vernos anoche.

payment n pago m

payphone n teléfono público m

PC n (= personal computer) PC m

PE n (= physical education) educación física f ▷ We do PE twice a week. Tenemos educación física dos veces a la semana.

pea n guisante m

peace n paz f; **peace talks** conversaciones de paz; **a peace treaty** un tratado de paz

peaceful adj ❶ (non-violent) pacífico(-a) ▷ a peaceful protest una manifestación pacífica ❷ (restful) apacible ▷ a peaceful afternoon una tarde apacible

peach n melocotón m (pl melocotones)

peacock n pavo real m

peak n ❶ (of mountain) cumbre f ❷ apogeo m ▷ She's at the peak of her career. Está en el apogeo de su carrera profesional.; **in peak season** en temporada alta

peanut n cacahuete m (maní m LatAm)

peanut butter n crema de cacahuete f

pear n pera f

pearl n perla f

pebble n guijarro m

peculiar adj raro(-a)

pedal n pedal m

pedestrian n peatón m (pl peatones)

pedestrian crossing n paso de peatones m

pee n **to have a pee** hacer [26] pis

peel n piel f
▶ vb pelar [25] ▷ Shall I peel the potatoes? ¿Pelo las patatas?

peg n ❶ (for coats) gancho m ❷ (clothes peg) pinza f ❸ (tent peg) estaca f

pelvis n pelvis f (pl pelvis)

pen n ❶ (ballpoint pen) bolígrafo m ❷ (fountain pen) pluma f ❸ (felt-tip pen) rotulador m

penalty n ❶ pena f; **the death penalty** la pena de muerte ❷ (in football) penalty m (pl penaltys); **a penalty shoot-out** una tanda de penaltys ❸ (in rugby) golpe de castigo m

pence npl **24 pence** 24 peniques

pencil n lápiz m (pl lápices) (lapicero m LatAm); **to write in pencil** escribir [58] a lápiz

pencil case n estuche m

pencil sharpener n sacapuntas m (pl sacapuntas)

penfriend n amigo por correspondencia m, amiga por correspondencia f

penguin n pingüino m

penicillin n penicilina f

penis n pene m

penknife n navaja f

penny n penique m

pension n pensión f (pl pensiones)

pensioner n pensionista mf

people npl ❶ gente f ▷ The people were nice. La gente era simpática. ▷ A lot of people mucha gente ❷ personas fpl ▷ six people seis personas; **People say that...** Dicen que...; **How many people are there in your family?** ¿Cuántos sois en tu familia?; **Spanish people** los españoles

pepper n ❶ pimienta f ▷ Pass the pepper, please. ¿Me pasas la pimienta? ❷ pimiento m (chile m LatAm) ▷ a green pepper un pimiento verde

peppermill n molinillo de pimienta m

peppermint n caramelo de menta m; **peppermint chewing gum** el chicle de menta

per prep por ▷ per person por persona; **per day** al día; **per week** a la semana

per cent adv por ciento ▷ 50 per cent 50 por ciento

percentage n porcentaje m

a b c d e f g h i j k l m n o p q r s t u v w x y z

percussion n percusión f ▷ I play percussion. Toco la percusión.

perfect adj perfecto(-a) ▷ Dave speaks perfect Spanish. Dave habla un español perfecto.

perfectly adv perfectamente ▷ You know perfectly well what happened. Sabes perfectamente lo que ocurrió.; **a perfectly normal child** un niño completamente normal

perform vb (a play) representar **[25]** ▷ to perform Hamlet representar Hamlet; **The team performed brilliantly.** El equipo tuvo una brillante actuación.

performance n ❶ espectáculo m ▷ The performance lasts two hours. El espectáculo dura dos horas. ❷ interpretación f (pl interpretaciones) ▷ his performance as Hamlet su interpretación de Hamlet

perfume n perfume m

perhaps adv quizás ▷ Perhaps they were tired. Quizás estaban cansados.

> Use the present subjunctive after **quizás** to refer to the future.

▷ Perhaps he'll come tomorrow. Quizás venga mañana.; **perhaps not** quizás no

period n ❶ periodo m ▷ for a limited period por un periodo limitado ❷ clase f ▷ Each period lasts forty minutes. Cada clase dura cuarenta minutos. ❸ época f ▷ the Victorian period la época victoriana ❹ regla f ▷ I'm having my period. Estoy con la regla.

perm n permanente f ▷ She's got a perm. Lleva permanente.

permanent adj ❶ permanente ▷ a permanent state of tension un estado permanente de tensión ❷ fijo(-a) ▷ a permanent job un trabajo fijo

permission n permiso m ▷ Could I have permission to leave early? ¿Tengo permiso para salir antes?

permit n permiso m ▷ a work permit un permiso de trabajo

person n persona f ▷ She's a very nice person. Es muy buena persona.; **in person** en persona

personal adj personal ▷ Those letters are personal. Son cartas personales.; **He's a personal friend of mine.** Es amigo íntimo mío.

personality n personalidad f

personally adv personalmente ▷ Personally I don't agree. Yo personalmente no estoy de acuerdo.; **I don't know him personally.** No lo conozco en persona.; **Don't take it personally.** No te lo tomes como algo personal.

personal stereo n walkman® m

perspiration n transpiración f

persuade vb convencer **[12]**

> Use the subjunctive after **convencer de que** when translating 'to persuade somebody to do something'.

to persuade sb to do sth convencer **[12]** a alguien de que haga algo ▷ She persuaded me to go with her. Me convenció de que fuera con ella.

Peru n Perú m

Peruvian adj peruano(-a)
▶ n peruano m, peruana f

pessimistic adj pesimista ▷ Don't
be so pessimistic! ¡No seas tan
pesimista!

pest n pesado m, pesada f ▷ He's a
real pest! ¡Es un pesado!

pester vb dar [**14**] la lata a ▷ He's
always pestering me. Siempre me
está dando la lata.

pet n animal doméstico m; **Have
you got a pet?** ¿Tenéis algún
animal en casa?; **She's the
teacher's pet.** Es la enchufada del
profesor.

petrol n gasolina f; **unleaded
petrol** gasolina sin plomo; **4-star
petrol** gasolina súper

petrol station n gasolinera f

pharmacy n farmacia f
    Pharmacies in Spain are
    identified by a green cross
    outside the shop.

pheasant n faisán m (pl faisanes)

philosophy n filosofía f

phobia n fobia f

phone n teléfono m; **by phone** por
teléfono; **to be on the phone**
(1) (talking) estar [**22**] al teléfono
▷ She's on the phone at the moment.
Ahora mismo está al teléfono.
(2) (to have a phone) tener [**53**]
teléfono; **Can I use the phone,
please?** ¿Puedo hacer una
llamada?
▶ vb llamar [**25**] ▷ I'll phone you
tomorrow. Mañana te llamo.

phone bill n factura del teléfono f

phone book n guía telefónica f

phone box n cabina telefónica f

phone call n llamada de teléfono f;
to make a phone call hacer [**26**]
una llamada

phonecard n tarjeta telefónica f

phone number n número de
teléfono m

photo n foto f
    Although **foto** ends in -o, it is
    actually a feminine noun.
to take a photo hacer [**26**] una
foto ▷ I took a photo of the bride and
groom. Les hice una foto a los
novios.

photocopier n fotocopiadora f

photocopy n fotocopia f
▶ vb fotocopiar [**25**]

photograph n fotografía f; **to
take a photograph** hacer [**26**] una
fotografía ▷ I took a photograph of
the bride and groom. Les hice una
fotografía a los novios.
▶ vb fotografiar [**21**]

photographer n fotógrafo m,
fotógrafa f ▷ She's a photographer.
Es fotógrafa.

photography n fotografía f ▷ My
hobby is photography. Mi hobby es la
fotografía.

phrase n frase f

phrase book n manual de
conversación m

physical adj físico(-a)
▶ n (US) reconocimiento médico m

physicist n físico m, física f ▷ a
nuclear physicist un físico nuclear

physics n física f ▷ She teaches
physics. Enseña física.

physiotherapist n
fisioterapeuta mf

physiotherapy n fisioterapia f

pianist n pianista mf

piano n piano m ▷ I play the piano.
Toco el piano.

pick n Take your pick! ¡Elige el que quieras!

> Replace **el que** with **la que**, **los que** or **las que** as appropriate to agree with the thing or things you can take your pick of.

▶ vb ❶ (choose) elegir [18] ▷ I picked the biggest piece. Elegí el trozo más grande. ❷ (for team) seleccionar [25] ▷ I've been picked for the team. Me han seleccionado para el equipo. ❸ (fruit, flowers) recoger [7]; **to pick on somebody** meterse [8] con alguien ▷ She's always picking on me. Siempre se está metiendo conmigo.

pick out vb escoger [7]

pick up vb ❶ recoger [7] ▷ We'll come to the airport to pick you up. Iremos a recogerte al aeropuerto. ❷ (learn) aprender [8]

pickpocket n carterista mf

picnic n picnic m (pl picnics); **to have a picnic** irse [27] de picnic

picture n ❶ ilustración f (pl ilustraciones) ❷ (photo) foto f

> Although **foto** ends in -o, it is actually a feminine noun.

> My picture was in the paper. Mi foto salió en el periódico. ❸ (painting) cuadro m ❹ (drawing) dibujo m; **to draw a picture of something** dibujar [25] algo; **to paint a picture of something** pintar [25] algo; **the pictures** el

cine ▷ Shall we go to the pictures?
¿Vamos al cine?

picture message n mensaje con foto m

pie n ❶ (sweet) tarta f ▷ an apple pie una tarta de manzana ❷ (of meat) pastel m ▷ a meat pie un pastel de carne

piece n ❶ trozo m ▷ a piece of cake un trozo de tarta; **A small piece, please.** Un trocito, por favor. ❷ (individual) pieza f ▷ a 500-piece jigsaw un puzzle de 500 piezas ❸ (of something larger) pedazo m ▷ A piece of plaster fell from the roof. Un pedazo de yeso se cayó del tejado.; **a piece of furniture** un mueble; **a piece of advice** un consejo; **a 10p piece** una moneda de 10 peniques

pier n muelle m

pierced adj I've got pierced ears. Tengo los agujeros hechos en las orejas.

pig n cerdo m

pigeon n paloma f

piggyback n to give somebody a piggyback llevar [25] a alguien a cuestas

piggy bank n hucha f

pigtail n trenza f

pile n ❶ (untidy heap) montón m (pl montones) ▷ a pile of dirty laundry un montón de ropa sucia ❷ (tidy stack) pila f; **Put your books in a pile on my desk.** Apilad vuestros cuadernos en mi mesa.

pill n píldora f; **to be on the pill** tomar [25] la píldora

pillow n almohada f

pilot n piloto mf ▷ He's a pilot. Es piloto.

pimple n grano m

PIN n (= personal identification number) número secreto m

pin n alfiler m; **pins and needles** tengo hormigueo ▷ I've got pins and needles. Tengo hormigueo.

pinball n máquina de bolas f; **They're playing pinball.** Juegan a la máquina.

pinch vb ❶ pellizcar [48] ▷ He pinched me! ¡Me ha pellizcado! ❷ birlar [25] (informal) ▷ Who's pinched my pen? ¿Quién me ha birlado el bolígrafo?

pine n pino m ▷ a pine table una mesa de pino

pineapple n piña f

pink adj rosa

pint n pinta f

In Spain measurements are in litres and centilitres. A pint is about 0.6 litres.

to have a pint tomarse [25] una cerveza ▷ He's gone out for a pint. Ha salido a tomarse una cerveza.

pipe n ❶ tubería f ▷ The pipes froze. Se helaron las tuberías. ❷ pipa f ▷ He smokes a pipe. Fuma en pipa.; **the pipes** la gaita ▷ He plays the pipes. Toca la gaita.

pirate n pirata mf

pirated adj pirata ▷ a pirated video un vídeo pirata

Pisces n (sign) Piscis m; **I'm Pisces.** Soy piscis.

pistol n pistola f

pitch n campo m (cancha LatAm) ▷ a football pitch un campo de fútbol

▷ vb montar [25] ▷ We pitched our tent near the beach. Montamos la tienda cerca de la playa.

pity n compasión f ▷ They showed no pity. No demostraron ninguna compasión.; **What a pity!** ¡Qué pena!

▷ vb compadecer [12] ▷ I don't hate him, I pity him. No lo odio, lo compadezco.

pizza n pizza f

place n ❶ lugar m ▷ It's a quiet place. Es un lugar tranquilo. ❷ plaza f ▷ Book your place for the trip now. Reserve ya su plaza para el viaje. ▷ a university place una plaza en la universidad ❸ (in sports) puesto m ▷ Britain won third place in the games. Gran Bretaña consiguió el tercer puesto en los juegos.; **a parking place** un sitio para aparcar; **to change places** cambiarse [25] de sitio; **to take place** tener [53] lugar ▷ Elections will take place on November 25th. Las elecciones tendrán lugar el 25 de noviembre.; **at your place** en tu casa ▷ Shall we meet at your place? ¿Nos vemos en tu casa?; **Do you want to come round to my place?** ¿Quieres venir a mi casa?

▷ vb colocar [48] ▷ He placed his hand on hers. Colocó su mano sobre la de ella.

plain adj, adv ❸ (not patterned) liso(-a) ▷ a plain tie una corbata lisa ❷ (not fancy) sencillo(-a) ▷ a plain white blouse una blusa blanca sencilla; **It was plain to see.** Era obvio.

▷ n llanura f

plain chocolate n chocolate amargo m

plait n trenza f ▷ She wears her hair in plaits. Lleva trenzas.

plan n ➊ plan m ▷ What are your plans for the holidays? ¿Qué planes tienes para las vacaciones?; **to make plans** hacer [26] planes; **Everything went according to plan.** Todo fue según lo previsto. ➋ plano m ▷ a plan of the campsite un plano del camping; **my essay plan** el esquema de mi trabajo
▶ vb ➊ (make plans for) planear [25] ▷ We're planning a trip to France. Estamos planeando hacer un viaje a Francia. ➋ (schedule) planificar [48] ▷ Plan your revision carefully. Tienes que planificar bien el repaso.; **to plan to do something** tener [53] la intención de hacer algo ▷ I'm planning to get a job in the holidays. Tengo la intención de encontrar un trabajo para las vacaciones.

plane n avión m (pl aviones) ▷ by plane en avión

planet n planeta m
▌ Although **planeta** ends in **-a**, it is actually a masculine noun.

plant n planta f; **a chemical plant** una planta química
▶ vb plantar [25] ▷ We planted fruit trees and vegetables. Plantamos árboles frutales y hortalizas.

plaster n ➊ (for cut) tirita f ➋ (for broken limb) escayola f; **Her leg's in plaster.** Lleva la pierna escayolada.

plastic n plástico m ▷ It's made of plastic. Es de plástico.
▶ adj de plástico ▷ a plastic bag una bolsa de plástico

plate n plato m

platform n ➊ (in railway station) andén m (pl andenes) ➋ (for speaker, performer) estrado m

play n obra de teatro f; **a play by Shakespeare** una obra de Shakespeare; **to put on a play** montar [25] una obra
▶ vb ➊ jugar [28] ▷ He's playing with his friends. Está jugando con sus amigos. ➋ jugar [28] contra ▷ Spain will play Scotland next month. España juega contra Escocia el mes que viene. ➌ jugar [28] a ▷ Can you play pool? ¿Sabes jugar al billar americano? ➍ tocar [48] ▷ I play the guitar. Toco la guitarra. ▷ What sort of music do they play? ¿Qué clase de música tocan? ➎ poner [41] ▷ She's always playing that CD. Siempre está poniendo ese CD. ➏ hacer [26] de ▷ I would love to play Cleopatra. Me encantaría hacer de Cleopatra.

play down vb quitar [25] importancia a ▷ He tried to play down his illness. Trató de quitarle importancia a su enfermedad.

player n ➊ jugador m, jugadora f ▷ a game for four players un juego para cuatro jugadores; **a football player** un futbolista ➋ (musician) músico m, música f; **a piano player** un pianista; **a saxophone player** un saxofonista

playground n ❶ (at school) patio de recreo m ❷ (in park) columpios mpl

playgroup n guardería f

playing card n naipe m

playing field n campo de deportes m (cancha de deportes f LatAm)

playtime n recreo m

pleasant adj agradable ▷ We had a very pleasant evening. Pasamos una tarde muy agradable.

please excl por favor ▷ Two coffees, please. Dos cafés, por favor.

> por favor is not as common as 'please' and can be omitted in many cases. Spanish speakers may show their politeness by their intonation, or by using usted.

Can we have the bill please? ¿Nos puede traer la cuenta?; **Please come in.** Pase.; **Would you please be quiet?** ¿Quieres hacer el favor de callarte?

pleased adj **My mother's not going to be very pleased.** A mi madre no le va a hacer mucha gracia.; **It's beautiful: she'll be very pleased with it.** Es precioso: le va a gustar mucho.; **Pleased to meet you!** ¡Encantado!

pleasure n placer m ▷ I read for pleasure. Leo por placer.

plenty pron **I've got plenty.** Tengo de sobra.; **That's plenty, thanks.** Así está bien, gracias.; **plenty of** (1) (lots of) mucho ▷ He's got plenty of energy. Tiene mucha energía. (2) (more than enough) de sobra ▷ We've got plenty of time. Tenemos tiempo de sobra.

pliers n alicates mpl

plot n ❶ (of story, play) argumento m ❷ (conspiracy) complot m (pl complots) ▷ a plot against the president un complot contra el presidente ❸ (for vegetables) huerto m
> vb conspirar [25]

plough n arado m
> vb arar [25]

plug n ❶ (electrical) enchufe m ❷ (for sink) tapón m (pl tapones)

plug in vb enchufar [25] ▷ Is the iron plugged in? ¿Está enchufada la plancha?

plum n ciruela f

plumber n fontanero m, fontanera f ▷ He's a plumber. Es fontanero.

plump adj rechoncho(-a)

plural n plural m

plus prep, adj más ▷ 4 plus 3 equals 7. 4 más 3 son 7.; **three children plus a dog** tres niños y un perro; **I got a B plus.** Saqué un notable alto.

p.m. abbr
> Use de la tarde if it's light and de la noche if it's dark.
▷ at 2 p.m. a las dos de la tarde ▷ at 9 p.m. a las nueve de la noche

pneumonia n pulmonía f

pocket n bolsillo m ▷ He had his hands in his pockets. Tenía las manos en los bolsillos.

pocket money n paga f ▷ How much pocket money do you get? ¿Cuánto te dan de paga?

podcast n podcast m (pl podcasts)

poem n poema m
> Although **poema** ends in -a, it is actually a masculine noun.

a b c d e f g h i j k l m n o p q r s t u v w x y z

poet n poeta m, poetisa f

poetry n poesía f

point n ❶ punto m ▷ They scored five points. Sacaron cinco puntos. ❷ momento m ▷ At that point, we decided to leave. En aquel momento decidimos marcharnos. ❸ (of pencil) punta f ❹ comentario m ▷ He made some interesting points. Hizo algunos comentarios de interés.; **They were on the point of finding it.** Estaban a punto de encontrarlo.; **a point of view** un punto de vista; **That's a good point!** ¡Tiene razón!; **That's not the point.** Eso no tiene nada que ver.; **There's no point.** No tiene sentido. ▷ There's no point in waiting. No tiene sentido esperar.; **What's the point?** ¿Para qué? ▷ What's the point of leaving so early? ¿Para qué salir tan pronto?; **Punctuality isn't my strong point.** La puntualidad no es mi fuerte.; **two point five (2.5)** dos coma cinco (2,5)
▶ vb señalar [25] con el dedo ▷ Don't point! ¡No señales con el dedo!; **to point at somebody** señalar [25] a alguien con el dedo ▷ She pointed at Anne. Señaló a Anne con el dedo.; **to point a gun at somebody** apuntar [25] a alguien con una pistola

point out vb ❶ señalar [25] ▷ The guide pointed out the Alhambra to us. El guía nos señaló la Alhambra. ❷ indicar [48] ▷ I should point out that... Me gustaría indicar que...

pointless adj inútil ▷ It's pointless arguing. Es inútil discutir.

poison n veneno m
▶ vb envenenar [25]

poisonous adj ❶ (animal, plant) venenoso(-a) ❷ (chemical) tóxico(-a) ▷ poisonous gases gases tóxicos

poke vb **He poked me in the eye.** Me metió un dedo en el ojo.

poker n póker m ▷ I play poker. Juego al póker.

Poland n Polonia f

polar bear n oso polar m

Pole n (person) polaco m, polaca f

pole n ❶ poste m ▷ a telegraph pole un poste de teléfonos; **a tent pole** un mástil de tienda; **a ski pole** un bastón de esquí; **the North Pole** el Polo Norte; **the South Pole** el Polo Sur

police npl policía f ▷ We called the police. Llamamos a la policía.

police car n coche de policía m

policeman n policía m (agente m LatAm)

police officer n policía mf (agente mf LatAm)

police station n comisaría f

policewoman n policía f (agente f LatAm)

Polish adj polaco(-a)
▶ n (language) polaco m

polish n ❶ (for shoes) betún m ❷ (for furniture) cera f
▶ vb (shoes, glass) limpiar [25]; **to polish the furniture** sacar [48] brillo a los muebles

polite adj educado(-a) ▷ a polite child un niño educado

political adj político(-a)

politician n político m, política f

politics n política f ▷ I'm not interested in politics. No me interesa la política.

pollution n contaminación f

polo-necked sweater n suéter de cuello alto m

polythene bag n bolsa de plástico f

pond n ❶ (natural) charca f ❷ (artificial) estanque m

pony n poney m

ponytail n coleta f ▷ He's got a ponytail. Lleva coleta.

pony trekking n to go pony trekking ir [27] de excursión en poney

poodle n caniche m

pool n ❶ (pond) estanque m ❷ (swimming pool) piscina f ❸ (game) billar americano m; **a pool table** una mesa de billar; **the pools** las quinielas ▷ I do the pools every week. Juego a las quinielas todas las semanas.

poor adj ❶ pobre

> pobre goes after the noun when it means that someone has not got very much money. It goes before the noun when you want to show that you feel sorry for someone.

▷ a poor family una familia pobre ▷ Poor David, he's very unlucky! ¡Pobre David, tiene muy mala suerte!; **the poor** los pobres ❷ malo(-a)

> Use **mal** before a masculine singular noun.

▷ He's a poor actor. Es un mal actor. ▷ a poor mark una mala nota

pop adj pop ▷ pop music la música pop ▷ a pop star una estrella pop; **a pop group** un grupo de música pop

pop in vb entrar [25] un momento

pop out vb salir [49] un momento

popcorn n palomitas de maíz fpl

poppy n amapola f

popular adj popular ▷ Football is the most popular game in this country. El fútbol es el deporte más popular de este país.; **She's a very popular girl.** Es una chica que cae bien a todo el mundo.; **This is a very popular style.** Este estilo está muy de moda.

population n población f (pl poblaciones)

porch n porche de entrada m

pork n carne de cerdo f (carne de puerco f LatAm); **a pork chop** una chuleta de cerdo

porridge n gachas de avena fpl

port n (harbour, town) puerto m

portable adj portátil ▷ a portable TV un televisor portátil

porter n ❶ (in hotel) portero m, portera f ❷ (at station) mozo de equipajes m, moza de equipajes f

portion n ❶ porción f (pl porciones) ❷ (of food) ración f (pl raciones) ▷ a large portion of chips una ración grande de patatas fritas

portrait n retrato m

Portugal n Portugal m

Portuguese adj portugués (f portuguesa, pl portugueses) ▶ n (language) portugués m; **the Portuguese** los portugueses

posh adj de lujo ▷ a posh car un coche de lujo

position n posición f (pl posiciones)

positive adj ❶ positivo(-a) ▷ a positive attitude una actitud positiva ❷ (sure) seguro(-a) ▷ I'm positive. Estoy completamente seguro.

possession n Have you got all your possessions? ¿Tienes todas tus pertenencias?

possibility n posibilidad f ▷ There were several possibilities. Había varias posibilidades.

possible adj posible; **as soon as possible** lo antes posible

> **es posible que** has to be followed by a verb in the subjunctive.

▷ It's possible that he's gone away. Es posible que se haya ido.

possibly adv tal vez ▷ Are you coming to the party? — Possibly. ¿Vas a venir a la fiesta? — Tal vez.; **... if you possibly can.** ... si es que puedes.; **I can't possibly go.** Me es del todo imposible ir.

post n ❶ correo m ▷ Has the post arrived yet? ¿Ha llegado ya el correo?; **by post** por correo; **Is there any post for me?** ¿Tengo alguna carta? ❷ poste m ▷ The ball hit the post. El balón dio en el poste. ❸ (on blog, social network) post m (pl posts)

▷ vb ❶ mandar [25] por correo ▷ You could post it. Puedes mandarlo por correo.; **I've got some cards to post.** Tengo que mandar algunas postales.; **Would you post this letter for me?** ¿Me

echas esta carta al correo? ❷ colgar [28] ▷ She posted it on my wall. Lo colgó en mi muro.

postbox n buzón m (pl buzones)

postcard n postal f

postcode n código postal m

poster n ❶ (public) cartel m ▷ There are posters all over town. Hay carteles por toda la ciudad. ❷ (personal) póster m (pl pósters) ▷ I've got posters on my bedrooms walls. Tengo pósters en las paredes de mi cuarto.

postman n cartero m ▷ He's a postman. Es cartero.

post office n oficina de correos f ▷ Where's the post office, please? ¿Sabe dónde está la oficina de correos?; **She works for the post office.** Trabaja en correos.

postpone vb aplazar [13] ▷ The match has been postponed. El partido ha sido aplazado.

postwoman n cartera f ▷ She's a postwoman. Es cartera.

pot n ❶ tarro m (pote m LatAm) ▷ a pot of jam un tarro de mermelada; **a pot of paint** un bote de pintura; **the pots and pans** las cacerolas ❷ (teapot) tetera f; **a coffeepot** una cafetera ❸ maría f (informal) ▷ to smoke pot fumar maría

potato n patata f (papa f LatAm); **mashed potatoes** el puré de patatas

pottery n cerámica f

pound n ❶ libra f

> In Spain measurements are in grams and kilograms. One pound is about 450 grams.

▷ *a pound of carrots* una libra de zanahorias ❷ **libra esterlina** *f*; **20 pounds** 20 libras; **a pound coin** una moneda de una libra ▶*vb* latir [**58**] con fuerza

pour *vb* ❶ echar [**25**] ▷ *She poured some water into the pan.* Echó un poco de agua en la olla. ❷ llover [**31**] a cántaros ▷ *It's pouring.* Está lloviendo a cántaros.; **in the pouring rain** bajo una lluvia torrencial

poverty *n* pobreza *f*

powder *n* polvo *m*; **a fine white powder** un polvillo blanco

power *n* ❶ (electrical) corriente *f* ▷ *The power's off.* Se ha ido la corriente.; **a power point** un enchufe ❷ energía *f* ▷ *nuclear power* la energía nuclear ❸ poder *m* ▷ *They were in power for 18 years.* Estuvieron 18 años en el poder.

power cut *n* apagón *m* (*pl* apagones)

powerful *adj* ❶ (person, organization) poderoso(-a) ❷ (machine, substance) potente

power station *n* central eléctrica *f*

practical *adj* práctico(-a)

practically *adv* prácticamente ▷ *It's practically impossible.* Es prácticamente imposible.

practice *n* ❶ práctica *f* ▷ *You'll get better with practice.* Mejorarás con la práctica.; **in practice** en la práctica; **It's normal practice in our school.** Es lo normal en nuestro colegio. ❷ entrenamiento *m* ▷ *football practice* entrenamiento de fútbol; **I'm out of practice.** Estoy desentrenado.; **I've got to do my piano practice.** Tengo que hacer los ejercicios de piano.; **a medical practice** una consulta médica

practise (US **practice**) *vb* ❶ practicar [**48**] ▷ *I practised my Spanish when we were on holiday.* Practiqué el español cuando estuvimos de vacaciones. ❷ (train) entrenarse [**25**] ▷ *The team practises on Thursdays.* El equipo se entrena los jueves.

praise *vb* elogiar [**25**] ▷ *Everyone praises her cooking.* Todo el mundo elogia cómo cocina.

pram *n* cochecito de niño *m*

prawn *n* gamba *f*

pray *vb* rezar [**13**] ▷ *to pray for something* rezar por algo

prayer *n* oración *f* (*pl* oraciones)

precious *adj* precioso(-a) ▷ *a precious stone* una piedra preciosa

precise *adj* preciso(-a) ▷ *at that precise moment* en aquel preciso instante; **to be precise** para ser exacto

precisely *adv* precisamente ▷ *That is precisely what it's meant for.* Para eso precisamente está hecho.; **Precisely!** ¡Exactamente!; **at 10 a.m. precisely** a las diez en punto de la mañana

predict *vb* predecir [**15**]

predictable *adj* previsible

prefect *n* (in school) monitor *m*, monitora *f*

prefer *vb* preferir [**51**] ▷ *Which would you prefer?* ¿Tú cuál prefieres? ▷ *I prefer chemistry to maths.*

Prefiero la química a las matemáticas.

pregnant adj embarazada ▷ She's six months pregnant. Está embarazada de seis meses.

prejudice n prejuicio m ▷ That's just a prejudice. Eso no es más que un prejuicio.; **There's a lot of racial prejudice.** Hay muchos prejuicios raciales.

prejudiced adj **to be prejudiced against somebody** tener [53] prejuicios contra alguien

premature adj prematuro(-a) ▷ a premature baby un bebé prematuro

Premier League n primera división f

premises npl local m ▷ They're moving to new premises. Se cambian de local.

prep n deberes mpl ▷ history prep los deberes de historia

prepare vb preparar [25] ▷ He was preparing dinner. Estaba preparando la cena.; **to prepare for something** hacer [26] los preparativos para algo ▷ We're preparing for our holiday. Estamos haciendo los preparativos para las vacaciones.

prepared adj **to be prepared to do something** estar [22] dispuesto a hacer algo ▷ I'm prepared to help you. Estoy dispuesto a ayudarte.

prescribe vb recetar [25] ▷ The doctor prescribed a course of antibiotics for me. El doctor me recetó antibióticos.

prescription n receta f ▷ a prescription for penicillin una receta

de penicilina; **on prescription** con receta médica

present adj ❶ presente ▷ He wasn't present at the meeting. No estuvo presente en la reunión. ❷ actual ▷ the present situation la situación actual; **the present tense** el presente
▶ n ❶ regalo m; **to give somebody a present** hacer [26] un regalo a alguien ▷ He gave me a lovely present. Me hizo un precioso regalo. ❷ presente m ▷ to live in the present vivir el presente; **at present** actualmente; **for the present** por el momento; **up to the present** hasta el momento presente
▶ vb **to present somebody with something** entregar [37] algo a alguien ▷ The Mayor presented the winner with a medal. El alcalde le entregó una medalla al vencedor.; **He agreed to present the show.** Aceptó presentar el espectáculo.

presenter n presentador m, presentadora f

president n presidente m, presidenta f

press n prensa f ▷ The story appeared in the press last week. La historia salió en la prensa la semana pasada.
▶ vb apretar [39] ▷ Don't press too hard! ¡No aprietes muy fuerte!; **He pressed the accelerator.** Pisó el acelerador.

press-up n **to do press-ups** hacer [26] flexiones

pressure n presión f (pl presiones); **a pressure group** un grupo de presión; **to be under pressure** estar [22] presionado ▷ *She was under pressure from the management.* Estaba presionada por la dirección.; **He's been under a lot of pressure recently.** Últimamente ha estado muy agobiado.

presume vb suponer [41] ▷ *I presume he'll come.* Supongo que vendrá.

pretend vb **to pretend to do something** fingir [16] hacer algo; **to pretend to be asleep** hacerse [26] el dormido

Be careful not to translate **to pretend** by **pretender**.

pretty adj, adv ❶ bonito(-a) ▷ *She wore a pretty dress.* Llevaba un vestido bonito. ❷ guapo(-a) ▷ *She's very pretty.* Es muy guapa. ❸ bastante ▷ *That film was pretty bad.* La película era bastante mala.; **The weather was pretty awful.** Hacía un tiempo horroroso.; **It's pretty much the same.** Es más o menos lo mismo.

prevent vb evitar [25] ▷ *Every effort had been made to prevent the accident.* Se había hecho todo lo posible para evitar el accidente.

evitar que has to be followed by a verb in the subjunctive.

to prevent something happening evitar [25] que pase algo ▷ *I want to prevent this happening again.* Quiero evitar que esto se repita.

impedir a alguien que has to be followed by a verb in the subjunctive.

to prevent somebody from doing something impedir [38] a alguien que haga algo ▷ *My only thought was to prevent him from speaking.* Mi única idea era impedirle que hablara.

previous adj anterior ▷ *the previous night* la noche anterior; **He has no previous experience.** No tiene experiencia previa.

previously adv antes

price n precio m ▷ *What price is this painting?* ¿Qué precio tiene este cuadro?; **to go up in price** subir [58] de precio; **to come down in price** bajar [25] de precio

price list n lista de precios f

prick vb pinchar [25] ▷ *I've pricked my finger.* Me he pinchado un dedo.

pride n orgullo m

priest n sacerdote m

primary school n escuela primaria f

prime minister n primer ministro m, primera ministra f

prince n príncipe m ▷ *the Prince of Wales* el príncipe de Gales

princess n princesa f ▷ *Princess Victoria* la princesa Victoria

principal adj principal
▶ n director m, directora f

principle n principio m ▷ *the basic principles of physics* los principios básicos de física; **in principle** en principio; **on principle** por principio

a
b
c
d
e
f
g
h
i
j
k
l
m
n
o
p
q
r
s
t
u
v
w
x
y
z

print n ❶ foto f

> Although **foto** ends in **-o**, it is actually a feminine noun.

▷ colour prints fotos a color ❷ letra f ▷ in small print en letra pequeña ❸ huella f ▷ The police officer took his prints. El policía le tomó las huellas. ❹ grabado m ▷ a framed print un grabado enmarcado

printer n impresora f

printout n copia impresa f

priority n prioridad f ▷ My family takes priority over my work. Mi familia tiene prioridad sobre mi trabajo.

prison n cárcel f ▷ to send somebody to prison for 5 years condenar a alguien a 5 años de cárcel; **in prison** en la cárcel

prisoner n ❶ (in prison) preso m, presa f ❷ (captive) prisionero m, prisionera f; **to take somebody prisoner** hacer [26] prisionero a alguien

private adj ❶ privado(-a); **private life** la vida privada ❷ (for one person only) particular ▷ private lessons clases particulares; **a private bathroom** un baño individual; **'private'** (on envelope) 'confidencial'; **in private** en privado

prize n premio m ▷ to win a prize ganar un premio

prize-giving n entrega de premios f

prizewinner n premiado m, premiada f

pro n **the pros and cons** los pros y los contras

probable adj probable

probably adv probablemente ▷ He'll probably come tomorrow. Probablemente vendrá mañana.

problem n problema m

> Although **problema** ends in **-a**, it is actually a masculine noun.

▷ the drug problem el problema de la droga; **No problem! (1)** (of course) ¡Por supuesto! ▷ Can you repair it? — No problem! ¿Lo puedes arreglar? — ¡Por supuesto! **(2)** (it doesn't matter) ¡No importa! ▷ I'm sorry about that — No problem! Lo siento — ¡No importa!; **What's the problem?** ¿Qué pasa?

process n proceso m ▷ the peace process el proceso de paz; **We're in the process of painting the kitchen.** Ahora mismo estamos pintando la cocina.

procession n procesión f (pl procesiones)

produce vb ❶ (manufacture, create) producir [9] ❷ (on stage) montar [25]

producer n ❶ (of film, record, TV programme) productor m, productora f ❷ (of play, show) director m, directora f

product n producto m

production n ❶ producción f (pl producciones) ▷ They're increasing production of luxury models. Están aumentando la producción de modelos de lujo. ❷ montaje m ▷ a production of 'Hamlet' un montaje de 'Hamlet'

profession n profesión f (pl profesiones)

professional n profesional mf
▶ adj profesional ▷ a professional musician un músico profesional

professor n catedrático m, catedrática f

Be careful not to translate **professor** by the Spanish word **profesor**.

profit n beneficios mpl ▷ to make a profit sacar beneficios ▷ a profit of £10,000 unos beneficios de 10.000 libras

profitable adj rentable

program n programa m

Although **programa** ends in -a, it is actually a masculine noun.

▷ a computer program un programa informático; **a TV program** (US) un programa de televisión
▶ vb programar [25]

programme n programa m

Although **programa** ends in -a, it is actually a masculine noun.

▷ a TV programme un programa de televisión

programmer n programador m, programadora f ▷ She's a programmer. Es programadora.

progress n progreso m ▷ You're making progress! ¡Estás haciendo progresos!

prohibit vb prohibir [42] ▷ Smoking is prohibited. Está prohibido fumar.

project n ① (scheme, plan) proyecto m ② (research) trabajo m ▷ I'm doing a project on the greenhouse effect. Estoy haciendo un trabajo sobre el efecto invernadero.

projector n proyector m

promise n promesa f ▷ He made me a promise. Me hizo una promesa.; **That's a promise!** ¡Lo prometo!
▶ vb prometer [8] ▷ He didn't do what he promised. No hizo lo que prometió.; **She promised to write.** Prometió que escribiría.; **I'll write, I promise!** ¡Escribiré, lo prometo!

promote vb (employee, team) ascender [20] ▷ She was promoted six months later. La ascendieron seis meses después.

promotion n ascenso m

prompt adj, adv ① rápido(-a) ▷ a prompt reply una rápida respuesta ② puntual ▷ He's always very prompt. Siempre es muy puntual.; **at eight o'clock prompt** a las ocho en punto

pronoun n pronombre m

pronounce vb pronunciar [25]
▷ How do you pronounce that word? ¿Cómo se pronuncia esa palabra?

pronunciation n pronunciación f (pl pronunciaciones)

proof n prueba f; **I've got proof that he did it.** Tengo pruebas de que lo hizo.

proper adj ① (genuine) de verdad ▷ It's difficult to get a proper job. Es difícil conseguir un trabajo de verdad. ② (suitable) adecuado(-a) ▷ You have to have the proper equipment. Tienes que tener el equipo adecuado.; **If you had come at the proper time...** Si hubieras llegado a tu hora...

properly adv correctamente
▷ You're not doing it properly. No lo estás haciendo correctamente.

property n propiedad f; **'private property'** 'propiedad privada'; **stolen property** objetos robados

propose vb proponer [**41**] ▷ I propose a new plan. Propongo un cambio de planes. ▷ What do you propose to do? ¿Qué te propones hacer?

▌ **proponer que** has to be followed by a verb in the subjunctive.

▷ He proposed that we stay at home. Propuso que nos quedáramos en casa.; **to propose to somebody** (for marriage) declararse [**25**] a alguien

prosecute vb They were prosecuted for murder. Les procesaron por asesinato.

prostitute n prostituta f

protect vb proteger [**7**]

protection n protección f

protein n proteína f

protest n protesta f; **a protest march** una manifestación
▶ vb protestar [**25**]

Protestant n protestante mf ▷ I'm a Protestant. Soy protestante.
▶ adj protestante

protester n manifestante mf

proud adj orgulloso(-a) ▷ Her parents are proud of her. Sus padres están orgullosos de ella.

prove vb probar [**11**] ▷ The police couldn't prove it. La policía no pudo probarlo.

proverb n proverbio m ▷ a Chinese proverb un proverbio chino

provide vb proporcionar [**25**]; **to provide somebody with something** proporcionar [**25**] algo a alguien ▷ They provided us with maps. Nos proporcionaron mapas.

provide for vb mantener [**53**]

provided conj siempre que

▌ **siempre que** has to be followed by a verb in the subjunctive.

▷ He'll play in the next match provided he's fit. Jugará el próximo partido siempre que esté en condiciones.

prune n ciruela pasa f

psychiatrist n psiquiatra mf

psychological adj psicológico(-a)

psychologist n psicólogo m, psicóloga f

psychology n psicología f

PTO abbr (= please turn over) sigue

pub n bar m

public n the public el público
▷ open to the public abierto al público; **in public** en público
▶ adj público(-a); **a public holiday** un día festivo (un día feriado LatAm); **public opinion** la opinión pública; **the public address system** la megafonía; **to be in the public eye** ser [**52**] un personaje público

publicity n publicidad f

public school n colegio privado m

public transport n transporte público m

publish vb publicar [**48**]

publisher n ❶ (person) editor m, editora f ❷ (company) editorial f

pudding n postre m ▷ What's for pudding? ¿Qué hay de postre?; **rice pudding** el arroz con leche; **black pudding** la morcilla

puddle n charco m

puff pastry n hojaldre m

pull vb ❶ (to make something move) tirar [25] ▷ Pull as hard as you can. Tira con todas tus fuerzas. ❷ (to tug at something) tirar [25] de (jalar [25] LatAm) ▷ She pulled my hair. Me tiró del pelo.; **He pulled the trigger.** Apretó el gatillo.; **I pulled a muscle when I was training.** Me dio un tirón mientras entrenaba.; **You're pulling my leg!** ¡Me estás tomando el pelo!; **Pull yourself together!** ¡Tranquilízate!

pull down vb echar [25] abajo ▷ The old school was pulled down last year. El año pasado echaron abajo la vieja escuela.

pull out vb ❶ (remove) sacar [48] ▷ to pull a tooth out sacar una muela ❷ (car) echarse [25] a un lado ▷ The car pulled out to overtake. El coche se echó a un lado para adelantar. ❸ (from competition) retirarse [25] ▷ She pulled out of the tournament. Se retiró del torneo.

pull through vb recuperarse [25] ▷ They think he'll pull through. Creen que se recuperará.

pull up vb (car) parar [25] ▷ A black car pulled up beside me. Un coche negro paró a mi lado.

pullover n jersey m (pl jerseys)

pulse n pulso m ▷ The nurse took his pulse. La enfermera le tomó el pulso.

pump n ❶ bomba f ▷ a bicycle pump una bomba de bicicleta ❷ zapatilla f ▷ She was wearing a black leotard and black pumps. Llevaba malla y zapatillas negras.
▶ vb bombear [25]; **to pump up a tyre** inflar [25] una rueda

pumpkin n calabaza f

punch n ❶ (blow) puñetazo m ❷ (drink) ponche m
▶ vb dar [14] un puñetazo a ▷ He punched me! ¡Me ha dado un puñetazo!

punctual adj puntual

punctuation n puntuación f

puncture n pinchazo m ▷ I had a puncture on the motorway. Tuve un pinchazo en la autopista.

punish vb castigar [37] ▷ They were severely punished for their disobedience. Les castigaron severamente por su desobediencia.; **to punish somebody for doing something** castigar [37] a alguien por haber hecho algo

punishment n castigo m

punk n punki mf; **a punk rock band** un grupo punk

pupil n alumno m, alumna f

puppet n títere m

puppy n cachorro m

purchase vb adquirir [2]

pure adj puro(-a)

purple adj morado(-a)

purpose n objetivo m ▷ What is the purpose of these changes? ¿Cuál es el objetivo de estos cambios?; **his purpose in life** su meta en la vida; **It's being used for military**

a
b
c
d
e
f
g
h
i
j
k
l
m
n
o
p
q
r
s
t
u
v
w
x
y
z

purposes. Se está usando con fines militares.; **on purpose** a propósito ▷ He did it on purpose. Lo hizo a propósito.

purr vb ronronear **[25]**

purse n ❶ (for money) monedero m ❷ (US: handbag) bolso m

push n empujón m (pl empujones); **to give somebody a push** dar **[14]** un empujón a alguien ▶ vb empujar **[25]** ▷ Don't push! ¡No empujes!; **to push a button** pulsar **[25]** un botón; **to push drugs** pasar **[25]** droga; **I'm pushed for time today.** Hoy ando fatal de tiempo.; **Push off!** ¡Lárgate!; **Don't push your luck!** ¡No tientes a la suerte!

push around vb dar **[14]** órdenes a ▷ He likes pushing people around. Le gusta dar órdenes a la gente.

pushchair n silla de paseo f

put vb poner **[41]** ▷ Where shall I put my things? ¿Dónde pongo mis cosas? ▷ Don't forget to put your name on the paper. No te olvides de poner tu nombre en la hoja.; **She's putting the baby to bed.** Está acostando al niño.

put aside vb apartar **[25]** ▷ Can you put this aside for me till tomorrow? ¿Me lo puede apartar hasta mañana?

put away vb ❶ guardar **[25]** ▷ Can you put the dishes away, please? ¿Guardas los platos? ❷ (in prison) encerrar **[39]** ▷ I hope they put him away for a long time. Espero que lo encierren por muchos años.

put back vb ❶ (in place) poner **[41]** en su sitio ▷ Put it back when you've

finished with it. Ponlo en su sitio cuando hayas terminado. ❷ (postpone) aplazar **[13]** ▷ The meeting has been put back till 2 o'clock. La reunión ha sido aplazada hasta las 2.

put down vb ❶ soltar **[11]** ▷ I'll put these bags down for a minute. Voy a soltar estas bolsas un momento. ❷ (note) apuntar **[25]** ▷ I've put down a few ideas. He apuntado algunas ideas.; **to have an animal put down** sacrificar **[48]** a un animal ▷ We had to have our dog put down. Tuvimos que sacrificar a nuestro perro.; **to put the phone down** colgar **[28]**

put forward vb (clock) adelantar **[25]**

put in vb (install) poner **[41]** ▷ We're going to get central heating put in. Vamos a poner calefacción central.; **He has put in a lot of work on this project.** Ha dedicado mucho trabajo a este proyecto.; **I've put in for a new job.** He solicitado otro empleo.

put off vb ❶ (light, TV) apagar **[37]** ▷ Shall I put the light off? ¿Apago la luz? ❷ (delay) aplazar **[13]** ▷ I keep putting it off. No hago más que aplazarlo. ❸ (distract) distraer **[54]** ▷ Stop putting me off! ¡Deja ya de distraerme! ❹ (discourage) desanimar **[25]** ▷ He's not easily put off. No es de los que se desaniman fácilmente.

put on vb ❶ (clothes, lipstick) ponerse **[41]** ▷ I put my coat on. Me puse el abrigo. ❷ (CD, DVD) poner **[41]** ▷ Put on some music. Pon algo de música. ❸ *(light, TV)* encender [20] ▷ *Shall I put the heater on?* ¿Enciendo el radiador? ❹ *(play, show)* representar [25] ▷ *We're putting on 'Bugsy Malone'.* Estamos representando 'Bugsy Malone'.; **I'll put the potatoes on.** Voy a poner a hacer las patatas.; **to put on weight** engordar [25] ▷ *He has put on a lot of weight.* Ha engordado mucho.; **She's not ill: she's just putting it on.** No está enferma: es puro teatro.

put out *vb* apagar [37] ▷ *It took them five hours to put out the fire.* Tardaron cinco horas en apagar el incendio.; **He's a bit put out that nobody came.** Le sentó mal que no viniera nadie.

put through *vb* poner [41] (comunicar [48] *LatAm*) ▷ *Can you put me through to the manager?* ¿Me pone con el director? ▷ *I'm putting you through.* Le pongo.

put up *vb* ❶ *(on wall)* colgar [28] ▷ *I'll put the poster up on my wall.* Colgaré el póster en la pared. ❷ montar [25] ▷ *We put up our tent in a field.* Montamos la tienda en un prado. ❸ subir [58] ▷ *They've put up the price.* Han subido el precio.; **My friend will put me up for the night.** Me quedaré a dormir en casa de mi amigo.; **to put one's hand up** levantar [25] la mano ▷ *If you have any questions, put your hand up.* Quien tenga alguna pregunta que levante la mano.; **to put up with something** aguantar [25] algo ▷ *I'm not going to put up with it*

any longer. No pienso aguantarlo más.; **to put something up for sale** poner [41] algo en venta ▷ *They're going to put their house up for sale.* Van a poner la casa en venta.

puzzle *n* rompecabezas *m* (*pl* rompecabezas)

puzzled *adj* perplejo(-a)

pyjamas *npl* pijama *m* (piyama *m* *LatAm*) ▷ *my pyjamas* mi pijama; **a pair of pyjamas** un pijama

▌ Although **pijama** ends in **-a**, it is actually a masculine noun.

pyramid *n* pirámide *f*

Pyrenees *npl* **the Pyrenees** los Pirineos

a
b
c
d
e
f
g
h
i
j
k
l
m
n
o
p
q
r
s
t
u
v
w
x
y
z

q

qualification n título m ▷ *He left school without any qualifications.* Dejó la escuela sin sacarse ningún título.

qualified adj ❶ cualificado(-a) ▷ *a qualified driving instructor* un profesor de autoescuela cualificado ❷ titulado(-a) ▷ *a qualified teacher* un profesor titulado; **She was well qualified for the position.** Estaba suficientemente capacitada para el puesto.

qualify vb ❶ sacarse [**48**] el título (recibirse [**58**] *LatAm*) ▷ *She qualified as a teacher last year.* Se sacó el título de profesora el año pasado. ❷ clasificarse [**48**] ▷ *Our team didn't qualify for the finals.* Nuestro equipo no se clasificó para la final.

quality n ❶ calidad f ▷ *good-quality paper* el papel de calidad ❷ cualidad f ▷ *She's got lots of good qualities.* Tiene un montón de buenas cualidades.

quantity n cantidad f

quarantine n cuarentena f ▷ *in quarantine* en cuarentena

quarrel n pelea f; **We had a quarrel.** Nos peleamos.
▶ vb pelearse [**25**]

quarry n (for stone) cantera f

quarter n cuarto m; **three quarters** tres cuartos; **a quarter of an hour** un cuarto de hora; **a quarter past ten** las diez y cuarto; **a quarter to eleven** las once menos cuarto

quarter-finals npl cuartos de final mpl

quartet n cuarteto m ▷ *a string quartet* un cuarteto de cuerda

quay n muelle m

queen n ❶ reina f ▷ *Queen Elizabeth* la reina Isabel ❷ dama f ▷ *the queen of hearts* la dama de corazones; **the Queen Mother** la reina madre

query n pregunta f
▶ vb poner [**41**] en duda ▷ *No one queried my decision.* Nadie puso en duda mi decisión.; **They queried the bill.** Pidieron explicaciones sobre la factura.

question n ❶ pregunta f ▷ *Can I ask a question?* ¿Puedo hacer una pregunta? ❷ cuestión f (pl cuestiones) ▷ *It's just a question of...* Tan solo es cuestión de...; **It's out**

of the question. Es imposible.
▶ vb **interrogar** [**37**] ▷ *He was questioned by the police.* Lo interrogó la policía.

question mark n **signo de interrogación** m

questionnaire n **cuestionario** m

queue n **cola** f ▷ *People were standing in a queue outside the cinema.* La gente hacía cola a las puertas del cine.
▶ vb **hacer** [**26**] **cola** ▷ *We had to queue for tickets.* Tuvimos que hacer cola para comprar los billetes.

quick adj, adv **rápido(-a)** ▷ *It's quicker by train.* Se va más rápido en tren.; **She's a quick learner.** Aprende rápido.; **Quick, phone the police!** ¡Rápido, llama a la policía!; **Be quick!** ¡Date prisa!

quickly adv **rápidamente** ▷ *It was all over very quickly.* Se acabó todo muy rápidamente.

quiet adj ① **callado(-a)** ▷ *You're very quiet today.* Hoy estás muy callado hoy. ② **silencioso(-a)** ▷ *The engine's very quiet.* El motor es muy silencioso. ③ **tranquilo(-a)** ▷ *a quiet little town* un pueblecito tranquilo; **Be quiet!** ¡Cállate!; **Quiet!** ¡Silencio!

quietly adv ① **en voz baja** ▷ *'She's dead,' he said quietly.* 'Está muerta,' dijo en voz baja. ② **sin hacer ruido** ▷ *He quietly opened the door.* Abrió la puerta sin hacer ruido.

quilt n **edredón** m (pl **edredones**)

quit vb ① **dejar** [**25**] ▷ *I quit my job last week.* Dejé mi trabajo la semana pasada. ② **marcharse** [**25**] ▷ *I've*

been given notice to quit. Me han dado el aviso para que me marche.

quite adv ① (rather) **bastante** ▷ *It's quite warm today.* Hoy hace bastante calor. ▷ *It's quite a long way.* Está bastante lejos. ▷ *I quite liked the film.* La película me gustó bastante.; **How was the film?** — **Quite good.** ¿Qué tal la película? — No está mal. ② (completely) **totalmente** ▷ *It's quite different.* Es totalmente distinto. ▷ *I quite agree with you.* Estoy totalmente de acuerdo contigo.; **It's quite clear that this plan won't work.** Está clarísimo que este plan no va a funcionar.; **not quite...** no del todo... ▷ *I'm not quite sure.* No estoy del todo seguro.; **It's not quite the same.** No es exactamente lo mismo.; **quite a...** todo un ▷ *It was quite a shock.* Fue todo un susto.; **quite a lot** bastante ▷ *I've been there quite a lot.* He estado allí bastante. ▷ *quite a lot of money* bastante dinero ▷ *It costs quite a lot to go abroad.* Es bastante caro ir al extranjero.; **There were quite a few people there.** Había bastante gente allí.

quiz n **concurso** m ▷ *a quiz show* un programa concurso

quotation n **cita** f ▷ *a quotation from Shakespeare* una cita de Shakespeare

quotation marks npl **comillas** fpl

quote n **1** cita f ▷ *a Shakespeare quote* una cita de Shakespeare **2** presupuesto m ▷ *Can you give me a quote for the work?* ¿Puede darme un presupuesto por el trabajo?; **quotes** las comillas ▷ *in quotes* entre comillas
▶ *vb* citar [**25**]

rabbi n rabino m, rabina f
rabbit n conejo m; **rabbit hutch** la conejera
race n **1** carrera f; **a cycle race** una carrera ciclista **2** raza f; **race relations** las relaciones interraciales
▶ *vb* **1** correr [**8**] ▷ *We raced to get there on time.* Corrimos para llegar allí a tiempo. **2** echarle [**25**] una carrera a ▷ *I'll race you!* ¡Te echo una carrera!
racecourse n hipódromo m
racer n bicicleta de carreras f
racetrack n **1** (*for cars*) circuito m **2** (*for cycles*) velódromo m
racial *adj* racial ▷ *racial discrimination* la discriminación racial

racing car n coche de carreras m

racing driver n piloto de carreras mf

racism n racismo m

racist adj racista
▸ n racista mf ▷ He's a racist. Es racista.

rack n (for luggage) portaequipajes m (pl portaequipajes)

racket n ❶ (for sport) raqueta f ▷ my tennis racket mi raqueta de tenis ❷ (informal: noise) jaleo m ▷ They're making a terrible racket. Están armando muchísimo jaleo.

racquet n raqueta f

radar n radar m

radiation n radiación f

radiator n radiador m

radio n radio f

> Although **radio** ends in -o, it is actually a feminine noun.

on the radio por la radio; **a radio station** una emisora de radio

radioactive adj radiactivo(-a)

radish n rábano m

RAF abbr (= Royal Air Force) fuerzas aéreas británicas fpl ▷ He's in the RAF. Está en las fuerzas aéreas británicas.

raffle n rifa f ▷ a raffle ticket una papeleta de rifa

raft n balsa f

rag n trapo m

rage n rabia f ▷ mad with rage loco de rabia; **to be in a rage** estar [22] furioso; **It's all the rage.** Es el último grito.

rail n ❶ (on stairs, bridge, balcony) barandilla f ❷ (for curtains) riel m; **by rail** por ferrocarril

railroad n (US) ferrocarril m;
railroad line la línea ferroviaria;
railroad station la estación de ferrocarril

railway n ferrocarril m; **railway line** la línea ferroviaria; **railway station** la estación de ferrocarril

rain n lluvia f ▷ in the rain bajo la lluvia
▸ vb llover [31] ▷ It rains a lot here. Aquí llueve mucho.; **It's raining.** Está lloviendo.

rainbow n arco iris m (pl arco iris)

raincoat n impermeable m

rainforest n selva tropical f

rainy adj lluvioso(-a)

raise vb ❶ levantar [25] ▷ He raised his hand. Levantó la mano. ❷ mejorar [25] ▷ They want to raise standards in schools. Quieren mejorar el nivel escolar. ❸ aumentar [25] ▷ to raise interest rates aumentar los tipos de interés; **to raise money** recaudar [25] fondos ▷ The school is raising money for a new gym. El colegio está recaudando fondos para un gimnasio nuevo.

raisin n pasa f

rally n ❶ (of people) concentración f (pl concentraciones) ❷ (sport) rally m (pl rallys) ❸ (in tennis) peloteo m

Ramadan n ramadán m

rambler n excursionista mf

ramp n rampa f

ran vb see **run**

rang vb see **ring**

range n (selection, variety) variedad f ▷ There's a wide range of colours. Hay una gran variedad de colores.;

It's out of my price range. Está fuera de mis posibilidades.; **a range of mountains** una cadena montañosa

▶ *vb* **to range from...to...** oscilar [25] entre...y... ▷ *Temperatures in summer range from 20 to 35 degrees.* En verano las temperaturas oscilan entre los 20 y los 35 grados.; **Tickets range from £5 to £20.** El precio de las entradas va de 5 a 20 libras esterlinas.

rap *n* rap *m*

rape *n* violación *f* (*pl* violaciones)

▶ *vb* violar [25]

rare *adj* ① (*unusual*) raro(-a) ② (*steak*) poco hecho(-a)

rash *adj* precipitado(-a)

rasher *n* **a rasher of bacon** una loncha de bacon

raspberry *n* frambuesa *f*

rat *n* rata *f*

rate *n* ① tarifa *f* ▷ *There are reduced rates for students.* Hay tarifas reducidas para estudiantes. ② tipo *m* ▷ *a high rate of interest* un tipo de interés elevado

▶ *vb* considerar [25]

rather *adv* bastante ▷ *I was rather disappointed.* Quedé bastante decepcionado.; **rather a lot of** mucho ▷ *I've got rather a lot of homework to do.* Tengo muchos deberes que hacer.; **I'd rather...** Preferiría... ▷ *I'd rather stay in tonight.* Preferiría no salir esta noche.

▌ **preferiría que** has to be followed by a verb in the subjunctive.

▷ *I'd rather he didn't come to the party.* Preferiría que no viniera a la fiesta.; **rather than...** en lugar de... ▷ *We decided to camp, rather than stay at a hotel.* Decidimos acampar, en lugar de quedarnos en un hotel.

raw *adj* (*food*) crudo(-a); **raw material** la materia prima

razor *n* maquinilla de afeitar *f*; **razor blade** la hoja de afeitar

RE *abbr* (= *Religious Education*) religión *f*

reach *n* **out of reach** fuera del alcance ▷ *Keep medicine out of reach of children.* Guárdense los medicamentos fuera del alcance de los niños.; **within easy reach of** a poca distancia de ▷ *The hotel is within easy reach of the town centre.* El hotel está a poca distancia del centro de la ciudad.

▶ *vb* ① llegar [37] a ▷ *We reached the hotel at seven o'clock.* Llegamos al hotel a las siete. ② (*get in touch*) ponerse [41] en contacto con ▷ *How can I reach you?* ¿Cómo puedo ponerme en contacto contigo?

reaction *n* reacción *f* (*pl* reacciones)

reactor *n* reactor *m* ▷ *a nuclear reactor* un reactor nuclear

read *vb* leer [30]

read out *vb* leer [30] ▷ *I was reading it out to the children.* Se lo estaba leyendo a los niños.

reading *n* lectura *f* ▷ *Reading is one of my hobbies.* La lectura es una de mis aficiones.; **I like reading.** Me gusta leer.

ready adj preparado(-a) ▷ The meal is ready. La comida está preparada.; **She's nearly ready.** Está casi lista.; **He's always ready to help.** Siempre está dispuesto a ayudar.; **to get ready** prepararse [25]; **to get something ready** preparar [25] algo ▷ He's getting the dinner ready. Está preparando la cena.

real adj ❶ verdadero(-a) ▷ the real reason el verdadero motivo ▷ It was a real nightmare. Fue una verdadera pesadilla.; **in real life** en la vida real ❷ auténtico(-a) ▷ It's real leather. Es piel auténtica.

realistic adj realista

reality n realidad f

reality TV n telerrealidad f

realize vb **to realize that...** darse [14] cuenta de que... ▷ We realized that something was wrong. Nos dimos cuenta de que algo iba mal.

really adv de verdad ▷ I'm learning German. — Really? Estoy aprendiendo alemán. — ¿De verdad?; **Do you really think so?** ¿Tú crees?; **She's really nice.** Es muy simpática.; **Do you want to go? — Not really.** ¿Quieres ir? — La verdad es que no.

realtor n (US) agente inmobiliario m, agente inmobiliaria f

reason n razón f (pl razones) ▷ There's no reason to think that he's dangerous. No hay razón para pensar que es peligroso.; **for security reasons** por motivos de seguridad; **That was the main reason I went.** Fui mayormente por eso.

reasonable adj ❶ razonable ▷ Be reasonable! ¡Sé razonable! ❷ bastante aceptable ▷ He wrote a reasonable essay. Escribió una redacción bastante aceptable.

reasonably adv bastante ▷ The team played reasonably well. El equipo jugó bastante bien.; **reasonably priced accommodation** alojamiento a precios razonables

reassure vb tranquilizar [13]

reassuring adj tranquilizador(a)

rebellious adj rebelde

receipt n ❶ (for goods bought) ticket m ❷ (for work done) recibo m

> Be careful not to translate **receipt** by receta.

receive vb recibir [58]

receiver n auricular m; **to pick up the receiver** descolgar [28]

recent adj reciente ▷ recent scientific discoveries los recientes descubrimientos científicos; **in recent weeks** en las últimas semanas

recently adv últimamente ▷ I haven't seen him recently. No lo he visto últimamente.; **until recently** hasta hace poco

reception n recepción f (pl recepciones)

receptionist n recepcionista mf ▷ She's a receptionist in a hotel. Es recepcionista en un hotel.

recipe n receta f

reckon vb creer [30] ▷ What do you reckon? ¿Tú qué crees?

recognize vb reconocer [**12**]

recommend vb recomendar [**39**]
▷ What do you recommend? ¿Qué me recomienda?

reconsider vb reconsiderar [**25**]

record n ❶ (sport) récord m (pl récords) ▷ the world record el récord mundial ❷ (music) disco m; **in record time** en un tiempo récord; **criminal record** los antecedentes penales ▷ He's got a criminal record. Tiene antecedentes penales.; **There is no record of your booking.** No tenemos constancia de su reserva.; **records** los archivos ▷ I'll check in the records. Miraré en los archivos.
▶ vb grabar [**25**] ▷ They've just recorded their new album. Acaban de grabar su nuevo álbum.

> Be careful not to translate **to record** by recordar.

recorded delivery n **to send something recorded delivery** enviar [**21**] algo por correo certificado

recorder n (musical instrument) flauta dulce f; **video recorder** el vídeo

recording n grabación f (pl grabaciones)

record player n tocadiscos m (pl tocadiscos)

recover vb recuperarse [**25**] ▷ He's recovering from a knee injury. Se está recuperando de una lesión de rodilla.

recovery n mejora f; **Best wishes for a speedy recovery!** ¡Que te mejores pronto!

rectangle n rectángulo m

rectangular adj rectangular

recycle vb reciclar [**25**]

recycling n reciclaje m

red adj rojo(-a) ▷ a red rose una rosa roja; **Gavin's got red hair.** Gavin es pelirrojo.; **to go through a red light** saltarse [**25**] un semáforo en rojo; **red wine** vino tinto

Red Cross n Cruz Roja f

redcurrant n grosella f

redecorate vb ❶ (with paint) volver [**59**] a pintar ❷ (with wallpaper) volver [**59**] a empapelar

red-haired adj pelirrojo(-a)

redo vb rehacer [**26**]

reduce vb reducir [**9**] ▷ at a reduced price a precio reducido; **'reduce speed now'** 'disminuya la velocidad'

reduction n reducción f (pl reducciones); **a five per cent reduction** un descuento del cinco por ciento; **'huge reductions!'** '¡grandes rebajas!'

redundant adj **to be made redundant** ser [**52**] despedido

refer vb **to refer to** referirse [**51**] a ▷ What are you referring to? ¿A qué te refieres?

referee n árbitro m, árbitra f

reference n ❶ referencia f ▷ He made no reference to the murder. No hizo referencia al homicidio. ❷ referencias fpl ▷ Would you please give me a reference? ¿Me podría facilitar referencias?; **a reference book** un libro de consulta

refill vb volver [59] a llenar ▷ He refilled my glass. Volvió a llenarme el vaso.

reflect vb ❶ (image) reflejar [25] ❷ (think) reflexionar [25]

reflection n (image) reflejo m

reflex n reflejo m

reflexive adj reflexivo(-a) ▷ a reflexive verb un verbo reflexivo

refreshing adj ❶ refrescante ▷ a refreshing drink una bebida refrescante ❷ estimulante ▷ It was a refreshing change. Fue un cambio estimulante.

refreshments npl refrigerio m

refrigerator n frigorífico m

refuge n refugio m

refugee n refugiado m, refugiada f

refund n reembolso m
▶ vb reembolsar [25]

refuse vb negarse [34] ▷ He refused to comment. Se negó a hacer comentarios.
▶ n basura f; **refuse collection** la recogida de basuras

regain vb to regain consciousness recobrar [25] el conocimiento

regard n with regard to con respecto a; **Give my regards to Alice.** Dale recuerdos a Alice.; **'with kind regards'** 'un cordial saludo'
▶ vb **They regarded it as unfair.** Lo consideraron injusto.; **as regards...** en lo que se refiere a...

regiment n regimiento m

region n región f (pl regiones)

regional adj regional

register n (in hotel) registro m; **to call the register** pasar [25] lista

▶ vb (to enrol) inscribirse [58]; **The car was registered in his wife's name.** El coche estaba matriculado a nombre de su esposa.

registered adj a registered letter una carta certificada

registration n (number) número de matrícula m

regret n I've got no regrets. No me arrepiento.
▶ vb arrepentirse [51] ▷ Try it, you won't regret it! ¡Pruébalo! ¡No te arrepentirás!; **to regret doing something** arrepentirse [51] de haber hecho algo ▷ I regret saying that. Me arrepiento de haber dicho eso.

regular adj ❶ regular ▷ at regular intervals a intervalos regulares; **to take regular exercise** hacer [26] ejercicio con regularidad ❷ normal ▷ a regular portion of fries una porción normal de patatas fritas

regularly adv con regularidad

rehearsal n ensayo m; **dress rehearsal** el ensayo general

rehearse vb ensayar [25]

reindeer n reno m

reject vb ❶ (proposal, invitation) rechazar [13] ❷ (idea, advice) desechar [25]; **I applied but they rejected me.** Presenté una solicitud, pero no me aceptaron.

related adj We're related. (by family) Somos parientes.; **Are you related to her?** ¿Eres pariente suyo?; **The two events are not related.** (connected) Los dos sucesos no están relacionados.

a b c d e f g h i j k l m n o p q r s t u v w x y z

relation n ❶ pariente mf ▷ He's a distant relation. Es un pariente lejano mío. ❷ relación f (pl relaciones) ▷ It has no relation to reality. No guarda ninguna relación con la realidad.; **in relation to** con relación a

relationship n relación f (pl relaciones) ▷ We have a good relationship. Tenemos una buena relación.; **I'm not in a relationship at the moment.** No tengo relaciones sentimentales con nadie en este momento.

relative n pariente mf

relatively adv relativamente

relax vb relajarse [25] ▷ I relax listening to music. Me relajo escuchando música.; **Relax! Everything's fine.** ¡Tranquilo! No pasa nada.

relaxation n esparcimiento m

relaxed adj relajado(-a)

relaxing adj relajante ▷ Having a bath is very relaxing. Darse un baño es muy relajante.; **I find cooking relaxing.** Cocinar me relaja.

release vb ❶ (prisoner) poner [41] en libertad ❷ (report, news) hacer [26] público ❸ (CD, DVD) sacar [48] a la venta
▶ n puesta en libertad f ▷ the release of the prisoners la puesta en libertad de los presos; **the band's latest release** el último trabajo del grupo

relevant adj (documents) pertinente; **That's not relevant.** Eso no viene al caso.; **to be relevant to something** guardar [25] relación con algo ▷ Education

should be relevant to real life. La educación debería guardar relación con la vida real.

reliable adj fiable ▷ He's not very reliable. No es una persona muy fiable.

relief n alivio m ▷ That's a relief! ¡Es un alivio!

relieved adj to be relieved sentir [51] un gran alivio ▷ I was relieved to hear he was better. Sentí un gran alivio al saber que estaba mejor.

religion n religión f (pl religiones) ▷ What religion are you? ¿De qué religión eres?

religious adj religioso(-a) ▷ I'm not religious. No soy religioso.

reluctant adj reacio(-a); **to be reluctant to do something** ser [52] reacio a hacer algo ▷ They were reluctant to help us. Eran reacios a ayudarnos.

reluctantly adv de mala gana ▷ She reluctantly accepted. Aceptó de mala gana.

rely on vb confiar [21] en ▷ I'm relying on you. Confío en ti.

remain vb permanecer [12] ▷ to remain silent permanecer callado

remaining adj restante ▷ the remaining ingredients los ingredientes restantes

remark n comentario m

remarkable adj extraordinario(-a)

remarkably adv extraordinariamente

remember vb ❶ acordarse [11] ▷ I don't remember. No me acuerdo. ❷ acordarse [11] de ▷ I can't *remember his name.* No me acuerdo de su nombre. ▷ *I don't remember saying that.* No me acuerdo de haber dicho eso.

> In Spanish you often say **no te olvides** – 'don't forget' – instead of 'remember'.
> ▷ *Remember to write your name on the form.* No te olvides de escribir tu nombre en el impreso.

remind *vb* recordar [25] ▷ *The scenery here reminds me of Scotland.* Este paisaje me recuerda a Escocia.

> When talking about reminding someone to do something, **recordar a alguien que** has to be followed by a verb in the subjunctive.
> ▷ *Remind me to speak to Daniel.* Recuérdame que hable con Daniel.

remote *adj* remoto(-a) ▷ *a remote village* un pueblo remoto

remote control *n* mando a distancia m

remove *vb* quitar [25] ▷ *Please remove your bag from my seat.* Por favor, quite su bolsa de mi asiento.

renew *vb* (passport, licence) renovar [11]

renewable *adj* renovable

renovate *vb* renovar [11] ▷ *The building's been renovated.* Han renovado el edificio.

rent *n* alquiler m
▶ *vb* alquilar [25] ▷ *We rented a car.* Alquilamos un coche.

reorganize *vb* reorganizar [13]

rep *n* (= representative) representante *mf*

repaid *vb see* **repay**

repair *vb* reparar [25] ▷ *I got the washing machine repaired.* Me repararon la lavadora.
▶ *n* reparación *f* (pl reparaciones)

repay *vb* (money) devolver [59]; **I don't know how I can ever repay you.** No sé cómo podré devolverle el favor.

repeat *vb* repetir [38]
▶ *n* reposición *f* (pl reposiciones)

repeatedly *adv* repetidamente

repetitive *adj* repetitivo(-a)

replace *vb* ❶ sustituir [10]
❷ (batteries) cambiar [25]

replay *n* **There will be a replay on Friday.** El partido se volverá a jugar el viernes.
▶ *vb* ❶ (match) volver [59] a jugar ❷ (track) volver [59] a poner

reply *n* respuesta *f*
▶ *vb* responder [8]

report *n* ❶ (of event) informe m ❷ (news report) reportaje m ▷ *a report in the paper* un reportaje en el periódico ❸ (at school) notas fpl; **I got a good report this term.** He sacado buenas notas este trimestre.
▶ *vb* ❶ dar [14] parte de ▷ *I reported the theft to the police.* Di parte del robo a la policía. ❷ presentarse [25] ▷ *Report to reception when you arrive.* Preséntese en recepción cuando llegue.; **I'll report back as soon as I hear anything.** En cuanto tenga noticias, te lo haré saber.

reporter *n* periodista *mf*

represent vb ❶ (client, country) representar [25] a ❷ (change, achievement) representar [25]

representative adj representativo(-a)

reptile n reptil m

republic n república f

reputation n reputación f (pl reputaciones)

request n petición f (pl peticiones)
▸ vb solicitar [25]

require vb requerir [51] ▷ Her job requires a lot of patience. Su trabajo requiere mucha paciencia.

rescue vb rescatar [25]
▸ n rescate m ▷ a rescue operation una operación de rescate; **to come to somebody's rescue** ir [27] en auxilio de alguien

research n investigación f (pl investigaciones) ▷ He's doing research. Realiza trabajos de investigación.; **She's doing some research in the library.** Está investigando en la biblioteca.

resemblance n parecido m

resent vb I resent being dependent on her. Me molesta tener que depender de ella.

reservation n reserva f ▷ I've got a reservation for two nights. Tengo una reserva para dos noches.; **I've got reservations about the idea.** Tengo mis reservas al respecto.

reserve n ❶ (place) reserva f ▷ a nature reserve una reserva natural ❷ (person) suplente mf ▷ I was reserve in the game last Saturday. Yo era suplente en el partido del sábado.

▸ vb reservar [25] ▷ I'd like to reserve a table for tomorrow evening. Quisiera reservar una mesa para mañana por la noche.

reserved adj reservado(-a) ▷ He's quite reserved. Es bastante reservado.

resident n vecino m, vecina f ▷ local residents los vecinos del lugar

residential adj residencial ▷ a residential area una zona residencial

resign vb dimitir [58]

resit vb volver [59] a presentarse a ▷ I'm resitting the exam in December. Me vuelvo a presentar al examen en diciembre.

resolution n propósito m ▷ Have you made any New Year's resolutions? ¿Has hecho algún buen propósito para el Año Nuevo?

resort n centro turístico m ▷ a resort on the Costa del Sol un centro turístico en la Costa del Sol; **as a last resort** como último recurso

resource n recurso m

respect n respeto m; **in some respects** en algunos aspectos
▸ vb respetar [25]

respectable adj ❶ respetable ▷ a respectable family una familia respetable ❷ decente ▷ My marks were quite respectable. Mis notas eran bastante decentes.

responsibility n responsabilidad f

responsible adj responsable ▷ You should be more responsible! ¡Deberías ser más responsable!; **to be responsible for something** ser [52] responsable de algo

▷ *He's responsible for booking the tickets.* Es responsable de reservar las entradas.; **It's a responsible job.** Es un puesto de responsabilidad.

rest n ❶ descanso m ▷ *five minutes' rest* cinco minutos de descanso; **to have a rest** descansar [**25**] ▷ *We stopped to have a rest.* Nos paramos a descansar. ❷ resto m ▷ *the rest of the money* el resto del dinero; **the rest of them** los demás ▷ *The rest of them went swimming.* Los demás fueron a nadar.

▷ *vb* ❶ descansar [**25**] ▷ *She's resting in her room.* Está descansando en su habitación.; **He has to rest his knee.** Tiene que descansar la rodilla. ❷ apoyar [**25**] ▷ *I rested my bike against the window.* Apoyé la bicicleta en la ventana.

restaurant n restaurante m; **restaurant car** el vagón restaurante

restore *vb* (building, painting) restaurar [**25**]

restrict *vb* limitar [**25**]

rest room n (US) servicios mpl

result n resultado m ▷ *my exam results* los resultados de mis exámenes

résumé n (US) currículum vitae m

retire *vb* jubilarse [**25**]

retired *adj* jubilado(-a) ▷ *She's retired.* Está jubilada.

retirement n **since his retirement** desde que se jubiló

return n ❶ regreso m ▷ *his sudden return home* su repentino regreso a casa; **the return journey** el viaje

de vuelta ❷ billete de ida y vuelta m ▷ *A return to Bilbao, please.* Un billete de ida y vuelta a Bilbao, por favor.; **in return** a cambio ▷ *She helps me and I help her in return.* Me ayuda y yo la ayudo a cambio.; **in return for** a cambio de; **Many happy returns!** ¡Que cumplas muchos más!

▷ *vb* ❶ volver [**59**] ▷ *He returned to Spain the following year.* Volvió a España al año siguiente. ❷ *(give back)* devolver [**59**]

reunion n reunión f (pl reuniones) ▷ *We had a big family reunion at Christmas.* Tuvimos una gran reunión familiar en Navidad.

reuse *vb* reutilizar [**13**]

reveal *vb* revelar [**25**]

revenge n venganza f ▷ *in revenge* como venganza; **to take revenge** vengarse [**37**] ▷ *They planned to take revenge on him.* Planearon vengarse de él.

reverse *vb* (car) dar [**14**] marcha atrás ▷ *He reversed without looking.* Dio marcha atrás sin mirar.; **to reverse the charges** llamar [**25**] a cobro revertido

▷ *adj* inverso(-a) ▷ *in reverse order* en orden inverso; **in reverse gear** en marcha atrás; **reverse charge call** llamada a cobro revertido

review n ❶ *(of policy, salary)* revisión f (pl revisiones) ❷ *(of subject)* repaso m

revise *vb* estudiar [**25**] para un examen ▷ *I haven't started revising yet.* Todavía no he empezado a estudiar para el examen.

a
b
c
d
e
f
g
h
i
j
k
l
m
n
o
p
q
r
s
t
u
v
w
x
y
z

ENGLISH > SPANISH

revision n **Have you done a lot of revision?** ¿Has estudiado mucho para el examen?

revolting adj repugnante

revolution n revolución f (pl revoluciones)

reward n recompensa f

rewarding adj gratificante ▷ a rewarding job un trabajo gratificante

rewind vb rebobinar [25] ▷ to rewind a cassette rebobinar una cinta

rhinoceros n rinoceronte m

rhubarb n ruibarbo m

rhythm n ritmo m

rib n costilla f

ribbon n cinta f

rice n arroz m; **rice pudding** el arroz con leche

rich adj rico(-a); **the rich** los ricos

rid vb to **get rid of** deshacerse [26] de ▷ I want to get rid of some old clothes. Quiero deshacerme de algunas ropas viejas.

ridden vb see **ride**

ride n **to go for a ride** (1) (on horse) montar [25] a caballo (2) (on bike) dar [14] un paseo en bicicleta ▷ We went for a bike ride. Fuimos a dar un paseo en bicicleta.; **It's a short bus ride to the town centre.** El centro de la ciudad queda cerca en autobús.
▶ vb montar [25] a caballo ▷ I'm learning to ride. Estoy aprendiendo a montar a caballo.; **to ride a bike** ir [27] en bicicleta ▷ Can you ride a bike? ¿Sabes ir en bicicleta?

rider n ❶ jinete m ▷ She's a good rider. Ella monta muy bien a caballo. ❷ (cyclist) ciclista mf

ridiculous adj ridículo(-a)

riding n (as sport) equitación f ▷ a riding school una escuela de equitación; **to go riding** montar [25] a caballo

rifle n rifle m

right adj, adv

> There are several ways of translating 'right'. Scan the examples to find one that is similar to what you want to say.

❶ correcto(-a) ▷ the right answer la respuesta correcta ❷ (place, time) adecuado(-a) ▷ We're on the right train. Estamos en el tren adecuado.; **Is this the right road for Ávila?** ¿Vamos bien por aquí para Ávila?; **to be right** (1) (person) tener [53] razón ▷ You were right! ¡Tenías razón! (2) (statement, opinion) ser [52] verdad ▷ That's right! ¡Es verdad!; **Do you have the right time?** ¿Tienes hora? ❸ bien ▷ Am I pronouncing it right? ¿Lo pronuncio bien?; **I think you did the right thing.** Creo que hiciste bien. ❹ (not left) derecho(-a) ▷ my right hand mi mano derecha ❺ (turn, look) a la derecha ▷ Turn right at the traffic lights. Cuando llegues al semáforo dobla a la derecha.; **Right! Let's get started!** ¡Bueno! ¡Empecemos!; **right away** enseguida ▷ I'll do it right away. Lo haré enseguida.
▶ n ❶ derecho m ▷ You've got no

right to do that. No tienes derecho de hacer eso. ❷ derecha f; **on the right** a la derecha ▷ *on the right of Mr Yates* a la derecha del Sr. Yates

right-hand adj **the right-hand side** la derecha ▷ *It's on the right-hand side.* Está a la derecha.

right-handed adj diestro(-a)

ring n ❶ anillo m ▷ *a gold ring* un anillo de oro; **a wedding ring** una alianza ❷ círculo m ▷ *to stand in a ring* formar un círculo ❸ (at door) timbrazo m; **After three or four rings the door was opened.** Después de tres o cuatro timbrazos la puerta se abrió.; **There was a ring at the door.** Se oyó el timbre de la puerta.; **to ring somebody** llamar [25] a alguien por teléfono

▶ vb ❶ llamar [25] ▷ *Your mother rang this morning.* Tu madre llamó esta mañana.; **to ring somebody** llamar [25] a alguien ❷ sonar [11] ▷ *The phone's ringing.* El teléfono está sonando.; **to ring the bell** tocar [48] el timbre

ring back vb volver [59] a llamar ▷ *I'll ring back later.* Volveré a llamar más tarde.

ring up vb llamar [25] por teléfono

ring binder n carpeta de anillas f

ringtone n tono de llamada m

rinse n enjuagar [37]

riot n disturbio m

▶ vb causar [25] disturbios

rip vb rasgar [37] ▷ *I've ripped my jeans.* Me he rasgado los vaqueros. ▷ *My shirt's ripped.* Mi camisa está rasgada.

rip off vb (informal) timar [25] ▷ *The hotel ripped us off.* En el hotel nos timaron.

rip up vb hacer [26] pedazos ▷ *He read the note and then ripped it up.* Leyó la nota y la hizo pedazos.

ripe adj maduro(-a)

rip-off n **It's a rip-off!** (informal) ¡Es un timo!

rise n ❶ (in prices, temperature) subida f ▷ *a sudden rise in temperature* una repentina subida de las temperaturas ❷ (pay rise) aumento m

▶ vb ❶ (increase) subir [58] ▷ *Prices are rising.* Los precios están subiendo. ❷ salir [49] ▷ *The sun rises early in June.* En junio el sol sale temprano.

risk n riesgo m; **to take risks** correr [8] riesgos; **It's at your own risk.** Es a tu propia cuenta y riesgo.

▶ vb arriesgarse [37] ▷ *I wouldn't risk it if I were you.* Yo en tu lugar no me arriesgaría.

rival n rival mf

▶ adj ❶ rival ▷ *a rival gang* una banda rival ❷ competidor(a) ▷ *a rival company* una empresa competidora

river n río m

road n ❶ carretera f ▷ *There's a lot of traffic on the roads.* Hay mucho tráfico en las carreteras. ▷ *a road accident* un accidente de carretera ❷ (street) calle f ▷ *They live across the road.* Viven al otro lado de la calle.

road map n mapa de carreteras m
▮ Although **mapa** ends in -a, it is
actually a masculine noun.

road rage n conducta agresiva al
volante f

road sign n señal de tráfico f

roadworks npl obras fpl ▷ There are
roadworks on the motorway. Hay
obras en la autopista.

roast adj asado(-a) ▷ roast chicken
pollo asado; **roast pork** el asado
de cerdo; **roast beef** el rosbif

rob vb to rob somebody robar [25]
a alguien ▷ I've been robbed. Me han
robado.

robber n ladrón m, ladrona f; **a
bank robber** un asaltante de
bancos (f una asaltante de bancos)

robbery n robo m; **a bank robbery**
un asalto a un banco; **an armed
robbery** un asalto a mano armada

robin n petirrojo m

robot n robot m (pl robots)

rock n ❶ roca f ▷ I sat on a rock. Me
senté encima de una roca.
❷ (stone) piedra f ❸ rock m ▷ a rock
concert un concierto de rock; **rock
and roll** el rock and roll; **a stick of
rock** una barra de caramelo

rocket n (spacecraft, firework)
cohete m

rocking chair n mecedora f

rocking horse n caballo de
balancín m

rod n (for fishing) caña de pescar f

rode vb see **ride**

role n papel m ▷ to play a role hacer
un papel

role play n juego de roles m ▷ to do
a role play hacer un juego de roles

roll n ❶ rollo m ▷ a toilet roll un rollo
de papel higiénico; ❷ panecillo m
▷ a cheese roll un panecillo de queso
▶ vb (ball, bottle) rodar [11]

rollercoaster n montaña rusa f

roller skates npl patines de
ruedas mpl

roller-skating n patinaje sobre
ruedas m; **to go roller-skating** ir
[27] a patinar

Roman adj, n romano(-a) ▷ the
Roman empire el imperio romano;
the Romans los romanos

Roman Catholic n católico m,
católica f ▷ He's a Roman Catholic.
Es católico.

romance n ❶ (novels) novelas
románticas fpl ▷ I read a lot of
romance. Leo muchas novelas
románticas. ❷ romanticismo m
▷ the romance of Paris el
romanticismo de París; **a holiday
romance** un romance de verano

Romania n Rumania f

Romanian adj rumano(-a)

romantic adj romántico(-a)

roof n techo m

roof rack n baca f

room n ❶ habitación f (pl
habitaciones) ▷ She's in her room.
Está en su habitación.; **a single
room** una habitación individual;
a double room una habitación
doble ❷ (in school) sala f ▷ the music
room la sala de música ❸ espacio m
▷ There's no room for that box. No
hay espacio para esa caja.

root n raíz f (pl raíces)

rope n cuerda f

rose vb see **rise**
▶ n (flower) rosa f

rot vb pudrirse [58] ▷ The wood had started to rot. La madera había empezado a pudrirse.; **Sugar rots your teeth.** El azúcar pica los dientes.

rotten adj podrido(-a) ▷ A rotten apple una manzana podrida; **rotten weather** un tiempo asqueroso; **That's a rotten thing to do!** ¡Eso está fatal!; **to feel rotten** sentirse [51] fatal

rough adj, adv, ① áspero(-a) ▷ My hands are rough. Tengo las manos ásperas. ② violento(-a) ▷ Rugby's a rough sport. El rugby es un deporte violento. ③ peligroso(-a) ▷ It's a rough area. Es una zona peligrosa. ④ agitado(-a) ▷ The sea was rough. El mar estaba agitado. ⑤ aproximado(-a) ▷ I've got a rough idea. Tengo una idea aproximada.; **to feel rough** sentirse [51] mal; **to sleep rough** dormir [17] en la calle ▷ A lot of people sleep rough in London. Mucha gente duerme en la calle en Londres.

roughly adv aproximadamente ▷ It weighs roughly 20 kilos. Pesa aproximadamente 20 kilos.

round adj, adv, prep ① redondo(-a) ▷ a round table una mesa redonda ② alrededor de ▷ We were sitting round the table. Estábamos sentados alrededor de la mesa. ▷ She wore a scarf round her neck. Llevaba una bufanda alrededor del cuello.; **It's just round the corner.** Está a la vuelta de la esquina.; **to go round**

to somebody's house ir [27] a casa de alguien; **to have a look round** echar [25] un vistazo ▷ We had a look round the shoe department. Echamos un vistazo a la sección de zapatos.; **to go round a museum** visitar [25] un museo; **round here** por aquí cerca ▷ He lives round here. Vive aquí cerca. ▷ Is there a chemist's round here? ¿Hay alguna farmacia por aquí cerca?; **all round** por todos lados ▷ There were vineyards all round. Había viñedos por todos lados.; **all year round** todo el año; **round about** alrededor de ▷ It costs round about £100. Cuesta alrededor de 100 libras esterlinas.; **round about eight o'clock** hacia las ocho
▶ n ① (of tournament) vuelta f ② (of boxing match) round m (pl rounds); **a round of golf** una vuelta de golf; **a round of drinks** una ronda de bebidas ▷ He bought them a round of drinks. Les invitó a una ronda de bebidas.; **I think it's my round.** Creo que me toca pagar.

roundabout n ① (at junction) rotonda f ② (at funfair) tiovivo m

rounders nsg **Rounders is similar to baseball.** Rounders es parecido al béisbol

● Rounders is not played in Spain.

round trip n (US) viaje de ida y vuelta m; **a round-trip ticket** un billete de ida y vuelta

route n itinerario m ▷ We are planning our route. Estamos planeando el itinerario.; **bus route** el recorrido del autobús

a
b
c
d
e
f
g
h
i
j
k
l
m
n
o
p
q
r
s
t
u
v
w
x
y
z

routine n rutina f ▷ *my daily routine* mi rutina diaria

row (1) n ❶ (racket) jaleo m ▷ *What's that terrible row?* ¿Qué es ese jaleo tan tremendo? ❷ (quarrel) pelea f; **to have a row** pelearse [**25**] ▷ *They've had a row.* Se han peleado.

row (2) n ❶ (line) hilera f ▷ *a row of houses* una hilera de casas ❷ (of people, seats) fila f ▷ *in the front row* en primera fila; **five times in a row** cinco veces seguidas

row (3) vb (boat) remar [**25**]

rowboat n (US) barca de remos f

rowing n remo m ▷ *My hobby is rowing.* Mi hobby es el remo.; **rowing boat** la barca de remos

royal adj real ▷ *the royal family* la familia real

rub vb ❶ (stain) frotar [**25**] ❷ (part of body) restregarse [**37**] ▷ *Don't rub your eyes.* No te restriegues los ojos.

rubber n ❶ goma f ▷ *rubber soles* suelas de goma ❷ (eraser) goma de borrar f ▷ *Can I borrow your rubber?* ¿Me prestas la goma?; **a rubber band** una goma elástica

rubbish n ❶ basura f ▷ *They sell a lot of rubbish at the market.* Venden mucha basura en el mercado.; **That magazine is rubbish!** ¡Esa revista es una porquería! (*informal*) ❷ estupideces fpl ▷ *Don't talk rubbish!* ¡No digas estupideces!; **That's a load of rubbish!** ¡Son puras tonterías!; **rubbish bin** el cubo de la basura; **rubbish dump** el vertedero
▶ adj **They're a rubbish team!** ¡Es un equipo que no vale nada!

rucksack n mochila f

rude adj grosero(-a) ▷ *He was very rude to me.* Fue muy grosero conmigo.; **It's rude to interrupt.** Es de mala educación interrumpir.; **a rude joke** un chiste verde; **a rude word** una palabrota

rug n ❶ (carpet) alfombra f ❷ (travelling rug) manta de viaje f

rugby n rugby m ▷ *He enjoys playing rugby.* Le gusta jugar al rugby.

ruin n ruina f ▷ *the ruins of the castle* las ruinas del castillo; **in ruins** en ruinas
▶ vb ❶ estropear [**25**] ▷ *It ruined my holiday.* Nos estropeó las vacaciones. ❷ (financially) arruinar [**25**]

rule n ❶ regla f ▷ *the rules of grammar* las reglas de la gramática; **as a rule** por regla general ❷ norma f ▷ *It's against the rules.* Va en contra de las normas.

ruler n regla f

rum n ron m

rumour (US rumor) n rumor m

run n **to go for a run** salir [**49**] a correr ▷ *I go for a run every morning.* Salgo a correr todas las mañanas.; **I did a 10-kilometre run.** Corrí 10 kilómetros.; **The criminals are still on the run.** Los delincuentes están todavía en fuga.; **in the long run** a la larga
▶ vb ❶ correr [**8**] ▷ *I ran five kilometres.* Corrí cinco kilómetros.; **to run a marathon** correr [**8**] un maratón ❷ dirigir [**16**] ▷ *He runs a large company.* Dirige una gran empresa. ❸ organizar [**13**] ▷ *They*

run music courses in the holidays. Organizan cursos de música en las vacaciones. ❹ *(by car)* llevar [25] ▷ I can run you to the station. Te puedo llevar a la estación.; **Don't leave the tap running.** No dejen el grifo abierto. (No dejen la llave abierta. *LatAm)*; **to run a bath** llenar [25] la bañera; **The buses stop running at midnight.** Los autobuses dejan de funcionar a medianoche.

run away *vb* huir [10] ▷ They ran away before the police came. Huyeron antes de que llegara la policía.

run out *vb* **Time is running out.** Queda poco tiempo.; **to run out of something** quedarse [25] sin algo ▷ We ran out of money. Nos quedamos sin dinero.

run over *vb* atropellar [25]; **to get run over** ser [52] atropellado

rung *vb see* **ring**

runner *n* corredor *m*, corredora *f*

runner-up *n* subcampeón *m* (*pl* subcampeones), subcampeona *f*

running *n* footing *m* ▷ Running is my favourite sport. El footing es mi deporte favorito.; **to go running** hacer footing

runway *n* pista de aterrizaje *f*

rush *n* prisa *f* ▷ I'm in a rush. Tengo prisa. ▷ There's no rush. No corre prisa.; **to do something in a rush** hacer [26] algo deprisa
▶ *vb* ❶ correr [8] ▷ Everyone rushed outside. Todos corrieron hacia fuera. ❷ precipitarse [25] ▷ There's no need to rush. No hay por qué precipitarse.

rush hour *n* hora punta *f* (hora pico *f LatAm*)

Russia *n* Rusia *f*

Russian *adj* ruso(-a)
▶ *n* ❶ *(person)* ruso *m*, rusa *f* ▷ the Russians los rusos ❸ *(language)* ruso *m*

rust *n* óxido *m*

rusty *adj* oxidado(-a)

rye *n* centeno *m*; **rye bread** el pan de centeno

S

sack n (bag) saco m ▷ a sack of potatoes un saco de patatas; **to give somebody the sack** despedir **[38]** a alguien; **He got the sack.** Lo despidieron.
▶ vb **to sack somebody** despedir **[38]** a alguien ▷ He was sacked. Lo despidieron.

sacred adj sagrado(-a)

sacrifice n sacrificio m

sad adj triste

saddle n ❶ (for horse) silla de montar f ❷ (on bike) sillín m

saddlebag n ❶ (on bike) cartera f ❷ (for horse) alforja f

safe n caja fuerte f (pl cajas fuertes)
▶ adj ❶ seguro(-a) ▷ This car isn't safe. Este coche no es seguro. ❷ a salvo ▷ You're safe now. Ya estás a salvo.; **to feel safe** sentirse **[51]**

protegido; **Is the water safe to drink?** ¿Es agua potable?; **Don't worry, it's perfectly safe.** No te preocupes, no tiene el menor peligro.; **safe sex** el sexo sin riesgo

safety n seguridad f; **safety belt** el cinturón de seguridad; **safety pin** el imperdible (el seguro LatAm)

Sagittarius n (sign) Sagitario m; **I'm Sagittarius.** Soy sagitario.

said vb see **say**

sail n vela f
▶ vb ❶ navegar **[37]** ▷ to sail around the world dar la vuelta al mundo navegando ❷ zarpar **[25]** ▷ The boat sails at eight o'clock. El barco zarpa a las ocho.

sailing n (sport) vela f; **to go sailing** hacer **[26]** vela; **sailing boat** el barco de vela

sailor n marinero m ▷ He's a sailor. Es marinero.

saint n santo m, santa f

When used before a man's name, the word **Santo** is shortened to **San**, the exceptions being **Santo Tomás** and **Santo Domingo**.

▷ Saint John San Juan

sake n **for the sake of the children** por el bien de los niños; **For goodness sake!** ¡Por el amor de Dios!

salad n ensalada f; **salad cream** la mayonesa; **salad dressing** el aliño para la ensalada

salary n sueldo m

sale n ❶ rebajas fpl ▷ There's a sale on at Harrods. En Harrods están de rebajas. ❷ venta f ▷ Newspaper sales have fallen. Ha descendido la venta de periódicos.; **on sale** a la venta; **The house is for sale.** La casa está en venta.; **'for sale'** 'se vende'

sales assistant n dependiente m, dependienta f

salesman n ❶ (commercial) representante m ▷ *an insurance salesman* un representante de seguros ❷ (sales assistant) dependiente m; **a car salesman** un vendedor de coches

saleswoman n ❶ (commercial) representante f ▷ *an insurance saleswoman* una representante de seguros ❷ (sales assistant) dependienta f

salmon n salmón m (pl salmones)

salon n salón m (pl salones) ▷ *beauty salon* salón de belleza

salt n sal f

salty adj salado(-a)

Salvation Army n Ejército de Salvación m

same adj mismo(-a) ▷ *the same model* el mismo modelo; **It's not the same.** No es lo mismo.; **They're exactly the same.** Son exactamente iguales.; **The house is still the same.** La casa sigue igual.

sample n muestra f ▷ *a free sample of perfume* una muestra gratuita de perfume

sand n arena f

sandal n sandalia f ▷ *a pair of sandals* unas sandalias

sand castle n castillo de arena m

sandwich n ❶ (with sliced bread) sandwich m (pl sandwiches) ❷ (with French bread) bocadillo m

sang vb see **sing**

sanitary towel n compresa f

sank vb see **sink**

Santa Claus n Papá Noel m

sarcastic adj sarcástico(-a)

sardine n sardina f

sat vb see **sit**

satchel n cartera f

satellite n satélite m ▷ *by satellite* vía satélite; **a satellite dish** una antena parabólica; **satellite television** la televisión vía satélite

satisfactory adj satisfactorio(-a)

satisfied adj satisfecho(-a)

Saturday n sábado m (pl sábados) ▷ *I saw her on Saturday.* La vi el sábado. ▷ *every Saturday* todos los sábados ▷ *last Saturday* el sábado pasado ▷ *next Saturday* el sábado que viene ▷ *on Saturdays* los sábados; **I've got a Saturday job.** Tengo un trabajo los sábados.

sauce n ❶ salsa f ▷ *tomato sauce* salsa de tomate ❷ crema f ▷ *chocolate sauce* crema de chocolate

saucepan n cazo m

saucer n platillo m

Saudi Arabia n Arabia Saudí f

sausage n salchicha f; **a sausage roll** un pastelito de salchicha

save vb ❶ (money, time) ahorrar [25] ▷ *I saved money by staying in youth hostels.* Ahorré dinero yendo a albergues juveniles. ▷ *I've saved £50 already.* Ya llevo ahorradas 50 libras. ▷ *It saved us time.* Nos

a b c d e f g h i j k l m n o p q r s t u v w x y z

ahorró tiempo.; **We went in a taxi to save time.** Para ganar tiempo fuimos en taxi. ❷ *(person in danger, lives)* salvar [**25**] ▷ *Doctors saved her from cancer.* Los médicos la salvaron del cáncer.; **Luckily, all the passengers were saved.** Afortunadamente, todos los pasajeros se salvaron. ❸ *(computing)* guardar [**25**] ▷ *Don't forget to save your work regularly.* No te olvides de guardar tu trabajo de vez en cuando.

save up *vb* ahorrar [**25**] ▷ *I'm saving up for a new bike.* Estoy ahorrando para una bici nueva.

savings *npl* ahorros *mpl*

savoury *adj* salado(-a) ▷ *Is it sweet or savoury?* ¿Es dulce o salado?

saw *vb* see **see**
▷ *n* sierra *f*

saxophone *n* saxofón *m* (*pl* saxofones)

say *vb* decir [**15**] ▷ *To say yes* decir que sí ▷ *What did he say?* ¿Qué dijo él?; **Could you say that again?** ¿Podrías repetir eso?

saying *n* dicho *m*

scale *n* escala *f* ▷ *a large-scale map* un mapa a gran escala; **He underestimated the scale of the problem.** Ha subestimado la envergadura del problema.

scales *npl* ❶ *(in kitchen)* peso *m* ❷ *(in shop)* báscula *f*; **bathroom scales** la báscula de baño

scampi *npl* gambas rebozadas *fpl*

scandal *n* ❶ *(outrage)* escándalo *m* ▷ *It caused a scandal.* Causó escándalo. ❷ *(gossip)* habladurías

fpl ▷ *It's just scandal.* No son más que habladurías.

scar *n* cicatriz *f* (*pl* cicatrices)

scarce *adj* escaso(-a) ▷ *scarce resources* recursos escasos; **Jobs are scarce.** Escasean los trabajos.

scarcely *adv* apenas ▷ *I scarcely knew him.* Apenas lo conocía.

scare *n* susto *m* ▷ *We got a bit of a scare.* Nos pegamos un susto.; **a bomb scare** una amenaza de bomba
▷ *vb* asustar [**25**] ▷ *You scared me!* ¡Me has asustado!

scarecrow *n* espantapájaros *m* (*pl* espantapájaros)

scared *adj* **to be scared** tener [**53**] miedo ▷ *Are you scared of him?* ¿Le tienes miedo?; **I was scared stiff.** Estaba muerto de miedo.

scarf *n* ❶ *(woollen)* bufanda *f* ❷ *(light)* pañuelo *m*

scary *adj* **It was really scary.** Daba verdadero miedo.; **a scary film** una película de miedo

scene *n* ❶ escena *f* ▷ *love scenes* las escenas de amor ❷ lugar *m* ▷ *at the scene of the crime* en el lugar del crimen; **to make a scene** montar [**25**] el número

scenery *n* paisaje *m*

schedule *n* programa *m*

> Although *programa* ends in -a, it is actually a masculine noun.

▷ *a production schedule* un programa de producción; **There's a tight schedule for this project.** Este proyecto tiene un calendario muy justo.; **a busy schedule** una agenda muy apretada; **on schedule** sin retraso; **to be behind schedule** ir [27] con retraso

scheduled flight n vuelo regular m

scheme n plan m ▷ a crazy scheme he dreamed up un plan descabellado que se le ocurrió

scholarship n beca f

school n ① (for children) colegio m ▷ at school en el colegio ▷ to go to school ir al colegio ② (at university) facultad f

schoolbook n libro de texto m

schoolboy n colegial m

schoolchildren npl colegiales mpl

schoolgirl n colegiala f

science n ciencia f

science fiction n ciencia ficción f

scientific adj científico(-a)

scientist n científico m, científica f

scissors npl tijeras fpl ▷ a pair of scissors unas tijeras

scooter n ① (motorcycle) Vespa® f ② (child's toy) patinete m

score n ① (in test, competition) puntuación f (pl puntuaciones) ② (in game, match) resultado m ▷ The score was three nil. El resultado fue de tres a cero.; **What's the score?** ¿Cómo van? ▶ vb ③ marcar [48] ▷ to score a goal marcar un gol; **to score a point** anotar [25] un punto; **to score six out of ten** sacar [48] una puntuación de seis sobre diez ④ llevar [25] el tanteo ▷ Who's going to score? ¿Quién va a llevar el tanteo?

Scorpio n (sign) Escorpio m; **I'm Scorpio.** Soy escorpio.

Scot n (person) escocés m, escocesa f

Scotch tape® n (US) celo m

Scotland n Escocia f

Scots adj escocés (f escocesa, pl escoceses) ▷ a Scots accent un acento escocés

Scotsman n escocés m (pl escoceses)

Scotswoman n escocesa f

Scottish adj escocés (f escocesa, pl escoceses) ▷ a Scottish accent un acento escocés

scout n explorador m, exploradora f

scrambled eggs npl huevos revueltos mpl

scrap n ① trocito m ▷ a scrap of paper un trocito de papel ② (fight) pelea f; **scrap iron** la chatarra ▶ vb desechar [25]

scrapbook n álbum de recortes m (pl álbumes de recortes)

scratch vb ① (when itchy) rascarse [48] ▷ Stop scratching! ¡Deja de rascarte! ② (cut) arañar [25] ▷ He scratched his arm on the bushes. Se arañó el brazo con las zarzas. ③ (scrape) rayar [25] ▷ You'll scratch the worktop with that knife. Vas a rayar la encimera con ese cuchillo. ▶ n (on skin, floor) arañazo m; **to start from scratch** partir [58] de cero; **a scratch card** una tarjeta de 'rasque y gane'

scream n grito m ▶ vb gritar [25]

screen n (television, cinema, computer) pantalla f

screw n tornillo m

screwdriver n destornillador m

scribble vb garabatear [25]

scrub vb fregar [34]

sculpture n escultura f

sea n mar m ▷ by sea por mar ▷ a house by the sea una casa junto al mar

> The word **mar** is masculine in most cases, but in some set expressions it is feminine.

▷ The fishermen put out to sea. Los pescadores se hicieron a la mar.

seafood n marisco m ▷ I don't like seafood. No me gusta el marisco.; **a seafood restaurant** una marisquería

seagull n gaviota f

seal n ❶ (animal) foca f ❷ (on letter) sello m
> ▶ vb sellar [25]

seaman n marinero m

search vb ❶ buscar [48] ▷ They're searching for the missing climbers. Están buscando a los alpinistas desaparecidos. ❷ registrar [25] ▷ The police searched him for drugs. La policía lo registró en busca de drogas.; **They searched the woods for the little girl.** Rastrearon el bosque en busca de la niña.
> ▶ n ❶ búsqueda f; **to go in search of** ir [27] en busca de ❷ (inspection) registro m

search party n equipo de búsqueda m

seashore n orilla del mar f ▷ on the seashore a la orilla del mar

seasick adj **to be seasick** marearse [25] ▷ n barco

seaside n playa f

season n estación f (pl estaciones) ▷ What's your favourite season? ¿Cuál es tu estación preferida?; **out of season** fuera de temporada; **during the holiday season** en la temporada de vacaciones; **a season ticket** un abono

seat n ❶ asiento m ▷ I was sitting in the back seat. Yo iba sentada en el asiento trasero.; **Are there any seats left?** ¿Quedan localidades? ❷ escaño m ▷ to win a seat at the election conseguir un escaño en las elecciones

seat belt n cinturón de seguridad m (pl cinturones de seguridad)

seaweed n alga marina f

> Although it's a feminine noun, remember that you use **el** and **un** with **alga**.

second adj, adv segundo(-a) ▷ the second time la segunda vez; **to come second** llegar [37] en segundo lugar; **the second of March** el dos de marzo
> ▶ n segundo m ▷ It'll only take a second. Es un segundo nada más.

secondary school n ❶ (state) instituto m ❷ (private) colegio m

second-class adj, adv (ticket, compartment) de segunda clase; **to travel second class** viajar [25] en segunda; **second-class postage**

> In Spain there is no first-class or second-class postage. If you want your mail to arive fast,

you must have it sent express – **urgente** – from a post office.

secondhand *adj* de segunda mano

secondly *adv* en segundo lugar

secret *adj* secreto(-a)
▶ n secreto m ▷ Can you keep a secret? ¿Me guardas un secreto?; **in secret** en secreto

secretary n secretario m, secretaria f

secretly *adv* en secreto

section n sección f (pl secciones)

security n seguridad f; **security guard** el/la guarda jurado

see *vb* ver [57] ▷ I can't see. No veo nada. ▷ I saw him yesterday. Lo vi ayer.; **You need to see a doctor.** Tienes que ir a ver a un médico.; **See you!** ¡Hasta luego!; **See you soon!** ¡Hasta pronto!

seed n semilla f ▷ poppy seeds semillas de amapola

seem *vb* parecer [12] ▷ She seems tired. Parece cansada.; **The shop seemed to be closed.** Parecía que la tienda estaba cerrada.; **It seems that...** Parece que... ▷ It seems you have no alternative. Parece que no tienes otra opción.; **It seems she's getting married.** Por lo visto se casa.; **There seems to be a problem.** Parece que hay un problema.

seen *vb* see **see**

seesaw n balancín m (pl balancines)

seldom *adv* rara vez

select *vb* seleccionar [25]

selection n ❶ selección f (pl selecciones) ▷ a selection test una prueba de selección ❷ surtido m ▷ the widest selection on the market el más amplio surtido del mercado

self-catering *adj* **self-catering apartment** el apartamento con cocina

self-confidence n confianza en uno mismo f ▷ I lost all my self-confidence. Perdí toda la confianza en mí mismo.

self-conscious *adj* ❶ cohibido(-a) ▷ She was really self-conscious at first. Al principio estaba muy cohibida. ❷ acomplejado(-a) ▷ She was self-conscious about her height. Estaba acomplejada por su estatura.

self-defence (US **self-defense**) n defensa personal f ▷ self-defence classes clases de defensa personal; **She killed him in self-defence.** Lo mató en defensa propia.

self-employed *adj* autónomo(-a); **to be self-employed** ser [52] autónomo; **the self-employed** los trabajadores autónomos

selfish *adj* egoísta

self-service *adj* de autoservicio

sell *vb* vender [8] ▷ He sold it to me. Me lo vendió.

sell off *vb* liquidar [25]

sell out *vb* **The tickets sold out in three hours.** Las entradas se agotaron en tres horas.

sell-by date n fecha de caducidad f

Sellotape® n celo m

semi n casa adosada f

semicircle n semicírculo m

semicolon n punto y coma m (pl punto y coma)

semi-detached house n casa adosada f ▷ We live in a semi-detached house. Vivimos en una casa adosada.; **a street of semi-detached houses** una calle de casas pareadas

semi-final n semifinal f

semi-skimmed milk n leche semidesnatada f

send vb mandar [25] ▷ She sent me a birthday card. Me mandó una tarjeta de cumpleaños.

send back vb devolver [59]

send off vb ❶ enviar [21] por correo ▷ We sent off your order yesterday. Le enviamos el pedido por correo ayer. ❷ expulsar [25] ▷ He was sent off. Lo expulsaron.

send out vb enviar [21]

senior adj, n alto(-a) ▷ senior management los altos directivos; **She's five years my senior.** Es cinco años mayor que yo.; **senior school** el instituto de enseñanza secundaria

senior citizen n persona de la tercera edad f

sensational adj sensacional

sense n sentido m ▷ the five senses los cinco sentidos ▷ Use your common sense! ¡Usa el sentido común!; **It makes sense.** Tiene sentido.; **It doesn't make sense.** No tiene sentido.; **a keen sense of smell** un olfato finísimo; **sense of humour** sentido del humor

sensible adj sensato(-a) ▷ Be sensible! ¡Sé sensato!

Be careful not to translate **sensible** by the Spanish word **sensible**.

sensitive adj sensible

sent vb see **send**

sentence n ❶ oración f (pl oraciones) ▷ What does this sentence mean? ¿Qué significa esta oración? ❷ sentencia f ▷ to pass sentence dictar sentencia ❸ condena f ▷ a sentence of 10 years una condena de 10 años; **the death sentence** la pena de muerte; **He got a life sentence.** Fue condenado a cadena perpetua.

▶ vb **to sentence somebody to life imprisonment** condenar [25] a alguien a cadena perpetua; **to sentence somebody to death** condenar [25] a muerte a alguien

sentimental adj sentimental

separate adj distinto(-a) ▷ separate changing rooms vestuarios distintos; **The children have separate rooms.** Los niños tienen cada uno su habitación.; **I wrote it on a separate sheet.** Lo escribí en una hoja aparte.; **on separate occasions** en diversas ocasiones

▶ vb ❶ separar [25] ▷ Police moved in to separate the two groups. La policía intervino para separar a los dos grupos. ❷ separarse [25] ▷ Her parents separated last year. Sus padres se separaron el año pasado.

separately adv por separado

separation n separación f (pl separaciones)

September n septiembre m
▷ in September en septiembre
▷ on 23 September el 23 de
septiembre

sequel n continuación f (pl
continuaciones)

sergeant n ❶ (army) sargento mf
❷ (police) oficial de policía mf

serial n ❶ (on TV, radio) serial m
❷ (in magazine) novela por
entregas f

series n serie f

serious adj ❶ serio(-a) ▷ You're
looking very serious. Estás muy
serio.; **Are you serious?** ¿Lo dices
en serio? ❷ grave ▷ a serious illness
una grave enfermedad

seriously adv en serio ▷ to take
somebody seriously tomar en serio a
alguien; **seriously injured**
gravemente herido; **Seriously?**
¿De verdad?

servant n criado m, criada f

serve vb ❶ servir [38] ▷ Dinner is
served. La cena está servida.; **It's
Murray's turn to serve.** Al servicio
Murray.; **Are you being served?**
¿Le atienden ya? ❷ cumplir [58]
▷ to serve a life sentence cumplir
cadena perpetua ▷ to serve time
cumplir [58] condena; **It serves
you right.** Te está bien empleado.
▶ n servicio m

service vb (car, washing machine)
revisar [25]
▶ n ❶ servicio m ▷ Service is
included. El servicio está incluido.;
a bus service una línea de autobús
❷ (of car, machine) revisión f (pl
revisiones) ❸ (at church) oficio

religioso m; **the armed services**
las fuerzas armadas

service charge n servicio m
▷ Service charge is included. El
servicio va incluido.

service station n estación de
servicio f (pl estaciones de servicio)

serviette n servilleta f

session n sesión f (pl sesiones)

set n ❶ (of objects, tools) juego m ▷ a
set of keys un juego de llaves; **The
sofa and chairs are only sold as a
set.** El sofá y los sillones no se
venden por separado. ❷ (in tennis)
set m (pl sets) ▷ She was leading 5–1
in the first set. Iba ganando 5 a 1 en
el primer set.
▶ vb ❶ poner [41] ▷ I set the alarm
for seven o'clock. Puse el
despertador a las siete.
❷ establecer [12] ▷ The world record
was set last year. El récord mundial
se estableció el año pasado.
❸ ponerse [41] ▷ The sun was
setting. Se estaba poniendo el sol.;
The film is set in Morocco. La
película se desarrolla en
Marruecos.; **to set something on
fire** prender [8] fuego a algo; **to
set sail** zarpar [25]; **to set the
table** poner [41] la mesa

set off vb salir [49] ▷ We set off for
London at nine o'clock. Salimos para
Londres a las nueve.

set out vb salir [49] ▷ We set out for
London at nine o'clock. Salimos para
Londres a las nueve.

settee n sofá m (pl sofás)

settle vb ❶ zanjar [25] ▷ That should
settle the problem. Esto debería

a
b
c
d
e
f
g
h
i
j
k
l
m
n
o
p
q
r
s
t
u
v
w
x
y
z

zanjar el problema. ❷ pagar **[37]**
▷ *I'll settle the bill tomorrow.*
Mañana pagaré la cuenta.
settle down vb calmarse **[25]**
settle in vb adaptarse **[25]**
seven num siete ▷ *She's seven.* Tiene
siete años.
seventeen num diecisiete ▷ *He's
seventeen.* Tiene diecisiete años.
seventeenth adj
decimoséptimo(-a); **the
seventeenth floor** la planta
diecisiete; **the seventeenth of
April** el diecisiete de abril
seventh adj séptimo(-a) ▷ *the
seventh floor* el séptimo piso; **the
seventh of August** el siete de
agosto
seventy num setenta ▷ *She's
seventy.* Tiene setenta años.
several adj, pron varios (f varias)
▷ *several times* varias veces
sew vb coser **[8]**
sew up vb coser **[8]**
sewing n costura f ▷ *I like sewing.*
Me gusta la costura.; **sewing
machine** la máquina de coser
sewn vb see **sew**
sex n sexo m ▷ *the opposite sex* el
sexo opuesto; **to have sex with
somebody** tener **[53]** relaciones
sexuales con alguien; **sex
education** la educación sexual
sexism n sexismo m
sexist adj sexista
sexual adj sexual ▷ *sexual
discrimination* la discriminación
sexual
sexuality n sexualidad f
sexy adj sexy (pl sexy)

shabby adj (person, clothes)
andrajoso(-a)
shade n ❶ sombra f ▷ *It was 35
degrees in the shade.* Hacía 35
grados a la sombra. ❷ tono m
▷ *a beautiful shade of blue* un tono
de azul muy bonito
shadow n sombra f
shake vb ❶ sacudir **[58]** ▷ *She shook
the rug.* Sacudió la alfombra.;
'Shake well before use' 'Agítese
bien antes de usarse' ❷ temblar
[39] ▷ *He was shaking with cold.*
Temblaba de frío.; **Donald shook
his head.** Donald negó con la
cabeza.; **to shake hands with
somebody** dar **[14]** la mano a
alguien ▷ *They shook hands.* Se
dieron la mano.
shall vb **Shall I shut the window?**
¿Cierro la ventana?
shallow adj poco profundo(-a)
shambles n desastre m ▷ *It's a
complete shambles.* Es un desastre
total.
shame n vergüenza f ▷ *I'd die of
shame!* ¡Me moriría de
vergüenza!; **What a shame!**
¡Qué pena!

▌ **es una pena** has to be
followed by a verb in the
subjunctive.

▷ *It's a shame he isn't here.* Es una
pena que no esté aquí.
shampoo n champú m (pl
champús) ▷ *a bottle of shampoo* un
bote de champú
shandy n clara f
shape n forma f ▷ *in the shape of a
star* en forma de estrella; **to be in

good shape estar **[22]** en buena forma

share n **❶** acción f (pl acciones) ▷ They've got shares in many companies. Tienen acciones en muchas empresas. **❷** (portion) parte f ▷ He refused to pay his share of the bill. Se negó a pagar su parte de la factura. ▶ vb compartir **[58]** ▷ to share a room with somebody compartir habitación con alguien

share out vb repartir **[58]** ▷ They shared the sweets out among the children. Repartieron los caramelos entre los niños.

shark n tiburón m (pl tiburones)

sharp adj, adv **❶** afilado(-a) ▷ Be careful, that knife's sharp! ¡Cuidado con ese cuchillo que está afilado! **❷** (point, spike) puntiagudo(-a) **❸** (intelligent) listo(-a) ▷ She's very sharp. Es muy lista.; **at two o'clock sharp** a las dos en punto

shave vb afeitarse **[25]** ▷ He took a bath and shaved. Se dio un baño y se afeitó.; **to shave one's legs** depilarse **[25]** las piernas

shaver n **electric shaver** la maquinilla de afeitar eléctrica

shaving cream n crema de afeitar f

shaving foam n espuma de afeitar f

she pron ella

    'she' generally isn't translated unless it's emphatic.
▷ She's very nice. Es muy maja.
    Use **ella** for emphasis.
▷ She did it but he didn't. Ella lo hizo, pero él no.

shed n cobertizo m

she'd = **she had**; **she would**

sheep n oveja f

sheepdog n perro pastor m (pl perros pastores)

sheer adj puro(-a) ▷ It's sheer greed. Es pura codicia.

sheet n sábana f ▷ to change the sheets cambiar las sábanas; **a sheet of paper** una hoja de papel

shelf n **❶** (on wall, in shop) estante m **❷** (in oven) parrilla f

shell n **❶** (on beach, of tortoise, snail) concha f (caracol m LatAm) **❷** (of egg, nut) cáscara f **❸** (explosive) obús m (pl obuses)

she'll = **she will**

shellfish n marisco m

shelter n refugio m ▷ a bomb shelter un refugio antiaéreo; **to take shelter** refugiarse **[25]**

shelves npl see **shelf**

sherry n jerez m

she's = **she is**; **she has**

shift n turno m ▷ the night shift el turno de noche ▷ His shift starts at eight o'clock. Su turno empieza a las ocho.; **to do shift work** trabajar **[25]** por turnos
▶ vb trasladar **[25]** ▷ I couldn't shift the wardrobe on my own. No podía trasladar el armario yo solo.; **Shift yourself!** (informal) ¡Quita de ahí!

shin n espinilla f

shine vb brillar **[25]** ▷ The sun was shining. Brillaba el sol.

shiny adj brillante

ship n barco m ▷ by ship en barco

shirt n camisa f

shiver vb tiritar [25] ▷ to shiver with cold tiritar de frío

shock n ① conmoción f(pl conmociones) ▷ The news came as a shock. La noticia causó conmoción. ② calambre m ▷ I got a shock when I touched the switch. Me dio calambre al tocar el interruptor.
▶ vb ① (upset) horrorizar [13] ▷ They were shocked by the tragedy. Quedaron horrorizados por la tragedia. ② (scandalize) escandalizar [13] ▷ Nothing shocks me any more. Ya nada me escandaliza.

shocking adj escandaloso(-a) ▷ It's shocking! ¡Es escandaloso!

shoe n zapato m ▷ a pair of shoes un par de zapatos

shoelace n cordón m (pl cordones)

shoe polish n betún m

shoe shop n zapatería f

shone vb see **shine**

shook vb see **shake**

shoot vb ① (fire a shot) disparar [25] ▷ Don't shoot! ¡No disparen!; **to shoot at somebody** disparar [25] contra alguien; **He shot himself with a revolver.** Se pegó un tiro con un revólver.; **He was shot dead by the police.** Murió de un disparo de la policía. ② (execute) fusilar [25] ▷ He was shot at dawn. Lo fusilaron al amanecer. ③ rodar [11] ▷ The film was shot in Prague. La película se rodó en Praga. ④ (in football) chutar [25]

shooting n ① disparos mpl ▷ They heard shooting. Oyeron disparos.; **a shooting** un tiroteo ② caza f ▷ to go shooting ir de caza

shop n tienda f ▷ a sports shop una tienda de deportes

shop assistant n dependiente m, dependienta f

shopkeeper n comerciante mf

shoplifting n hurto en las tiendas m

shopping n compra f ▷ Can you get the shopping from the car? ¿Puedes sacar la compra del coche?; **to go shopping** (1) (for food) ir [27] a hacer la compra (2) (for pleasure) ir [27] de compras; **I love shopping.** Me encanta ir de compras.; **shopping bag** la bolsa de la compra; **shopping centre** el centro comercial

shop window n escaparate m

shore n orilla f ▷ on the shores of the lake a orillas del lago; **on shore** en tierra

short adj ① corto(-a) ▷ short hair pelo corto; **a short break** un pequeño descanso; **a short time ago** hace poco ② bajo(-a) ▷ She's quite short. Es bastante baja.; **to be short of something** andar [4] escaso de algo; **at short notice** con poco tiempo de antelación

shortage n escasez f ▷ a water shortage escasez de agua

short cut n atajo m

shortly adv dentro de poco ▷ I'll be there shortly. Estaré allí dentro de poco.; **She arrived shortly after**

midnight. Llegó poco después de la medianoche.

shorts npl pantalones cortos mpl
▷ a pair of shorts unos pantalones cortos

short-sighted adj miope

shot vb see **shoot**
▶n ❶ (from gun) tiro m ▷ to fire a shot disparar un tiro ▷ a shot at goal un tiro a puerta ❷ (photo) foto f

⬛ Although **foto** ends in -a, it is actually a feminine noun.

▷ a shot of Edinburgh Castle una foto del castillo de Edimburgo ❸ (vaccination) inyección f (pl inyecciones)

shotgun n escopeta f

should vb

⬛ When 'should' means 'ought to', use the conditional of **deber**.

deber [8] ▷ You should take more exercise. Deberías hacer más ejercicio. ▷ That shouldn't be too hard. Eso no debería ser muy difícil.

⬛ **tener que** is also a very common way to translate 'should'.

▷ I should have told you before. Tendría que habértelo dicho antes.

⬛ When 'should' means 'would', use the conditional.

▷ I should go if I were you. Yo que tú, iría.; **I should be so lucky!** ¡Ojalá!

shoulder n hombro m

shouldn't = **should not**

shout vb gritar [25] ▷ Don't shout! ¡No grites!
▶n grito m

shovel n pala f

show n ❶ (in theatre) espectáculo m
▷ to stage a show montar un espectáculo ❷ (on TV, radio) programa m

⬛ Although **programa** ends in -a, it is actually a masculine noun.

▷ a radio show un programa de radio; **fashion show** el pase de modelos; **motor show** el salón del automóvil
▶vb ❶ enseñar [25]; **to show somebody something** enseñar [25] algo a alguien ▷ Have I shown you my hat? ¿Te he enseñado ya mi sombrero? ❷ demostrar [11] ▷ She showed great courage. Demostró gran valentía.; **It shows.** Se nota.
▷ I've never been riding before. — It shows. Nunca había montado a caballo antes. — Se nota.

show off vb presumir [58]

show up vb presentarse [25] ▷ He showed up late as usual. Se presentó tarde, como de costumbre.

shower n ❶ ducha f; **to have a shower** ducharse [25] ❷ chubasco m ▷ scattered showers chubascos dispersos

shown vb see **show**

show-off n fantasmón m (pl fantasmones), fantasmona f

shrank vb see **shrink**

shriek vb chillar [25]

shrimps npl camarones mpl

shrink vb (clothes, fabric) encogerse [7]

Shrove Tuesday n martes de carnaval m

shrug vb **to shrug one's shoulders** encogerse **[7]** de hombros

shrunk vb see **shrink**

shuffle vb **to shuffle the cards** barajar **[25]** las cartas

shut vb cerrar **[39]** ▷ What time do the shops shut? ¿A qué hora cierran las tiendas?

shut down vb cerrar **[39]** ▷ The cinema shut down last year. El cine cerró el año pasado.

shut up vb callarse **[25]** ▷ Shut up! ¡Cállate!

shuttlecock n volante m

shy adj tímido(-a)

Sicily n Sicilia f

sick adj **❶** enfermo(-a) ▷ She looks after her sick mother. Cuida de su madre enferma. **❷** de mal gusto ▷ That's really sick! ¡Eso es muy mal gusto!; **to be sick** devolver **[59]** (arrojar LatAm) ▷ I was sick twice last night. Anoche devolví dos veces.; **I feel sick.** Tengo ganas de devolver.; **to be sick of something** estar **[22]** harto de algo ▷ I'm sick of your jokes. Estoy harto de tus bromas.

sickness n enfermedad f

side n **❶** (of object, building, car) lado m ▷ He was driving on the wrong side of the road. Iba por el lado contrario de la carretera.; **a house on the side of a mountain** una casa en la ladera de una montaña; **We sat side by side.** Nos sentamos uno al lado del otro. **❷** (of path, bed, road) borde m ▷ The car was abandoned at the side of the road. El coche estaba abandonado

al borde de la carretera.; **by the side of the lake** a la orilla del lago **❸** (of paper, tape) cara f ▷ Play side A. Pon la cara A. **❹** (team) equipo m ▷ He's on my side. Está en mi equipo.; **I'm on your side.** Yo estoy de tu parte.; **to take somebody's side** ponerse **[41]** de parte de alguien; **to take sides** tomar **[25]** partido; **the side entrance** la entrada lateral

sideboard n aparador m

side-effect n efecto secundario m

sidewalk n (US) acera f

sideways adv **to look sideways** mirar **[25]** de reojo; **to move sideways** moverse **[33]** de lado

sieve n **❶** (for liquids) colador m **❷** (for solids) criba f

sigh n suspiro m
▶ vb suspirar **[25]**

sight n **❶** vista f ▷ I'm losing my sight. Estoy perdiendo la vista.; **at first sight** a primera vista; **to know somebody by sight** conocer **[12]** a alguien de vista; **in sight** a la vista **❷** espectáculo m ▷ It was an amazing sight. Era un espectáculo asombroso.; **Keep out of sight!** ¡Que no te vean!; **the sights** las atracciones turísticas; **to see the sights of London** hacer **[26]** turismo por Londres

sightseeing n **to go sightseeing** hacer **[26]** turismo

sign n **❶** (notice) letrero m **❷** señal f ▷ She made a sign to the waiter. Le hizo una señal al camarero. ▷ There's no sign of improvement. No hay señales de mejoría.; **road**

sign la señal de tráfico; **What sign are you?** ¿De qué signo eres?
► vb firmar [25]

sign on vb apuntarse [25] al paro

signal n señal f
► vb **to signal to somebody** hacer [26] señas a alguien

signature n firma f

significance n importancia f

significant adj significativo(-a)

sign language n lenguaje por señas m

signpost n señal f

silence n silencio m

silent adj ① (place) silencioso(-a) ▷ a silent room una habitación silenciosa ② (person) callado(-a)

silk n seda f ▷ a silk scarf un pañuelo de seda

silky adj sedoso(-a)

silly adj tonto(-a)

silver n plata f ▷ a silver medal una medalla de plata

similar adj parecido(-a); **similar to** parecido a

simple adj ① sencillo(-a) ▷ It's very simple. Es muy sencillo. ② simple ▷ He's a bit simple. Es un poco simple.

simply adv sencillamente

sin n pecado m

since prep, adv, conj ① desde ▷ since then desde entonces; **I haven't seen him since.** Desde entonces no lo he vuelto a ver. ② desde que ▷ I haven't seen her since she left. No la he visto desde que se fue.; **It's a few years since I've seen them.** Hace varios años que no los veo. ③ como ▷ Since you're tired, let's stay

at home. Como estás cansado podemos quedarnos en casa.

sincere adj sincero(-a)

sincerely adv **Yours sincerely...** Atentamente...

sing vb cantar [25]

singer n cantante mf

singing n canto m ▷ singing lessons clases de canto

single adj ① individual ▷ a single room una habitación individual ▷ a single bed una cama individual ② soltero(-a) ▷ a single mother una madre soltera ③ solo(-a) ▷ She hadn't said a single word. No había dicho una sola palabra.; **not a single thing** nada de nada
► n ③ (ticket) billete de ida m
② single m ▷ a CD single un single en CD

single parent n **She's a single parent.** Es madre soltera.

singular n singular ▷ in the singular en singular

sink n ① (in the kitchen) fregadero m ② (in the bathroom) lavabo m
► vb ① hundir [58] ▷ We sank the enemy's ship. Hundimos el barco enemigo. ② hundirse [58] ▷ The boat was sinking fast. El barco se hundía rápidamente.

sir n señor m ▷ Yes sir. Sí, señor.

siren n sirena f

sister n ① hermana f ▷ my little sister mi hermana pequeña ② (nurse) enfermera jefe f

sister-in-law n cuñada f

sit vb sentarse [39] ▷ He sat in front of the TV. Se sentó frente a la tele.; **to be sitting** estar [22] sentado

a
b
c
d
e
f
g
h
i
j
k
l
m
n
o
p
q
r
s
t
u
v
w
x
y
z

▷ *He was sitting in front of the TV.*
Estaba sentado frente a la tele.; **to
sit an exam** presentar [25] a un
examen

sit down vb sentarse [39] ▷ *He sat
down at his desk.* Se sentó en su
escritorio.

site n ❶ lugar m ▷ *the site of the
accident* el lugar del accidente
❷ (*campsite*) camping m (pl
campings)

sitting room n sala de estar f
(pl salas de estar)

situation n situación f (pl
situaciones)

six num seis ▷ *He's six.* Tiene seis
años.

sixteen num dieciséis ▷ *He's sixteen.*
Tiene dieciséis años.

sixteenth adj decimosexto(-a);
the sixteenth floor la planta
dieciséis; **the sixteenth of
August** el dieciséis de agosto

sixth adj sexto(-a) ▷ *the sixth floor* el
sexto piso; **the sixth of August** el
seis de agosto

sixty num sesenta ▷ *She's sixty.*
Tiene sesenta años.

size n ❶ (*of object, place*) tamaño m
▷ *plates of various sizes* platos de
varios tamaños
   • Spain uses the European system
   • for clothing and shoe sizes.
❷ (*of clothing*) talla f ▷ *What size do
you take?* ¿Qué talla usas? ❸ (*of
shoes*) número m; **I take size five.**
Calzo un treinta y ocho.

skate vb patinar [25]

skateboard n monopatín m (pl
monopatines)

skateboarding n to go
skateboarding montar [25] en
monopatín

skates npl patines mpl

skating n patinaje m; **to go
skating** ir a patinar; **skating rink**
la pista de patinaje

skeleton n esqueleto m

sketch n boceto m
   ▶ vb esbozar [13]

ski vb esquiar [21]
   ▶ n esquí m ▷ *a pair of skis* unos
esquís; **ski boots** las botas de
esquí; **ski lift** el telesilla

   ▮ Although **telesilla** ends in -a,
   it is actually a masculine noun.

ski pants los pantalones de esquí;
ski pole el bastón de esquí (pl
bastones de esquí); **ski slope** la
pista de esquí; **ski suit** el traje de
esquí

skid vb patinar [25]

skier n esquiador m, esquiadora f

skiing n esquí m ▷ *I love skiing.* Me
encanta el esquí.; **to go skiing** ir
[27] a esquiar; **to go on a skiing
holiday** irse [27] de vacaciones a
esquiar

skilful adj hábil

skill n habilidad f ▷ *It requires a lot of
skill.* Requiere mucha habilidad.

skilled adj a **skilled worker** un
trabajador cualificado

skimmed milk n leche
desnatada f

skin n piel f; **skin cancer** el cáncer
de piel

skinhead n cabeza rapada mf (pl
cabezas rapadas)

skinny adj flaco(-a)

skip n contenedor de basuras m
▶ vb saltarse [25] ▷ *You should never skip breakfast.* No debes saltarte nunca el desayuno.; **to skip school** hacer [26] novillos

skirt n falda f

skive vb (informal) escaquearse [25]; **to skive off school** hacer [26] novillos

skull n ❶ (of corpse) calavera f ❷ (in anatomy) cráneo m

sky n cielo m

skyscraper n rascacielos m (pl rascacielos)

slam vb cerrar [39] de un portazo ▷ *She slammed the door.* Cerró la puerta de un portazo.; **The door slammed.** La puerta se cerró de un portazo.

slang n argot m

slap n bofetada f
▶ vb dar [14] una bofetada a

slate n teja de pizarra f

sledge n trineo m

sledging n **to go sledging** ir [27] en trineo

sleep n sueño m ▷ *lack of sleep* falta de sueño; **I need some sleep.** Necesito dormir.; **to go to sleep** dormirse [17]
▶ vb dormir [17] ▷ *I couldn't sleep last night.* Anoche no podía dormir.

sleep around vb irse [27] a la cama con cualquiera

sleep in vb dormir [17] hasta tarde

sleep together vb acostarse [11] juntos

sleeping bag n saco de dormir m

sleeping car n coche cama m (pl coches cama)

sleeping pill n somnífero m

sleepy adj **to feel sleepy** tener [53] sueño

sleet n aguanieve f

> Although it's a feminine noun, remember that you use **el** with **aguanieve**.

▶ vb **It's sleeting.** Está cayendo aguanieve.

sleeve n (of shirt, coat) manga f

slept vb see **sleep**

slice n ❶ (of bread) rebanada f ❷ (of cake) trozo m ❸ (of lemon, pineapple) rodaja f ❹ (of ham, cheese) loncha f
▶ vb cortar [25]

slide n ❶ (in playground) tobogán m (pl toboganes) ❷ (photo) diapositiva f ❸ (hair slide) pasador m
▶ vb deslizarse [13] ▷ *Tears were sliding down his cheeks.* Las lágrimas se deslizaban por sus mejillas.; **She slid the door open.** Corrió la puerta.

slight adj ligero(-a) ▷ *a slight improvement* una ligera mejoría; **a slight problem** un pequeño problema

slightly adv ligeramente ▷ *They are slightly more expensive.* Son ligeramente más caros.

slim adj delgado(-a)
▶ vb adelgazar [13] ▷ *I'm trying to slim.* Estoy intentando adelgazar.; **I'm slimming.** Estoy a régimen.

sling n cabestrillo m ▷ *She had her arm in a sling.* Llevaba el brazo en cabestrillo.

slip n ❶ (mistake) desliz m (pl deslices) ❷ (underskirt)

combinación f (pl combinaciones); **a slip of paper** un papelito; **a slip of the tongue** un lapsus
▶ vb resbalar [25] ▷ He slipped on the ice. Resbaló en el hielo.

slip up vb equivocarse [48]

slipper n zapatilla f

slippery adj resbaladizo(-a)

slope n ① (surface) cuesta f ▷ The street was on a slope. La calle era en cuesta. ② (angle) pendiente f ▷ a slope of 10 degrees una pendiente del 10 por ciento

slot n ranura f

slot machine n ① (for gambling) máquina tragaperras f (pl máquinas tragaperras) ② (vending machine) máquina expendedora f

slow adj, adv lento(-a) ▷ to go slow ir lento; **Drive slower!** ¡Conduce más despacio!; **My watch is slow.** Mi reloj se atrasa.

slow down vb reducir [9] la velocidad ▷ The car slowed down. El coche redujo la velocidad.

slowly adv lentamente

slug n babosa f

slum n barrio bajo m

smack n cachete m
▶ vb dar [14] un cachete a

small adj pequeño(-a) (chico LatAm) ▷ two small children dos niños pequeños

smart adj ① elegante ▷ a smart navy blue suit un elegante traje azul marino ② listo(-a) ▷ He thinks he's smarter than Sarah. Se cree más listo que Sarah.

smash n accidente de coche m
▶ vb ① romper [8] ▷ They smashed

windows. Rompieron ventanas.
② romperse [8] ▷ The glass smashed into tiny pieces. El vaso se rompió en pedazos.

smashing adj estupendo(-a)
▷ That's a smashing idea. Me parece una idea estupenda.

smell n olor m ▷ a smell of lemon un olor a limón; **the sense of smell** el olfato
▶ vb oler [36] ▷ That dog smells! ¡Cómo huele ese perro! ▷ I can't smell anything. No huelo nada.; **I can smell gas.** Me huele a gas.; **to smell of something** oler [36] a algo ▷ It smells of petrol. Huele a gasolina.

smelly adj maloliente ▷ The pub was dirty and smelly. El pub era sucio y maloliente.; **He's got smelly feet.** Le huelen los pies.

smile n sonrisa f
▶ vb sonreír [44]

smoke n humo m
▶ vb fumar [25] ▷ I don't smoke. No fumo.

smoker n fumador m, fumadora f

smoking n **Smoking is bad for you.** Fumar es malo para la salud.; **'no smoking'** 'prohibido fumar'

smooth adj liso(-a) ▷ a smooth surface una superficie lisa

SMS abbr (= short message service) SMS m

smudge n borrón m (pl borrones)

smuggle vb **to smuggle in** meter [8] de contrabando; **to smuggle out** sacar [48] de contrabando

smuggler n contrabandista mf

smuggling n contrabando m

snack n to have a snack picar [48] algo

snack bar n cafetería f

snail n caracol m

snake n serpiente f

snap vb partirse [58] ▷ The branch snapped. La rama se partió.; **to snap one's fingers** chasquear [25] los dedos

snatch vb arrebatar [25]; **to snatch something from somebody** arrebatar [25] algo a alguien ▷ He snatched the keys from my hand. Me arrebató las llaves de la mano.; **My bag was snatched.** Me robaron el bolso.

sneak vb to sneak in entrar [25] a hurtadillas; **to sneak out** salir [49] a hurtadillas

sneeze vb estornudar [25]

sniff vb ❶ sorberse [8] la nariz ▷ Stop sniffing! ¡Deja de sorberte la nariz! ❷ olfatear [25] ▷ The dog sniffed my hand. El perro me olfateó la mano.; **to sniff glue** esnifar [25] pegamento

snob n esnob mf (pl esnobs)

snooker n billar m

snooze n (informal) cabezadita f ▷ to have a snooze echar una cabezadita

snore vb roncar [48]

snow n nieve f
▶ vb nevar [39] ▷ It's snowing. Está nevando.

snowball n bola de nieve f

snowflake n copo de nieve m

snowman n muñeco de nieve m ▷ to build a snowman hacer un muñeco de nieve

so conj, adv ❶ (therefore) así que ▷ The shop was closed, so I went home. La tienda estaba cerrada, así que me fui a casa. ▷ So, have you always lived in London? Así que, ¿siempre has vivido en Londres?; **So what?** ¿Y qué? ❷ (so that) para que

para que has to be followed by a verb in the subjunctive.
▷ He took her upstairs so they wouldn't be overheard. La subió al piso de arriba para que nadie los oyera. ❸ (very, as) tan ▷ He was talking so fast I couldn't understand. Hablaba tan rápido que no le entendía. ▷ He's like his sister but not so clever. Es como su hermana pero no tan listo.; **It was so heavy!** ¡Pesaba tanto!; **How's your father? — Not so good.** ¿Cómo está tu padre? — No muy bien.; **so much** tanto ▷ I love you so much. Te quiero tanto. ▷ She's got so much energy. Tiene tanta energía.; **so many** tantos ▷ I've got so many things to do today. Tengo tantas cosas que hacer hoy.; **That's not so.** No es así. ❹ (also) también; **so do I** yo también ▷ I work a lot. — So do I. Trabajo mucho. — Yo también.; **I love horses. — So do I.** Me encantan los caballos. — A mí también.; **so have we** y nosotros también ▷ I've been waiting for ages! — So have we. ¡Llevo esperando un siglo! — Y nosotros también.; **I think so.** Creo que sí.; **... or so** ... o así ▷ at five o'clock or so

a las cinco o así ▷ **ten or so people**
diez personas o así
soak vb ❶ poner [41] en remojo
▷ Soak the beans for two hours.
Ponga las judías en remojo dos
horas. ❷ empapar [25] ▷ Water had
soaked his jacket. El agua le había
empapado la chaqueta.
soaking adj empapado(-a) ▷ By the
time we got back we were soaking.
Cuando regresamos estábamos
empapados.; **Your shoes are
soaking wet.** Tienes los zapatos
calados.
soap n jabón m
soap opera n telenovela f
soap powder n detergente en
polvo m
sob vb sollozar [13]
sober adj sobrio(-a)
sober up vb **He sobered up.** Se le
pasó la borrachera.
soccer n fútbol m ▷ to play soccer
jugar al fútbol; **soccer player** el/la
futbolista
social adj social ▷ social problems
problemas sociales; **I have a good
social life.** Tengo mucha vida
social.
socialism n socialismo m
socialist adj, n socialista
social network n red social f
social security n seguridad social
f; **to be on social security** cobrar
[25] de la seguridad social
social worker n asistente social
m, asistenta social f
society n ❶ sociedad f ▷ a
multi-cultural society una sociedad
pluricultural ❷ asociación f

(pl asociaciones) ▷ a drama society
una asociación de amigos del
teatro
sociology n sociología f
sock n calcetín m (pl calcetines)
(media f LatAm)
socket n enchufe m
sofa n sofá m (pl sofás)
soft adj ❶ suave ▷ a soft towel una
toalla suave ❷ blando(-a) ▷ The
mattress is too soft. El colchón es
demasiado blando.; **to be soft on
somebody** ser [52] blando con
alguien; **soft cheeses** los quesos
tiernos; **a soft drink** un refresco;
soft drugs las drogas blandas;
soft option la alternativa fácil
software n software m
soggy adj ❶ (bread, biscuits)
revenido(-a) ❷ (salad) pasado(-a)
soil n tierra f
solar power n energía solar f
sold vb see **sell**
soldier n soldado m
solicitor n ❶ (for lawsuits) abogado
m, abogada f ❷ (for wills, property)
notario m, notaria f
solid adj sólido(-a) ▷ a solid wall un
muro sólido; **solid gold** oro
macizo; **for three solid hours**
durante tres horas seguidas
solo n solo m ▷ a guitar solo un solo
de guitarra
solution n solución f (pl
soluciones)
solve vb resolver [33]
some adj, pron

> When 'some' refers to
> something you can't count,
> it usually isn't translated.

▷ Would you like some bread? ¿Quieres pan? ▷ Have you got some mineral water? ¿Tiene agua mineral? ▷ Would you like some coffee? — No thanks, I've got some coffee? — No gracias, ya tengo.; **I only want some of it.** Solo quiero un poco.

When 'some' refers to something you can count, use **alguno**, which is shortened to **algún** before a masculine singular noun.

▷ some day algún día ▷ some books algunos libros ▷ You have to be careful with mushrooms: some are poisonous. Cuidado con las setas: algunas son venenosas.; **I'm going to buy some stamps. Do you want some too?** Voy a por sellos. ¿Quieres que te traiga?; **some day next week** un día de la semana que viene; **Some people say that...** Hay gente que dice que...; **some of them** algunos ▷ I only sold some of them. Solo vendí algunos.

somebody pron alguien ▷ I need somebody to help me. Necesito que me ayude alguien.

somehow adv de alguna manera; **I'll do it somehow.** De alguna manera lo haré.; **Somehow I don't think he believed me.** Por alguna razón me parece que no me creyó.

someone pron alguien ▷ I need someone to help me. Necesito que me ayude alguien.

something pron algo ▷ something special algo especial; **It cost £100,**

or something like that. Costó 100 libras, o algo así.; **His name is Peter or something.** Se llama Peter o algo por el estilo.

sometime adv algún día ▷ You must come and see us sometime. Tienes que venir a vernos algún día.; **sometime last month** el mes pasado

sometimes adv a veces ▷ Sometimes I drink beer. A veces bebo cerveza.

somewhere adv en algún sitio ▷ I left my keys somewhere. Me he dejado las llaves en algún sitio.; **I'd like to go on holiday, somewhere exotic.** Me gustaría irme de vacaciones, a algún sitio exótico.

son n hijo m

song n canción f (pl canciones)

son-in-law n yerno m

soon adv pronto ▷ very soon muy pronto; **soon afterwards** poco después; **as soon as possible** cuanto antes

sooner adv antes ▷ Can't you come a bit sooner? ¿No puedes venir un poco antes?; **sooner or later** tarde o temprano; **the sooner the better** cuanto antes mejor

soprano n soprano f

Although **soprano** ends in -o, it is actually a feminine noun.

sore adj It's sore. Me duele.; **I have a sore throat.** Me duele la garganta.; **That's a sore point.** Ese es un tema delicado.
▷ n llaga f

sorry adj I'm sorry. Lo siento.
▷ I'm very sorry. Lo siento mucho.;

I'm sorry I'm late. Siento llegar tarde.; **Sorry!** ¡Perdón!; **I'm sorry about the noise.** Perdón por el ruido.; **You'll be sorry!** ¡Te arrepentirás!; **to feel sorry for somebody** sentir **[51]** pena por alguien

sort n tipo m ▷ *What sort of bike have you got?* ¿Qué tipo de bicicleta tienes?; **all sorts of...** todo tipo de...

sort out vb ❶ ordenar **[25]** ▷ *Sort out all your books.* Ordena tus libros.; ❷ arreglar **[25]** ▷ *They have sorted out their problems.* Han arreglado sus problemas.

soul ❶ (spirit) alma f

> Although it's a feminine noun, remember that you use **el** and **un** with **alma**.

❷ soul m ▷ *a soul singer* una cantante de soul

sound n ❶ ruido m ▷ *the sound of footsteps* el ruido de pasos ❷ sonido m ▷ *at the speed of sound* a la velocidad del sonido
> vb sonar **[11]** ▷ *That sounds interesting.* Eso suena interesante.; **It sounds as if she's doing well at school.** Parece que le va bien en el colegio.; **That sounds like a good idea.** Eso me parece buena idea.
> adj, adv válido(-a) ▷ *His reasoning is perfectly sound.* Su argumentación es perfectamente válida.; **Julian gave me some sound advice.** Julian me dio un buen consejo.; **sound asleep** profundamente dormido

soundtrack n banda sonora f

soup n sopa f

sour adj agrio(-a)

south adj, adv ❶ del sur ▷ *a south wind* un viento del sur; **the south coast** la costa meridional ❷ hacia el sur ▷ *We were travelling south.* Viajábamos hacia el sur.; **south of** ▷ *It's south of London.* Está al sur de Londres.
> n sur m ▷ *the South of France* el sur de Francia

South Africa n Sudáfrica f

South America n Sudamérica f

South American adj sudamericano(-a)
> n sudamericano m, sudamericana f ▷ *South Americans* los sudamericanos

southeast n sudeste m; **southeast England** el sudeste de Inglaterra

southern adj **Southern England** el sur de Inglaterra

South Pole n Polo Sur m

southwest n sudoeste m

souvenir n recuerdo m ▷ *souvenir shop* la tienda de recuerdos

soya n soja f

space n espacio m ▷ *There isn't enough space.* No hay espacio suficiente.; **a parking space** un sitio para aparcar

spacecraft n nave espacial f

spade n pala f; **spades** (at cards) las picas ▷ *the ace of spades* el as de picas

> Be careful not to translate **spade** by **espada**.

Spain n España f

Spaniard n (person) español m, española f

spaniel n perro de aguas m

Spanish adj español(a)
▶ n español m
  * The official name for the Spanish language in Spain and Latin America is **el castellano** and is also the term many Spanish speakers prefer to use. Despite controversies, both **español** and **castellano** are perfectly acceptable.
  ▷ Spanish lessons las clases de español; **the Spanish** los españoles

spanner n llave inglesa f

spare adj ① de repuesto ▷ Take a few spare batteries. Llévate unas pilas de repuesto. ▷ spare wheel la rueda de repuesto ② de sobra ▷ Have you got a spare pencil? ¿Tienes un lápiz de sobra?; **spare part** el repuesto; **spare room** el cuarto de los huéspedes; **spare time** el tiempo libre
▶ vb Can you spare a moment? ¿Tienes un momento?; **I can't spare the time.** No tengo tiempo.; **They've got no money to spare.** No les sobra el dinero.; **We arrived with time to spare.** Llegamos con tiempo de sobra.
▶ n I've lost my key. — Have you got a spare? He perdido la llave. — ¿Tienes una de sobra?

sparkling adj con gas ▷ sparkling water agua con gas; **sparkling wine** vino espumoso

sparrow n gorrión m (pl gorriones)

spat vb see **spit**

speak vb hablar [**25**] ▷ Do you speak English? ¿Hablas inglés? ▷ Have you spoken to him? ¿Has hablado con él? ▷ She spoke to him about it. Habló de ello con él.; **Could I speak to Alison? — Speaking!** ¿Podría hablar con Alison? — ¡Soy yo!

speak up vb hablar [**25**] **más alto** ▷ You'll need to speak up — we can't hear you. Habla más alto que no te oímos.

speaker n ① (loudspeaker) altavoz m (pl altavoces) ② (at conference) orador m, oradora f; **French speakers** los hablantes de francés

special adj especial

specialist n especialista mf

speciality n especialidad f

specialize vb especializarse [**13**] ▷ She specialized in Russian. Se especializó en ruso.; **We specialize in skiing equipment.** Estamos especializados en material de esquí.

specially adv especialmente ▷ It can be very cold here, specially in winter. Llega a hacer mucho frío aquí, especialmente en invierno.

species n especie f

specific adj ① específico(-a) ▷ certain specific issues ciertos temas específicos ② concreto(-a) ▷ Could you be more specific? ¿Podrías ser más concreto?

spectacular adj espectacular

spectator n espectador m, espectadora f

speech n discurso m ▷ to make a speech dar un discurso

speechless *adj* **I was speechless.** Me quedé sin habla.

speed *n* velocidad *f* ▷ **at top speed** a toda velocidad; **a three-speed bike** una bicicleta de tres marchas

speed up *vb* acelerar **[25]**

speedboat *n* lancha motora *f*

speeding *n* exceso de velocidad *m* ▷ *He was fined for speeding.* Lo multaron por exceso de velocidad.

speed limit *n* límite de velocidad *m*; **to break the speed limit** saltarse **[25]** el límite de velocidad

spell *vb* deletrear **[25]** ▷ *Can you spell that please?* ¿Me lo deletrea, por favor?; **How do you spell 'library'?** ¿Cómo se escribe 'library'?; **I can't spell.** Cometo faltas de ortografía.
　▶ *n* hechizo *m* ▷ *to be under somebody's spell* estar bajo el hechizo de alguien; **to cast a spell on somebody** hechizar **[13]** a alguien

spelling *n* ortografía *f* ▷ *My spelling is terrible.* Cometo muchas faltas de ortografía.; **a spelling mistake** una falta de ortografía

spend *vb* **①** gastar **[25]** ▷ *They spend enormous amounts of money on advertising.* Gastan cantidades enormes de dinero en publicidad. **②** dedicar **[48]** ▷ *He spends a lot of time and money on his hobbies.* Dedica mucho tiempo y dinero a sus aficiones. **③** pasar **[25]** ▷ *He spent a month in France.* Pasó un mes en Francia.

spice *n* especia *f*

spicy *adj* picante

spider *n* araña *f*

spill *vb* **You've spilled coffee on your shirt.** Se te ha caído café en la camisa.

spinach *n* espinacas *fpl*

spine *n* columna vertebral *f*

spire *n* aguja *f*

spirit *n* **①** espíritu *m* ▷ *a youthful spirit* un espíritu joven **②** valor *m* ▷ *Everyone admired her spirit.* Todos admiraban su valor. **③** brío *m* ▷ *They played with great spirit.* Jugaron con mucho brío.

spirits *npl* licores *mpl* ▷ *I don't drink spirits.* No bebo licores.; **to be in good spirits** estar **[22]** de buen ánimo

spiritual *adj* espiritual

spit *n* saliva *f*
　▶ *vb* escupir **[58]**

spite *n* **in spite of** a pesar de; **out of spite** por despecho
　▶ *vb* fastidiar **[25]** ▷ *He just did it to spite me.*

spiteful *adj* **①** (person) rencoroso(-a) **②** (action) malintencionado(-a)

splash *vb* salpicar **[48]** ▷ *Don't splash me!* ¡No me salpiques!; **He splashed water on his face.** Se echó agua en la cara.
　▶ *n* chapoteo *m* ▷ *I heard a splash.* Oí un chapoteo.; **a splash of colour** una mancha de color

splendid *adj* espléndido(-a)

splinter *n* astilla *f*

split *vb* **①** partir **[58]** ▷ *He split the wood with an axe.* Partió la madera con un hacha. **②** partirse **[58]** ▷ *The ship hit a rock and split in two.*

El barco chocó con una roca y se partió en dos. ❸ **dividir** [58] ▷ *a decision that will split the party* una decisión que se dividirá al partido; **They decided to split the profits.** Decidieron repartir los beneficios.

split up vb **separarse** [25]

spoil vb ❶ **estropear** [25] ▷ *It spoiled our holiday.* Nos estropeó las vacaciones. ❷ **mimar** [25] ▷ *Grandparents like to spoil their grandchildren.* A los abuelos les encanta mimar a los nietos.

spoiled adj **mimado(-a)** ▷ *a spoiled child* un niño mimado

spoilsport n **aguafiestas** mf (pl aguafiestas)

spoke vb see **speak**

spoken vb see **speak**

spokesman n **portavoz** m (pl portavoces) (**vocero** m LatAm)

spokeswoman n **portavoz** f (pl portavoces) (**vocera** f LatAm)

sponge n **esponja** f; **sponge bag** la bolsa de aseo; **sponge cake** el bizcocho

sponsor n **patrocinador** m, **patrocinadora** f
▷ vb **patrocinar** [25] ▷ *The tournament was sponsored by local firms.* El torneo fue patrocinado por empresas locales.

spontaneous adj **espontáneo(-a)**

spooky adj **The house is really spooky at night.** La casa te pone los pelos de punta de noche.

spoon n **cuchara** f

spoonful n **a spoonful** una cucharada

sport n **deporte** m; **sports bag** la bolsa de deporte; **sports car** el coche deportivo; **sports jacket** la chaqueta de sport

sportsman n **deportista** m

sportswear n **ropa de deporte** f

sportswoman n **deportista** f

sporty adj **deportista** ▷ *I'm not very sporty.* No soy muy deportista.

spot n ❶ **mancha** f ▷ *There's a spot on your shirt.* Tienes una mancha en la camisa. ❷ **lunar** m ▷ *a red dress with white spots* un vestido rojo con lunares blancos ❸ **grano** m ▷ *He's covered in spots.* Está lleno de granos. ❹ **sitio** m ▷ *It's a lovely spot for a picnic.* Es un sitio precioso para un picnic.; **on the spot** (1) (*immediately*) en el acto ▷ *They gave her the job on the spot.* Le dieron el trabajo en el acto. (2) (*at the same place*) en el mismo sitio ▷ *Luckily they were able to mend the car on the spot.* Afortunadamente consiguieron arreglar el coche en el mismo sitio.
▷ vb **notar** [25] ▷ *I spotted a mistake.* Noté un error.

spotlight n **foco** m

spotty adj **con granos**

sprain vb **torcerse** [6] ▷ *She's sprained her ankle.* Se ha torcido el tobillo.
▷ n **torcedura** f

spray n (*spray can*) **spray** m (pl sprays)
▷ vb ❶ **rociar** [21] ▷ *She sprayed perfume on my hand.* Me roció perfume en la mano. ❷ **fumigar** [37] ▷ *to spray against insects*

fumigar contra los insectos; **There was graffiti sprayed on the wall.** Había pintadas de spray en la pared.

spread vb ❶ extender [20] ▷ She spread a towel on the sand. Extendió una toalla sobre la arena. ❷ untar [25] ▷ Spread the top of the cake with whipped cream. Unte la parte superior de la tarta con nata montada. ❸ propagarse [37] ▷ The news spread rapidly. La noticia se propagó rápidamente.

spread out vb ❶ dispersarse [25] ▷ The soldiers spread out across the field. Los soldados se dispersaron por el campo. ❷ desplegar [34] ▷ He spread the map out on the table. Desplegó el mapa sobre la mesa.

spring n ❶ primavera f ▷ in spring en primavera ❷ (metal) muelle m ❸ (of water) manantial m

springtime n primavera f

sprint n carrera de velocidad f; **the women's 100 metres sprint** los cien metros lisos femeninos
▶ vb correr [8] a toda velocidad ▷ She sprinted for the bus. Corrió a toda velocidad para coger el autobús.

> Be very careful with the verb **coger**: in most of Latin America this is an extremely rude word that should be avoided. However, in Spain this verb is common and not rude at all.

sprouts npl **Brussels sprouts** las coles de Bruselas

spy n espía mf

spying n espionaje m

square n ❶ (shape) cuadrado m ❷ plaza f ▷ the town square la plaza mayor
▶ adj cuadrado(-a) ▷ two square metres dos metros cuadrados; **It's two metres square.** Mide dos por dos.

squash n (sport) squash m; **squash court** la cancha de squash; **squash racket** la raqueta de squash; **orange squash** la naranjada; **lemon squash** la limonada
▶ vb aplastar [25] ▷ You're squashing me. Me estás aplastando.

squeak vb ❶ (mouse, child) chillar [25] ❷ (door, wheel) chirriar [21] ❸ (shoes) crujir [58]

squeeze vb ❶ exprimir [58] ▷ Squeeze two large lemons. Exprima dos limones grandes. ❷ apretar [39] ▷ She squeezed my hand. Me apretó la mano.; **The thieves squeezed through a tiny window.** Los ladrones se colaron por una pequeña ventana.

squeeze in vb hacer [26] un hueco a

squirrel n ardilla f

stab vb apuñalar [25]

stable n cuadra f
▶ adj estable ▷ a stable relationship una relación estable

stack n pila f ▷ There were stacks of books on the table. Había pilas de libros sobre la mesa.; **They've got stacks of money.** Tienen cantidad de dinero.

stadium n estadio m

staff n ❶ (in company) personal m ❷ (in school) profesorado m

stage n ❶ etapa f ▷ in stages por etapas; **at this stage in the negotiations** a estas alturas de las negociaciones ❷ escenario m ▷ The band came on stage late. El grupo salió tarde al escenario.; **I always wanted to go on the stage.** Siempre quise dedicarme al teatro.

stain n mancha f
▶ vb manchar [25]

stainless steel n acero inoxidable m

stair n escalón m (pl escalones)

staircase n escalera f

stairs npl escaleras fpl

stale adj **stale bread** el pan duro

stalemate n punto muerto m ▷ to reach a stalemate llegar a un punto muerto; **The game ended in stalemate.** (in chess) La partida terminó en tablas.

stall n puesto m ▷ He's got a market stall. Tiene un puesto en el mercado.; **the stalls** (in theatre) la platea

stammer n tartamudeo m; **He's got a stammer.** Es tartamudo.

stamp n sello m (estampilla f LatAm) ▷ My hobby is stamp collecting. Mi afición es coleccionar sellos.; **stamp album** el álbum de sellos (pl álbumes de sellos)
▶ vb sellar [25] ▷ The file was stamped 'confidential'. El archivo iba sellado como 'confidencial'.; **The audience stamped their feet.** El público pateaba.

stand vb ❶ estar [22] de pie ▷ He was standing by the door. Estaba de pie junto a la puerta.; **What are you standing there for?** ¿Qué haces ahí de pie?; **They all stood when I came in.** Se pusieron de pie cuando entré. ❷ soportar [25] ▷ I can't stand all this noise. No soporto todo este ruido.

stand for vb ❶ significar [48] ▷ 'EU' stands for 'European Union'. 'EU' significa 'European Union'. ❷ consentir [51] ▷ I won't stand for it any more! ¡No pienso consentirlo más!

stand out vb destacar [48]

stand up vb ❶ ponerse [41] de pie ▷ I stood up and walked out. Me puse de pie y me fui. ❷ estar [22] de pie ▷ She has to stand up all day. Tiene que estar todo el día de pie.

standard adj normal ▷ the standard procedure el procedimiento normal; **standard equipment** el equipamiento de serie m
▶ n nivel m ▷ The standard is very high. El nivel es muy alto.; **She's got high standards.** Es muy exigente.; **standard of living** el nivel de vida

stands npl tribuna f

stank vb see **stink**

staple básico(-a) ▷ their staple food su alimento básico

stapler n grapadora f

star n estrella f ▷ a TV star una estrella de televisión; **the stars** el horóscopo
▶ vb **to star in a film** protagonizar [13] una película; **The film stars**

Sharon Stone. La protagonista de la película es Sharon Stone.; **starring Johnny Depp** ...con Johnny Depp

stare *vb* mirar **[25]** fijamente ▷ *Andy stared at him.* Andy lo miraba fijamente.

start *n* ❶ principio *m* ▷ *at the start of the film* al principio de la película ▷ *from the start* desde el principio; **for a start** para empezar; **Shall we make a start on the washing-up?** ¿Nos ponemos a fregar los platos? ❷ *(of race)* salida *f*
▶ *vb* ❶ empezar **[19]** ▷ *What time does it start?* ¿A qué hora empieza?; **to start doing something** empezar **[19]** a hacer algo ▷ *I started learning Spanish two years ago.* Empecé a aprender español hace dos años. ❷ *(business, organization, campaign)* montar **[25]** ▷ *He wants to start his own business.* Quiere montar su propio negocio. ❸ arrancar **[48]** ▷ *He couldn't start the car.* No conseguía arrancar el coche.

start off *vb* ponerse **[41]** en camino ▷ *We started off first thing in the morning.* Nos pusimos en camino pronto por la mañana.

starter *n (first course)* primer plato *m*

starve *vb* morirse **[32]** de hambre ▷ *People are starving.* La gente se muere de hambre.; **I'm starving!** ¡Me muero de hambre!

state *n* estado *m* ▷ *It's an independent state.* Es un estado independiente.; **He wasn't in a fit**

state to drive. No estaba en condiciones de conducir.; **Tim was in a real state.** Tim estaba de los nervios.; **the States** los Estados Unidos
▶ *vb* declarar **[25]** ▷ *He stated his intention to resign.* Declaró que tenía intención de dimitir.; **Please state your name and address.** Por favor indique su nombre y dirección.

statement *n* ❶ declaración *f* (*pl* declaraciones) ▷ *statements by witnesses* las declaraciones de testigos ❷ afirmación *f* (*pl* afirmaciones) ▷ *Andrew now disowns the statement he made.* Ahora Andrew desmiente la afirmación que hizo.; **a bank statement** un extracto de cuenta

station *n* estación *f* (*pl* estaciones); **bus station** la estación de autobuses; **police station** la comisaría; **radio station** la emisora de radio

stationer's *n* papelería *f*

statue *n* estatua *f*

stay *n* estancia *f* ▷ *my stay in Spain* mi estancia en España
▶ *vb* quedarse **[25]** ▷ *Stay here!* ¡Quédate aquí! ▷ *I'm going to be staying with friends.* Me voy a quedar en casa de unos amigos.; **Where are you staying? In a hotel?** ¿Dónde estás? ¿En un hotel?; **to stay the night** pasar **[25]** la noche; **We stayed in Belgium for a few days.** Pasamos unos días en Bélgica.

stay in *vb* quedarse **[25]** en casa

stay up vb quedarse [**25**] levantado ▷ *We stayed up till midnight.* Nos quedamos levantados hasta las doce.

steady adj ❶ fijo(-a) ▷ *a steady job* un trabajo fijo; **a steady boyfriend** un novio formal ❷ firme ▷ *a steady hand* un pulso firme ❸ constante ▷ *a steady pace* un ritmo constante; **Steady on!** ¡Calma!

steak n filete m

steal vb robar [**25**]

steam n vapor m ▷ *a steam engine* una máquina de vapor

steel n acero m

steep adj empinado(-a)

steeple n aguja f

steering wheel n volante m

step n ❶ paso m ▷ *He took a step forward.* Dio un paso adelante. ❷ peldaño m ▷ *She tripped over the step.* Tropezó con el peldaño. ▷ vb dar [**14**] un paso ▷ *I tried to step forward.* Traté de dar un paso adelante.; **Step this way, please.** Pase por aquí, por favor.

stepbrother n hermanastro m

stepdaughter n hijastra f

stepfather n padrastro m

stepladder n escalera de tijera f

stepmother n madrastra f

stepsister n hermanastra f

stepson n hijastro m

stereo n equipo de música m

sterling adj **pound sterling** la libra esterlina; **one hundred pounds sterling** cien libras esterlinas

stew n estofado m (guisado m LatAm)

steward n ❶ (on plane) auxiliar de vuelo m ❷ (on ship) camarero m

stewardess n ❶ (on plane) auxiliar de vuelo f ❷ (on ship) camarera f

stick n palo m; **a walking stick** un bastón (pl unos bastones) ▷ vb ❶ pegar [**37**] ▷ *Stick the stamps on the envelope.* Pegue los sellos en el sobre. ❷ pegarse [**37**] ▷ *The rice stuck to the pan.* El arroz se pegó a la olla. ❸ meter [**8**] ▷ *He picked up the papers and stuck them in his briefcase.* Recogió los papeles y los metió en el maletín.; **I can't stick it any longer.** Ya no lo aguanto más.

stick out vb sacar [**48**] ▷ *The little girl stuck out her tongue.* La niña sacó la lengua.

sticker n pegatina f

stick insect n insecto palo m

sticky adj ❶ pegajoso(-a) ▷ *to have sticky hands* tener las manos pegajosas ❷ adhesivo(-a) ▷ *a sticky label* una etiqueta adhesiva

stiff adj, adv rígido(-a); **to have a stiff neck** tener [**53**] tortícolis; **to feel stiff** estar [**22**] agarrotado; **to be bored stiff** estar [**22**] aburrido como una ostra; **to be frozen stiff** estar [**22**] tieso de frío; **to be scared stiff** estar [**22**] muerto de miedo

still adv ❶ todavía ▷ *I still haven't finished.* No he terminado todavía. ▷ *Are you still in bed?* ¿Todavía estás en la cama?; **Do you still live in Glasgow?** ¿Sigues viviendo en Glasgow?; **better still** mejor aún ❷ (even so) aun así ▷ *She knows*

I don't like it, but she still does it.
Sabe que no me gusta, pero aun
así lo hace. ❸ *(after all)* en fin ▷ *Still,
it's the thought that counts.* En fin, la
intención es lo que cuenta.
▶ adj quieto(-a) ▷ *He stood still.* Se
quedó quieto.; **Keep still!** ¡No te
muevas!

sting n picadura f ▷ *a bee sting* una
picadura de abeja
▶ vb picar [**48**]

stink vb apestar [**25**] ▷ *You stink of
garlic!* ¡Apestas al ajo!
▶ n tufo m ▷ *the stink of beer* el tufo a
cerveza

stir vb agitar [**25**]

stitch vb coser [**8**]
▶ n ❶ *(in sewing)* puntada f ❷ *(in
knitting, in wound)* punto m ▷ *I had
five stitches.* Me pusieron cinco
puntos.

stock n ❶ reserva f ▷ *stocks of
ammunition* reservas de munición
❷ existencias fpl ▷ *the shop's stock*
las existencias de la tienda; **Yes,
we've got your size in stock.** Sí,
nos quedan existencias de su
número.; **out of stock** agotado
▷ *I'm sorry, they're both out of stock.*
Lo siento, están los dos agotados.
❸ caldo m ▷ *chicken stock* caldo de
pollo
▶ vb vender [**8**] ▷ *Do you stock
camping stoves?* ¿Venden infiernillos?

stock up vb abastecerse [**12**]

stock cube n pastilla de caldo f

stocking n media f

stomach n estómago m

stone n ❶ piedra f ▷ *a stone wall* un
muro de piedra ❷ hueso m ▷ *an*

apricot stone un hueso de
albaricoque
  ● In Spain measurements are in
  grams and kilograms. One
  stone is about 6.3 kg.
I weigh eight stone. Peso unos
cincuenta kilos.

stood vb see **stand**

stool n taburete m

stop vb ❶ parar [**25**] ▷ *The bus
doesn't stop there.* El autobús no
para allí. ❷ pararse [**25**] ▷ *The music
stopped.* Se paró la música.; **This
has got to stop!** ¡Esto se tiene que
acabar!; **I think the rain's going
to stop.** Creo que va a dejar de
llover.; **to stop doing something**
dejar [**25**] de hacer algo ▷ *to stop
smoking* dejar de fumar ❸ acabar
[**25**] con ▷ *a campaign to stop
whaling* una campaña para acabar
con la caza de ballenas

> **impedir que** has to be
> followed by a verb in the
> subjunctive.

**to stop somebody doing
something** impedir [**38**] que
alguien haga algo ▷ *She would have
liked to stop us seeing each other.* Le
hubiera gustado impedir que nos
siguiéramos viendo.; **Stop!** ¡Alto!
▶ n parada f ▷ *a bus stop* una parada
de autobús; **This is my stop.** Yo
me bajo aquí.

stopwatch n cronómetro m

store n ❶ tienda f ▷ *a furniture store*
una tienda de muebles ❷ almacén
m (pl almacenes) ▷ *a grain store* un
almacén de grano
▶ vb ❶ guardar [**25**] ▷ *They store*

potatoes in the cellar. Guardan patatas en el sótano. ❸ **almacenar** [25] ▷ *to store information* almacenar información

storey n planta f ▷ *a three-storey building* un edificio de tres plantas

storm n tormenta f

stormy adj tormentoso(-a)

story n ❶ *(tale)* cuento m ❷ *(account)* historia f

stove n ❶ *(in kitchen)* cocina f ❷ *(camping stove)* infiernillo m

straight adj, adv ❶ recto(-a) ▷ *a straight line* una línea recta ❷ liso(-a) ▷ *straight hair* pelo liso ❸ *(not gay)* heterosexual; **He looked straight at me.** Me miró directamente a los ojos.; **straight away** enseguida; **I'll come straight back.** Vuelvo enseguida.; **Keep straight on.** Siga todo recto.

straightforward adj ❶ sencillo(-a) ▷ *It's very straightforward.* Es muy sencillo. ❷ sincero(-a) ▷ *She's very straightforward.* Es muy sincera.

strain n tensión f (pl tensiones); **It was a strain.** Fue muy estresante. ▶ vb **to strain one's eyes** forzar [3] la vista; **I strained my back.** Me dio un tirón en la espalda.; **to strain a muscle** sufrir [58] un tirón muscular

strange adj raro(-a) ▷ *That's strange!* ¡Qué raro!

■ **es raro que** has to be followed by a verb in the subjunctive. ▷ *It's strange that she doesn't talk to us anymore.* Es raro que ya no nos hable.

stranger n desconocido m, desconocida f ▷ *Don't talk to strangers.* No hables con desconocidos.; **I'm a stranger here.** Yo no soy de aquí.

strangle vb estrangular [25]

strap n ❶ *(of bra, dress)* tirante m ❷ *(of watch, camera, suitcase)* correa f ❸ *(of bag)* asa f

■ Although it's a feminine noun, remember that you use **el** and **un** with **asa**.

straw n ❶ paja f ▷ *a straw hat* un sombrero de paja ❷ pajita f ▷ *He was drinking his lemonade through a straw.* Se bebía la gaseosa con pajita.; **That's the last straw!** ¡Eso es la gota que colma el vaso!

strawberry n fresa f (frutilla f LatAm)

stray adj extraviado(-a) ▷ *a stray cat* un gato extraviado

stream n riachuelo m

street n calle f

streetcar n (US) tranvía m

■ Although **tranvía** ends in **-a**, it is actually a masculine noun.

streetlamp n farola f

streetwise adj **to be streetwise** sabérselas [47] todas

strength n fuerza f ▷ *with all his strength* con todas sus fuerzas

stress vb recalcar [48] ▷ *I would like to stress that...* Me gustaría recalcar que...

▶ n estrés m ▷ *She's under a lot of stress.* Está pasando mucho estrés.

stretch vb ❶ estirarse [25] ▷ *The dog woke up and stretched.* El perro se despertó y se estiró.; **I went out**

to stretch my legs. Salí a estirar las piernas.; **My jumper stretched after I washed it.** Se me dio de sí el jersey al lavarlo. ❷ *tender* **[20]** ▷ *They stretched a rope between two trees.* Tendieron una cuerda entre dos árboles.

stretcher n camilla f

stretchy adj elástico(-a)

strict adj estricto(-a)

strike n huelga f; **to be on strike** estar **[22]** en huelga; **to go on strike** hacer **[26]** huelga ▶ vb golpear **[25]** ▷ *She struck him across the mouth.* Le golpeó en la boca.; **The clock struck three.** El reloj dio las tres.; **to strike a match** encender **[20]** una cerilla

striker n ❶ (person on strike) huelguista mf ❷ (footballer) delantero m, delantera f

string n cuerda f; **a piece of string** una cuerda

strip vb desnudarse **[25]** ▶ n tira f; **strip cartoon** la tira cómica (la historieta LatAm)

stripe n franja f

striped adj a rayas; **a striped skirt** una falda de rayas

stroke vb acariciar **[25]** ▶ n derrame cerebral m ▷ *to have a stroke* sufrir un derrame cerebral; **a stroke of luck** un golpe de suerte

stroll n to go for a stroll ir **[27]** a dar un paseo

stroller n (US) silla de paseo f

strong adj fuerte

strongly adv **We strongly advise you to…** Te aconsejamos encarecidamente que…; **I don't**

feel strongly about it. Me da un poco igual.

struck vb see **strike**

struggle vb forcejear **[25]** ▷ *He struggled, but he couldn't escape.* Forcejeó, pero no pudo escapar.; **to struggle to do something** (1) (fight) luchar **[25]** por hacer algo ▷ *He struggled to get custody of his daughter.* Luchó por conseguir la custodia de su hija. (2) (have difficulty) pasar **[25]** apuros para hacer algo ▷ *They struggle to pay their bills.* Pasan apuros para pagar las facturas. ▶ n lucha f ▷ *a struggle for survival* una lucha por la supervivencia; **It was a struggle.** Nos costó mucho.

stubborn adj terco(-a)

stuck vb see **stick** ▶ adj atascado(-a) ▷ *The lid is stuck.* La tapadera está atascada.; **to get stuck** quedarse **[25]** atascado; **We got stuck in a traffic jam.** Nos metimos en un atasco.

stuck-up adj (informal) creído(-a)

stud n ❶ (earring) pendiente m ❷ (on football boots) taco m

student n estudiante mf

studio n estudio m ▷ *a TV studio* un estudio de televisión; **a studio flat** un estudio

study vb estudiar **[25]**

stuff n cosas fpl ▷ *Have you got all your stuff?* ¿Tienes todas tus cosas?; **I need some stuff for hay fever.** Me hace falta algo para la alergia al polen.

stuffy adj **It's stuffy in here.** Hay un ambiente muy cargado aquí.

stumble vb tropezar [**19**]

stung vb see **sting**

stunk vb see **stink**

stunned adj pasmado(-a) ▷ I was stunned. Me quedé pasmado.

stunning adj pasmoso(-a)

stupid adj estúpido(-a)

stutter vb tartamudear [**25**]
▶n tartamudeo m; **He's got a stutter.** Es tartamudo.

style n estilo m

subject n ❶ (topic, theme) tema m

Although **tema** ends in **-a**, it is actually a masculine noun.

▷ The subject of my project is the internet. El tema de mi trabajo es Internet. ❷ asignatura f ▷ What's your favourite subject? ¿Cuál es tu asignatura preferida? ❸ (of verb) sujeto m

submarine n submarino m

subscription n (to paper, magazine) suscripción f (pl suscripciones); **to take out a subscription to something** suscribirse [**58**] a algo

subsidy n subvención f (pl subvenciones)

substance n sustancia f

substitute n ❶ (replacement) sustituto m, sustituta f ❷ (in football, rugby) suplente mf
▶vb sustituir [**10**] ▷ to substitute A for B sustituir a B por A

subtitled adj subtitulado(-a)

subtitles npl subtítulos mpl ▷ a Spanish film with English subtitles una película española con subtítulos en inglés

subtle adj sutil

subtract vb restar [**25**] ▷ to subtract 3 from 5 restar 3 a 5

suburb n barrio residencial m ▷ a London suburb un barrio residencial de Londres; **They live in the suburbs.** Viven en las afueras.

subway n ❶ (underground) metro m ❷ (underpass) paso subterráneo m

succeed vb ❶ tener [**53**] éxito ▷ to succeed in business tener éxito en los negocios ❷ salir [**49**] bien ▷ The plan did not succeed. El plan no salió bien.; **to succeed in doing something** lograr [**25**] hacer algo

success n éxito m

Be careful not to translate **success** by **suceso**.

successful adj de éxito (exitoso LatAm) ▷ a successful lawyer un abogado de éxito; **a successful attempt** un intento fructífero; **to be successful** tener [**53**] éxito; **to be successful in doing something** lograr [**25**] hacer algo

successfully adv con éxito

such adj, adv ❶ tan ▷ such a long journey un viaje tan largo ❷ tal ▷ I wouldn't dream of doing such a thing. No se me ocurriría hacer tal cosa.; **such a lot** tanto ▷ such a lot of work tanto trabajo ▷ such a long time ago hace tanto tiempo; **such as** como; **as such** propiamente dicho ▷ She's not an expert as such, but... No es una experta propiamente dicha, pero...

such-and-such adj tal
▷ such-and-such a place tal lugar

suck vb chupar [**25**]; **to suck one's thumb** chuparse [**25**] el pulgar

sudden adj repentino(-a) ▷ a sudden change un cambio repentino; **all of a sudden** de repente

suddenly adv de repente

suede n ante m (gamuza f LatAm) ▷ a suede jacket una chaqueta de ante

suffer vb sufrir [58] ▷ She was really suffering. Sufría de verdad.; **to suffer from something** padecer [12] de algo ▷ I suffer from hay fever. Padezco de alergia al polen.

suffocate vb ahogarse [37]

sugar n azúcar m

suggest vb ❶ sugerir [51]

  Use the subjunctive after **sugerir que**.

  ▷ She suggested going out for a pizza. Sugirió que saliéramos a tomar una pizza. ❷ aconsejar [25]

  Use the subjunctive after **aconsejar que**.

  ▷ I suggested they set off early. Yo les aconsejé que salieran pronto.; **What are you trying to suggest?** ¿Qué insinúas?

suggestion n sugerencia f ▷ to make a suggestion hacer una sugerencia

suicide n suicidio m; **to commit suicide** suicidarse [25]

suit n ❶ (man's) traje m ❷ (woman's) traje de chaqueta m
  ▶ vb ❸ venir [56] bien a ▷ What time would you suit you? ¿Qué hora te vendría bien?; **That suits me fine.** Eso me viene estupendamente. ❷ sentar [39] bien a ▷ That dress really suits you. Ese vestido te

sienta la mar de bien.; **Suit yourself!** ¡Haz lo que te parezca!

suitable adj ❶ conveniente ▷ a suitable time una hora conveniente ❷ apropiado(-a) ▷ suitable clothing ropa apropiada

suitcase n maleta f (valija f LatAm)

suite n suite f ▷ a suite at the Paris Hilton una suite en el Hilton de París; **a bedroom suite** un dormitorio completo; **a three-piece suite** un tresillo

sulk vb estar [22] de mal humor

sultana n pasa de Esmirna f

sum n suma f ▷ a sum of money una suma de dinero

sum up vb resumir [58]; **To sum up...** Resumiendo...

summarize vb resumir [58]

summary n resumen m (pl resúmenes)

summer n verano m ▷ summer clothes ropa de verano ▷ the summer holidays las vacaciones de verano

summertime n verano m

summit n cumbre f

sun n sol m ▷ in the sun al sol

sunbathe vb tomar [25] el sol

sunblock n crema solar de protección total f

sunburn n quemadura f

sunburnt adj quemado por el sol (f quemada por el sol); **Mind you don't get sunburnt!** ¡Cuidado de quemarte con el sol!

Sunday n domingo m (pl domingos) ▷ I saw her on Sunday. La vi el domingo. ▷ every Sunday

todos los domingos ▷ *last Sunday*
el domingo pasado ▷ *next Sunday*
el domingo que viene ▷ *on Sundays*
los domingos

Sunday school n catequesis f
* The Spanish equivalent of
* Sunday school takes place
* during the week after school
* rather than on a Sunday.

sunflower n girasol m

sung vb *see* **sing**

sunglasses npl gafas de sol fpl

sunk vb *see* **sink**

sunlight n luz del sol f

sunny adj soleado(-a) ▷ *a sunny morning* una mañana soleada;
It's sunny. Hace sol.; **a sunny day** un día de sol

sunrise n salida del sol f

sunroof n techo corredizo m

sunscreen n protector solar m

sunset n puesta de sol f

sunshine n sol m ▷ *in the sunshine* al sol

sunstroke n insolación f (pl insolaciones)

suntan n bronceado m; **to get a suntan** broncearse [**25**]; **suntan lotion** la crema bronceadora;
suntan oil el aceite bronceador

super adj estupendo(-a)

supermarket n supermercado m

supernatural adj sobrenatural

superstitious adj supersticioso(-a)

supervise vb supervisar [**25**]

supervisor n supervisor m, supervisora f

supper n cena f

supplement n suplemento m

supplies npl provisiones fpl;
medical supplies material médico

supply vb suministrar [**25**]; **to supply somebody with something** suministrar [**25**] algo a alguien ▷ *The centre supplied us with all the equipment.* El centro nos suministró todo el material.
▶ n suministro m ▷ *the water supply* el suministro de agua; **a supply of paper** una remesa de papel

supply teacher n profesor interino m, profesora interina f

support vb ❶ (*emotionally*) apoyar [**25**] ▷ *My mum has always supported me.* Mi madre siempre me ha apoyado. ❷ (*financially*) mantener [**53**] ▷ *She had to support five children on her own.* Tenía que mantener a cinco niños ella sola.; **What team do you support?** ¿De qué equipo eres?

> Be careful not to translate **to support** by **soportar**.

▶ n apoyo m

supporter n ❶ hincha mf ▷ *a Liverpool supporter* un hincha del Liverpool ❷ partidario m, partidaria f ▷ *a supporter of the Labour Party* un partidario del partido laborista

suppose vb suponer [**41**] ▷ *I suppose he'll be late.* Supongo que llegará tarde. ▷ *Suppose you win the lottery...* Supón que te toca la lotería...;
I suppose so. Supongo que sí.;
You're supposed to show your passport. Tienes que enseñar el pasaporte.; **You're not supposed to smoke in the toilet.** No está

permitido fumar en el servicio.; **It's supposed to be the best hotel in the city.** Dicen que es el mejor hotel de la ciudad.

supposing *conj*

| **suponiendo que** has to be followed by a verb in the subjunctive.

▷ *Supposing you won the lottery...* Suponiendo que te tocara la lotería...

sure *adj* seguro(-a) ▷ *Are you sure?* ¿Estás seguro?; **Sure!** ¡Claro!; **to make sure that...** asegurarse **[25]** de que... ▷ *I'm going to make sure the door's locked.* Voy a asegurarme de que la puerta está cerrada con llave.

surely *adv* Surely you don't believe that? ¿No te creerás eso, no?

surf *n* espuma de las olas *f*
▶ *vb* (in sea) hacer **[26]** surf

surface *n* superficie *f*

surfboard *n* tabla de surf *f*

surfing *n* surf *m* ▷ *to go surfing* hacer surf

surgeon *n* cirujano *m*, cirujana *f*

surgery *n* ❶ (room) consultorio médico *m* ❷ (treatment) cirugía *f*

surname *n* apellido *m*

surprise *n* sorpresa *f*

surprised *adj* I was surprised to see him. Me sorprendió verlo.; **I'm not surprised that ...** No me sorprende que...

surprising *adj* sorprendente

surrender *vb* rendirse **[38]**

surround *vb* rodear **[25]** ▷ *surrounded by trees* rodeado de árboles

surroundings *npl* entorno *m* ▷ *a hotel in beautiful surroundings* un hotel en un hermoso entorno

survey *n* encuesta *f* ▷ *They did a survey of a thousand students.* Hicieron una encuesta a mil estudiantes.

survivor *n* superviviente *mf*
▷ *There were no survivors.* No hubo supervivientes.

suspect *vb* sospechar **[25]**
▶ *n* sospechoso *m*, sospechosa *f*

suspend *vb* ❶ (from school) expulsar **[25]** temporalmente ❷ (from team) excluir **[10]** ❸ (from job) suspender **[8]**

suspense *n* ❶ incertidumbre *f*
▷ *The suspense was terrible.* La incertidumbre era terrible.
❷ suspense *m* ▷ *a film with lots of suspense* una película llena de suspense

suspicious *adj* ❶ (mistrustful) receloso(-a) ▷ *He was suspicious at first.* Al principio estaba receloso.
❷ (suspicious-looking) sospechoso(-a) ▷ *a suspicious person* un individuo sospechoso

swallow *vb* tragar **[37]**

swam *vb* see **swim**

swan *n* cisne *m*

swap *vb* cambiar **[25]** ▷ *to swap A for B* cambiar A por B; **Do you want to swap?** ¿Quieres que cambiemos?

swear *vb* ❶ jurar **[25]** ▷ *to swear allegiance to* jurar fidelidad a
❷ decir **[15]** palabrotas ▷ *It's wrong to swear.* No se deben decir palabrotas.

swearword n palabrota f

sweat n sudor m
▶ vb sudar [25]

sweater n jersey m (pl jerseys) (suéter m LatAm)

Swede n (person) sueco m, sueca f

Sweden n Suecia f

Swedish adj, n sueco(-a)

sweep vb barrer [8] ▷ to sweep the floor barrer el suelo

sweet n ❶ caramelo m ▷ a bag of sweets una bolsa de caramelos ❷ postre m ▷ Are you going to have a sweet? ¿Vas a tomar postre?
▶ adj ❶ dulce ▷ a sweet wine un vino dulce ❷ amable ▷ That was really sweet of you. Fue muy amable de tu parte.

sweetcorn n maíz dulce m

swept vb see **sweep**

swerve vb girar [25] bruscamente ▷ I swerved to avoid the cyclist. Giré bruscamente para esquivar al ciclista.

swim n to go for a swim ir [27] a nadar
▶ vb nadar [25] ▷ Can you swim? ¿Sabes nadar?; **She swam across the river.** Cruzó el río a nado.

swimmer n nadador m, nadadora f

swimming n natación f
▷ swimming lessons clases de natación; **Do you like swimming?** ¿Te gusta nadar?; **to go swimming** ir [27] a nadar; **swimming cap** el gorro de baño; **swimming costume** el traje de baño; **swimming pool** la piscina; **swimming trunks** el bañador

swimsuit n traje de baño m

swing vb ❶ (on a swing) columpiarse [25] ❷ balancearse [25] ▷ Her bag swung as she walked. El bolso se balanceaba según iba andando.; **He was swinging on a rope.** Se balanceaba colgado de una cuerda. ❸ colgar [28] ▷ A large key swung from his belt. Le colgaba una gran llave del cinturón. ❹ balancear [25] ▷ He was swinging his bag back and forth. Balanceaba la bolsa de un lado al otro.
▶ n columpio m

Swiss adj, n suizo(-a); **the Swiss** los suizos

switch n interruptor m
▶ vb cambiar [25] de ▷ We switched partners. Cambiamos de pareja.

switch off vb (TV, machine, engine) apagar [37]

switch on vb (TV, machine, engine) encender [20] (prender [8] LatAm)

Switzerland n Suiza f

swollen adj hinchado(-a) ▷ My ankle is very swollen. Tengo el tobillo muy hinchado.

swop vb cambiar [25]

sword n espada f

swot n empollón m, empollona f
▶ vb empollar [25]

swum vb see **swim**

swung vb see **swing**

syllabus n programa de estudios m
   Although **programa** ends in -a, it is actually a masculine noun.

symbol n símbolo m

sympathetic adj comprensivo(-a)
   Be careful not to translate **sympathetic** by simpático.

sympathize *vb* to sympathize with somebody (1) *(feel sorry for)* compadecerse [**12**] de alguien (2) *(understand)* comprender [**8**] a alguien

sympathy *n* ❶ *(sorrow)* compasión *f* ❷ *(understanding)* comprensión *f*

symptom *n* síntoma *m*

> Although **síntoma** ends in **-a**, it is actually a masculine noun.

syringe *n* jeringuilla *f*

system *n* sistema *m*

> Although **sistema** ends in **-a**, it is actually a masculine noun.

table *n* mesa *f*; to lay the table poner [**41**] la mesa

tablecloth *n* mantel *m*

tablespoon *n* cuchara de servir *f*

tablet *n* ❶ *(medicine)* pastilla *f* ❷ *(computer)* tableta

table tennis *n* tenis de mesa *m*
> *to play table tennis* jugar al tenis de mesa

tackle *n* ❶ *(in football)* entrada *f* ❷ *(in rugby)* placaje *m*
> *vb* to tackle somebody (1) *(in football)* entrar [**25**] a alguien (2) *(in rugby)* placar [**48**] a alguien; to tackle a problem abordar [**25**] un problema

tact *n* tacto *m*

tactful *adj* diplomático(-a)

tactics *npl* táctica *sg*

tadpole *n* renacuajo *m*

tag n (label) etiqueta f
 ▶ vb (label) etiquetar [25]

tail n ❶ (of horse, bird, fish) cola f ❷ (of dog, bull, ox) rabo m; **Heads or tails?** ¿Cara o cruz?

tailor n sastre m

take vb ❶ tomar [25] ▷ Do you take sugar? ¿Tomas azúcar?; **He took a plate out of the cupboard.** Sacó un plato del armario. ❷ (take with you) llevar [25] ▷ When will you take me to London? ¿Cuándo me llevarás a Londres? ▷ Don't forget to take your camera. No te olvides de llevarte la cámara. ▷ It takes about one hour. Se tarda más o menos una hora. ▷ It won't take long. No tardaré mucho tiempo.; **That takes a lot of courage.** Hace falta mucho valor para eso. ❸ (bear) soportar [25] ▷ He can't take being criticized. No soporta que le critiquen. ❹ (exam, subject at school) hacer [26] ▷ Have you taken your driving test yet? ¿Ya has hecho el examen de conducir? ▷ I decided to take French instead of German. Decidí hacer francés en vez de alemán. ❺ aceptar [25] ▷ We take credit cards. Aceptamos tarjetas de crédito.

take after vb parecerse [12] a ▷ She takes after her mother. Se parece a su madre.

take apart vb to take something apart desmontar [25] algo

take away vb ❶ llevarse [25] ▷ They took away all his belongings. Se llevaron todas sus pertenencias. ❷ quitar [25] ▷ She was afraid her children would be taken

away from her. Tenía miedo de que le quitaran a los niños.; **hot meals to take away** platos calientes para llevar

take back vb devolver [59] ▷ I took it back to the shop. Lo devolví a la tienda.; **I take it all back!** ¡Retiro lo dicho!

take down vb quitar [25] ▷ She took down the painting. Quitó el cuadro.

take in vb ❶ comprender [8] ▷ I didn't really take it in. La verdad es que no lo comprendí. ❷ engañar [25] ▷ They were taken in by his story. Se dejaron engañar por la historia que les contó.

take off vb ❶ despegar [37] ▷ The plane took off 20 minutes late. El avión despegó con 20 minutos de retraso. ❷ quitar [25] ▷ Take your coat off. Quítate el abrigo.

take out vb sacar [48] ▷ He opened his wallet and took out some money. Abrió la cartera y sacó dinero.; **He took her out to the theatre.** La invitó al teatro.

take over vb hacerse [26] cargo de ▷ He took over the running of the company last year. Se hizo cargo del control de la empresa el año pasado.; **to take over from somebody** (1) (replace) sustituir [10] a alguien (2) (in shift work) relevar [25] a alguien

takeaway n (meal) comida para llevar f

takeoff n (of plane) despegue m

tale n cuento m

talent n talento m ▷ He's got a lot of talent. Tiene mucho talento.;

to have a talent for something
tener [53] talento para algo; **He's
got a real talent for languages.**
Tiene verdadera facilidad para los
idiomas.

talented adj **She's a talented
pianist.** Es una pianista de
talento.

talk n ① conversación f (pl
conversaciones) ▷ *We had a long
talk about her problems.* Tuvimos
una larga conversación acerca de
sus problemas.; **I had a talk with
my Mum about it.** Hablé sobre
eso con mi madre.; **to give a talk
on something** dar [14] una charla
sobre algo ▷ *She gave a talk on
ancient Egypt.* Dio una charla sobre
el antiguo Egipto. ② (gossip)
habladurías fpl ▷ *It's just talk.* Son
solo habladurías.
▶ vb hablar [25] ▷ *What did you talk
about?* ¿De qué hablasteis?; **to talk
to somebody** hablar [25] con
alguien; **to talk to oneself** hablar
[25] consigo mismo; **to talk
something over with somebody**
discutir [58] algo con alguien

talkative adj hablador(a)

tall adj alto(-a); **to be two metres
tall** medir [38] dos metros

tame adj (animal) domesticado(-a)

tampon n tampón m (pl
tampones)

tan n bronceado m; **to get a tan**
broncearse [25]

tangerine n mandarina f

tank n ① (for water, petrol) depósito
m ② (on truck) cisterna f ③ (military)
tanque m

tanker n ① (ship) petrolero m
② (truck) camión cisterna m (pl
camiones cisterna); **an oil tanker**
un petrolero; **a petrol tanker** un
camión cisterna

tap n ① (for water) grifo m (llave f
LatAm) ▷ *the hot tap* el grifo de agua
caliente ② (gentle knock) golpecito
m ▷ *I heard a tap on the window.* Oí
un golpecito en la ventana.; **There
was a tap on the door.** Llamaron
a la puerta.

tap-dancing n claqué m ▷ *I do
tap-dancing.* Bailo claqué.

tape n ① (music) cinta f ② (sticky
tape) cinta adhesiva f

tape measure n cinta métrica f

target n ① (board) diana f ② (goal)
objetivo m

tart n tarta f ▷ *an apple tart* una
tarta de manzana

tartan adj escocés (f escocesa,
pl escoceses) ▷ *a tartan scarf* una
bufanda escocesa

task n tarea f

taste n ① sabor m ▷ *It's got a really
strange taste.* Tiene un sabor muy
extraño. ② gusto m ▷ *His joke was
in bad taste.* Su broma fue de mal
gusto.; **Would you like a taste?**
¿Quiere probarlo?
▶ vb probar [11] ▷ *Would you like to
taste it?* ¿Quiere probarlo?; **to
taste of something** saber [47]
a algo ▷ *It tastes of fish.* Sabe a
pescado.; **You can taste the
garlic in it.** Se le nota el sabor a
ajo.

tasty adj sabroso(-a)

tattoo n tatuaje m

taught vb see **teach**

Taurus n (sign) Tauro m; **I'm Taurus.** Soy tauro.

tax n impuesto m; **I pay a lot of tax.** Pago muchos impuestos.; **income tax** el impuesto sobre la renta

taxi n taxi m; **a taxi driver** un/una taxista

taxi rank n parada de taxis f

TB abbr (= tuberculosis) tuberculosis f

tea n ① té m ▷ Would you like some tea? ¿Te apetece un té?; **a cup of tea** una taza de té ② (afternoon tea) merienda f; **to have tea** merendar [39] ▷ We had tea at the Savoy. Merendamos en el Savoy. ③ (evening meal) cena f; **to have tea** cenar [25] ▷ We're having sausages and beans for tea. Vamos a cenar salchichas con alubias.

tea bag n bolsita de té f

teach vb ① enseñar [25] ▷ My sister taught me to swim. Mi hermana me enseñó a nadar. ② (subject) dar [14] clases de p ▷ She teaches physics. Da clases de física.; **That'll teach you!** ¡Así aprenderás!

teacher n ① (in secondary school) profesor m, profesora f ▷ a maths teacher un profesor de matemáticas ▷ She's a teacher. Es profesora. ② (in primary school) maestro m, maestra f

team n equipo m ▷ a football team un equipo de fútbol

teapot n tetera f

tear n lágrima f; **She was in tears.** Estaba llorando.

▶ vb ① romper [8] ▷ Be careful or you'll tear the page. Ten cuidado que vas a romper la página.; **He tore his jacket.** Se rasgó la chaqueta.; **Your shirt is torn.** Tu camisa está rota. ② romperse [8] ▷ It won't tear, it's very strong. No se rompe, es muy resistente.

tear up vb hacer [26] pedazos ▷ He tore up the letter. Hizo pedazos la carta.

tease vb ① atormentar [25] ▷ Stop teasing that poor animal! ¡Deja de atormentar al pobre animal! ② tomar [25] el pelo a ▷ He's teasing you. Te está tomando el pelo.; **I was only teasing.** Lo decía en broma.

teaspoon n cucharita f

teatime n (in evening) hora de cenar f ▷ It was nearly teatime. Era casi la hora de cenar.; **Teatime!** ¡A la mesa!

tea towel n paño de cocina m

technical adj técnico(-a); **technical college** el centro de formación profesional (la escuela politécnica LatAm)

technician n técnico m, técnica f

technological adj tecnológico(-a)

technology n tecnología f

teddy bear n osito de peluche m

teenage adj a teenage magazine una revista para adolescentes; **She has two teenage daughters.** Tiene dos hijas adolescentes.

teenager n adolescente mf

teens npl **She's in her teens.** Es adolescente.

tee-shirt n camiseta f

teeth npl see **tooth**

telephone n teléfono m ▷ on the telephone al teléfono; **a telephone box** una cabina telefónica; **a telephone call** una llamada telefónica; **a telephone directory** una guía telefónica; **a telephone number** un número de teléfono

telescope n telescopio m

television n televisión f ▷ The match is on television tonight. Ponen el partido en televisión esta noche.

tell vb decir [15]; **to tell somebody to do something** decir [15] a alguien que haga algo ▷ He told me to wait a moment. Me dijo que esperara un momento.

> Use the subjunctive after **decir a alguien que** when translating 'to tell somebody to do something'.

to tell lies decir [15] mentiras; **to tell a story** contar [11] un cuento; **I can't tell the difference between them.** No puedo distinguirlos.; **You can tell he's not serious.** Se nota que no se lo toma en serio.

tell off vb regañar [25]

telly n (informal) tele f ▷ to watch telly ver la tele

temper n genio m ▷ He's got a terrible temper. Tiene muy mal genio.; **to be in a temper** estar [22] de mal humor; **to lose one's temper** perder [20] los estribos

temperature n temperatura f; **to have a temperature** tener [53] fiebre

temple npl ❶ (building) templo m ❷ (on head) sien f

temporary adj temporal

temptation n tentación f (pl tentaciones)

tempting adj tentador(a)

ten num diez ▷ She's ten. Tiene diez años.

tend vb **to tend to do something** tener [53] tendencia a hacer algo ▷ He tends to arrive late. Tiene tendencia a llegar tarde.

tennis n tenis m ▷ to play tennis jugar al tenis; **a tennis ball** una pelota de tenis; **a tennis court** una pista de tenis; **a tennis racket** una raqueta de tenis

tennis player n tenista mf ▷ He's a tennis player. Es tenista.

tenor n tenor m

tenpin bowling n bolos mpl ▷ to go tenpin bowling jugar a los bolos

tense adj tenso(-a)
▶ n tiempo m; **the present tense** el presente; **the future tense** el futuro

tension n tensión f (pl tensiones)

tent n tienda de campaña f

tenth adj décimo(-a) ▷ the tenth floor el décimo piso; **the tenth of August** el diez de agosto

term n ❶ (at school) trimestre m ▷ It's nearly the end of term. Ya casi es final de trimestre. ❷ plazo m ▷ in the long term a largo plazo; **to come to terms with something** aceptar [25] algo ▷ He hasn't yet come to terms with his disability. Todavía no ha aceptado su invalidez.

terminal adj (illness, patient) terminal

▶ **terminal** (of computer) terminal m;
airport terminal la terminal del
aeropuerto; **bus terminal** la
terminal de autobuses

terminally adv **to be terminally ill**
estar [**22**] en fase terminal

terrace n ❶ (patio) terraza f ❷ (row
of houses) hilera de casas adosadas
f; **the terraces** (in stadium) las
gradas

terraced adj **a terraced house** una
casa adosada

terrible adj espantoso(-a) ▷ This
coffee is terrible. Este café es
espantoso.; **I feel terrible.** Me
siento fatal.

terrific adj (wonderful)
estupendo(-a) ▷ That's terrific!
¡Estupendo!; **You look terrific!**
¡Estás guapísima!

terrified adj aterrorizado(-a) ▷ I
was terrified! ¡Estaba aterrorizado!

terrorism n terrorismo m

terrorist n terrorista mf; **a
terrorist attack** un atentado
terrorista

test n ❶ prueba f ▷ a spelling test
una prueba de ortografía ❷ (of
blood, urine) análisis m (pl análisis)
▷ a blood test un análisis de sangre
❸ (driving test) examen de conducir
m ▷ He's just passed his test. Acaba
de aprobar el examen de conducir.
▶ vb probar [**11**]; **to test
something out** probar [**11**] algo;
**He tested us on the new
vocabulary.** Nos hizo una prueba
del vocabulario nuevo.; **She was
tested for drugs.** Le hicieron la
prueba antidóping.

text n (text message) SMS m
▶ vb enviar [**21**] un SMS a ▷ I'll text
you when I get there. Te envío un
SMS cuando llegue.

textbook n libro de texto m ▷ a
Spanish textbook un libro de texto
de español

text message n SMS m

Thames n Támesis m

than conj ❶ que ▷ She's taller than
me. Es más alta que yo. ❷ de ▷ more
than 10 years más de 10 años

thank vb dar [**14**] las gracias a
▷ Don't forget to write and thank
them. Acuérdate de escribirles y
darles las gracias.; **thank you**
gracias; **thank you very much**
muchas gracias

thanks excl ¡Gracias!; **thanks to**
gracias a ▷ Thanks to him, everything
went OK. Gracias a él, todo salió
bien.

that adj ❶ ese(-a) ▷ that man ese
hombre ▷ that road esa carretera

> To refer to something more
> distant, use **aquel** and
> **aquella**.

❷ aquel (f aquella) ▷ Look at that
car over there! ¡Mira aquel coche!
▷ THAT road there aquella
carretera; **that one** ese(-a) ▷ This
man? — No, that one. ¿Este hombre?
— No, ese. ❸ Do you like this photo?
— No, I prefer that one. ¿Te gusta
esta foto? — No, prefiero esa.

> To refer to something more
> distant, use **aquel** and **aquella**.

❸ aquel (f aquella) ▷ That one over
there is cheaper. Aquel es más
barato. ▷ Which woman? — That one

over there. ¿Qué mujer? —Aquella.
▶ *pron* **①** ese(-a) (*neut* eso) ▷ *That's impossible.* Eso es imposible. ▷ *What's that?* ¿Qué es eso?; **Who's that?** (*who is that man*) ¿Quién es ese?; **Who's that?** (*who is that woman*) ¿Quién es esa?; **Who's that?** (*on the telephone*) ¿Con quién hablo?

> To refer to something more distant, use **aquel, aquella** and **aquello**.

② aquel (*f* aquella, *neut* aquello) ▷ *That's my French teacher over there.* Aquel es mi profesor de francés. ▷ *That's my sister over by the window.* Aquella de la ventana es mi hermana. ▷ *That was a silly thing to do.* Aquello fue una tontería.; **Is that you?** ¿Eres tú? **③** (*in relative clauses*) que ▷ *the man that saw us* el hombre que nos vio ▷ *the dog that she bought* el perro que ella compró ▷ *the man that we saw* el hombre que vimos

> After a preposition **que** becomes **el que, la que, los que, las que** to agree with the noun.

▷ *the man that we spoke to* el hombre con el que hablamos ▷ *the women that she was chatting to* las mujeres con las que estaba hablando
▶ *conj* que ▷ *He thought that Henry was ill.* Creía que Henry estaba enfermo. ▷ *I know that she likes chocolate.* Sé que le gusta el chocolate.
▶ *adv* **It was that big.** Era así de grande.; **It's about that high.**

Es más o menos así de alto.; **It's not that difficult.** No es tan difícil.
the *def art* **①** el m (*pl* los) ▷ *the boy* el niño ▷ *the cars* los coches

> **a + el** changes to **al** and **de + el** changes to **del**.

▷ *They went to the theatre.* Fueron al teatro. ▷ *the soup of the day* la sopa del día **②** la f (*pl* las) ▷ *the woman* la mujer ▷ *the chairs* las sillas
theatre (*US* **theater**) *n* teatro *m*
theft *n* robo *m*
their *adj* su (*pl* sus) ▷ *their house* su casa ▷ *their parents* sus padres

> 'Their' is usually translated by the definite article **el/los** or **la/las** when it's clear from the sentence who the possessor is, particularly when referring to clothing or parts of the body.

▷ *They took off their coats.* Se quitaron los abrigos. ▷ *after washing their hands* después de lavarse las manos ▷ *Someone stole their car.* Alguien les robó el coche.
theirs *pron* **①** el suyo m (*pl* los suyos) ▷ *Is this their car? — No, theirs is red.* ¿Es este su coche? — No, el suyo es rojo. ▷ *my parents and theirs* mis padres y los suyos **②** la suya f (*pl* las suyas) ▷ *Is this their house? — No, theirs is white.* ¿Es esta su casa? — No, la suya es blanca. ▷ *my sisters and theirs* mis hermanas y las suyas

> Use **de ellos** (masculine) or **de ellas** (feminine) instead of **suyo** if you want to be specific about a masculine or feminine group.

▷ It's not our car, it's theirs. No es nuestro coche, es suyo. ▷ The suitcase is theirs. La maleta es suya. ▷ Whose is this? — It's theirs. ¿De quién es esto? — Es de ellos.; **Isobel is a friend of theirs.** Isobel es amiga suya.

them pron ❶ los (f las)

Use **los** or **las** when 'them' is the direct object of the verb in the sentence.

▷ I didn't know them. No los conocía. ▷ Look at them! ¡Míralos! ▷ I had to give them to her. Tuve que dárselos. ❷ se

Use **les** when 'them' means 'to them'.

▷ I gave them some brochures. Les di unos folletos. ▷ You have to tell them the truth. Tienes que decirles la verdad. ❸ se

Use **se** not **les** when 'them' is used in combination with a direct-object pronoun.

▷ Give it to them. Dáselo. ❹ ellos (f ellas)

Use **ellos** or **ellas** after prepositions, in comparisons, and with the verb 'to be'.

▷ It's for them. Es para ellos. ▷ We are older than them. Somos mayores que ellos. ▷ It must be them. Deben de ser ellos.

theme park n parque temático m

themselves pron ❶ (reflexive) se ▷ Did they hurt themselves? ¿Se hicieron daño? ❷ (after preposition) sí mismos (f sí mismas) ▷ They talked mainly about themselves. Hablaron sobre todo de sí mismos.

❸ (for emphasis) ellos mismos (f ellas mismas) ▷ They built it themselves. Lo construyeron ellos mismos.; **by themselves** por sí mismos (f por sí mismas) ▷ The girls did it all by themselves. Las chicas lo hicieron todo por sí mismas.

then adv, conj ❶ (next) después ▷ I get dressed. Then I have breakfast. Me visto. Después desayuno. ❷ (in that case) pues ▷ My pen's run out. — Use a pencil then! Se me ha acabado el bolígrafo. — ¡Pues usa un lápiz! ❸ (in those days) en aquella época ▷ There was no electricity then. En aquella época no había electricidad.; **now and then** de vez en cuando ▷ Do you play chess? — Now and then. ¿Juegas al ajedrez? — De vez en cuando.; **By then it was too late.** Para entonces ya era demasiado tarde.

there adv ahí ▷ Put it there, on the table. Ponlo ahí, en la mesa.; **over there** allí; **in there** ahí dentro; **on there** ahí encima; **up there** ahí arriba; **down there** ahí abajo; **There he is!** ¡Ahí está!; **there is** hay ▷ There's a factory near my house. Hay una fábrica cerca de mi casa.; **there are** hay ▷ There are 20 children in my class. Hay 20 niños en mi clase.; **There has been an accident.** Ha habido un accidente.

therefore adv por lo tanto

there's = **there is**; **there has**

thermometer n termómetro m

these adj estos (f estas) ▷ these shoes estos zapatos ▷ these houses estas casas

▶ pron **estos** (f **estas**) ▷ I want these! ¡Quiero estos!

they pron **ellos** (f **ellas**)

1 'they' generally isn't translated unless it's emphatic.
▷ They're fine, thank you. Están bien, gracias.

2 Use **ellos** or **ellas** as appropriate for emphasis.
▷ We went to the cinema but they didn't. Nosotros fuimos al cine pero ellos no. ▷ I spoke to my sisters. THEY agree with me. Hablé con mis hermanas. Ellas estaban de acuerdo conmigo.; **They say that...** Dicen que... ▷ They say that the house is haunted. Dicen que la casa está embrujada.

they'd = they had; they would

they'll = they will

they're = they are

they've = they have

thick adj **1** (wall, slice) **grueso(-a)**
▷ Give him a thick slice. Dále una rebanada gruesa.; **The walls are one metre thick.** Las paredes tienen un metro de grosor.
2 (soup) **espeso(-a)** ▷ My soup turned out too thick. La sopa me quedó demasiado espesa.
3 (informal: stupid) **corto(-a)**

thief n **ladrón** m (pl **ladrones**), **ladrona** f

thigh n **muslo** m

thin adj **1** **fino(-a)** ▷ a thin slice una rebanada fina **2** **delgado(-a)**
▷ She's very thin. Está muy delgada.

thing n **cosa** f ▷ Where shall I put my things? ¿Dónde pongo mis cosas?; **How's things?** ¿Qué tal?; **What's**

that thing called? ¿Cómo se llama eso?; **You poor thing!** ¡Pobrecito!; **The best thing would be to leave it.** Lo mejor sería dejarlo.

think vb **1** **pensar [39]** ▷ What do you think about it? ¿Qué piensas? ▷ What are you thinking about? ¿En qué estás pensando?; **I'll think it over.** Lo pensaré. **2** **creer [30]** ▷ I think you're wrong. Creo que estás equivocado.; **I think so.** Creo que sí.; **I don't think so.** Creo que no. **3** **imaginar [25]** ▷ Think what life would be like without cars. Imagínate cómo sería la vida sin coches.

third adj, adv **tercero(-a)**

Use **tercer** before a masculine singular noun.
▷ the third prize el tercer premio ▷ the third time la tercera vez; **the third of March** el tres de marzo
▶ n (fraction) **tercio** m; **a third of the population** una tercera parte de la población

thirdly adv en tercer lugar

Third World n **Tercer Mundo** m

thirst n **sed** f

thirsty adj **to be thirsty** tener **[53]** sed

thirteen num **trece** ▷ I'm thirteen. Tengo trece años.

thirteenth adj **decimotercero(-a)**; **the thirteenth floor** la planta trece; **the thirteenth of January** el trece de enero

thirty num **treinta** ▷ He's thirty. Tiene treinta años.

this adj **este(-a)** ▷ this boy este niño ▷ this road esta carretera; **this one**

este(-a) ▷ Pass me that pen. — This one? Acércame ese bolígrafo. — ¿Este? ▷ This is my room and this one's my sister's. Esta es mi habitación y esta es la de mi hermana.

▶ pron este(-a) (neut esto) ▷ This is my office and this is the meeting room. Este es mi despacho y esta es la sala de reuniones. ▷ What's this? ¿Qué es esto?; This is my mother. (introduction) Te presento a mi madre.; This is Gavin speaking. (on the phone) Soy Gavin.

thistle n cardo m

thorough adj minucioso(-a) ▷ a thorough check un control minucioso; She's very thorough. Es muy meticulosa.

thoroughly adv minuciosamente ▷ I checked the car thoroughly. Revisé el coche minuciosamente.; Mix the ingredients thoroughly. Mézclense bien los ingredientes.; I thoroughly enjoyed myself. Me divertí muchísimo.

those adj ❶ esos (f esas) ▷ those shoes esos zapatos ▷ those girls esas chicas

> To refer to something more distant, use **aquellos** and **aquellas**.

❷ aquellos (f aquellas) ▷ THOSE shoes aquellos zapatos ▷ those houses over there aquellas casas

▶ pron ❶ esos (f esas) ▷ I want those! ¡Quiero esos!

> To refer to something more distant, use **aquellos**.

❷ aquellos (f aquellas) ▷ Ask those children. — Those over there?

Pregúntales a esos niños. — ¿A aquellos?

though conj, adv aunque ▷ Though she was tired she stayed up late. Aunque estaba cansada, se quedó levantada hasta muy tarde.; It's difficult, though, to put into practice. Pero es difícil llevarlo a la práctica.

thought vb see think

▶ n idea f ▷ I've just had a thought. Se me ocurre una idea.; He kept his thoughts to himself. No le dijo a nadie lo que pensaba.; It was a nice thought, thank you. Fue muy amable de tu parte, gracias.

thoughtful adj ❶ (deep in thought) pensativo(-a) ▷ You look thoughtful. Pareces pensativo. ❷ (considerate) considerado(-a) ▷ She's very thoughtful. Es muy considerada.

thoughtless adj desconsiderado(-a) ▷ She's very thoughtless. Es muy desconsiderada.; It was thoughtless of her to mention it. Fue una falta de consideración por su parte mencionarlo.

thousand num a thousand mil ▷ a thousand euros mil euros; two thousand pounds dos mil libras; thousands of people miles de personas

thread n hilo m

threat n amenaza f

threaten vb amenazar [13] ▷ He threatened me. Me amenazó.; to threaten to do something (person) amenazar [13] con hacer algo

three num tres ▷ She's three. Tiene tres años.

threw vb see **throw**

thrilled adj I was thrilled. Estaba emocionada.

thriller n ❶ (film) película de suspense f (película de misterio f LatAm) ❷ (novel) novela de suspense f (novela de misterio f LatAm)

thrilling adj emocionante

throat n garganta f ▷ I have a sore throat. Me duele la garganta.

through adj, adv, prep ❶ a través de ▷ to look through a telescope mirar a través de un telescopio ▷ I know her through my sister. La conozco a través de mi hermana.; **I saw him through the crowd.** Lo vi entre la multitud.; **The window was dirty and I couldn't see through.** La ventana estaba sucia y no podía ver nada. ❷ por ▷ The thief got in through the kitchen window. El ladrón entró por la ventana de la cocina. ▷ to go through Birmingham pasar por Birmingham ▷ to walk through the woods pasear por el bosque; **to go through a tunnel** atravesar [39] un túnel; **He went straight through to the dining room.** Pasó directamente al comedor.; **a through train** un tren directo; **'no through road'** 'calle sin salida'; **all through the night** durante toda la noche; **from May through to September** desde mayo hasta septiembre

throughout prep throughout Britain en toda Gran Bretaña;

throughout the year durante todo el año

throw vb tirar [25] ▷ He threw the ball to me. Me tiró la pelota.; **to throw a party** dar [14] una fiesta; **That really threw him.** Eso lo desconcertó por completo.

throw away vb ❶ (rubbish) tirar [25] ❷ (chance) desperdiciar [25]

throw out vb ❶ (throw away) tirar [25] ❷ (person) echar [25] ▷ I threw him out. Lo eché.

throw up vb devolver [59]

thumb n pulgar m

thumb tack n (US) chincheta f

thump vb to thump somebody pegar [37] un puñetazo a alguien

thunder n truenos mpl

thunderstorm n tormenta f

Thursday n jueves m (pl jueves) ▷ I saw her on Thursday. La vi el jueves. ▷ every Thursday todos los jueves ▷ last Thursday el jueves pasado ▷ next Thursday el jueves que viene ▷ on Thursdays los jueves

tick n ❶ señal f ▷ Place a tick in the appropriate box. Marque con una señal la casilla correspondiente. ❷ tictac m ▷ The clock has a loud tick. El reloj tiene un tictac muy fuerte.; **in a tick** en un instante ▶ vb ❶ marcar [48] ▷ Tick the appropriate box. Marque la casilla correspondiente. ❷ (clock) hacer [26] tictac

tick off vb ❶ (on form, list) marcar [48] ▷ The teacher ticked the names off in the register. El profesor marcó los nombres de la lista con una señal. ❷ (scold) regañar [25]

▷ *He was ticked off for being late.* Le regañaron por llegar tarde.

ticket n ① *(for bus, train, tube)* billete m *(boleto m LatAm)* ② *(for plane)* billete m *(pasaje m LatAm)* ③ *(for cinema, theatre, concert, museum)* entrada f ④ *(for baggage, coat, parking)* ticket m *(pl tíckets)*; **a parking ticket** *(fine)* una multa de aparcamiento

ticket inspector n revisor m, revisora f

ticket office n taquilla f

tickle vb hacer [26] cosquillas a ▷ *She enjoyed tickling the baby.* Le gustaba hacer cosquillas al niño.

tide n marea f; **high tide** la marea alta; **low tide** la marea baja

tidy adj ordenado(-a) ▷ *Your room is very tidy.* Tu habitación está muy ordenada.
▶ vb *(room)* ordenar [25]

tidy up vb *(toys)* recoger [7] ▷ *Don't forget to tidy up afterwards.* No os olvidéis de recoger las cosas después.

tie n ① *(necktie)* corbata f ② *(in sport)* empate m
▶ vb *(shoelaces, parcel)* atar [25]; **to tie a knot in something** hacer [26] un nudo en algo ② empatar [25] ▷ *They tied three all.* Empataron a tres.

tie up vb ① *(person, shoelaces, parcel)* atar [25] ② *(boat)* atracar [48]

tiger n tigre m

tight adj ① *(fitting)* ceñido(-a) ▷ *tight jeans* vaqueros ceñidos ② *(too small)* estrecho(-a) ▷ *This dress is a bit tight.* Este vestido es un poco estrecho.

tighten vb ① *(rope)* tensar [25] ② *(screw)* apretar [39]

tightly adv tightly closed fuertemente cerrado; **She held his hand tightly.** Le agarró la mano con fuerza.

tights npl medias fpl ▷ *a pair of tights* unas medias

tile n ① *(on roof)* teja f ② *(for wall)* azulejo m ③ *(for floor)* baldosa f

till n caja f
▶ prep, conj ① hasta ▷ *I waited till 10 o'clock.* Esperé hasta las 10.; **till then** hasta entonces ② hasta que ▷ *We stayed there till the doctor came.* Nos quedamos allí hasta que vino el médico.

> **hasta que** has to be followed by a verb in the subjunctive when referring to an event in the future.

▷ *Wait till I come back.* Espera hasta que yo vuelva.

time n ① hora f ▷ *What time is it?* ¿Qué hora es? ▷ *What time do you get up?* ¿A qué hora te levantas? ▷ *It was two o'clock, Spanish time.* Eran las dos, hora española.; **on time** a la hora ▷ *He never arrives on time.* Nunca llega a la hora. ② tiempo m ▷ *I'm sorry, I haven't got time.* Lo siento, no tengo tiempo. ▷ *We waited a long time.* Esperamos mucho tiempo. ▷ *Have you lived here for a long time?* ¿Hace mucho tiempo que vives aquí?; **from time to time** de vez en cuando; **in time** a tiempo ▷ *We arrived in time for lunch.* Llegamos a tiempo para el almuerzo.; **just in time** justo a tiempo ❸ momento m ▷ *This isn't a good time to ask him.* Este no es buen momento para preguntarle.; **for the time being** por el momento; **in no time** en un momento ▷ *It was ready in no time.* Estuvo listo en un momento. ❹ vez f (pl veces) ▷ *this time esta vez* ▷ *How many times?* ¿Cuántas veces?; **at times** a veces; **two at a time** de dos en dos; **in a week's time** dentro de una semana; **Come and see us any time.** Ven a vernos cuando quieras.; **to have a good time** pasarlo [25] bien ▷ *Did you have a good time?* ¿Lo pasaste bien?; **Two times two is four.** Dos por dos son cuatro.

time off n tiempo libre m

timetable n ❶ (for train, bus, school) horario m ❷ (schedule of events) programa m

Although **programa** ends in -a, it is actually a masculine noun.

tin n ❶ lata f ▷ *a tin of beans* una lata de alubias ❷ (metal) estaño m

tin opener n abrelatas m (pl abrelatas)

tiny adj minúsculo(-a)

tip n ❶ (money) propina f ▷ *to leave a tip* dejar propina ❷ (advice) consejo m ▷ *a useful tip* un consejo práctico ❸ (end) punta f ▷ *It's on the tip of my tongue.* Lo tengo en la punta de la lengua.; **a rubbish tip**; **This place is a complete tip!** ¡Esto es una pocilga!

▷ vb dar [14] una propina a ▷ *Don't*

forget to tip the waiter. No te olvides de darle una propina al camarero.

tiptoe n **on tiptoe** de puntillas

tired adj cansado(-a) ▷ *I'm tired.* Estoy cansado.; **to be tired of something** estar [22] harto de algo

tiring adj cansado(-a)

tissue n Kleenex® m (pl Kleenex)

title n (of novel, film) título m

to prep ❶ a

a + el changes to al.

▷ *to go to school* ir al colegio ▷ *to go to Portugal* ir a Portugal ▷ *the train to London* el tren a Londres; **I've never been to Valencia.** Nunca he estado en Valencia.; **from...to...** de...a... ▷ *from nine o'clock to half past three* de las nueve a las tres y media ❷ de ▷ *It's easy to do.* Es fácil de hacer. ▷ *the key to the front door* la llave de la puerta principal ❸ hasta ▷ *to count to ten* contar hasta diez ❹ (in order to) para ▷ *I did it to help you.* Lo hice para ayudarte. ▷ *She's too young to go to school.* Es muy pequeña para ir al colegio. ▷ *ready to go* listo para irse ❺ con ▷ *to be kind to somebody* ser amable con alguien ▷ *They were very kind to me.* Fueron muy amables conmigo.; **Give it to her!** ¡Dáselo!; **That's what he said to me.** Eso fue lo que me dijo.; **I've got things to do.** Tengo cosas que hacer.; **ten to nine** las nueve menos diez

toad n sapo m

toast n ❶ (bread) pan tostado m; **a piece of toast** una tostada

❷ *(speech)* brindis m *(pl* brindis); **to drink a toast to somebody** brindar [25] por alguien

toaster n tostadora f

tobacco n tabaco m

tobacconist's n estanco m (tabaquería f *LatAm*)

today *adv* hoy

toddler n niño pequeño m, niña pequeña f

toe n dedo del pie m *(pl* dedos de los pies) ▷ *The dog bit my big toe.* El perro me mordió el dedo gordo del pie.

toffee n caramelo m

together *adv* ❶ juntos *(f* juntas) ▷ *Are they still together?* ¿Todavía están juntos? ❷ *(at the same time)* a la vez ▷ *Don't all speak together!* ¡No habléis todos a la vez!; **together with** junto con

toilet n ❶ *(in public place)* servicios mpl ❷ *(in house)* wáter m

toilet paper n papel higiénico m

toiletries npl artículos de perfumería mpl

toilet roll n rollo de papel higiénico m

told *vb see* **tell**

toll n *(on bridge, motorway)* peaje m

tomato n tomate m ▷ *tomato soup* sopa de tomate

tomorrow *adv* mañana ▷ *tomorrow morning* mañana por la mañana ▷ *tomorrow night* mañana por la noche; **the day after tomorrow** pasado mañana

ton n tonelada f ▷ *a ton of coal* una tonelada de carbón; **That old bike weighs a ton.** Esa bici vieja pesa una tonelada.

tongue n lengua f; **to say something tongue in cheek** decir [15] algo en plan de broma

tonic n tónica f; **a gin and tonic** un gin-tonic

tonight *adv* esta noche ▷ *Are you going out tonight?* ¿Vas a salir esta noche?

tonsillitis n amigdalitis f ▷ *She's got tonsillitis.* Tiene amigdalitis.

tonsils npl amígdalas fpl

too *adv* ❶ *(as well)* también ▷ *My sister came too.* Mi hermana también vino. ❷ *(excessively)* demasiado ▷ *The water's too hot.* El agua está demasiado caliente.; **too much** demasiado(-a) ▷ *too much butter* demasiada mantequilla ▷ *At Christmas we always eat too much.* En Navidades siempre comemos demasiado.; **too many** demasiados *(f* demasiadas) ▷ *too many chairs* demasiadas sillas; **Too bad!** *(what a pity)* ¡Qué pena!

took *vb see* **take**

tool n herramienta f; **a tool box** una caja de herramientas

tooth n diente m

toothache n dolor de muelas m ▷ *These pills are good for toothache.* Estas pastillas son buenas para el dolor de muelas.; **I've got toothache.** Me duele una muela.

toothbrush n cepillo de dientes m

toothpaste n dentífrico m

top n ❶ parte de arriba f ▷ *at the top of the page* en la parte de arriba de la página ❷ *(of mountain)* cima f ❸ *(of box, jar)* tapa f ❹ *(of bottle)*

a
b
c
d
e
f
g
h
i
j
k
l
m
n
o
p
q
r
s
t
u
v
w
x
y
z

tapón m (pl tapones); **a bikini top** la parte de arriba del bikini; **the top of the table** el tablero de la mesa; **on top of the cupboard** encima del armario; **There's a surcharge on top of that.** Hay un recargo, además.; **from top to bottom** de arriba abajo ▷ *I searched the house from top to bottom.* Busqué en la casa de arriba abajo.

▶ adj ❶ *(shelf)* de arriba ▷ *It's on the top shelf.* Está en la estantería de arriba.; **the top layer of skin** la capa superior de la piel; **the top floor** el último piso ❷ eminente ▷ *a top surgeon* un eminente cirujano; **a top model** una top model; **a top hotel** un hotel de primera; **He always gets top marks in French.** Siempre saca excelentes notas en francés.; **at top speed** a máxima velocidad

topic n tema m

Although **tema** ends in -a, it is actually a masculine noun.

▷ *The essay can be on any topic.* La redacción puede ser sobre cualquier tema.

torch n *(electric)* linterna f

tortoise n tortuga f

torture n tortura f ▷ *It was pure torture.* Fue una tortura.

▶ vb torturar **[25]** ▷ *Stop torturing that poor animal!* ¡Deja de torturar al pobre animal!

total adj total ▷ *The total cost was very high.* El coste total fue muy alto.; **the total amount** el total

▶ n total m; **the grand total** la suma total

totally adv totalmente

touch n to get in touch with somebody ponerse **[41]** en contacto con alguien; **to keep in touch with somebody** mantenerse **[53]** en contacto con alguien; **Keep in touch! (1)** *(write)* ¡Escribe de vez en cuando! **(2)** *(phone)* ¡Llama de vez en cuando!; **to lose touch** perder **[20]** el contacto; **to lose touch with somebody** perder **[20]** el contacto con alguien

▶ vb tocar **[48]** ▷ *Don't touch that!* ¡No toques eso!

tough adj ❶ difícil ▷ *It was tough, but I managed then.* Fue difícil, pero me las arreglé.; **It's a tough job.** Es un trabajo duro. ❷ duro(-a) ▷ *The meat is tough.* La carne está dura. ❸ resistente ▷ *tough leather gloves* guantes de cuero resistentes; **He thinks he's a tough guy.** Le gusta hacerse el duro.; **Tough luck!** ¡Mala suerte!

tour n ❶ recorrido turístico m ▷ *We went on a tour of the city.* Hicimos un recorrido turístico por la ciudad.; **a package tour** un viaje organizado; **a bus tour** un viaje en autobús ❷ *(of building, exhibition)* visita f ❸ *(by band)* gira f; **to go on tour** ir **[27]** de gira ▶ vb **Robbie Williams is touring Europe.** Robbie Williams está haciendo una gira por Europa.

tour guide n guía turístico m, guía turística f

tourism n turismo m

tourist n turista mf; **tourist information office** la oficina de información y turismo

towards prep hacia ▷ He came towards me. Vino hacia mí.

towel n toalla f

tower n torre f

tower block n ❶ (of flats) bloque de pisos m ❷ (of offices) bloque de oficinas m

town n ciudad f ▷ the town centre el centro de la ciudad

town hall n ayuntamiento m

tow truck n (US) grúa f

toy n juguete m; **a toy shop** una juguetería; **a toy car** un coche de juguete

trace n rastro m ▷ There was no trace of the robbers. No había rastro de los ladrones.
▷ vb ❶ (draw) trazar [13] ❷ (locate) encontrar [11]

tracing paper n papel de calco m

track n ❶ (dirt road) camino m ❷ (railway line) vía f ❸ (in sport) pista f ❹ (song) canción f (pl canciones) ▷ This is my favourite track. Esta es mi canción preferida. ❺ (trail) huella f ▷ They followed the tracks for miles. Siguieron las huellas durante millas.

track down vb encontrar [11] ▷ The police never tracked down the killer. La policía nunca encontró al asesino.

tracksuit n chándal m (pl chándals)

tractor n tractor m

trade n oficio m ▷ to learn a trade aprender un oficio

trade union n sindicato m

tradition n tradición f (pl tradiciones)

traditional adj tradicional

traffic n tráfico m ▷ There was a lot of traffic. Había mucho tráfico.

traffic circle n (US) rotonda f

traffic jam n atasco m

traffic lights npl semáforo m

traffic warden n guardia de tráfico mf ▷ I'm a traffic warden. Soy guardia de tráfico.

tragedy n tragedia f

tragic adj trágico(-a)

trailer n ❶ (for luggage, boat) remolque m ❷ (of film) tráiler m (pl tráilers)

train n tren m
▷ vb entrenar [25] ▷ to train for a race entrenar para una carrera; **to train as a teacher** estudiar [25] magisterio; **to train an animal to do something** enseñar [25] a un animal a hacer algo

trained adj cualificado(-a) (calificado LatAm) ▷ highly trained workers los trabajadores altamente cualificados; **She's a trained nurse.** Es enfermera diplomada.

trainee n (apprentice) aprendiz m (pl aprendices), aprendiza f ▷ He's a trainee plumber. Es aprendiz de fontanero.; **She's a trainee teacher.** Es profesora de prácticas.

trainer n ❶ (sports) entrenador m, entrenadora f ❷ (of animals) amaestrador m, amaestradora f

trainers npl zapatillas de deporte fpl

training n ❶ formación f ▷ a
training course un curso de
formación ❷ (in sport)
entrenamiento m; **He strained a
muscle in training.** Se hizo un
esguince entrenando.

tram n tranvía m

Although **tranvía** ends in **-a**,
it is actually a masculine noun.

tramp n vagabundo m,
vagabunda f

trampoline n cama elástica f

transfer n ❶ transferencia f ▷ a
bank transfer una transferencia
bancaria ❷ (sticker) calcomanía f

translate vb traducir [9] ▷ to
translate something into English
traducir algo al inglés

translation n traducción f (pl
traducciones)

translator n traductor m,
traductora f ▷ Anita's a translator.
Anita es traductora.

transparent adj transparente

transplant n trasplante m ▷ a
heart transplant un trasplante de
corazón

transport n transporte m ▷ public
transport el transporte público
▶ vb transportar [25]

trap n trampa f

trash n (US) basura f; **the trash
can** el cubo de la basura

travel n **Air travel is relatively
cheap.** Viajar en avión es
relativamente barato.
▶ vb viajar [25] ▷ I prefer to travel by
train. Prefiero viajar en tren.; **I'd
like to travel round the world.**
Me gustaría dar la vuelta al

mundo.; **We travelled over 800
kilometres.** Hicimos más de 800
kilómetros.; **News travels fast!**
¡Las noticias vuelan!

travel agency n agencia de
viajes f

travel agent n **She's a travel
agent.** Es empleada de una
agencia de viajes.

traveller (US traveler) n viajero m,
viajera f

traveller's cheque (US traveler's
check) n cheque de viaje m (pl
cheques de viaje)

travelling (US traveling) n I love
travelling. Me encanta viajar.

travel sickness n mareo m

tray n bandeja f

tread vb pisar [25]; **to tread on
something** pisar [25] algo ▷ He
trod on her foot. Le pisó el pie.

treasure n tesoro m

treat n **As a birthday treat, I'll
take you out to dinner.** Como es
tu cumpleaños, te invito a cenar.;
**She bought a special treat for
the children.** Les compró algo
especial a los niños.; **I'm going to
give myself a treat.** Me voy a dar
un gusto.
▶ vb tratar [25] ▷ The hostages were
well treated. Los rehenes fueron
tratados bien.; **She was treated
for a minor head wound.** La
atendieron de una leve herida en la
cabeza.; **to treat somebody to
something** invitar [25] a alguien a
algo ▷ I'll treat you! ¡Te invito yo!

treatment n ❶ (medical)
tratamiento m ▷ an effective

treatment for eczema un tratamiento efectivo contra el eccema ❷ *(of person)* trato *m* ▷ *We don't want any special treatment.* No queremos ningún trato especial.

treble *vb* triplicarse **[48]** ▷ *The cost of living has trebled.* El coste de la vida se ha triplicado.

tree *n* árbol *m*

tremble *vb* temblar **[39]**

trend *n* ❶ *(tendency)* tendencia *f* ❷ *(fashion)* moda *f* ▷ *the latest trend* la última moda

trendy *adj* moderno(-a)

trial *n (in law)* juicio *m*

triangle *n* triángulo *m*

tribe *n* tribu *f*

trick *n* ❶ broma *f* ▷ *to play a trick on somebody* gastar una broma a alguien ❷ truco *m* ▷ *It's not easy: there's a trick to it.* No es fácil: tiene un truco.

▶ *vb* **to trick somebody** engañar **[25]** a alguien

tricky *adj (problem)* peliagudo(-a)

tricycle *n* triciclo *m*

trip *n* viaje *m* ▷ *to go on a trip* ir de viaje ▷ *Have a good trip!* ¡Buen viaje!; **a day trip** una excursión de un día

▶ *vb (stumble)* tropezarse **[19]** ▷ *He tripped on the stairs.* Se tropezó en las escaleras.

triple *adj* triple

triplets *npl* trillizos *mpl* (*f* trillizas)

trivial *adj* insignificante

trolley *n* carrito *m*

trombone *n* trombón *m* (*pl* trombones)

troops *npl* tropas *fpl*

trophy *n* trofeo *m*

tropical *adj* tropical

trouble *n* problema *m*

> Although **problema** ends in **-a**, it is actually a masculine noun. ▷ *The trouble is, it's too expensive.* El problema es que es demasiado caro.; **What's the trouble?** ¿Qué pasa?; **to be in trouble** tener **[53]** problemas; **stomach trouble** problemas de estómago; **to take a lot of trouble over something** poner **[41]** mucho cuidado en algo; **Don't worry, it's no trouble.** No te preocupes, no importa.

troublemaker *n* alborotador *m*, alborotadora *f*

trousers *npl* pantalones *mpl* ▷ *a pair of trousers* unos pantalones

trout *n* trucha *f*

truant *n* **to play truant** hacer **[26]** novillos

truck *n* camión *m* (*pl* camiones)

truck driver *n* camionero *m*, camionera *f* ▷ *He's a truck driver.* Es camionero.

true *adj (love, courage)* verdadero(-a); **It's true.** Es verdad.; **to come true** hacerse **[26]** realidad ▷ *I hope my dream will come true.* Espero que mi sueño se haga realidad.

trumpet *n* trompeta *f*

trunk *n* ❶ *(of tree)* tronco *m* ❷ *(of elephant)* trompa *f* ❸ *(luggage)* baúl *m* ❹ *(US: of car)* maletero *m*

trunks *npl* **swimming trunks** el traje de baño

trust *n* confianza *f* ▷ *to have trust in somebody* tener confianza en alguien

a
b
c
d
e
f
g
h
i
j
k
l
m
n
o
p
q
r
s
t
u
v
w
x
y
z

▶ vb Don't you trust me? ¿No tienes confianza en mí?; **Trust me!** ¡Confía en mí!; **I don't trust him.** No me fío de él.

truth n verdad f

try n intento m ▷ his third try su tercer intento; **to give something a try** intentar [25] algo; **It's worth a try.** Vale la pena intentarlo.; **Have a try!** ¡Inténtalo!
▶ vb ① intentar [25] ▷ to try to do something intentar hacer algo; **to try again** volver [59] a intentar ② (product, machine) probar [11] ▷ Would you like to try some? ¿Quieres probar un poco?

try on vb (clothes) probarse [11]

try out vb (product, machine) probar [11]

T-shirt n camiseta f

tube n tubo m; **the Tube** (underground) el Metro

tuberculosis n tuberculosis f ▷ He's got tuberculosis. Tiene tuberculosis.

Tuesday n martes m (pl martes) ▷ I saw her on Tuesday. La vi el martes. ▷ every Tuesday todos los martes ▷ last Tuesday el martes pasado ▷ next Tuesday el martes que viene ▷ on Tuesdays los martes

tuition n clases fpl ▷ private tuition clases particulares

tulip n tulipán m (pl tulipanes)

tumble dryer n secadora f

tummy n tripa f (informal); **He has tummy ache.** Le duele la tripa.

tuna n atún m (pl atunes)

tune n (melody) melodía f; **to play in tune** tocar [48] bien

Tunisia n Túnez m

tunnel n túnel m

Turk n turco m, turca f ▷ the Turks los turcos

Turkey n Turquía f

turkey n pavo m

Turkish adj turco(-a)
▶ n (language) turco m

turn n (bend in road) curva f; **'no left turn'** 'prohibido girar a la izquierda'; **to take turns** turnarse [25]; **It's my turn!** ¡Me toca a mí!
▶ vb ① girar [25] ▷ Turn right at the lights. Gira a la derecha al llegar al semáforo. ② (become) ponerse [41] ▷ When he's drunk he turns nasty. Cuando se emborracha se pone desagradable.; **The weather turned cold.** Empezó a hacer frío.; **to turn into something** convertirse [51] en algo ▷ The holiday turned into a nightmare. Las vacaciones se convirtieron en una pesadilla.

turn back vb volver [59] hacia atrás ▷ We turned back. Volvimos hacia atrás.

turn down vb ① rechazar [13] ▷ He turned down the offer. Rechazó la oferta. ② bajar [25] ▷ Shall I turn the heating down? ¿Bajo la calefacción?

turn off vb ① (light, radio) apagar [37] ② (tap) cerrar [39] ③ (engine) parar [25]

turn on vb ① (light, radio) encender [20] ② (tap) abrir [58] ③ (engine) poner [41] en marcha

turn out vb resultar [25] ▷ It turned out to be a mistake. Resultó ser un error. ▷ *It turned out that she was right.* Resultó que ella tenía razón.

turn round vb ❶ (car) dar [**14**] la vuelta ❷ (person) darse [**14**] la vuelta

turn up vb ❶ aparecer [**12**] ▷ *She never turned up.* No apareció. ❷ subir [**58**] ▷ *Could you turn up the radio?* ¿Puedes subir la radio?

turning n *We took the wrong turning.* **(1)** (in the country) Nos equivocamos de carretera. **(2)** (in the city) Nos equivocamos de bocacalle.

turnip n nabo m

turquoise adj turquesa

turtle n tortuga de mar f

tutor n (private teacher) profesor particular m, profesora particular f

tuxedo n (US) esmoquin m (pl esmóquines)

TV n tele f

tweezers npl pinzas fpl ▷ *a pair of tweezers* unas pinzas

twelfth adj duodécimo(-a) ▷ *the twelfth floor* el duodécimo piso; **the twelfth of August** el doce de agosto

twelve num doce ▷ *She's twelve.* Tiene doce años.; **twelve o'clock** las doce

twentieth adj vigésimo(-a); **the twentieth floor** la planta veinte; **the twentieth of May** el veinte de mayo

twenty num veinte ▷ *He's twenty.* Tiene veinte años.

twice adv dos veces ▷ *He had to repeat it twice.* Tuvo que repetirlo dos veces.; **twice as much** el

doble ▷ *He gets twice as much pocket money as me.* Le dan el doble de paga que a mí.

twin n mellizo m, melliza f ▷ *my twin brother* mi hermano mellizo; **identical twins** gemelos; **a twin room** una habitación con dos camas

twinned adj hermanado(-a) ▷ *Nottingham is twinned with Minsk.* Nottingham está hermanada con Minsk.

twist vb ❶ torcer [**6**]; **He's twisted his ankle.** Se ha torcido el tobillo. ❷ tergiversar [**25**] ▷ *You're twisting my words.* Estás tergiversando lo que he dicho.

two num dos ▷ *She's two.* Tiene dos años.; **The two of them can sing.** Los dos saben cantar.

type n tipo m ▷ *What type of camera have you got?* ¿Qué tipo de cámara tienes?
▶ vb escribir [**58**] a máquina ▷ *to type a letter* escribir una carta a máquina

typewriter n máquina de escribir f

typical adj típico(-a)

tyre (US tire) n neumático m

a b c d e f g h i j k l m n o p q r s t u v w x y z

u

UFO abbr (= Unidentified Flying Object) OVNI m (= el Objeto Volador No Identificado)

ugly adj feo(-a)

UK abbr (= United Kingdom) RU m (= el Reino Unido)

ulcer n úlcera f; **a mouth ulcer** una llaga en la boca

Ulster n Ulster m

umbrella n paraguas m (pl paraguas)

umpire n árbitro m, árbitra f

UN abbr (= United Nations) ONU f (= la Organización de las Naciones Unidas)

unable adj **to be unable to do something** no poder [**40**] hacer algo ▷ He was unable to come. No ha podido venir.

unanimous adj unánime

unavoidable adj inevitable

unbearable adj insoportable

unbelievable adj increíble

uncertain adj incierto(-a) ▷ The future is uncertain. El futuro es incierto.; **to be uncertain about something** no estar [**22**] seguro de algo; **She was uncertain how to begin.** No sabía muy bien cómo empezar.

uncle n tío m; **my uncle and aunt** mis tíos

uncomfortable adj incómodo(-a)

unconscious adj inconsciente

under prep

> When something is located under something, use **debajo de**. When there is movement involved, use **por debajo de**.

❶ debajo de ▷ The cat's under the table. El gato está debajo de la mesa. ❷ por debajo de ▷ The tunnel goes under the Channel. El túnel pasa por debajo del Canal.; **under there** ahí debajo ▷ What's under there? ¿Qué hay ahí debajo? ❸ menos de ▷ under 20 people menos de 20 personas; **children under 10** niños menores de 10 años

underage adj **He's underage.** Es menor de edad.

underground adv bajo tierra ▷ Moles live underground. Los topos viven bajo tierra.

▶ n metro m ▷ Is there an underground in Barcelona? ¿Hay metro en Barcelona?

underline vb subrayar [**25**]

underneath prep, adv

> When something is located underneath something, use **debajo de**. When there is movement involved, use **por debajo de**.

① debajo de ▷ *underneath the carpet* debajo de la moqueta ▷ *I got out of the car and looked underneath.* Bajé del coche y miré debajo. **②** por debajo de ▷ *I walked underneath a ladder.* Pasé por debajo de una escalera.

underpants npl calzoncillos mpl
▷ *a pair of underpants* unos calzoncillos

underpass n paso subterráneo m

undershirt n (US) camiseta f

understand vb entender [**20**] ▷ *Do you understand?* ¿Entiendes? ▷ *I don't understand the question.* No entiendo la pregunta.; **Is that understood?** ¿Está claro?

understanding adj comprensivo(-a) ▷ *She's very understanding.* Es muy comprensiva.

understood vb see **understand**

undertaker n empleado de una funeraria m, empleada de una funeraria f; **the undertaker's** la funeraria

underwater adj, adv
① subacuático(-a) ▷ *underwater photography* fotografía subacuática **②** bajo el agua
▷ *This sequence was filmed underwater.* Esta secuencia se filmó bajo el agua.

underwear n ropa interior f

undo vb **①** (button, blouse) desabrochar [**25**] **②** (knot, parcel, shoe laces) desatar [**25**] **③** (zipper) abrir [**58**]

undress vb (get undressed) desnudarse [**25**] ▷ *The doctor told me to undress.* El médico me dijo que me desnudase.

unemployed adj parado(-a) (desempleado LatAm); **He's been unemployed for a year.** Lleva parado un año.; **the unemployed** los parados (los desempleados LatAm)

unemployment n desempleo m

unexpected adj inesperado(-a)
▷ *an unexpected visitor* una visita inesperada

unexpectedly adv de improviso
▷ *This law is unfair to women.* Esta ley es injusta para las mujeres.

unfair adj injusto(-a) ▷ *This law is unfair to women.* Esta ley es injusta para las mujeres.

unfamiliar adj desconocido(-a)
▷ *I heard an unfamiliar voice.* Oí una voz desconocida.

unfashionable adj pasado de moda (f pasada de moda)

unfit adj **I'm unfit at the moment.** En este momento no estoy en forma.

unfold vb desplegar [**34**] ▷ *She unfolded the map.* Desplegó el mapa.

unforgettable adj inolvidable

unfortunately adv desafortunadamente

unfriendly adj antipático(-a)
▷ *The waiters are a bit unfriendly.* Los camareros son un poco antipáticos.

a
b
c
d
e
f
g
h
i
j
k
l
m
n
o
p
q
r
s
t
u
v
w
x
y
z

ungrateful adj desagradecido(-a)

unhappy adj infeliz (pl infelices)
▷ He was very unhappy as a child. De niño fue muy infeliz.; **to look unhappy** parecer [12] triste

unhealthy adj ❶ (food) malo para la salud (f mala para la salud) ❷ (ill) con mala salud ❸ (atmosphere) malsano(-a)

uniform n uniforme m; **school uniform** el uniforme de colegio

uninhabited adj ❶ (house) deshabitado(-a) ❷ (island) despoblado(-a)

union n (trade union) sindicato m

Union Jack n bandera del Reino Unido f

unique adj único(-a)

unit n unidad f ▷ a unit of measurement una unidad de medida; **a kitchen unit** un módulo de cocina

United Kingdom n Reino Unido m

United Nations n Naciones Unidas fpl

United States n Estados Unidos mpl

universe n universo m

university n universidad f ▷ She's at university. Está en la universidad. ▷ Lancaster University la Universidad de Lancaster

unleaded petrol n gasolina sin plomo f

unless conj a no ser que

▌ **a no ser que** has to be followed by a verb in the subjunctive.

▷ I won't come unless you phone me.

No vendré a no ser que me llames.; **Unless I am mistaken, we're lost.** Si no me equivoco, estamos perdidos.

unlikely adj poco probable ▷ That's possible, but unlikely. Es posible pero poco probable.

▌ **es poco probable que** has to be followed by a verb in the subjunctive.

▷ He's unlikely to come. Es poco probable que venga.

unload vb descargar [37] ▷ We unloaded the furniture. Descargamos los muebles.

unlock vb abrir [58] ▷ He unlocked the door of the car. Abrió la puerta del coche.

unlucky adj to be unlucky
(1) (be unfortunate) tener [53] mala suerte ▷ Did you win? — No, I was unlucky. ¿Ganaste? — No, tuve mala suerte. **(2)** (bring bad luck) traer [54] mala suerte ▷ They say thirteen is an unlucky number. Dicen que el número trece trae mala suerte.

unmarried adj soltero(-a) ▷ an unmarried mother una madre soltera; **an unmarried couple** una pareja no casada

unnatural adj poco natural

unnecessary adj innecesario(-a)

unpack vb deshacer [26] ▷ I unpacked my suitcase. Deshice la maleta.; **I haven't unpacked my clothes yet.** Todavía no he sacado la ropa de la maleta.

unpleasant adj desagradable

unplug vb desenchufar [25]

unpopular adj impopular ▷ It was an unpopular decision. Fue una decisión impopular.; **She's an unpopular child.** Tiene muy pocos amigos.

unrealistic adj poco realista

unreasonable adj poco razonable

unreliable adj poco fiable ▷ The car was slow and unreliable. El coche era lento y poco fiable.; **He's completely unreliable.** Es muy informal.

unroll vb desenrollar [25]

unscrew vb ① (screw) destornillar [25] ② (lid) desenroscar [48]

unsuccessful adj (attempt) fallido(-a); **to be unsuccessful in doing something** no conseguir [50] hacer algo; **an unsuccessful artist** un artista sin éxito

unsuitable adj (clothes, equipment) inapropiado(-a)

untidy adj ① (disorganized) desordenado(-a) ▷ Your bedroom is really untidy. Tu cuarto está muy desordenado. ② (writing) descuidado(-a); **She always looks so untidy.** Siempre va tan desaliñada.

untie vb ① (knot, parcel) deshacer [26] ② (shoelace, animal) desatar [25]

until prep, conj ① hasta ▷ I waited until ten o'clock. Esperé hasta las 10.; **until now** hasta ahora ▷ It's never been a problem until now. Hasta ahora nunca ha sido un problema.; **until then** hasta entonces ▷ Until then I'd never been to Italy. Hasta entonces no había estado nunca

en Italia. ② hasta que ▷ We stayed there until the doctor came. Nos quedamos allí hasta que vino el médico.

> **hasta que** has to be followed by a verb in the subjunctive when referring to a future event.
> ▷ Wait until I come back. Espera hasta que yo vuelva.

unusual adj ① poco común ▷ an unusual shape una forma poco común ② raro(-a)

> **es raro que** has to be followed by a verb in the subjunctive.
> ▷ It's unusual to get snow at this time of year. Es raro que nieve en esta época del año.

unwilling adj He was unwilling to help me. No estaba dispuesto a ayudarme.

unwrap vb abrir [58] ▷ After the meal we unwrapped the presents. Después de comer abrimos los regalos.

up prep, adv

> For other expressions with 'up', see the verbs 'come', 'put', 'turn' etc.

arriba ▷ up on the hill arriba de la colina ▷ up there allí arriba; **up north** en el norte; **They live up the road.** Viven en esta calle, un poco más allá.; **to be up** estar [22] levantado ▷ He's not up yet. Todavía no se ha levantado.; **What's up?** ¿Qué hay?; **What's up with her?** ¿Qué le pasa?; **to go up** subir [58] ▷ The bus went up the hill. El autobús subió la colina.; **to go up**

to somebody acercarse [48] a alguien ▷ *She came up to me.* Se me acercó.; **up to** hasta ▷ *up to now* hasta ahora; **It's up to you.** Depende de ti.

uphill adj **It was an uphill struggle.** Fue una tarea muy difícil.

upper adj superior

upright adj **to stand upright** tenerse [53] derecho

upset n **I had a stomach upset.** Tenía mal el estómago.
▶ adj disgustado(-a) ▷ *She's still a bit upset.* Todavía está un poco disgustada.; **Don't get upset.** No te enfades.; **I had an upset stomach.** Tenía mal el estómago.
▶ vb **to upset somebody** disgustar [25] a alguien; **Don't upset yourself.** No te disgustes.

upside down adv al revés ▷ *The painting was hung upside down.* El cuadro estaba colgado al revés.

upstairs adv arriba ▷ *Where's your coat? — It's upstairs.* ¿Dónde está tu abrigo? — Está arriba.; **the people upstairs** los de arriba; **He went upstairs to bed.** Subió para irse a la cama.

up-to-date adj ❶ (car, stereo) moderno(-a) ❷ actualizado(-a) ▷ *an up-to-date timetable* un horario actualizado; **to bring somebody up-to-date on something** poner [41] a alguien al corriente de algo; **to bring something up-to-date** actualizar [13] algo

upwards adv hacia arriba ▷ *to look upwards* mirar hacia arriba

urgent adj urgente

urine n orina f

US abbr (= United States) EEUU mpl (= los Estados Unidos)

us pron ❶ nos

> Use **nos** to translate 'us' when it is the direct object of the verb in the sentence, or when it means 'to us'.

▷ *They helped us.* Nos ayudaron.
▷ *Look at us!* ¡Míranos! ❷ nosotros (f nosotras)

> Use **nosotros** or **nosotras** after prepositions, in comparisons, and with the verb 'to be'.

▷ *Why don't you come with us?* ¿Por qué no vienes con nosotras? ▷ *They are older than us.* Son mayores que nosotros. ▷ *It's us.* Somos nosotros.

USA abbr (= United States of America) EEUU mpl (= los Estados Unidos)

use n uso m; 'directions for use' 'modo de empleo'; **It's no use shouting, she's deaf.** Es inútil gritar, es sorda.; **It's no use, I can't do it.** No hay manera, no puedo hacerlo.; **to make use of something** usar [25] algo
▶ vb usar [25] ▷ *Can I use your phone?* ¿Puedo usar tu teléfono?; **I used to go camping as a child.** De pequeño solía ir de acampada.; **I didn't use to like maths, but now I love it.** Antes no me gustaban las matemáticas, pero ahora me encantan.; **to be used to something** estar [22] acostumbrado a algo ▷ *He wasn't*

used to driving on the right. No estaba acostumbrado a conducir por la derecha.

use up vb **We've used up all the paint.** Hemos acabado toda la pintura.

useful adj útil

useless adj inútil ▷ a piece of useless information una información inútil; **You're useless!** ¡Eres un inútil!; **This computer is useless.** Este ordenador no sirve para nada.; **It's useless asking her.** No sirve de nada preguntarle.

user n usuario m, usuaria f

user-friendly adj fácil de usar

usual adj habitual; **as usual** como de costumbre

usually adv normalmente ▷ I usually get to school at about half past eight. Normalmente llego al colegio sobre las ocho y media.

vacancy n ❶ (job) vacante f ❷ (in hotel) habitación libre f; **'no vacancies'** 'completo'

vacant adj libre ▷ a vacant seat un asiento libre

vacation n (US) vacaciones fpl ▷ to be on vacation estar de vacaciones ▷ to take a vacation tomarse unas vacaciones

vaccinate vb vacunar [25]

vacuum vb pasar [25] la aspiradora ▷ to vacuum the hall pasar la aspiradora por el vestíbulo

vacuum cleaner n aspiradora f

vagina n vagina f

vague adj ❶ vago(-a) ▷ I've only got a vague idea what he means. Tengo solo una vaga idea de lo que quiere decir. ❷ distraído(-a) ▷ He's getting a bit vague in his old age. Se está poniendo un poco distraído en su vejez.

vain adj vanidoso(-a) ▷ He's so vain! ¡Es más vanidoso!; **in vain** en vano

Valentine card n tarjeta del día de los enamorados f

Valentine's Day n día de los enamorados m

valid adj válido(-a) ▷ a valid passport un pasaporte válido; **This ticket is valid for three months.** Este billete tiene una validez de tres meses.

valley n valle m

valuable adj ① de valor ▷ a valuable painting un cuadro de valor ② valioso(-a) ▷ valuable help una valiosa ayuda

value n valor m

van n furgoneta f

vandal n vándalo m

vandalism n vandalismo m

vandalize vb destrozar [13]

vanilla n vainilla f ▷ a vanilla ice cream un helado de vainilla

vanish vb desaparecer [12]; **to vanish into thin air** esfumarse [25]

variety n variedad f

various adj varios (f varias) ▷ We visited various villages in the area. Visitamos varias aldeas de la zona.

vary vb variar [21]

vase n jarrón m (pl jarrones)

VAT n IVA m

| Although IVA ends in -A, it is actually a masculine noun.

VCR n (= video cassette recorder) vídeo m

veal n carne de ternera f

vegan n vegetariano estricto m, vegetariana estricta f

vegetable n ① (to be cooked) verdura f ▷ vegetable soup sopa de verduras ② (for salads) hortaliza f ▷ peppers, tomatoes and other vegetables pimientos, tomates y otras hortalizas

vegetarian n vegetariano m, vegetariana f ▷ I'm a vegetarian. Soy vegetariano.
▶ adj vegetarian lasagne lasaña vegetariana

vehicle n vehículo m

vein n vena f

velvet n terciopelo m

vending machine n máquina expendedora f

verb n verbo m

verdict n veredicto m

vertical adj vertical

vertigo n vértigo m ▷ I get vertigo. Tengo vértigo.

very adv muy ▷ very tall muy alto; **It's very cold.** Hace mucho frío.; **not very interesting** no demasiado interesante; **very much** muchísimo; **We were thinking the very same thing.** Estábamos pensando exactamente lo mismo.
▶ adj mismo(-a) ▷ in this very house en esta misma casa

vest n ① (underclothing) camiseta f ② (US: waistcoat) chaleco m

vet n veterinario m, veterinaria f ▷ She's a vet. Es veterinaria.

via prep ① por ▷ We drove to Lisbon via Salamanca. Fuimos a Lisboa por Salamanca. ❷ **vía** ▷ *a flight via Brussels* un vuelo vía Bruselas

vicar n párroco m

vice n (tool) tornillo de banco m

vicious adj ❶ brutal ▷ *a vicious attack* una brutal agresión ❷ feroz ▷ *a vicious dog* un perro feroz; **He was a vicious man.** Era un hombre despiadado.; **a vicious circle** un círculo vicioso

victim n víctima f ▷ *He was the victim of a mugging.* Fue víctima de un atraco.

victory n victoria f

video vb grabar [25] en vídeo (grabar [25] en video LatAm) ▷ *They videoed the whole wedding.* Grabaron en vídeo toda la boda. ▷ n vídeo m (video m LatAm) ▷ *to watch a video* ver un vídeo; **a video camera** una videocámara; **a video game** un videojuego

view n ❶ vista f ▷ *There's an amazing view.* La vista es magnífica. ❷ opinión f (pl opiniones) ▷ *in my view* en mi opinión

viewer n telespectador m, telespectadora f

viewpoint n punto de vista m

vile adj repugnante

villa n chalet m

village n ❶ (large) pueblo m ❷ (small) aldea f

vine n ❶ (trailing) vid f ❷ (climbing) parra f

vinegar n vinagre m

vineyard n viñedo m

viola n viola f

violence n violencia f

violent adj violento(-a)

violin n violín m (pl violines)

violinist n violinista mf

virgin n virgen f (pl vírgenes) ▷ *to be a virgin* ser virgen

Virgo n (sign) Virgo m; **I'm Virgo.** Soy virgo.

virtual reality n realidad virtual f

virus n (also computing) virus m (pl virus)

visa n visado m (visa f LatAm)

visible adj visible

visit n visita f ▷ *my last visit to my grandmother* la última visita que le hice a mi abuela; **I saw him on my latest visit to Spain.** Lo vi la última vez que estuve en España. ▷ vb visitar [25]

visitor n ❶ (tourist) visitante mf ❷ (guest) visita f ▷ *to have a visitor* tener visita

visual adj visual

vital adj vital

vitamin n vitamina f

vivid adj vivo(-a) ▷ *vivid colours* colores vivos; **to have a vivid imagination** tener [53] una imaginación desbordante

vocabulary n vocabulario m

vocational adj **a vocational course** un curso de formación profesional

vodka n vodka m

Although **vodka** ends in -**a**, it is actually a masculine noun.

voice n voz f (pl voces)

voicemail n buzón de voz m

volcano n volcán m (pl volcanes)

volleyball n voleibol m

volt n voltio m

voluntary *adj* voluntario(-a); **to do voluntary work** hacer [26] voluntariado

volunteer *n* voluntario *m*, voluntaria *f*
▸ *vb* **to volunteer to do something** ofrecerse [12] a hacer algo

vomit *vb* vomitar [25]

vote *vb* votar [25] ▸ *Who did you vote for?* ¿A quién votaste?
▸ *n* voto *m*

voucher *n* vale *m* ▸ *a gift voucher* un vale de regalo

vowel *n* vocal *f*

vulgar *adj* vulgar

wage *n* paga *f* ▸ *He collected his wages.* Recogió la paga.

waist *n* cintura *f*

waistcoat *n* chaleco *m*

wait *vb* esperar [25] ▸ *I'll wait for you.* Te esperaré. ▸ *Wait a minute!* ¡Espera un momento!; **to keep somebody waiting** hacer [26] esperar a alguien ▸ *They kept us waiting for hours.* Nos hicieron esperar durante horas.; **I can't wait for the holidays.** Estoy deseando que lleguen las vacaciones.; **I can't wait to see him again.** Me muero de ganas de verlo otra vez.

wait up *vb* esperar [25] levantado

waiter *n* camarero *m*

waiting list *n* lista de espera *f*

waiting room *n* sala de espera *f*

waitress n camarera f

wake up vb despertarse **[39]** ▷ I woke up at six o'clock. Me desperté a las seis.; **to wake somebody up** despertar **[39]** a alguien ▷ Please would you wake me up at seven o'clock? ¿Podría despertarme a las siete, por favor?

Wales n Gales m; **the Prince of Wales** el Príncipe de Gales; **I'm from Wales.** Soy de Gales.

walk vb ❶ andar **[4]** ▷ We walked 10 kilometres. Anduvimos 10 kilómetros. ❷ (go on foot) ir **[27]** a pie ▷ Are you walking or going by bus? ¿Vas a ir a pie o en autobús? ❸ (for fun) pasear **[25]** ▷ I like walking through the park. Me gusta pasear por el parque.; **to walk the dog** pasear **[25]** el perro
▶ n paseo m; **to go for a walk** ir **[27]** a pasear; **It's 10 minutes' walk from here.** Está a 10 minutos de aquí a pie.

walking n (hill walking) senderismo m; **Walking is good for your health.** Andar es bueno para la salud.

walking stick n bastón m (pl bastones)

wall n ❶ (of room, building) pared f ❷ (freestanding) muro m ❸ (of castle, city) muralla f

wallet n cartera f

wallpaper n papel pintado m

walnut n nuez f (pl nueces)

want vb querer **[43]** ▷ Do you want some cake? ¿Quieres un poco de pastel?; **to want to do something** querer **[43]** hacer algo ▷ What do you want to do tomorrow? ¿Qué quieres hacer mañana?

▌**querer que** has to be followed by a verb in the subjunctive.

to want somebody to do something querer **[43]** que alguien haga algo ▷ They want us to wait here. Quieren que esperemos aquí.

war n guerra f; **to be at war** estar **[22]** en guerra

ward n sala f

wardrobe n armario m

warehouse n almacén m (pl almacenes)

warm adj ❶ caliente ▷ warm water agua caliente ❷ caluroso(-a) ▷ a warm day un día caluroso ▷ a warm welcome una calurosa bienvenida; **warm clothing** ropa de abrigo; **This jumper is very warm.** Este jersey es muy calentito.; **He's a very warm person.** Es una persona muy afectuosa.; **It's warm in here.** Aquí dentro hace calor.; **I'm too warm.** Tengo demasiado calor.

warn vb advertir **[51]** ▷ Well, I warned you! ¡Ya te lo había advertido!

▌Use the subjunctive after **aconsejar a alguien que.**

to warn somebody to do something aconsejar **[25]** a alguien que haga algo

warning n advertencia f

Warsaw n Varsovia f

wart n verruga f

was vb see **be**

wash n **to have a wash** lavarse **[25]**; **to give something a wash**

lavar **[25]** algo; **The car needs a wash.** Al coche le hace falta un lavado.

▶ vb ❶ lavar **[25]** ▷ *to wash the car* lavar el coche ❷ *(have a wash)* **lavarse [25]** ▷ *Every morning I get up, wash and get dressed.* Todas las mañanas me levanto, me lavo y me visto.; **to wash one's hands** lavarse **[25]** las manos; **to wash up** lavar **[25]** los platos

washbasin n lavabo m

washcloth n (US) toallita para lavarse f

washing n (clean laundry) ropa lavada f; **to do the washing** lavar **[25]** la ropa; **dirty washing** la ropa para lavar; **Have you got any washing?** ¿Tienes ropa para lavar?

washing machine n lavadora f

washing powder n detergente m

washing-up n **to do the washing-up** lavar **[25]** los platos

washing-up liquid n lavavajillas m (pl lavavajillas)

wasn't = was not

wasp n avispa f

waste n ❶ desperdicio m ▷ *It's such a waste!* ¡Qué desperdicio!; **It's a waste of time.** Es una pérdida de tiempo. ❷ residuos pl ▷ *nuclear waste* residuos radioactivos

▶ vb (food, space, opportunity) desperdiciar **[25]**; **to waste time** perder **[20]** el tiempo ▷ *There's no time to waste.* No hay tiempo que perder.; **I don't like wasting money.** No me gusta malgastar el dinero.

wastepaper basket n papelera f

watch n reloj m

▶ vb ❶ mirar **[25]**; **Watch me!** ¡Mírame! ❷ ver **[57]** ▷ *to watch TV* ver la tele ❸ vigilar **[25]** ▷ *The police were watching the house.* La policía vigilaba la casa.

watch out vb tener **[53]** cuidado; **Watch out!** ¡Cuidado!

water n agua f

> Although it's a feminine noun, remember that you use **el** with **agua**.

▶ vb regar **[34]** ▷ *He was watering his tulips.* Estaba regando los tulipanes.

waterfall n cascada f

watering can n regadera f

watermelon n sandía f

waterproof adj impermeable; **a waterproof watch** un reloj sumergible

water-skiing n esquí acuático m ▷ *to go water-skiing* hacer esquí acuático

wave n ola f

▶ vb **to wave to somebody (1)** (say hello) saludar **[25]** a alguien con la mano **(2)** (say goodbye) hacer **[26]** adiós con la mano

wax n cera f

way n ❶ manera f ▷ *She looked at me in a strange way.* Me miró de manera extraña.; **This book tells you the right way to do it.** Este libro explica cómo hay que hacerlo.; **You're doing it the wrong way.** Lo estás haciendo mal.; **in a way...** en cierto sentido...; **a way of life** un estilo de vida ❷ (route) camino m

▷ *We stopped for lunch on the way.* Paramos a comer en el camino.; **Which way is it?** ¿Por dónde es?; **The supermarket is this way.** El supermercado es por aquí.; **Do you know the way to the hotel?** ¿Sabes cómo llegar al hotel?; **He's on his way.** Está de camino.; **It's a long way.** Está lejos. ▷ *It's a long way from the hotel.* Está lejos del hotel.; **'way in'** 'entrada'; **'way out'** 'salida'; **by the way...** a propósito...

we pron nosotros (f nosotras)

■ 'we' generally isn't translated unless it is emphatic.

▷ *We were in a hurry.* Teníamos prisa.

■ Use **nosotros** or **nosotras** as appropriate for emphasis.

▷ *They went but we didn't.* Ellos fueron pero nosotros no.

weak adj ❶ débil ❷ (tea, coffee) poco cargado(-a)

wealthy adj rico(-a)

weapon n arma f

■ Although it's a feminine noun, remember that you use **el** and **un** with **arma**.

wear vb llevar [**25**] ▷ *She was wearing a hat.* Llevaba un sombrero.; **She was wearing black.** Iba vestida de negro.

weather n tiempo m ▷ *What's the weather like?* ¿Qué tiempo hace?

weather forecast n pronóstico del tiempo m

Web n the Web la Web

web browser n navegador de Internet m

webcam n webcam f

web page n página web f

website n sitio web m

we'd = **we had**; **we would**

wedding n boda f; **wedding anniversary** el aniversario de boda; **wedding dress** el vestido de novia

Wednesday n miércoles m (pl miércoles) ▷ *I saw her on Wednesday.* La vi el miércoles. ▷ *every Wednesday* todos los miércoles ▷ *last Wednesday* el miércoles pasado ▷ *next Wednesday* el miércoles que viene ▷ *on Wednesdays* los miércoles

weed n hierbajo m ▷ *The garden's full of weeds.* El jardín está lleno de hierbajos.

week n semana f ▷ *in a week's time* dentro de una semana; **a week on Friday** el viernes de la semana que viene; **during the week** durante la semana

weekday n día entre semana m

■ Although **día** ends in -a, it is actually a masculine noun.

on weekdays los días entre semana

weekend n fin de semana m; **next weekend** el próximo fin de semana

weigh vb pesar [**25**] ▷ *How much do you weigh?* ¿Cuánto pesas?; **to weigh oneself** pesarse [**25**]

weight n peso m; **to lose weight** adelgazar [**13**]; **to put on weight** engordar [**25**]

weightlifting n levantamiento de pesas m

a b c d e f g h i j k l m n o p q r s t u v w x y z

weird adj raro(-a)

welcome n bienvenida f ▷ *They gave her a warm welcome.* Le dieron una calurosa bienvenida.; **Welcome!** ¡Bienvenido!

> If you're addressing a woman remember to use the feminine form: **¡Bienvenida!** If you're addressing more than one person use the plural form **¡Bienvenidos!** or **¡Bienvenidas!**

▶ vb **to welcome somebody** dar [14] la bienvenida a alguien; **Thank you! — You're welcome!** ¡Gracias! — ¡De nada!

well adj, adv ❶ bien ▷ *You did that really well.* Lo hiciste realmente bien. ▷ *She's doing really well at school.* Le va muy bien en el colegio.; **to be well** estar [22] bien ▷ *I'm not very well at the moment.* No estoy muy bien en este momento.; **Get well soon!** ¡Que te mejores!; **Well done!** ¡Muy bien! ❷ bueno ▷ *It's enormous! Well, quite big anyway.* ¡Es enorme! Bueno, digamos que bastante grande.; **as well** también ▷ *We worked hard, but we had some fun as well.* Trabajamos mucho, pero también nos divertimos.; **as well as** además de ▷ *We went to Gerona as well as Sitges.* Fuimos a Gerona, además de Sitges.

▶ n pozo m

we'll = **we will**

well-behaved adj **to be well-behaved** portarse [25] bien

wellingtons npl botas de agua fpl

well-known adj conocido(-a) ▷ *a well-known film star* un conocido actor de cine

well-off adj adinerado(-a)

Welsh adj galés (f galesa)
▶ n (language) galés m; **the Welsh** los galeses

Welshman n galés m (pl galeses)

Welshwoman n galesa f

went vb see **go**

were vb see **be**

we're = **we are**

weren't = **were not**

west n oeste m
▶ adj, adv ❶ occidental ▷ *the west coast* la costa occidental; **west of** al oeste de ▷ *Stroud is west of Oxford.* Stroud está al oeste de Oxford. ❷ hacia el oeste ▷ *We were travelling west.* Viajábamos hacia el oeste.; **the West Country** el sudoeste de Inglaterra

western n western m
▶ adj occidental ▷ *the western part of the island* la parte occidental de la isla; **Western Europe** Europa Occidental

West Indian adj antillano(-a); **She's West Indian.** Es antillana.
▶ n antillano m, antillana f

West Indies npl the West Indies las Antillas

wet adj mojado(-a) ▷ *wet clothes* ropa mojada; **to get wet** mojarse [25]; **dripping wet** chorreando; **wet weather** el tiempo lluvioso; **It was wet all week.** Llovió toda la semana.

wetsuit n traje de buzo m

we've = **we have**

whale n ballena f

what adj, pron ➊ qué

Use **qué** (with an accent) in direct and indirect questions and exclamations.

▷ *What subjects are you studying?* ¿Qué asignaturas estudias? ▷ *What's it for?* ¿Para qué es? ▷ *I don't know what to do.* No sé qué hacer. ▷ *What a mess!* ¡Qué desorden!

Only translate 'what is' by **qué es** if asking for a definition or explanation.

▷ *What is it?* ¿Qué es? ▷ *What's a tractor, Daddy?* ¿Qué es un tractor, papá? ➋ cuál (pl cuáles)

Translate 'what is' by **cuál es** when not asking for a definition or explanation.

▷ *What's her telephone number?* ¿Cuál es su número de teléfono? ➌ lo que

Use **lo que** (no accent) when 'what' isn't a question word. ▷ *I saw what happened.* Vi lo que pasó.; *What?* **(1)** *(what did you say?)* ¿Cómo? **(2)** *(shocked)* ¿Qué?; *What's your name?* ¿Cómo te llamas?

wheat n trigo m

wheel n rueda f; **steering wheel** el volante

wheelchair n silla de ruedas f

when adv cuándo

Remember the accent on **cuándo** in direct and indirect questions.

▷ *When did he go?* ¿Cuándo se fue? ▷ *I asked her when the next bus was.*

Le pregunté cuándo salía el próximo autobús.

▶ conj cuando ▷ *She was reading when I came in.* Cuando entré ella estaba leyendo.

cuando has to be followed by a verb in the subjunctive when referring to an event in the future.

▷ *Call me when you get there.* Llámame cuando llegues.

where adv dónde

Remember the accent on **dónde** in direct and indirect questions.

▷ *Where do you live?* ¿Dónde vives? ▷ *Where are you from?* ¿De dónde eres? ▷ *She asked me where I had bought it.* Me preguntó dónde lo había comprado.; **Where are you going?** ¿Adónde vas?

▶ conj donde ▷ *a shop where you can buy coffee* una tienda donde se puede comprar café

whether conj si ▷ *I don't know whether to go or not.* No sé si o no.

which adj, pron ➊ cuál (pl cuáles)

Remember the accent on **cuál** and **cuáles** in direct and indirect questions.

▷ *I know his sister. —Which one?* Conozco a su hermana. —¿A cuál? ▷ *Which would you like?* ¿Cuál quieres? ▷ *Of the five pairs, which were sold?* De los cinco pares, ¿cuáles se vendieron? ➋ qué

Use **qué** (with an accent) before nouns.

▷ *Which flavour do you want?* ¿Qué sabor quieres? ➌ *(that)* que ▷ *It's an illness which causes nerve damage.* Es una enfermedad que daña los nervios. ▷ *This is the skirt which Daphne gave me.* Esta es la falda que me dio Daphne. ▷ *Our uniform, which is green, is quite nice.* Nuestro uniforme, que es verde, está bastante bien.

▌After a preposition **que** becomes **el que, la que, los que, las que** to agree with the noun.

▷ *That's the film which I was telling you about.* Esa es la película de la que te hablaba. ❷ **lo cual** ▷ *The cooker isn't working, which is a nuisance.* La cocina no funciona, lo cual es un fastidio.

while conj ❶ mientras ▷ *You hold the torch while I look inside.* Aguanta la linterna mientras yo miro por dentro. ❷ mientras que ▷ *Isobel is very dynamic, while Kay is more laid-back.* Isobel es muy dinámica, mientras que Kay es más tranquila.

▸ n a **while** un rato ▷ *after a while* después de un rato; **a while ago** hace un momento ▷ *He was here a while ago.* Hace un momento estaba aquí.; **for a while** durante un tiempo ▷ *I lived in London for a while.* Viví en Londres durante un tiempo.; **quite a while** mucho tiempo ▷ *I haven't seen him for quite a while.* Hace mucho tiempo que no lo veo.

whip n (for horse) fusta f
▸ vb ❶ (animal) fustigar [**37**]
❷ (person) azotar [**25**] ❸ (eggs, cream) batir [**58**]

whipped cream n nata montada f

whiskers npl (of animal) bigotes mpl

whisky n whisky m (pl whiskys)

whisper vb susurrar [**25**]

whistle n silbato m ▷ *The referee blew his whistle.* El árbitro tocó el silbato.
▸ vb ❶ (with a whistle) pitar [**25**]
❷ (with mouth) silbar [**25**]

white adj blanco(-a) ▷ *He's got white hair.* Tiene el cabello blanco.; **white bread** el pan blanco; **white coffee** el café con leche; **a white man** un hombre blanco; **white people** los blancos; **white wine** el vino blanco

whiteboard n pizarra blanca f; **an interactive whiteboard** una pizarra digital

Whitsun n Pentecostés m

who pron ❶ quién (pl quiénes)

▌Remember the accent on **quién** and **quiénes** in direct and indirect questions.

▷ *Who said that?* ¿Quién dijo eso? ▷ *Who is it?* ¿Quién es? ▷ *We don't know who broke the window.* No sabemos quién rompió la ventana. ❷ que ▷ *the people who know us* las personas que nos conocen

▌After a preposition **que** becomes **el que, la que, los que, las que** to agree with the noun.

▷ *the women who she was chatting with* las mujeres con las que estaba hablando

▌Note that **a + el que** becomes **al que.**

▷ *the boy who I gave it to* el chico al que se lo di

whole *adj* entero(-a) ▷ *two whole days* dos días enteros; **the whole afternoon** toda la tarde; **the whole world** todo el mundo

▶ *n* **The whole of Wales was affected.** Todo Gales se vio afectado.; **on the whole** en general

wholemeal *adj* integral

▷ *wholemeal bread* pan integral

wholewheat *adj* (US) integral

whom *pron* ❶ quién (*pl* quiénes)

Remember the accent on **quién** and **quiénes** in direct and indirect questions.

▷ *With whom did you go?* ¿Con quién fuiste? ❷ quien ▷ *the man whom I saw* el hombre a quien vi

whose *adj* ❶ (*in questions*) de quién (*pl* de quiénes)

Remember the accent on **quién** and **quiénes** in direct and indirect questions.

▷ *Whose books are these?* ¿De quiénes son estos libros? ❷ (*relative*) cuyo(-a) ▷ *the girl whose picture was in the paper* la muchacha cuya foto venía en el periódico

▶ *pron* de quién (*pl* de quiénes)

Remember the accent on **quién** and **quiénes** in direct and indirect questions.

▷ *Whose is this?* ¿De quién es esto?

why *adv* por qué

Remember to write **por qué** as two words with an accent on **qué** when translating 'why'.

▷ *Why did you do that?* ¿Por qué hiciste eso?; **Why not?** ¿Por qué no?; **That's why he did it.** Por eso lo hizo.

wicked *adj* ❶ (*evil*) malvado(-a) ❷ (*really great*) sensacional

wide *adj, adv* ancho(-a) ▷ *a wide road* una carretera ancha ▷ *How wide is the room? — It's five metres wide.* ¿Cómo es de ancha la habitación? — Tiene cinco metros de ancho.; **wide open** abierto de par en par ▷ *The door was wide open.* La puerta estaba abierta de par en par.; **wide awake** completamente despierto

widow *n* viuda *f* ▷ *She's a widow.* Es viuda.

widower *n* viudo *m* ▷ *He's a widower.* Es viudo.

width *n* anchura *f*

wife *n* esposa *f*

wig *n* peluca *f*

wild *adj* ❶ salvaje ▷ *a wild animal* un animal salvaje ❷ silvestre ▷ *wild flowers* flores silvestres ❸ loco(-a) ▷ *She's a bit wild.* Es un poco loca.

wildlife *n* flora y fauna *f*

will *n* (*document*) testamento *m*

▶ *vb*

'will' can often be translated by the present tense, as in the following examples.

▷ *Come on, I'll help you.* Venga, te ayudo. ▷ *We'll talk about it later.* Hablamos luego. ▷ *Will you help me?* ¿Me ayudas?

Use **voy a**, **va a**, and so on + the infinitive to talk about plans and intentions.

▷ *What will you do?* ¿Qué vas a hacer? ▷ *We'll be having lunch late.* Vamos a comer tarde.

▌ Use the future tense when guessing what will happen or when making a supposition.

▷ *It won't take long.* No llevará mucho tiempo. ▷ *We'll probably go out later.* Seguramente saldremos luego. ▷ *I'll always love you.* Te querré siempre. ▷ *That will be the postman.* Será el cartero.

▌ Use **querer** for 'to be willing' in emphatic requests, and invitations.

▷ *Tom won't help me.* Tom no me quiere ayudar. ▷ *Will you be quiet!* ¿Te quieres callar? ▷ *Will you have some tea?* ¿Quieres tomar un té?

willing *adj* **to be willing to do something** estar [**22**] dispuesto a hacer algo

win *vb* ganar [**25**] ▷ *Did you win?* ¿Ganaste? ▷ *to win a prize* ganar un premio
 ▶ *n* victoria *f*

wind *vb* (rope, wire) enrollar [**25**]
 ▶ *n* viento *m*; **a wind instrument** un instrumento de viento; **wind power** la energía eólica

window *n* ❶ (of building) ventana *f* ❷ (in car, train) ventanilla *f*; **a shop window** un escaparate ❸ (window pane) cristal *m* (vidrio *m* LatAm) ▷ *to break a window* romper un cristal

windscreen *n* parabrisas *m* (pl parabrisas)

windscreen wiper *n* limpiaparabrisas *m* (pl limpiaparabrisas)

windshield *n* (US) parabrisas *m* (pl parabrisas)

windshield wiper *n* (US) limpiaparabrisas *m* (pl limpiaparabrisas)

windy *adj* **a windy day** un día de viento; **It's windy.** Hace viento.

wine *n* vino *m* ▷ **white wine** el vino blanco ▷ **red wine** el vino tinto; **a wine bar** un bar especializado en vinos; **a wine glass** una copa de vino; **the wine list** la carta de vinos

wing *n* ala *f*

▌ Although it's a feminine noun, remember that you use **el** and **un** with **ala**.

wink *vb* **to wink at somebody** guiñar [**25**] el ojo a alguien

winner *n* ganador *m*, ganadora *f*

winning *adj* vencedor(a) ▷ *the winning team* el equipo vencedor; **the winning goal** el gol de la victoria

winter *n* invierno *m*

wipe *vb* limpiar [**25**]; **to wipe one's feet** limpiarse [**25**] los zapatos; **to wipe one's nose** limpiarse [**25**] la nariz; *Did you wipe up that water you spilled?* ¿Recogiste el agua que derramaste?

wire *n* alambre *m*; **copper wire** el hilo de cobre; **the telephone wire** el cable del teléfono

wisdom tooth *n* muela del juicio *f*

wise *adj* sabio(-a)

wish *vb* **to wish for something** desear [**25**] algo ▷ *What more could you wish for?* ¿Qué más podrías desear?; **to wish to do something**

desear [**25**] hacer algo ▷ I wish to make a complaint. Deseo hacer una reclamación.; **I wish you were here!** ¡Ojalá estuvieras aquí!; **I wish you'd told me!** ¡Me lo podrías haber dicho!; **to wish somebody happy birthday** desear [**25**] a alguien un feliz cumpleaños
▶ n deseo m ▷ to make a wish pedir un deseo; **'best wishes'** (on birthday card) 'felicidades'; **'with best wishes, Kathy'** 'un abrazo, Kathy'

wit n ingenio m

with prep ❶ con ▷ He walks with a stick. Camina con un bastón. ▷ Come with me. Ven conmigo. ❷ de ▷ a woman with blue eyes una mujer de ojos azules ▷ Fill the jug with water. Llena la jarra de agua.; **We stayed with friends.** Nos quedamos en casa de unos amigos.

within prep dentro de ▷ I want it back within three days. Quiero que me lo devuelvas dentro de tres días.; **The police arrived within minutes.** La policía llegó a los pocos minutos.; **The shops are within easy reach.** Las tiendas están cerca.

without prep sin ▷ without a coat sin abrigo ▷ without speaking sin hablar

witness n testigo mf ▷ There were no witnesses. No había testigos.

witty adj ingenioso(-a)

wives npl see **wife**

woke up vb see **wake up**

wolf n lobo m

woman n mujer f; **a woman doctor** una doctora

won vb see **win**

wonder vb preguntarse [**25**] ▷ I wonder why she said that. Me pregunto por qué dijo eso.; **I wonder where Caroline is.** ¿Dónde estará Caroline?

wonderful adj maravilloso(-a)

won't = **will not**

wood n ❶ madera f ▷ It's made of wood. Es de madera. ❷ (for fire) leña f ❸ bosque m ▷ We went for a walk in the wood. Fuimos a pasear por el bosque.

wooden adj de madera ▷ a wooden chair una silla de madera

woodwork n carpintería f

wool n lana f ▷ It's made of wool. Es de lana.

word n palabra f; **What's the word for 'shop' in Spanish?** ¿Cómo se dice 'shop' en español?; **in other words** en otras palabras; **to have a word with somebody** hablar [**25**] con alguien ▷ Can I have a word with you? ¿Puedo hablar contigo?; **the words** (lyrics) la letra

word processing n procesamiento de textos m

word processor n procesador de textos m

wore vb see **wear**

work n trabajo m ▷ She's looking for work. Está buscando trabajo.; **It's hard work.** Es duro.; **at work** en el trabajo ▷ He's at work until five o'clock. Está en el trabajo hasta las cinco.; **He's off work today.** Hoy

tiene el día libre.; **to be out of work** estar [22] sin trabajo
▶ vb ❶ trabajar [25] ▷ *She works in a shop.* Trabaja en una tienda.
❷ funcionar [25] ▷ *The heating isn't working.* La calefacción no funciona.

work out vb ❶ (exercise) hacer [26] ejercicio ▷ *I work out twice a week.* Hago ejercicio dos veces a la semana. ❷ (turn out) salir [49] ▷ *I hope it will work out well.* Espero que salga bien. ❸ (calculate) calcular [25] ▷ *I worked it out in my head.* Lo calculé en mi cabeza. ❹ (understand) entender [20] ▷ *I just couldn't work it out.* No lograba entenderlo.; **It works out at £10 each.** Sale a 10 libras esterlinas por persona.

worker n trabajador m, trabajadora f ▷ *She's a good worker.* Trabaja bien.

work experience n **I'm going to do my work experience in a factory.** Voy a hacer las prácticas en una fábrica.

working-class adj de clase obrera ▷ *a working-class family* una familia de clase obrera

workman n obrero m

worksheet n hoja de ejercicios f

workshop n taller m ▷ *a drama workshop* un taller de teatro

workstation n terminal de trabajo f

world n mundo m; **the world champion** el campeón mundial; **the World Cup** la Copa del Mundo

worm n gusano m

worn vb *see* **wear**
▶ adj gastado(-a) ▷ *The carpet is a bit worn.* La moqueta está un poco gastada.; **worn out** agotado ▷ *We were worn out after the long walk.* Estábamos agotados después de andar tanto.

worried adj preocupado(-a) ▷ *to be worried about something* estar preocupado por algo

worry vb preocuparse [25]; **Don't worry!** ¡No te preocupes!

worse adj, adv peor ▷ *It was even worse than mine.* Era incluso peor que el mío.

worst adj peor ▷ *the worst student in the class* el peor alumno de la clase; **Maths is my worst subject.** Las matemáticas es la asignatura que peor se me da.
▶ n **The worst of it is that...** Lo peor es que...; **at worst** en el peor de los casos; **if the worst comes to the worst** en el peor de los casos

worth adj **to be worth** valer [55] ▷ *It's worth a lot of money.* Vale mucho dinero.; **It's worth it.** (worthwhile) Vale la pena.

would vb

The conditional is often used to translate 'would' + verb.
▷ *I said I would do it.* Dije que lo haría. ▷ *If you asked him he'd do it.* Si se lo pidieras, lo haría. ▷ *If you had asked him he would have done it.* Si se lo hubieras pedido, lo habría hecho.

When 'would you' is used to make requests, translate using **poder** in the present.

▷ *Would you close the door please?* ¿Puedes cerrar la puerta, por favor?

es una pena que has to be followed by a verb in the subjunctive.

▷ *It's a shame he isn't here.* Es una pena que no esté aquí.; **I'd like ... (1)** *(it would be good)* Me gustaría ... ▷ *I'd like to go to China.* Me gustaría ir a China. **(2)** *(can I have)* Quería ... ▷ *I'd like three tickets please.* Quería tres entradas.; **Would you like a biscuit?** ¿Quieres una galleta?

Use the subjunctive after **querer que**.

▷ *Would you like me to iron your jeans for you?* ¿Quieres que te planche los pantalones?; **Would you like us to go to the cinema?** ¿Quieres ir al cine?

wouldn't = **would not**

wound vb herir [**51**] ▷ *He was wounded in the leg.* Fue herido en la pierna.
▶ n herida f

wrap vb envolver [**59**] ▷ *She's wrapping her Christmas presents.* Está envolviendo los regalos de Navidad.

wrap up vb ❶ *(parcel)* envolver [**59**] ❷ *(put on warm clothes)* abrigarse [**37**]

wrapping paper n papel de regalo m

wreck n cacharro m ▷ *That car is a wreck!* ¡Ese coche es un cacharro!; **After the exams I was a complete wreck.** Después de los exámenes estaba hecho polvo.
▶ vb ❶ destruir [**10**] ▷ *The explosion*

wrecked the whole house. La explosión destruyó toda la casa. ❷ *(car)* destrozar [**13**] ❸ echar [**25**] por tierra ▷ *The bad weather wrecked our plans.* El mal tiempo echó por tierra nuestros planes.

wrestler n luchador m, luchadora f

wrestling n lucha libre f

wrinkled adj arrugado(-a)

wrist n muñeca f

write vb escribir [**58**] ▷ *to write a letter* escribir una carta

write down vb anotar [**25**] ▷ *Can you write it down for me, please?* ¿Me lo puedes anotar, por favor?

writer n escritor m, escritora f

writing n letra f ▷ *I can't read your writing.* No entiendo tu letra.; **in writing** por escrito

written vb see **write**

wrong adj, adv ❶ incorrecto(-a) ▷ *the wrong answer* la respuesta incorrecta; **You've got the wrong number.** Se ha equivocado de número. ❷ mal ▷ *You've done it wrong.* Lo has hecho mal.; **to go wrong** *(plan)* ir [**27**] mal; **to be wrong** estar [**22**] equivocado ▷ *You're wrong about that.* En eso estás equivocado.; **What's wrong?** ¿Qué pasa? ▷ *What's wrong with her?* ¿Qué le pasa?

wrote vb see **write**

a
b
c
d
e
f
g
h
i
j
k
l
m
n
o
p
q
r
s
t
u
v
w
x
y
z

X   y

Xmas n (= Christmas) Navidad f
X-ray vb hacer [**26**] una radiografía
de ▷ They X-rayed my arm. Me
hicieron una radiografía del brazo.
▶ n radiografía f ▷ I had an X-ray
taken. Me hicieron una radiografía.

yacht n yate m
yawn vb bostezar [**13**]
year n año m ▷ last year el año
pasado; **to be 15 years old** tener
[**53**] 15 años; **an eight-year-old
child** un niño de ocho años; **She's
in the fifth year.** Está en quinto.
yell vb gritar [**25**]
yellow adj amarillo(-a)
yes adv sí ▷ Do you like it? — Yes.
¿Te gusta? — Sí.
yesterday adv ayer ▷ yesterday
morning ayer por la mañana
yet adv todavía ▷ Have you eaten?
— Not yet. ¿Ya has comido? —
Todavía no. ▷ It's not finished yet.
Todavía no está terminado.
▷ There's no news as yet. Todavía no
se tienen noticias.; **Have you
finished yet?** ¿Has terminado ya?

yoghurt n yogur m

yolk n yema f

you pron

> There are formal and informal ways of saying 'you' in Spanish. As you look down the entry, choose the informal options if talking to people your own age or that you know well. Otherwise use the formal options. Note that subject pronouns are used less in Spanish – for emphasis and in comparisons.

❶ (informal: 1 person) tú ▷ What do YOU think about it? ¿Y tú qué piensas? ▷ She's younger than you. Es más joven que tú.; **You don't understand me.** No me entiendes. **❷** (informal: 2 or more people) vosotros mpl, vosotras fpl ▷ You've got kids but we haven't. Vosotros tenéis hijos pero nosotros no. ▷ They're younger than you. Son más jóvenes que vosotros. ▷ I'd like to speak to you. (ie all female) Quiero hablar con vosotras.; **How are you?** ¿Qué tal estáis? **❸** (formal: 1 person) usted ▷ They're younger than you. Son más jóvenes que usted. ▷ This is for you. Esto es para usted.; **How are you?** ¿Cómo está? **❹** (formal: 2 or more people) ustedes

> **ustedes** is always used in Latin America instead of **vosotros**.

> ▷ They're younger than you. Son más jóvenes que ustedes. ▷ This is for you. Esto es para ustedes.; **How are you?** ¿Cómo están?

> When 'you' means 'one' or 'people' in general, the impersonal **se** is often used.

> ▷ I doubt it, but you never know. Lo dudo, pero nunca se sabe.

> When 'you' is the object of the sentence, you have to use different forms from the ones above. See translations 5 to 10 below.

❺ (informal: 1 person) te ▷ I love you. Te quiero. ▷ Shall I give it to you? ¿Te lo doy?; **This is for you.** Esto es para ti.; **Can I go with you?** ¿Puedo ir contigo? **❻** (informal: 2 or more people) os ▷ I saw you. Os vi. ▷ I gave you the keys. Os di las llaves.; **I gave them to you.** Os los di. **❼** (formal: 1 person – direct object) lo msg, la fsg ▷ May I help you? ¿Puedo ayudarlo? ▷ I saw you, Mrs Jones. La vi, señora Jones. **❽** (formal: 1 person – indirect object) le ▷ I gave you the keys. Le di las llaves.

> Change **le** to **se** before another object pronoun.

I gave them to you. Se las di. **❾** (formal: 2 or more people – direct object) los mpl, las fpl ▷ May I help you? ¿Puedo ayudarlos? **❿** (formal: 2 or more people – indirect object) les pl

> Change **les** to **se** before another object pronoun.

> ▷ I gave you the keys. Les di las llaves.; **I gave them to you.** Se las di.

young adj joven (pl jóvenes); **young people** los jóvenes; **He's younger than me.** Es menor

a
b
c
d
e
f
g
h
i
j
k
l
m
n
o
p
q
r
s
t
u
v
w
x
y
z

que yo.; **my youngest brother** mi hermano pequeño

your adj

Use **tu** and **vuestro/vuestra** etc with people your own age or that you know well, and **su/ sus** otherwise.

❶ (informal: 1 person) **tu** (pl **tus**)

Remember there's no accent on **tu** meaning 'your'.

▷ your house tu casa ▷ your books tus libros ▷ your sisters tus hermanas ❷ (informal: 2 or more people) **vuestro(-a)**

Remember to make **vuestro** agree with the person or thing it describes.

▷ your dog vuestro perro ▷ These are your keys. Estas son vuestras llaves. ❸ (formal) **su** (pl **sus**)

Use **su** when talking to one person or to a group of people. **su** is used in Latin America instead of **vuestro**.

▷ Can I see your passport, sir? ¿Me enseña su pasaporte, señor? ▷ your uncle and aunt sus tíos

Use **el**, **la**, **los**, **las** as appropriate with parts of the body and to translate 'your' referring to people in general.

▷ Have you washed your hair? ¿Te has lavado el pelo?; **It's bad for your health.** Es malo para la salud.

yours pron

Use **tuyo/tuya** etc and **vuestro/vuestra** etc with people your own age or that you know well, and **su/sus** otherwise.

---

❶ (informal: 1 person) **tuyo(-a)**

Remember to make **tuyo** agree with the person or thing it describes.

▷ That's yours. Eso es tuyo. ▷ Is that box yours? ¿Esa caja es tuya?

Add the definite article when 'yours' means 'your one' or 'your ones'.

I've lost my pen. Can I use yours? He perdido el bolígrafo. ¿Puedo usar el tuyo?; **These are my keys and those are yours.** Estas son mis llaves y esas son las tuyas. ❷ (informal: 2 or more people) **vuestro(-a)**

Remember to make **vuestro** agree with the person or thing it describes.

▷ That's yours. Eso es vuestro.

Add the definite article when 'yours' means 'your one' or 'your ones'.

These are my keys and those are yours. Estas son mis llaves y esas son las vuestras. ❸ (formal) **suyo(-a)**

Use **suyo** in more formal situations with one person or a group of people, and remember to make it agree with the person or thing it describes. **suyo** is always used instead of **vuestro** in Latin America.

▷ That's yours. Eso es suyo.

Add the definite article when 'yours' means 'your one' or 'your ones'.

I've lost my pen. Can I use yours?

He perdido el bolígrafo. ¿Puedo usar el suyo?; **These are my keys and those are yours.** Estas son mis llaves y esas son las suyas.; **Yours sincerely...** Le saluda atentamente...

yourself pron

Use **te**, **tú mismo** and **ti mismo** when you are talking to someone of your own age or that you know well and **se** and **usted mismo** otherwise.

❶ (reflexive) te ▷ Have you hurt yourself? ¿Te has hecho daño? **❷** (for emphasis) tú mismo(-a) ▷ Do it yourself! ¡Hazlo tú mismo! **❸** (after a preposition) ti mismo(-a) ▷ You did it for yourself. Lo hiciste para ti mismo. **❹** (reflexive) se ▷ Have you hurt yourself? ¿Se ha hecho daño? **❺** (after a preposition, for emphasis) usted mismo(-a) ▷ You did it for yourself. Lo hizo para usted mismo. ▷ Do it yourself! ¡Hágalo usted mismo!

yourselves pron

In Spain use **os** and **vosotros mismos** when talking to people your own age or that you know well, and **se** or **ustedes mismos** otherwise. In Latin America **se** and **ustedes mismos** replace both **os** and **vosotros mismos**.

❶ (reflexive) os ▷ Did you enjoy yourselves? ¿Os divertisteis? **❷** (after a preposition, for emphasis) vosotros mismos (f vosotras mismas) ▷ Did you make it yourselves? ¿Lo habéis hecho vosotros mismos?

❸ (reflexive) se ▷ Did you enjoy yourselves? ¿Se divirtieron? **❹** (after a preposition, for emphasis) ustedes mismos (f ustedes mismas) ▷ Did you make it yourselves? ¿Lo han hecho ustedes mismos?

youth club n club juvenil m (pl clubs juveniles)

youth hostel n albergue juvenil m

Yugoslavia n Yugoslavia f ▷ in the former Yugoslavia en la antigua Yugoslavia

a
b
c
d
e
f
g
h
i
j
k
l
m
n
o
p
q
r
s
t
u
v
w
x
y
z

Z

zany *adj* estrafalario(-a)
zebra *n* cebra *f*
zebra crossing *n* paso de cebra *m*
zero *n* cero *m*
zip *n* cremallera *f*
zip code *n* (US) código postal *m*
zipper *n* (US) cremallera *f*
zodiac *n* zodíaco *m* ▷ the signs of the
    zodiac los signos del zodíaco
zone *n* zona *f*
zoo *n* zoo *m*
zoom lens *n* zoom *m*
zucchini *n* (US) calabacín *m*
    (*pl* calabacines)

VERB TABLES

Introduction

The following section contains 59 tables of Spanish verbs (some regular and some irregular) in alphabetical order. Each table shows the following tenses and forms: **Present**, **Preterite**, **Future**, **Present Subjunctive**, **Imperfect**, **Conditional**, **Imperative**, **Past Participle** and **Gerund**. At the bottom of each table are several examples to help you see how the verb is used.

On the Spanish side of the dictionary, Spanish verbs are followed by a number (e.g. hablar [**25**] *vb* <u>to speak</u>). This number corresponds to a page number in the verb tables where the pattern the verb follows is shown. When you come across cambiar [**25**] *vb* <u>to change</u>, for example, you will know that cambiar follows the same pattern as that of hablar shown in verb table **25**.

The regular verbs shown in these tables are:

hablar (regular –ar verb, verb table **25**)
comer (regular –er verb, verb table **8**)
vivir (regular –ir verb, verb table **58**)
lavarse (regular –ar reflexive verb, verb table **29**)

Some Spanish verbs are regular except for their past participles.

Escribir (to write) and abrir (to open) follow the pattern for vivir in verb table **58** except that the past participle for escribir is escrito and that of abrir is abierto. Imprimir (to print) also follows the pattern for vivir but can either have the regular past participle imprimido or the irregular one impreso.

Romper (to break) follows the pattern for comer in verb table **8** except that it has the irregular past participle roto.

Table
1

actuar *to act*

PRESENT		PRESENT SUBJUNCTIVE	
(yo)	actúo	(yo)	actúe
(tú)	actúas	(tú)	actúes
(él/ella/usted)	actúa	(él/ella/usted)	actúe
(nosotros/as)	actuamos	(nosotros/as)	actuemos
(vosotros/as)	actuáis	(vosotros/as)	actuéis
(ellos/ellas/ustedes)	actúan	(ellos/ellas/ustedes)	actúen

PRETERITE		IMPERFECT	
(yo)	actué	(yo)	actuaba
(tú)	actuaste	(tú)	actuabas
(él/ella/usted)	actuó	(él/ella/usted)	actuaba
(nosotros/as)	actuamos	(nosotros/as)	actuábamos
(vosotros/as)	actuasteis	(vosotros/as)	actuabais
(ellos/ellas/ustedes)	actuaron	(ellos/ellas/ustedes)	actuaban

FUTURE		CONDITIONAL	
(yo)	actuaré	(yo)	actuaría
(tú)	actuarás	(tú)	actuarías
(él/ella/usted)	actuará	(él/ella/usted)	actuaría
(nosotros/as)	actuaremos	(nosotros/as)	actuaríamos
(vosotros/as)	actuaréis	(vosotros/as)	actuaríais
(ellos/ellas/ustedes)	actuarán	(ellos/ellas/ustedes)	actuarían

IMPERATIVE	PAST PARTICIPLE
actúa / actuad	actuado

GERUND
actuando

--- EXAMPLE PHRASES ---

Actúa de una forma muy rara.　　He's acting very strangely.
Actuó en varias películas.　　He was in several films.
¿Quién **actuará** en su próxima　　Who will be in his next film?
　película?

PRESENT

(yo)	adquiero
(tú)	adquieres
(él/ella/usted)	adquiere
(nosotros/as)	adquirimos
(vosotros/as)	adquirís
(ellos/ellas/ustedes)	adquieren

PRESENT SUBJUNCTIVE

(yo)	adquiera
(tú)	adquieras
(él/ella/usted)	adquiera
(nosotros/as)	adquiramos
(vosotros/as)	adquiráis
(ellos/ellas/ustedes)	adquieran

PERFECT

(yo)	adquirí
(tú)	adquiriste
(él/ella/usted)	adquirió
(nosotros/as)	adquirimos
(vosotros/as)	adquiristeis
(ellos/ellas/ustedes)	adquirieron

IMPERFECT

(yo)	adquiría
(tú)	adquirías
(él/ella/usted)	adquiría
(nosotros/as)	adquiríamos
(vosotros/as)	adquiríais
(ellos/ellas/ustedes)	adquirían

FUTURE

(yo)	adquiriré
(tú)	adquirirás
(él/ella/usted)	adquirirá
(nosotros/as)	adquiriremos
(vosotros/as)	adquiriréis
(ellos/ellas/ustedes)	adquirirán

CONDITIONAL

(yo)	adquiriría
(tú)	adquirirías
(él/ella/usted)	adquiriría
(nosotros/as)	adquiriríamos
(vosotros/as)	adquiriríais
(ellos/ellas/ustedes)	adquirirían

IMPERATIVE

adquiere / adquirid

PAST PARTICIPLE

adquirido

GERUND

adquiriendo

=============== EXAMPLE PHRASES ===============

Hemos adquirido una colección de sellos.

Al final **adquirirán** los derechos de publicación.

¿Lo **adquirirías** por ese precio?

We've bought a stamp collection.

They will get the publishing rights in the end.

Would you buy it for that price?

| Table 3 |

almorzar *to have lunch*

PRESENT

(yo)	almuerzo
(tú)	almuerzas
(él/ella/usted)	almuerza
(nosotros/as)	almorzamos
(vosotros/as)	almorzáis
(ellos/ellas/ustedes)	almuerzan

PRESENT SUBJUNCTIVE

(yo)	almuerce
(tú)	almuerces
(él/ella/usted)	almuerce
(nosotros/as)	almorcemos
(vosotros/as)	almorcéis
(ellos/ellas/ustedes)	almuercen

PRETERITE

(yo)	almorcé
(tú)	almorzaste
(él/ella/usted)	almorzó
(nosotros/as)	almorzamos
(vosotros/as)	almorzasteis
(ellos/ellas/ustedes)	almorzaron

IMPERFECT

(yo)	almorzaba
(tú)	almorzabas
(él/ella/usted)	almorzaba
(nosotros/as)	almorzábamos
(vosotros/as)	almorzabais
(ellos/ellas/ustedes)	almorzaban

FUTURE

(yo)	almorzaré
(tú)	almorzarás
(él/ella/usted)	almorzará
(nosotros/as)	almorzaremos
(vosotros/as)	almorzaréis
(ellos/ellas/ustedes)	almorzarán

CONDITIONAL

(yo)	almorzaría
(tú)	almorzarías
(él/ella/usted)	almorzaría
(nosotros/as)	almorzaríamos
(vosotros/as)	almorzaríais
(ellos/ellas/ustedes)	almorzarían

IMPERATIVE

almuerza / almorzad

PAST PARTICIPLE

almorzado

GERUND

almorzando

EXAMPLE PHRASES

¿A qué hora **almuerzas**?	*What time do you have lunch?*
Almorcé en un bar.	*I had lunch in a bar.*
Mañana **almorzaremos** todos juntos.	*We'll all have lunch together tomorrow.*

PRESENT

(yo)	ando
(tú)	andas
(él/ella/usted)	anda
(nosotros/as)	andamos
(vosotros/as)	andáis
(ellos/ellas/ustedes)	andan

PRESENT SUBJUNCTIVE

(yo)	ande
(tú)	andes
(él/ella/usted)	ande
(nosotros/as)	andemos
(vosotros/as)	andéis
(ellos/ellas/ustedes)	anden

PRETERITE

(yo)	anduve
(tú)	anduviste
(él/ella/usted)	anduvo
(nosotros/as)	anduvimos
(vosotros/as)	anduvisteis
(ellos/ellas/ustedes)	anduvieron

IMPERFECT

(yo)	andaba
(tú)	andabas
(él/ella/usted)	andaba
(nosotros/as)	andábamos
(vosotros/as)	andabais
(ellos/ellas/ustedes)	andaban

FUTURE

(yo)	andaré
(tú)	andarás
(él/ella/usted)	andará
(nosotros/as)	andaremos
(vosotros/as)	andaréis
(ellos/ellas/ustedes)	andarán

CONDITIONAL

(yo)	andaría
(tú)	andarías
(él/ella/usted)	andaría
(nosotros/as)	andaríamos
(vosotros/as)	andaríais
(ellos/ellas/ustedes)	andarían

IMPERATIVE

anda / andad

PAST PARTICIPLE

andado

GERUND

andando

─────────── EXAMPLE PHRASES ───────────

Voy andando al trabajo todos los días.

I walk to work every day.

Anduvimos al menos 10 km.

We walked at least 10 km.

No sé por dónde **andará**.

I don't know where he will be.

Table
5

caer *to fall*

PRESENT		
(yo)	caigo
(tú)	caes
(él/ella/usted)	cae
(nosotros/as)	caemos
(vosotros/as)	caéis
(ellos/ellas/ustedes)	caen

PRESENT SUBJUNCTIVE	
(yo)	caiga
(tú)	caigas
(él/ella/usted)	caiga
(nosotros/as)	caigamos
(vosotros/as)	caigáis
(ellos/ellas/ustedes)	caigan

PRETERITE	
(yo)	caí
(tú)	caíste
(él/ella/usted)	cayó
(nosotros/as)	caímos
(vosotros/as)	caísteis
(ellos/ellas/ustedes)	cayeron

IMPERFECT	
(yo)	caía
(tú)	caías
(él/ella/usted)	caía
(nosotros/as)	caíamos
(vosotros/as)	caíais
(ellos/ellas/ustedes)	caían

FUTURE	
(yo)	caeré
(tú)	caerás
(él/ella/usted)	caerá
(nosotros/as)	caeremos
(vosotros/as)	caeréis
(ellos/ellas/ustedes)	caerán

CONDITIONAL	
(yo)	caería
(tú)	caerías
(él/ella/usted)	caería
(nosotros/as)	caeríamos
(vosotros/as)	caeríais
(ellos/ellas/ustedes)	caerían

IMPERATIVE
cae / caed

PAST PARTICIPLE
caído

GERUND
cayendo

EXAMPLE PHRASES

Me caí por las escaleras.
Ese edificio **se está cayendo**.
Se me ha caído un guante.

I fell down the stairs.
That building is falling down.
I've dropped one of my gloves.

PRESENT

(yo)	cuezo
(tú)	cueces
(él/ella/usted)	cuece
(nosotros/as)	cocemos
(vosotros/as)	cocéis
(ellos/ellas/ustedes)	cuecen

PRESENT SUBJUNCTIVE

(yo)	cueza
(tú)	cuezas
(él/ella/usted)	cueza
(nosotros/as)	cozamos
(vosotros/as)	cozáis
(ellos/ellas/ustedes)	cuezan

PRETERITE

(yo)	cocí
(tú)	cociste
(él/ella/usted)	coció
(nosotros/as)	cocimos
(vosotros/as)	cocisteis
(ellos/ellas/ustedes)	cocieron

IMPERFECT

(yo)	cocía
(tú)	cocías
(él/ella/usted)	cocía
(nosotros/as)	cocíamos
(vosotros/as)	cocíais
(ellos/ellas/ustedes)	cocían

FUTURE

(yo)	coceré
(tú)	cocerás
(él/ella/usted)	cocerá
(nosotros/as)	coceremos
(vosotros/as)	coceréis
(ellos/ellas/ustedes)	cocerán

CONDITIONAL

(yo)	cocería
(tú)	cocerías
(él/ella/usted)	cocería
(nosotros/as)	coceríamos
(vosotros/as)	coceríais
(ellos/ellas/ustedes)	cocerían

IMPERATIVE
cuece / coced

PAST PARTICIPLE
cocido

GERUND
cociendo

--- EXAMPLE PHRASES ---

Cuécelo a fuego lento.   *Cook it over a gentle heat.*
Aquí nos **estamos cociendo**.   *It's boiling in here.*
No lo **cuezas** demasiado.   *Don't overcook it.*

Table
7

coger   *to take, to catch*

PRESENT

(yo)	cojo
(tú)	coges
(él/ella/usted)	coge
(nosotros/as)	cogemos
(vosotros/as)	cogéis
(ellos/ellas/ustedes)	cogen

PRESENT SUBJUNCTIVE

(yo)	coja
(tú)	cojas
(él/ella/usted)	coja
(nosotros/as)	cojamos
(vosotros/as)	cojáis
(ellos/ellas/ustedes)	cojan

PRETERITE

(yo)	cogí
(tú)	cogiste
(él/ella/usted)	cogió
(nosotros/as)	cogimos
(vosotros/as)	cogisteis
(ellos/ellas/ustedes)	cogieron

IMPERFECT

(yo)	cogía
(tú)	cogías
(él/ella/usted)	cogía
(nosotros/as)	cogíamos
(vosotros/as)	cogíais
(ellos/ellas/ustedes)	cogían

FUTURE

(yo)	cogeré
(tú)	cogerás
(él/ella/usted)	cogerá
(nosotros/as)	cogeremos
(vosotros/as)	cogeréis
(ellos/ellas/ustedes)	cogerán

CONDITIONAL

(yo)	cogería
(tú)	cogerías
(él/ella/usted)	cogería
(nosotros/as)	cogeríamos
(vosotros/as)	cogeríais
(ellos/ellas/ustedes)	cogerían

IMPERATIVE

coge / coged

PAST PARTICIPLE

cogido

GERUND

cogiendo

--- EXAMPLE PHRASES ---

La **cogí** entre mis brazos.
Estuvimos cogiendo setas.
¿Por qué no **coges** el tren de
las seis?

I took her in my arms.
We were picking mushrooms.
*Why don't you get the six o'clock
train?*

PRESENT

(yo)	como
(tú)	comes
(él/ella/usted)	come
(nosotros/as)	comemos
(vosotros/as)	coméis
(ellos/ellas/ustedes)	comen

PRESENT SUBJUNCTIVE

(yo)	coma
(tú)	comas
(él/ella/usted)	coma
(nosotros/as)	comamos
(vosotros/as)	comáis
(ellos/ellas/ustedes)	coman

PRETERITE

(yo)	comí
(tú)	comiste
(él/ella/usted)	comió
(nosotros/as)	comimos
(vosotros/as)	comisteis
(ellos/ellas/ustedes)	comieron

IMPERFECT

(yo)	comía
(tú)	comías
(él/ella/usted)	comía
(nosotros/as)	comíamos
(vosotros/as)	comíais
(ellos/ellas/ustedes)	comían

FUTURE

(yo)	comeré
(tú)	comerás
(él/ella/usted)	comerá
(nosotros/as)	comeremos
(vosotros/as)	comeréis
(ellos/ellas/ustedes)	comerán

CONDITIONAL

(yo)	comería
(tú)	comerías
(él/ella/usted)	comería
(nosotros/as)	comeríamos
(vosotros/as)	comeríais
(ellos/ellas/ustedes)	comerían

IMPERATIVE
come / comed

PAST PARTICIPLE
comido

GERUND
comiendo

──────────── EXAMPLE PHRASES ────────────

No **come** carne.	He doesn't eat meat.
No **comas** tan deprisa.	Don't eat so fast.
Se ha comido todo.	He's eaten it all.

Table
9

conducir *to drive*

PRESENT	
(yo)	conduzco
(tú)	conduces
(él/ella/usted)	conduce
(nosotros/as)	conducimos
(vosotros/as)	conducís
(ellos/ellas/ustedes)	conducen

PRESENT SUBJUNCTIVE	
(yo)	conduzca
(tú)	conduzcas
(él/ella/usted)	conduzca
(nosotros/as)	conduzcamos
(vosotros/as)	conduzcáis
(ellos/ellas/ustedes)	conduzcan

PRETERITE	
(yo)	conduje
(tú)	condujiste
(él/ella/usted)	condujo
(nosotros/as)	condujimos
(vosotros/as)	condujisteis
(ellos/ellas/ustedes)	condujeron

IMPERFECT	
(yo)	conducía
(tú)	conducías
(él/ella/usted)	conducía
(nosotros/as)	conducíamos
(vosotros/as)	conducíais
(ellos/ellas/ustedes)	conducían

FUTURE	
(yo)	conduciré
(tú)	conducirás
(él/ella/usted)	conducirá
(nosotros/as)	conduciremos
(vosotros/as)	conduciréis
(ellos/ellas/ustedes)	conducirán

CONDITIONAL	
(yo)	conduciría
(tú)	conducirías
(él/ella/usted)	conduciría
(nosotros/as)	conduciríamos
(vosotros/as)	conduciríais
(ellos/ellas/ustedes)	conducirían

IMPERATIVE
conduce / conducid

PAST PARTICIPLE
conducido

GERUND
conduciendo

=== EXAMPLE PHRASES ===

Conduces muy bien.
You are a really good driver.

¿**Condujiste** tú?
Was it you driving?

Él los **conducirá** a la mesa.
He'll show you to your table.

PRESENT

(yo)	construyo
(tú)	construyes
(él/ella/usted)	construye
(nosotros/as)	construimos
(vosotros/as)	construís
(ellos/ellas/ustedes)	construyen

PRESENT SUBJUNCTIVE

(yo)	construya
(tú)	construyas
(él/ella/usted)	construya
(nosotros/as)	construyamos
(vosotros/as)	construyáis
(ellos/ellas/ustedes)	construyan

PRETERITE

(yo)	construí
(tú)	construiste
(él/ella/usted)	construyó
(nosotros/as)	construimos
(vosotros/as)	construisteis
(ellos/ellas/ustedes)	construyeron

IMPERFECT

(yo)	construía
(tú)	construías
(él/ella/usted)	construía
(nosotros/as)	construíamos
(vosotros/as)	construíais
(ellos/ellas/ustedes)	construían

FUTURE

(yo)	construiré
(tú)	construirás
(él/ella/usted)	construirá
(nosotros/as)	construiremos
(vosotros/as)	construiréis
(ellos/ellas/ustedes)	construirán

CONDITIONAL

(yo)	construiría
(tú)	construirías
(él/ella/usted)	construiría
(nosotros/as)	construiríamos
(vosotros/as)	construiríais
(ellos/ellas/ustedes)	construirían

IMPERATIVE
construye / construid

PAST PARTICIPLE
construido

GERUND
construyendo

=== EXAMPLE PHRASES ===

Están construyendo una escuela.
Yo solo **construí** el puzzle.
Aquí **construirán** una autopista.

They are building a new school.
I did the jigsaw puzzle on my own.
They're going to build a new motorway here.

Table
11

contar *to tell, to count*

PRESENT			PRESENT SUBJUNCTIVE	
(yo)	cuento		(yo)	cuente
(tú)	cuentas		(tú)	cuentes
(él/ella/usted)	cuenta ·		(él/ella/usted)	cuente
(nosotros/as)	contamos		(nosotros/as)	contemos
(vosotros/as)	contáis		(vosotros/as)	contéis
(ellos/ellas/ustedes)	cuentan		(ellos/ellas/ustedes)	cuenten

PRETERITE			IMPERFECT	
(yo)	conté		(yo)	contaba
(tú)	contaste		(tú)	contabas
(él/ella/usted)	contó		(él/ella/usted)	contaba
(nosotros/as)	contamos		(nosotros/as)	contábamos
(vosotros/as)	contasteis		(vosotros/as)	contabais
(ellos/ellas/ustedes)	contaron		(ellos/ellas/ustedes)	contaban

FUTURE			CONDITIONAL	
(yo)	contaré		(yo)	contaría
(tú)	contarás		(tú)	contarías
(él/ella/usted)	contará		(él/ella/usted)	contaría
(nosotros/as)	contaremos		(nosotros/as)	contaríamos
(vosotros/as)	contaréis		(vosotros/as)	contaríais
(ellos/ellas/ustedes)	contarán		(ellos/ellas/ustedes)	contarían

IMPERATIVE
cuenta / contad

PAST PARTICIPLE
contado

GERUND
contando

--------- EXAMPLE PHRASES ---------

Venga, **cuéntamelo**.
Nos **contó** un secreto.
Prométeme que no se lo **contarás**
   a nadie.

Come on, tell me.
He told us a secret.
Promise you won't tell anyone.

PRESENT

(yo)	crezco
(tú)	creces
(él/ella/usted)	crece
(nosotros/as)	crecemos
(vosotros/as)	crecéis
(ellos/ellas/ustedes)	crecen

PRESENT SUBJUNCTIVE

(yo)	crezca
(tú)	crezcas
(él/ella/usted)	crezca
(nosotros/as)	crezcamos
(vosotros/as)	crezcáis
(ellos/ellas/ustedes)	crezcan

PRETERITE

(yo)	crecí
(tú)	creciste
(él/ella/usted)	creció
(nosotros/as)	crecimos
(vosotros/as)	crecisteis
(ellos/ellas/ustedes)	crecieron

IMPERFECT

(yo)	crecía
(tú)	crecías
(él/ella/usted)	crecía
(nosotros/as)	crecíamos
(vosotros/as)	crecíais
(ellos/ellas/ustedes)	crecían

FUTURE

(yo)	creceré
(tú)	crecerás
(él/ella/usted)	crecerá
(nosotros/as)	creceremos
(vosotros/as)	creceréis
(ellos/ellas/ustedes)	crecerán

CONDITIONAL

(yo)	crecería
(tú)	crecerías
(él/ella/usted)	crecería
(nosotros/as)	creceríamos
(vosotros/as)	creceríais
(ellos/ellas/ustedes)	crecerían

IMPERATIVE
crece / creced

PAST PARTICIPLE
crecido

GERUND
creciendo

--- EXAMPLE PHRASES ---

Esas plantas **crecen** en Chile.	*Those plants grow in Chile.*
Crecimos juntos.	*We grew up together.*
Cuando **crezca**, ya verás.	*You'll see, when he grows up.*

Table
13

cruzar *to cross*

PRESENT

(yo)	cruzo
(tú)	cruzas
(él/ella/usted)	cruza
(nosotros/as)	cruzamos
(vosotros/as)	cruzáis
(ellos/ellas/ustedes)	cruzan

PRESENT SUBJUNCTIVE

(yo)	cruce
(tú)	cruces
(él/ella/usted)	cruce
(nosotros/as)	crucemos
(vosotros/as)	crucéis
(ellos/ellas/ustedes)	crucen

PRETERITE

(yo)	crucé
(tú)	cruzaste
(él/ella/usted)	cruzó
(nosotros/as)	cruzamos
(vosotros/as)	cruzasteis
(ellos/ellas/ustedes)	cruzaron

IMPERFECT

(yo)	cruzaba
(tú)	cruzabas
(él/ella/usted)	cruzaba
(nosotros/as)	cruzábamos
(vosotros/as)	cruzabais
(ellos/ellas/ustedes)	cruzaban

FUTURE

(yo)	cruzaré
(tú)	cruzarás
(él/ella/usted)	cruzará
(nosotros/as)	cruzaremos
(vosotros/as)	cruzaréis
(ellos/ellas/ustedes)	cruzarán

CONDITIONAL

(yo)	cruzaría
(tú)	cruzarías
(él/ella/usted)	cruzaría
(nosotros/as)	cruzaríamos
(vosotros/as)	cruzaríais
(ellos/ellas/ustedes)	cruzarían

IMPERATIVE

cruza / cruzad

PAST PARTICIPLE

cruzado

GERUND

cruzando

--- EXAMPLE PHRASES ---

No **cruces** la calle con el semáforo en rojo.
Cruzaron la carretera.
Hace tiempo que no **me cruzo** con él.

Don't cross the road when the signal's at red.
They crossed the road.
I haven't seen him for a long time.

PRESENT

(yo)	doy
(tú)	das
(él/ella/usted)	da
(nosotros/as)	damos
(vosotros/as)	dais
(ellos/ellas/ustedes)	dan

PRESENT SUBJUNCTIVE

(yo)	dé
(tú)	des
(él/ella/usted)	dé
(nosotros/as)	demos
(vosotros/as)	deis
(ellos/ellas/ustedes)	den

PRETERITE

(yo)	di
(tú)	diste
(él/ella/usted)	dio
(nosotros/as)	dimos
(vosotros/as)	disteis
(ellos/ellas/ustedes)	dieron

IMPERFECT

(yo)	daba
(tú)	dabas
(él/ella/usted)	daba
(nosotros/as)	dábamos
(vosotros/as)	dabais
(ellos/ellas/ustedes)	daban

FUTURE

(yo)	daré
(tú)	darás
(él/ella/usted)	dará
(nosotros/as)	daremos
(vosotros/as)	daréis
(ellos/ellas/ustedes)	darán

CONDITIONAL

(yo)	daría
(tú)	darías
(él/ella/usted)	daría
(nosotros/as)	daríamos
(vosotros/as)	daríais
(ellos/ellas/ustedes)	darían

IMPERATIVE
da / dad

PAST PARTICIPLE
dado

GERUND
dando

--- EXAMPLE PHRASES ---

Me **da** miedo la oscuridad.
I'm scared of the dark.

Nos **dieron** un par de entradas gratis.
They gave us a couple of free tickets.

Te **daré** el número de mi móvil.
I'll give you my mobile phone number.

Table
15

decir *to say, to tell*

PRESENT			PRESENT SUBJUNCTIVE	
(yo)	digo		(yo)	diga
(tú)	dices		(tú)	digas
(él/ella/usted)	dice		(él/ella/usted)	diga
(nosotros/as)	decimos		(nosotros/as)	digamos
(vosotros/as)	decís		(vosotros/as)	digáis
(ellos/ellas/ustedes)	dicen		(ellos/ellas/ustedes)	digan

PRETERITE			IMPERFECT	
(yo)	dije		(yo)	decía
(tú)	dijiste		(tú)	decías
(él/ella/usted)	dijo		(él/ella/usted)	decía
(nosotros/as)	dijimos		(nosotros/as)	decíamos
(vosotros/as)	dijisteis		(vosotros/as)	decíais
(ellos/ellas/ustedes)	dijeron		(ellos/ellas/ustedes)	decían

FUTURE			CONDITIONAL	
(yo)	diré		(yo)	diría
(tú)	dirás		(tú)	dirías
(él/ella/usted)	dirá		(él/ella/usted)	diría
(nosotros/as)	diremos		(nosotros/as)	diríamos
(vosotros/as)	diréis		(vosotros/as)	diríais
(ellos/ellas/ustedes)	dirán		(ellos/ellas/ustedes)	dirían

IMPERATIVE
di / decid

GERUND
diciendo

PAST PARTICIPLE

dicho

— EXAMPLE PHRASES —

Pero ¿qué **dices**?
Me lo **dijo** ayer.
¿Te **ha dicho** lo de la boda?

What are you saying?
He told me yesterday.
Has he told you about the wedding?

PRESENT

(yo)	dirijo
(tú)	diriges
(él/ella/usted)	dirige
(nosotros/as)	dirigimos
(vosotros/as)	dirigís
(ellos/ellas/ustedes)	dirigen

PRESENT SUBJUNCTIVE

(yo)	dirija
(tú)	dirijas
(él/ella/usted)	dirija
(nosotros/as)	dirijamos
(vosotros/as)	dirijáis
(ellos/ellas/ustedes)	dirijan

PRETERITE

(yo)	dirigí
(tú)	dirigiste
(él/ella/usted)	dirigió
(nosotros/as)	dirigimos
(vosotros/as)	dirigisteis
(ellos/ellas/ustedes)	dirigieron

IMPERFECT

(yo)	dirigía
(tú)	dirigías
(él/ella/usted)	dirigía
(nosotros/as)	dirigíamos
(vosotros/as)	dirigíais
(ellos/ellas/ustedes)	dirigían

FUTURE

(yo)	dirigiré
(tú)	dirigirás
(él/ella/usted)	dirigirá
(nosotros/as)	dirigiremos
(vosotros/as)	dirigiréis
(ellos/ellas/ustedes)	dirigirán

CONDITIONAL

(yo)	dirigiría
(tú)	dirigirías
(él/ella/usted)	dirigiría
(nosotros/as)	dirigiríamos
(vosotros/as)	dirigiríais
(ellos/ellas/ustedes)	dirigirían

IMPERATIVE
dirige / dirigid

PAST PARTICIPLE
dirigido

GERUND
dirigiendo

--- EXAMPLE PHRASES ---

Dirijo esta empresa desde hace dos años.

I've been running this company for two years.

Hace días que no me **dirige** la palabra.

He hasn't spoken to me for days.

Se dirigía a la parada del autobús.

He was making his way to the bus stop.

Table
17

dormir *to sleep*

PRESENT		PRESENT SUBJUNCTIVE	
(yo)	duermo	(yo)	duerma
(tú)	duermes	(tú)	duermas
(él/ella/usted)	duerme	(él/ella/usted)	duerma
(nosotros/as)	dormimos	(nosotros/as)	durmamos
(vosotros/as)	dormís	(vosotros/as)	durmáis
(ellos/ellas/ustedes)	duermen	(ellos/ellas/ustedes)	duerman

PRETERITE		IMPERFECT	
(yo)	dormí	(yo)	dormía
(tú)	dormiste	(tú)	dormías
(él/ella/usted)	durmió	(él/ella/usted)	dormía
(nosotros/as)	dormimos	(nosotros/as)	dormíamos
(vosotros/as)	dormisteis	(vosotros/as)	dormíais
(ellos/ellas/ustedes)	durmieron	(ellos/ellas/ustedes)	dormían

FUTURE		CONDITIONAL	
(yo)	dormiré	(yo)	dormiría
(tú)	dormirás	(tú)	dormirías
(él/ella/usted)	dormirá	(él/ella/usted)	dormiría
(nosotros/as)	dormiremos	(nosotros/as)	dormiríamos
(vosotros/as)	dormiréis	(vosotros/as)	dormiríais
(ellos/ellas/ustedes)	dormirán	(ellos/ellas/ustedes)	dormirían

IMPERATIVE
duerme / dormid

GERUND
durmiendo

PAST PARTICIPLE

dormido

--- EXAMPLE PHRASES ---

No **duermo** muy bien.	*I don't sleep very well.*
Nos dormimos en el cine.	*We fell asleep at the cinema.*
Durmió durante doce horas.	*He slept for twelve hours.*

PRESENT

(yo)	elijo
(tú)	eliges
(él/ella/usted)	elige
(nosotros/as)	elegimos
(vosotros/as)	elegís
(ellos/ellas/ustedes)	eligen

PRESENT SUBJUNCTIVE

(yo)	elija
(tú)	elijas
(él/ella/usted)	elija
(nosotros/as)	elijamos
(vosotros/as)	elijáis
(ellos/ellas/ustedes)	elijan

PRETERITE

(yo)	elegí
(tú)	elegiste
(él/ella/usted)	eligió
(nosotros/as)	elegimos
(vosotros/as)	elegisteis
(ellos/ellas/ustedes)	eligieron

IMPERFECT

(yo)	elegía
(tú)	elegías
(él/ella/usted)	elegía
(nosotros/as)	elegíamos
(vosotros/as)	elegíais
(ellos/ellas/ustedes)	elegían

FUTURE

(yo)	elegiré
(tú)	elegirás
(él/ella/usted)	elegirá
(nosotros/as)	elegiremos
(vosotros/as)	elegiréis
(ellos/ellas/ustedes)	elegirán

CONDITIONAL

(yo)	elegiría
(tú)	elegirías
(él/ella/usted)	elegiría
(nosotros/as)	elegiríamos
(vosotros/as)	elegiríais
(ellos/ellas/ustedes)	elegirían

IMPERATIVE

elige / elegid

PAST PARTICIPLE

elegido

GERUND

eligiendo

--- EXAMPLE PHRASES ---

Nosotros no **elegimos** a nuestros padres, ni ellos nos **eligen** a nosotros.

We don't choose our parents and neither do they choose us.

Creo que **ha elegido** bien.

I think he's made a good choice.

No lo **eligieron** ellos.

They didn't choose it.

Table
19

empezar *to start, to begin*

PRESENT		
(yo)	empiezo	
(tú)	empiezas	
(él/ella/usted)	empieza	
(nosotros/as)	empezamos	
(vosotros/as)	empezáis	
(ellos/ellas/ustedes)	empiezan	

PRESENT SUBJUNCTIVE	
(yo)	empiece
(tú)	empieces
(él/ella/usted)	empiece
(nosotros/as)	empecemos
(vosotros/as)	empecéis
(ellos/ellas/ustedes)	empiecen

PRETERITE	
(yo)	empecé
(tú)	empezaste
(él/ella/usted)	empezó
(nosotros/as)	empezamos
(vosotros/as)	empezasteis
(ellos/ellas/ustedes)	empezaron

IMPERFECT	
(yo)	empezaba
(tú)	empezabas
(él/ella/usted)	empezaba
(nosotros/as)	empezábamos
(vosotros/as)	empezabais
(ellos/ellas/ustedes)	empezaban

FUTURE	
(yo)	empezaré
(tú)	empezarás
(él/ella/usted)	empezará
(nosotros/as)	empezaremos
(vosotros/as)	empezaréis
(ellos/ellas/ustedes)	empezarán

CONDITIONAL	
(yo)	empezaría
(tú)	empezarías
(él/ella/usted)	empezaría
(nosotros/as)	empezaríamos
(vosotros/as)	empezaríais
(ellos/ellas/ustedes)	empezarían

IMPERATIVE
empieza / empezad

PAST PARTICIPLE
empezado

GERUND
empezando

─────────── EXAMPLE PHRASES ───────────

Empieza por aquí.

¿Cuándo **empiezas** a trabajar en el sitio nuevo?

La semana que viene **empezaremos** un curso nuevo.

Start here.

When do you start work at the new place?

We'll start a new course next week.

PRESENT

(yo)	entiendo
(tú)	entiendes
(él/ella/usted)	entiende
(nosotros/as)	entendemos
(vosotros/as)	entendéis
(ellos/ellas/ustedes)	entienden

PRESENT SUBJUNCTIVE

(yo)	entienda
(tú)	entiendas
(él/ella/usted)	entienda
(nosotros/as)	entendamos
(vosotros/as)	entendáis
(ellos/ellas/ustedes)	entiendan

PRETERITE

(yo)	entendí
(tú)	entendiste
(él/ella/usted)	entendió
(nosotros/as)	entendimos
(vosotros/as)	entendisteis
(ellos/ellas/ustedes)	entendieron

IMPERFECT

(yo)	entendía
(tú)	entendías
(él/ella/usted)	entendía
(nosotros/as)	entendíamos
(vosotros/as)	entendíais
(ellos/ellas/ustedes)	entendían

FUTURE

(yo)	entenderé
(tú)	entenderás
(él/ella/usted)	entenderá
(nosotros/as)	entenderemos
(vosotros/as)	entenderéis
(ellos/ellas/ustedes)	entenderán

CONDITIONAL

(yo)	entendería
(tú)	entenderías
(él/ella/usted)	entendería
(nosotros/as)	entenderíamos
(vosotros/as)	entenderíais
(ellos/ellas/ustedes)	entenderían

IMPERATIVE
entiende / entended

PAST PARTICIPLE
entendido

GERUND
entendiendo

EXAMPLE PHRASES

No lo **entiendo**.
¿**Entendiste** lo que dijo?
Con el tiempo lo **entenderás**.

I don't understand.
Did you understand what she said?
You'll understand one day.

Table
21

enviar *to send*

PRESENT

(yo)	envío
(tú)	envías
(él/ella/usted)	envía
(nosotros/as)	enviamos
(vosotros/as)	enviáis
(ellos/ellas/ustedes)	envían

PRESENT SUBJUNCTIVE

(yo)	envíe
(tú)	envíes
(él/ella/usted)	envíe
(nosotros/as)	enviemos
(vosotros/as)	enviéis
(ellos/ellas/ustedes)	envíen

PRETERITE

(yo)	envié
(tú)	enviaste
(él/ella/usted)	envió
(nosotros/as)	enviamos
(vosotros/as)	enviasteis
(ellos/ellas/ustedes)	enviaron

IMPERFECT

(yo)	enviaba
(tú)	enviabas
(él/ella/usted)	enviaba
(nosotros/as)	enviábamos
(vosotros/as)	enviabais
(ellos/ellas/ustedes)	enviaban

FUTURE

(yo)	enviaré
(tú)	enviarás
(él/ella/usted)	enviará
(nosotros/as)	enviaremos
(vosotros/as)	enviaréis
(ellos/ellas/ustedes)	enviarán

CONDITIONAL

(yo)	enviaría
(tú)	enviarías
(él/ella/usted)	enviaría
(nosotros/as)	enviaríamos
(vosotros/as)	enviaríais
(ellos/ellas/ustedes)	enviarían

IMPERATIVE
envía / enviad

PAST PARTICIPLE
enviado

GERUND
enviando

EXAMPLE PHRASES

Envíe todos sus datos personales.   *Send all your personal details.*
La han **enviado** a Guatemala.   *They've sent her to Guatemala.*
Nos **enviarán** más información.   *They'll send us further information.*

PRESENT

(yo)	estoy
(tú)	estás
(él/ella/usted)	está
(nosotros/as)	estamos
(vosotros/as)	estáis
(ellos/ellas/ustedes)	están

PRESENT SUBJUNCTIVE

(yo)	esté
(tú)	estés
(él/ella/usted)	esté
(nosotros/as)	estemos
(vosotros/as)	estéis
(ellos/ellas/ustedes)	estén

PRETERITE

(yo)	estuve
(tú)	estuviste
(él/ella/usted)	estuvo
(nosotros/as)	estuvimos
(vosotros/as)	estuvisteis
(ellos/ellas/ustedes)	estuvieron

IMPERFECT

(yo)	estaba
(tú)	estabas
(él/ella/usted)	estaba
(nosotros/as)	estábamos
(vosotros/as)	estabais
(ellos/ellas/ustedes)	estaban

FUTURE

(yo)	estaré
(tú)	estarás
(él/ella/usted)	estará
(nosotros/as)	estaremos
(vosotros/as)	estaréis
(ellos/ellas/ustedes)	estarán

CONDITIONAL

(yo)	estaría
(tú)	estarías
(él/ella/usted)	estaría
(nosotros/as)	estaríamos
(vosotros/as)	estaríais
(ellos/ellas/ustedes)	estarían

IMPERATIVE
está / estad

PAST PARTICIPLE

estado

GERUND
estando

──────── EXAMPLE PHRASES ────────

Estoy cansado.
Estuvimos en casa de mis padres.
¿A qué hora **estarás** en casa?

I'm tired.
We went to my parents' house.
What time will you be home?

Table
23

freír *to fry*

PRESENT

(yo)	frío
(tú)	fríes
(él/ella/usted)	fríe
(nosotros/as)	freímos
(vosotros/as)	freís
(ellos/ellas/ustedes)	fríen

PRESENT SUBJUNCTIVE

(yo)	fría
(tú)	frías
(él/ella/usted)	fría
(nosotros/as)	friamos
(vosotros/as)	friais
(ellos/ellas/ustedes)	frían

PRETERITE

(yo)	freí
(tú)	freíste
(él/ella/usted)	frio
(nosotros/as)	freímos
(vosotros/as)	freísteis
(ellos/ellas/ustedes)	frieron

IMPERFECT

(yo)	freía
(tú)	freías
(él/ella/usted)	freía
(nosotros/as)	freíamos
(vosotros/as)	freíais
(ellos/ellas/ustedes)	freían

FUTURE

(yo)	freiré
(tú)	freirás
(él/ella/usted)	freirá
(nosotros/as)	freiremos
(vosotros/as)	freiréis
(ellos/ellas/ustedes)	freirán

CONDITIONAL

(yo)	freiría
(tú)	freirías
(él/ella/usted)	freiría
(nosotros/as)	freiríamos
(vosotros/as)	freiríais
(ellos/ellas/ustedes)	freirían

IMPERATIVE
fríe / freíd

PAST PARTICIPLE
frito

GERUND
friendo

————————————— EXAMPLE PHRASES —————————————

Fríelo en esta sartén. *Fry it in this pan.*
He frito el pescado. *I've fried the fish.*
Nos freíamos de calor. *We were roasting in the heat.*

PRESENT

(yo)	he
(tú)	has
(él/ella/usted)	ha
(nosotros/as)	hemos
(vosotros/as)	habéis
(ellos/ellas/ustedes)	han

PRESENT SUBJUNCTIVE

(yo)	haya
(tú)	hayas
(él/ella/usted)	haya
(nosotros/as)	hayamos
(vosotros/as)	hayáis
(ellos/ellas/ustedes)	hayan

PRETERITE

(yo)	hube
(tú)	hubiste
(él/ella/usted)	hubo
(nosotros/as)	hubimos
(vosotros/as)	hubisteis
(ellos/ellas/ustedes)	hubieron

IMPERFECT

(yo)	había
(tú)	habías
(él/ella/usted)	había
(nosotros/as)	habíamos
(vosotros/as)	habíais
(ellos/ellas/ustedes)	habían

FUTURE

(yo)	habré
(tú)	habrás
(él/ella/usted)	habrá
(nosotros/as)	habremos
(vosotros/as)	habréis
(ellos/ellas/ustedes)	habrán

CONDITIONAL

(yo)	habría
(tú)	habrías
(él/ella/usted)	habría
(nosotros/as)	habríamos
(vosotros/as)	habríais
(ellos/ellas/ustedes)	habrían

IMPERATIVE
not used

PAST PARTICIPLE
habido

GERUND
habiendo

─────────── EXAMPLE PHRASES ───────────

¿**Has visto** eso?
Ya **hemos ido** a ver esa película.
Eso nunca **había pasado** antes.

Did you see that?
We've already been to see that film.
That had never happened before.

Table
25

hablar   *to speak, to talk*

PRESENT		PRESENT SUBJUNCTIVE	
(yo)	hablo	(yo)	hable
(tú)	hablas	(tú)	hables
(él/ella/usted)	habla	(él/ella/usted)	hable
(nosotros/as)	hablamos	(nosotros/as)	hablemos
(vosotros/as)	habláis	(vosotros/as)	habléis
(ellos/ellas/ustedes)	hablan	(ellos/ellas/ustedes)	hablen

PRETERITE		IMPERFECT	
(yo)	hablé	(yo)	hablaba
(tú)	hablaste	(tú)	hablabas
(él/ella/usted)	habló	(él/ella/usted)	hablaba
(nosotros/as)	hablamos	(nosotros/as)	hablábamos
(vosotros/as)	hablasteis	(vosotros/as)	hablabais
(ellos/ellas/ustedes)	hablaron	(ellos/ellas/ustedes)	hablaban

FUTURE		CONDITIONAL	
(yo)	hablaré	(yo)	hablaría
(tú)	hablarás	(tú)	hablarías
(él/ella/usted)	hablará	(él/ella/usted)	hablaría
(nosotros/as)	hablaremos	(nosotros/as)	hablaríamos
(vosotros/as)	hablaréis	(vosotros/as)	hablaríais
(ellos/ellas/ustedes)	hablarán	(ellos/ellas/ustedes)	hablarían

IMPERATIVE
habla / hablad

GERUND
hablando

PAST PARTICIPLE

hablado

—————————————— EXAMPLE PHRASES ——————————————

Hoy **he hablado** con mi hermana.	*I've spoken to my sister today.*
No **hables** tan alto.	*Don't talk so loud.*
No **se hablan**.	*They don't talk to each other.*

PRESENT

(yo)	hago
(tú)	haces
(él/ella/usted)	hace
(nosotros/as)	hacemos
(vosotros/as)	hacéis
(ellos/ellas/ustedes)	hacen

PRESENT SUBJUNCTIVE

(yo)	haga
(tú)	hagas
(él/ella/usted)	haga
(nosotros/as)	hagamos
(vosotros/as)	hagáis
(ellos/ellas/ustedes)	hagan

PRETERITE

(yo)	hice
(tú)	hiciste
(él/ella/usted)	hizo
(nosotros/as)	hicimos
(vosotros/as)	hicisteis
(ellos/ellas/ustedes)	hicieron

IMPERFECT

(yo)	hacía
(tú)	hacías
(él/ella/usted)	hacía
(nosotros/as)	hacíamos
(vosotros/as)	hacíais
(ellos/ellas/ustedes)	hacían

FUTURE

(yo)	haré
(tú)	harás
(él/ella/usted)	hará
(nosotros/as)	haremos
(vosotros/as)	haréis
(ellos/ellas/ustedes)	harán

CONDITIONAL

(yo)	haría
(tú)	harías
(él/ella/usted)	haría
(nosotros/as)	haríamos
(vosotros/as)	haríais
(ellos/ellas/ustedes)	harían

IMPERATIVE

haz / haced

PAST PARTICIPLE

hecho

GERUND

haciendo

——————————— EXAMPLE PHRASES ———————————

Lo **haré** yo mismo.	I'll do it myself.
¿Quién **hizo** eso?	Who did that?
Quieres que **haga** las camas?	Do you want me to make the beds?

Table
27

ir *to go*

PRESENT		PRESENT SUBJUNCTIVE	
(yo)	voy	(yo)	vaya
(tú)	vas	(tú)	vayas
(él/ella/usted)	va	(él/ella/usted)	vaya
(nosotros/as)	vamos	(nosotros/as)	vayamos
(vosotros/as)	vais	(vosotros/as)	vayáis
(ellos/ellas/ustedes)	van	(ellos/ellas/ustedes)	vayan

PRETERITE		IMPERFECT	
(yo)	fui	(yo)	iba
(tú)	fuiste	(tú)	ibas
(él/ella/usted)	fue	(él/ella/usted)	iba
(nosotros/as)	fuimos	(nosotros/as)	íbamos
(vosotros/as)	fuisteis	(vosotros/as)	ibais
(ellos/ellas/ustedes)	fueron	(ellos/ellas/ustedes)	iban

FUTURE		CONDITIONAL	
(yo)	iré	(yo)	iría
(tú)	irás	(tú)	irías
(él/ella/usted)	irá	(él/ella/usted)	iría
(nosotros/as)	iremos	(nosotros/as)	iríamos
(vosotros/as)	iréis	(vosotros/as)	iríais
(ellos/ellas/ustedes)	irán	(ellos/ellas/ustedes)	irían

IMPERATIVE
ve / id

PAST PARTICIPLE
ido

GERUND
yendo

--- EXAMPLE PHRASES ---

¿**Vamos** a comer al campo? — *Shall we have a picnic in the country?*
El domingo **iré** a Edimburgo. — *I'll go to Edinburgh on Sunday.*
Yo no **voy** con ellos. — *I'm not going with them.*

PRESENT

(yo)	juego
(tú)	juegas
(él/ella/usted)	juega
(nosotros/as)	jugamos
(vosotros/as)	jugáis
(ellos/ellas/ustedes)	juegan

PRESENT SUBJUNCTIVE

(yo)	juegue
(tú)	juegues
(él/ella/usted)	juegue
(nosotros/as)	juguemos
(vosotros/as)	juguéis
(ellos/ellas/ustedes)	jueguen

PRETERITE

(yo)	jugué
(tú)	jugaste
(él/ella/usted)	jugó
(nosotros/as)	jugamos
(vosotros/as)	jugasteis
(ellos/ellas/ustedes)	jugaron

IMPERFECT

(yo)	jugaba
(tú)	jugabas
(él/ella/usted)	jugaba
(nosotros/as)	jugábamos
(vosotros/as)	jugabais
(ellos/ellas/ustedes)	jugaban

FUTURE

(yo)	jugaré
(tú)	jugarás
(él/ella/usted)	jugará
(nosotros/as)	jugaremos
(vosotros/as)	jugaréis
(ellos/ellas/ustedes)	jugarán

CONDITIONAL

(yo)	jugaría
(tú)	jugarías
(él/ella/usted)	jugaría
(nosotros/as)	jugaríamos
(vosotros/as)	jugaríais
(ellos/ellas/ustedes)	jugarían

IMPERATIVE

juega / jugad

PAST PARTICIPLE

jugado

GERUND

jugando

=========== EXAMPLE PHRASES ===========

Juego al fútbol todos los domingos.	*I play football every Sunday.*
Están jugando en el jardín.	*They're playing in the garden.*
Jugarán contra el Real Madrid.	*They'll play Real Madrid.*

Table
29

lavarse *to wash oneself*

PRESENT		PRESENT SUBJUNCTIVE	
(yo)	me lavo	(yo)	me lave
(tú)	te lavas	(tú)	te laves
(él/ella/usted)	se lava	(él/ella/usted)	se lave
(nosotros/as)	nos lavamos	(nosotros/as)	nos lavemos
(vosotros/as)	os laváis	(vosotros/as)	os lavéis
(ellos/ellas/ustedes)	se lavan	(ellos/ellas/ustedes)	se laven

PRETERITE		IMPERFECT	
(yo)	me lavé	(yo)	me lavaba
(tú)	te lavaste	(tú)	te lavabas
(él/ella/usted)	se lavó	(él/ella/usted)	se lavaba
(nosotros/as)	nos lavamos	(nosotros/as)	nos lavábamos
(vosotros/as)	os lavasteis	(vosotros/as)	os lavabais
(ellos/ellas/ustedes)	se lavaron	(ellos/ellas/ustedes)	se lavaban

FUTURE		CONDITIONAL	
(yo)	me lavaré	(yo)	me lavaría
(tú)	te lavarás	(tú)	te lavarías
(él/ella/usted)	se lavará	(él/ella/usted)	se lavaría
(nosotros/as)	nos lavaremos	(nosotros/as)	nos lavaríamos
(vosotros/as)	os lavaréis	(vosotros/as)	os lavaríais
(ellos/ellas/ustedes)	se lavarán	(ellos/ellas/ustedes)	se lavarían

IMPERATIVE	PAST PARTICIPLE
lávate / lavaos	lavado

GERUND
lavándose

--- EXAMPLE PHRASES ---

Se lava todos los días.	He washes every day.
Ayer **me lavé** el pelo.	I washed my hair yesterday.
Nos lavaremos con agua fría.	We'll wash in cold water.

PRESENT

(yo)	leo
(tú)	lees
(él/ella/usted)	lee
(nosotros/as)	leemos
(vosotros/as)	leéis
(ellos/ellas/ustedes)	leen

PRESENT SUBJUNCTIVE

(yo)	lea
(tú)	leas
(él/ella/usted)	lea
(nosotros/as)	leamos
(vosotros/as)	leáis
(ellos/ellas/ustedes)	lean

PRETERITE

(yo)	leí
(tú)	leíste
(él/ella/usted)	leyó
(nosotros/as)	leímos
(vosotros/as)	leísteis
(ellos/ellas/ustedes)	leyeron

IMPERFECT

(yo)	leía
(tú)	leías
(él/ella/usted)	leía
(nosotros/as)	leíamos
(vosotros/as)	leíais
(ellos/ellas/ustedes)	leían

FUTURE

(yo)	leeré
(tú)	leerás
(él/ella/usted)	leerá
(nosotros/as)	leeremos
(vosotros/as)	leeréis
(ellos/ellas/ustedes)	leerán

CONDITIONAL

(yo)	leería
(tú)	leerías
(él/ella/usted)	leería
(nosotros/as)	leeríamos
(vosotros/as)	leeríais
(ellos/ellas/ustedes)	leerían

IMPERATIVE
lee / leed

PAST PARTICIPLE
leído

GERUND
leyendo

--- EXAMPLE PHRASES ---

Hace mucho tiempo que no **leo**.   _I haven't read anything for ages._
¿**Has leído** esta novela?   _Have you read this novel?_
Lo **leí** hace tiempo.   _I read it a while ago._

Table
31

llover *to rain*

PRESENT		PRESENT SUBJUNCTIVE	
	llueve		llueva

PRETERITE		IMPERFECT	
	llovió		llovía

FUTURE		CONDITIONAL	
	lloverá		llovería

IMPERATIVE	PAST PARTICIPLE	
not used		llovido

GERUND
lloviendo

─────── EXAMPLE PHRASES ───────

Está lloviendo.	*It's raining.*
Llovió sin parar.	*It rained non-stop.*
Hace semanas que no **llueve**.	*It hasn't rained for weeks.*

PRESENT

(yo)	muero
(tú)	mueres
(él/ella/usted)	muere
(nosotros/as)	morimos
(vosotros/as)	morís
(ellos/ellas/ustedes)	mueren

PRESENT SUBJUNCTIVE

(yo)	muera
(tú)	mueras
(él/ella/usted)	muera
(nosotros/as)	muramos
(vosotros/as)	muráis
(ellos/ellas/ustedes)	mueran

PRETERITE

(yo)	morí
(tú)	moriste
(él/ella/usted)	murió
(nosotros/as)	morimos
(vosotros/as)	moristeis
(ellos/ellas/ustedes)	murieron

IMPERFECT

(yo)	moría
(tú)	morías
(él/ella/usted)	moría
(nosotros/as)	moríamos
(vosotros/as)	moríais
(ellos/ellas/ustedes)	morían

FUTURE

(yo)	moriré
(tú)	morirás
(él/ella/usted)	morirá
(nosotros/as)	moriremos
(vosotros/as)	moriréis
(ellos/ellas/ustedes)	morirán

CONDITIONAL

(yo)	moriría
(tú)	morirías
(él/ella/usted)	moriría
(nosotros/as)	moriríamos
(vosotros/as)	moriríais
(ellos/ellas/ustedes)	morirían

IMPERATIVE
muere / morid

PAST PARTICIPLE
muerto

GERUND
muriendo

= EXAMPLE PHRASES =

Murió a las cinco de la madrugada.

Cuando **me muera**...

Se le **ha muerto** el gato.

He died at five in the morning.

When I die...

His cat has died.

Table
33

mover *to move*

PRESENT		PRESENT SUBJUNCTIVE	
(yo)	muevo	(yo)	mueva
(tú)	mueves	(tú)	muevas
(él/ella/usted)	mueve	(él/ella/usted)	mueva
(nosotros/as)	movemos	(nosotros/as)	movamos
(vosotros/as)	movéis	(vosotros/as)	mováis
(ellos/ellas/ustedes)	mueven	(ellos/ellas/ustedes)	muevan

PRETERITE		IMPERFECT	
(yo)	moví	(yo)	movía
(tú)	moviste	(tú)	movías
(él/ella/usted)	movió	(él/ella/usted)	movía
(nosotros/as)	movimos	(nosotros/as)	movíamos
(vosotros/as)	movisteis	(vosotros/as)	movíais
(ellos/ellas/ustedes)	movieron	(ellos/ellas/ustedes)	movían

FUTURE		CONDITIONAL	
(yo)	moveré	(yo)	movería
(tú)	moverás	(tú)	moverías
(él/ella/usted)	moverá	(él/ella/usted)	movería
(nosotros/as)	moveremos	(nosotros/as)	moveríamos
(vosotros/as)	moveréis	(vosotros/as)	moveríais
(ellos/ellas/ustedes)	moverán	(ellos/ellas/ustedes)	moverían

IMPERATIVE
mueve / moved

PAST PARTICIPLE
movido

GERUND
moviendo

——————————— EXAMPLE PHRASES ———————————

Mueve la mesa hacia la derecha.   *Move the table over to the right.*
Se está moviendo.   *It's moving.*
No **se movieron** de casa.   *They didn't leave the house.*

PRESENT

(yo)	niego
(tú)	niegas
(él/ella/usted)	niega
(nosotros/as)	negamos
(vosotros/as)	negáis
(ellos/ellas/ustedes)	niegan

PRESENT SUBJUNCTIVE

(yo)	niegue
(tú)	niegues
(él/ella/usted)	niegue
(nosotros/as)	neguemos
(vosotros/as)	neguéis
(ellos/ellas/ustedes)	nieguen

PRETERITE

(yo)	negué
(tú)	negaste
(él/ella/usted)	negó
(nosotros/as)	negamos
(vosotros/as)	negasteis
(ellos/ellas/ustedes)	negaron

IMPERFECT

(yo)	negaba
(tú)	negabas
(él/ella/usted)	negaba
(nosotros/as)	negábamos
(vosotros/as)	negabais
(ellos/ellas/ustedes)	negaban

FUTURE

(yo)	negaré
(tú)	negarás
(él/ella/usted)	negará
(nosotros/as)	negaremos
(vosotros/as)	negaréis
(ellos/ellas/ustedes)	negarán

CONDITIONAL

(yo)	negaría
(tú)	negarías
(él/ella/usted)	negaría
(nosotros/as)	negaríamos
(vosotros/as)	negaríais
(ellos/ellas/ustedes)	negarían

IMPERATIVE

niega / negad

PAST PARTICIPLE

negado

GERUND

negando

—— EXAMPLE PHRASES ——

No lo **niegues**.
Se negó a venir con nosotros.
No me **negarás** que es barato.

Don't deny it.
She refused to come with us.
You can't say it's not cheap.

Table
35

oír *to hear*

PRESENT			PRESENT SUBJUNCTIVE	
(yo)	oigo		(yo)	oiga
(tú)	oyes		(tú)	oigas
(él/ella/usted)	oye		(él/ella/usted)	oiga
(nosotros/as)	oímos		(nosotros/as)	oigamos
(vosotros/as)	oís		(vosotros/as)	oigáis
(ellos/ellas/ustedes)	oyen		(ellos/ellas/ustedes)	oigan

PRETERITE			IMPERFECT	
(yo)	oí		(yo)	oía
(tú)	oíste		(tú)	oías
(él/ella/usted)	oyó		(él/ella/usted)	oía
(nosotros/as)	oímos		(nosotros/as)	oíamos
(vosotros/as)	oísteis		(vosotros/as)	oíais
(ellos/ellas/ustedes)	oyeron		(ellos/ellas/ustedes)	oían

FUTURE			CONDITIONAL	
(yo)	oiré		(yo)	oiría
(tú)	oirás		(tú)	oirías
(él/ella/usted)	oirá		(él/ella/usted)	oiría
(nosotros/as)	oiremos		(nosotros/as)	oiríamos
(vosotros/as)	oiréis		(vosotros/as)	oiríais
(ellos/ellas/ustedes)	oirán		(ellos/ellas/ustedes)	oirían

IMPERATIVE
oye / oíd

PAST PARTICIPLE
oído

GERUND
oyendo

=== EXAMPLE PHRASES ===

No **oigo** nada. — I can't hear anything.
Si no **oyes** bien, ve al médico. — If you can't hear properly, go and see the doctor.

¿**Has oído** eso? — Did you hear that?

PRESENT

(yo)	huelo
(tú)	hueles
(él/ella/usted)	huele
(nosotros/as)	olemos
(vosotros/as)	oléis
(ellos/ellas/ustedes)	huelen

PRESENT SUBJUNCTIVE

(yo)	huela
(tú)	huelas
(él/ella/usted)	huela
(nosotros/as)	olamos
(vosotros/as)	oláis
(ellos/ellas/ustedes)	huelan

PRETERITE

(yo)	olí
(tú)	oliste
(él/ella/usted)	olió
(nosotros/as)	olimos
(vosotros/as)	olisteis
(ellos/ellas/ustedes)	olieron

IMPERFECT

(yo)	olía
(tú)	olías
(él/ella/usted)	olía
(nosotros/as)	olíamos
(vosotros/as)	olíais
(ellos/ellas/ustedes)	olían

FUTURE

(yo)	oleré
(tú)	olerás
(él/ella/usted)	olerá
(nosotros/as)	oleremos
(vosotros/as)	oleréis
(ellos/ellas/ustedes)	olerán

CONDITIONAL

(yo)	olería
(tú)	olerías
(él/ella/usted)	olería
(nosotros/as)	oleríamos
(vosotros/as)	oleríais
(ellos/ellas/ustedes)	olerían

IMPERATIVE

huele / oled

PAST PARTICIPLE

olido

GERUND

oliendo

——— EXAMPLE PHRASES ———

Huele a pescado.
Olía muy bien.
Con esto ya no **olerá**.

It smells of fish.
It smelled really nice.
This will take the smell away.

Table
37

pagar *to pay*

PRESENT			PRESENT SUBJUNCTIVE	
(yo)	pago		(yo)	pague
(tú)	pagas		(tú)	pagues
(él/ella/usted)	paga		(él/ella/usted)	pague
(nosotros/as)	pagamos		(nosotros/as)	paguemos
(vosotros/as)	pagáis		(vosotros/as)	paguéis
(ellos/ellas/ustedes)	pagan		(ellos/ellas/ustedes)	paguen

PRETERITE			IMPERFECT	
(yo)	pagué		(yo)	pagaba
(tú)	pagaste		(tú)	pagabas
(él/ella/usted)	pagó		(él/ella/usted)	pagaba
(nosotros/as)	pagamos		(nosotros/as)	pagábamos
(vosotros/as)	pagasteis		(vosotros/as)	pagabais
(ellos/ellas/ustedes)	pagaron		(ellos/ellas/ustedes)	pagaban

FUTURE			CONDITIONAL	
(yo)	pagaré		(yo)	pagaría
(tú)	pagarás		(tú)	pagarías
(él/ella/usted)	pagará		(él/ella/usted)	pagaría
(nosotros/as)	pagaremos		(nosotros/as)	pagaríamos
(vosotros/as)	pagaréis		(vosotros/as)	pagaríais
(ellos/ellas/ustedes)	pagarán		(ellos/ellas/ustedes)	pagarían

IMPERATIVE
paga / pagad

PAST PARTICIPLE
pagado

GERUND
pagando

--- EXAMPLE PHRASES ---

¿Cuánto te **pagan** al mes?   *How much do they pay you a month?*
Lo **pagué** en efectivo.   *I paid for it in cash.*
Yo te **pagaré** la entrada.   *I'll pay for your ticket.*

PRESENT

(yo)	pido
(tú)	pides
(él/ella/usted)	pide
(nosotros/as)	pedimos
(vosotros/as)	pedís
(ellos/ellas/ustedes)	piden

PRESENT SUBJUNCTIVE

(yo)	pida
(tú)	pidas
(él/ella/usted)	pida
(nosotros/as)	pidamos
(vosotros/as)	pidáis
(ellos/ellas/ustedes)	pidan

PRETERITE

(yo)	pedí
(tú)	pediste
(él/ella/usted)	pidió
(nosotros/as)	pedimos
(vosotros/as)	pedisteis
(ellos/ellas/ustedes)	pidieron

IMPERFECT

(yo)	pedía
(tú)	pedías
(él/ella/usted)	pedía
(nosotros/as)	pedíamos
(vosotros/as)	pedíais
(ellos/ellas/ustedes)	pedían

FUTURE

(yo)	pediré
(tú)	pedirás
(él/ella/usted)	pedirá
(nosotros/as)	pediremos
(vosotros/as)	pediréis
(ellos/ellas/ustedes)	pedirán

CONDITIONAL

(yo)	pediría
(tú)	pedirías
(él/ella/usted)	pediría
(nosotros/as)	pediríamos
(vosotros/as)	pediríais
(ellos/ellas/ustedes)	pedirían

IMPERATIVE
pide / pedid

PAST PARTICIPLE
pedido

GERUND
pidiendo

— EXAMPLE PHRASES —

No nos **pidieron** el pasaporte.
Hemos pedido dos cervezas.
Pídele el teléfono.

They didn't ask us for our passports.
We've ordered two beers.
Ask her for her telephone number.

Table
39

pensar *to think*

PRESENT			PRESENT SUBJUNCTIVE	
(yo)	pienso		(yo)	piense
(tú)	piensas		(tú)	pienses
(él/ella/usted)	piensa		(él/ella/usted)	piense
(nosotros/as)	pensamos		(nosotros/as)	pensemos
(vosotros/as)	pensáis		(vosotros/as)	penséis
(ellos/ellas/ustedes)	piensan		(ellos/ellas/ustedes)	piensen

PRETERITE			IMPERFECT	
(yo)	pensé		(yo)	pensaba
(tú)	pensaste		(tú)	pensabas
(él/ella/usted)	pensó		(él/ella/usted)	pensaba
(nosotros/as)	pensamos		(nosotros/as)	pensábamos
(vosotros/as)	pensasteis		(vosotros/as)	pensabais
(ellos/ellas/ustedes)	pensaron		(ellos/ellas/ustedes)	pensaban

FUTURE			CONDITIONAL	
(yo)	pensaré		(yo)	pensaría
(tú)	pensarás		(tú)	pensarías
(él/ella/usted)	pensará		(él/ella/usted)	pensaría
(nosotros/as)	pensaremos		(nosotros/as)	pensaríamos
(vosotros/as)	pensaréis		(vosotros/as)	pensaríais
(ellos/ellas/ustedes)	pensarán		(ellos/ellas/ustedes)	pensarían

IMPERATIVE
piensa / pensad

PAST PARTICIPLE
pensado

GERUND
pensando

───────── EXAMPLE PHRASES ─────────

No lo **pienses** más.

Está pensando en comprarse
un piso.

Pensaba que vendrías.

Don't think any more about it.

He's thinking of buying a flat.

I thought you'd come.

PRESENT

(yo)	puedo
(tú)	puedes
(él/ella/usted)	puede
(nosotros/as)	podemos
(vosotros/as)	podéis
(ellos/ellas/ustedes)	pueden

PRESENT SUBJUNCTIVE

(yo)	pueda
(tú)	puedas
(él/ella/usted)	pueda
(nosotros/as)	podamos
(vosotros/as)	podáis
(ellos/ellas/ustedes)	puedan

PRETERITE

(yo)	pude
(tú)	pudiste
(él/ella/usted)	pudo
(nosotros/as)	pudimos
(vosotros/as)	pudisteis
(ellos/ellas/ustedes)	pudieron

IMPERFECT

(yo)	podía
(tú)	podías
(él/ella/usted)	podía
(nosotros/as)	podíamos
(vosotros/as)	podíais
(ellos/ellas/ustedes)	podían

FUTURE

(yo)	podré
(tú)	podrás
(él/ella/usted)	podrá
(nosotros/as)	podremos
(vosotros/as)	podréis
(ellos/ellas/ustedes)	podrán

CONDITIONAL

(yo)	podría
(tú)	podrías
(él/ella/usted)	podría
(nosotros/as)	podríamos
(vosotros/as)	podríais
(ellos/ellas/ustedes)	podrían

IMPERATIVE
puede / poded

PAST PARTICIPLE
podido

GERUND
pudiendo

=== EXAMPLE PHRASES ===

¿**Puedo** entrar?
Puedes venir cuando quieras.
¿**Podrías** ayudarme?

Can I come in?
You can come when you like.
Could you help me?

Table
41

poner *to put*

PRESENT	
(yo)	pongo
(tú)	pones
(él/ella/usted)	pone
(nosotros/as)	ponemos
(vosotros/as)	ponéis
(ellos/ellas/ustedes)	ponen

PRESENT SUBJUNCTIVE	
(yo)	ponga
(tú)	pongas
(él/ella/usted)	ponga
(nosotros/as)	pongamos
(vosotros/as)	pongáis
(ellos/ellas/ustedes)	pongan

PRETERITE	
(yo)	puse
(tú)	pusiste
(él/ella/usted)	puso
(nosotros/as)	pusimos
(vosotros/as)	pusisteis
(ellos/ellas/ustedes)	pusieron

IMPERFECT	
(yo)	ponía
(tú)	ponías
(él/ella/usted)	ponía
(nosotros/as)	poníamos
(vosotros/as)	poníais
(ellos/ellas/ustedes)	ponían

FUTURE	
(yo)	pondré
(tú)	pondrás
(él/ella/usted)	pondrá
(nosotros/as)	pondremos
(vosotros/as)	pondréis
(ellos/ellas/ustedes)	pondrán

CONDITIONAL	
(yo)	pondría
(tú)	pondrías
(él/ella/usted)	pondría
(nosotros/as)	pondríamos
(vosotros/as)	pondríais
(ellos/ellas/ustedes)	pondrían

IMPERATIVE
pon / poned

PAST PARTICIPLE
puesto

GERUND
poniendo

--- EXAMPLE PHRASES ---

Ponlo ahí encima. *Put it on there.*
Lo **pondré** aquí. *I'll put it here.*
Todos **nos pusimos** de acuerdo. *We all agreed.*

PRESENT

(yo)	prohíbo
(tú)	prohíbes
(él/ella/usted)	prohíbe
(nosotros/as)	prohibimos
(vosotros/as)	prohibís
(ellos/ellas/ustedes)	prohíben

PRESENT SUBJUNCTIVE

(yo)	prohíba
(tú)	prohíbas
(él/ella/usted)	prohíba
(nosotros/as)	prohibamos
(vosotros/as)	prohibáis
(ellos/ellas/ustedes)	prohíban

PRETERITE

(yo)	prohibí
(tú)	prohibiste
(él/ella/usted)	prohibió
(nosotros/as)	prohibimos
(vosotros/as)	prohibisteis
(ellos/ellas/ustedes)	prohibieron

IMPERFECT

(yo)	prohibía
(tú)	prohibías
(él/ella/usted)	prohibía
(nosotros/as)	prohibíamos
(vosotros/as)	prohibíais
(ellos/ellas/ustedes)	prohibían

FUTURE

(yo)	prohibiré
(tú)	prohibirás
(él/ella/usted)	prohibirá
(nosotros/as)	prohibiremos
(vosotros/as)	prohibiréis
(ellos/ellas/ustedes)	prohibirán

CONDITIONAL

(yo)	prohibiría
(tú)	prohibirías
(él/ella/usted)	prohibiría
(nosotros/as)	prohibiríamos
(vosotros/as)	prohibiríais
(ellos/ellas/ustedes)	prohibirían

IMPERATIVE

prohíbe / prohibid

PAST PARTICIPLE

prohibido

GERUND

prohibiendo

=========== EXAMPLE PHRASES ===========

Le **prohibieron** la entrada en el bingo.

Han prohibido el acceso a la prensa.

Te **prohíbo** que me hables así.

She was not allowed into the bingo hall.

The press have been banned.

I won't have you talking to me like that!

Table
43

querer *to want*

PRESENT	
(yo)	quiero
(tú)	quieres
(él/ella/usted)	quiere
(nosotros/as)	queremos
(vosotros/as)	queréis
(ellos/ellas/ustedes)	quieren

PRESENT SUBJUNCTIVE	
(yo)	quiera
(tú)	quieras
(él/ella/usted)	quiera
(nosotros/as)	queramos
(vosotros/as)	queráis
(ellos/ellas/ustedes)	quieran

PRETERITE	
(yo)	quise
(tú)	quisiste
(él/ella/usted)	quiso
(nosotros/as)	quisimos
(vosotros/as)	quisisteis
(ellos/ellas/ustedes)	quisieron

IMPERFECT	
(yo)	quería
(tú)	querías
(él/ella/usted)	quería
(nosotros/as)	queríamos
(vosotros/as)	queríais
(ellos/ellas/ustedes)	querían

FUTURE	
(yo)	querré
(tú)	querrás
(él/ella/usted)	querrá
(nosotros/as)	querremos
(vosotros/as)	querréis
(ellos/ellas/ustedes)	querrán

CONDITIONAL	
(yo)	querría
(tú)	querrías
(él/ella/usted)	querría
(nosotros/as)	querríamos
(vosotros/as)	querríais
(ellos/ellas/ustedes)	querrían

IMPERATIVE
quiere / quered

PAST PARTICIPLE
querido

GERUND
queriendo

--- EXAMPLE PHRASES ---

Te **quiero**.
Quisiera preguntar una cosa.
No **quería** decírmelo.

I love you.
I'd like to ask something.
She didn't want to tell me.

PRESENT

(yo)	río
(tú)	ríes
(él/ella/usted)	ríe
(nosotros/as)	reímos
(vosotros/as)	reís
(ellos/ellas/ustedes)	ríen

PRESENT SUBJUNCTIVE

(yo)	ría
(tú)	rías
(él/ella/usted)	ría
(nosotros/as)	riamos
(vosotros/as)	riais
(ellos/ellas/ustedes)	rían

PRETERITE

(yo)	reí
(tú)	reíste
(él/ella/usted)	rio
(nosotros/as)	reímos
(vosotros/as)	reísteis
(ellos/ellas/ustedes)	rieron

IMPERFECT

(yo)	reía
(tú)	reías
(él/ella/usted)	reía
(nosotros/as)	reíamos
(vosotros/as)	reíais
(ellos/ellas/ustedes)	reían

FUTURE

(yo)	reiré
(tú)	reirás
(él/ella/usted)	reirá
(nosotros/as)	reiremos
(vosotros/as)	reiréis
(ellos/ellas/ustedes)	reirán

CONDITIONAL

(yo)	reiría
(tú)	reirías
(él/ella/usted)	reiría
(nosotros/as)	reiríamos
(vosotros/as)	reiríais
(ellos/ellas/ustedes)	reirían

IMPERATIVE

ríe / reíd

PAST PARTICIPLE

reído

GERUND

riendo

--- EXAMPLE PHRASES ---

No **te rías** de mí.	*Don't laugh at me.*
Si **ríes** mucho te saldrán arrugas.	*If you laugh too much you'll get lines.*
Se ríe de cualquier cosa.	*She laughs at anything.*

Table
45

reñir *to tell off*

PRESENT

(yo)	riño
(tú)	riñes
(él/ella/usted)	riñe
(nosotros/as)	reñimos
(vosotros/as)	reñís
(ellos/ellas/ustedes)	riñen

PRESENT SUBJUNCTIVE

(yo)	riña
(tú)	riñas
(él/ella/usted)	riña
(nosotros/as)	riñamos
(vosotros/as)	riñáis
(ellos/ellas/ustedes)	riñan

PRETERITE

(yo)	reñí
(tú)	reñiste
(él/ella/usted)	riñó
(nosotros/as)	reñimos
(vosotros/as)	reñisteis
(ellos/ellas/ustedes)	riñeron

IMPERFECT

(yo)	reñía
(tú)	reñías
(él/ella/usted)	reñía
(nosotros/as)	reñíamos
(vosotros/as)	reñíais
(ellos/ellas/ustedes)	reñían

FUTURE

(yo)	reñiré
(tú)	reñirás
(él/ella/usted)	reñirá
(nosotros/as)	reñiremos
(vosotros/as)	reñiréis
(ellos/ellas/ustedes)	reñirán

CONDITIONAL

(yo)	reñiría
(tú)	reñirías
(él/ella/usted)	reñiría
(nosotros/as)	reñiríamos
(vosotros/as)	reñiríais
(ellos/ellas/ustedes)	reñirían

IMPERATIVE
riñe / reñid

PAST PARTICIPLE
reñido

GERUND
riñendo

--- EXAMPLE PHRASES ---

Les **riñó** por llegar tarde a casa.

Nos **reñía** sin motivo.

She told them off for getting home late.

She used to tell us off for no reason.

PRESENT

(yo)	
(tú)	
(él/ella/usted)	
(nosotros/as)	
(vosotros/as)	
(ellos/ellas/ustedes)	

PRESENT SUBJUNCTIVE

(yo)	reúna
(tú)	reúnas
(él/ella/usted)	reúna
(nosotros/as)	reunamos
(vosotros/as)	reunáis
(ellos/ellas/ustedes)	reúnan

PRETERITE

(yo)	reuní
(tú)	reuniste
(él/ella/usted)	reunió
(nosotros/as)	reunimos
(vosotros/as)	reunisteis
(ellos/ellas/ustedes)	reunieron

IMPERFECT

(yo)	reunía
(tú)	reunías
(él/ella/usted)	reunía
(nosotros/as)	reuníamos
(vosotros/as)	reuníais
(ellos/ellas/ustedes)	reunían

FUTURE

(yo)	reuniré
(tú)	reunirás
(él/ella/usted)	reunirá
(nosotros/as)	reuniremos
(vosotros/as)	reuniréis
(ellos/ellas/ustedes)	reunirán

CONDITIONAL

(yo)	reuniría
(tú)	reunirías
(él/ella/usted)	reuniría
(nosotros/as)	reuniríamos
(vosotros/as)	reuniríais
(ellos/ellas/ustedes)	reunirían

IMPERATIVE
reúne / reunid

GERUND
reuniendo

PAST PARTICIPLE

reunido

========= EXAMPLE PHRASES =========

Han reunido suficientes pruebas.

No **reúne** las condiciones
necesarias.
Se reunían una vez por semana.

They have gathered enough evidence.
He doesn't meet the necessary
requirements.
They used to meet once a week.

Table
47

saber *to know*

PRESENT

(yo)	sé
(tú)	sabes
(él/ella/usted)	sabe
(nosotros/as)	sabemos
(vosotros/as)	sabéis
(ellos/ellas/ustedes)	saben

PRESENT SUBJUNCTIVE

(yo)	sepa
(tú)	sepas
(él/ella/usted)	sepa
(nosotros/as)	sepamos
(vosotros/as)	sepáis
(ellos/ellas/ustedes)	sepan

PRETERITE

(yo)	supe
(tú)	supiste
(él/ella/usted)	supo
(nosotros/as)	supimos
(vosotros/as)	supisteis
(ellos/ellas/ustedes)	supieron

IMPERFECT

(yo)	sabía
(tú)	sabías
(él/ella/usted)	sabía
(nosotros/as)	sabíamos
(vosotros/as)	sabíais
(ellos/ellas/ustedes)	sabían

FUTURE

(yo)	sabré
(tú)	sabrás
(él/ella/usted)	sabrá
(nosotros/as)	sabremos
(vosotros/as)	sabréis
(ellos/ellas/ustedes)	sabrán

CONDITIONAL

(yo)	sabría
(tú)	sabrías
(él/ella/usted)	sabría
(nosotros/as)	sabríamos
(vosotros/as)	sabríais
(ellos/ellas/ustedes)	sabrían

IMPERATIVE
sabe / sabed

PAST PARTICIPLE
sabido

GERUND
sabiendo

───────────── EXAMPLE PHRASES ─────────────

No lo **sé**.
¿**Sabes** una cosa?
Pensaba que lo **sabías**.

I don't know.
Do you know what?
I thought you knew.

PRESENT

(yo)	saco
(tú)	sacas
(él/ella/usted)	saca
(nosotros/as)	sacamos
(vosotros/as)	sacáis
(ellos/ellas/ustedes)	sacan

PRESENT SUBJUNCTIVE

(yo)	saque
(tú)	saques
(él/ella/usted)	saque
(nosotros/as)	saquemos
(vosotros/as)	saquéis
(ellos/ellas/ustedes)	saquen

PRETERITE

(yo)	saqué
(tú)	sacaste
(él/ella/usted)	sacó
(nosotros/as)	sacamos
(vosotros/as)	sacasteis
(ellos/ellas/ustedes)	sacaron

IMPERFECT

(yo)	sacaba
(tú)	sacabas
(él/ella/usted)	sacaba
(nosotros/as)	sacábamos
(vosotros/as)	sacabais
(ellos/ellas/ustedes)	sacaban

FUTURE

(yo)	sacaré
(tú)	sacarás
(él/ella/usted)	sacará
(nosotros/as)	sacaremos
(vosotros/as)	sacaréis
(ellos/ellas/ustedes)	sacarán

CONDITIONAL

(yo)	sacaría
(tú)	sacarías
(él/ella/usted)	sacaría
(nosotros/as)	sacaríamos
(vosotros/as)	sacaríais
(ellos/ellas/ustedes)	sacarían

IMPERATIVE
saca / sacad

PAST PARTICIPLE
sacado

GERUND
sacando

=== EXAMPLE PHRASES ===

Ya **he sacado** las entradas.
Saqué un 7 en el examen.
No **saques** la cabeza por la
ventanilla.

I've already bought the tickets.
I got 7 points in the exam.
Don't lean out of the window.

Table
49

salir *to come out, to go out*

PRESENT

(yo)	salgo
(tú)	sales
(él/ella/usted)	sale
(nosotros/as)	salimos
(vosotros/as)	salís
(ellos/ellas/ustedes)	salen

PRESENT SUBJUNCTIVE

(yo)	salga
(tú)	salgas
(él/ella/usted)	salga
(nosotros/as)	salgamos
(vosotros/as)	salgáis
(ellos/ellas/ustedes)	salgan

PRETERITE

(yo)	salí
(tú)	saliste
(él/ella/usted)	salió
(nosotros/as)	salimos
(vosotros/as)	salisteis
(ellos/ellas/ustedes)	salieron

IMPERFECT

(yo)	salía
(tú)	salías
(él/ella/usted)	salía
(nosotros/as)	salíamos
(vosotros/as)	salíais
(ellos/ellas/ustedes)	salían

FUTURE

(yo)	saldré
(tú)	saldrás
(él/ella/usted)	saldrá
(nosotros/as)	saldremos
(vosotros/as)	saldréis
(ellos/ellas/ustedes)	saldrán

CONDITIONAL

(yo)	saldría
(tú)	saldrías
(él/ella/usted)	saldría
(nosotros/as)	saldríamos
(vosotros/as)	saldríais
(ellos/ellas/ustedes)	saldrían

IMPERATIVE

sal / salid

PAST PARTICIPLE

salido

GERUND

saliendo

--- EXAMPLE PHRASES ---

Hace tiempo que no **salimos**.
Por favor, **salgan** por la puerta
de atrás.
Salió un par de veces con
nosotros.

We haven't been out for a while.
Please leave via the back door.

He went out with us a couple of
times.

PRESENT

(yo)	sigo
(tú)	sigues
(él/ella/usted)	sigue
(nosotros/as)	seguimos
(vosotros/as)	seguís
(ellos/ellas/ustedes)	siguen

PRESENT SUBJUNCTIVE

(yo)	siga
(tú)	sigas
(él/ella/usted)	siga
(nosotros/as)	sigamos
(vosotros/as)	sigáis
(ellos/ellas/ustedes)	sigan

PRETERITE

(yo)	seguí
(tú)	seguiste
(él/ella/usted)	siguió
(nosotros/as)	seguimos
(vosotros/as)	seguisteis
(ellos/ellas/ustedes)	siguieron

IMPERFECT

(yo)	seguía
(tú)	seguías
(él/ella/usted)	seguía
(nosotros/as)	seguíamos
(vosotros/as)	seguíais
(ellos/ellas/ustedes)	seguían

FUTURE

(yo)	seguiré
(tú)	seguirás
(él/ella/usted)	seguirá
(nosotros/as)	seguiremos
(vosotros/as)	seguiréis
(ellos/ellas/ustedes)	seguirán

CONDITIONAL

(yo)	seguiría
(tú)	seguirías
(él/ella/usted)	seguiría
(nosotros/as)	seguiríamos
(vosotros/as)	seguiríais
(ellos/ellas/ustedes)	seguirían

IMPERATIVE

sigue / seguid

PAST PARTICIPLE

seguido

GERUND

siguiendo

--- EXAMPLE PHRASES ---

Siga por esta calle hasta el final.
Go on till you get to the end of the street.

Nos seguiremos viendo.
We will go on seeing each other.

Nos **siguió** todo el camino.
He followed us all the way.

Table
51

sentir *to feel*

PRESENT

(yo)	siento
(tú)	sientes
(él/ella/usted)	siente
(nosotros/as)	sentimos
(vosotros/as)	sentís
(ellos/ellas/ustedes)	sienten

PRESENT SUBJUNCTIVE

(yo)	sienta
(tú)	sientas
(él/ella/usted)	sienta
(nosotros/as)	sintamos
(vosotros/as)	sintáis
(ellos/ellas/ustedes)	sientan

PRETERITE

(yo)	sentí
(tú)	sentiste
(él/ella/usted)	sintió
(nosotros/as)	sentimos
(vosotros/as)	sentisteis
(ellos/ellas/ustedes)	sintieron

IMPERFECT

(yo)	sentía
(tú)	sentías
(él/ella/usted)	sentía
(nosotros/as)	sentíamos
(vosotros/as)	sentíais
(ellos/ellas/ustedes)	sentían

FUTURE

(yo)	sentiré
(tú)	sentirás
(él/ella/usted)	sentirá
(nosotros/as)	sentiremos
(vosotros/as)	sentiréis
(ellos/ellas/ustedes)	sentirán

CONDITIONAL

(yo)	sentiría
(tú)	sentirías
(él/ella/usted)	sentiría
(nosotros/as)	sentiríamos
(vosotros/as)	sentiríais
(ellos/ellas/ustedes)	sentirían

IMPERATIVE
siente / sentid

PAST PARTICIPLE
sentido

GERUND
sintiendo

——————————————— EXAMPLE PHRASES ———————————————

Siento mucho lo que pasó.

Sentí un pinchazo en la pierna.
No creo que lo **sienta**.

*I'm really sorry about what
happened.*
I felt a sharp pain in my leg.
I don't think she's sorry.

PRESENT

(yo)	soy
(tú)	eres
(él/ella/usted)	es
(nosotros/as)	somos
(vosotros/as)	sois
(ellos/ellas/ustedes)	son

PRESENT SUBJUNCTIVE

(yo)	sea
(tú)	seas
(él/ella/usted)	sea
(nosotros/as)	seamos
(vosotros/as)	seáis
(ellos/ellas/ustedes)	sean

PRETERITE

(yo)	fui
(tú)	fuiste
(él/ella/usted)	fue
(nosotros/as)	fuimos
(vosotros/as)	fuisteis
(ellos/ellas/ustedes)	fueron

IMPERFECT

(yo)	era
(tú)	eras
(él/ella/usted)	era
(nosotros/as)	éramos
(vosotros/as)	erais
(ellos/ellas/ustedes)	eran

FUTURE

(yo)	seré
(tú)	serás
(él/ella/usted)	será
(nosotros/as)	seremos
(vosotros/as)	seréis
(ellos/ellas/ustedes)	serán

CONDITIONAL

(yo)	sería
(tú)	serías
(él/ella/usted)	sería
(nosotros/as)	seríamos
(vosotros/as)	seríais
(ellos/ellas/ustedes)	serían

IMPERATIVE

sé / sed

PAST PARTICIPLE

sido

GERUND

siendo

——————————— EXAMPLE PHRASES ———————————

Soy español.
¿**Fuiste** tú el que llamó?
Era de noche.

I'm Spanish.
Was it you who phoned?
It was dark.

Table
53

tener *to have*

PRESENT		PRESENT SUBJUNCTIVE	
(yo)	tengo	(yo)	tenga
(tú)	tienes	(tú)	tengas
(él/ella/usted)	tiene	(él/ella/usted)	tenga
(nosotros/as)	tenemos	(nosotros/as)	tengamos
(vosotros/as)	tenéis	(vosotros/as)	tengáis
(ellos/ellas/ustedes)	tienen	(ellos/ellas/ustedes)	tengan

PRETERITE		IMPERFECT	
(yo)	tuve	(yo)	tenía
(tú)	tuviste	(tú)	tenías
(él/ella/usted)	tuvo	(él/ella/usted)	tenía
(nosotros/as)	tuvimos	(nosotros/as)	teníamos
(vosotros/as)	tuvisteis	(vosotros/as)	teníais
(ellos/ellas/ustedes)	tuvieron	(ellos/ellas/ustedes)	tenían

FUTURE		CONDITIONAL	
(yo)	tendré	(yo)	tendría
(tú)	tendrás	(tú)	tendrías
(él/ella/usted)	tendrá	(él/ella/usted)	tendría
(nosotros/as)	tendremos	(nosotros/as)	tendríamos
(vosotros/as)	tendréis	(vosotros/as)	tendríais
(ellos/ellas/ustedes)	tendrán	(ellos/ellas/ustedes)	tendrían

IMPERATIVE
ten / tened

PAST PARTICIPLE
tenido

GERUND
teniendo

=== EXAMPLE PHRASES ===

Tengo sed.
No **tenía** suficiente dinero.
Tuvimos que irnos.

I'm thirsty.
She didn't have enough money.
We had to leave.

PRESENT

(yo)	traigo
(tú)	traes
(él/ella/usted)	trae
(nosotros/as)	traemos
(vosotros/as)	traéis
(ellos/ellas/ustedes)	traen

PRESENT SUBJUNCTIVE

(yo)	traiga
(tú)	traigas
(él/ella/usted)	traiga
(nosotros/as)	traigamos
(vosotros/as)	traigáis
(ellos/ellas/ustedes)	traigan

PRETERITE

(yo)	traje
(tú)	trajiste
(él/ella/usted)	trajo
(nosotros/as)	trajimos
(vosotros/as)	trajisteis
(ellos/ellas/ustedes)	trajeron

IMPERFECT

(yo)	traía
(tú)	traías
(él/ella/usted)	traía
(nosotros/as)	traíamos
(vosotros/as)	traíais
(ellos/ellas/ustedes)	traían

FUTURE

(yo)	traeré
(tú)	traerás
(él/ella/usted)	traerá
(nosotros/as)	traeremos
(vosotros/as)	traeréis
(ellos/ellas/ustedes)	traerán

CONDITIONAL

(yo)	traería
(tú)	traerías
(él/ella/usted)	traería
(nosotros/as)	traeríamos
(vosotros/as)	traeríais
(ellos/ellas/ustedes)	traerían

IMPERATIVE

trae / traed

PAST PARTICIPLE

traído

GERUND

trayendo

——————————— EXAMPLE PHRASES ———————————

¿**Has traído** lo que te pedí?
No **trajo** el dinero.
Trae eso.

Have you brought what I asked?
He didn't bring the money.
Give that here.

Table
55

valer *to be worth*

PRESENT		PRESENT SUBJUNCTIVE	
(yo)	valgo	(yo)	valga
(tú)	vales	(tú)	valgas
(él/ella/usted)	vale	(él/ella/usted)	valga
(nosotros/as)	valemos	(nosotros/as)	valgamos
(vosotros/as)	valéis	(vosotros/as)	valgáis
(ellos/ellas/ustedes)	valen	(ellos/ellas/ustedes)	valgan

PRETERITE		IMPERFECT	
(yo)	valí	(yo)	valía
(tú)	valiste	(tú)	valías
(él/ella/usted)	valió	(él/ella/usted)	valía
(nosotros/as)	valimos	(nosotros/as)	valíamos
(vosotros/as)	valisteis	(vosotros/as)	valíais
(ellos/ellas/ustedes)	valieron	(ellos/ellas/ustedes)	valían

FUTURE		CONDITIONAL	
(yo)	valdré	(yo)	valdría
(tú)	valdrás	(tú)	valdrías
(él/ella/usted)	valdrá	(él/ella/usted)	valdría
(nosotros/as)	valdremos	(nosotros/as)	valdríamos
(vosotros/as)	valdréis	(vosotros/as)	valdríais
(ellos/ellas/ustedes)	valdrán	(ellos/ellas/ustedes)	valdrían

IMPERATIVE
vale / valed

PAST PARTICIPLE
valido

GERUND
valiendo

--- EXAMPLE PHRASES ---

¿Cuánto **vale** eso?	How much is that?
No **valía** la pena.	It wasn't worth it.
Valga lo que valga, lo compro.	I'll buy it, no matter how much it costs.

PRESENT

(yo)	vengo
(tú)	vienes
(él/ella/usted)	viene
(nosotros/as)	venimos
(vosotros/as)	venís
(ellos/ellas/ustedes)	vienen

PRESENT SUBJUNCTIVE

(yo)	venga
(tú)	vengas
(él/ella/usted)	venga
(nosotros/as)	vengamos
(vosotros/as)	vengáis
(ellos/ellas/ustedes)	vengan

PRETERITE

(yo)	vine
(tú)	viniste
(él/ella/usted)	vino
(nosotros/as)	vinimos
(vosotros/as)	vinisteis
(ellos/ellas/ustedes)	vinieron

IMPERFECT

(yo)	venía
(tú)	venías
(él/ella/usted)	venía
(nosotros/as)	veníamos
(vosotros/as)	veníais
(ellos/ellas/ustedes)	venían

FUTURE

(yo)	vendré
(tú)	vendrás
(él/ella/usted)	vendrá
(nosotros/as)	vendremos
(vosotros/as)	vendréis
(ellos/ellas/ustedes)	vendrán

CONDITIONAL

(yo)	vendría
(tú)	vendrías
(él/ella/usted)	vendría
(nosotros/as)	vendríamos
(vosotros/as)	vendríais
(ellos/ellas/ustedes)	vendrían

IMPERATIVE

ven / venid

PAST PARTICIPLE

venido

GERUND

viniendo

--- EXAMPLE PHRASES ---

Vengo andando desde la playa.

I've walked all the way from the beach.

¿**Vendrás** conmigo al cine?

Will you come to see a film with me?

Prefiero que no **venga**.

I'd rather he didn't come.

Table
57

ver to see

PRESENT

(yo)	veo
(tú)	ves
(él/ella/usted)	ve
(nosotros/as)	vemos
(vosotros/as)	veis
(ellos/ellas/ustedes)	ven

PRESENT SUBJUNCTIVE

(yo)	vea
(tú)	veas
(él/ella/usted)	vea
(nosotros/as)	veamos
(vosotros/as)	veáis
(ellos/ellas/ustedes)	vean

PRETERITE

(yo)	vi
(tú)	viste
(él/ella/usted)	vio
(nosotros/as)	vimos
(vosotros/as)	visteis
(ellos/ellas/ustedes)	vieron

IMPERFECT

(yo)	veía
(tú)	veías
(él/ella/usted)	veía
(nosotros/as)	veíamos
(vosotros/as)	veíais
(ellos/ellas/ustedes)	veían

FUTURE

(yo)	veré
(tú)	verás
(él/ella/usted)	verá
(nosotros/as)	veremos
(vosotros/as)	veréis
(ellos/ellas/ustedes)	verán

CONDITIONAL

(yo)	vería
(tú)	verías
(él/ella/usted)	vería
(nosotros/as)	veríamos
(vosotros/as)	veríais
(ellos/ellas/ustedes)	verían

IMPERATIVE

ve / ved

PAST PARTICIPLE

visto

GERUND

viendo

=== EXAMPLE PHRASES ===

No **veo** muy bien.
Los **veía** a todos desde la ventana.
¿**Viste** lo que pasó?

I can't see very well.
I could see them all from the window.
Did you see what happened?

Table
58

to live **vivir**

PRESENT

(yo)	vivo
(tú)	vives
(él/ella/usted)	vive
(nosotros/as)	vivimos
(vosotros/as)	vivís
(ellos/ellas/ustedes)	viven

PRESENT SUBJUNCTIVE

(yo)	viva
(tú)	vivas
(él/ella/usted)	viva
(nosotros/as)	vivamos
(vosotros/as)	viváis
(ellos/ellas/ustedes)	vivan

PRETERITE

(yo)	viví
(tú)	viviste
(él/ella/usted)	vivió
(nosotros/as)	vivimos
(vosotros/as)	vivisteis
(ellos/ellas/ustedes)	vivieron

IMPERFECT

(yo)	vivía
(tú)	vivías
(él/ella/usted)	vivía
(nosotros/as)	vivíamos
(vosotros/as)	vivíais
(ellos/ellas/ustedes)	vivían

FUTURE

(yo)	viviré
(tú)	vivirás
(él/ella/usted)	vivirá
(nosotros/as)	viviremos
(vosotros/as)	viviréis
(ellos/ellas/ustedes)	vivirán

CONDITIONAL

(yo)	viviría
(tú)	vivirías
(él/ella/usted)	viviría
(nosotros/as)	viviríamos
(vosotros/as)	viviríais
(ellos/ellas/ustedes)	vivirían

IMPERATIVE

vive / vivid

PAST PARTICIPLE

vivido

GERUND

viviendo

--- EXAMPLE PHRASES ---

Vivo en Valencia.
Vivieron juntos dos años.
Hemos vivido momentos
difíciles.

I live in Valencia.
They lived together for two years.
We've had some difficult times.

Table
59

volver *to return*

PRESENT

(yo)	vuelvo
(tú)	vuelves
(él/ella/usted)	vuelve
(nosotros/as)	volvemos
(vosotros/as)	volvéis
(ellos/ellas/ustedes)	vuelven

PRESENT SUBJUNCTIVE

(yo)	vuelva
(tú)	vuelvas
(él/ella/usted)	vuelva
(nosotros/as)	volvamos
(vosotros/as)	volváis
(ellos/ellas/ustedes)	vuelvan

PRETERITE

(yo)	volví
(tú)	volviste
(él/ella/usted)	volvió
(nosotros/as)	volvimos
(vosotros/as)	volvisteis
(ellos/ellas/ustedes)	volvieron

IMPERFECT

(yo)	volvía
(tú)	volvías
(él/ella/usted)	volvía
(nosotros/as)	volvíamos
(vosotros/as)	volvíais
(ellos/ellas/ustedes)	volvían

FUTURE

(yo)	volveré
(tú)	volverás
(él/ella/usted)	volverá
(nosotros/as)	volveremos
(vosotros/as)	volveréis
(ellos/ellas/ustedes)	volverán

CONDITIONAL

(yo)	volvería
(tú)	volverías
(él/ella/usted)	volvería
(nosotros/as)	volveríamos
(vosotros/as)	volveríais
(ellos/ellas/ustedes)	volverían

IMPERATIVE
vuelve / volved

PAST PARTICIPLE
vuelto

GERUND
volviendo

=============== EXAMPLE PHRASES ===============

Mi padre **vuelve** mañana.
No **vuelvas** por aquí.
Ha vuelto a casa.

My father's coming back tomorrow.
Don't come back here.
He's gone back home.